# NAVAL ACCIDENTS

Since 1945

by

**Malcolm Maclean**

First published in the United Kingdom in 2008 by Maritime Books, Lodge Hill, Liskeard, Cornwall, PL14 4EL

# FOREWORD

# Captain Mark Slawson, Royal Navy
# BSc(Hons) C Eng MI MarEST

*Captain Slawson is a senior Engineer Officer in the Royal Navy and from 2004 to 2006 was responsible for the maintenance and repair of all Portsmouth based naval vessels.*

I am delighted to have been asked to write the foreword for this highly detailed and well-researched analysis of accidental losses since World War Two. This book will be a very useful reference for everyone associated with not only the operation, but also the design and repair of warships. The details of the many tragic events within these covers confirm the ever-present requirement for the maritime environment to be treated with care, respect and with the knowledge that accidents, frequently life threatening and always costly, are never too far away from even the careful mariner.

The compilation of the knowledge contained here will ease the recognition of the lessons that can be learned from the past and, hopefully, assist in their not having to be re-learned following some future avoidable shipping loss. There are a great many causes of incidents and accidents. It would be comforting to think that the more fundamental failures of specification, design and manufacturing had, over many years of man's maritime experience, have been removed from the accident-causing equation, leaving only the frailties of man himself, or the vagaries of the weather, to be the cause of the later incidents in this collection. Unfortunately, the introduction of new technology and labour-saving devices bring its own inherent risks, which need to be assessed and managed. While there has long been a drive to reduce the numbers of naval personnel in ships and automate many of the functions previously required of the crew, this has reduced the number of personnel available to react to a major incident. The number of incidents within this book where major loss of life and disaster have been averted by the quality of training and courage of the ships' companies, reacting in a manner, and in circumstances, beyond the design envelope of any machine, are noteworthy. This may give pause to the headlong drive for through life cost reduction in the design of warships.

All countries carry out analysis of accidents in their own warships. It is vital that this detailed and stringent analysis continues and that the lessons identified are made freely available to all those involved with the design and safety of naval shipping. Greater openness in the West, and in the hitherto Eastern Bloc, has enabled Malcolm Maclean to gain access to the comprehensive information presented in this book, and I commend it to all those associated with the engineering and operation of warships.

# INTRODUCTION

Peacetime accidents over the past sixty years have resulted in hundreds of naval vessels either being stricken from active service as constructive total losses, being declared as beyond economical repair, or being lost completely - often with heavy loss of life. The reasons for these tragic accidents are numerous, sometimes being a combination of human error and 'acts of God'. To quote an old expression: "The sea lies in wait for the merely unwary; it stalks the careless."

All ships, and in particular warships, are constantly exposed to the perils of storms, fires, collisions, grounding or structural failure, whilst submarines are subject to the additional risks associated with loss of control or flooding whilst submerged. Furthermore, the large quantities of ammunition and volatile fuels carried aboard naval vessels present a fervent hazard when safety precautions are not stringently adhered to.

Almost every vessel is at some time in her service career involved in some kind of accident. For instance, in 1960, the Royal Navy suffered a total of 25 groundings, 17 collisions and 68 berthing accidents, involving almost one third of all ships then in commission. However, in the vast majority of cases, the damage sustained is minimal and the vessel is repaired for further service. In other cases, the vessel is declared beyond repair or is lost completely. Sometimes a vessel's remaining planned service life is so short that it is not deemed economically viable to commit funds to repair the damage, resulting in it being paid off and sold for scrap or to commercial ownership.

The aim of this book is to explain why and how these accidents have occurred, being categorised by their primary cause, and to try to cover some of the lessons which have and can be learnt. In many cases however, the accident may be attributed to a proliferation of many seemingly insignificant incidents which individually may have gone unnoticed, but which together have resulted in a chain reaction which has had disastrous consequences for the vessel and her crew. In many such cases, providence, or the lack of it, has been a major contributing factor in determining the ultimate outcome.

Other circumstances may also determine whether vessels are subsequently repaired or are paid off and scrapped. For example, following the cessation of hostilities with the formal surrender of Japan aboard the battleship USS *Missouri* (BB-63) on 2 September 1945, most navies - and particularly those of the Allies - found that they possessed massive fleets which far exceeded the requirements of their peacetime roles. Most of the vessels had been hard worked during years of conflict and many had sustained structural damage which, whilst being acceptable during wartime, would require extensive repairs to prepare them for their peacetime functions. Furthermore, many of the pre-war and early war-built warships were suddenly declared obsolete by the advent of new weapons and construction techniques, despite the fact that most were only a few years old.

These factors, taken individually or collectively, resulted in a number of vessels being 'prematurely' scrapped following damage sustained in post-war accidents. The higher value of sophisticated naval vessels in recent decades has resulted in many vessels being rebuilt after sustaining extensive damage that in the immediate post-war years would almost certainly have resulted in their disposal.

My intention here has been to examine the circumstances surrounding dozens of individual incidents and to describe the findings of the subsequent inquiries, the general lessons that have been learnt, and the actions - both procedural and material - that have been taken by the relevant authorities to prevent a recurrence of the accident.  This book is not concerned with vessels lost as a direct result of enemy action during times of conflict - such as those ships lost during the Vietnam, Arab-Israeli or Falklands conflicts - although I have included minor details of some incidents where I have felt that the details of the incident serve to extrapolate on the case in point.  The prime scope of this book is the loss, or critical damage of warships and naval auxiliaries as a result of accidents or misfortune since the end of World War Two.

In my extensive research I have contacted representatives of over fifty countries, the number of individual sources numbering several hundred.  These sources have included a large number of official government offices and history departments, as well as private contributors, many of whom were actually involved in the individual incidents.  Most of my sources, especially those connected professionally with navies world-wide, have shown extreme interest and enthusiasm in the fact that someone is at last tackling this particular subject. Many, including senior officers serving with navies world-wide - as far afield as South Korea, South Africa and the United States - have stated that anyone even remotely connected with, or interested in, naval activities would be interested in such a book.

Some organisations have been unable to provide me with research assistance and material due to the constraints being forced upon them in times of financial restraint, whilst other sources have shown a reluctance to discuss such embarrassing incidents and the acquisition of material has been a little like 'pulling teeth'. Consequently, many instances of ships being paid-off and scrapped, or merely disappearing from fleet lists, have gone unexplained.  Nevertheless, many of the personal accounts included here, as well as several of the photographs, have never been published before.

The incidence of the loss of naval vessels is reducing significantly, due to a number of factors, such as better training of crews, improved navigational aids, improved construction techniques, and the mere fact that the number of ships possessed by individual navies is far smaller than those in the post-war years. Nevertheless, as long as vessels plough the world's seaways, there will always be accidents involving human error or the wrath of the sea.

# ACKNOWLEDGEMENTS

During my extensive research for this book, I have been in contact with many sources, both private and official, representing over fifty countries. Understandably, many countries have been unwilling to discuss accidents involving their naval vessels and some have been less than forthcoming with material regarding such incidents. Nevertheless, many others have kindly provided much useful material, whilst many individuals have given eye-witness accounts of incidents in which they have been personally involved. Without such assistance this book could not have been written and I therefore wish to express my gratitude to the following individuals, organisations and authorities:

United Kingdom

*Aberdeen Herald & Post*, Aberdeen; Mr Jim Allaway, *Navy News*, Portsmouth, Hampshire, http://www.navynews.co.uk; Mrs M.J.A. Bidmead, Royal Navy Submarine Museum, Gosport, Hampshire, http://www.rnsubmus.co.uk; Mr David Blewett, St. Austell, Cornwall; Mr Brock Brearley, Dunfermline, Fife Mr L.A. Bridge, Coastal Forces Veterans' Association, http://www.inadee.btinternet.co.uk/coastal.htm; Mr Lesley Brown, Fareham, Hampshire; Mr John Carter, Northolt, Middlesex; Mr Simon Cobley, Marine Salvage School, Rosyth, Fife; Mr Maurice P. Cocker, Cleveleys, Lancashire; Mr Jim J. Colledge, Wanstead, London; Mr Kenneth Collins, Wincanton, Somerset; Mr Malcolm Craigen, Dunfermline, Fife; Mr Dennis Doherty, Wigan, Lancashire; *The Dundee Courier & Advertiser*, Dundee; Mr Neil F. Ebbutt, Hextable, Kent; Mr Allan J. Francis, Naval Historical Branch, London (Now Portsmouth); Mr Bob Fredericks, Plymouth, Devon; Mr Dennis N. Gibson, Braunton, North Devon; Mr Peter Hansford, Suffolk; *The Herald & Evening Times*, Glasgow; Mr Geoffrey Hudson, Halifax, Yorkshire; Mr Warwick Jacobs, Hovercraft Museum Trust, Lee on Solent, Gosport, Hampshire, http://www.hovercraft-museum.org; Mr D. Jones, Swansea, West Glamorgan; Mr Eric Lovering, Bideford, Devon; Lieutenant Commander John Maber (RN Retd.), Corsham, Wiltshire; Mr C. Maxwell, The LST & Landing Craft Association, http://www.lstlandingcraftassoc.org; Mrs Jacky Melhuish, Minster Shearness, Kent; Reverend Micheal J. Melvin, BEM, Harlow, Essex; Rear Admiral R.O. Morris, CB, Taunton, Somerset; *The News*, Portsmouth, Hampshire; *The North Devon Gazette*, Devon; Dr R.H. Osborne and D. Sowdon: The World Ship Society, http://www.worldshipsociety.org; Mr George Ransome, Manchester; Mr Len Reynolds, Maidenhead, Berkshire; Mr John D.A. Robbie and Mr Jack Worth: Ton Class Association, http://www.tca2000.co.uk; *Scottish Daily Record & Sunday Mail Ltd*, Glasgow; Officer In Charge, Royal Navy Sea Survival Training Centre, Portsmouth; Mr E.W. Shannon, Shearness, Kent; Mr John Shearn, Ilfracombe, Devon; *The Shearness Times and Guardian*, Shearness on Sea, Kent; Mr Allan Southall, Beaufort Air-Sea Equipment Ltd, Merseyside; Mr Deryck Swetnam, Portsmouth, Hampshire; Mr Robin Tapply, Isle of Mull, Argyll; Ms Kate Tildesley, Curator, Naval Historical Branch, Portsmouth, Hampshire; Mr. Richard J. Wardrope, Inverkeithing, Fife; Mr Adrian Vicary, Maritime Photo Library; Mr Berry Vissers, Arbroath, Scotland; Mr Chris White, Portsmouth, Hampshire; Mr Jack Williams, The Algerines Association, Bishop Aukland, Durham, http://www.minesweepers.org.uk.

Algeria

Direction des Relations Exterieures et de Coopération, Ministére de la Défense Nationale, Algiers
Group Captain K. Gowing, British Embassy, Algiers

Australia

Fiona Burn, David Wagland, Holly Schulte:  National Archives of Australia, Canberra, ACT,
http://www.naa.gov.au
Australian Archives, Victorian Regional Office, Melbourne, Victoria
Australian Government Publishing Service, Canberra, ACT
Jenny Norberry and Fee Jensen:  Australian War Memorial, Canberra, ACT, http://www.awm.gov.au
Lyndsey Shaw, Australian National Maritime Museum, Darling Harbour, NSW, http://www.anmm.gov.au
Mr John Bastock, Penshurst, New South Wales
Mr Michael J. Fogarty, Weston ACT
Dr Tom Frame, Monash, ACT
Mr Colin Jones, Middle Park, Victoria
The Naval Historical Society, Garden Island, New South Wales, http://www.navyhistory.org.au
The Naval Photographic Unit, Darlinghurst, New South Wales
Mr Terry Quinn, Queensland Newspapers Pty Ltd, Brisbane, QLD
Lieutenant Commander J.H. Straczek, RAN, Directorate of Public Information, Dept. of Defence (Navy),
Canberra, ACT

Bahamas

Royal Bahamas Defence Force Headquarters, Nassau
Mr Frederick R. Sturrup, The Nassau Gardian Ltd, Nassau

Belgium

Mr Leo Van Ginderen, Antwerp

Brazil

Mr George A. Gratz, Rio de Janeiro
Ministério da Marinha, Servico de Documentacão Geralda Marinha, Rio de Janeiro
Capitafio-de-Fragata Mônica Hartz Oliviera Moitrel, Chefe do Dpto. De História Marítima e Naval

Canada

BGM Photo Centre Limited, Ottawa, Ontario
Canadian Forces Photographic Unit, Ottawa, Ontario
Mr R. Brown and Mr Paul Marsden:  National Archives of Canada, Ottawa, Ontario,
http://museum.gov.ns.ca/mikmaq/nac
Mr Malcolm B. Mackay, Halifax, Nova Scotia
Maritime Museum of the Atlantic, Halifax, Nova Scotia, http://museum.gov.ns.ca/mma
The Public Archives of Nova Scotia, Halifax, Nova Scotia, http://www.gov.ns.ca
Mr Cecil S. Woods, Burnaby, British Columbia

Chile

  Eduardo Rivera Silva, Vina del Mar

Denmark

  Mr J Balvsed, Copenhagen
  Kommandørkaptajn A. Holm, Marinens Bibliotek, Copenhagen
  http://forsvaret.dk/FAK/Fakulteter+og+Centre/Biblioteker/MAB
  Mr Anthony H. Standish, Odense, Fyn

Ecuador

  Veronica Ruiz, Defence Assistant, Ecuadorian Navy


Finland
  Captain Stig Lõthner, Helsinki

France

  B Castel, Editions Photographiques Marius Bar, Toulon, http://www.mariusbar-photo.com
  Alain Morgat, Isabel le Toquin, G Rueda, Chef du Service Historique de la Marine, Vincennes,
  http://www.servicehistorique.sga.defense.gouv.fr
  Mr P.J.F. Roullet, Paris

Germany

  Dr. jur. Achim Borchert, Hamburg
  Bundesarchiv-Militärarchiv, Frieburg, http://www.bundesarchiv.de/aufgaben
  Bundesarchiv, Militärisches Zwischenarchiv, Potsdam  http://www.bundesarchiv.de/aufgaben
  Prof Dr Jurgen Rowher and Mr Thomas Weis: Bibliothek Fur Zeitgeschichte, Stuttgart,
  http://www.ifz-muenchen.de

Greece

  Rear-Admiral (S) D. Yiakoumakis and Captain (S) P. Georgoulakis: Hellenic Navy,
  Navy History Service, Athens, http://www.hellenicnavy.gr/history_en.asp
  Lt. (E) S.J. Haratsis HN (Retd.), Athens

Israel

  Uri Dotan Bochner, Israeli Navy

Italy

  Ufficio Storico, Stato Maggiore Della Marina, Rome, http://www.leg.it/antiqua/sme_25

Japan

    Mr Y. Fukawa, Hiratsuka-Shi, Kangawa-Ken
    Mr Rinya Takayama, Hirosaki-shi, Aomori-ken

The Netherlands

    Dr P.C. van Royen, Koninklijke Marine, Afdeling, http://www.marine.nl
    Maritieme Historie van de Marinestaf, Gravenhage

Norway

    Mr Frank Abelsen, Greáker
    Ms Sissel Amundsen, the Norwegian Defence Museum
    Forsvarets Overkommando, Presse & Informasjonsavdelingen, Oslo, http://www.mil.no
    Mr Hans Petter Oset, Mvh, Marinemuseet, Tlf, http://www.fmu.mil.no/marine
    Mr Anthony I. Tandberg, Bønes

Philippines

    Lieutenant Commander Anselmo C. Cabingan, PN, The Naval Public Information Officer, Philippine Navy, Manila
    Lieutenant Pelipe Bautista, Philippine Navy

Poland

    Muzeum Marynarki Wojennej, Gydynia, http://www.mw.mil

Russia

    Rashid Alimov and Igor Kudrik:  Bellona, Saint Petersburg, http://www.bellona.no
    Andrei Lubchenko, http://rpf.ru/alf/galery/

South Africa

    Captain Richard Stephen, PRO of the SA Navy, Pretoria

Sweden

    Pär Frohnert, Stockholm
    Sjöhistoriska Muséet, Stockholm, http://www.sjohistoriska.se

Taiwan

    Mr Larry Lin

Turkey

    Devrim Yaylali, Turkish Navy Website http://www.turkishnavy.net/

U.S.A.

Mr Darryl L Baker, San Francisco, California
Mr John Barber, USMC/Combat Helicopter Association, http://www.popasmoke.com Weymouth, Massachussetts
Mr Melvin D. Barger, Toledo, Ohio
Mr Wally Beddoe, USMC/Combat Helicopter Association
Mr Wally Bengston, Dahlgren, Virginia
Mr Kermit H. Bonner, Fair Oaks, California
Mr Bob Daly, Milford, Connecticut
Mr David Dieter
Mr Vic DiMaio, Ridley Park, Pennsylvania
Mr Thoralf Doehring
Mr Gordon D. Dorian
Mr Edward R. Emanuel, Marysville, Washington
Mrs Thelma Gurske
Mr Allan Harris, International Naval Research Organisation, Toledo, Ohio, http://www.warship.org
Mr Zane Healy
Mr Albert B. Howe, Orinda, California
Mr Hugh Hudson
Mr John Hummel, Langhorne, Pennsylvania
Mr David Jourdan, President, Nauticos, http://www.nauticos.com
Captain Alex Andrew Kerr, USN (Retd.), Seattle, Washington
Commander George W. Kingston, USN (Retd.), Foley, Alabama
Mr Brian Kroenung
Mr Dick Lewis
Mr Bob Langrill
Mr Dennis McDowell, Middleton, Wisconsin
Mr R. Stan Melman, Honolulu, Hawaii
Janea Milburn and Mr Glenn Helm: US Navy Historical Centre, Washington Navy Yard, Washington DC, http://www.history.navy.mil
Mr Vernon J. Miller, Arbutus, Maryland
Mr Jim Myers, Cuyahoga Falls, Ohio
Office of the Chief of Information, Department of the Navy, Washington, DC
Office of The Judge Advocate General, Alexandria, Virginia
Mr John Payne, USNR (Retd.), Grand Rapids, Michigan
Mr Paul Perris
Mr Joe Radigan, Mr Gary Priolo and Mr Fabio Pena: Navsource, http://www.navsource.org
Mr Ernie Shea
Mr Paul Sherbo, San Mateo, California
Commander Harry E. Simms, USNR (Retd.), St. Micheals, Maryland
Mr Rick Szpyrka, Navy MSO Association, http://minesweep.org
Mr John Taflinger
Mr Paul Ulsan, Boynton Beach, Florida
United States Naval Institute, Annapolis, Maryland, http://www.usni.org
Kathy Vinson and Neva Lawson, The Defense Visual Information Center (DVIC), March Air Reserve Base, Moreno Valley, California, http://www.dodmedia.osd.mil
Mr Tom Warning, Williamston, Michigan
World War II Naval Journal, San Diego, California

Thanks are also due to the following staff of foreign embassies and high commissions in London:

Captain Izidério de Almeida Mendes, The Brazilian Naval Attaché
Rear Admiral Hugo Bruna, Head of the Naval Mission, Chilean Embassy
Mr Soteris Georgallis, Press Counsellor, The Cyprus High Commission
Miss Gunnarsdóttir, The Embassy of Iceland
Captain Sung Joong Kim, The Defence Attaché, The Embassy of the Republic of Korea

The acquisition of photographs has been a particularly arduous task and I have endeavoured to credit each photograph to the person or organisation to which the copyright belongs. For any errors in such credits, or for the omission of any individuals in my acknowledgements, I sincerely apologise in advance.


Malcolm Maclean
2008

# CONTENTS

# Chapter One

# THE CRUEL FORCE OF NATURE

The element in which all vessels have to operate is one of this planet's most powerful forces - the sea. It demands the respect of all seafarers, is untameable and cruel and notoriously unforgiving, especially when whipped up by high winds. Individually, the sea and the wind are formidable foes which, when acting in alliance are invincible. Once caught in a storm there is little that a vessel can do except attempt to ride it out or to seek shelter. The seabed and the coasts of every country and island are littered with the wrecks of vessels that have lost their duels with the legendary Neptune over the centuries.

Hurricanes generally form within 20 degrees of the equator, near the Inter-tropical Convergence Zone. Warm tropical air causes large volumes of water to be evaporated from the sea's surface, forming a layer of warm moist air. This warm air rises, forming a deep depression, until it meets with the layer of cooler, dry air at around 10,000 feet, where the water vapour condenses, adding massive clouds of rain to the spiralling winds being drawn into the depression. Wind speeds of up to 200 mph may be experienced in a hurricane, which can cover an area up to 300 miles across and travel at about 20 mph. At the heart of the storm lies a region of calm, low pressure air called the 'eye', which is ringed by howling winds and towering clouds. In the Caribbean Sea and the Atlantic Ocean, hurricanes usually form in early autumn.

Similar storms are known by different names according to the part of the world in which they occur. In the Pacific they are called typhoons, in the Arabian Sea, Bay of Bengal and South Indian Ocean they are known as tropical cyclones, whilst around the northern and western coasts of Australia they have been amusingly dubbed 'willy-willies'.

In the North Pacific, typhoons can occur as often as twenty times a year, with an occasional superimpose which can cover an area the size of continental USA. The southwest area of the North Pacific has the greatest number of typhoons, which often surpass the Atlantic hurricanes in intensity.

It was one of these typhoons that devastated Admiral William F. Halsey's Task Force 38 on 18 December 1944. Typhoon Cobra, as it became known, sent three of the fleet's destroyers - *USSs Hull* (DD-350), *Monoghan* (DD-354) and *Spence* (DD-512) - to the bottom of the Philippine Sea, with heavy loss of life amongst their crews. In total, 790 men lost their lives that night and, apart from the ill-fated destroyers, the fleet also suffered damage to twenty-eight ships and the loss of about 200 aircraft. The destroyers had capsized due to the effect of high beam winds and rolling beam seas. So many other ships were damaged that the task force was unable to participate in the attack on Luzon. A Court of Inquiry blamed Admiral H alsey for turning into the typhoon instead of heading away from it.

The disaster induced the US Navy to investigate the stability criteria of many of their newer destroyer classes, the results later being utilised by many western navies. Several US Navy destroyer designs had been plagued by stability problems, notably the Gridley, Somers and Farragut classes, two of the three ships lost in Typhoon Cobra belonging to the latter class. Early impressions of the *Farragut*s showed them to have excellent sea-keeping qualities, but their stability margin, like that of most warships during the war, was slowly eroded by the added

top-weight of increased anti-aircraft batteries and the addition of radar suites. Such additions also had the effect of increasing the longitudinal stresses imposed on the keel in a seaway, which in extreme cases could result in structural distress or even failure. One precaution quickly incorporated to prevent overloading of the ships was the painting of a 'Plimsoll Mark' at the waterline amidships on all destroyers built after the mid-1930s. The later *Fletcher* class also incorporated water-compensated wing fuel tanks that could be filled with seawater as the fuel was consumed, thereby maintaining a low centre of gravity.

The events of that fateful day in December 1944 were soon to be overshadowed by a series of typhoons the following year.

*USS LST-555 on the beach at Wakayama, Honshu Island, Japan. The ship was blown onto the beach by a typhoon during the night of 17-18 September 1945.*
*(US Navy/Melvin Barger)*

One of the US tank landing ships built in large numbers between 1942 and 1945, *LST-555* survived hostilities in the Far East theatre and was one of the large fleet of ships present in the Okinawa area when the Japanese surrendered in Tokyo Bay on 2 September 1945.

*LST-555s* first mission after the cessation of hostilities was to transport a cargo of aviation gasoline in drums to Kagoshima Bay, Kyushu, following which she returned to Okinawa. The ship was then ordered to proceed to Wakayama and then on to Nagasaki. However, a day after leaving Wakayama, the ship was ordered to reverse course due to the imminent approach of a ferocious typhoon which was already leaving a trail of destruction in it's path across the southern-most Japanese islands. Arriving back in the bay at Wakayama on the afternoon of 17 September, *LST-555* anchored and her crew began to fill her capacious ballast tanks to improve the vessel's stability.

The typhoon approached with terrifying speed and in just a couple of hours the barometric pressure dropped dramatically. By 2000 the ship, not yet fully ballasted and so still possessing a high freeboard, was being buffeted by the high winds and had begun to drag her anchor. Even with her engines running, it proved impossible to prevent the ship being blown towards the nearby beach. The LST's shallow draught and flat bottom made these vessels difficult to handle even in calm weather, but the heavy swell caused *LST-555s* propellers to momentarily come out of the water, which resulted in the engines over-speeding and tripping out.

Although the engine room crew were quick to restart the engines each time they shut down, and endeavoured to devise a way to bypass the tripping mechanism, the bridge crew were unable to prevent their ship drifting nearer and nearer to the shore. Just after midnight, *LST-555* was driven heavily aground on the rocky beach. The jagged rocks pierced the hull

in several places and Motor Machinist's Mate, 2nd Class, Melvin Barger recalls *"in the engine room, I could hear and feel the scraping against the rocks and water began to seep over the deck plates as the bilges filled up."* It was not long before the generators were flooded and all electrical power was lost and soon afterwards the machinery spaces were evacuated.

There was little the damage-control teams could do to stem the flow of water into the ship, so extensive was the perforation of the hull plating. The main concern of the ship's officers was that their vessel would slip stern-first off of her jagged perch and sink completely. However, this fear proved unfounded, as the ship was now lodged firmly on the rocks. Nevertheless, plans were made for evacuating some of the crew to the shore, only twenty yards away. The evacuation however was fraught with danger, and so the commanding officer, Lieutenant James I. Mooney, USN, decided that his crew, none of whom had been seriously injured, should remain on board until daylight.

By morning the storm was abating and a large crowd of Japanese civilians gathered on the hilltop above the stricken vessel. All but a skeleton crew were evacuated from the ship later that day, and the hull was surveyed to ascertain the extent of the damage. The rocks had penetrated almost every one of the ship's ballast tanks and her hull plating was badly distorted and holed. All main and auxiliary machinery, including main engines, generators and electrical equipment had been flooded. The damage was so extensive that the 1,600-ton ship vessel was deemed to be irreparable and attempts to salvage her proved futile. *LST-555* was decommissioned where she lay in January the following year and, on the 26th of that month, her hull temporarily patched, she was towed out to sea and sunk by gunfire from US Navy destroyers.

Ironically, several small craft at

Wakayama were berthed in a small bay which Japanese fishing vessels used to shelter safely from typhoons. Had the crew of *LST-555* known of this sheltered anchorage, it is possible that they could have saved their ship. Other ships, including a hospital ship, anchored in deeper water in the bay, managed to ride out the storm, but several PBY flying boats were sunk and a minesweeper was driven ashore. Two other LSTs were also driven aground, but they beached on soft sand and so were easily re-floated. The typhoon had also claimed three minesweepers, *YMS-98*, *YMS-341* and *YMS-472*, among its victims as it rampaged across Okinawa less than 48 hours before. Later, the storm raged on over the Japanese island of Kyushu sending at least a half-dozen ex-Japanese naval vessels to a watery grave.

This was the fiercest typhoon to strike elements of the US Fleet since Typhoon Cobra. However, much worse still was to come in October 1945 as yet another typhoon struck the Japanese islands.

The nucleus of a major storm front was first tracked on 3 October to the southeast of the Mariana Islands, and it quickly grew in ferocity. By the time it blasted past the island of Saipan two days later, it had grown into typhoon proportions and had gained the title of Typhoon Louise. Louise then banked south-westward towards the Philippine Islands, before again changing course to the north-west, with wind speeds increasing to up to 100 knots.

A US troop convoy, consisting of units of FastTransDiv 54 and comprising eight transports and the amphibious command ship *USS Estes* (AGC-12), escorted by the patrol ship *PC-555*, was only a day out of San Fernando in the Philippine Islands, destined for Jinsen (Inchon) in Korea, when they found themselves in the path of the typhoon. Whilst the *Estes*, displacing some 7,400-tons, and the large transports were able to ride the mountainous waves, the small patrol ship quickly found herself being overwhelmed and had to reduce speed, falling behind the convoy she was supposed to be escorting.

At only 173 feet in length and displacing a mere 280-tons, *PC-555* had never been intended as an ocean escort, and she was now bearing the full brunt of one of the most violent typhoons ever to strike the western Pacific. During the night of 6 October, the small submarine chaser began flooding through almost every hatch as the tiny hull was battered and twisted by the massive waves. So mountainous were the waves that, during the night, a lookout aboard one of the transports reported spotting a periscope, the sighting later being identified as the mast of the struggling *PC-555*, the only part of her visible above the huge waves.

The storm pulverised the convoy for three days before it finally overtook them and the prayers of the crew of *PC-555* were finally answered. With their hulls

*USS PC-555 - October 1945. Some of the damage to the ship's forward structure and 3.5-inch gun mount can be clearly seen.*

*(E. Emanuel)*

and superstructures battered and dented and with many of their upper-deck fitting wrenched off by the force of the waves, the ships of the convoy eventually reached their destination.

As the typhoon neared Formosa (now Taiwan), it encountered an area of high pressure that deflected it north-north-eastward, towards Japan. The typhoon was still gathering speed and ferocity with winds gusting up to 150 knots being recorded. With the course of the typhoon changing so often, typhoon warnings were being transmitted all over the area from Formosa northwards, and vessels were being redirected to supposed 'safe' anchorages with each update. By the time Louise slammed into the first of the Japanese islands on the night of Monday, 8 October, it's size and strength was terrifying and the sea had been whipped into a frenzy of gigantic waves. At Wakanura, the mountainous seas claimed their first victim that night, when US Navy minesweeper *YMS-478* was driven aground and wrecked. The battered hulk was later destroyed where it lay.

In Buckner Bay, off the city of Okinawa, a massive US Navy fleet of several hundred vessels was assembled, comprising almost every type of ship, including cruisers, escorts, mine-warfare vessels, amphibious ships and a vast array of auxiliary vessels. Operational considerations had deemed this site the most suitable for the gathering of this huge fleet - part of the enormous force mustered in the closing stages of the Pacific war for the invasion of the Japanese islands - despite the fact that ships anchored within the bay would be vulnerable to heavy weather.

As the eye of the typhoon passed over Okinawa, Louise turned north-eastward, but then circled back to blast the island a second time on Wednesday 10th. During these two days the storm had only abated slightly, the tail end of the typhoon having hardly departed before the full force of it struck the island again. Winds were still increasing, with 170-knot gusts now being recorded.

The fleet was devastated. There being no appreciable port facilities at Okinawa, most of the vessels were anchored or moored offshore in a position which offered little protection against the imminent onslaught of Louise. As ships were torn from their moorings or anchorages, many of them were smashed together. The patrol yacht *USS Southern Seas* (PY-32) was struck by several drifting vessels and sank, along with thirteen of her crew, as a result of the damage inflicted by the impacts. The barracks ship *USS Ocelot* (IX-110), flagship of Service Squadron 10, was struck by at least three other ships, one of whose depth charges detonated. There was a series of massive explosions and the 6,000-ton *Ocelot* was blown in two. Further indignity was forced upon the devastated *Ocelot* when the battle repair ship *USS Nestor* (ARB-6), a converted LST, slammed into her, the bow of the repair ship penetrating the *Ocelot's* hull. The *Nestor*, which had already been holed in a collision with the lighter *YF1079*, quickly flooded and settled in 24 feet of water.

One of the smaller vessels anchored in Buckner Bay on Tuesday 9th was the submarine chaser *PC-590*, a sister-ship to *PC-555*, which had already encountered the mounting ferocity of Louise. The wind had reached force 11 and the barometer had fallen to 978 millibars when, at about 1145, *PC-590s* anchor chain finally snapped under the tremendous strain being applied to it by the monstrous waves. The ship, her engines already running, was forced to get underway, although with her fuel supplies already depleted, her crew knew that they would have to operate the main engines sparingly if they were to maintain steerage way.

Their intention was to make for shelter to the leeward side of Tsuken Shima Island to the east, further out into the bay. Unfortunately, they found themselves

*Her structure bent and twisted, USS PC-590 lies aground on a reef off Tsuken Shima Island, along with other victims of Typhoon Louise.*

*(E. Emanuel)*

heading directly into the eye of the storm and the ship was making little headway. Evasion action had to be taken several times to avoid collisions with other ships either at anchor, underway or drifting.

With all the heavy manoeuvring, shutting down and re-starting engines to conserve fuel, and the inhalation of a large quantity of water through the engine exhausts, both main engines were overheating, and the commanding officer ordered that the assistance of a tug be urgently requested. Shortly afterwards, one of her engines now out of action, *PC-590* grounded on the reef off Tsuken Shima Island and another futile request for immediate assistance was transmitted. Amazingly, despite a ruptured fuel tank, the crew managed to quickly re-float their ship.

Nevertheless, the relief of the crew was to be short-lived as, just before 1600, the fuel supplies were finally exhausted and the ship found herself at the complete mercy of Louise's wrath. The wind was now reaching force 15-16, gusting to force 17, and the barometer had reached a low of 952 millibars. Soon afterwards the

little ship struck the reef again, tearing large gashes in the 173-feet long hull. The machinery spaces flooded rapidly and had to be evacuated, leaving the ship without electrical power.

Two other vessels, *LSM-143* and *YTM-146*, could also be seen aground on the same reef. Just when it appeared that matters couldn't get any worse, the crew of *PC-590* spotted a much larger vessel apparently being blown directly towards them. The crew made preparations to abandon their ship, but it soon became evident that the larger ship, now identified as the 5,800-ton repair ship *USS Mona Island* (ARG-9), was approaching for a rescue attempt.

The *Mona Island* had earlier been ripped from her moorings by immense waves and was now being driven towards the spot where *PC-590* was stranded. Her Executive Officer, Lt. Cdr. John Payne, USNR, recalled: *"We had very little clue as to where we were headed as the wind was blowing the wave crests into a misty fog and as the visibility was zero, I could only imagine where the harbor entrance was (the wind had long since carried*

*The rescue of PC-590's crew by USS Mona Island.*
*(J.B. Payne)*

away our radar antenna so we could only guess as the location of the harbor entrance). I had merely an instinct as to the location of the entrance and ordered the helmsman to steer in that direction but no sooner had we got part way into the turn, all motion stopped. It was just like we were on dry land which was partially the case. We had run hard aground on a reef! We tried backing off, but we were high and dry and firmly grounded.

As our eyes became more accustomed to the fog, the lookout reported a ship standing in our stern. We signalled over to her, "stand clear of us, we are aground". She replied "you are not telling us any-thing, we have been aground for hours". We discovered later that this vessel was one of the ships we had had to cast off when our cable parted and she, like us, was aground on a

nearby pinnacle and broken in two and apparently in imminent danger of foundering. This vessel was *PC-590*, whose crew's preparations for abandoning ship were not wasted as her hull had now begun to buckle and crack as she was tossed up and down on the rocky pinnacle. In an amazing feat of seamanship, the crew of the *Mona Island* passed a line to

*The barograph reading from USS Mona Island, indicating a low of 952 millibars.*
*(J.B. Payne)*

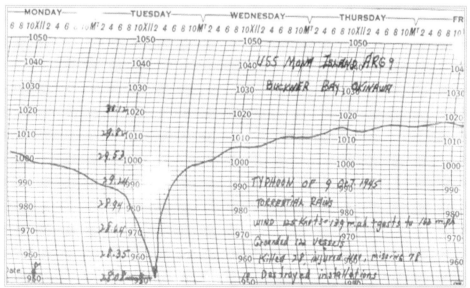

the *PC-590* which, with a great deal of daring on behalf of the submarine chaser's crew, was secured to the funnel. A breeches buoy was set up and, over the next couple of hours, with waves crashing over the mangled superstructure of the ship, the entire crew were hauled aboard Mona Island.

*PC-590* finally split in two amidships, the stern half settling on the bottom of the reef and the forward half listing to an obscene angle at about 2015, almost as the feet of the last man, the Commanding Officer, left the ship. The fact that there was no loss of life amongst the ill-fated *PC-590's* 51-man crew can only be attributed to the determination and bravery of her crew and to the seamanship skills of the crew of *USS Mona Island*.

Whilst this drama was unfolding, the crew of another small patrol ship anchored nearby were fighting to save their ship from a similar fate. Like *PC-590*, the strain on *PGM-27's* anchor chain had been steadily increasing and at about 1300, the Commanding Officer ordered the craft's main engines started and

engaged. Despite careful manoeuvring, the strain on the anchor chain increased and at about 1535 it finally parted and the ship momentarily swung beam-on to the seas, before the crew managed to steer the bow into the sea and wind.

For the next three hours, *PGM-27* struggled to make headway and, her radar confused by the 30-foot waves with visibility almost zero the ship became increasing difficult to handle. The only thing visible was the port running light of a ship, but it soon became evident that this ship was aground. Shortly after, at 1845, *PGM-27* was driven on to the beach. Main engines were shut down and the Commanding Officer ordered the running lights turned off and break-down lights switched on. Damage control checks determined that the ship's hull was intact and watertight and that there were no casualties, so no attempt was made to abandon ship. For the moment, the crew of the beleaguered *PGM-27* were relatively safe.

However, a drifting pontoon barge struck another PC-461-class submarine chaser, *PC-1126*, anchored nearby. With a large hole punched in the starboard side of the hull, *PC-1126's* machinery room began flooding and the engines had to be shut down. Both anchors were slipped and the ship drifted towards the beach. At 2012, *PC-1126* slammed into the starboard quarter of *PGM-27*, wrecking the latter ship's rudders and propeller shafts. However, of the two ships, *PGM-27* remained the most watertight and so the 72-man crew of *PC-1126* evacuated to *PGM-27*, where they remained to ride out the rest of the storm.

Only a thousand yards to the southwest of Tsuken Shima, the destroyer-minesweeper *USS Southard* (DMS-10) was driven onto a reef and was wrecked, whilst the high-speed transport *USS Greene* (APD-36) was driven aground at nearby Kutaka.

All around the bay, other vessels were being torn from their moorings and either

*USS PC-1126 and USS PGM-27 were beached in a storm off Okinawa. (Bob Daly/Emil Hale)*

driven aground or foundering in the mountainous seas. The salvage ship *USS Extricate* (ARS-16), who's crew had fought so valiantly to assist crippled vessels during the September typhoons, was finally driven ashore herself, her wooden hull ripped open by the force of the grounding. At 1518 on the afternoon of the 9th, the 9,600-ton tanker *USS Vandalia* (IX-191) was driven aground about 200 yards from the Miyegusuku Lighthouse on Naha Island. The crew stayed with their ship overnight and were finally rescued at 0740 the following morning.

The Apache-class tug *USS Wateree* (ATF-117) had arrived in Buckner Bay earlier that afternoon with a Mission-class tanker under tow. Having assisted the disabled tanker to lay out her two anchors, *Wateree* herself went to anchor, keeping her diesel-electric motor running in order to maintain some headway and so reduce the strain on the chains. As huge waves battered the 1,200-ton tug, carrying away both of her boats and most of her life rafts, the bridge watchkeepers, all dressed in life jackets and flotation belts, peered through the almost impenetrable sheets of rain.

With visibility reduced to almost zero, Quartermaster 2nd Class Albert Howe, on the tug's bridge, suddenly saw the bow of the tanker, who's anchor chains had apparently snapped under the horrendous strain of the massive waves, bearing down on them. It was almost impossible to take evasive action and the tanker struck *Wateree* port side amidships, the force of the collision holing her engine room and causing both of her anchor cables to part.

As the wind and waves carried the tanker towards a nearby beach at an astounding speed of about 10-12 knots, *Wateree's* engine room was rapidly flooding, the loss of her main engine leaving her totally helpless. At 1528, she herself grounded on a reef, half a mile from shore, the jagged coral ripping a wide gash along the vessel's starboard side. Albert Howe recalls: *"All power was gone and she was going down fast. We hoped she would hang up on the reef but she didn't - she just kept on going down. The guys started riding the breakers like a bunch of Southern California beach bums - across the reef and to shore. The waves were breaking clear over the top of the bridge. I picked a wave and took a ride over the reef."*

*Wateree's* crew had been ordered to abandon ship at 1555, the ill-fated vessel sinking some 15 minutes later in water eight fathoms deep, taking with her the Commanding Officer, Executive Officer and six of the crew.

*USS Vandalia driven aground and sinking at Okinawa.*
*(G.D. Dorian)*

The crew of the Alianthus-class netlayer *USS Snowbell* (AN-52) were extremely lucky to escape with their lives when they were trapped aboard their ship after it was driven aground at about 1630 that afternoon. Cold and wet, they were eventually rescued the following morning. Only thirty minutes after the *Snowbell* grounded, the Salem-class minelayer *USS Weehawken* (CM-12) was also driven onto rocks and later broke up.

The fleet assembled in Buckner Bay included a large number of amphibious craft and landing ships. *LSM-15*'s anchor cable parted during the afternoon and the ship was driven onto a nearby reef, the jagged pinnacles ripping open the vessel's hull and causing rapid and extensive flooding. The waves continued to pound the stricken ship and she was later blown off of the reef, the crew quickly abandoning her as she sank at 2100 outside the channel entrance. Over twenty of *LSM-15*'s sister-ships were also driven aground, with *LSM-137* and *LSM-361* subsequently being declared total losses.

In all, over a dozen ships were sunk, whilst over 200 more had been driven aground and many others were seriously damaged. Those ships sunk or totally destroyed at Okinawa included two destroyers, six amphibious landing ships, sixteen patrol vessels, ten mine-warfare vessels and over a dozen auxiliaries and army freighters. The US Coast Guard lost the cutters *CG-83301* and *CG-83306*, and several Liberty ships were also wrecked or sunk. Considering the number of ships lost and the carnage caused across the island, casualties, although high with 83 men killed or missing and over 400 injured, could have been much worse.

Typhoon Louise had not yet fully vented her wrath however, and turned her attention towards Nagasaki, her strength slowly waning as she blasted a path over the island of Shikoku and then over the mainland of Honshu on 11 October, damaging several vessels of the now demobilised Japanese Fleet en route, before running into cold air and petering out over the Sea of Japan.

*LSM-137 beached in Buckner Bay, 9 October 1945.*

*(P. Ulsan)*

*Stranded vessels seen in Buckner Bay, Okinawa on 10 October 1945.*
*(P. Ulsan)*

Over the following weeks, a massive salvage and rescue operation was undertaken. The exhaustive USAF effort to re-supply the stranded garrison was thwarted by the destruction caused at the naval air base on Okinawa, and feverish work was required to clear and repair the runways and buildings. By mid-November, almost eighty ships had been re-floated and over a hundred more were under repair. However, many vessels were wrecked completely or declared as constructive total losses and were either destroyed by explosives to prevent them becoming navigational hazards, scrapped where they lay or were towed out to sea and either scuttled or sunk by gunfire.

A full and accurate list of the vessels wrecked is difficult to ascertain as some of the vessels scuttled or scrapped were probably already carrying their war scars or had reached their fatigue life and so were destined to be disposed of anyway. That said, this remains the worst peace-time disaster, in terms of material loss, of the post-war era.

There are many reasons why this storm proved so devastating. Firstly, it has to be appreciated that Louise was one of the fiercest typhoons to strike the area this century, classed by some as a "super-typhoon". It could not have struck at a worse time. Most of the ships of the massive fleet gathered in Buckner Bay had been built during the war years using mass production techniques and had been hard worked over the previous four years. The fatigue lives of their hulls had in many cases already been reached or surpassed. Added to this, many of the ships were unmanned or had only skeleton crews aboard, thousands of servicemen having already been demobilised and ferried back to the USA as part of Operation Magic Carpet.

Even whilst the wreckage of Typhoon Louise was being cleared, another typhoon struck the Okinawa area and claimed a further US Navy victim. During the early hours of 1 December 1945, *LST-767* was beached at Kana Wan, Okinawa, when she was torn from her moorings by crashing waves and high winds. Dawn found the 2366-ton landing ship broached on the rocky shore, her hull ripped open and most of the underwater compartments flooded. During the day the crew escaped ashore via a breeches buoy, whilst the engineers surveyed the damage. Salvage was likely to take several months, whilst damage to the hull was mounting with each passing day. The ship was stripped of any valuable material and equipment and de-commissioned where she lay in March 1946, the hulk being scrapped the following year.

The vessels of the defeated Japanese Navy also suffered a great many casualties to storms in the first year or two following the cessation of hostilities. Apart from the fact that almost all of their naval vessels had suffered some form of damage in the face of the overwhelming might of the allied war machine, their war-built vessels had born the brunt of the hardships of the war years.

The increasing scarcity of high quality materials to sustain their massive shipbuilding programme resulted in inferior materials being used instead, whilst the use of electric arc welding to speed the building process was hampered by the loss of much of their skilled labour force as almost every able-bodied Japanese male had been shipped to the front line.

Post-war, a large number of Japanese vessels were pressed into service with the allied minesweeping service to clear the extensive minefields laid around the Japanese islands. Due to the complete destruction of the Japanese engineering and shipbuilding industries, as well as the urgency of the task, many of these vessels received little or no repairs or maintenance to their hulls or machinery. In such circumstances some losses were almost inevitable. Apart from the increasing number of ships that simply sank at their moorings in their neglected state, several were lost at sea, incurring a significant loss of life amongst their crews. Notable amongst these was the loss on 17 November of the Natsushima-class ex-minelayer *Ashizaki* after being driven aground in a storm at Hayakawa. Her sister ship, *Kurosaki*, suffered a similar fate off Hachinohe the following day, later breaking up and becoming a total loss. In April of the following year the 240-ton patrol ship *Pa.No.176* was driven aground and wrecked in rough weather near Yoshimi.

As the veil of peace settled over the western Pacific, the allies returned to many of their former colonies, and long-established naval bases were rebuilt. At Hong Kong, the River-class frigate *HMS Aire* (K262) was employed as the colony's guardship, being temporarily named *HMS Tamar* from March 1946, the name held by the colony's shore establishment for many years before the Japanese invasion of 1942. In December 1946 the frigate, having reverted to her original name of *HMS Aire*, departed from Hong Kong with only a reduced steaming watch on board and set course for Singapore where she was to be paid off for scrapping.

Whilst transiting the South China Sea the frigate was caught in a fierce typhoon. The 1,400-ton ship was tossed around in the tempestuous seas, the strong stern tide causing her to be blown 30 miles off her intended course. Just before 0500 on 20

*Even as the wrecage from Typhoon Louise was being cleared LST-767 found herself beached when another typhoon hit the area on 1 December. (U.S. Naval Historical Centre)*

*The River-class frigate HMS Aire at anchor. The ship was driven aground and wrecked on Bombay Reef in December 1946.*
*(Neil Ebbutt)*

December the ship was driven aground on Bombay Reef, a treacherous atoll south of Hainan. The impact caused the generators to fail and knocked off all power. The ship flooded rapidly in several compartments, including the engine room.

With her radio out of action, there was no way of contacting Singapore or Hong Kong. Having lain at Hong Kong in a reduced state for several months, much of her equipment had been neglected and it was found that all of the life belts were in a perished state. Following the initial flurry of damage control activity there was little the crew could do in the darkness except huddle together and ponder their fate. Leading Stoker Mechanic Denis Docherty, who had just finished his watch in the engine-room when the ship struck the reef, remembers that, after the initial panic, the crew settled down and started a sing-song to while away the hours and to keep up their morale.

When daylight broke the tide had receded, leaving *Aire* high and dry. An inspection revealed that the ship was lodged on the reef with her port propeller shaft 'A' bracket embedded in the coral, and that

she was holed in seven compartments. In the engine room, fuel and oil had escaped into the bilges and a fire had started. With no power to supply the fire pumps, the fire-fighting effort was limited to the use of buckets, mess tins and pans to provide water to quench the flames. It was over 24 hours before the fire was finally extinguished.

When the danger of the fire was finally overcome, the Commanding Officer mustered his exhausted crew on the upper deck and briefed them on their situation. Being 30 miles off the nearest shipping lane, with no radio and little food or water on board and even the rum ration exhausted, their chances of rescue were slim. A service was held and the Lord's Prayer recited, and in the tradition of the Navy, their souls were commended to the deep. A keen watch on the horizon resulted in several false and wishful sightings of 'ships', but as the days passed hope faded and morale began to wane. Their position was becoming more perilous as the tides rose and fell, smashing and rocking the ship deeper into the coral.

However, fate was to take a hand and, at

about 1620 on 23 December, the depot ship *HMS Bonaventure* (F139), herself blown off course by the tail end of the typhoon, spotted what was at first thought to be a destroyer under way on the horizon. The depot ship attempted to contact the vessel by radio and signal lamp, but as *Aire*'s radio was smashed and she was not carrying signal gear, or a rating trained in this skill, they were unable to reply. The lack of response puzzled the crew of *Bonaventure* and they decided to close the contact to investigate. It was soon realised that, by pure chance, they had stumbled across the stricken *HMS Aire*.

The *Aire* could not be reached from the seaward side of the reef, which appeared as a solid line of white surf breaking over the submerged coral. The stranded ship could be seen, waves breaking over it, some eight miles beyond the seemingly impenetrable barrier. As night was closing in, and the weather was still stormy, the Commanding Officer of *Bonaventure*, Captain W.R Fell, decided to stand by at a safe distance and prepare a plan for a rescue attempt at dawn.

The following morning, Christmas Eve, the whole southern extent of the reef was surveyed for an entry point into the lagoon. At the south-western tip a small entrance, no more than a few feet deep, was spotted which would be just passable for a small motor launch.

Under the command of Commander G. Arbuthnot, one of *Bonaventure*'s 32 ft cutters inched its way through the entrance. This required a superb act of seamanship due to the turbulence of the water being ripped up by the breaking surf and the strong tidal currents prevailing. Added to this, jagged rocks threatened to rip the bottom out of the launch should the crew drop their guard for a moment. Once inside the lagoon, the sheltered water was flat calm and crystal clear, and the launch began its eight-mile transit towards the *Aire*. The mother ship followed its course on the seaward side of the reef, monitoring its progress.

When the cutter reached *Aire*, the members of the shipwrecked crew were able to wade out across the coral and climb aboard. One at a time, 51 crew and the

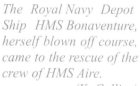

*The Royal Navy Depot Ship HMS Bonaventure, herself blown off course, came to the rescue of the crew of HMS Aire.*
*(K. Collins)*

ship's dog reached the launch before it began its long haul back through the lagoon, out through the reef and eventually to the safe haven of *Bonaventure*. A second trip saw the rest of the survivors picked up. Fortunately there were no serious casualties and all 85 crew were landed safely in Singapore a few days later.

Had the *Bonaventure* not happened upon the scene, or had she passed the stricken vessel in the dark, it is probable that the entire crew of *HMS Aire* would have perished through starvation or drowning over the next few days.

Before leaving the area, marker buoys were laid by *HMS Bonaventure* to mark the entrance of the channel into the lagoon in case of possible future salvage attempts. However, it is likely that Chinese pirates, eavesdropping on radio traffic, lay in wait until the *Bonaventure* had departed before scrambling aboard the wreck and stripping it of all that may have been valuable. The wreck was never recovered and it eventually disintegrated where it lay.

*HMS Aire* was not the only British vessel lost in the South China Sea in December 1946. On the 21st, the day after *Aire* struck a reef south of Hainan, the naval Envoy-class tug *Enticer* (W166) was lost in the same storm whilst endeavouring to take over the tow, from the ocean salvage vessel *HMS King Salvor* (W191), of the Swedish merchant ship *ss Rosebank*, in difficulties in the heavy seas. The tug's civilian master and chief engineer were drowned.

The alarming regularity with which these powerful typhoons strike the western Pacific has ensured a steady stream of victims amongst the navies operating in the area. On 15 October 1951, the United Nations troopship *ss Kongo Maru* was caught in a typhoon and wrecked off southern Japan.

Some navies have appeared to suffer a number of warship casualties out of all proportion to the size of the force. For

example, the Philippine Navy has lost several patrol vessels and at least two frigates in typhoons.

The Bostwick-class frigate *USS Bowers* (APD-40) was transferred to the Philippine Navy in April 1961 and was taken in hand at Bataan for conversion to a command ship. The ship, renamed *RPS Rajah Soliman* (D66), was berthed at the dockyard in June 1962 when yet another typhoon struck the area. The ship was battered against the wharf, holing her hull in several places and soon afterwards she capsized and sank. Raised in December 1964, *Rajah Soliman* was deemed to be beyond repair and was stricken.

This was not to be the only frigate lost by the Philippine Navy to the awesome power of a typhoon. On 20 September 1981 the 1,300-ton *RPS Datu Kalatiaw* (PS76) was driven aground and capsized

*Survivors from HMS Aire are brought alongside Bonaventure after their rescue.*

*(K. Collins)*

*The Philippino warship RPS Datu Kalantiaw lies on her port side having been driven aground.*
*(US DoD, DVIC)*

near Calayan Island, 340 miles south of Manila, by 127 mph winds and mountainous seas whipped up by Typhoon Clara. A massive rescue operation was launched by units of the Philippine and US Navies, but the only men of the 97 crew to survive were the 18 rescued by helicopters from the ammunition ship *USS Mount Hood* (AE-29).

On 11 November 1962, only five months after the loss of *Rajah Soliman*, the ex-US PC-461 class submarine chaser *RPS Negros Oriental* (C26) was berthed alongside a former sister-ship, the South Korean Navy patrol ship *ROKN Han Ra San* (PC705), in the inner harbour at Guam when Typhoon Karen struck. Both vessels were sunk and nine other harbour craft were driven aground. Winds gusting up to 180 knots caused complete devastation across the island.

The salvage operation was the most extensive conducted by the US Navy since the end of the Second World War. First priority went to refloating the service craft, most of which were beached around the inner harbour. The two patrol craft, required greater resources as they were

sunk in 35 feet of water alongside the ship repair facility, where they had been undergoing refits. The US Navy salvage ships *Deliver* (ARS-23), *Bolster* (ARS-38) and *Reclaimer* (ARS-42) arrived at Guam over the next three weeks. Using the salvage ships and a floating crane, the *Han Ra San* and *Negros Oriental* were raised during December. Following a period as salvage training hulks, both were sold for scrapping in 1963 and 1964.

More recently, another *PC-461* class patrol vessel, the *RPS Nueva Viscaya* (PS80), sank at Cebu in the Philippines during a typhoon in March 1993.

All of these Philippine vessels were ex-US Navy ships of World War Two vintage, whose hull states were, at best, questionable. The Philippine Navy has been known to buy surplus vessels from other navies, notably Japan and South Vietnam, and then refit and modernise them for further service. Whilst providing them with vessels at a very affordable price, this practice has resulted in their naval personnel operating obsolete ships that may have been laid up and neglected, having had no maintenance carried out on them, for some considerable time. In the case of ex-South Vietnamese vessels, they may never have been dry-docked for hull survey since the day they had been acquired from the US Navy and, in the case of those handed over to the Philippines in 1975-76, may have received significant battle damage during the Vietnam War.

Several vessels of the Philippines Navy have, in fact, changed hands more times than the average motorcar. An example of this is the US Navy landing ship *LSSL-9*, which was completed in 1944 and was transferred to France in 1951 as *FS Hallabarde* (L9023). The ship was sold to Japan five years later and returned to the USA in 1964. The following year the ship was resold to South Vietnam for spares to support their other ex-US Navy landing ships, but was subsequently overhauled and operated as *Doan Ngoc Tang*. In 1975 the ship was bought by the Philippines for spares, but was again overhauled and returned to service, operating as *RPS La Union* (LF50) until finally scrapped in the late 1980s!

The seaworthiness of vessels such as this must be in some doubt, especially when confronted with the violence of a full-blown typhoon.

Nevertheless, as of 2007 there is still a large, though steadily decreasing, number of Second World War vintage warships and auxiliaries, mostly of US origin, in service with many navies around the world. It has to be said that, apart from those that foundered in the immediate post-war years after being laid up without preservation, vessels that have been in constant operation have generally given reliable service. Their robust construction and simple propulsion plants have allowed their effective operation by many of the less technologically advanced navies. However, when neglected or poorly maintained, the age of these ships makes them increasingly more expensive to operate, and can quickly lead to a ship that is no longer seaworthy or structurally sound.

Other vessels of western Pacific navies have also succumbed to typhoons. On 23 January 1952 the South Korean landing ship *Andong* (LST803) was driven aground and wrecked during a typhoon.

The Japanese Kagero-class destroyer *Yukikaze* was ceded to China on 6 July 1947 in a disarmed state and renamed *Tan Yang*. After the Republic of China claimed independence in 1949, the vessel became part of the Taiwanese Navy and was rearmed to a near-original configuration during a major refit that began in 1951, becoming Taiwan's largest operational warship. Tragically, *Tan Yang* was driven around in a typhoon in May 1970

*The South Korean patrol boat RoKN Han Ra San is lifted by the USN salvage ships Deliver, Bolster and Reclaimer.*

*(USN/Bob Daly)*

and, partly due to her age, was written off and scrapped.

The Vietnam War saw a large proportion of the US Pacific Fleet deployed in the South China Sea. Although the US Navy suffered little at the hands of the North Vietnamese, the sea was to take its toll. Between November 1966 and October 1967 three minor patrol craft were sunk in heavy weather off South Vietnam. The most significant weather related loss however, occurred on New Years Day 1967.

In 1966 the LST511-1152 class vessel *USS Mahnomen County* (LST-912) was attached to Landing Ship Squadron 2 in the western Pacific, employed mainly in the task of supplying cargo to US forces engaged in the Vietnam War. On 30 December of that year the ship, along with her sister ship *USS New London County* (LST-1066), dropped anchor off Chu Lai, Republic of Vietnam, to await orders to proceed to the LST ramp inside the harbour and deposit their cargoes.

Having on previous occasions encountered difficulties in finding good holding ground whilst anchoring off the inlet, the Commanding Officer of *Mahnomen County*, Lieutenant W. S. Arbuckle, decided on this occasion to anchor in eight fathoms of water 1,100 yards from the shoreline, somewhat closer than usual.

*New London County* was anchored some 700 yards east and to seaward of *Mahnomen County* in about nine fathoms of water. A modified steaming watch was set, including a skeleton engine room watch and upperdeck sentries. Although a rating was detailed as anchor watch, he had not been properly instructed regarding this duty and was in effect just an augmentation of the anti-hostile swimmer watch.

Over the next two days the weather slowly deteriorated. By 1800 on New Year's Eve, the wind had risen to nearly 30 knots, gusting inshore from an easterly/north-easterly direction, with waves of 12-14 feet high and continuous heavy rain and fog, which reduced visibility considerably. Weather reports transmitted on 4445kHz had earlier warned of the approach of the weakening tropical storm Pamela, which was centred some 180 miles to the south.

Although the warnings were heard aboard *Mahnomen County*, her officers failed to make use of the ship's SPS-21D radar to assist in monitoring their ship's position, relying instead on visual bearings taken on three lights ashore every thirty minutes. Only one of these lights, atop a dome, was shown on the charts being used by the ship, the other two being unidentified. At 0030 on the morning of 1 January the Officer of the Deck (OOD), Lieutenant Junior Grade T.J. Fitzgerald, began to suspect that the ship's position had changed. Bearings of two of the lights had altered significantly, one by 22-degrees, the other by 44-degrees.

Failing to appreciate the significance of this, he did not inform his superiors. Even when the Executive/Navigating Officer, Lieutenant Junior Grade J.F.W. Neal, visited the bridge fifteen minutes later, Lt. Fitzgerald didn't bring the matter to his attention.

Surprisingly, Lt. Neal, having taken his own set of bearings from lights pointed out to him by the OOD, himself failed to check them against the ship's previous position on the chart, so further adding to the OOD's uncertainty. Lt. Neal then informed the Commanding Officer that the ship's position was satisfactory. It is probable that the ship actually started dragging her anchor shortly before 0030, although nothing untoward was noted by the inexperienced rating sheltering from the weather on the forecastle.

At 0050, *New London County* requested that *Mahnomen County* energise her radar and provide her with radar ranges from the shore. Although the reason for this request was not given at the time, the OOD aboard *New London County* had already suspected that his ship was dragging her anchor.

When, at 0100, Lt. Fitzgerald took another set of bearings, he was horrified to find that one of them differed by 100-degrees from the readings taken thirty minutes earlier. At about the same time, the radar operator, having energised his equipment to provide readings requested by the *New London County*, reported that he estimated the beach to be only 400-500 yards away!

Meanwhile, the *New London County* was nearly astern of the *Mahnomen County* and was less than 100 yards from the surf line. However, the *New London County's* OOD had already alerted his Commanding Officer of the danger and had got his ship's engines started, with the result that the *New London County* was already under way and, at 0101, began using her engines and rudder to turn to starboard and to seaward.

At 0103, the quartermaster on the bridge of *Mahnomen County* reported that he had sighted the surf line, at which time the OOD decided to alert his superiors and order starting of the main engines. Two minutes later, the bow sentry reported that he thought he had heard the anchor chain parting. The Commanding Officer dashed to the forecastle to check the anchor, whilst the Executive Officer proceeded to the bridge, where he ordered that the word be passed to 'Set the Special Sea and Anchor Detail'.

Arriving on the bridge a couple of minutes later the Commanding Officer assumed the 'conn' and immediately ordering engine and rudder movements in an attempt to extricate his ship from what was now an almost impossible situation. *Mahnomen County* was, by this time, only 400 yards from, and parallel to, the surf line. Without the aid of it's anchor to pull the bow round, the condemned ship continued to be driven beam-on towards the shore by the offshore winds until, at 0110, she struck the rocks.

No attempt was made to let go the stern

*The landing ship USS Mahnomen County (LST-912) after being driven aground and wrecked off Chu Lai, Republic of Vietnam, in the early hours of 1 January 1967. The ship eventually broke in two and was abandoned.*

*(US Navy)*

anchor, although it is doubtful if, at this late stage, such an action would have had any appreciable effect. Lt. Arbuckle continued to attempt to break his ship free of the rocks, but soon realised that she was hard aground and at 0117 he ordered 'stop' on main engines and that a distress call and request for assistance be transmitted.

Meanwhile, at 0111, *New London County's* anchor chain had also parted. However, by this time the Commanding Officer had managed to heave in on the chain and manoeuvre his ship so that her bow was facing away from the shore and she was soon heading to seaward.

At daylight it could be seen that *Mahnomen County* was hard aground between the shoreline and an area of offshore rocks, with further rocks hemming the ship in ahead and astern. Her main engine room, auxiliary engine room, pump room and shaft passageways were all flooding, which had necessitated the shutting down of the ship's generators, leaving her without power to supply pumps. Although power cables were supplied from shore that afternoon, the continuous pounding of the ship against the rocks by the waves was resulting in further compartments and tanks being opened to the sea with each passing hour.

Over the coming weeks it proved impossible to re-float her as she was further battered against the rocks and eventually her hull was snapped in two by the force of the sea's onslaught. The salvage operation was called off on 31 January and the ship abandoned in position 15° 28'30"N, 108° 42'25"E.

The salvage operation on *Mahnomen County* was to be one of the first occasions that polyurethane foam was used, the expanding 'Styrofoam' being injected into the ship's void spaces and ballast tanks to assist in expelling water from the flooded compartments. However, the use of the foam under water caused fluorocarbon and $CO_2$ gases to form on the surface of the water, resulting in three ratings being overcome by the toxic fumes, one fatally.

These fluorocarbon gases, Freon 11 (fluorotrichloromethane), Freon 12 (dichlorodifluoromethane) and $CO_2$ were classed as non-toxic substances unless present in the atmosphere in concentrations greater than 1%. Such a condition would have been found in the enclosed compartments aboard *Mahnomen County* in which the foam was used. Inhalation of the gases causes narcosis followed by unconsciousness. Adequate ventilation of the compartment prior to entry by the ratings was hampered by the lack of power aboard the vessel and by the construction of the tank deck.

The Formal Board of Investigation into the grounding and loss of *USS Mahnomen County*, convened by Commander Service Group Three at Sasebo on 6 February 1967, found that the Officer of the Deck was negligent in that he failed to take the appropriate action when he first suspected that the position of his ship was changing and failed to notify his superiors. The Executive Officer was also found negligent in that he failed to check the bearings that he took at about 2345 and that he failed to ensure the use of radar to check the ship's position.

The Commanding Officer was found negligent in that he failed to ensure the use of radar and that he failed to check his ship's position as the weather worsened. The Board also found that Lt(JG) Fitzgerald was not professionally competent to hold the post of Officer of the Deck and that the two senior officers were negligent by having so qualified him.

All three officers were court martialed. Lt. Fitzgerald was found guilty, through negligence, of hazarding his vessel, for which he was reprimanded, fined and ordered to lose seniority points. Lt. Neal was found guilty of dereliction of duty and was admonished, fined and ordered to lose seniority points, while Lt. Arbuckle

*An aerial view of the forward section of the wreck of the landing ship USS Mahnomen County (LST-912), seen several months after the ship was driven aground off Chu Lai, Republic of Vietnam, in the early hours of 1 January 1967. The ship broke in two and was abandoned.*

*(Tom Warning)*

was convicted of dereliction of duty which led to the loss of his ship, was reprimanded and ordered to lose seniority points.

When anchoring adjacent to a lee shore, a hazardous undertaking even in calm conditions, the minimum requirements are that at least one main engine be available for immediate use with a skeleton steaming watch closed up. Although the senior officers of USS Mahnomen County had, quite correctly, taken these prudent precautions, the delegation of the posts of OOD and the anchor watch to junior and inexperienced personnel, as well as the failure to use radar to supplement visual bearings, were entirely avoidable mistakes that contributed to the loss of the ship. Complacency had resulted in the sea snatching another unsuspecting vessel from the control of its crew.

Examination of the anchor chains of both LSTs revealed that a large proportion of the links were worn beyond the tolerance established by the NAVSHIPS Technical Manual. The environment in which anchor chains are used and stowed results in a natural tendency for them to

erode and corrode and the importance of their regular survey for signs of cracking and elongation, as well as measurement of the percentage of wear on each link, cannot be overemphasised.

In the case of USSs Mahnomen County and New London County, already weakened chains were subjected to excessive strain in the prevailing weather conditions, with the result that they parted. That the anchor chains of both vessels parted within a few minutes of each other suggests that an unusually large swell or wave had bodily lifted the ships and provided the additional breaking strain. Failure by the crew of USS Mahnomen County to recognise the signs of the anchor dragging and the subsequent parting of the chain resulted in their vessel being driven against the rocks, whilst USS New London County was successfully extricated from a similar fate.

The US Navy was to suffer a further storm related loss at Okinawa when, two days before Christmas 1968, the landing ship LST-600 was critically damaged after being driven aground in tempestuous seas.

Less than three years later, on the night

of 16/17 August 1971, the 8,000-dwt Denebola-class stores ship *Regulus* (AF-57) grounded on Kau Yi Chau Island near Hong Kong during Typhoon Rose. Despite attempts to salvage the ship, severe damage to the vessel's hull forced the operation to be abandoned and she was written off as a constructive total loss. The wreck was later cut in three and the fore and aft sections re-floated and towed to Junk Bak for scrapping, whilst the sunken midship section was broken up where it lay. Although only commissioned in February 1954, *Regulus* had in fact been launched almost ten years earlier as the *Escanaba Victory*, but was laid up post-war in an incomplete state. The fact, therefore, that both *LST-600* and *Regulus* were of World War Two vintage probably contributed to the decision to dispose of them.

In the southern Pacific such violent storms are known as tropical cyclones. These tempests are normally born within about 7-degrees of the Equator, but never in its immediate vicinity, and consist of small depressions, circulating under the influence of the Earth's rotation in a clockwise direction in the northern hemisphere and anti-clockwise in the southern.

Tropical cyclones, which are often referred to as the most deadly storms on earth, are most frequent and powerful in the South Pacific and South Indian Ocean, especially between June and mid-November in the northern hemisphere, mid December to early May in the southern. Their characteristics include high winds and mountainous seas, with visibility often reduced by torrential rain and spray. In the Arabian Sea they are most frequent at the change of the monsoon, usually in May-June and October-November, whilst in the Indian Ocean they normally occur in late spring and early autumn approximately a half-dozen times per year.

On 21 December 1974, weather satellite pictures indicated that a large mass of clouds in the Arafura Sea, between New Guinea and northern Australia, had taken on the ominous circular form of a developing tropical cyclone. Over the next three days the storm intensified and travelled slowly and steadily southwest over open water toward the Indian Ocean, forecasters predicting that it would pass harmlessly sixty miles offshore.

However, on 24 December Cyclone Tracy, as it was named, suddenly intensified and changed course to the southeast, slamming into the city of Darwin at 0400 on Christmas morning. The 150 mph winds caused devastation in the city and killed fifty people.

In the harbour, *HMAS Arrow* (P88), an Attack-class patrol boat of 146-tons full load displacement, struggled for four hours to reach her berth against the increasingly blustery winds. As the ship was battered by the waves, her anchor windlass disintegrated and the Commanding Officer, realising that his vessel was in imminent danger of foundering, decided to make for the wharf with all abandon so that his crew may be saved. However, as the ship neared the wharf she was dashed against it with such force that ammunition in the magazine was detonated, killing two of the crew. As *Arrow* began rapidly sinking and the survivors took to a life raft the craft was rammed beneath the wharf.

For thirteen hours the survivors clung to the raft for all they were worth before they were finally rescued later that afternoon. One of *Arrow*'s sister ships, *HMAS Attack* (P90), was driven ashore and badly damaged, but was later salvaged and towed to Cairns for repair.

It was no secret that the Royal Australian Navy (RAN) was less than satisfied with the Attack-class boats in the role in which they were used, especially in areas such as the Bass Strait where they were used for oil rig patrol, an area of wild and unpredictable seas where firms use large ocean-going tugs to re-supply their oil rigs. In fact, the boats' unsuitability for this task was reported in the Australian press on more than one occasion.

It was partly in response to their request for a more suitable vessel that in 1977 the RAN gained approval for the construction of a new class of patrol boat of the Brooke-Marine 'PCF 420' design to replace the Attack-class. The lead ship of the Fremantle-class, as they became known, was delivered from the UK in 1979, and fourteen other units were handed over by the local builders North Queensland Engineering Agents (NQEA) by the end of 1984. This class has given the Australian Navy a better, faster and more seaworthy boat for northern surveillance tasks compared to the Attack-class. However, even these vessels are inoperable for 30% of the time in the Bass Strait due to winds of over 35 knots.

The Dibb report of 1986 recommended the building of eight 1,200-tonne corvettes for EEZ patrol in place of the Fremantle-class, stating that such vessels would have sea-keeping, endurance and reconnaissance capabilities that patrol boats do not have and yet be less expensive to acquire and maintain than destroyers. Similarly, the commanders of the Australian Mine Warfare and Patrol Boat flotillas wanted the follow-on class to be twice the size of the 42-metre Fremantles, and if possible possess helicopter-handling facilities as well. For such duties designs such as the British River, the Italian Cassiopea, or the Danish Osprey designs would have seemed ideal. After many years of deliberation, the Australian Navy finally ordered twelve 56.8-metre *Armidale-class* boats in August 2003. These 270-tonne boats are now (2008) replacing the Freemantles.

Most of the storm-related naval losses in this area are of relatively small vessels. In fact, *HMAS Arrow* was the second patrol craft of the post-war Australian Navy to fall victim of heavy weather.

*The small patrol boat HMAS Arrow fell victim to the power of the wind and sea.*

*(Navy Photographic Unit - Sydney)*

In mid-1952, the Australian Navy decided to transfer the 54-ton Seaward Defence Motor Launches *SDML1322* and *SDML1327* from Sydney to the naval base at Manus, on Manus Island, for use as local patrol craft and tenders. Whilst *SDML1327* was transferred during July, *SDML1322*'s journey was delayed whilst repairs were carried out to damage sustained in a minor collision with a floating dock. The craft had been in reserve and, from 21 July, *SDML1322* was crewed with seven ratings - under the command of the coxswain, petty officer A.H. Dickson - and restored with fuel, ammunition and victuals, prior to being prepared for the long tow to the Bismarck Archipelago. On 1 August, custody of *SDML1322* was handed over to the 800-ton fleet tug *HMAS Reserve* (W149).

*HMAS Reserve*, with *SDML1322* in tow, left Sydney at 0140 on Monday, 5 August, a slight delay being encountered due to *Reserve*'s other harbour duties and to the repair of defects on *SDML1322*'s starboard engine. As the two vessels cleared Sydney harbour 1½ hours later, a force 3-4 wind was blowing from a heading of 170°, whipping up a large swell, sea state 5. The SDML's engines were then shut down and the two ships settled on a course of 050°. *Reserve*'s commanding officer, Lieutenant Commander H.J. Hull, RANR, had intended that, should weather conditions deteriorate, the two ships would shelter in Broken Bay, about 30 miles north of Sydney. However, by 0500, rising wind and reduced visibility caused by heavy rain forced a decision to alter course to the southward in order to head into the wind and sea.

Continuing bad weather prevented the ships from returning to Sydney during the afternoon, as this would have necessitated turning to starboard and putting the sea on their beam. Consequently, the southerly course was maintained throughout the day until, at 1715, it was decided that the weather had moderated sufficiently to allow them to alter course to the north and head for the shelter of Port Jackson. Bailey Point Light was sighted 20 minutes later and a land fix was obtained.

Throughout the day there had been no serious problems with the 90 fathom-long, 3½ inch tow wire, but at 1745 the SDML appeared to have slewed at an angle to the tow and it was soon apparent that the 3½ inch towing bridle, which surrounded the hull of the craft, had broken free and had fouled on the craft's hull aft. Whilst crew of *Reserve* recovered the bridle, the craft's two mechanics started the SDML's port engine with ease, but it was some time before the starboard engine could be started by trailing the propeller.

Both vessels then proceeded together under their own power until, at 2100 - as they approached Sydney Harbour heads - P.O. Dickson reported that both main engines had stopped due to salt-water contamination of the fuel. This fuel contamination had also resulted in the craft's auxiliary generators being out of action since about 1630, thereby preventing recharging of the now exhausted engine starting batteries. Although the engine fuel lines were cleared, the starting batteries contained insufficient charge to re-start the engines.

Nevertheless, *Reserve*'s crew successfully managed to pass a 6-inch manila towrope, which was secured to the drifting patrol craft's capstan, and both vessels continued on their course for Port Jackson.

Over the next hour the wind speed increased - gusting up to 49-mph - whilst heavy rain squalls significantly reduced visibility. At 2215, the towrope snapped due to the extra strain imparted on it by the increased swell then running, once more casting *SDML1322* adrift, in a position approximately 1,400 yards from Hornby Light.

As waves were constantly washing over *Reserve*'s tow deck, Lt. Cdr. Hull manoeuvred the bow of his ship close to the drifting craft while his crew attempted, unsuccessfully, to re-establish the tow.

With the two vessels drifting perilously close to the lee shore, Lt. Cdr. Hull decided that the crew of *SDML1322* should be evacuated, but all attempts to pass a towrope or evacuate the crew were thwarted by the increasingly violent swell.

Within yards of the shoreline, Lt. Cdr. Hull ordered his ship to reverse away from *SDML1322* and shortly afterwards, at 2235, the small craft was dashed onto a rocky ledge close to a cliff face in the vicinity of Old Man's Hat, Inner North Head. Although the crew had managed to release both of the craft's Carley rafts, there was insufficient time to let go an anchor. Thankfully, all crewmen managed to scramble ashore and clamber up the steep cliff to safety and thence made their way to the nearby Quarantine Station, where they were able to contact the Naval Headquarters to inform them of their predicament.

Meanwhile, unable to render any further assistance to the stranded craft, *Reserve* entered Sydney Harbour and berthed alongside the boom defence vessel *HMAS Kangaroo* (P80) at the West Dock wall.

Inspections of the wrecked *SDML1322* over the next few days revealed that she was lying on her starboard side, which was badly holed aft and in the vicinity of the engine room, and that her starboard propeller shaft was badly buckled. Declared a constructive total loss, *SDML1322* was stripped of her engines and 40mm gun mounting and her hull was later broken up where it lay.

The primary reason for the loss of *SDML1322* was similar to that which resulted in the loss of twelve *Fairmile 'D'* craft in the Mediterranean in January 1946 (described later in this chapter) - that the vessels were sent to sea in the face of deteriorating storm conditions. Stress of weather initially resulted in the failure of the wire lashing at the forward end of the SDML's towing bridle, which had in turn resulted in undue strain being put on the stops leading to the forward bollards which, combined with the violent motions of the craft due to the heavy swell, had caused them to slip from the bollards, an action which had gone unnoticed by the crew due to seasickness and fatigue.

Failure of the craft's auxiliary generators and then of her main engines had been due to salt-water contamination of the fuel tanks. Heavy spray washing over the craft's forecastle had caused seawater to enter the fuel tanks via their upper-deck breather pipes, situated forward of the bridge. Water had also been leaking into the engine room via the skylights on the starboard side. Continuous attempts to start the main engine then drained the power of the engine starting batteries and had been hindered by fouling of the starboard engine by the towing bridle.

The New South Wales Weather Bureau had issued a storm and gale warning at 2330 on 4 August, but although this report was passed to *Reserve* prior to her sailing, the staff of Flag Officer In Charge Eastern Area did not see it until 0900 the next morning.

As the weather within Sydney Harbour was not particularly inclement, *Reserve* was ordered to sail as previously ordered. Furthermore, whilst the weather at sea worsened throughout the day, the confused sea in the entrance to Sydney Harbour, exaggerated by the heavy swell rebounding from North Head and Middle Head, would have made manoeuvring of the vessels extremely difficult.

Harbour defence motor launches had not been designed for service in the open ocean and it was considered, with hindsight, that the sailing of *Reserve* and *SDML1322* should have been deferred until more favourable weather conditions for the journey could have been assured. Alternatively, the ships should have remained hove to, or proceeded slowly into the sea, rather than attempt to enter Sydney Harbour.

Another similarly sized patrol craft to succumb to the force of the sea in this area was the Malaysian Kedah-class boat *KD Sri Perak* (P3140), which foundered in a storm in January 1984.

Taking into account the three US Swift-class patrol craft which foundered during the Vietnam War and the numerous small craft lost by other navies, it has thus been shown over the years that many of the craft operating in the Western Pacific are either too small for the roles in which they serve, are in an ill-maintained or decrepit condition, or are operated by poorly trained personnel.

The destructive force of tropical cyclones regularly hits the countries bordering the Indian Ocean. The coastal areas of these generally poor countries suffer such devastation and misery in the face of these storms that the people and the economy barely have time to recover before the next disaster strikes.

On 22 December 1964 the worst cyclone to strike Ceylon (later renamed Sri Lanka) for sixty years devastated the port of Trincomalee. Vessels of all shapes and sizes were either swamped by the waves and sank, or were driven aground, including several vessels of the Royal

Ceylon Navy. The seaward defence boat *Kotiya* was wrecked and sank and the ex-RN Algerine-class minesweeper *Viyaya* (M370) was beached and broached. Four naval tugs - the TANAC class *YTM1*, *YTM2* and *YTM3*, and the Empire-class boat *Behest* - were also either driven ashore or sunk.

*Viyaya*, which had been transferred to the Royal Ceylon Navy in 1949 (previously named *HMS Flying Fish*), was returned to Britain and scrapped the following year.

The low-lying coastal plains of Bangladesh are particularly susceptible to the ravages of the violent storms that rip through the area with terrifying regularity.

The Bangladeshi Navy, which consists mainly of unsophisticated Chinese-designed vessels, elderly ex-RN frigates and ex-Indian and Yugoslav gunboats, has suffered a series of disasters, notably between 1989 and 1991. The first of these was the damaging of several Hegu-class missile boats and Huchuan-class torpedo boats when a Japanese-registered merchant ship rammed the Chittagong naval pier where they were berthed in high winds in October 1989. A similar incident occurred on the evening of 21 September

*The Malaysian patrol boat KD Sri Perek (P3140), which foundered in a storm in January 1984.*
*(Maritime Photo Library)*

2003, when eight naval vessels, a substantial portion of the Bangladeshi Navy, were damaged in Chittagong Harbour following a collision between two merchant vessels. The impact of the initial collision forced one of the merchantmen to hit the berthed naval vessels, causing significant damage and injuring at least 20 personnel.

In August 1991, the new Jianghu-class frigate *Osman* (F18) - which had only been commissioned in November 1989 - was badly damaged in a collision with a merchant ship. However, these accidents were overshadowed by the cyclone that struck the country on 29 April 1991. The port of Chittagong was devastated, with the wreckage of merchant and naval vessels strewn around the area and sunken vessels blocking the port and hampering the relief effort by American and British naval units operating in the Gulf area. Extensive damage was inflicted on the Naval Stores and Armament Depots near the port, with the result that several missiles and torpedoes were found floating in the streets of the naval base!

A Huangfen-class missile armed fast attack craft was sunk and a further thirteen small naval craft were badly damaged, including five of the Navy's eight missile-armed fast attack craft, two of the four Huchuan-class torpedo-armed fast attack craft, four patrol vessels and two of the four operational Yuchin-class landing craft. The majority of these were relatively new Chinese-built vessels commissioned in the 1980s.

Most of the damaged craft were later repaired, but one Hegu-class missile boat was scrapped. It also appears that the Hainan-class patrol craft *Durjoy* (P212) and the Yuchin-class *LCT L103* were not fully repaired and were paid off in 1995 and 1994 respectively. New vessels, of the same types, were transferred from China in June 1992 to replace the two missile boats destroyed by the typhoon.

The Indian Navy is one of the very few naval forces in the world that is currently expanding, with the addition of a large number of locally built Soviet- and indigenously-designed warships to the inventory annually. The ultimate aim of the Indian Navy is to achieve naval supremacy over the northern Indian Ocean, the Bay of Bengal and the eastern Arabian Sea areas, an ambition which is growing nearer to realisation as the US and Russian navies curtail the deployment of their shrinking naval fleets to the area.

This efficient and disciplined force suffered a minor set-back to their expansion plans on 22 August 1990, when the Project 159A ('Petya II'-class) light frigate *INS Andaman* (P74) sank in heavy seas in the Bay of Bengal with the tragic loss of fourteen of her crew of around a hundred men. However, *Andaman* was one of a class of twelve Soviet-built ships which were in the process of being deleted and whose build quality had always been regarded as poor. During their delivery voyages from Vladivostok in 1970, several of the frigates had to receive repairs at the Royal Navy base, *HMS Terror* at Singapore, as a result of damage occasioned by bad weather. Personnel carrying out the repairs were surprised at the unsatisfactory state in which these vessels were being handed over to their new Indian owners.

Nevertheless, despite the large number of vessels of such calibre the Indian Navy have operated over the years, they appear to have suffered relatively few accidental losses, a fact which must bear testimony to the professionalism of the naval personnel that operate them.

Although not subject to the ravages of hurricanes, typhoons or cyclones, the land-locked waters of the Mediterranean are prone to the effects of many strange offshore wind conditions unique to this area, including levanters, libeccios and mistrals. Nevertheless, violent gales and storms still occur in the area and from time to time vessels become victims, as in any other sea.

At the end of World War Two, a large number of Royal Navy motor gunboats and motor torpedo-boats, which had served with great distinction in the Mediterranean against the Axis forces, were laid up at Malta in Category 'B' Reserve in Pieta Creek near the Coastal Forces Base, *HMS Grecale*, where they were looked after by a small care and maintenance party.

In January 1946, twelve of these boats were sold to the Egyptian Government, presumably for service within the Egyptian Navy or Coast Guard. The vessels, by now minus their armament and some with their engines removed for preservation ashore, were prepared for tow to Alexandria.

The Fairmile 'D' type boats *MTB633*, *MTB634*, *MTB637*, *MTB638*, *MGB642*, *MGB643*, *MGB658*, *MGB659*, *MTB670*, *MGB674*, *MTB698* and *MTB700* left Marsamaxett under tow of the four destroyers - *HM Ships Jervis* (G00), *Chevron* (D51), *Chaplet* (D52) and *Chequers* (D61) - at the end of January, under the command of Commander Maitland-Makgill-Crichton in H MS *Jervis*.

Each destroyer was towing three boats in line astern behind them, with two sailors aboard the leading vessel in each line to tend the tow wires. The boats were riding high in the water due to their light condition and even in the relatively calm seas then prevailing, were seen to be wallowing unpleasantly.

Despite a request from Commander Maitland-Makgill-Crichton to delay the journey due to expected bad weather in the central Mediterranean, they were curtly told by Flag Officer, Malta, to *"sail in accordance with my orders."*

A few hours later, the weather began to deteriorate as the expected storm closed in on the small flotilla. As the boats began to corkscrew wildly in the mounting seas the ratings aboard the lead boats were evacuated to the destroyers. The weather continued to worsen during the night, deteriorating into storm conditions, and some of the Fairmile 'Ds' could now be seen to be broaching.

One after the other, some of the vessels broke loose from their tow. Other tows were deliberately slipped to prevent damage to the towing ships. The commanding officer of *HMS Chequers* ordered that the events be collated and relayed to Malta in a series of signals throughout the night.

Battered by the heavy seas, some of the boats were overwhelmed by the towering waves and sank, while others drifted helplessly. *Chevron* was the first destroyer to lose all three of her charges and so, when a distress call was received from a troopship foundering near Crete, she was hastily despatched to render assistance.

In the Operations Office in *HMS Grecale*, the Duty Officer listened in dismay to the 'blow by blow' account of the disaster as it happened. By daylight, the boats still afloat were considered to be a hazard to navigation and the decision was reluctantly taken to sink them by gunfire, a task quickly and efficiently executed by the destroyers. By 30 January, within 36 hours of leaving Malta, the entire group of twelve Fairmile 'D's had disappeared, the last some distance north of Benghazi.

Incidentally, when *HMS Chevron* arrived off Gavdhos Island, south of Crete, she found that the troopship that she had been despatched to assist, the ex-Italian hospital ship *ss Gradisca*, had been wrecked after running aground, although all the troops had been safely evacuated by two British cruisers which had arrived some time earlier. The Italian crew later mutinied, the uprising being quashed by an armed boarding party from *Chevron*.

There is no doubt that the decision to proceed with the tow of the twelve Fairmile 'D's with the stormy weather forecast was, at best, ill advised, particularly with the vessels in such a light displacement condition. In hindsight, the tow should not have been attempted in anything but fine weather. A Court of Enquiry was held into the incident, but the results have not yet been made public. If a Court Martial resulted, then no records can be found, but in any case, they would be closed for a period of 75 years to protect the consequences to the subject and his immediate family.

The Egyptian Navy was to suffer the loss of another ex-Royal Navy ship when, on 7 March 1953, the Bangor-class corvette *ENS Sollum* sank in heavy weather off Alexandria with the loss of 54 of her crew. The ship, built as the ocean minesweeper *HMS Wedgeport*, had been transferred to the Egyptian Navy in 1946, the same year as the ill-fated Fairmile 'D' vessels already mentioned.

A few months later, the Royal Navy was to suffer a further loss near Malta when, on 22 October 1953, the small naval motor fishing vessel *Recasoli* (MFV26), one of about 1,400 of the type built for service with the Royal Navy during the war, foundered in heavy weather.

The mighty US Navy has also suffered the indignity of storm-related ship losses in the Mediterranean. On 15 December 1952 the stores ship *USNS Grommet Reefer* (T-AF-53) was wrecked in a gale

on a reef off Leghorn, northern Italy. As the stranded vessel began to break in two the following day, the forty crewmen were rescued via a breeches buoy rigged to another ship. Shortly after, the stern section sank. The bow section, along with the cargo contained therein, was later salvaged and handed over to the Maritime Administration.

On 6 February 1968, the Fletcher-class destroyer *USS Bache* (DD-470) was driven aground on a reef off the Greek island of Rhodes after her anchor chain snapped in a gale.

Within minutes, the ship's hull was holed and several after compartments were flooded. As the ship broached onto the beach, waves continued to crash over her and it soon became evident that there was little the crew could do to save their ship. The order was given to abandon ship and over the next few hours all of the crew managed to make their way ashore in life rafts, to be met by local people eager to assist the cold, wet sailors.

Over the following weeks, the *Bache* suffered severe damage to her hull plating and extensive flooding whilst being further ravaged by storms. The critically damaged ship was decommissioned on 1

*The destroyer USS Bache awash off Crete after being driven aground in February 1968.*

*(D. Dieter)*

March and subsequently written off as a constructive total loss and, after being re-floated, was sunk in deeper water.

The countries bordering the Mediterranean have not escaped the ravages of the sudden storms that strike viper-like from the land masses. An Israeli warship is reported to have sunk in a storm in the eastern Mediterranean in November 1952. Only sixteen months later, on 25 March 1954, the Spanish Bidasoa-class minesweeper *SNS Guadalete* (DM2) was on a routine patrol, bolstering the hard-pressed coastguard when she was caught up in the tempest of a fierce gale. The 775-ton ship was soon in extreme difficulties and eventually foundered 20 miles east of Gibraltar.

The turbulent and sometimes capricious waters of the Aegean Sea have also claimed their fair share of victims, one of which was the Turkish tank landing craft *C136*. The six-year-old craft, one of several vessels of the French EDIC design built for the Turkish Navy between 1966 and 1980 to replace British and US war-built vessels, succumbed to heavy weather and sank on 30 January 1985.

Even in the more serene waters of the Black Sea, the sea waits to stake its claim on the unwary. During the Soviet era, the Soviet Black Sea Fleet was the largest naval force in the region. In 1952 the fleet suffered the loss of the Project 73-K ('Polukhin'-class) ocean minesweeper *Pavel Golovin* (T-450). The 850-ton vessel was driven aground and wrecked in a storm near the port of Tuapse with the loss of several of her crew.

Mystery surrounds the fact that not a single hurricane has ever been reported in the South Atlantic. Amongst the theories for this strange phenomenon is that the ocean area may be too small, or the sea water too cold, or that the wind patterns may not be conducive to the formation of hurricanes. There are, however, certain areas of the South Atlantic that are notorious for severe gales and storms, often

exceeding force eight or nine. One such area, which has been the scourge of mariners for centuries, is in the region of Cape Horn, the very southern tip of the South American continent.

The Drake Passage is littered with the wrecks of sailing ships sunk or smashed on the thousands of small islands whilst attempting to 'round the Horn'. However, maritime traffic has been significantly reduced since the opening of the Panama Canal in 1914, which links the Atlantic and Pacific Oceans. Traffic now consists mainly of local vessels, or the occasional challenger to the sea's potency, such as the late Sir Francis Chichester.

The Chilean Navy was particularly ravaged by savage storms in the area in the 1960s. On 25 May 1964, the 130-tonne harbour tug *Yagan* (YT126) was despatched to Punta Arenas to assist the British merchant ship *ss Hornby Grande*, which had run aground on a sandbank. Unfortunately, having accomplished her mission, the tug was overwhelmed by mountainous seas and capsized, with the loss of three of her crew. Although she was re-floated the following year, the hulk foundered on 7 June 1965 whilst under tow to Talcahuano by the patrol vessel *Lautoro* (PP62).

In August of the following year, the grounding of one of *Lautoro's* sister ships was to be the catalyst for one of the worst catastrophes in the history of the Chilean Navy. Although this incident occurred further up the Pacific coast, it deserves mention at this point.

On the 1st of that month, *Leucoton* (PP61) departed her home port of Talcahuano, for a routine visit to the lighthouses off Chiloé, near Puerto Montt, then to return to Talcahuano to tow the ferry *Alonso de Ercilla*. However, during her voyage south the following day, she encountered a fierce northerly storm and her commanding officer, Capitàn de Corbeta Pedro Fierro Herreros, decide to steer for Caleta Lliuco, in San Pedro Bay, south of Corral, where his ship could shelter from the rising seas and effect repairs to a fault on the starboard engine. Just as *Leucoton* dropped anchor, an immense wave struck, bodily lifting the 800-tonne ship and depositing her 250 metres nearer the shore across a sandbank.

The stranded ship immediately radioed for assistance, in response to which the survey ship *Janequeo* (AGS65) - formerly the US Navy Apache-class fleet tug *USS Potawatomi* (ATF-109), transferred to Chile in August 1963 - and the tugs *Cabrales* (ATA71) and *Galvarino* (ATA72) were dispatched from Talcahuano to begin a salvage operation. By the time they arrived in the area later that night, the worsening weather conditions necessitated the despatch of the *Galverino* to Puerto Montt to undertake the duties previously assigned to the *Leucoton*.

Over the following nine days, the salvage operation, under the overall command of Capitàn de Fregata Claudio Hemmerdinger Lambert, was hampered by the persistent storm-force winds and high seas and little progress was made beyond the attachment of a towing cable to the stranded *Leucoton*.

Late on the afternoon of the 11th, as the *Janequeo* was being tossed around at anchor, her towing cable became entangled around her propeller shaft and, despite unsuccessful attempts by her divers to remove the cable the following day, the ship remained crippled. Consequently, the Flag Officer of the 2nd Naval District at Talcahuano ordered that *Janequeo*'s sister ship *Yelcho* (AGS64) and the Flower-class corvette *Casma* be despatched to San Pedro Bay, where they were to assist in the salvage of *Leucoton* and tow *Janequeo* back to Talcahuano for docking.

Meanwhile, the storm had rounded to the east and continued to increase in intensity. When the *Casma* arrived early on 15 August she was unable to enter the bay because of the 40-knot winds and mountainous seas.

Inside the bay, the *Janequeo*'s anchor began to drag and, at 0854, the chain finally snapped under the strain of the heavy swell. Minutes later, the ship was smashed against the Campanario rocks by waves 15 metres in height.

As his ship rapidly flooded and listed to over 60-degrees, the Commanding Officer, Capitàn de Corbeta Marcelo Léniz Bennett, realised that there was little that could be done to save his vessel and so ordered that preparations be made to abandon ship. Being relentlessly impelled against the rocks, the ship soon began breaking up and, at 0921, her hull broke in two amidships. As their ship began to sink, the crew were compelled to jump onto the rocks in an attempt to save themselves, but many, including Capitàns Hemmerdinger and Léniz, went down with their ship.

Watching the tragedy of the *Janequeo* unfold before his eyes, *Leucoton*'s Commanding Officer decided that he should attempt to put his crew ashore. Despite being constantly battered by the waves that continued to smash into her starboard side, *Leucoton* remained firmly embedded in the sand, broadside onto the shore 100 metres away, near to the mouth of the River Lliuco.

Although two brave enlisted men managed to swim ashore and rig a safety line from the ship's forecastle to the beach, this was soon ripped away by the mountainous waves. The crew of the *Leucoton* now had little choice but to remain with their ship, whilst ashore the two enlisted men were assisted by local villagers in dragging ashore survivors - and bodies - from the crew of the *Janequeo*.

When the storm began to abate the following day, the cruiser *O'Higgins* (CL02) and the destroyer *Williams* (DD19) arrived in the area to pick up survivors from the two stricken ships, assisted by several helicopters. Of *Janequeo*'s crew of 73 men, 46 lost their lives, of which only 13 bodies were recovered. Additionally, one of *Leucoton*'s crew died trying to save the lives of fellow mariners from the *Janequeo*. *Leucoton* was later declared a constructive total loss.

Heroes of the tragedy were later honoured by having Chilean warships named after them: one of the two ex-US LSTs transferred in 1973 was named *Hemmerdinger*; whilst two patrol craft built in Chile in 1966/67 were named *Marinero Fuentealba* (WPC75) and *Cabo Odger* (WPC76) - after a *Leucoton* sailor who lost his life rescuing *Janequeo* survivors and a *Janequeo* Corporal who - despite serious injuries - saved at least one of his shipmates, respectively.

Yet another Chilean warship was to be wrecked in a storm-related incident, almost fifteen years later. The tank landing ship *Aguila* (ARV135) had been undergoing repairs to her port engine and gearbox at Valparaiso when, on 10 April 1980, a violent storm struck the area. Even though repairs to the port machinery plant were incomplete, her Commanding Officer, Capitàn de Fregata Frederick Corthorn Besse, decided that, rather than have his ship smashed against the jetty, it would be prudent to take his vessel to sea, where she could ride out the storm. The *Aguila* had barely got under way when the starboard engine developed a serious fault and had to be shut down. Without propulsive power, there was little that the crew could do to prevent their ship drifting towards the rocks, near to the University Frederico Santa Maria.

The inevitable impact with the rocks ripped open a massive hole in the ship's hull, rapidly flooding the engine room and shaft passageways. As the generators became submerged, the ship was plunged into darkness and the crew were deprived of pumps with which to control the flooding. As the water level rose in the tank deck, the crew spent many hours huddled aboard their crippled ship whilst a rescue

operation was initiated.

Although the ship was later re-floated, the extensive damage to her hull, machinery and shafting rendered her irreparable. Consequently, the ship's shattered hull was patched and she was towed to Talcahuano, were she was de-commissioned on 13 June and, after all useful equipment and materials had been stripped from her, the hulk was towed out to sea and demolition charges used to scuttle her.

*Aguila* had been built towards the end of World War Two as the US Navy *LST-1092* and was later converted to a repair ship, being renamed *USS Aventinus* (ARVE-3). Transferred to the Chilean Navy in August 1963, the *Aguila* was seriously damaged in a grounding incident during an amphibious exercise in August 1974, which necessitated a major overhaul of her sand- and salt water-contaminated engines and gearboxes. Re-designated as a submarine support ship following this accident, *Aguila* was plagued by constant problems with her propulsion plant, problems which were exacerbated by the postponement of refits throughout the Chilean fleet during an increased state of tension with their Argentine neighbours in 1978/79.

In hindsight, the decision to proceed to sea in storm conditions with only one engine operable, especially given the elderly machinery's notorious unreliability, can best be described as an error of judgement, although it had appeared to be the safest option then open to the Commanding Officer.

Reverting our attention back to the South Atlantic, the Argentine Navy too, has suffered it's fair share of victims in the area, one such example being the loss, without trace, of the Ona-class naval tug *Guarani* in the Strait of Magellan on 15 October 1958.

Compared to the other oceans of the world, the number of naval vessels lost in the South Atlantic due to heavy weather is relatively small. This is partly due to the smaller number of storms of hurricane proportions in the area, but it must also be remembered that there are fewer significant navies operating in the region. The only truly 'blue water' navies bordering the South Atlantic today are those of Argentina, Brazil, Chile and Peru, whilst that of South Africa is the only sizeable naval force possessed by those countries situated on the African South Atlantic coast.

The navies of other Latin American and West African coastal countries consist of mainly coastal or riverine patrol craft, which are probably more susceptible to loss through inadequate crew training and maintenance than to the stress of the sea. Nevertheless, these navies are not invulnerable to the destructive force of coastal storms and losses, such as that of two Shanghai II-class patrol boats belonging to Zaire that sank at their moorings in a storm in 1990. However, the number of vessels owned by these countries is very small compared to those bordering the rest of the world's oceans and seas and so such incidents are relatively rare.

Notwithstanding the above, ships of the major naval powers such as Britain and the USA frequently patrol the ocean and, inevitably, these navies have not gone totally unscathed. The US research ship *Bowditch* (AGS-21) was extensively damaged at Rio de Janeiro, Brazil, after being rammed by two other ships which had broken adrift in a storm on 26 May 1987. On return to her home port of New Orleans the damage to the vessel's hull was surveyed, but was judged to be beyond economical repair and the ship was laid up until stricken in January the following year.

Moving our attentions northwards, the Caribbean Sea is frequently ravaged by fierce hurricanes. Like the great typhoons of the Pacific and the tropical cyclones of the Indian Ocean, these storms form within 20-degrees of the Equator. They are most frequent between the months of June and November, although they have been known to occur at almost any time of the year. Gaining in strength as they travel westwards from the Atlantic Ocean until they reach the Caribbean, they then either gouge a path of destruction across the Gulf of Mexico or, more usually, bank northwards along the string of islands

*HMCS Kamsack (K171) - Later to become the Venezuelan Carabobo. (BGM Photo Centre)*

commonly known as the West Indies, before slamming into the US state of Florida, wreaking a trail of carnage as it passes up the US eastern seaboard. Such hurricanes are commonly given girls names, such as 'Hurricane Mary'.

Within the Caribbean Sea and the Gulf of Mexico, these hurricanes tend to cause more damage to the towns and settlements on the hundreds of small islands within the Greater Antilles chain or on the mainland regions of Mexico or Florida. Nevertheless, they have also been the cause of many losses among the vessels of the large number of small navies and defence forces within the area.

The Flower-class corvette *HMCS Asbestos* (K358) was one of the later vessels of the class built for the Canadian Navy, commissioning on 16 June 1944. Following her brief war service on convoy escort duties in the North Atlantic the ship was de-stored at Sydney, Nova Scotia, and was paid off for disposal at Sorel on 8 July 1945, having been in service a little over a year. A large number of these corvettes were sold to Central and South American navies in 1946-47, *Asbestos* and five of her sisters going to the Dominican Republic. Given the new pennant number of C106, ex-*Asbestos* never reached her new owners as she broke her tow during a storm on her delivery voyage and was wrecked on the north coast of Cuba. The vessel was later salved and towed to New Orleans, where she was scrapped in March 1949. Her sisters served in the Dominican Republic Navy until they were discarded in the 1970s. However, one of them, *Cristobal Colon*, fell victim to another hurricane en route to the scrapyard on 31 August 1979, when she was driven aground and wrecked.

Other Canadian Flower-class corvettes, laid up at Sorel, were sold to the Venezuelan Navy on 17 October 1945. The vessels, *HMCSs Algoma* (K127), *Amherst* (K148), *Wetaskiwin* (K175), *Battleford* (K165), *Dunvegan* (K177),

*Kamsack* (K171) and *Oakville* (K178), were renamed *Constitution*, *Federacion*, *Victoria*, *Libertad*, *Independencia*, *Carabobo* and *Patria* respectively. Most of these vessels reached their destination safely, but one of them, *Carabobo*, broke her tow in rough weather and ran aground on a sandbar one mile east of Cape Brule near Gaspe on 5 December. All of the passage crew, including a Venezuelan national, abandoned ship and were rescued by one of the other corvettes on passage. The ship was declared a total loss and, over the next few years, was plundered by local inhabitants as she lay on the sandbank.

There was no formal investigation by the Canadians into the incident. The Venezuelan Consul at Montreal later contacted the firm of C.C. Prat and Co. of Canada Ltd, agents for the sale, offering the vessel for scrap, but the ship was never salvaged. However, there seems some doubt as to the vessel's Canadian identity, as the name *Amherst* was given by the Venezuelan Consul, although most other sources, including *"Jane's Fighting Ships"*, identify her as ex-*HMCS Kamsack*.

Further vessels of the small Dominican Republic Navy were to be lost in bad weather, with the tank landing craft *Samana* (LA2), the launch *LR102* and the tug *Hercules* (R2) all being lost in 1956, followed by the wrecking of the ex-US Ashville-class frigate *Juan Pablo Duarte* (F102) the following year.

Numerous other storm-related losses have occurred amongst the area's naval forces, including the Mexican naval tug *Rio Blanca* in February 1955, the Haitian landing craft *Vertieres* (GC6) in 1956, the Mexican naval tug *R4* in 1973, and four Nicaraguan craft - a Sin Hung-class and two Zhuk-class patrol boats and a Yevgenya-class minesweeper - which sank in a hurricane in October 1989.

More recently, the Bahamian patrol craft *P106* was sunk in a hurricane in

1992. Three ex-US PT-boats of the Cuban Navy were also sunk in a hurricane on 5 October 1948, although they were all later salvaged and repaired.

The St. Vincent patrol boat *Chatoyer* was tied up at her berth in Kingston harbour in 1979 when a hurricane struck the area. The vessel was battered against the jetty and later sank due to the damage sustained. The boat was subsequently raised and scrapped. *Chatoyer* was not strictly a warship, as she was under the control of the police force and as such was a tool of civil, and not military, authority. The craft, the only vessel of the Marine Wing of the St. Vincent Police Force, was replaced in March 1981 by the larger 70-tonne Vosper-built patrol craft *George Mackintosh* (SCG05).

There have also been a few losses amongst the major navies operating in the area, with the foundering of the Royal Navy drifter *Onyx* (Z79) in Bermuda dockyard on 21 March 1947 and several small auxiliaries of the US Navy operating out of the US Gulf coast naval bases in the following years.

A larger vessel was seriously damaged in a hurricane whilst under construction for the US navy at New Orleans on 9 September 1965. The survey ship *USS Kellar* (T-AGS-25) broke loose from her moorings and capsized, the damage inflicted causing her completion to be delayed until the end of 1968.

The east coast of the North American continent is not only ravaged by the hurricanes that sweep up from the Caribbean, but are also subjected to the notorious North Atlantic gales, which occur throughout the year. Vessels under tow are particularly susceptible to such ravages.

The Gleaves-class destroyer *USS Baldwin* (DD-624) was one of several Reserve Fleet vessels transferred from the Philadelphia Reserve Group to the Boston Reserve Group in April 1961. At 0637 on the 16th of that month, whilst about 23 miles off Montauk Point, Long Island, the towing rig swivel of the tug USNS *Keywadin* (ATA-213) fractured, casting the destroyer adrift.

The *Baldwin*, with no machinery running and no crew aboard, was carried towards the coast by gale force winds gusting at up to 40 mph. Repeated attempts by the tug's personnel to board the destroyer were thwarted by the large swell then running and assistance was promptly requested from the nearest naval base. Soon afterwards the larger tug *USNS Luiseno* (ATF-156) was despatched from Newport, Rhode Island. Nevertheless, it appeared that the ship might be blown into the calmer waters of Long Island Sound, where she could be safely boarded and the tow re-secured, but the outgoing tide from the Sound altered the course of the drifting vessel a little to the south and, soon after noon, the 1,600-ton *Baldwin* ran aground on rocks about two miles south-west of Montauk Point. The destroyer, impaled on the rocky shore directly beneath high cliffs, was lifted bodily inshore with each wave that crashed in from the Atlantic and it soon became apparent that any salvage attempt would have to wait until the weather had abated.

Later that afternoon, responsibility for the salvage was passed to Commander Service Force, US Atlantic Fleet, who assembled the salvage Task Unit 48.7.6 for the purpose. This task unit comprised, in addition to *Keywadin* and *Luiseno* already on the scene, the salvage vessels *USNSs Hoist* (ARS-40), *Salvager* (YMLC-3) and *Windlass* (YMLC-4) and the lighter *YFNB-17*. However, by the time salvage experts were able to undertake a survey two days later, the ship was firmly embedded in deep sand and was badly holed below the waterline, with the result that she was flooded almost throughout her length.

Over the next few days, continued bad weather limited salvage work to the pumping out of most of the flooded compartments and preparations for pulling the destroyer free of the rocks. De-fuelling of the ship in order to lighten her proved impossible, as a barge could not be brought close enough to her due to the number of large rocks lurking in the shallow water.

On the evening of the 24th, *Windlass* and *Hoist* made the first of many attempts to pull *Baldwin* free of the beach, but only succeeded in hauling her about fifty feet to seaward before the beach gear anchors began dragging, partly due to continued flooding of the destroyer's compartments. Further attempts over the next week resulted in the *Baldwin* being moved a mere sixty feet, before the weather and poor visibility again forced a halt in the operation. It was realised that, in order to haul the stranded vessel completely free it would be necessary to first clear a path through the jagged rocks which were tearing further holes in the hull with each movement. Blasting of a clear channel began on 1 May.

The next pull on 7 May only managed to move *Baldwin* a few yards and it wasn't until the 16th that the ship was at last afloat, although still surrounded by rocks. Inspections at this point revealed extensive damage to the ship's hull plating, with several sections forward completely flooded.

Despite the horrendous weather conditions over the following weeks, the salvage operation continued, but with only limited success as anchors were dragged and cables parted. The *Baldwin* was finally hauled free of the rocks late on the afternoon of 4 June, but the damage caused to the hull and machinery was so extensive that the ship was judged to be beyond economical repair, even for sale as scrap. The hulk was towed by *Luiseno* about 85 miles to the south-south-east where, at 1310 the following day, she was scuttled in 258 fathoms of water in position 39° 56'N, 71° 17'W.

Apart from the inclement weather conditions, several other factors had contributed to the grounding of the *Baldwin* and the complexity of the salvage operation. The fact that the ship was being towed in a 'dead' condition meant that personnel were not aboard at the critical time to assist in re-securing the severed tow and that the ship's engines were not available to allow her to steer clear of the remote rocky headland. The shallow rocky water and the close vicinity of steep cliffs then complicated the subsequent salvage operation. Also, the extent of the flooding was made worse by additional holes that had been cut in the ship's internal structures to assist the mothballing process.

Nevertheless, the fact remains that, had the gale force winds, which persisted for a total of over four weeks during the seven week operation, not hampered the salvage operation to such an extent, it is probable that the ship may have been salvaged. Nature however, is not always so considerate.

Less than a year after the *USS Baldwin* incident, another US Navy destroyer was lost in almost identical circumstances. The Fletcher-class destroyer *USS Monssen* (DD-798) was being towed to

*Another USN Reserve Fleet destroyer, USS Monssen, seen driven aground at Beach Haven Inlet, New Jersey, on 6 March 1962.*

*(Navsource)*

Philadelphia to join the Reserve Group on 6 March 1962, when the towing cable parted in heavy seas. As the destroyer was blown towards the coast by 50-knot winds, attempts to regain the tow were frustrated by the heavy swell, with waves reaching 15-feet in height.

was eventually driven aground at Beach Haven Inlet, New Jersey. Although the badly damaged ship was re-floated in mid-April, it was declared as beyond economical repair and was sold to the Union Minerals and Alloys Corporation of New York for scrapping the following year.

The Atlantic gales affect the eastern freeboard of the North American continent as far north as the Labrador Sea. It was in this latter area that another US Navy ship came to grief in 1949. The survey vessel *USS Simon Newcomb* (AGSc-14), a converted minesweeper (ex-YMS-263), was driven aground on 9 August 1949 at Mother Burns Cove, Labrador. The ship was re-floated and towed to Norfolk, where she was surveyed, declared a constructive total loss and stricken, finally being sold on 25 April 1950 to BFM Industries, Brooklyn, for scrapping.

During the height of the 'Cold War' many ships of the Soviet Merchant Marine were built to allow swift conversion to military use should the need arise, including the provision of damage control, pre-wetting, and comprehensive electronic and radio equipment. Some also carried a large military contingent among their crew.

One such vessel was the 6,130-dwt Mekhanik-class Ro-Ro ship *Mekhanik Tarasov*. Whilst off Newfoundland on 16 February 1982, the 124.2-metre long vessel foundered in heavy weather, with the loss of thirty-two crewmen. Tragically, most of these could have been saved had they not refused to allow themselves to be rescued by a non-Soviet ship.

The stormy depressions of the Western Atlantic tend to follow the track of the jet

stream, maturing as they are driven eastwards across the ocean, whipping up the surface of the sea to form mountainous waves as it reaches the shallower waters of the continental shelves. The toll of mariners and their ships that have fallen foul of the sea's wrath over the centuries on the busy North Atlantic shipping routes is endless, and will no doubt continue to grow.

The treacherous coastline of the United Kingdom is strewn with the shattered wreckage of ships that have lost their battle with the sea. Several British naval vessels and auxiliaries have succumbed to such gale-whipped seas in post-war years, the incidents highlighting the terrible conditions aboard the vessels at the time of their loss, with tales of amazing tenacity and seamanship amongst their crews.

Scotland's rugged west coast is particularly renowned for it's weather-beaten landscapes. A winter gale that battered the eastern isles in 1968 resulted in the loss of a Royal Fleet Auxiliary tug, fortunately without loss of life amongst her crew.

The 274-ton Empire-class tug *Empire Ace* was completed in December 1942 and later served at Malta, where she was sunk in an air raid on 15 March 1944. Raised

*The 274-ton Empire Ace was driven aground on the Mull of Kintyre in a storm on 11 November 1968. Although refloated four months later, the vessel was declared a constructive total loss and was scrapped.*

*(Maritime Photo Library)*

and repaired in May the same year, the vessel was renamed *Diligent* in August 1947. In July 1960 she was temporarily laid up in reserve at Pembroke Dock, before undergoing a refit at Rosyth and being re-commissioned for service with the RFA in January 1961.

Reverting to her original name, *Empire Ace* was based at Greenock and served in the Clyde area. However, her new career came to an abrupt end when, on 11 November 1968, she was blown aground on Davaar Island, off the Mull of Kintyre, four miles south of Campbeltown (55°20'25"N, 05° 27'00"W). Attempts to free their vessel from rocks proved futile and the crew decided to abandon ship, escaping to the shore only 70 yards away, whilst the salvage vessel *RMAS Mandarin* (P192) stood by.

It proved impossible to re-float *Empire Ace* at that time and a salvage attempt was postponed until the spring. The vessel was re-floated on 28 March the following year by the *Mandarin* and *MFV64*, but was found to be a constructive total loss.

The wreck was sold in September 1969 to A Hood & Co. of Helensburgh for scrapping where she lay, but was later resold for demolition to Archibald Macfadyen and part of it now lies in 34 metres of water.

In the latter stages of the Second World War, the Spithead anchorage off Portsmouth was utilised for the storage of a large number of surplus and obsolete Royal Navy warships awaiting disposal at the country's busy scrapyards. A series of severe gales in late-1945 took their toll on these vessels, vulnerable as they were lying at their exposed moorings.

On 25 October the Ancient-class paddle tug *Swarthy* (W12) was towing the rusting hulk of the old Hunt-class minesweeper *Saltburn* (N58) to a scrapyard in a gale off Spithead when she fouled a defence obstruction near Horse Sand Fort and was blown ashore. The towing hawser was parted and *Saltburn* also struck the obstruction and foundered. Both vessels were later salvaged. *Swarthy* was repaired and remained in service until

*The minesweeper Saltburn, perched on rocks at Speaks Mouth, near Hartland Point, Devon, after having been driven on to rocks during a storm. The ship was being towed in rough weather when it broke adrift.*

*(T. Ferrers-Walker Collection)*

*Already seriously damaged by a machinery space fire, the British torpedo boat MTB1602 was under tow to Anglesey for repair on 31 January 1952 when she foundered and sank in a gale.*

*(World Ship Photo Library)*

1961, whilst *Saltburn* was eventually scrapped in 1948.

A series of other British vessels were lost after breaking their tows over the following year. In December the ZZ-class minesweeper *ZZ13*, one of thirty 'Z' lighters that had been converted to a minesweeping role a year earlier, foundered in a gale. A similar fate befell one of her sisters, *ZZ12*, a few months later when, on 5 May, she broke her tow and sank in 58 metres of water off St. Abbs Head in position 56° 09'00"N, 02° 13'07"W. The wreck was never recovered.

Then, on 20 September 1946, the Admiralty TID (Tug Inshore & Dock) tug *TID62*, completed in May 1944, was being towed from Portsmouth to Sheerness by the larger Assurance-class tug *Tenacity* (W18), when a fierce gale forced the tow to part. The tow was recovered and taken up again by the destroyer *HMS Zephyr* (D19) , but the tug hove-to, took in water, capsized and sank off Beachy Head, 5 miles south-east of Folkstone pier.

In September 1951 the Vosper 73ft Fast Patrol Boat *MTB1602*, built the previous year as the prototype *MGB539*, was badly damaged by an explosion at Portsmouth.

The explosion occurred in the engine exhaust system, damaging the engines and systems and causing the compartment to flood. Emergency repairs were carried out at *HMS Hornet* at Gosport, preparing her for the tow to the Saunders-Roe shipyard at Beaumaris, Anglesey, where she had been built, for refit and repair.

However, whilst under tow off Smalls on the night of 30/31 January 1952, the weather deteriorated and the boat took on water with the result that the main tow parted. The second, emergency tow took the strain but only 2 miles off North Anglesey the force 10 southerly gale caused this second tow to also break and *MTB1602* foundered.

The design of *MTB1602* was not a successful one. A major inadequacy discovered during the vessel's short career was her weak alloy structure which permitted heavy leakage of water into the hull through the upper deck, especially in bad weather or when the craft was operating at speed.

Three 3,800-dwt Ranger-class tankers were built for the Royal Navy in 1941 by Caledon Shipyard, Dundee, and named *Gold Ranger*, *Gray Ranger* and *Green Ranger*. Following successful war serv-

*RFA Green Ranger, her hull broken in two, lies on rocks at Hartland Point on 18 November 1962.*

*(Freeman's Press Agency)*

ice, *RFA Green Ranger* (A152) was laid up in reserve at Devonport in the late 1950's. In 1962 it was decided to refit the ship for further service, the Welsh Barry Yard of Cardiff winning the contract, which included the towing of the vessel to the yard.

On the morning of 17 November 1962, *RFA Green Ranger* left Plymouth under tow of the small commercial tug *Caswell* (ex-*Empire Sybil*), with a skeleton crew of seven men aboard the tanker to tend the tow. H aving successfully rounded the notorious Land's End the weather rapidly deteriorated and the two vessels took shelter and anchored in St. Ives Bay.

As the weather temporarily improved, it

was decided to resume the tow. *Green Ranger's* steam machinery was still inoperative, and so a portable diesel compressor had been fitted to her forecastle to permit operation of the anchor winch. Unfortunately, the crew were unable to start the compressor and so, after spending several hours struggling with the machinery, it was decided to remove a shackle pin and jettison the anchor.

The tow was resumed shortly after, but the weather again took a turn for the worse, with a force 8 north-north-east gale blowing. The *Caswell* was clearly too small for the task and had insufficient propulsive power to keep the tanker from drifting towards Hartland Point. At 1530 several distress signals fired by the tug brought an RAF Whirlwind helicopter from the RAF Station at Chivenor to investigate, but neither it, nor two lifeboats which had also been scrambled, could reach the tanker, now being tossed around wildly by the tempestuous seas.

The crew of the *Caswell* tried feverishly over the next few hours to maintain control of the ship, but, at around 2030 the tow finally parted and *Green Ranger* was blown onto the rocks near Hartland Point, half a mile south of Longpeak.

Preparations for the rescue operation were by this time well in hand, with members of the Coast Guard and volunteers of the Hartland Lifesaving Company already in position on the cliffs above the stricken vessel. Attempts to fire a line onto the stranded vessel from this position failed and it was decided that a team of rescuers would have to descend the 400-foot cliff to a position nearer the ship.

The Battle-class destroyer *HMS Agincourt* (D86) was now standing off to lend assistance, but could do little more than illuminate the scene with her searchlights and act as a communications link in the deteriorating weather conditions, now reaching gale force 10. The stranded tanker could by now be seen to be listing to port with her hull badly holed by the rocks.

Soon after midnight the rescue team were on the rocks below and, battered by the wind, sleet and sea spray, made another attempt to pass a line aboard *Green Ranger*. They could see the stern of the ship only 120 yards away, heavy seas now breaking over her forward section. After much perseverance, a line was passed and secured and a breeches buoy rigged. Whilst all this was going on, nobody noticed the Appledore lifeboat coming alongside but, after being battered against the tanker's side and with the jagged rocks only yards away, the lifeboat had to withdraw. Nevertheless, the breeches buoy was successfully rigged and by 0400 both

rescued and rescuers were safely back at the top of the cliff.

Later that day, following several unsuccessful attempts to reach the ship from seaward, an RAF Search and Rescue helicopter was employed to winch four Admiralty construction and salvage experts aboard, a particularly precarious operation with the strong offshore wind still howling and the heavy seas still battering the tanker, now listing at an angle of over 35-degrees. A salvage plan was subsequently prepared. However, by 9 December, after sustained battering by tempestuous seas, *Green Ranger* had broken in two and any salvage was confined to valuable fixtures and fittings.

The wreck was sold as a constructive total loss in June 1963 to Mr Robb of Newcastle who carried out some salvage work. The hulk was resold in 1965 to Mr Henry Wright and finally sold in 1970 to Mr Clifford of Bude, but remnants of the wreck remain to this day.

Much had been mentioned in this chapter about vessels being lost whilst under tow, due primarily to the ravages of the sea. However, the subject of towing operations will resurrect itself throughout this book and so this may be a good time to discuss some of the rudiments of this task.

The requirement to take another vessel in tow at short notice is an evolution practised regularly by the majority of naval vessels, as they may be called upon to undertake this task at any time with little or no warning, particularly in the case of assisting a vessel in distress. Nevertheless, the taking in tow of a vessel by a warship will only be regarded a temporary measure undertaken in an emergency, until relieved by a vessel more suited to the task, namely a tug, naval or civilian.

In the case of a vessel in distress, whether because of damage or mechanical defect, there will be little choice but for the nearest vessel of suitable size to undertake the task. In the case of naval

vessels being transferred from one port to another to undertake repairs or refit however, there is no real substitute for the employment of a tug of suitable size and power rating.

Tugs are generally of short, beamy design with a high propulsive power to displacement ratio. These characteristics, together with the common use of Voith-Schneider propulsors instead of propellers, make these vessels highly manoeuvrable. Their low and expansive quarter-decks permit the towing winches to be located as near to the vessel's centre of gravity as possible and eases the handling of towing hawsers.

When determining the method to be utilised in taking in tow another vessel, there are several factors which need to be taken into consideration: type of vessel undertaking the tow; type of vessel to be towed; weather conditions prevailing; expected duration of the towing operation; urgency of the situation; and the locality of any navigational hazards.

A towing hawser, or towrope, should be strong enough for the task and, ideally,

should comprise primarily of a suitable rope such as polyamide or polyester, rather than wire cable, because of its better elastic properties. The towrope may be connected to a short length of anchor cable to keep the towrope free of the towed vessel's hawse pipe. However, tugs fitted with self-tensioning or self-rendering towing winches may use a wire hawser secured to a length of the disabled vessel's anchor cable. Such winches automatically heave-in or render the towing wire to compensate for the strain on it.

To prevent subjecting the towing hawser to unnecessary, strain with the resultant risk of parting, the strain on the hawser should be taken up gradually by the towing vessel going ahead slowly, increasing speed gradually until a safe and satisfactory towing speed is reached. Other factors, such as the disabled ship's freeboard, draught, trim, list and extent of hull damage, will also greatly affect the strain on the towing hawser. It should also be noted that a lightly laden vessel will tend to yaw, or stray, either side of the towed track more than would a heavily laden ship. The effect of yaw can be reduced by altering the speed or course of the tow, or by altering the trim or draught of the towed ship, an option which will be dependant on its material state. A vessel trimmed heavily by the stern will generally be a better towed 'patient'.

For a vessel trimmed by the bow, for instance when damaged, consideration will be given to towing her stern first. Another method which has in the past achieved some success in reducing the effect of yaw is using a second vessel 'towed' astern of the dead vessel to act as a form of active rudder, steadying the towed ship on a set course. Trailing a drogue, in the form of an anchor cable or cargo nets, astern of the towed ship will have a similar effect.

The length of the tow may be determined by the length of any swell running, it being desirable that both vessels rise and fall together on the crests and in the troughs of the swell. Every precaution should be taken to prevent over-stressing of the towing hawser, such as close monitoring of the condition of the hawser for signs of chafing or parting, undertaking changes of course slowly and adjusting of the towing speed to match the prevailing weather conditions, especially in confined areas or where navigational hazards or other shipping are present. In such circumstances the risk of the vessel grounding or being involved in a collision should the towing hawser part are greatly increased as it may take some time to recover the tow and, particularly when neither the towing nor the towed vessel is a tug, it is unlikely that a spare hawser will be carried.

Changes in the course of the tow should be carried out a few degrees at a time, sufficient time being taken to acquire the new heading before undertaking further steps. The difficulty of such manoeuvres is greatly eased if the towed vessel has the ability to steer itself.

The recovery of a slipped or parted towrope, especially during adverse weather conditions, can be a difficult and time consuming operation, during which the disabled vessel may be left to the mercy of the wind and sea. The drifting craft will then be a danger to herself and to others due to the increased risk of grounding or collision. Heavy weather is probably the most common cause of parting of towing hawsers. In such conditions, it may be desirable to alter the course of the tow before the wind and sea to reduce the strain on the towrope. However, should the towrope be subjected to excessive strain, it may be preferable to slip the tow and allow the disabled vessel to drift, using the towrope as a drogue, rather then risk damage to, or loss of, the towing gear, so permitting tow to be taken up again once the weather abates.

Should it be necessary to slip a towrope in an emergency, especially in shallow water, efforts should be made to attach a buoy to the free end of it in order to ease the task of recovery. Failure to buoy the towrope, and the inability of the disabled ship to use her own windlass, may make the recovery of the tow extremely difficult. Alternatively, if the disabled ship is able to slip an anchor, this may prevent her from straying into further difficulties.

*HMS Berkeley Castle overturned in dock at Sheerness.*
*(J. Melhuish)*

*In No.1 Dock at Sheerness, the submarine HMS Sirdar lies on her side after being knocked from the dock blocks by the same wave that struck HMS Berkeley Castle.*

*(J. Melhuish)*

more suitable vessel with a lesser draught or better manoeuvrability before the beaching operation commences.

Thus, it can be seen that a towing operating is a complex and specialised task, which must be practised regularly if the necessary skills are to be maintained by ships' crews.

Gales are not only a danger to be overcome by ships at sea, as they can also strike out at ships in the comparative haven of harbours or naval bases. During the night of 31 January/1 February 1953, a violent storm struck the Thames area. Despite warnings of an abnormally high tide of ten feet above normal level, there was little that could be done to protect the low-lying area of Sheerness, where a number of Royal Navy Reserve Fleet vessels were either laid up or in refit at the Naval Dockyard.

As high tide approached, the storm blew up a huge tidal wave that washed over the 22-feet high wall of the dockyard's Great Basin. Thousands of tons of water flooded over the gates of all three dry docks. In No.2 dock the Castle-class frigate *HMS Berkeley Castle* (F387) was undergoing a refit. The 1,000-ton ship was lifted bodily off of her blocks by the force of the water cascading into the dock and capsized, her keel coming to rest on the dock steps above the broad altar with her bows protruding over the end of the dock. Her mast barely missed a dockside crane as the ship came to rest on her port side. The only man aboard *Berkeley Castle* at the time of the tidal wave managed to escape by jumping from the ship onto a Carley float, which was washed away, depositing the shaken watchman near the dockyard's Main Gate.

In the neighbouring No.1 dock the submarine *HMS Sirdar* (S76), with much of her hull plating removed, was also lifted off of her blocks and became totally submerged. The boat had been undergoing an extensive refit that was to include streamlining of her conning tower and the

In the event of the towed ship taking in water and being in danger of sinking, the only option may be to beach her. Such an option will be dependant on the value of the towed vessel and the vicinity of a suitable sheltered bay, preferably with a gently sloping beach free of jagged rocks. The beaching operation is inherently dangerous to the towing ship, as it entails recovery of the tow and securing the sinking ship on the leeward side before pushing it as far as possible towards the selected beaching point before backing off. Obviously, should the towing vessel be of greater draught than the disabled ship, she herself will be in danger of grounding. Consideration should therefore be given to passing the tow of the sinking ship to a removal of her gun mounting and pedestal.

Several other vessels, including the salvage vessel *RMAS Uplifter* (W06) in No.3 dock, the water tanker *Freshwater* in No.4 dock and a number of RNVR minesweepers in the now tidal basin were also slightly damaged. Amazingly, there were no serious casualties among the naval or dockyard personnel.

Others were not to be so lucky. That terrible storm caused the loss of eleven vessels in the North and Irish Seas that night, nine of them with all hands. Most of the vessels lost were fishing boats and small coastal merchant ships. The car ferry *Princess Victoria* sank with heavy loss of life in the Irish Sea and a tanker under tow from Singapore to Blyth for scrap was wrecked off Clacton after the tow parted. Vast areas of south-eastern England and southern Holland were flooded by waves that completely overwhelmed normally impregnable sea defences.

There was little that could be done at Sheerness that evening until the flooding had subsided. The scene on Sunday morning revealed extensive damage, including the submergence of all generating stations under several feet of water, and debris deposited in huge quantities around the area. Over 2,000 employees spent the next few days working feverishly to restore electrical power supplies and clear up the mess. The cost of the damage to the dockyard was estimated at around £1.5-million and was regarded at the time as the worst catastrophe in the dockyard's history.

Following inspection of *Berkeley Castle* by the Naval Constructor and salvage experts, her stem was burned off. The dock was then flooded leaving the ship floating on her side. Attempts were made to pull her upright, but this was unsuccessful as she rolled over onto the opposite beam, sending dockyard workers scattering for their lives. The ship was then ballasted, rivet holes plugged and the ves-

sel re-docked in the middle of February. As the vessel's collision bulkhead had failed, a temporary bow of steel tubing and fairing plates was fitted. Further inspections of the hull resulted in the conclusion that the ship was beyond economical repair and she was later towed to Chatham, where she was laid up. The ship was sold to Grays, Essex, on 26 September 1955, where she arrived on 29 February the following year.

*HMS Sirdar* was re-floated on 15 February, but damage to machinery systems was found to be so severe that she too was deemed beyond economical repair. After being laid up in unmaintained reserve at Sheerness, *Sirdar* was towed to Portsmouth a year later by the tug *RMAS Enforcer* (W177). In 1959 the submarine was used in experiments at Rosyth by the Naval Construction Research Establishment and in May 1965 her battered hulk was sold to the shipbreakers P.W. McLellan of Bo'ness for breaking up.

Although not a storm-related incident, a further accident involving a dry dock that occurred in the nearby Chatham dockyard the following year deserves mention here.

The T-class submarine *HMS Talent* was almost lost on 15 December 1954, when she was swept into the River Medway after the caisson of No.3 dock collapsed, coming to rest aground on the opposite bank. Three dockyard workers were killed and a further 31 injured in the incident.

The caisson was normally held in position during a rising tide by allowing water to flow into the tidal chamber through the flooding holes, the additional water adding to the ballast already contained within it. However, at the time of the accident, maintenance was being carried out on the caisson, during which the flooding holes were plugged. The exceptionally high tide that day caused the caisson to become buoyant and rise slightly, allowing water to cascade into the dock,

*The minesweeper HMS Belton aground at Lochmaddy on 23 October 1971.*
*(Richard Wardrope)*

due to the caisson having been insufficiently ballasted. The caisson broke free and ended up alongside *Talent* in the dock, smashing into her stern on the way, before the submarine was swept out of the dock.

*Talent* was later pumped out and secured to the salvage vessel *Swin*. Following re-docking, a hull survey revealed extensive damage to the boat's bow, stern and ballast tanks. Luckily, there was only superficial damage to the keel, pressure hull, torpedo tubes and propulsion mountings and the boat was later repaired and returned to service.

If a vessel is caught at anchor when a gale strikes, there is often little option but to weigh anchor and ride out the waves in open water, where the ship has room to manoeuvre its bows into the oncoming sea.

In October 1971, the Royal Navy minesweeper *HMS Belton* (M1199) went to the rescue of a female scientist, working for the Nature Conservancy Council, who was studying grey seals one of the small uninhabited Monarch islands in the

Outer Hebrides and had been stranded for nine days with only a tent for shelter. Nothing had been heard from her for several days and there was some concern for her safety, rough weather having prevented local fishermen from establishing contact. Having successfully rescued the woman, *HMS Belton* proceeded to the small ferry terminal at Lochmaddy where the scientist was disembarked.

The minesweeper's crew had been exceedingly busy during the previous few days and were looking forward to a rest period alongside. However, shortly after berthing the Commanding Officer was informed that the normal Caledonian-Macbrayne ferry had run aground, and that the timetable had been amended for the standby ferry, which would require the use of the jetty during the night. Rather than move in the dark when the ferry arrived, it was decided that the minesweeper would move to an anchorage in a small bay to the south of the jetty.

In the early hours of Saturday, 23 October, a force 9 southerly gale blew up and the crew were awakened by the sounds of the ship's anchor dragging. There was little room available in the bay to weigh and re-anchor, so the decision was made to proceed to sea and ride the weather out. The manoeuvre required a 90-degree turn to starboard, which put the ship across the wind, blowing from astern, with the rocks of an island close to leeward. In the prevailing conditions it is probable that a navigational error was made and the turn was left too late. The ship was blown, virtually broadside on, onto the rocks, holing her along her starboard side in the vicinity of the engine and generator rooms.

Efforts to re-float were unavailing and as the tide ebbed it became apparent the ship would heel over dangerously. The local mountain rescue team had been called out and were in attendance, so the order was given to 'abandon ship'.

The first ashore was the ship's dog, closely followed by the rest of the ship's company and the ship's other mascot, a brown and white rat. Rescued, rescuers and pets then adjourned to the local Lochmaddy Hotel to recuperate from their ordeal.

The following day moves were made to prepare for the ship to be re-floated. The salvage officer from Greenock was flown to North Uist, while charter arrangements were made to employ the tug *Flying Falcon*, fortunately still in the area after having earlier assisted in the re-floating of the stranded ferry. Another Ton-class vessel, the minehunter *HMS Bildeston* (M1110), with her divers, was diverted to the area, as was the minesweeper *HMS Wasperton* (M1189).

When *Bildeston* arrived at dawn on the 24th, *Belton* was high and dry on the rocks. The main damage to the vessel, after grounding and being bounced by the rise and fall of three successive tides, was a badly holed hull, and therefore fully flooded engine room. The rest of the ship appeared in to be in a sound condition. A copper patch was fitted over the gaping hole in *Belton's* side and it was decided that an attempt would be made to re-float her during the next high tide at around 1000 that day.

The salvage officer was dubious whether the minesweeper had retained enough buoyancy to float in her damaged condition but it was felt that the ship was at greater risk of further damage if left on the rocks to be 'bounced' by another tide, especially in the deteriorating weather conditions. Shortly after 1000, the tug took the strain on the towing hawser and *Belton* was dragged from the rocks. After making arrangements for a proper towing bridle, the tug and *Belton*, escorted by *Bildeston*, made their way slowly towards Greenock.

Following a detailed survey of the vessel, it was decided that the cost of replacing *Belton's* flood-damaged machinery and wiring and repairing her hull damage would be prohibitively high, even though the rest of the hull was in such good condition that, prior to the grounding, the ship's life was expected to extend into the 1980's. The ship had been completed only fourteen years earlier, and as the damage was not too extensive, it would have been feasible to re-commission her after repairs. Nonetheless, owing to the large number of Ton-class vessels then available - over 50 of the original 117 built were still in commission with the Royal Navy - it was decided to scrap the vessel and cannibalise her to provide spares for her sister ships. Following a period laid up at Rosyth she was sold to Davies and Newman Ltd. of London on behalf of M.H. Gonzalez of Gijon, Spain, on 25 November 1974 for break-up.

As is customary when a ship of the Royal Navy is damaged, a Board of Inquiry was convened. While many coincidences combined to make an accident almost inevitable, one aspect that immediately became apparent was the failure of those aboard *Belton* to receive the gale

*The Dutch naval tug RS21, which sank after being torn from her moorings by gale force winds on 23 December 1949.*

*(Afdeling Maritieme Historie van de Marinestaf)*

warning for their area. This was partly due to an error in procedures on board whereby the Quartermaster was supposed to be provided with a loudspeaker to listen for calls on 2182kHz. If this had been in force the gale warning might have been heard.

It was stated as naval doctrine that once a ship was anchored, the Navigating Officer should automatically prepare an exit plan for use in case of an emergency. If this had been done, the hurried exit in the dark might have been completed safely.

At the subsequent court martial, the Commanding Officer of *HMS Belton*, Lieutenant S. Taylor, RN, pleaded guilty to the charge of negligently endangering his ship and was 'reprimanded'. Nevertheless, due to his previously unblemished naval record, he was immediately given command of *HMS Chawton* (M1209), the ship which was taken out of reserve at Gibraltar to take over *Belton's* fishery protection duties.

The North Sea is noted for its savage weather conditions and for being one of the busiest shipping areas of the world. It is therefore inevitable that dozens of vessels are lost in the North Sea every year.

The vast majority of these are small private pleasure or fishing craft, but larger merchant ships can also find themselves victims of the sea's venom. Occasionally, the loss of a naval vessel, often with heavy loss of life, hits the headlines.

Built in 1916 at Rotterdam as the ocean-going tug *Marie*, the Dutch naval tug *RS21* had a varied service career. In 1918 she had been purchased by the Dutch Navy for conversion to a minesweeper. Renamed *M1*, the vessel served in this role until seized by the Kriegsmarine in May 1940. Having survived the war, the vessel was returned to the Dutch Navy in 1945 and employed in the purpose for which she was built.

Whilst lying at an anchorage in the Schluchter, west of Norderney, two days before Christmas 1949, *RS21* was torn from her moorings in a gale and stranded. Fortunately, all of her crew were saved, but the ship sank soon afterwards and was never recovered.

The German MAL Type II logistic landing craft *MAL44* and *MAL46* were captured by the Allies in May 1945 and were employed post-war on German Minesweeping Administration (GM/SA) duties with the 18th Mine-flotilla. Later, as the Allied minesweeping operations were wound down, the vessels were utilised as transport barges. On 18 March 1948, in transit between Bremerhaven and the River Rhine in tow of the tugs *Fairplay XIV* and *Fairplay XII* respectively, *MAL44* and *MAL46* capsized and were lost in a gale near Terschelling in position 53°23'20"N, 05°00'00"E.

Like their British counterparts of the ZZ-class, the extra load of modifications in this design had reduced the already low freeboard of the craft and, together with the square, blunt bow and flat bottom, made for very poor handling and seakeeping ability. Thus, it had been the sea which claimed the first wartime loss of this type, when the Type I vessel *MAL8* was lost in the Sea of Azov through stress of weather on 1 September 1943.

Another former Kriegsmarine vessel was later to be the subject of the West German Navy's worst post-war disaster. Originally commissioned in March 1945 at the Deutche Werft shipyard in Hamburg, the Type XXIII submarine *U2365* was scuttled in the Kattegat in position 56° 51'N, 11° 49'E, after being struck by bombs during an air attack on 8 May that year, in which her entire crew of nineteen men were killed.

Along with her sister-boat *U2367*, the submarine was raised in June 1956 from a depth of over 50 metres by the salvage vessel *John Beckendorf* and refitted for service with the underwater weapons school of the Federal German Navy under the pennant number UW20, re-commissioning on 15 August 1957 as *FGS Hai* (S170).

She followed *U2367*, now renamed *FGS Hecht* (S171), into the Submarine Training Group at Neustadt on 31 August 1960. Both boats were extensively rebuilt between 1961 and 1963 at the Blohm and Voss shipyard during which they were lengthened by 1.45 metres in the region of the engine room to accommodate new diesel engines. Further minor modifications followed, including the streamlining of their conning tower fairings.

Whilst crossing the Dogger Bank on her way to visit Aberdeen on 14 September 1966 as part of the Submarine Training Group, *Hai* sank in a heavy storm in the approximate position of 55°15'N, 04°22'E. The submarine had been transiting on the surface and it was some time before the two other submarines and two escorts of the group realised that she had disappeared and raised the alarm. The tender *Lech* had lost radar contact with the submarine at 1742, after having received a message that the boat was on a course of 300° and was listing. *Lech*'s commanding officer, Fregattenkapitan Mahrholz, ordered his ship to turn to a starboard to a course of 220° to investigate, believing

that *Hai* may have changed course in order to better ride out the violent south-westerly force 7-8 gale.

When it was realised that *Hai* may have foundered, a huge search was instigated by ships of several navies, including the frigate *HMS Blackwood* (F78), the submarine *HMS Opportune* (S20), the mine-hunters *HM Ships Bronington* (M1115) and *Iveston* (M1151) and four minesweepers of the Royal Navy. Only one of *Hai's* twenty-one man crew, Obermaat Peter Silbermann, survived the accident, having been plucked from the sea by one of the searching ships. Her captain, Oberleutnant Wiedersheim, who had only taken over command of the boat in June of that year, was among those lost when the ship sank, presumably at around 1800.

The *Hai* was raised five days later from a depth of 47 metres by the heavy-lift crane vessel *Magnus III* and beached in the Ems Estuary on the 24th, from where she was officially paid off.

A close examination at the Rheinstahl-Nordseewerke shipyard at Emden initially indicated that a seam in the engine room may had split due to a fault in the welding, allowing water to stream into the boat. However, no such attributable defects on the pressure hull could be found and following trials and an official inquiry into the tragedy, it was announced by the Minister of Justice of Schleswig-Holstein at Kiel in August 1967 that the sinking had in fact been the result of water entering the boat through the retracted schnorkel, situated less than a metre above the main deck level. As the water level in the engine room bilge rose, un-noticed by the watch-keepers, the boat's already meagre freeboard would have been steadily eroded, until water eventually cascaded into the boat through the open conning tower hatch. Flooding of the submarine was so rapid that there was no time to transmit a distress signal before she sank.

The sole survivor of the tragedy stated that OLzS Wiedersheim, realising that his boat was foundering, gave the order to abandon ship, an order which, although judged by the inquiry to have been hasty, was considered justified by the situation as he saw it at the time.

Although *Hai* had not carried a suitable life raft or a distress buoy during her fateful voyage, it was not considered that provision of such equipment would have resulted in any further members of her crew being saved.

The public prosecutor in Lubeck decided to discontinue inquiries into the tragedy, as it was determined that there was no criminal liability by any living members of the Federal German Navy. The accident had been the result of a number of unconnected factors and was unique in U-boat history. Neither the officer in charge of the Training Group, Fregattenkapitan Mahrholz, the commander of the Group's Flagship, the tender *FGS Lech*, nor the Blohm and Voss yard which had carried out her recent reconstruction, were judged as being criminally negligent.

*Hai* was broken up in 1968-69. Following the conclusion of enquiries into her loss, her sister boat *Hecht* was decommissioned on 30 September 1968 and laid up at Kiel before being broken up from July 1969.

Often referred to as the 'little brother' of the larger Type XXI submarines, the Type XXIII was derived from the Type XXII coastal U-boats and was the earliest all-external ballast tank, single-hull class. This was a result of the unusually large battery capacity within a hull in which internal space was at a premium. The design had almost no surface buoyancy, a slight in-rush of water through the lower hatch being sufficient to sink the boats abruptly.

Trials showed that, even when diving without forward motion, the highest part of the conning tower was below the water's surface after just twenty seconds. The danger of sinking was thus extremely high and, indeed, such mishaps occurred several times: *U2331* sank accidentally off Hela on 10 October 1944; *U2344* sank after a collision with *U2336* on 18 February 1945; the French *N35* (ex-*U2326*) disappeared off Toulon on 6 December 1946; and *Hai* (ex-*U2365*) on 14 September 1966. In most cases the submarines sank so rapidly that their entire crew perished.

Nearby, the Baltic Sea also bears the brunt, from time to time, of the gales blasting in form the eastern Atlantic and North Sea. One such gale resulted in the sinking of the East German Habicht I-class minesweeper *MLR6-33* off Sassnitz in April 1958. The 500-tonne ship was raised the following year and, although not returned to service in her previous role, was repaired for use as a salvage vessel.

In the waters north of the Arctic Circle, mariners have not only had to contend with the wild storms which batter their vessels, but also with the dangers of ice flows in the winter months, and the knowledge that, should they have to abandon ship, the deadly spectre of the sub-zero temperatures is waiting to take it's toll amongst the survivors.

The *Razumny* had been completed as a destroyer of the Russian Type 7 design at the Baltic Nikolayev Dalzavod shipyard during the gloomy year of 1941 and was later transferred to the Northern Fleet via the Siberian Sea route. Having survived the ravages of the war years, the ship was converted into an electronic survey vessel between 1958 and 1959. Not long afterwards *Razumny* was operating off Murmansk in a storm when she was driven ashore and wrecked.

Russia had employed Italian assistance in the design of the Type 7 destroyers, but the ships proved deficient in sea-keeping qualities for the more exacting weather conditions within the Arctic Circle.

During the war, structural failures resulted in *Gromky* losing her bow, and *Sokrushitelny* foundering due to stress of weather in the Barents Sea on 22 November 1942. It is probable that a further vessel of the class, *Spokoiny*, also succumbed to the weather in the final winter of the war, as there appear to be no war records to suggest an alternative reason for her deletion.

Although warmed by the North Atlantic Drift, the waters around Iceland are still whipped by severe gales throughout the year. The island does not possess a navy, but the Icelandic Coast Guard operates several ocean-going patrol vessels in the fishery protection and offshore patrol roles. These vessels were often referred to as 'gunboats' during the 'Cod War' with Britain in 1975-76.

The 200-tonne patrol boat *Hermódur* was built at Finnboda Varv, Stockholm in 1947 as a lighthouse tender for the Icelandic Government and was occasionally used as a Coast Guard vessel, in which duty it was armed with a 47mm calibre gun. During a patrol off the southwest coast of the island on 18 February 1959 the ship foundered in a gale off Reykjanes with her entire crew of twelve men.

Greenland, the earth's largest island, is almost entirely covered with ice and snow. Its tiny population is mainly scattered around the south coast. Colonised by the Danes in the early 1700s, the island became a Danish county in 1953. The Danish Navy, therefore, has the responsibility of patrolling the iceberg-strewn waters around the coast and for this purpose has built several designs of patrol vessel based on ocean-going trawlers. Whilst employed on such duties, at least two Danish Navy vessels have been lost.

Whilst en route between the weather station Aputiteq to Angmagssalik in October 1948, the patrol cutter *HDMS Alken* disappeared. Despite an extensive air and sea search operation, no traces of the vessel or her nine-man crew were ever found. It is assumed that she foundered in the southerly gale blowing up the east coast of Greenland at the time of her disappearance. However, an incident involving her sister ship *HDMS Maagen* a couple of years later may lend credence to another theory as to the cause of her loss.

*Maagen* set sail from Godthåb in Greenland on Sunday, 9 January 1950 and set a southerly course towards Ivigtut. The Naval Base at Godthåb received two radio reports from the ship, one four hours after sailing and the other at 1330 the following afternoon. Concern was raised

*The Icelandic patrol boat/tender Hermodur, which foundered with all hands in a gale off Reykjanes on 18 February 1959. (Icelandic Coast Guard)*

when the ship failed to arrive at Ivigtut at her expected time of 1700 on Monday evening. As it was already dark, it was Tuesday morning before the massive search operation could be initiated, involving dozens of Danish and American ships and aircraft. Despite the intensity of the search, it was over a week before anyone was to see the ship again.

After her first radio report on Sunday afternoon, *Maagen* had steamed into an increasingly deteriorating weather front. On Monday the high winds were joined by heavy snow that rapidly gathered on the vessel's decks and was frozen by the sub-zero temperatures. Late that night the crew were experiencing difficulties with the ship's steering as the rudder and steering gear began to freeze up. The wind and snow also affected the ship's radio, so it proved impossible to inform Godthåb that they were already in difficulties.

The gale continued to intensify, with winds reaching storm force 11 until by the early hours of Wednesday the 11th. Fuel was running low and at 0500 it was estimated that there was only enough left for about one hour's steaming, leaving the Commanding Officer no choice but to order the engines stopped. Gale force winds persisted throughout the day and overnight and, with the ship being tossed about violently, it proved impossible for the crew to keep the decks and superstructure clear of the ever-increasing build-up of snow and ice. The situation deteriorated further still when, late on Wednesday evening, the vessel lost all electrical lighting.

During the Thursday morning, the weather abated slightly, allowing the crew to clear some of the ice from the ship, but the respite was to be short-lived as the winds intensified again that afternoon from the north-west. During the next two days the crew tried, unsuccessfully, to rig a distress antenna, but hopes rose on Saturday afternoon when land was at last sighted 25 miles to the north, quickly identified as Kap Thorvaldsen, south of Arsuk. At least they now knew where they were!

As the ship continued to drift southward for yet another night the winds blew fiercer than ever. On Sunday morning an attempt to restart the main engines failed as all the ship's compressed air had been exhausted. Throughout the previous days the crew had been busy pumping out their waterlogged vessel using hand pumps, but the pipework fractured and the rest of the day was spent repairing it. On Monday morning, with the gale blowing force 7 from the south-east, a massive wave struck the ship stern-on, smashing a door and the windows of the wheelhouse, and destroying the already waterlogged generator and dynamo. The water, knee-deep in the shattered wheelhouse, had to be drained by opening the opposite door. That night, the winds reached hurricane force.

At 0600 the next morning a searchlight was sighted to the south-west and the crew mustered on deck and released rockets and signal flares. Their hopes were dashed once again though when, as daylight dawned, no help was in sight. However, as the wind decreased that afternoon they were able to rig some sails on the mast and they were able to make some headway towards land. Later that afternoon they arrived off Støren, the entrance to Ivigtut and, at 2030 on Tuesday, 17 January - eight days late - *Maagen* finally reached her destination, a 'ghost ship' covered in ice and without lights.

Although cold, wet and exhausted, the crew of *Maagen* survived their terrifying ordeal, as did their ship, which continued in service in the Danish Navy until 1958, when she was sold to the Royal Greenland Trade Department and renamed *Nauja*. In 1976 the cutter changed hands yet again when she was sold to a private owner.

The truth regarding the loss of the *Alken* will probably never be known, although it is likely that she suffered the fate that her sister ship *Maagen* narrowly escaped - succumbing to a combination of hurricane force winds and the build-up of ice on her superstructure and upper-deck fittings.

There is no doubt however, that the effects of ice build-up caused the loss of another Danish Navy vessel some years later. The 82-ton patrol cutter *HDMS Ternen* (Y381) sank off Ravns Storø, west Greenland in January 1957 with her entire crew of eight after capsizing due to the weight of ice on her upper deck.

*Ternen*, under the command of Lieutenant Commander Erik Erling Olsen, had entered the port of Godtháb on 23 January with a heavy list to port due to her superstructure being iced over. The vessel was de-iced and sailed the following day to Færingehavn where she anchored overnight. Early next morning *Ternen* weighed anchor and sailed south towards the anchorage of Ravns Storø, a large basin 3km inland along one of the many fjords along the serrated Greenland coast. The weather was bitterly cold, the chill factor of the already freezing -18°C temperature being compounded by the strong force 6-7 north-westerly wind. At 1833 that night, a signal was received by Greenland Command stating that *Ternen* had not arrived at her destination.

Nothing more was heard from *Ternen* and when there was no response to signals from Greenland Command the following day, an intensive air and sea search was instigated to find her, including US aircraft from their base at Narssarssuaq and the Danish patrol cutters *HDMS Skarven* (Y382) and *HDMS Teisten* (Y383). The initial search was concentrated around Ravns Storø and widened to the south towards Kap Farvel, along the route Ternen was expected to have sailed. No trace of the missing ship could be found.

Six days after the receipt of *Ternen*'s last transmission, a telegram to Greenland Command from the Greenland Government cutter *H.J. Rink* stated: "*Have found marine cutter Ternen in the*

*harbour of Ravns Storø 13.30 hours. The ship is laying on the bottom. Can see foremast with crows nest above the water and can see mizzen masts with flag. Have not seen any people yet. Will go inland now and search for men.*"

The *Teisten* was despatched to the area immediately and on arrival anchored over the sunken cutter. Naval and civilian divers carried out a search of the wreck over the next couple of days, but hope of finding any survivors from the eight-man crew had long since faded. *Ternen*, her hull intact, was lying in twelve metres of water with a heavy list to port 200 metres from shore and 75 metres from some jagged rocks. Ice still clung to the submerged vessel's port side, her anchor barely discernible. Her engines had been at ' ¾ ' speed when she sank and her rudder was positioned hard to port.

It was evident that the end had come quickly for the crew as all the lifebelts were still in their stowages. A copy of *Ternen*'s final signal, despatched at 1832 on 25 January, was found in the radio room, where the clock had stopped only a minute later.

The bodies of three of the crew were found near their ship. Two more corpses were found 100 metres away, but the other three crew were never found. Even a search of the few houses in the area, unoccupied in the winter months, showed no signs of recent visitation.

A Board of Inquiry was later held into the loss. Examination of *Ternen*'s logbook indicated that she had arrived at the anchorage at 1800 on 25 January and that engines were kept running as the anchor was having trouble restraining the vessel. It is thought that the ship's upperworks were already showing signs of ice build-up when she departed Færingehavn.

Formation of ice would have been minimal whilst the ship was heading south, but once she had changed course to the north-east on the transit up the fjord towards the anchorage, the freezing wind and snow would have been on her port side and ice would have begun accumulating. It is probable that she grounded on the submerged rocks and that the effects of this, the ice build-up on her port side and a strong gust of wind, caused the ship to capsize so suddenly that her crew would have had no chance to react. Strong gusts of mountain wind, known as 'fjedkast', are a common phenomenon in the area. The eight-man crew would have stood little chance in the freezing waters and would have been quickly overcome by the shock of the intense cold.

*Ternen* was later raised and sold and, under the name *Serfaq*, was employed as a coaster off the west coast of Greenland from 1959 until 1968.

The potentially serious effects of ice on the superstructure of any surface ship should not be underestimated. The subsequent raising of the vessel's centre of gravity will result in the ship becoming top-heavy and, particularly in rough weather, presents a danger of capsizing. The trend for modern warships to be top-heavy, especially following in-service weapon and electronic modifications, makes it even more imperative that the build-up of ice on upper decks and fittings be closely monitored whilst operating in arctic conditions.

Minor war vessels and naval auxiliaries are often transported between overseas builders/refitters and their owner countries on 'piggy back' ships, it being more desirable to charter special heavy lift ships for the purpose rather than risk their loss to heavy seas. However, it has been known for such vessels to be lost overboard when their transport ship itself incurs the wrath of the sea.

The Japanese tug *YAS-4* was one of several YTL-class tugs transferred from the USA in the 1950s. Having been replaced by a newer craft, *YAS-4* was sold to the Philippines. Unfortunately, the tug never reached her new owners as she was lost overboard from a transport ship during her delivery voyage from Japan in September 1976 and was never recovered.

In 1972 Brooke Marine completed three 37.5-metre fast patrol craft for the Omani Navy. All three of these craft were returned to the UK yard for modernisation and refit in November 1977, work which included their complete rebuild from the main deck upwards and the addition of two Exocet MM38 missiles to their armament, as well as the installation of a Sea

*The Omani missile boat Al Bushra was washed overboard and lost from the heavylift vessel Trautenfels on 28 December 1978.*
*(Maritime Photo Library)*

Archer fire control system. On completion of the refit, *Al Bushra* (B1) crossed the English Channel to Rotterdam on 12 December 1978, where she was loaded aboard the Hansa Line heavy lift vessel *Trautenfels* for the long journey back to Oman. During this deliver voyage *Al Bushra* was washed overboard by hurricane winds in the Bay of Biscay on 28 December and sank without trace.

The craft was later replaced by one of the larger Province-class, ordered from Vosper Thornycroft, Southampton, in 1980.

The Omani Navy suffered a second loss in almost identical circumstances when, in 1990, one of two Van Damen Push Cat 1500 tugs, *T1*, was lost overboard from a transport ship whilst en route to Oman. Like the *Al Bushra*, *T1* was also lost without trace and was replaced by a sister ship, *T3*, later that year.

Again in similar circumstances, the Egyptian October-class missile boat *No.791* was washed overboard from a merchant ship on return from refit at Vosper Thornycroft on 16 December 1980. Fortunately, this vessel was recovered six months later and returned to Portsmouth for refit. Following repairs the vessel again left the UK for Alexandria on 13 August 1982.

High winds are not the only cause of huge waves. In the Pacific Ocean, underwater seismic shocks instigated by volcanic eruptions, earthquakes or landslides, occasionally result in a phenomenon known as a tsunami - the Hawaiian name for a seismic sea wave. Sometimes incorrectly referred to as tidal waves, the height and strength of a tsunami tends to increase as it approaches shallower water at speeds of up to 720 km/h (450 mph) and can totally engulf small ships and low-lying coastal areas. On 2 November 1946, a tsunami that struck the south coast of the Japanese mainland caused the sinking of the Japanese former-torpedo-boat *No.223* at Toba.

Such a phenomenon was probably also responsible for the disappearance of the Japanese Maritime Safety Agency (JMSA) survey ship *Kaiyo No.5* in the Autumn of 1952. The ship had been despatched to investigate the erupting submarine volcano Myojin-Sho. Contact was lost with the 211-ton ship on 24 September and, following the discovery of a sole lifebuoy, she was later located in position 31°56'N, 140°0.5'E. None of her crew survived.

Although found mainly in the Pacific, they do very occasionally occur elsewhere in the world. In fact, a tsunami in the Caribbean in August 1916 was responsible for the wrecking of the armoured cruiser *USS Memphis*, when the ship was dashed against the rocks off San Domingo in the Dominican Republic.

Centred at Honolulu, in the middle of the Pacific Ocean, the Tsunami Warning system consists of six buoys that monitor changes in water pressure that would indicate seismic activities and subsequently alerts the Pacific Rim countries when signs of a tsunami are detected. Following the devastating tsunami that hit the countries bordering the Indian Ocean, on 26 December 2004, the Indian Ocean Tsunami Warning and Mitigation System (IOTWS), was quickly established and became active in late June 2006. The system consists of 25 seismographic stations relaying information to 26 national tsunami information centres, as well as three deep-ocean sensors. However, further coordination between governments and improved methods of relaying information from the centres to the civilians at risk are required to make the system fully effective. The December 2004 phenomenon was triggered by the shifting of the tectonic plates that run north-to-south off the west coast of Sumatra, six miles under the surface of the sea. The earthquake, measuring 9.3 on the Richter scale and centred just north of the island of Simeulue, caused a massive 20-foot wall of water to surge across the ocean, swamping first Sumatra, then continuing its trail of destruction along the coastlines of Malaysia, Thailand, Burma, India and Sri Lanka. The final death toll may never be known, but is estimated at around 230,000.

Entire areas were wiped out, with thousands of vessels swept up to a mile inland.

Although most of the craft sunk or wrecked were small pleasure and fishing craft, it was inevitable that a number of smaller naval vessels also succumbed to nature's fury on that terrible day. One such vessel was the small Thai Navy patrol boat *T215*, which sank near the main Andaman Sea naval base at Phangnga, with the loss of two of the 19.8-metre vessel's crew.

The Phangnga Naval Base, where two frigates and six patrol craft were stationed, was almost completely destroyed, whilst the frigate *HTMS Kra Buri* (457) was grounded at Thap Lamu, and three patrol boats were washed aground on rocks. The 34-metere patrol craft *T94* was partially flooded. It was several months before these vessels were salvaged and even the most rudimentary services restored to the naval base, where four officers were missing and 14 others injured.

In Sri Lanka, the naval base at Trincomalee was severely damaged and those at Nilaweli and Magella wiped out. In the Dakshina naval base at Galle the Haiqing-class fast attack craft *SNS Parakramabahu* (P351) capsized and sank, along with several inshore patrol craft. The *Parakramabahu* was raised in May 2005 and scrapped.

The problem of survivability of vessels in severe weather conditions and mountainous seas is constantly being addressed by ship designers the world over. Better hull design results in better sea-keeping, therefore increased crew efficiency, increased availability of the ship making more efficient use of resources, and less structural damage to the ship, at a moderate increase in cost.

The seaworthiness of new hull designs is assessed by using scale models in test tanks, although this method, though valuable, is expensive and limited. A later method was instrumented ship trials at sea, which although even more limited, is essential to validate other methods by confirming the way ships actually react in various sea states. A method called the Strip Theory is now well established in the testing of hull forms. Computers are also widely utilised as a design aid.

Any ship designer must take into account several factors, such as the primary role of the ship, speed required in a seaway and the areas in which the vessel will be expected to operate. Consequently, the designers must take into account limits on motion, realising that a cure for one may expose another limit. The effects of varying dimensions on the motion of the ship must be appreciated. For instance, increased hull length will result in a reduction in pitch and heave, increased draft will result in reduced bow 'slamming' in heavy seas and increase propeller efficiency, while the beam of the vessel will effect it's stability and motion characteristics.

In November 1986 the Lloyds Register of Shipping was commissioned by the British Secretary of State for Defence to carry out a study into the advantages and disadvantages of the short/fat S90 hull form, in accordance with the Naval Staff Requirement NSR 7069. The S90, or 'Sirius' hull form, had first been advocated some years earlier by Thornycroft, Giles and Associates (TGA) as an alternative hull form for future anti-submarine frigates.

Although the subject of much controversy at the time, the Lloyds inquiry found that this hull form held no distinct advantages over the standard long/thin hull form. Advantages in the S90 design were improved stability and manoeuvrability, but it was also determined that these were outweighed by higher building and operating costs, increased propulsive power requirements, increased hull noise and reduced sea-keeping performance. Consequently, the Royal Navy stuck with the well-tried and tested standard hull form for their next class of anti-submarine frigates, the Type 23.

In August 1998, the UK Ministry of Defence awarded Vosper Thornycroft a contract for the construction of a trimaran research vessel. The *RV Triton*, a two-thirds scale representative of a proposed future warship design, was delivered two years later. The vessel was subjected to extensive trials over the next two years to determine the concept's suitability as the hull form for the Royal Navy's Future Surface Combatant frigate requirement. This was followed by a further 18-months of trials with a variety of military and commercial equipment, including weapons, sensors and propulsion systems. With a length of 90-metres and beam of 22-metres, the trials sought to prove the advantages of a trimaran hull form over a monohull in terms of reduced through-life costs, hull resistance and signature and increased stability and deck space. Although the vessel proved the suitability of the hull form, the design failed to attract the expected level of interest from other navies The vessel was put up for sale in March 2004 and now serves with the Australian Customs Service.

Various hull fittings also have a significant effect on a vessel's sea-keeping qualities. Bilge keels add greatly to the damping of roll at all speeds, while active stabiliser fins are very effective, especially at speeds above 8 knots. Tank stabilisers are fitted in very few ships, but these are not considered to be as effective as active stabiliser fins and are only really effective at low speeds.

Increased freeboard forward contributes to reduced deck wetness, although excessive freeboard can cause handling difficulties, particularly in high winds. The fitting of bulwark structures in way of the bow is another effective way of increasing freeboard and has been used to great effect in many ship classes. For example, from 1979 the US Navy's Knox-class frigates were given spray strakes and 3.5-feet higher bow bulwarks to reduce deck wetness and improve seaworthiness.

Generally, ships can sink in one of three ways: on an even keel, or bodily; by plunging bow or stern first; or by capsizing. The latter, when a vessel suffers from a loss of stability to such an extent that she rolls over, accounts for about 80% of ship sinkings.

As far as possible a hull should be compartmentalised to contain flooding, the ability of a ship to survive flooding of at least two adjacent sections without sinking or capsizing being a requirement of most modern warship designs. Hull subdivision, which also serves to increase a vessel's structural strength, can be effected by the use of decks, transverse and longitudinal bulkheads and, to a certain extent, double bottoms. The latter can restrict damage as a result of grounding and minor collisions, especially if the double-bottom is itself divided into smaller compartments. These spaces are often used for the storage of fuel, although water compensation will probably be required in ships of destroyer size and below, to prevent a dangerous rise in the centre of gravity of the ship as the fuel is consumed.

In a damaged ship, these compartments can provide a means of righting a list by the transference of liquids from one side to the other. However, the flooding of these spaces by rupturing of the hull can actually be the cause of a ship to heel. When the above-water structure is longitudinally subdivided, the flooding of a port or starboard compartment can lead to the ship listing and, ultimately, capsizing. This being so, the flooding of large compartments which span the beam of the ship can cause a state of loll when the water is allowed to flow back and forth across the ship - one of the most dangerous conditions for a vessel to be in. This problem can be solved by dividing the flooded area up longitudinally, so reducing the effect, by draining the free-surface water to a lower deck, so lowering the centre of gravity, or by pumping the fluid overboard. Depending on the circumstances, each choice can have detrimental effects on the stability of the ship before the situation improves and must be carefully considered by the Damage-control Officer before hasty decisions are made.

Many navies are now following the lead taken by the US Navy in the design and installation of computerised ballast management systems. Development of the US Navy's PACER Ballast System was prompted by the near-capsize of the frigate *USS Stark* (FFG-31) after she was hit by Iraqi Exocet missiles in the Persian Gulf in 1987. The system, which calculates rapid counter-flooding solutions to overcome ship stability problems caused by large masses of free-flooding water, such as that resulting from fire-fighting or from hull damage, was later trialed in one of *Stark's* sister ships, *USS Reid* (FFG-30) and in the assault ship *USS Belleau Wood* (LHA-3), before being installed operationally in several ship classes.

The Royal Navy also approached John Brown Engineers and Constructors in 1988 regarding the development of software to allow warship crews to assess the effects of flooding on the ship's stability and, although much delayed by budgetary constraints, such systems are now in service in a variety of formats on most Royal Navy ships of frigate size and larger.

Analysis of ship damage reports show that approximately 80% of structural problems involve cracking. This is frequently as a result of poor construction or design, as with vessels hurriedly constructed during World War Two. Sharp corners form high stress points and a tendency to crack. Cracking can occur on

ships in their first few months of service or on ships newly undocked after refit. Research into brittle fractures at the naval Construction Research Establishment at Rosyth, Scotland, in 1969 found that at a temperature of minus-10°C a small crack in a vessel's hull could be propagated at a speed of a mile per second.

Similarly, although corrosion takes some time to develop into a problem, only minimal corrosion allowances are built into modern warship design. Corrosion rates can be controlled by the application of advanced preservation methods and coatings. Zinc coatings and high duty paints are two very effective, but expensive alternatives.

Fatigue affects hulls by the continuous flexing of a ship's structure due to the passage of waves, and is accumulative, with larger waves taking a bigger toll than smaller ones. To this end, a vessel working continuously in the North Atlantic will approach its fatigue limit some 3-4 times faster than one serving world-wide, due to the higher average wave heights and lengths in this ocean. Also, the increased pressures put on navies to cover the same operational commitments with fewer ships means that each vessel will spend more time at sea, and so reach its fatigue limit at an earlier age. This is then exacerbated by the fact that defence cuts mean that ships are being kept in service much longer than originally intended when they were designed and built. This makes a vessel even more susceptible to loss when receiving accidental damage, for instance in a collision or grounding.

These effects can be prevented by a good Hull Health Monitoring procedure, both by ships' staffs and by dockyards, in order to spot likely weak points before they become critical.

The vast majority of warship hulls are still built of steel. The hull is coated with an anti-fouling paint, preventing organisms adhering to the hull and also protecting the hull from corrosion. These paints have improved vastly over the years, with the result that vessels require fewer dockings for bottom cleans. Further protection can also be provided by the use of a cathodic protection system, first used by the Royal Navy in the 1960s.

Different metals in the hull, such as the steel of the hull and the alloys in the propellers, rudders, sea inlets and other hull fittings, will become anodic and cathodic. The sea water in which the vessel is floating will form an electrolyte, thus allowing an small electric current to flow between the anodes and cathodes formed by the dissimilar metals, resulting in erosion of the hull. A cathodic protection system measures this current via a reference electrode and, through a control box, provides an output current of the opposite potential to a series of electrodes situated at strategic points around the ship's underwater area, thus cancelling out the residual current. The output current is controlled by increasing or decreasing the voltage to the anodes, usually in the region of 500-800mV. Also fitted are a series of zinc sacrificial anodes on fittings such as rudders and sea inlets, manufactured of a lower electrolytic value so as to erode before the hull fittings. Fittings such as rudders and stabilisers should also be 'earthed' to the ship's hull.

The material used in the building of the vessel will also have a great effect on its survivability. The designer may use high tensile steel in areas of known stress such as in the way of bilge and shear strakes, although such steels are obviously more expensive and more difficult to weld and shape. The choice of which grade of high tensile steel to use must also take into consideration its compatibility with the mild steel which they complement so as not to build in areas of weakness.

More use is now being made of glass reinforced plastic (GRP), especially in the building of mine-countermeasures vessels and patrol craft, the former mainly because of GRP's non-magnetic qualities,

but also for its great strength and ease of maintenance. However, the cost of building vessels of GRP is sometimes prohibitive, especially for smaller navies.

A simple answer to better sea-keeping is increased hull size. The cost of increased hull size, strength and design is very small when considering the benefits in through-life maintenance cost to keep the hull seaworthy. The very light hull of the British Leander-class frigate design, for instance, resulted in considerable work to constantly check deterioration and the later Type 21 frigate and Type 42 destroyer designs have both required extensive strengthening of their hull due to structural cracking problems. As the cost of the hull is only some 10% of total warship costs, then surely a small increase in investment for a larger and more seaworthy hull would lead to through-life savings, as well as providing a comfortable margin for 'stretch'. It appears that this lesson has been learnt with the larger 'stretch' margin being built into the Royal Navy's new Type 45 destroyers.

This may help to alleviate the problems of warships being modernised to the stage where they are top-heavy and consequently unstable, and susceptible to stress and cracking, particularly in areas of maximum stress such as engine uptakes/downtakes, machinery removal routes, hatches, towed array winch mountings, and hull in way of slamming/bending/wave stress, the latter of which has an accumulative effect.

A longer hull will also result in savings in fuel costs, which for a ship of destroyer/frigate size can be a sizeable annual sum. The larger ship will be easier to lay out; in particular the arrangement of sensors and weapons so as to avoid mutual interference will be eased. The more spacious hull will also allow the superstructures to be smaller, reducing the windage that upsets stability and handling at low speeds, another benefit being a lower radar-reflective area.

Probably the most effective way of saving ships from the fury of storms is, of course, to warn them in plenty of time of its imminent approach. To ensure an accurate forecast of weather in the North Atlantic, it was agreed by several countries at an International Conference in 1946 that a number of weather ships would be utilised for this purpose. These would be stationed throughout the North Atlantic in set patrol areas to monitor weather patterns and also to act as rescue vessels for ships or aircraft in distress. They would also be ideally positioned to give navigational aid to transatlantic airlines. The thirteen weather stations in the North Atlantic were operated by the USA, Canada, UK, France, Norway, Sweden, Belgium and Holland. The British ships, under the control of the Ocean Weather Service and based at Greenock, carried out 27-day missions, being relieved on station every 21 days. Similar organisations were set up in all ocean areas by a large variety of authorities.

Because of the severe sea conditions in which these vessels would be expected to operate, ex-naval corvettes were usually used, notably those of the Flower-class. The ships were extensively modified, with the removal of all armament and the addition of numerous masts and deckhouses, to accommodate the many aerials, loops and balloons for which to obtain the necessary meteorological data, increasing their displacement from around 1,000 to over 1,400 tons. Elaborate communications systems were also added to allow the ships to keep in constant contact with their shore stations. Because of the conditions in which the ships would be expected to operate throughout their patrols their accommodation was also much improved.

As technology advanced, the work of these vessels was taken over more and more by radar, and later still by a large number of weather satellites. By the late-1980s most maritime nations had abandoned or severely cut back the use of weather ships. However, whilst there is no denying the photographic assistance provided by satellite surveillance, the basis of synoptic charts are actual measurements of pressure, temperature, wind speed and direction, etc. For the ocean environment this data can best be provided by weather ships, stationed off the established trade routes in areas that are not normally visited.

A small fleet of vessels is still maintained by the Japanese Meteorological Agency for this purpose, with older vessels being replaced by newer ships, such as the *Chofu Maru*, completed in 1987 and the slightly modified sister ship, the *Kofu Maru*, completed in July 1988.

The technology used in predicting weather patterns is improving all the time, much effort being devoted to computer programmes capable of digesting everything known about storms, their formation and patterns. This is greatly assisted by the use of satellites, although as we all know, the forecasters don't always get it right!

One final quirk of nature deserves a brief mention here. Until recently, the disappearance of ships and aircraft, without warning or trace, in the area known as the Bermuda Triangle has formed a legend, along with strange lights and sea disturbances and the appearance and disappearance of small 'islands'. However, a scientific explanation for these phenomenon now exists.

The oil and gas industry is familiar with a phenomenon known as a 'blowout', when a drilling rig suddenly ruptures and releases a large pocket of highly explosive methane gas. It is now realised that the continental shelf areas are subject to the formation of gas hydrates which normally only form when water and gas together are subjected to low temperatures and high pressures. Such characteristics are natural in areas where permafrost exists, but may also be found deep in the ocean at depths exceeding 500 metres. Where the continental shelf ends and the ocean floor suddenly drops away, a build-up of sediment from rotting sea life can, if disturbed, eventually result in massive landslides, measuring many miles across, which can scour upper rock layers of the seabed and the layer of hydrates to rupture pockets of methane gas trapped beneath.

Massive clouds of the gas, formed from decomposing sea life, crystallised by the high pressure, can therefore be released, rising to the surface and causing the sea to become extremely gaseous. It is not difficult to imagine that, given such gasified water conditions, a vessel floating in such water will lose buoyancy, due to the reduction of the specific gravity of the water. The ship will therefore 'sink' deeper in the water and may be swamped.

On falling to the ocean floor, the wreck may land in the newly created crater and will quickly be covered by the settling cloud of silt and mud blown up by the gas cloud. Crewmen jumping overboard, even when wearing life jackets, will similarly be unable to maintain flotation and will sink, as will any lifeboats, rafts or wreckage. If a source of ignition aboard the ship ignited the gas cloud, a massive explosion would rip the ship apart without warning. This theory then would explain why ships would effectively 'disappear' without warning and with no traces of their existence to be found.

The methane gas, being lighter than air, will rise into the atmosphere. If the highly explosive cloud then comes into contact with hot exhaust gases from aircraft engines, there may be a mighty explosion. The aircraft wreckage may then fall into the gasified sea and, just as in the case of the ship, sink without trace. Such circumstances may explain the sudden 'disappearance' of aircraft in the 'Bermuda Triangle' and other sea areas where, until now, the disappearance of ships and aircraft have gone unexplained.

The strange behaviour of radio and compass equipment in some areas can also be explained by such gas releases. The gasified and agitated water surface will cause the immediate air above it to become ionised, thus producing a negative electrical charge, and therefore a magnetic source, which can effect magnetic compasses or ship's equipment. Strange lights can be explained by the burning gas, and the appearance and disappearance of 'islands' by the white-coloured boiling of the water's surface.

Seventy percent of the world's surface is covered in water, much of which is still unexplored and remains as unfamiliar to us as the surface of the moon. Man has learned over the centuries never to underestimate the power of the sea to surprise us.

# Chapter Two

# FIRE AND EXPLOSIONS

Apart from the sea, the most terrifying enemy of the seafarer is fire, the effects of which can be catastrophic. Fires in warships are all the more dangerous due to the large quantities of fuel and ammunition carried on board. A 4,000-tonne frigate can be expected to carry around 500-700 tonnes of fuel, 50 tonnes of ammunition and 100 tonnes of miscellaneous inflammable materials. Added to this are the large amounts of inflammable cabling, furnishings, stationary and personal belongings carried on board, although many improvements in these areas, particularly as a result of the 1982 Falklands conflict, have been incorporated in recent years.

Considering the regularity with which they occur aboard ships and submarines, fire, on its own, seldom sinks a vessel, but the damage wreaked can be devastating, especially with the incapacitating effect on the crew of thick, acrid and toxic black smoke. Saving a ship in difficulties, either as a result of fire or any other cause, is very much dependent on the fire-fighting and damage-control skills of the crew. Their lives, and the survival of their ship, may well depend on these skills, bearing in mind that over half of the fires aboard naval vessels occur whilst the ship is at sea, where assistance of any kind may be hundreds of miles distant.

Even when a vessel is secured alongside in harbour, it will be incumbent upon the ship's duty personnel to provide the initial fire-fighting response. Their primary aim, should first-aid appliances fail to extinguish the fire, will be to contain the blaze until assistance can arrive and to ensure the safety of the crew. At sea however, the emphasis may well shift to the survival of the ship, upon which the lives of the crew may depend, especially when the ship is involved in military operations.

A third of all fires occur whilst a ship is in refit or undergoing major overhaul, when even the reduced crew assigned to the vessel may not be resident aboard. In such circumstances, the fire-fighting responsibility will fall to the dockyard's fire-fighting organisation or to the local civilian fire department. These cases will be discussed later, in Chapter Six.

Personnel using first-aid fire-fighting appliances such as portable extinguishers successfully extinguish well over 90% of all fires. The cause of fires are numerous, with around half being electrical in nature, whilst welding, machinery malfunction and fuel or oil leaks are also major contributors. Accidents involving munitions will be dealt with later, in Chapter Seven.

The most common location of shipboard blazes is in machinery compartments, within which the three ingredients required for a fire are contained in copious quantities - namely fuel, heat and oxygen.

The removal of any one of these components from the equation will cause a fire to die.

Most of the major warships built during the Second World War were propelled by steam-powered machinery - either reciprocating engines or turbines. Steam to operate this machinery was provided mostly by oil-fired boilers, the ancient coal-burning vessels fast being resigned to the scrap yard.

Probably the most dangerous occurrence with regard to a ship's boilers is that of an iron-in-steam fire. This phenomenon occurs when the tubes of a boiler are starved of water, quickly allowing them to overheat, unless the boiler flame is immediately extinguished or the correct water level restored. When the temperature of steel exceeds 700°C - at which temperature it will begin to glow to a 'cherry-red' colour - the iron will burn in the steam, utilising the oxygen released by the iron/steam reaction. This reaction will also release hydrogen, which, if the temperature is high enough, will ignite spontaneously on contact with the air, resulting in a self-regenerating fire that can only be quenched by the use of copious quantities of water to remove the heat element of the equation.

Such fires often rage for many hours before being brought under control, with the consequence that irreparable damage is inflicted on the machinery, necessitating many months of work to replace the useless components. The inside of a boiler after an iron-in-steam fire will resemble an underground cavern, the molten tubes forming metal stalactites and stalagmites protruding from the furnace brickwork. Such a blaze occurred in the early-1970s aboard the British commando carrier HMS Bulwark (R08), due to incorrect interpretation of the water level indicated by the local gauge glass, as the normal remote-indicating IGEMA gauge glass was out-of-action at the time.

Boilers are also susceptible to explosions, commonly caused when excess fuel leaks or is injected into, the furnace before the flame is introduced. Such an explosion caused extensive damage to the Japanese landing ship SB-110 in October 1945. The Type 103 LST was considered beyond repair and lay at Hataka until being broken up three years later.

Most recently, a major boiler room explosion aboard a Spanish frigate has resulted in the ship's premature disposal. SNS Extremadura (F75) was berthed in the El Ferrol naval base at 0220 on 19 December 2005 when the crew were roused from their slumber by the blast that ripped through the bowels of the ship, instantly killing two naval ratings. The ship was rapidly evacuated and fire and rescue services arrived promptly on the scene, where they found several injuring sailors suffering from steam burns.

One of five ships built in Spain in the 1970s to the U.S. Knox-class design, the vessels are in the process of being replaced by the Alvaron de Bazan-class frigates. The Extremadura was due to decommission in the Autumn of 2006, but the damage inflicted on the ship by the fire and explosion was so extensive that she was deemed beyond economical repair and paid off in early-2006.

Although few vessels have been written off as a result of boiler room fires, several have been seriously damaged and deserve mention here. On 26 January 1953, the newly commissioned Daring-class destroyer HMS Duchess (D154) suffered a boiler room explosion at Portland. A petty officer and three junior ratings were killed in the blast and the resultant fire took several hours to extinguish.

The early career of the Royal Navy's sole Type 82 destroyer HMS Bristol (D23) was dogged by ill fortune. In November 1974 a major fire practically destroyed her steam plant, leading to initial fears that the ship, which had only been commissioned the year before, may be scrapped. However, the flexibility of her CoSAG

(Combined Steam And Gas) propulsion system permitted her to continue with her trials programme using her two Rolls Royce Olympus TM1A gas turbines. The damaged steam plant was repaired during her major refit during 1976-77.

Fate was to deal another vicious blow to *HMS Bristol* when, immediately prior to her next refit, she suffered a major explosion and fire in her boiler room. The ship was lying at anchor off Portsmouth Naval Base on the night of 16/17 July 1984 when, a little after midnight, a fire broke out in the steam turbine room after a fractured pipe on a boiler fuel pump sprayed high pressure fuel into hot pipework. On-watch engineers promptly shut down the boiler, but a series of other minor blunders by the crew soon led to a situation whereby the loss of the ship was narrowly averted.

The intensity of the fire was magnified by the failure to isolate the fuel supply or to crash-stop ventilation systems to the compartment, while the steam drench fixed fire-fighting system was not available due to the shutting down of the boiler. As the fire grew out of control the space was evacuated and the crew set up hoses to boundary cool the bulkheads and decks of adjacent compartments. However, secondary fires were soon breaking out in several other compartments, adding to the confusion.

In their eagerness to contain the fire, the crew were pumping thousands of gallons of seawater into the ship, much of it into the superstructure, whilst little thought was initially paid to controlling or removing it. This free-surface water was soon causing stability problems by raising the ship's centre of gravity. By 0330, three hours after the fire had broken out, *Bristol* was listing 5-degrees to starboard and, as the list increased to 8-degrees, the crew attempted to compensate by partially filling trimming tanks. However, this only compounded the problem as the ship quickly lurched to port.

*Bristol* was now in a state of loll, a dangerous condition caused when floodwater is allowed to flow freely from one side of the vessel to the other, so causing her to list unpredictably from side to side. In this condition, any attempt to compensate for the list at a particular moment will result in an increased list as the ship rolls onto the other beam. If the condition of loll is not combated, or another external force, such as beam waves, is introduced, the vessel could capsize.

There are four methods of combating loll: remove weight from high in the ship; add weights lower in the ship; move weights from high up to low down in the ship; or reduce the surface area, especially the breadth, of the free-surface water. The first three of these methods have the effect of lowering the vessel's centre of gravity, whilst the fourth prevents the free-surface water from flowing athwartships.

The preferred option in the case of *Bristol*, whose underwater hull was undamaged, was to remove the water, which would not only lower the centre of gravity, but also increase her reserve of buoyancy. As the boundary cooling water was pumped out, the ship returned to a stable condition. The fire in the boiler room was eventually extinguished at 0630 by pumping high expansion foam into the compartment.

Fortunately, there were no fatalities among *HMS Bristol's* crew - although three were seriously injured - and the ship was later repaired and returned to service. Nevertheless, the subsequent inquiries into the incident revealed that many rudimentary lessons, learnt at such a high cost during the recent Falklands conflict, had to be re-learnt, so reinforcing the value of constant training and drilling in damage-control and fire-fighting methods, as well as the basic principles of stability.

The Dutch Friesland-class destroyer *HrMS Drenthe* (D816) was operating north of the Venezuelan coast, half way between the islands of Barbados and Curacao, on the afternoon of 12 November 1980, when a major fire broke out in her forward boiler room and forward engine room. A burst fuel conduit, allowing high-pressure fuel to be sprayed onto nearby hot pipes, caused the huge fireball and subsequent blaze, which killed two men and wounded a further seven. Extensive damage was caused to both compartments and, owing to the ship's 1957 vintage, repair was judged to be uneconomical and *Drenthe* was officially withdrawn from service twelve days later. Authorised for scrapping in May the following year, the ship was reprieved when she was sold to the Peruvian Navy the following month to join her seven sister ships, serving as *BAP Guise* (DD72) until stricken four years later.

The fate of the *Drenthe* echoed that of another Dutch warship, the aircraft carrier *HrMS Karel Doorman* (R81). The ship was berthed at the Den Helder Naval Base on the evening of 29 April 1968, when a fire broke out in the forward engine room. This fire was barely extinguished when a similar blaze started in the after engine room. Fortunately, there were no casualties, but damage to both compartments was so extensive that the Dutch Admiralty decided to advance the vessel's decommissioning from the planned date of January 1970 to 8 October 1968. Six days later the damaged carrier was sold to the Argentine Navy and, following a refit at the Wilton-Fijnoord shipyard, was commissioned as *ARA Vienticinco de Mayo* (V2). The ship served in this guise until being laid up after the 1982 Falklands conflict due to lack of funds for her refit. She was subsequently scrapped in the 1990s.

Similar fires in the engine rooms of steam-driven ships have cost hundreds of lives, quite apart from the operational loss of valuable maritime assets and the financial drain on ever-tightening defence budgets whilst the vessels undergo repair or even extensive rebuilds.

In June 1964, the engine room of the British Leopard-class frigate *HMS Puma* (F34) was gutted by fire, whilst three years later two crewmen were killed by an explosion in the engine room of the destroyer *HMS Hampshire* (D06), both occurring whilst the ships were berthed alongside at Portsmouth Naval Base.

More recently, six crewmen were killed and a further five injured when a fire swept through the engine room of the Mars-class supply ship *USNS White Plains* (AFS-4) whilst she was transiting the South China Sea towards her home base of Guam on 9 May 1989. Whilst the fierce blaze was being fought for more than an hour, the injured personnel were airlifted to the US military hospital at Clark Air Force Base in the Philippines. Her propulsion plant out-of-action, *White Plains* was later towed to the US Naval Base at Subic Bay in the Philippines where temporary repairs were carried out.

Since the early-1970s, the advent of the gas turbine has resulted in a sharp decrease in the number of vessels propelled by steam-driven machinery. Few navies now contemplate the installation of such plants into new-build ships, save for nuclear-powered vessels such as aircraft carriers and submarines. In fact, the only naval surface vessels currently being built with steam turbines, apart from aircraft carriers, are the Project 956 (Sovremenny-class) guided-missile destroyers under construction in Russia for the Chinese Navy.

Boilers and steam turbines have now given way to gas turbines and diesel engines, the former for their performance, flexibility and light weight, the latter for their ease of maintenance and fuel economy. Many vessels, from fast patrol craft upwards, now incorporate a combination of these prime-movers, thereby combining the impressive sprint speed performance of gas turbines with the economy of the diesel engines at cruising speeds.

The latest 'innovation' is the use of electric motors as prime movers for surface vessels, utilising electric power supplied by diesel- or gas turbine-driven generators. This is by no means a new idea, as electric motors have been used to propel submarines since the early part of the 20th century, while over 300 turbo-electric and diesel-electric driven destroyer-escorts of the Evans, Buckley, Rudderow and Cannon classes were built for the US Navy during the Second World War.

Although the machinery spaces of vessels fitted with gas turbines or diesel propulsion machinery constitute immeasurably more pleasant working and watchkeeping environments, the three components required to sustain a fire - fuel, heat and oxygen - are still present in considerable quantities. Fires, therefore, still pose a considerable danger in such vessels.

Engine room fires have damaged a large number of front line warships in recent years. On 12 December 1980, one crewman was killed by a machinery space fire aboard the Soviet Project 61 (NATO designation 'Kashin'-class) destroyer *Komsomolets Ukrainy*. The Danish frigate *Herluf Trolle* (F353) required some fifteen months of repair work following a major engine room fire in July 1982, while the Ecuadorian missile corvette *El Oro* (GM14) was out-of-action for almost two years following a similar fire on 14 April 1985. A major blaze aboard the Venezuelan tank landing ship *Goajira* (T63) in June of the following year put her out of action for nearly six years, the vessel being laid up for a considerable time before being repaired.

Extensive damage resulting from a fire involving the CoDAG (Combined Diesel and Gas) propulsion plant of the Turkish frigate *TCG Gemlik* (D361, ex-*FGS Emden*) in 1989 led to speculation that she may be scrapped and replaced by one of her ex-West German Navy Köln-class sisters. While the *Gemlik* was later considered worthy of repair, the logistic support ship *Erkin* (A590) was not to have such an auspicious future. The ship, built in 1955, had been acquired by the Turkish Navy in 1982 to replace the previous ship of the same name, but only four years later her engine room was totally destroyed by fire. The *Erkin* was considered beyond repair and was scrapped in Spain in December 1986.

*Gemlik's* reprieve was, however, to be short-lived. Following a second major fire in 1991, the ship was declared a total loss and later scrapped, her identity being assumed by the former-*FGS Braunschweig*, which had been sold to Turkey in 1989 to provide a source of spares to maintain her sisters in an operable condition. This practice of giving identical replacement vessels the name, and sometimes pennant number, of a decommissioned vessel is performed by many navies. Whilst its purpose is, in most cases, purely a way of carrying forward a traditional ship's name, it also serves as a means of disguising the disposal of a vessel following an accident.

*The Turkish frigate TCG Gemlik (D361, ex-FGS Emden) was repaired following a propulsion fire in 1989. However, another major fire in 1991 sealed the ship's fate and she was declared a total loss and later scrapped. Her identity was assumed by the former-FGS Braunschweig, which had been sold to Turkey in 1989 to provide a source of spares to maintain her sisters in an operable condition.*

*(Devrim Yaylali)*

More recently, major fire damage has resulted in the scrapping of one of the Russian Navy's most modern, and powerful, fighting ships. The Pacific Fleet Project 1155 (Udaloy-class) destroyer *Admiral Zakharov* was operating in Ussuriy Bay, off Vladivostok, on 17 February 1992, when a serious fire broke out in one of the ship's engine rooms. During the fire-fighting operation, one crewman was killed and a further seven injured. The damaged ship limped into Vladivostok, where she was laid up awaiting repair. Partly because of the extent of the damage, and partly due to the rundown of the post-'Cold War' Russian Navy and the lack of available funds, the *Admiral Zakharov*, which had only been commissioned in October 1983, was paid-off the following year and ultimately scrapped as beyond economical repair. One of *Admiral Zakharov's* sister ships, *Admiral Tributs*, almost suffered the same fate after she too was severely damaged by a machinery compartment fire whilst in refit in September 1995, but the destroyer was repaired and re-commissioned in 1999.

A major fire aboard an Argentinean naval ship will result in her being under repair for at least two years. At 2000 on the night of 11 April 2007, the icebreaking survey ship *ARA Almirante Irizar* (Q5) was conducting her regular annual patrols of the Antarctic, 140 miles east of Puerto Madryn, in support of the Argentine Antarctic outposts, when a blaze broke out in one of her generator rooms. The fire quickly grew out of control and, 90 minutes later, the Commanding Officer, Captain Guillermo Tarapow, was forced to order the abandoning of his ship. Fortunately, all 296 personnel aboard were evacuated to a Panamanian tanker and two Uruguayan and Argentine fishing vessels. The 15,000-tonne ship was later towed to Puerto Belgrano, where the damage was assessed.

The cause of the fire was determined to have been ignition of fuel from a ruptured fuel pipe, resulting in a blaze that had quickly grown out of control, threatening the ship's fuel tanks. The after end of the ship was extensively damaged, with the generator room, engine room and ship's laboratories burnt out, whilst in the fire-ravaged hangar two H-3 Sea King helicopters were also destroyed. Although the Argentine Navy has pledged to repair the 29-year old ship - a veteran of the 1982 Falklands conflict during which she acted as a hospital ship - the extent of the damage may bring into doubt the cost-effectiveness of the repairs.

Gearbox explosions are relatively rare and, as far as is known, have not resulted in the loss of any major warships in the post-war period. Nevertheless, the destructive force of such a blast can cause catastrophic damage to a vessel's machinery plant and result in her being withdrawn from service for repairs for a considerable period or, if the machinery is considered beyond economical repair, may possibly result in the ship's service life being prematurely terminated. As an example, the severe gearcase fire aboard the aircraft carrier *HMS Illustrious* (R06) in April 1986 caused damage costing some £4 million to repair.

A series of gearcase explosions aboard Royal Navy and Royal Canadian Navy ships during the 1960s prompted the appointment of a working party to investigate their cause. Under the auspices of the Royal Navy, the working party, established in July 1970, employed representatives from the Admiralty Oil and Materials Laboratories, as well as gearing manufacturers David Brown Gear Industries, GEC Marine and Industrial Gears and Vickers.

Although the Royal Navy had experienced minor explosions aboard several vessels, including two of the then new County-class guide-missile destroyers and the supply ship *RFA Regent* (A486) , the worst incident was that suffered by the Canadian frigate *HMCS Kootenay*

(DDE528) during the previous year. Not only was this the first such explosion to have occurred aboard a Canadian warship in post-war years, but it also surpassed in magnitude those experienced by the vessels of most other navies.

On 23 October 1969, *Kootenay*, in company with the aircraft carrier *HMCS Bonaventure* (CVL22) and the frigate *HMCS Saugenay* (DDE206), was heading home to Canada for a refit and was about 200 miles south-west of the English coast when the explosion occurred. The frigate had detached from the rest of the task force shortly before, in order to carry out a routine full-power trial of her propulsion plant. Only eleven minutes after reaching full power, the starboard gearbox exploded, the entire engine room being consumed by a massive fireball. Of the ten men within the compartment at the time of the blast, only four escaped with their lives, one of which later died of his injuries. Two men outside of the compartment were also killed.

With her main engine throttles jammed at 50% power and the fire in the engine room being constantly fed by oil from the gearbox-driven lubricating oil pump, the ship was for some time out of control and in an extremely dire situation. However, the blaze was eventually brought under control and the machinery systems isolated, but the ship was left adrift without propulsive power.

Five crewmen, suffering from the effects of smoke inhalation, were transferred to *Bonaventure*, while *Saugenay* took the crippled *Kootenay* under tow. *Saugenay* was eventually relieved of the painfully slow towing operation on 16 November by the Dutch tug *Elbe*, the group arriving in Halifax twelve days later.

*Kootenay* was re-commissioned in January 1972 after completion of repairs and her anti-submarine capability enhancement conversion. Meanwhile, the enquiry into the incident revealed that bearings within the gearcase had been incorrectly assembled, the bearing shells being installed the wrong way round. This resulted in the bearing oil-ways being obstructed, the lack of lubrication at full power causing them to overheat and ignite the atomised oil within the gearcase.

As the gearbox explosion working party continued their research, they were furnished with further valuable data from a succession of incidents during 1971. The US Navy oiler *USS Caliente* (AO-53) suffered minor damage from a gearcase explosion during April, followed in June by incidents aboard the Canadian frigates *HMCS Skeena* (DDE207) and *HMCS Chaudiere* (DDE235) and another aboard the British frigate *HMS Zulu* (F124) in November, none of which caused any serious damage.

That Canadian frigates should experience so many gearcase explosions within such a short period of time was a cause for extreme concern. In fact, the gearbox primary pinions of the early St. Laurent-class frigates had been a source of problems during contractor's sea trials and the installation of thermocouples within the gearcases was an attempt to detect overheating bearings before they developed into serious defects. Bearing failure is by far the most common cause of gearcase explosions. Other causes include the failure of gearwheel teeth, clutch failure, oil starvation and oil ignition.

Mineral oils commonly used in marine gearcases are not highly flammable and will not burn freely in air unless sufficiently heated, with a spontaneous ignition temperature greater than 300°C. Excessive heat from a defective or oil starved bearing may cause oil to be vaporised, the resultant oil mist and air mixture forming a highly combustible cocktail which may ignite, resulting in an explosion, the magnitude of which will be dependant on the temperature of the bearing and the amount of oil mist present.

Such an explosion is often followed by a major fire due to the large quantity of hot oil cast around the machinery compartment by the blast.

An initial explosion may also be followed by a contraction of the gases within the gearcase, drawing in more air and providing oxygen to produce a second explosion. This secondary explosion is often of a far greater magnitude than the initial ignition. Care should be taken by ship's crews to ensure that, should overheating of bearings or an explosion be suspected, the gearcase is not opened before it has sufficiently cooled to remove the danger of an ignition of any gases present within.

The exhaustive investigations of gearcase explosions carried out by a number of authorities have resulted in many design changes and the refinement of operating procedures, not least of which has been the awareness of operators to the dangers of such disasters. As with any other form of accident, prevention is by far the best form of defence. The close monitoring of gearcase bearing and oil temperatures at all engine powers is essential if bearing defects are to be detected in good time to prevent serious damage. However, it should be noted that a 'wiped' bearing may initially be indicated by a drop in bearing and oil outlet temperature due to increased oil flow through the enlarged bearing clearance. Routine analysis of vibration levels will also provide an early warning of impending bearing failure, while close attention to the hygiene of lubricating oil will minimise the occurrence of bearing defects.

When prevention fails, minimising the damage caused by an explosion is paramount. This could be achieved in a number of ways. Ideally, gearcases could be built of armoured construction, with sufficient strength to contain an explosion, but as pressures of up to $150 lb/in^2$ may be created by a detonation, the size and weight of such a structure makes this an impractical solution. Gearcases have, however, been strengthened within the design and cost constraints of some vessels, in an effort to minimise the extent of damage resulting from an explosion.

The fitting of explosion relief valves within gearcases is also impractical, due to their excessive size, the Lloyd's Register ruling that such fixtures should possess a cross-sectional area of at least $0.0115m^2$ per cubic metre of the gearcase volume. There is also the fear that they may act as flame-throwers in the event of an explosion.

The only viable alternative is the suppression of flames in the immediate vicinity of the ignition by the use of fixed fire-fighting systems within the machinery compartment to limit the extent of the damage. Almost all vessels now have some form of fixed fire-fighting system fitted within main machinery compartments.

Whilst few major warships or auxiliary vessels are lost or written off following fire damage, smaller vessels are often completely destroyed when a major fire breaks out. This is partly because a major engine room fire aboard a small craft can also result in critical damage to the structure and hull of the vessel, rendering it a constructive total loss. The smaller operational value of such vessels will also mean they are more readily discarded in favour of replacement rather than repair.

The torpedo-boat *HS Kataigis* (P51) was one of a number of craft of the Jaguar-class transferred from Germany to the Greek Navy during 1976-77. On the morning of 25 September 1980, *Kataigis* together with five other craft of the First Torpedo Boat Division, was participating in exercises in the Saronikos Gulf, south of Piraeus, with other naval vessels and helicopters. The boat was about eight miles west-south-west of Cape Sounion when, at 0835, the Commanding Officer ordered a gradual increase in speed from 23 to 36 knots. *Kataigis* never reached her ordered speed, as a few minutes later a fireball erupted from the port side of No. 2 main engine in the forward engine room.

As the compartment quickly filled with dense black smoke, the Petty Officer engineer on watch in the machinery control room immediately stopped the engines, before entering the compartment to attempt to extinguish the flames. However, by this time the fire had gained a firm hold and the incapacitating effect of the thick smoke forced him to order an evacuation of the compartment.

On deck, crewmen were rigging fire-fighting equipment, while others were attempting to fight the blaze from the hatches, but the fire-fighting effort was stalled a few minutes later when the generators had to be stopped. With no electrical power to run the main pumps, the supply of salt water was limited to that which could be provided by the single portable P-250 fire pump. Other vessels, including three destroyers, quickly closed the blazing *Kataigis* in order to render assistance and supply her with additional fire-fighting equipment, a task that was hampered by the swell caused by the strong force 5-6 breeze that was blowing at the time. Conditions aboard the burning craft were made even more arduous by the fire-fighting water now slopping around in the forward engine room, the free surface effect causing *Kataigis* to roll sluggishly and unpredictably from side to side. Fearing that the stability of his vessel was reaching a critical state, the Commanding Officer ordered that the minimum of water be used to fight the blaze. Nevertheless, high temperatures indicated in the forward magazine forced the flooding of that compartment and, at about 1030, a fire broke out in the after engine room.

Nevertheless, the crew continued to aggressively fight the fires and, by about 1145, managed to contain its spread and began to regain lost territory. Soon afterwards, the fires were extinguished and the

crippled torpedo boat was taken alongside one of the attending destroyers, where her engine rooms and forward magazine were pumped out and her crew were at last allowed to draw a breath.

Although there had been no serious casualties in the incident, the feverish fire-fighting effort had left them all exhausted. A naval tug despatched from the Salamis naval base then towed the *Kataigis* into port, where three crewmen were taken to hospital suffering from the effects of smoke inhalation.

Following a survey of the damage inflicted upon the machinery and on the wooden hull and light metal frames and beams, it was decided that repairs would be disproportionately costly and the *Kataigis* was declared a constructive total loss and scrapped.

The subsequent investigations revealed that the fire had resulted from a loose fuel return pipe from one of the main engine fuel injectors, allowing high pressure fuel to be sprayed directly onto the engine exhaust manifold. It is likely that the connection had been leaking for some time and that, as the lagging around the exhaust manifold became saturated, the cloud of vaporised fuel was ignited by the high temperature of the casting. Although it could not be determined whether the connection had been improperly tightened during maintenance or whether it had been loosened by the vibrations, inspection of maintenance schedules, together with the fact that the leak occurred when the craft was operating in relatively rough weather and at the moment that engine speed was being increased, led to the acceptance of the latter theory.

Inability to effectively fight the blaze was due primarily to the lack of a permanent sprinkler system, compounded by the early loss of all electrical power to the boat's main salt water pumps. However, even the existence of a fixed fire-suppression system could not prevent the loss of another Hellenic Navy patrol craft in similar circumstances less than three years later.

The coastal patrol craft *N.I. Goulandris II* was, like her sister boat *N.I. Goulandris I*, named after the Greek shipping magnate who donated the two vessels to the Navy in 1977. At 0700 on the morning of 24 June 1983, the 24-metre craft departed from her home port of Mytilene, on the island of Lesbos, on a routine training and fishery protection patrol. The weather was fair and calm and, as the craft reached open water, engine speed was increased to 1,500 rpm and then, at 0745, to 1,800 rpm, for a speed of about 18 knots.

Shortly after 0800, the on-watch mechanic in the engine room spotted flames flickering over the top of the starboard main engine, in the vicinity of the exhaust manifold and supercharger. As he raised the alarm the chief engineer promptly requested to the bridge that the engines be shut down, in response to which the Commanding Officer lowered engine speed to idle and pressed the emergency 'stop' button on the bridge. He was quickly joined by the chief engineer, who visually checked that both engine revolution counters had reduced to zero, before shutting off the lubrication oil supply. Both then attempted to activate the engine room fire-suppression system, while the on-watch mechanic shut off ventilation to the compartment and, together with other crewmen, attempted to fight the fire with portable extinguishers.

Up to this point, it appeared that the fire-fighting effort was proceeding in accordance with practised drills, but an unfortunate chain of events was to thwart the crew's efforts to fight the blaze.

It quickly became evident that the engines were still running and so still feeding the fire with fuel. The chief engineer tried to reach and shut the main engine fuel supply valves, but the fire was now producing so much heat and dense black smoke that it was impossible for anyone to enter the engine room. There

was little choice but to fight the fire from the upper deck, using water supplied by the boat's single P-250 portable fire pump. Coincidentally, the P-250 pump had been placed directly above the starboard main engine and, at 0814, the aluminium deck melted and gave way, casting the pump into the inferno. The fire-fighting effort was now reduced to throwing buckets of water through the hatches and the hole in the deck.

The situation now appeared hopeless and orders from the command ashore, contacted via a battery-powered radio, were that, if the fire could not be extinguished, the crew were to abandon ship. At 0825, as ammunition boxes were being jettisoned, the engines were heard to suddenly increase in speed and, fearing an explosion, the Commanding Officer had little choice but to order his crew to take to the Zodiac inflatable raft, already secured at the craft's side. A nearby fishing vessel approached, but could render little assistance other than to rescue the crew of the *Goulandris* from the raft. Soon afterwards they transferred to a Coast Guard boat and thence to a Navy patrol craft.

The *Goulandris II* continued to burn, her aluminium superstructure and decks slowly being consumed by the intense heat of the fire until, at 1010, she finally sank, 1.8 miles west-south-west of the Mersinia islets on the south coast of Lesbos.

As with the *Kataigis*, the Board of Enquiry determined that the fire had been the result of a loose connection on a fuel return pipe from one of the main injectors, allowing atomised fuel to be sprayed onto the exhaust manifold, where it was ignited. However, the reason for the failure of the emergency 'stop' button on the bridge to shut down the main engines was not determined, although it was surmised that, rather than being defective, it had not been operated properly in the confusion. Also, it was never ascertained whether or not the Halon fire-suppression system had actually operated, although it is assumed that it had been activated by the automatic fire-detection system. Its failure to extinguish the fire was attributed to the flames being continuously fed with fuel by the running engines. The fate of the *Goulandris II* had finally been sealed by the loss of the P-250 fire pump.

In 1988 a Naval Court Martial found the patrol craft's Commanding Officer, a conscripted sub-lieutenant, guilty of negligence, handing down the punishment of a four month sentence suspended for three years. This sentence was later quashed by the Military Appeal Court which, due to lack of evidence to support such a conviction, found him innocent by three votes to two.

Soon after its formation in March 1980, the Royal Bahamas Defence Force suffered the destruction by fire of two of its patrol craft in quick succession. Four 60-foot glass-reinforced plastic patrol craft, built by the Vosper Thornycroft boatyard in the United Kingdom, had been delivered to the Royal Bahamas Marine Police Force in February 1971, followed by a further three sister craft in December 1977.

At 0930 on Friday, 22 August 1980, *HMBS Acklins* (P21) left Coral Harbour, the main base for the naval arm of the Bahamian Defence Force on Providence Island, for its destination of Prince George Wharf. Thirty minutes later a huge explosion wracked the engine room. Efforts to contain the blaze failed and the fire soon spread throughout the craft. Realising that the fire was out of control, the commanding officer, Sub-Lieutenant R. Rolle, gave the order to his twelve man crew to abandon ship. All reached the nearby South Ocean shore safely aboard a life raft. Two sister vessels, *HMBSs Abaco* (P25) and *Inagua* (P27) arrived on the scene soon afterwards, but found the *Acklins* burned to the waterline, the intensity of the blaze forcing them to remain at a safe distance.

A second boat of the class, *HMBS San Salvador* (P24), sank three miles off Great Harbour Cay in the Berry Islands on Wednesday, 25 November 1981, after a fire that is believed to have been started by a fuel leak.

*San Salvador* had departed her Coral Harbour base early that morning for what was to be a routine patrol. Just after noon there was an explosion in the vessel's engine room. The resultant fire quickly grew out of control and, at 1345, the crew transmitted a distress call, stating that they were abandoning ship. This signal was intercepted by the US Coast Guard, who promptly alerted Miami, from where a helicopter and a C-131 aircraft were immediately despatched.

Meanwhile, thirteen of the vessel's fourteen crew safely evacuated the burning boat, but one marine was missing, presumed drowned in the choppy sea conditions. He had last been sighted swimming towards the life raft on which the rest of the survivors were huddled, but had then disappeared beneath the surface. When the aircraft arrived on the scene an hour later they found that the survivors had been picked up by a private pleasure boat. A search involving vessels and aircraft of the Royal Bahamas Defence Force and the

*Her superstructure completely consumed by fire, the Bahamian patrol craft HMBS Acklins continues to burn after an engine room fire on 22 August 1980.*

*(The Nassau Guardian)*

US Coast Guard continued until nightfall, but there was no sign of the missing marine.

The Royal Bahamas Defence Force later received insurance payments totalling US$356,707.50 for the *Acklins* and US$1,102,500 in compensation for the loss of the *San Salvador*. Subsequently, an ex-US Coast Guard Cape-class patrol boat transferred to the Royal Bahamas Defence Force in November 1989 was assigned the name *San Salvador II*.

A further victim of such an incident was the Turkish patrol craft *TCG Yilderim* (P338), which was destroyed by an explosion on 11 April 1985 near Mitilíni, Lesbos. The ex-US Ashville-class vessel was broken up at Aliaga in 1989.

An oil leak in the engine room was also determined to have been the cause of the destruction of one of the Royal Norwegian Navy's newest vessels.

*KNM Orkla* (M353) was one of a class of five Alta-class air-cushion catamaran minesweepers commissioned in the mid-1990s, along with four almost identical Oksøy-class minehunters. At 0700 on the morning of Tuesday 19 November 2002, the GRP-constructed vessel was about seven miles north of Vigra, near Ålesund, when the crew heard a loud noise emanating from the engine-room, followed immediately afterwards by fire detection alarms. The blaze quickly took hold and spread, engulfing the entire ship within minutes and forcing the bridge to be abandoned.

Twenty-two of the 33 crewmen were ordered to evacuate the ship, whilst the others remained to fight the blaze. Four others were evacuated by the fast ferry *Fjortoft* soon afterwards. Although the remaining seven crewmen fought valiantly to save their ship - and after an hour thought that they had it under control - the fire continued to take hold and despite assistance from other ships with fire-fighting equipment, they too were forced to abandon their vessel.

The 26 crew members in the life rafts were rescued by 0900 by the car ferry *Solskjel*. Two rescue helicopters were also scrambled and a casualty receiving station set up in nearby Ålesund. By early-afternoon, all of the crew had been rescued and were later transferred to Brattvaag, where eleven of them were treated for the effects of smoke inhalation.

The fires continued to rage throughout the night, fuelled by the vessel's breached fuel storage tanks. Finally, 24 hours after the fire had started, the *Orkla* capsized. The ferocity of the fire had consumed all of the ship's fuel and oil, thereby preventing any significant pollution.

On 22 November, the crew were transferred to the Oksøy-class minehunter, *KNM Måløy* (M342), which had recently been laid up in reserve as a cost-saving measure.

The upturned vessel was initially towed to shallower waters on the afternoon of 20 November. The civilian firm Eide Marine Services were contracted by the Norwegian Navy to recovery the wreck and hoped to lift the entire hulk onto a barge. However, the destruction caused by the fire was so intense that the wreck broke into three sections when attempts were made to hoist it. The sections were eventually recovered on Sunday and Monday 24/25 November and the barges towed to Bergen, where two military commissions were set up to investigate the cause of the fire. Meanwhile, all of the other Oksøy and Alta-class ships were promptly ordered to return to port pending the results of the investigations.

The investigations determined that the fire had started when an oil line fractured in the engine room and the hot oil quickly ignited. The commission considered that the use of non-fire-retardant paint and inflammable insulation materials in the ship's construction had contributed to the rapid spread of the fire. Amongst the recommendations were that stricter control be exercised and tests be conducted regarding the choice of materials in future ship construction, employing independent authorities, and that the Navy improve training in the fighting of fires on vessels built of composite materials.

The choice of materials in everything from paint to a vessel's structure can have a significant impact on the safety. For example, an unapproved type of flexible hose on the fuel system of the starboard engine of the Australian Navy's replenishment tanker *HMAS Westralia* (AO195) was determined to be the source of a fire that claimed the lives of four members of the ship's crew on 5 May 1998.

Fuel leaking from the burst hose sprayed onto the hot engine and ignited, resulting in a major explosion aboard the 40,870-ton vessel, whilst operating west of Rottnest Island, Western Australia. The resultant fireball ship killed one female and three male crew members in the engine room before the compartment was sealed and $CO_2$ injected to extinguish the fire. Five further crew members were injured. The extensive damage to the ship's engine room was repaired and *Westralia* returned to service.

The subsequent Board of Inquiry blamed the tragedy on poor quality assurance, determining that the fuel hoses, fitted during a recent maintenance period, were not fit for purpose.

Fires and explosions resulting from oil or diesel fuel leaks are hazardous enough, but many of the motor torpedo and gun boats built by the Allies during the war were powered by petrol engines, utilising a far more inflammable and volatile fuel. This gave them a distinct disadvantage when pitted against their German diesel-engined counterparts - the E-boats - as they were considerably more liable to catch fire and explode should their fuel tanks be penetrated by enemy gunfire.

However, even when not involved in the heat of battle, these craft were prone to devastating fires and explosions, such as that which destroyed twelve Allied MTBs on 14 February 1945, whilst berthed at Ostend. Most of the boats belonged to the Canadian 29th Flotilla. The engine room crew of one of these boats was attempting to remove water that had contaminated the fuel tanks, but instead of pumping the contaminated fuel into 40-gallon oil drums provided, the fuel was pumped overboard. It only required a cigarette or a backfire from one of the boats to ignite the floating fuel, engulfing and destroying twelve MTBs with the loss of 60 lives.

Three months later, on 19 May, whilst berthed at Fosnavag, a massive explosion in the engine room of the Norwegian Navy *MTB715* completely wrecked the Fairmile 'D' type boat and seriously damaged her sister vessel *MTB709*. Both craft were later returned to the Royal Navy for repair, but were scrapped soon after.

A large number of these craft continued to serve in many navies throughout the world in the post-war years, having been transferred from the Royal Navy in the closing stages of the war or immediately afterwards. That further accidents would occur was inevitable, with many of the craft suffering petrol-related fires and explosions of varying magnitude. The Norwegian motor torpedo-boat *HMNS Hauk* was one of the craft whose career with her new owners was destined to be short-lived.

*Hauk* sailed from her berth at Nordnestangen near Bergen at 1500 on 23 November 1948, having just refuelled with 14,000 litres of 91-octane gasoline, to take part in an exercise with other boats of the flotilla. Thirty-five minutes later a violent explosion ripped through the boat, ejecting a plume of fire and smoke from the torpedo tubes on either beam. Seven crewmen immediately took to a dinghy whilst the rest tried to contain the blaze. Less than ten minutes after the explosion, the fire had grown totally out of control and the Commanding Officer had little option but to order the rest of his crew to abandon ship by jumping into the sea. All were soon rescued by the other vessels in company.

Considering the ferocity of the fire, it was miraculous that none of the crew were killed or seriously injured, although all but the engine room crew had been on the upper deck at the time of the explosion. At about 1600, *Hauk* sank in 17 metres of water in Byfjorden, near Laksevag.

The cause of the explosion has not been positively ascertained, but the most likely explanation is that a fuel leak resulted in highly flammable petrol gases collecting unnoticed in pockets in the bilges of the craft. It would only have taken a minor spark, from an electrical fitting, or from a careless crewman, to ignite the gasses, with devastating consequences.

The burnt-out hulk was raised and, in October the following year, was sold for scrapping.

The British motor torpedo-boat *MTB1023* (ex-*MTB523*) was moored in Århus harbour on 17 May 1953, when a fire broke out in her engine room. Shortly afterwards the craft exploded, wounding one crewman and hurling burning wreckage onto the new fast patrol boat *HMS Gay Archer* (FPB1041) , causing minor damage to her hull.

This was the third loss of a British MTB in a little over a year. In September 1951 the British fast patrol boat *MTB1602* was badly damaged at Portsmouth by an explosion in the engine exhaust system, wrecking the engines and causing extensive flooding of the engine room. Four months later the ill-fated craft was under tow to Anglesey to be repaired when she sank in a storm. Only two months later *MTB1030*, a sister boat to *MTB1023*, sank after a collision in the North Sea.

Nonetheless, these small craft were not the only vessels that were susceptible to explosions involving petrol or the fumes emanating from its storage tanks, a fact all too tragically illustrated by the loss of the escort carrier *HMS Dasher* on 27 March 1943. The carrier had been preparing for her next convoy escort mission and her Swordfish aircraft were being refuelled when the explosion occurred without warning. The crippled ship sank almost immediately in 170 metres of water, taking all but 149 of her crew of nearly 800 men with her.

There had been doubts as to the *Dasher's* structural safety, as her conversion from the American passenger/cargo ship *ss Rio de Janeiro* in 1941 had been hurriedly completed, her presence being urgently required for convoy escort duties as the Battle of the Atlantic intensified. The previous year, off Iceland, a large split had opened up the ship's side, although she reached the River Clyde safely where repairs were carried out. Her loss, with so many lives was a tragic end of what was considered an unlucky ship.

However, this had not been the first occasion of the explosion of petrol fumes. Another of the mercantile conversions, *HMS Avenger*, had suffered a similar fate on 15th November 1942 when petrol exploded after the ship had been torpedoed by *U-155* west of Gibraltar. The loss of these two escort carriers raised considerable doubts as to the safety of arrangements for working and stowing of aviation spirit. Subsequently, *HM Ships Archer* and *Biter* were taken out of service to have their petrol systems modified and extra ballast fitted, as the British disliked the American practice of filling empty fuel tanks with sea water. This added a further 24 to 30 weeks to the time between the handover from America of US-built escort carriers to them being considered ready for active duty by the Royal Navy, causing much reproachment from the Americans.

A further such loss was that of the Japanese aircraft carrier *Taiho* during the Battle of the Philippine Sea on 19 June 1944. The ship was dealt her final crippling blow by the explosion of petrol vapour that had spread through the ship because of inept damage control, after she was struck by a single torpedo from the submarine *USS Albacore* (SS-218).

Post-war, the ignition of petrol vapours resulted in an explosion aboard the 1,850-ton US Navy *Patapsco*-class gasoline tanker *Chehalis* (AOG-48). The vessel was at her berth on Tutuila, in the American Samoa Islands, on 7 October 1949, when she was ripped apart by a massive blast that killed six of her crew. The resultant fire quickly grew out of control and *Chehalis* capsized and sank in a cloud of smoke and steam soon afterwards. The probable cause of the explosion was the ignition of gasoline fumes in one of the ship's tanks.

Only a few months later, another vessel was to fall victim to a similar incident, when the ignition of petrol vapours resulted in an explosion aboard the Australian Navy landing ship *HMAS Tarakan* (L3017) whilst in refit at the Garden

*On 21 August 1947 the Italian patrol vessel VAS 246 caught fire whilst berthed at Venice.*

*(Ufficio Storico Della Marina Militaire)*

Island Naval Dockyard, Sydney. Eight crewmen lost their lives in the accident and the ship was subsequently scrapped as a result of the damage caused by the explosion and the resulting fire. (Details of this incident are covered in Chapter Six).

Three years later, on 3 February 1953, the aircraft carrier *HMS Indomitable* (R92) was damaged by a fire and explosion off Malta, killing eight crewmen and injuring a further 32. The incident was caused by the ignition of petrol vapour from a leaky valve near the hangar entrance by a lighted cigarette. A large area of the starboard side beneath the island was gutted by the resultant fireball. Subsequently ten gallantry awards, including two George Medals, were presented to members of the ship's company.

*Indomitable* paid off later that year into low degree reserve and was towed to the River Forth. Her early departure from operational service was partly due to

structural damage caused in the explosion, but mainly because of the manpower shortage in the Royal Navy at that time, crews being required for the new aircraft carriers *HM Ships Ark Royal* (R09), *Centaur* (R06), *Albion* (R07), and *Bulwark* (R08), which were then in the later stages of construction. *Indomitable* was scrapped in 1955.

Explosive fumes and vapours from most fuels can be easily ignited in any number of ways, but most commonly through human carelessness or by sparks from machinery or equipment. Diesel fuel is relatively stable in its liquid form, but the explosive mixture of fuel vapour and air can be ignited by the slightest spark. When the presence of such a mixture goes unnoticed or is not treated with the courtesy it demands, its retribution can be swift and deadly.

The submarine chaser *MAS 438*, commissioned into the Italian Navy in 1935, served principally on anti-submarine

*The US Navy oiler USNS Potomac (T-AO-150) following a fire and explosion in one of her fuel storage bunkers on 26 September 1961at the Aviation Fuels Terminal Pier at Morehead City, North Carolina.*
*(D. McDowell)*

duties in the Jonio waters during the war. Her name was changed in June 1943 to *ME39* and again post-war to *AS26*, but she sank on 5 August 1946 after being ripped apart by an explosion of vapours within her fuel tanks whilst steaming off Cape Miseno. Twelve months later the Italian patrol vessel *VAS246* was also destroyed in an explosion. Then, on 26 July 1950, the Egyptian minesweeper *Gaza* sank off Mersa Metrouh, after ignition of fuel vapours caused her fuel tanks to explode.

On 26 September 1961, the US Navy oiler *Potomac* (T-AO-150) was virtually destroyed by a fire and explosion in one of her fuel storage bunkers at the Aviation Fuels Terminal Pier at Morehead City, North Carolina. Two crewmen were killed and severe damage was caused to the terminal, although the fire, which burned for 5 days, was prevented from escalating into what could have been a disaster of cataclysmic proportions. The forward and midships sections of the ship were completely destroyed and later, in March 1963, sold for scrap. Meanwhile, the stern section was raised, refurbished and towed to Newport News Shipbuilding, Virginia, where it was utilised in the construction of a virtually new ship for merchant service, named *ss Shenandoah*. On 1 December 1964, the *Shenandoah* was chartered by the US Navy for service with the Military Sea Lift Command, later to be purchased and reinstated on the Navy List, renamed *Potomac* (T-AO-181) on 12 January 1976.

This was not to be the only US Navy tanker was to succumb to a fuel tank explosion. On 7 March 1982, the *USNS Golden Dolphin* (AO/T8), under charter to the US Navy Military Sealift Command, exploded and sank whilst transiting the Atlantic. A similar fate befell the Russian Navy's Project 160 (Altay-class) replenishment tanker *Izhora*, which sank after an explosion in Vladivostok on 17 July 1991.

The ease with which undetected vapours can be ignited and the speed with which a fire can grow out of control, even in the face of a determined fire-fighting effort, was graphically illustrated in the early hours of 25 June 1966, when a major fire broke out aboard the Aggressive-class fleet minesweeper *USS Stalwart* (MSO-493).

The minesweeper, moored at the northeast end of the tender pier at the US Naval Station San Juan, Puerto Rico, was in port to effect repairs to the ship's diesel generators and so was being supplied with electrical power from the shore-side power plant within the Naval Station. Most of her machinery was shut down, except for lighting, ventilation and heating systems - a condition known as 'cold iron status'.

A rating carrying out routine rounds of the boiler compartment, situated above the main machinery rooms, at about 0320 noticed nothing amiss, the only item of machinery running being a portable electric fan located to the port side of No.2. boiler. However, five minutes later another rating walking forward in the starboard passageway past the boiler space detected a strong smell of smoke and, on investigation, discovered a fire already well established within the compartment. After raising the alarm, the rating tried to locate a portable $CO_2$ fire extinguisher with which to attack the fire, the nearest of which was known to be located in the galley.

Unfortunately the galley door was locked and so the rating had to go to the forward machinery room to collect an extinguisher. The resulting delay allowed the heat and smoke to develop to such an extent that the compartment door had to be secured to contain the fire.

Sounding of the general alarm alerted the rest of the crew, who immediately set about setting up fire fighting equipment and isolating systems in order to contain the fire until further assistance could arrive from shore-side.

The base of the fire was located on the port side of the boiler space at about frame

50, in close proximity to the boiler fuel oil service tank. The deck of the compartment consisted of an open metal grill, so allowing the fire to spread downwards into the main machinery space where most of the ship's machinery was located, including the four Packard diesel propulsion engines. Immediately below the base of the fire was located the ships main electrical distribution boards. It was, correctly, realised that the fire could not be attacked with water due to the risk of electric shock to the fire-fighters from the distribution boards and so the justifiable decision was taken to isolate the shore electrical supply.

The consequences of this action was the loss of the ship's main salt water pumps, reducing the vessel's fire-fighting capacity to portable extinguishers and water supplied from portable salt water pumps. Two of these were carried - one small P-60 and one larger P-500 petrol engine-driven pumps. Unfortunately, the latter had been out of commission for several days due to a defective carburettor, a replacement being unavailable, so reducing the fire-fighting capacity to one small hose supplied by the smaller P-60 unit. This was totally inadequate to tackle the ever-growing ferocity of the flames, which were by now breaking out of the compartment, or even to provide cooling of bulkheads and decks of adjacent compartments.

Nevertheless, the alarm had been quickly raised and within minutes two crash trucks and two pump trucks from the Naval Station Fire Department were on the scene. However, each vehicle was crewed only by a driver, so relying heavily on the ship's company for manpower. Furthermore, the foam pump on one of the crash trucks proved to be defective, so limiting the fire-fighting capability to just one crash truck.

Whilst the fire-fighting efforts were being controlled by Stalwart's Commanding Officer, Lieutenant Henry

G. Vargo, USN, the co-ordination of supporting forces was exercised by Lt. Cdr. E.M. Papio, USN, Commanding Officer of the nearby landing ship USS Wahkiakum County (LST-1162). Such support included the supply of further portable pumps, breathing apparatus and manpower from other ships in the vicinity and from the shore facilities.

The fire continued to grow out of control, spreading rapidly through the forward engine room and upwards through the uptakes to the funnel and also via the ladder wells to engulf the wooden bridge superstructure. As the fire spread forward, a decision was taken to remove the ammunition from the ship's magazine and ready-use lockers, a task that was successfully accomplished between 0930 and 1030.

The continued spread of the blaze presented the fire-fighters with a dilemma. The ferocity of the fire required massive quantities of water to be sprayed onto and into the ship to quell the flames. Such volumes of water could not be matched by the capacity of the available portable pumps, a large proportion of which proved to be defective, to remove it from the ship. It was therefore decided that the damage being caused to the ship by the fire outweighed the risk of sinking the ship due to the volume of fire-fighting water being pumped into her.

The option of deliberately scuttling the ship to reduce the fire damage was dismissed. However, the continued inflow of water was such that the ship finally capsized on to her starboard beam and sank in the shallow water of the berth at 1210, with the still burning port side of her hull protruding above the water's surface. The fire-fighting effort continued until 1245 when the flames in the exposed parts of the ship were finally extinguished. Thankfully, casualties were limited to a few minor cases of smoke inhalation.

The ship was later raised, but the cost of repair of the extensive damage, estimated at US$3,500,000, was such that the ship was declared beyond economical repair. *Stalwart* was stricken from the Naval Vessel Register on 1 July 1967 and authorised for destruction as a fleet target.

Due to the almost total destruction caused to the ship's wooden hull, bulkheads and decks, as well as much of her equipment and cabling, the exact cause of the fire could not be conclusively determined by the subsequent Board of Investigation, convened by Commander Mine Force, US Atlantic Fleet. It was determined that all concerned with the fire-fighting effort had acted professionally. The investigation concluded that the most like cause of the fire was the ignition of fuel vapour by a spark from an electrical fault, such as a short circuit, probably originating from either the electric fan or the starter panel of No.1 boiler within the boiler space. This conclusion stemmed from the close locality of both electrical units and the boiler fuel oil service tank, which contained some 77 gallons of JP-5 fuel at the time, to the estimated seat of the fire. JP-5 fuel has a flash point - the point at which spontaneous ignition will occur - of 140-150° F and a fire point of 190-210° F, temperatures which would easily have been reached by the arcing and spattering of molten metal in an electrical contact or motor.

It was recommended that the design of all future electrical installations be improved to comply with safety specification for spaces where explosive vapours may be present. It was also recommended that adequate ventilation systems should be fitted to these compartments in order to purge them of any vapour present. Sight glasses, a point of weakness on fuel and oil service tanks, were to be fitted with guards to protect them from accidental damage. In Royal Navy ships, all such sight glasses are now fitted with isolation valves, either of the spring-loaded or screw-down type, to prevent tank leakage should the glass be broken.

The rapid spread of the fire was facilitated by the open grill construction of the boiler space's deck and the lack of any means of isolating the natural ventilation grills, such as a stainless steel damper mechanism. The fire would quickly have spread to the oil-soaked wooden bilges of the main machinery space before spreading upwards via the uptakes and ladder wells, which formed convenient 'chimneys' through which the flames could travel, consuming the dry wooden structures as it went. It was recommended that all passages and ladder wells should be fitted with lightweight flame arrestor doors and hatches and that all wooden structures be treated with a fire-retardant coating and bilges be coated with epoxy paint to prevent oil impregnation of the wood.

The lack of electrical power with which to run the ship's salt water pumps, due to the isolation of the shore supply, had allowed the fire to gain a strong foothold before effective fire-fighting efforts could be brought to bear. The design of the Agile/Aggressive-class ships was such that a fire in the main machinery spaces, where all of the ship's electrical generating and distribution facilities, as well as fire and bilge pumps were located, would deny the ship of virtually its entire capacity to combat it. The location of main electrical distribution boards within the main machinery spaces, where they were susceptible to the ingress of water, was a particularly bad design factor. This had been a common practice in the design of small warships at that time - the main switchboard of the British Ton-class minesweeper design was itself located in the generator room, along with all of the vessel's generators. In later designs, such as the British *Hunt-class* and the French/Dutch/Belgian Tripartite type, the switchboard is located in the machinery control room and emergency salvage generators are provided in the superstructure, well away from the main machinery

*USS Enhance was one of at least six US Navy oceangoing minesweepers of the Agile and Aggressive classes which suffered major fires - three of which resulted in total losses.*
*(US Navy)*

spaces.

Heating in future classes of ship would be all electric, eliminating the need for oil fired boilers that had been the source of a large number of fires in wooden-hulled ships of many navies.

The lack of any fixed fire-main outlets at the berth was also criticised and in future all berths at US naval installations would be so fitted.

Further improvements were to be incorporated with regard to fire-fighting equipment and training, including: an increase in the number of breathing apparatus sets and spare canisters carried on board; the provision of asbestos fire-fighting suits; the provision of more $CO_2$ extinguishers, particularly in the vicinity of high risk areas; improvements to the ship's fixed $CO_2$ fire-fighting installations to allow remote operation and cross-connection of systems; the provision of connections on the fixed spray systems to facilitate the connection of hoses supplied from portable salt water pumps; the ability to flood all magazines from the ship's fire-main; the provision of two medium sized portable pumps (P-250), instead of the one small (P-60) and one large (P-500) already carried on fleet minesweepers;

and an increased emphasis by fire-fighting schools on wood-based fires and on the effects of free-surface water within a ship resulting from fire-fighting efforts.

All of these improvements were to be actioned as a matter of urgency and, in particular, were to be incorporated in the design of the new MSO-523-class minesweepers, the first of which was planned for the Financial Year 1966 programme. These ships were subsequently cancelled as a result of budgetary constraints. It was suggested by Commander Mine Force that, had the above recommendations been incorporated earlier, the fire in *Stalwart*, and an earlier fire aboard *USS Kingbird* (MSC-194), "would possibly not have occurred or would certainly have been less severe."

A total of 58 vessels of the generally similar Aggressive and Agile classes were built for the US Navy, plus another 35 for various NATO navies. Of the US Navy vessels, at least six suffered major fires, three of which were total losses. As well as *USS Stalwart*, these included *Exultant* (MSO-441), which caught fire after an explosion off the coast of Savannah, Georgia, and was later repaired; *Avenge* (MSO-423) in dry dock on 1 February

1970; and *Force* (MSO-445), which sank at sea en route from Subic Bay, Philippine Islands, to Guam on 24 April 1973. In the latter case, the fire started at about 0340 that morning on No.1 main engine, but failure by the engine-room watch to shut down the engine or crash-stop the ventilation fans allowed the fire to gain a firm hold before fire-fighting efforts began. Ineffectual fire-fighting procedures and the failure to spray foam into the compartment allowed the fire to grow out of control. The ship's fate was finally sealed when the generator failed, depriving the ship of fire-main pressure. At 0415, the Commanding Officer ordered his ship to be abandoned. *USS Force* sank at about 1053 in position 13°14' North, 131°57' East in 3,200 fathoms of water. The crew were picked up that evening by the British merchant ship *mv Spraynes*, 820 miles west of Guam.

Less than two years later, *USS Enhance* (MSO-437) was disabled off San Diego by a fire in her engine room. The fire-damaged machinery compartment was later repaired and the ship served on until 1991. Incidentally, another two units were scrapped following grounding incidents.

These were not the only vessels prone to explosions and fires. The vulnerability of MTBs to such phenomenon has already been discussed, but other craft of wooden construction were, in effect, tinderboxes just waiting to be lit.

Motor minesweepers (MMSs), known affectionately as 'Mickey Mouses' to those who served on them, were built in large numbers during the Second World War, with 276 units completed in boatyards both in the United Kingdom and abroad, together with a further 87 of a slightly larger design. These craft, desperately needed to supplement the pitifully under-strength Royal Navy minesweeping flotillas, were ordered to a simple design based on trawler lines, thus permitting their construction by a large number of small private boatyards. The scarcity of materials meant that many motor minesweepers were constructed of inferior green timber and were propelled by a wide variety of diesel engines, many of which were not specifically marine engines, but rather modified generating plant.

Other equipment was based on that used in coal-burning steam trawlers, with coal or oil-fired stoves utilised for heating in the forward and after messdecks and the wardroom. The galley stove was also oil-fired, heated by diesel oil sprayed into the oven, while water was heated by diesel oil dripped onto a hotplate that was initially heated by an open flame. This latter archaic monstrosity was located on the starboard side of the engine room, which also contained, apart from the main engine, the generators and the open-fronted electrical switchboard! Flues from these oil-fired units frequently belched clouds of smoke and sparks onto the weather decks. Fire restraint around this equipment was limited to asbestos sheeting, while the main engine exhaust was lagged with asbestos as it passed up through the wooden superstructure.

Few of these ships were modified to any great extent post-war, although they continued to serve for many years with numerous navies, with a few of the later units remaining operational into the early 1960s. It is hardly surprising therefore, that these vessels frequently caught fire and that some were inevitably lost.

In 1947 the Turkish MMS *TCG Kavak* was lost, presumably as a result of a fire, whilst the Royal Navy craft *MMS1534* was destroyed by fire off the coast of Tunisia on 2 June 1952, the wreck later being sold in October 1955.

*MMS58* (M1558) suffered a similar fate less than two years later. Having served with the Greek Navy as the danlayer *Argyrokastron* from 1946 until 1951, *MMS58* was then returned to the UK, where she was refitted at Millwall prior to being loaned to London Division RNVR to replace *MMS1785* and *MMS1789* in February 1954. On the evening of 16 April of that year, *MMS58* sailed from the Thames under the command of Lt. Cdr. P.W.T. Warren, RNVR, for a training cruise. Soon after the vessel sailed, the weather deteriorated and the ship was being battered by winds reaching gale force 9. The ship began leaking badly, and loose items were thrown around the ship. Not long after, a fire began in the engine room, with flames rising 10 feet into the air from the funnel.

All attempts to extinguish the blaze failed, the fire-fighters being beaten back by smoke and the intense heat. In atrocious conditions, the crew continued throughout the night to fight the blaze, but, at 0740 the following morning, 15 miles off Dunkirk, *MMS58* finally capsized and sank. Fortunately, all 31 London Division RNVR crewmen were rescued by the French steamer *Tunisie* and the Dutch merchant vessel *Phoenix* and were later landed at Flushing and Antwerp, although one able seaman was taken to hospital.

The Court of Inquiry concluded that the

*Firefighters aboard the guided missile destroyer USS Claude V. Ricketts (DDG5) direct spray from their hoses onto the fire aboard the guided missile cruiser USS Belknap (CG26). The Belknap was heavily damaged and caught fire when it collided with the aircraft carrier USS John F. Kennedy (CV67) during night operations.*
*(US Navy)*

vessel had been unseaworthy for the weather conditions prevailing on that night and that the fire resulted from electrical arcing caused by salt water coming into contact with the switchboard. The crew were absolved of all blame for loss of their vessel.

A major factor in many of these incidents was the material of which the vessels were constructed. Wood, especially that not treated with a fire-retardant coating, will obviously burn more readily than steel.

Aluminium was adopted in the construction of superstructures on several classes of major warship during the 1960s and 1970s, its light weight offering reductions in top-weight which could be more beneficially utilised in the fitting of further electronic equipments and weapons. However, aluminium will soften when subjected to temperatures of 550°C, melting at around 650°C. When an aluminium structure is subjected to such heat, a high-pressure water jet from a fire-fighting hose might easily puncture a deck or bulkhead, thus allowing the spread of a fire that may otherwise have been contained. Aluminium also splinters more readily than steel, resulting in horrific injuries to personnel in the event of an explosion. It was not until several major accidents highlighted these drawbacks, that the merits of this material were seriously questioned.

During the Vietnam War, a fire on board a US destroyer nearly grew out of control when the fire-fighting effort was hampered by the melting of aluminium ladders. Even more devastating was the damage caused to the cruiser *USS Belknap* (CG-26) following her collision with the aircraft carrier *USS John F. Kennedy* (CV-67) in the Mediterranean on 22 November 1975. Eight crewmen were killed and 25 more wounded by the resultant blaze, which almost completely destroyed her largely alloy superstructure. Although it was originally feared that the ship would

*Following a collision between the aircraft carrier USS John F Kennedy (CV67) and the cruiser USS Belknap (CG26) off Sicily on 22 November 1975, the US Navy reconsidered its policy of constructing warship superstructures from aluminium. Belknap's upperworks were almost totally destroyed by fire as fuel cascaded down onto her from the carrier's flight deck and ignited, resulting in the ship being out of action for over four years.*

*(J. Hummel)*

have to be scrapped, she was eventually returned to service some 4½ years later after a refit that cost an estimated US$213 million. Meanwhile, the Royal Navy frigate *HMS Amazon* (F169) suffered serious structural damage after a fire in 1978 whilst operating in the Far East.

Although the cause of the explosion that ripped through a Soviet Project 266 ('Yurka'-class) fleet minesweeper in the Black Sea on 19 August 1989 is unclear, the fact that the vessel's hull was constructed of aluminium alloy was probably a major factor in the ship's subsequent foundering. Two crewmen were killed and a third injured in the explosion. These incidents, amongst others, drew attention to the risk of building warships with all-aluminium superstructures, a risk further underlined during the Falklands War in 1982.

Designers of such vessels maintained that they could not have met the requirements to raise weapon and sensor loads without saving as much top-weight as possible, to which their critics replied that the flimsiness of aluminium accentuates the vulnerability of modern warships to relatively minor damage. What ever the merits of the arguments, after the construction of the Type 21s the British Naval Staff changed their minds about aluminium, and stipulated that future ships use steel only, whilst, in order to avoid such catastrophic damage as that suffered by the *USS Belknap* occurring in the future, the US Navy also returned to more traditional materials.

The Arleigh Burke-class destroyers were built almost entirely of steel, except for their aluminium funnels, whilst some 130 tons of Kevlar armour has also been fitted to protect vital spaces. Kevlar, along with refractory felt, has also been used in recent years to clad the aluminium structures of older vessels in vital areas to reduce the effects of damage. A consequence of this however, is a negating of the top-weight advantages, with the result that increased ballast has had to be fitted. Nevertheless, it is a more viable alternative to the replacement of the aluminium superstructure, or of the ship in total.

Other navies have resorted to the modification of those warship designs already in the course of production at the time of the Falklands conflict. For instance, ships of the Japanese Hatsuyuki-class from *Yamayuki* (129 - laid down on 25 February 1983) onwards have been constructed with steel superstructures instead of the aluminium structures of their earlier sisters, adding 100 tons to their displacement.

Modern warships are more susceptible to fire due to the more prevalent use of high-pressure oil and fuel systems and the smaller crew available to fight an outbreak of fire, coupled with the practice of having unmanned machinery spaces. However, these factors are counteracted by the use of more fire-retardant materials, the more widespread use of fixed fire detection and fire-fighting/suppression systems, and improved crew damage control training, including the employment of damage control simulators.

Even in merchant ships, some 60% of fires originate in the engine-room. Whilst this is not surprising due to the large quantities of combustible material and pressurised fluid systems in use in these spaces, these compartments should also be the best protected with fixed and portable fire-fighting/suppression systems. Also, the fact that watch-keepers should usually be in the vicinity of the compartment, or be remotely monitoring pressure and temperature parameters, should permit prompt and effective action to be taken to extinguish a fire before it gets out of hand.

Various substances have been utilised in fire-fighting, for example water, steam, foam, $CO_2$ and inert gases in the Halon group such as Bromochlorodifluoro methane (BCF) or Bromotrifluoro methane (BTM).

The first of these is usually supplied from a ship's high pressure salt water main, via hoses or fixed hose reels. The disadvantages of the use of salt water is the damage caused to equipment, especially electrical, and the danger of stability problems if its use is not controlled or it is not pumped out quickly. However, it is very effective for combating most fires and is available in never-ending quantities as long as the ship's fire pumps and salt water ringmain are operable and undamaged. Newer systems under development use small bore pipework, discharging water in an atomised spray in the vicinity of the fire only, rapidly extinguishing the flames and cooling the area, without the need to completely close down or evacuate the compartment.

Steam was for many years used as the primary fixed fire-fighting system within main machinery spaces, used to smother the fire by starving it of oxygen, but the demise of steam as the primary form of propulsion for major warships had largely necessitated its replacement with foam and inert gas systems.

Protein foam was itself replaced in the 1970s by the far more effective Aqueous Film Forming Foam (AFFF). Injected into a compartment using portable or fixed inductors, or by foam generators, it is extremely effective against liquid fires, especially in machinery spaces and on flight decks, as it forms a film over the top of a burning substance, so choking the fire into extinction. It has become common practice during the early stages of any main machinery space fire to inject AFFF into the bilges from the compartments above via fixed foam injection tubes.

During the Second World War, the Germans fitted their first aircraft carrier, the *Graf Zeppelin*, with a variety of fixed fire-fighting systems to protect the main machinery compartments and the aircraft hangar. Besides the high-pressure sea water main supplied by the ship's hull and fire pumps, and steam drenching, there were twenty gaseous extinguisher units that could flood compartments with Ardixine gas to smother fire. Ardixine fire-suppression systems were also fitted to other major combatants of the German Navy. However, the highly noxious nature of this gas was all too tragically demonstrated aboard the heavy cruiser *Admiral Hipper* when, the morning after fire-fighting activities, several crewmen were discovered dead in their hammocks. Post-mortem examinations revealed that they had been asphyxiated after Ardixine gas had seeped invisibly from defective glands and seals into adjacent mess-decks.

Most other navies adopted the less toxic $CO_2$ for fire-suppression purposes which, although less toxic than Ardixine, will still be harmful to personnel in relatively small concentrations. The use of $CO_2$ dilutes the oxygen in the air, without which combustion will cease. This medium has the advantage that it does not damage equipment and its use against electrical fires is clearly preferable to the use of sea water. Prior to the operation of fixed $CO_2$ fire-suppression systems it is necessary to 'crash-stop' ventilation fans and to close down a compartment before the gas is manually injected in order that an effective concentration can be built up to extinguish the fire, a procedure which may take several valuable minutes. As with inert gases, it has very little cooling ability, and so a reasonable time must be allowed for the area to cool before a re-entry can safely be effected, if re-ignition is to be avoided.

$CO_2$ has generally been replaced by inert gases such as BCF (Halon 1211) and BTM (Halon 1301). Neither of these gases are new, BTM having been used by the US Navy in the 1950s. As opposed to $CO_2$, inert gases extinguish a fire by chemically preventing the chain reaction that maintains combustion. Apart from being more effective in extinguishing flames, less gas is required for the same effect. For example, the 5% concentration of BTM necessary to extinguish a fire can be injected into a machinery compartment from the storage bottles via a high-level spray system in under ten seconds. These gases are also less toxic to personnel - $CO_2$ in a concentration of 16% can kill, whilst for BCF and BTM, concentrations of 35% and 83% respectively are required before they are considered lethal.

From the above, it can be seen that an ideal fire-fighting arrangement could be provided by a combination of BTM drench systems, high-level foam and water spray systems and low-level foam tubes. Older $CO_2$ drench systems can be adapted to allow water to be injected via $CO_2$ spray pipework. However, alternatives to these substances are urgently required, as the embodiment of Halon-based gases on new-build ships was banned on 1 July 1992 under an environmentally induced International Maritime Organisation resolution.

New automatic fire-suppression systems are also entering service. In the late 1980s, the Royal Navy carried out extensive trials of automatic BTM systems, both at Horsea Island, Portsmouth, and on the 'HULVUL' vessel - the decommissioned Leander-class frigate *HMS Naiad* used for hull vulnerability trials to test the effects of fire, explosion and shock on modern warships and to develop and test new equipment to combat them. With regards to fire-fighting, an extremely effective system was trialled, whereby small BTM bottles with their own fire detectors are dispersed around high-risk compartments. On the detection of a fire, a localised high concentration of gas is injected from the bottles to suppress it within a fraction of a second. Such a system possesses several advantages over previous arrangements: smaller quantities of gas are required to provide a higher local density for fire suppression; the compartment does not have to be evacuated prior to its operation; and a suitable supply of spare BTM bottles can be carried on board. The speed with which such a system can be activated will also result in an obvious reduction in damage to equipment and injury to personnel.

Older systems require large banks of bulky bottles in order to provide enough gas to completely drench the compartments they serve, therefore only a limited number of 'shots' are available to extinguish a blaze, their size rendering the prospect of used bottle replenishment during an incident impracticable. However, such systems do still not meet the latest IMO legislation.

Whatever medium is used for the extinguishing of a fire, systems must be operable from a remote position and it is imperative that their operation be proven at regular intervals. Warships built in the Second World War incorporated fire-fighting isolating facilities and methods of remote operation and isolation of flood and spray systems. Nevertheless, the investigations subsequent to a major fire frequently reveal new shortcomings in fire-fighting systems and procedures. Lack of sufficient remote operating and isolating arrangements on salt water, flood and spray systems was one of the criticisms of Royal Navy ships following the Falkland conflict, whilst similar conclusions were drawn after the frigate *USS Stark* was crippled by two Iraqi Exocet missiles whilst patrolling in the Persian Gulf in May 1987.

Ships' flight decks and hangars also constitute a major fire risk but, thankfully, serious fires are a relatively rare occurrence, due not only to the presence of extensive fire-suppression systems and fire-fighting equipment, but also the high level of fire-conscious manpower generally available in these areas during flying operations. Nevertheless, there have been a number of notable fires, mainly involving the accidental firing or detonation of live weapons, as in the case of the flight deck blazes aboard the US carriers *Forrestal* (CV-59) and *Enterprise* (CVN-65) in 1967 and 1969 respectively, both of which resulted in heavy loss of life. The *Forrestal* fire, in particular, was to have a major impact, with instructional videos

depicting the incident still being used today as part of the fire-fighting training syllabus in many navies.

As a direct result of the fire, flight deck fire-fighting arrangements were augmented with the provision of a number of carts equipped with fire-retardant chemicals, but the *Enterprise* blaze further highlighted a requirement for high-pressure water cannons that could spray large volumes of water and/or foam over the immediate area of the fire. Fixed foam guns have now been adopted by the Royal Navy, located above the hangar on new-build frigates. Trials have also been carried out on Halon fire-suppression systems for hangars, intended to replace the presently fitted salt water spray systems.

One of the worst post-war aircraft carrier blazes was that aboard *USS Bennington* (CV-20). Whilst cruising off Newport on 26 May 1954, one of the hydraulic accumulators serving the port catapult burst. By the time the resultant fire was brought under control, 103 men were dead and a further 201 injured. The badly damaged ship was later repaired and, in 1959, was converted to an anti-submarine carrier (CVS).

It is not just machinery spaces and hangars that must be protected by fixed fire detection and suppression systems, but other high-risk compartments such as magazines and inflammable material stores must also be covered by automatic and/or manual spray systems. After machinery spaces and electrical and electronic compartments, the most common locations for ship-board fires are galleys and accommodation spaces. A high proportion of galley fires result from the ignition of hot cooking oil or other combustibles near high temperature cooking ranges. Any attempt to tackle a cooking oil fire with water will inevitably result in the eruption of a deadly fireball that will consume all in its path and cause severe, and often fatal, injuries to personnel. One such fire resulted in the Bundesmarine's worst peacetime fire of recent years.

Whilst transiting the English Channel on return from the Mediterranean in December 1987, a fire broke out in the galley of the West German Lutjens-class destroyer *FGS Möelders* (D186). As the blaze grew quickly out of control it filled the ship with thick clouds of heavy smoke that spread via cable conduits and ventilation trunking. Despite assistance from the accompanying frigate *Niedersachsen* (F208) and the auxiliary *Freiburg* (A1413), the blaze burned fiercely for several hours before being brought under control. *Möelders* was then later towed by *Niedersachsen* to her home port of Wilhelmshaven, where she was repaired and returned to service.

Accommodation fires are normally the result of carelessness, the large quantities of combustible materials contained therein often serving to make such fires the most costly in terms of human lives. Following lessons learnt from the *Stark* incident, the US Navy has stipulated that all crew living compartments are to be equipped with auto-sprinkler systems, the Arleigh Burke-class destroyers being the

first so fitted.

One factor of fire-fighting that cannot be overemphasised is that of smoke clearance. Thick, toxic smoke not only has a severe incapacitating effect on personnel, but its transference to areas remote from the fire via ventilation trunking, cable passages or cavities formed behind false bulkheads, or by re-ingestion into the ship via ventilation intakes, can result in confusion as to the location of the seat of the fire, leading to the damage-control effort being misdirected. This in turn can result in a drastic delay in the fire-fighting effort and may even prove fatal should the source of the smoke be misinterpreted and two teams attack a fire from opposing directions, as an influx of oxygen from one direction may propel a fireball in the direction of unprepared personnel.

It has to be said, therefore, that the ability to control the spread of smoke may be the deciding factor between the saving or loss of a vessel and her crew. It is for this reason that, on detection of a fire, the first reaction of the crew in the damage control HQ is to 'crash-stop' all ventilation systems throughout the ship. Thereafter, the

*A port quarter view of the guided missile frigate USS Stark listing to port after being struck by an Iraqi-launched Exocet missile in May 1987.*

*As a consequence of such incidents cable insulation materials which gave off toxic fumes when burnt have now been replaced by less toxic materials.*

*(US Navy)*

starting of specific exhaust fans for the purpose of smoke clearance must be strictly controlled.

The fitting of smoke detectors within ventilation trunking that would automatically trip the fans serving them was recommended by the US National Transportation Board following an engine room fire aboard the Bahamian registered passenger vessel *Scandinavian Star* off St. Petersburg on 15 March 1988. Although this authority was primarily concerned with passenger vessels operating out of US ports or carrying US citizens, its adoption in warship design would clearly be of considerable value in controlling the spread of smoke.

The trend in modern warship designs is the division of the ship's structure into distinct boundaries, or zones, each with its own autonomous ventilation, pumping and fire-fighting systems. Some vessels, such as the British Type 23 frigates, have dedicated smoke clearance fans within each zone, the sole purpose of which is the removal of smoke from the compartments and passageways surrounding a fire, so permitting rapid identification of the source of the blaze and reducing the effects of the smoke on personnel. The fitting of easily-rigged smoke curtains around doors throughout the vessel also restricts the spread of smoke.

The greatest source of toxic smoke during a shipboard fire is the burning of electrical cabling, lagging and furnishings, a fact that was all too clearly illustrated during the Falklands War. As a consequence of lessons learnt during this conflict and following fires aboard the US Navy frigates *USS Stark* and *USS Samuel B. Roberts* (FFG58) in the Persian Gulf, cable insulation materials such as polyvinyl chloride (PVC), polychloroprene (PCP) and chloro-sulphated polythene (CSP) have largely been replaced by materials like Zerohal, which has a high resistance to melting and so reduces the level of smoke produced from smouldering cables. Smoke produced from the burning of Zerohal also has a toxicity level around twelve times less than that produced from PVC. Consequently, it has been widely adopted by the Royal Navy and the Royal Netherlands Navy, both in new-build vessels and to replace cabling renewed during refits. The US Navy is reducing the amount of cabling in its Arleigh Burke-class destroyers by adopting fibre optics for machinery control and CIC systems.

New low-smoke lagging materials, such as polymid, polyphosphazine or fibre-glass, are also being developed and fitted, whilst foam-based furnishings are being replaced with fire-retardant materials and foam mattresses by interior sprung alternatives. Taken together, these actions considerably reduce the amount of toxic fumes produced and so will undoubtedly reduce casualty rates amongst crews during shipboard fires.

The ability to rapidly identify the source of a fire is being aided by the increasing adoption of technological aids such as thermal imaging cameras, which are also a valuable tool for the location of casualties within smoke filled compartments, the ultimate design being a helmet-mounted variant such as that now in service with the Royal Navy. Further improvements to fearnought suits and breathing apparatus are also serving to improve the efficiency of fire-fighting teams.

The ever-increasing complexity of these fire detection and suppression systems, ship design specifications and fire-fighting equipments have one major drawback - their expense. Nevertheless, when considered against the cost of repairs resulting from shipboard fires, they form a cost-effective and necessary insurance policy. Failure to invest in sufficient resources in these areas can leave a crew totally ill-prepared for an unexpected fire.

The Chinese South Sea Fleet Project EF4 (Luda-class) destroyer *No.160* (names were not given to Chinese destroyers until after the Deng Xiao-Ping modernisation programme was started in 1985) was devastated by an explosion at Guangzhuo in August 1978. Her after section completely wrecked, the hulk was later scrapped as a constructive total loss. Most post-war Chinese naval vessels have been almost direct copies of already obsolete Soviet designs. However, the build quality of Chinese shipyards has been notoriously poor. It has not been unusual for even newly-commissioned ships to experience premature failure of welds and other symptoms of poor quality control such as ill-fitting 'watertight' doors.

The People's Liberation Army Navy (PLAN) also appears to have learned little from the experiences of other major navies, such as those encountered by the Royal Navy in the Falklands war. Until recently their warships were fitted out with flammable cables and furnishings and were almost barren of even the most rudimentary damage-control equipments such as fire hydrants, fixed fire-fighting systems and breathing apparatus and did not even have a centralised damage control station from which to direct fire-fighting and flooding control parties.

Damage control training also appears to be granted a very low priority. In such circumstances, even a minor fire aboard one of their vessels may quickly grow out of control should it not be tackled extremely quickly with portable extinguishers, poisonous fumes from low standard cable insulation and flammable materials adding to the hazards encountered by the crew. It is therefore probable that the PLAN, as well as many similarly equipped navies such as that of North Korea, have lost more vessels to fire than will ever be admitted by their Admiralty, given their craving for secrecy, particularly regarding subjects which may cause them some embarrassment.

Whilst fires aboard surface vessels can be uncompromisingly destructive, fires aboard submarines present a whole host of additional hazards and complications. A small fire in a submarine, even when quickly brought under control, can cause serious problems, especially when the boat is submerged. In a very short space of time, the most precious commodity in a submarine - oxygen - will be consumed beyond the ability of the regeneration equipment to replace it, thereby forcing the boat to surface.

The constituents of a normal breathable atmosphere are nitrogen and oxygen, together with small quantities of argon, carbon dioxide ($CO_2$) and other gases. As humans breath in oxygen, they breathe out almost pure $CO_2$, which is highly poisonous. The air is further polluted by other sources such as machinery exhausts, smoking and cooking. On a surface vessel, this would not present much of a problem, as the atmosphere is constantly being rejuvenated with fresh air to dilute the content of $CO_2$ and other pollutants. However, a submerged submarine cannot draw fresh air constantly from the atmosphere and so must rely on air purification equipment to cleanse the boat's artificial atmosphere.

The atmosphere within a submerged submarine may be rejuvenated either by filtering the contaminated air of the harmful $CO_2$ element or by admitting fresh oxygen into the boat. Filtering of the $CO_2$ may be achieved in a number of ways, the easiest of which is by passing used air through a series of soda lime canisters. However, whilst this is suitable for the shorter submerged periods of conventionally powered submarines, nuclear boats may remain submerged for months on end and so a far more efficient process is necessary. Many nuclear boats are quipped with Monothanolamine absorption units, which utilise an organic chemical to remove $CO_2$.

Gaseous oxygen stored in tanks either internal or external to the pressure hull may be used to replenish the oxygen supply within a submerged submarine.

However, whilst this method may be suitable for civilian research boats, the longer submerged duration of the military submarine renders the carriage of such large and cumbersome containers impracticable. Therefore, oxygen has to be produced within the boat, the simplest method being the use of oxygen candles, made of a mixture of sodium chlorate and potassium chloride, which when burned inside an oxygen generator create a chemical reaction which releases neat oxygen.

Extraction of oxygen from seawater many be achieved by the process of electrolysis, which uses electrical energy to split the water ($H_2O$) into its basic chemical components of hydrogen (H) and oxygen (O), the excess hydrogen being discharged overboard. Generally, conventional submarines use oxygen generators whilst nuclear boats use electrolysis for oxygen generation, with sodium chlorate candles reserved for emergencies. Development work is well underway (2008) of artificial gills for submarines, which will use new membrane technology to extract dissolved oxygen from seawater. Such a system would be smaller and have a lower power requirement than electrolysis, so making it suitable for conventional submarines.

Conventional submarines rely on huge banks of batteries for propulsive power whilst submerged, stowed low in the boat where their weight contributes to stability. Most common is the lead-acid type, but other versions include silver-zinc and silver-cadmium, which are lighter and smaller, but much more expensive. Also, silver-zinc does not react well to recharging from a partially-charged condition.

All batteries give off heat and gases during the recharging process, including carbon monoxide and high explosive hydrogen gas. Battery ventilation blowers are used to remove these dangerous substances during charging operations, whilst any particles remaining are filtered out of the boat's atmosphere by catalytic burn-

ers, thereby maintaining a hydrogen concentration of less than 2% by volume and a carbon monoxide concentration of under 15-parts-per-million. Batteries are recharged using diesel-powered generators whilst the boat is surfaced or whilst snorkelling, when the excess hydrogen can be discharged safely to the atmosphere along with the diesel engine exhaust fumes.

A fire in a battery compartment is probably one of the worst scenarios that can be faced by the crew of a conventionally-powered submarine. I t will almost inevitably result in a requirement by the control room crew to don emergency breathing apparatus, thus complicating an already difficult situation, whilst any contamination of the batteries by sea water will result in the production of highly poisonous chlorine gas. Consequently, in the event of a fire breaking out whilst submerged, the boat will have little choice but to surface immediately.

The valour of one of her crewmen undoubtedly saved the British submarine *HMS Stoic* (P231) from a watery grave on 8 August 1949, after she suffered a battery explosion whilst submerged. As the boat took on water, deadly chlorine gas was given off from the batteries. Luckily, a brave rating managed to reach the pump room and start the main ballast pump, which gave the submarine sufficient buoyancy to surface. However, whilst the loss of this submarine was narrowly averted, the US submarine *USS Cochino* (SS-345) was not so lucky when she too suffered a battery explosion later that same month.

On 25 August 1949, *Cochino* was taking part in naval exercises 100 miles north of Hammerfest, Norway. The boat had carried out a partial charge of her main batteries overnight, but had been submerged for several hours when her Commanding Officer ordered her to a snorkelling depth of 52 feet a little after 1030. Sea state at that time was 4-5, a condition that made

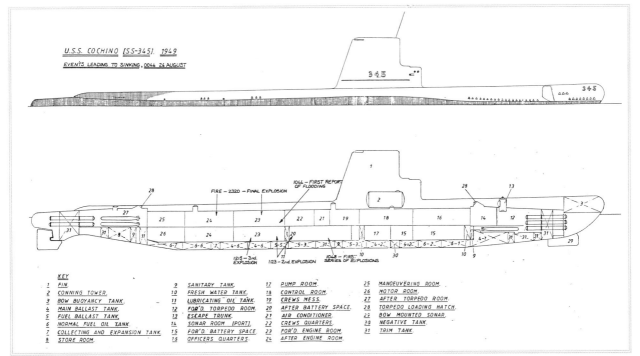

U.S.S. COCHINO [SS-345]. 1949
EVENTS LEADING TO SINKING, 0046 26 AUGUST

| KEY | | | |
|---|---|---|---|
| 1 FIN. | 9 SANITARY TANK. | 17 PUMP ROOM. | 25 MANOEUVERING ROOM. |
| 2 CONNING TOWER. | 10 FRESH WATER TANK. | 18 CONTROL ROOM. | 26 MOTOR ROOM. |
| 3 BOW BUOYANCY TANK. | 11 LUBRICATING OIL TANK. | 19 CREWS MESS. | 27 AFTER TORPEDO ROOM. |
| 4 MAIN BALLAST TANK. | 12 FOR'D TORPEDO ROOM. | 20 AFTER BATTERY SPACE. | 28 TORPEDO LOADING HATCH. |
| 5 FUEL BALLAST TANK. | 13 ESCAPE TRUNK. | 21 AIR CONDITIONER. | 29 BOW MOUNTED SONAR. |
| 6 NORMAL FUEL OIL TANK. | 14 SONAR ROOM [PORT]. | 22 CREWS QUARTERS. | 30 NEGATIVE TANK. |
| 7 COLLECTING AND EXPANSION TANK. | 15 FOR'D BATTERY SPACE. | 23 FOR'D ENGINE ROOM. | 31 TRIM TANK. |
| 8 STORE ROOM. | 16 OFFICERS QUARTERS. | 24 AFTER ENGINE ROOM. | |

depth-keeping extremely difficult, causing the boat to alternatively broach and then dive below snorkel depth. At 1044, the Commanding Officer despatched the Executive Officer to investigate a report of flooding of the forward engine room through the snorkel induction valve. No evidence of flooding was found, but a couple of minutes later engines Nos.1 and 2 cut out due to their drawing a high air intake vacuum, at which time the Commanding Officer ordered that the boat cease snorkelling and proceed under the propulsive power of the main motor.

No sooner had he given this order than, at 1048, a muffled thud was heard in the control room, emanating from the direction of the after battery compartment. The Commanding Officer immediately ordered the Diving Officer to surface and as the boat broke surface, reports reached him that there was a fire in the after battery compartment and that fire-fighting equipment was being rigged. Simultaneously, the occurrence of three or four small explosions was detected in the manoeuvring room by a watch-keeper,

who noted electrical discharge surges on numbers 3 and 4 ammeters in the battery circuit and that the overload relays for Nos.3 and 4 batteries had tripped, upon which the electrician's mate proceeded to transfer all auxiliary electrical load from the after to the forward batteries.

Personnel evacuating the after battery compartment managed to close the bulkhead supply and exhaust ventilation flaps as they left, but were unable to open the battery disconnect switches or close the battery ventilation intake covers due to the build-up of smoke and gases. These personnel reported that they had seen a series of flashes in the vicinity of the series parallel switch in the port after corner of the compartment.

At about 1100, the Executive Officer opened the door from the forward engine room and tossed four open $CO_2$ fire extinguishers into the battery compartment before immediately securing the door, but five minutes later the Electrician's Mate noted that No.4 battery appeared to be charging No.3 battery at a rate of up to 3,500 amperes and he duly advised the

*Following a series of battery explosions, USS Cochino sank in the early hours of 26 August 1949, 100 miles north of Hammerfest.*

*(John Lambert)*

Commanding Officer that this process had to be terminated by opening either of the battery disconnect switches, located within the compartment.

Meanwhile, the Executive Officer was taking charge of the situation locally, conducting a muster of personnel in the after section of the boat and making preparations to attack the fire from aft, whilst requesting that the seal on the forward bulkhead be maintained to ensure that the disastrous situation of two teams tackling the incident from two different directions at the same time did not occur.

Before the compartment could be entered, Nos.1 and 2 main engines were restarted for the purpose of clearing the compartment of smoke and gases, whilst the chief electrician's mate proceeded to don rescue breathing apparatus. As the Executive Officer partially unclipped the door to bleed excess pressure within the after battery compartment at 1123, the engines were heard to accelerate, compelling the throttlemen to trip them. However, No.1 engine failed to respond and continued to accelerate, causing flames to issue forth from the relief valve on No.16 cylinder. Then, as the door to the battery compartment was swung open, an explosion occurred in the after battery and another in the vicinity of the blower of No.1 engine, the searing heat of the blasts injuring several of those within the engine room.

The blast also caused the ventilation flap between the after battery room and the control room to leak, forcing smoke and gases into that compartment too. Although the battery compartment door was immediately closed, it was only partially secured before the forward engine room was itself evacuated. Despite the dangers, the Chief Electrician's Mate and the Chief Engineman re-entered the forward engine room a few minutes later and extinguished several small fires.

Although these two men took steps to secure the forward engine room, they left open the sea suction and discharge valves to the main engine coolers. Neither did they fully secure the door to the after battery compartment, even though it was now hot and gases could be seen leaking from around its gasket. After they left the compartment and closed the door between the engine rooms, pressure quickly built up on the forward side of the door until, at 1215, the concussion of a further violent explosion was felt throughout the boat.

Meanwhile, the Commanding Officer had ordered all personnel not involved in damage control duties to proceed topside onto the submarine's casing. One of the crewmen emerging from the after torpedo room hatch was promptly washed overboard by a wave. Although he was quickly rescued, the Commanding Officer decided that the danger of personnel being lost overboard was too great and so he ordered that they muster in the forward torpedo room instead. This order had itself to be countermanded soon after midday, as the build-up of gases throughout the boat was reaching a dangerous level. As the crew again headed for the upper deck, the boat shuddered under the influence of the third major explosion.

By 1230, several of the injured personnel being treated in the after torpedo room were in a critical condition and so the Commanding Officer was forced to request that another submarine operating in the area, *USS Tusk* (SS-426), come alongside and evacuate them. However, the heavy swell running at the time made such a manoeuvre too perilous and so the assistance was limited to the transference of medical supplies by inflatable raft.

At about 1420, this same raft was utilised to transfer two men across to *Tusk* in order that they may inform Commander Submarine Development Group Two (ComSubDevGru2) of the worsening situation aboard *Cochino*, but before they reached their destination they were thrown into the icy cold water as the raft was capsized. Both men were quickly pulled towards the *Tusk*, but one of them sustained severe head injuries and drowned before he could be hauled from the water. Further tragedy struck a few minutes later as, whilst trying to revive the drowned sailor, two large waves washed over the casing of *Tusk*, casting eleven of her crew, and the casualty, into the water. Despite a search that lasted until nearly 1700, only five of *Tusk's* crewmen were recovered.

Meanwhile, several further attempts had been made aboard *Cochino* to enter the forward torpedo room via the escape hatch on the casing in order to vent the compartment of gases, whilst other crewmen attempted to ventilate the after battery compartment, all to no avail. The engines had to be stopped at 1610 due to lack of fuel in the ready-use tanks, which could not be replenished as auxiliary power had been lost thirty minutes earlier when a short circuit tripped the breaker from the forward batteries. Nevertheless, personnel eventually managed to enter the boat and restore auxiliary power by running a series of emergency cables. At about 1800, Nos.3 and 4 main engines were restarted and *Cochino* turned towards Hammerfest at a speed of ten knots, initially steering by main engines until power to the steering gear was restored at 1910.

For the next couple of hours, as *Cochino* followed *Tusk* towards the Norwegian coast, it appeared that the crew were winning the battle to save their boat but, at 2320, another explosion racked the forward engine room, instantly engulfing the after engine room in flames and gases through the buckled door and via ventilation ducts, thereby forcing the evacuation of the compartment. As smoke and poisonous gases were gusted into the manoeuvring room, it too had to be evacuated and all crewmen aft made their way topside via the after torpedo room hatch. The fire in the after engine room quickly grew out of control.

Shortly after midnight, the Commanding Officer ordered all remaining personnel topside and the *Tusk* came alongside a few minutes later, whereby personnel were transferred from *Cochino*. The intention was that *Tusk* would take *Cochino* in tow but, as the submarine was developing an increasing list to starboard, it was apparent that the pressure hull had been breached in some way and the Commanding Officer reluctantly gave the order to abandon ship. Ten minutes later, at 0046 on 26 August 1946, *USS Cochino* slipped stern first beneath the waves, sinking to the bottom 170 fathoms below in position 71°35'N, 23°35'E.

The subsequent inquiry concluded that the initial series of flashes were caused by the ignition of hydrogen gases by sparks emanating from the series-parallel switch in the port after corner of the after battery compartment. This relatively minor incident should have prompted the crew of *Cochino* to immediately disconnect the batteries and positively purge the compartment of hydrogen gases, which had probably been present since the end of the battery charging period at 0800 on the morning of the 25th. As the engine sucked air from within the boat when the snorkel mast became submerged at about 1046, the vacuum caused within the boat would have had the effect of lowering the oxygen-hydrogen ratio to such an extent that the hydrogen level momentarily rose to well above the 2% danger level, making this initial explosion almost inevitable.

A further compendium of errors caused the situation to follow a downward spiral. Precious time was lost as the Executive Officer mustered personnel aft, the delay and subsequent failure to reach the battery disconnect switches allowing the charging of No.3 battery by No.4 battery to continue unabated and thereby accelerating the build-up of hydrogen gas. Had these switches been opened immediately following the initial explosions, it is most unlikely that the situation would have deteriorated further. Nevertheless, the decision to re-enter the after battery room when the compartment was obviously pressurised was clearly an error in judgement and led directly to the second blast.

Consequently, the failure to fully re-secure the after battery compartment door and the forward engine room, specifically the sea water suction and discharge valves, allowed further leakage of hydrogen and exposed a weak link in the boat's watertight integrity. It is probably that the final explosion resulted from continued leakage of hydrogen into the forward engine room, the blast rupturing sea water pipework, so flooding this compartment, the after battery room and the after engine room, leading ultimately to the boat sinking.

A number of material and operational improvements were recommended. The development of a hydrogen detector system which would respond to a concentration in any part of the battery ventilation system and thereby prevent pockets of the gas going unnoticed, was urgently pursued, whilst it was recommended that battery disconnect switches be modified so that they be operable from both a local and remote position. This latter recommendation was subsequently overtaken by the installation of circuit breakers - already under development for the Tang class boats - in place of disconnect switches, which are operable from remote positions and incorporate automatic tripping mechanisms. Operationally, all future drills simulating battery fires would include the practice of opening the battery disconnect switches immediately.

Also, as a result of the loss of the *Tusk's* crewmen, all US submarines were fitted with a safety track, running the full length of the upper casing, onto which crewmen can attach a safety line to permit them to move freely and safely in rough weather.

*Cochino* was one of a large number of US submarines converted in the late 1940s under the GUPPY - Greater

Underwater Propulsive Power - project. Proposed in 1946 by the Bureau of Ships, the aim of the GUPPY project was to modify fleet submarines for higher submerged speed by increasing storage battery power and by radical streamlining of both hull and superstructure, including many features of the German Type XXI boats. Sacrifices included all of the gun armament and, it was believed, some considerable measure of surfaced sea-keeping capability.

Converted submarines had four 126-cell GUPPY batteries, in place of the previous two 126-cell SARGO batteries, taking up space previously used for torpedo reloads, fresh water tanks and magazines. These batteries - type TPX67 Gould versions in *Cochino* - provided about twice the power of those originally fitted which, together with the effect of streamlining, gave them a submerged speed in excess of 16 knots, as opposed to the 10 knots previously achievable. However, the extra cost, and the fact that GUPPY batteries required twice as much lead, threatened to limit the number of GUPPY conversions. A study concluded that funds should be used to combine the snorkel with streamlining, foregoing the GUPPY battery in future conversions. Consequently, the GUPPY II boats were followed by two batches of conversions using modified SARGO batteries (SARGO II) known as the GUPPY IA, leading in turn to the GUPPY IIA and GUPPY III types.

The true cause of the explosion that led to the loss of the Soviet Project 629A ballistic missile-armed submarine *K-129* may never be known. Accusations of a collision with the Skate-class submarine *USS Swordfish* (SSN-579) proved unfounded, but the theory favoured by the Soviet Navy was that of a flooding incident resulting in the explosion of hydrogen gases from the boat's batteries. *K-129* had been tracked by the US Navy for several days after leaving her base in Vladivostok, when, on 11 April 1968, *USS Swordfish* detected the sound of a massive underwater explosion, emanating from the area of the boat. As the blast ripped open her hull, the boat sank to the ocean floor 16,800 feet below, along with her entire crew of 86 men, about 800 miles northwest of Hawaii. A massive search was quickly instigated by the Soviets, involving a large number of ships and aircraft, but it was some time before the wreck was located and photographed four months later by the submarine *USS Halibut* (SSN-587). Then, in July 1974, a 38ft forward section of the boat, including six of her doomed crew and two nuclear torpedo warheads, was raised in an incredible salvage mission reputed to have cost some US$350-million, dubbed Operation Jennifer, by the US Navy and the CIA using the purpose-built *Glomar Explorer* 'mining ship'.

The 618ft *Glomar Explorer*, along with a 350ft barge, was completed in mid-1973 by Howard Hughes for the Summa Corporation and was fitted with a derrick with a lifting capacity of 800 tons. It is claimed by the US Navy that the missile section broke away and was irretrievably lost as the boat was raised from its resting place to a depth of 8,000ft. The *K-129* was believed to be carrying her full load of three liquid-fuelled R-21 (SS-N-5) missiles when lost, but the whole operation is still shrouded in secrecy.

Experts examining the recovered section of the boat were reportedly surprised to find so much evidence of poor engineering practices, such as the wide variations in thickness of the inner and outer hull plating with exceptionally poor quality of welds, not all of which could be attributed to the five years the *K-129* had spent on the seabed. It was also alleged that wooden beams of 4 x 2-inch cross-section were used internally for structural support. In this and other incidences, it is clear that the Soviet Navy, in its haste to construct a numerically superior fleet to those of the west, had scrimped on quality

control, safety and habitability measures. This qualitative gap has however been reduced since the late-1980s to an uncomfortably low level, especially with the introduction of the latest Soviet/Russian submarines, such as the Project 941 ('Typhoon'-class), Project 949 ('Oscar'-class), Project 945 ('Sierra'-class) and Project 971 ('Akula'-class) designs.

In July 1989 the Soviet Navy approached the US Government requesting details of the submarine's crew and, if internment had taken place, the exact location of their resting places so that the families of the lost men could be informed and to satisfy their Orthodox religious beliefs. Incidentally, it appears that an article in the Russian weekly illustrated magazine the *Ogonyok* was the first disclosure of the *K-129* incident to the Russian public.

Although no other submarine losses have been directly attributed to battery explosions, it is highly probable that at least some of the unexplained submarine disappearances may have been the result of such incidents. For instance, reports of explosions featured prominently in the investigations into the loss of the two French Daphne-class submarines *Minerve* (S647) and *Eurydice* (S644) in 1968 and 1970 respectively.

Of half a dozen British boats affected by battery explosions since 1945, the worst incident occurred on board the A-class submarine *HMS Alliance* (S67) on 29 July 1971 whilst alongside at Portland, killing one crewman and injuring 14 others. Neither this nor the other incidents, however, resulted in the subsequent loss of a Royal Navy submarine.

Construction of conventional submarines for the US Navy ceased with the completion of the three Barbel-class boats in 1959, one of which *USS Bonefish* (SS-582), tragically ended a long service career with a battery explosion. The *Bonefish* was operating submerged in the Caribbean on 24 April 1988, some 160 miles from the coast

of Florida, when a battery explosion caused a fire that rapidly swept through the crew berthing quarters. Eighty-nine crewmen - eighteen of them injured - were later picked up by a US Navy frigate after they abandoned the boat, but three men were not accounted for. The boat was eventually towed into port, where the damage was judged to be beyond economical repair, primarily due to the fact that she was already earmarked for disposal.

*Bonefish* was retired from active service on 28 September 1988 and used for trials of fire-suppression equipment. In June of the following year, one of her sister boats, *USS Blueback* (SS-581), was forced to surface after a propulsion fire and was later towed into San Diego for repairs. The last two diesel-powered boats, *USS Barbel* (SS-580) and *USS Blueback*, were in turn decommissioned from Pacific Fleet service on 4 December 1989 and 30 June 1990 respectively, leaving the US

Navy with a totally nuclear-powered attack submarine force.

After this time, the US Navy's only diesel-electric submarine was the *USS Dolphin* (AGSS-555). Commissioned in 1968, she was a 950-ton unarmed deep-diving research and development boat and held the world deep-diving record for submarines, able to descend to depths in excess of 900-metres. On 21 May 2002, the *Dolphin* was operating on the surface off the coast of California, about 100 miles from San Diego, when heavy seas swamped the boat through the single hatch, which could not be properly closed due to a defect. The water level within the boat rose rapidly when all of the pumps failed, eventually reaching the boat's battery compartment and starting an electrical fire that quickly grew out of control. Despite the best efforts of the crew to keep a submersible pump running, the water level continued to rise.

Without power and adrift in heavy seas, the Commanding Officer had little choice but to transmit a distress signal at about 2330. Shortly afterwards, all 44 crew members, including two civilians, took to a life raft and managed to secure the conning tower hatch behind them to prevent further flooding. The oceanographic vessel *William McGaw* and the frigate *USS Thach* (FFG-43) were quickly on the scene and picked up all of the crew, although two had to be rescued from the water by a Coast Guard helicopter after falling overboard. Damage-control teams re-boarded the *Dolphin*, extinguishing the fire and stabilising the boat early the following morning. The submarine was later towed back to its berth at the Point Loma Submarine Base where an investigation into the cause of the fire was initiated. Repairs costing an estimated $9 million were completed in 2005.

A subsequent Board of Inquiry absolved the crew of any blame for the accident and several were later awarded commendations and medals.

Whilst the Americans concentrated on the GUPPY project to improve the submerged performance of their submarines post-war, the British and the Russians were more interested in the Walter-turbine propulsion system of captured German Type XVIIB boats. These boats were fitted with what was basically a closed cycle steam turbine, whereby a concentrated form of hydrogen peroxide, known as perhydrol, was decomposed by a catalyst to produce steam and oxygen at a temperature of 1,765°F, which in turn was burnt with oil fuel to produce a gas and steam mixture which was used to drive a conventional geared turbine. This system promised high underwater speeds in excess of 25 knots and improved underwater endurance without the need to 'snort', but the boats were limited by a short range, whilst the highly unstable perhydrol had to be stored in special fuel containers manufactured from Mipolan.

Perhydrol's reputation of being highly unstable was derived from its extremely corrosive nature, whilst even the slightest form of contamination would set off the oxygen-releasing chemical reaction. Any fire involving the substance could only be extinguished by the use of copious quantities of water, which in itself could prove disastrous in a submarine, especially while submerged.

Despite these drawbacks, Britain was determined to further develop the concept, initially using the ex-*U1407*, which was later renamed *HMS Meteorite* and operated until 1949. Two experimental boats followed. Ordered in 1947, the unarmed 1,000-ton displacement *HMS Explorer* (S30) and *HMS Excalibur* (S40) were completed in 1956 and 1958 respectively and were driven by two Vickers high-test peroxide (HTP) turbines. Although much safer in operation than the ex-U-boat they replaced, both suffered frequent fires and explosions with their propulsion plants, leading to their unfortunate nicknames of 'Exploder' and 'Excruciator'. Research and development work was finally abandoned in the early-1960s and both boats were scrapped soon after.

Meanwhile, the Russians were also experimenting with the Walter turbine, their research reputedly culminating in the equipping of the first few units of the

*USS Dolphin (AGSS-555) under tow on 22 May 2002, after a fire and flooding the previous night had disabled the boat. All crew members were evacuated safely with only a few minor injuries. Repairs costing an estimated $9 million were completed in 2005.*

*(U.S. Navy)*

Project 611 ('Zulu'-class) with such a propulsion system. However, their success was also limited and any boats originally itted with Walter turbines were either refitted with standard diesels or scrapped, as attention turned instead to other alternative forms of air-independent propulsion.

The single Soviet Project 617 submarine (NATO designation 'Whale') *S-99* was a 950-ton displacement prototype that had a speed of 11 knots on the surface and 20 knots submerged, a diving depth of 200 metres and an endurance of 45 days. Laid down at the Leningrad Sudomekh Yard 196 on 5 February 1951 and launched a year later, she entered operational service with the Soviet Baltic Fleet in early-1956, following a lengthy trials programme with her experimental closed-cycle propulsion plant. The hydrogen peroxide fuelled machinery had been assembled from captured parts from a German Type XXVI U-boat. The design never went into series production, as *S-99* was written off as a constructive total loss as the result of serious damage sustained in a machinery explosion on 19 May 1956 whilst submerged at a depth of 80 metres.

Like the larger Project 611 boats, the small coastal Project 615 ('Quebec'-class) boats followed from 1953, incorporating two conventional diesel engines and a single closed-cycle Kreislauf diesel system, but these vessels were also dogged by frequent fires and explosions, leading to them being nicknamed 'cigarette lighters'. Several of the improved Project A615 boats were damaged by explosions or fires involving their liquid oxygen-fuelled propulsion plant, one of which, *M-259*, was severely damaged in 1956 when her closed-cycle 32-D diesel exploded, killing four crewmen and injuring a further six. That same year, a machinery fire also damaged *M-257*. Worse was to follow when, on 26 September 1957, *M-256* suffered an explosion whilst submerged in the Baltic. The boat immediately surfaced

and the crew evacuated to the casing to continue damage-control efforts, but the fire quickly spread to adjacent compartments and the boat flooded and sank a few hours later. Only 7 of her 35 crewmen were rescued.

Only the previous month, one of *M-256's* sister boats, *M-351*, had flooded and sunk, although this boat was later salvaged and repaired, whilst another boat of the class which sank in 1957, *M-296*, was also raised and subsequently was erected as a naval memorial in Odessa. The damage sustained by *S-99* and the disastrous reputation of the Project A615 boats led the Soviets to scale down their experiments with air-independent propulsion systems in favour of the more promising nuclear propulsion and all such work stopped in 1960.

The Americans did, however, dabble briefly with HTP, with the completion in 1955 of the 36-ton midget submarine *X1*, inspired partly by the success of the British wartime X-craft. The boat originally incorporated a small hydrogen-peroxide engine for dived operations, backed up by a small electric motor. However, in February 1958 the craft suffered an internal explosion which fractured the hull and blew the bow section completely off. The rest of the crippled boat was backed away from the burning bow and pier before being salvaged and shipped to the Philadelphia Navy Yard, where it was rebuilt and a conventional diesel-electric propulsion plant fitted. With a bright orange paint-scheme, *X1* re-commissioned into the Navy on 14 December 1960 for use as a special test craft at NSRDC at Annapolis, where she served until 1973.

Interest in air-independent propulsion systems waned during the 1950s with the advent of nuclear power, although the concept has returned to favour since the 1980s as the cost of building and operating nuclear-powered boats has spiralled, not to mention the problem of disposing of the growing number of decommissioned nuclear hulks littering naval bases in the USA, UK and the former-Soviet Union.

Newer AIP systems are inherently safer and more efficient, with several countries actively involved in developing various concepts and even converting older submarines as trials vessels. The Swedish Navy converted the 1,000-ton *Näcken* to incorporate two 11kW V4-275R Stirling-cycle engines - giving a submerged endurance of over two weeks, whilst the Germans fitted the Type 205 boat *U1* with an oxygen/hydrogen fuel-cell closed-cycle propulsion system which produced 150kW of power to charge her batteries and give a submerged endurance of about 30 days. The latter has led to incorporation of air-independent propulsion systems in the German Navy's new Type 212A submarines, as well as two Type 212I and four units of the Type 214 variants currently (2008) being constructed for the Greek and Italian Navies respectively to commission between 2005 and 2010. The propulsion system combines a conventional diesel generator and lead acid battery system and an air-independent system consisting of nine polymer electrolyte membrane (PEM) hydrogen fuel cells.

Firms in the UK, the Netherlands and Italy are have also been involved in the development of closed-cycle diesel engines, whilst the French have sold their MESMA AIP-powered Agosta 90B class to the Pakistani Navy. All of these systems will undoubtedly be developed further over the coming years, as the prospect of acquiring conventional submarines with the operational flexibility of their larger nuclear-powered sisters is proving extremely attractive to the increasing number of submarine-operating navies.

Apart from the hazards associated with batteries or hybrid propulsion systems, the machinery compartments of all submarines contain all of the usual sources of fire or explosion found in surface vessels, such as the abundance of high-pressure and high-temperature liquids and gases, hot machinery and masses of electrical equipment. The incidence of fire and explosion are therefore just as commonplace in submarines as in surface ships although, thankfully, seldom result in the loss of the boat.

The British Porpoise-class boat *HMS Rorqual* (S02) suffered a serious engine room explosion whilst patrolling in the vicinity of Mozambique en route to Singapore during the Rhodesian UDI crisis in August 1966. Two men were killed and twenty others injured, but luckily the machinery was not badly damaged and the boat was able to reach Durban under her own power on 2 September. Two years later, in December 1968, *HMS Alliance* (S67) was nearly lost following a double explosion on board whilst she was running just below the surface off Gibraltar. A 22-year-old electrical rating managed to fight his way through dense smoke to slow down one of the electric motors, being injured in the event and later requiring treatment for leg burns on board the naval tanker *RFA Olwen* (A122). An immediate distress signal brought a French patrol aircraft to the scene, followed soon after by the destroyer *HMS Barrosa* (D68), which escorted the submarine into Gibraltar to undergo temporary repairs. For his bravery and quick thinking EM1 Derek Double later received an award.

On 4 August 1978, the French Narval-class submarine *FS Marsouin* (S632) was seriously damaged by fire, whilst on New Year's Day of the following year the Venezuelan Type 209 boat *Sabalo* (S31) also sustained extensive fire damage.

Another South American submarine was smitten by fire when, in the early hours of 2 February 2003, the crew of the Ecuadorian boat *BAE Shyri* (S101) were awoken by an alarm. Civilians living near to the Guayaquil naval base reported hearing several large explosions and huge clouds of smoke could be seen rising from the vicinity of the wharfs. The fire was quickly out of control and required the attendance of over a dozen fire appliances, whilst two naval craft sprayed foam onto the surrounding water to prevent the fire spreading to other vessels nearby, including the Navy's only other submarine, *BAE Huancavilca* (S102), berthed 500 metres away. By 0600, the smoke was towering 500 metres in to the morning sky.

It was not until after 1300 that that the fire was extinguished. One crewman had been killed whilst trying to extinguish the fire, which had started in the boat's accommodation area, and seven others were injured. Damage to the *Shyri,* commissioned in 1977, was so extensive that the boat was under repair until 2006.

More recently, a fire aboard a Canadian boat on 5 October 2004 cost the life of one its crew. *HMCS Chicoutimi* (878), the third of four ex-Upholder-class submarines bought from the Royal Navy, was 100 miles northwest of Ireland, en route to it's new home of Halifax, when the fire broke out. The boat was riding on the surface in a Force 9 gale whilst the crew

attempted to repair a defective air valve in the tower, when water cascaded into the boat through the open access hatch and caused shorts in the main electrical system. Whilst the crew bravely fought the blaze, all power and propulsion was lost throughout the boat. Although the crew quickly extinguished the fires, they would not be able to re-enter the boat until the smoke had cleared sufficiently the following day.

Early the next morning, the Royal Navy frigate *HMS Montrose* (F236) arrived on the scene to lend valuable assistance and evacuate three wounded submariners, but one officer later died of the effects of smoke inhalation.

The stricken boat was taken in tow by the British Coastguard tug *Anglian Prince* on the 7th and later by the US submarine support vessel *MV Carolyn Chouest*, arriving back at Faslane on 10 October. The boat was transported to Canada aboard a Norwegian transport vessel, finally arriving in Halifax on 1 February 2005. Damage to the boat's electrical systems and compartments was extensive and repairs to the *Chicoutimi* were originally expected to take at least a year. However,

*Fire damage to the submarine Chicoutimi was extensive as evidenced by this internal shot. (Canadian Navy)*

as cost estimates for the repairs continued to rise, there was speculation that the vessel would be cannibalised to keep her sister boats running. In April 2006 it was announced that the Chicoutimi would be laid up until commencing a refit in 2010 and she is not expected to be operational before 2012.

The ensuing Board of Inquiry relieved the crew of any blame for the fire, but recommended that further 'splash-prove' insulation be fitted to the boat's electrical systems to prevent further electrical fires and recommended amended procedures to keep conning tower hatches closed whist submarines are running on the surface.

Each of these boats were subsequently repaired and returned to service, and such incidents have undoubtedly occurred aboard boats of every submarine-operating nation in post-war years. Unfortunately, and perhaps understandably, details of such incidents are closely guarded by the navies of most countries, making quantification of the extent of any damage caused very difficult to ascertain with any degree of accuracy. Some of the numerically powerful, but technologically weak, submarine arms have probably even lost boats to machinery fire or explosion, their removal from the naval order going almost unnoticed.

Accounts of early post-war Soviet casualties are slowly coming to light as the walls of secrecy follow the same fate as the Berlin Wall, but some countries may never reveal such 'embarrassing' details. For example, from 1971 the Chinese began building their first indigenously designed submarines. One of these 2,113-ton Ming-class boats was reportedly scrapped following a serious fire in 1992, although the details and even the date of the accident are unknown. Similarly, the cause of the loss of one of North Korea's obsolescent Romeo-class boats off the country's eastern coast on 20 February 1985 is unknown, but fire or explosion is a distinct possibility.

Reports of even the smallest fires aboard nuclear powered submarines inevitably reach the ears of the press who, together with the ever-pessimistic anti-nuclear lobbyists, take every opportunity to stress how the incident 'might have' endangered the boat's reactor and caused a major disaster to equal that of the Three Mile Island or Chernobyl accidents. Official statements regarding fires aboard nuclear submarines, even if totally unconnected with the propulsion plant, invariably conclude with a comment to the effect that "the nuclear reactor was at no time endangered."

It is perhaps only natural that the public should require such reassurances, but the fact is, in western navies at least, the chances of a catastrophic disaster involving a reactor is almost non-existent, due to the number of safety back-up systems incorporated in their design. The numerous reported incidents of accidents involving the nuclear power plants of Soviet submarines have shown, however, that constant scrutiny of safety procedures and scrupulous attention to maintenance and design of the power plant, together with the total eradication of complacency, are essential if this excellent safety record is to be maintained.

Before going into series production of nuclear-powered submarines, the US Navy built two prototype boats with competing reactor designs. The world's first nuclear-powered submarine, *USS Nautilus* (SSN-571), completed in 1955, incorporated an S2W water-cooled reactor in which water heated by the nuclear fission reaction in the primary circuit was used to heat water in the secondary circuit, turning it to steam. This steam was then used to drive the main turbines to provide an almost unlimited source of power. The second boat, *USS Seawolf* (SSN-575), was completed two years later with a less successful liquid-metal (sodium) cooled S2G reactor. Liquid-metal reactors have several advantages over pressurised water reactors, being quieter, more compact and, because higher coolant temperatures are attainable, more thermal energy can be produced. However, they are far more dangerous to operate and so, following extensive trials, *Seawolf* was refitted in 1959 with a plant similar to that of *Nautilus*.

Extensive trials and evaluation of the advantages and disadvantages of each reactor design led ultimately to the adoption of the water-cooled S3W and S4W reactors in the Skate-class boats. These designs were later refined into the S5W reactor, which was incorporated in all US Navy SSNs and SSBNs up to the Surgeon-class boats. In the case of the UK, under agreement with the US government, a complete set of propulsion machinery, of the type fitted in *USS Skipjack* (SSN-585), was purchased for the first Royal Navy nuclear-powered submarine, *HMS Dreadnought* (S101), which was completed in 1963. In subsequent British nuclear-powered submarines, propulsion machinery was produced in Britain.

Britain's third nuclear submarine, *HMS Warspite (S103)*, suffered a serious fire whilst berthed in Liverpool on 2 May 1976. The blaze, which raged for 5 hours, began after a coupling fractured and the hot oil spraying from it ignited, putting the boat out of action for two years whilst the damage was repaired. This same boat was to be the subject of much speculation in the British press in 1990 after hairline cracks were reportedly discovered in the primary coolant circuit. A precautionary inspection programme was put in hand and all nuclear submarines in Royal Navy service were examined. However, since the independent Nuclear Powered Warships Safety Committee continued, against very stringent guidelines, to clear Royal Navy nuclear submarines to operate, one may safely assume that rapid progress was made in identifying the cause of the problem and in instigating remedial action. The American and French navies also share the seriousness with which the RN takes nuclear propulsion safety.

On the other hand, in their haste to match the US nuclear submarine programme, the Soviet Navy bypassed the prototype development stage and went straight into series production with the Project 627 ('November'-class) boats, incorporating pressurised water reactors and a teardrop hull form. This compressed development process is testimony to the dominance of Krushchev, who urged the building of innovative weapons systems in place of the more traditional fleet around a nucleus of major surface warships. This resulted in submarines being pressed into service without the opportunity to iron out any design flaws that may have serious consequences for the safety of the boat and it's crew, a fact that was to rear its ugly head on several occasions over the years of the vessels' service.

To compound this haste, by the time the Project 627 boats had been proved unreliable in service, two other classes of submarine had been designed and built around its rather leaky propulsion plant, namely the Project 658 ('Hotel'-class) and Project 659 ('Echo'-class) boats. Although Soviet submarine designs stabilised somewhat after Krushchev's demise in 1964, the reactors in these early boats (dubbed 'HEN' by NATO, an anagram derived from the NATO designations of the 'Hotel', 'Echo' and 'November'-class boats in which they were fitted) were the subject of numerous explosions and radiation leakages. In fact, the level of minor radiation leakage from Soviet nuclear submarines reportedly reached a peak in 1974 when they could be allegedly tracked by surface ships by the radiation trail they left. As a result of the regularity of such occurrences, these three classes of boats earned the nickname 'widowmakers', due to the poor quality of their reactor shielding.

Whilst on transit to a missile test range off Greenland on 4 July 1961 *K-19*, the Soviet Navy's first Project 658 ('Hotel'-class) SSBN, suffered a radiation leak from one of its two nuclear reactors after a coolant pipe failure. Eight men died in the efforts to repair the pipe and another six from radiation exposure before the rest of the crew were rescued by another submarine and the stricken vessel towed back to Polyarny. Ten years later, the same boat suffered another disaster, when a fire broke out in the 9th compartment, followed shortly afterwards by an explosion. Several men were killed instantly and twelve men became trapped in the aftermost section, compartment ten. As poisonous fumes spread forward throughout the boat, the rest of the crew mustered in the conning tower and on the casing, risking being washed overboard by the huge waves whipped up by the force 8 gale then blowing. *K-19* drifted westwards for several days, refusing assistance from American ships that had rushed to the rescue, until a Soviet tug arrived to take her in tow.

Most of the crew were evacuated by helicopters from a Soviet ship, but it still proved impossible to put out the fire in compartment nine and so the twelve crewmen remained trapped in the after torpedo compartment, with little food and no water, save for that which could be scavenged by collecting condensation as it accumulated on the bulkheads.

As the tug towed *K-19* back to her base, rescuers at last reached the trapped men and were amazed to find all of them were alive, although very weak, 23 days after the explosion. Twenty-eight men had perished in the disaster.

The Soviet Navy suffered its first known total loss of a nuclear-powered submarine on 12 April 1970. At about 2230 on 8 April, the Project 627 ('November'-class) attack boat *K-8* was operating off Cape Finisterre, Spain, participating in the massive Soviet naval exercise Okean, when an electrical fire broke out, quickly filling the control compartment with smoke. The boat surfaced immediately, but the fire, which had started in the 7th compartment, spread to the 5th, 6th and 8th compartments. Personnel in the 9th compartment were able to quickly evacuate via the hatch to the casing, but 15 men perished in the 8th compartment. A further 4 were killed in the 5th compartment. Dawn found the boat adrift with no communications as the fires continued to rage out of control. The following day, the Bulgarian merchant ship *Avior* arrived and rescued 46 crewmen, whilst later that night several other Soviet ships arrived and attempted to take the boat in tow. However, further damage control efforts proved fruitless and Captain Second Rank Bessonov was forced to abandon his boat before it eventually sank soon after 0600 on 12 April 1970. Fifty-two of *K-8*'s crew had perished.

The Project 659 ('Echo I'-class) attack boats and their converted cruise missile-armed Project 675 ('Echo II'-class) sisters, fared little better. One of the Project 659 SSNs, *K-66*, had to be towed into Vladivostok after sustaining severe fire damage on 20 August 1980 and was subsequently scrapped. Another boat of the class, *K-122* suffered a similar fate after a fire on 21 August 1983 that killed 14 crewmen. Then, on 10 August 1985, the Project 675 SSGN *K-431* was destroyed by an explosion whilst her reactor was being refuelled in Chazhma Bay.

Another Project 675 boat, *K-131*, suffered an electrical fire on 18 June 1984 that killed thirteen of her crew. Repaired and re-commissioned as *K-192*, the boat was again crippled by a fire off the Norwegian coast on 25 June 1989. The blaze aboard the Northern Fleet boat is believed to have been the result of a primary circuit coolant leak in one of her two reactors. Fortunately, the submarine managed to surface safely and, although

*On 25 June 1989, the Project 675 boat K-192 caught fire off the Norwegian coast and later limped into Severomorsk, where she was declared beyond economic repair.*

*(US Navy)*

clouds of smoke and steam were seen enveloping the boat, the fire was soon brought under control. Despite the best efforts of the crew and the assistance of the Soviet Navy Project 1151 ('Belyanka'-class) tanker *Amur* to bypass the system, the reactors had to be shut down to prevent a meltdown, but not before radioactive contaminated coolant had leaked into the sea. The Norwegian Nuclear Energy Safety Board later reported that they had discovered traces of Iodine 131, a by-product of nuclear fission, in water samples retrieved from the area of the incident, indicating that the coolant must have leaked from the reactor's primary coolant loop, possibly exposing the uranium fuel rods and causing them to overheat.

There appears to have been no serious casualties and *K-192* limped home on the surface under diesel-electric power, arriving at her base at Gadzhievo on 28 June, where she was de-commissioned and laid

up to await scrapping.

As a result of this accident, it was announced that all of these 'first generation' submarines - the NATO designated 'Hotel', 'Echo' and 'November' classes - were to be prematurely paid off and over the next two years around twenty of them were deleted.

The Soviet Navy has built few nuclear-powered surface ships, although they did build the world's first vessel of this type, the 17,000-ton ice-breaker *Lenin*, completed in September 1959. *Lenin* suffered a serious accident involving her original propulsion plant during 1966-67, including a meltdown of one of her three reactors, which resulted in her abandonment for more than a year and her withdrawal from service. She was subsequently re-commissioned in 1972 after undergoing a major rebuilt at Severodvinsk, during which she received a new propulsion plant based on two pressurised water reactors, each of which had a power rating of approximately 16MW (equivalent to 22,000shp). Since these reactors appear to have been readily available for installation, it is conceivable that they are derived from the reactor fitted in the Project 670 ('Charlie'-class) SSGNs.

Although the Western Navies have dismissed liquid-metal reactors as too dangerous to operate, the Soviet Navy have repeatedly returned to the concept. Liquid-metal reactors use substances such as liquid sodium or sodium-potassium alloys, which have the ability to soak up much more heat than water at a considerably lower pressure, as the coolant medium within the primary loop. These reactors thus have a much higher power-weight ratio, whilst being significantly smaller. However, the highly corrosive nature of these substances can culminate in leaks from the reactor heat exchanger, the increased risk of which was considered unacceptable in the West.

Nevertheless, in their quest for smaller, quieter and faster attack submarines to counter the superior Western boats, the Soviets accepted the higher risk of reactor leaks and explosions. The relatively high number of accidents involving submarines so fitted proves that the West were wise to reject such reactors.

*K-27*, completed in October 1963, was a liquid-metal reactor variant of the standard Project 627 nuclear-powered attack submarines, designated Project 645 ('November-mod'-class), the only vessel of the class. Nine members of her crew were killed in a serious reactor accident at sea on 24 May 1968. The boat was flooded with radiation from the reactor compartment and the reactor was so badly damaged that *K-27* was decommissioned and laid up. The boat was reportedly scuttled off Novaya Zemlya in 1981.

The Project 705 ('Alfa'-class) submarines combined a liquid-metal reactor with a pressure hull constructed of titanium, a combination that gave them a submerged speed and diving depth unparal-

leled by any other combatant submarines. The lead vessel of the class, *K-377*, was completed in 1969 but, following numerous problems during the extensive trials period - including a reported near melt-down of the reactor - this boat was broken up in the mid-1970s. Armed with the many lessons learned during the trials of the experimental craft, the series-production boats entered service from 1978 onwards. These boats in turn were all decommissioned during the early 1990s, the last one paying off in 1994. Current financial constraints imposed on the Russian military have probably resulted in the total abandonment of liquid-metal reactors in favour of the more reliable and proven pressurised-water designs.

The inferior design and construction quality of the first and second generation Soviet nuclear submarines was largely overcome with the later designs, a fact emphasised by the Commander-in-Chief of the Soviet Navy, Admiral Vladimir Chernavin, when he stated in an interview with the newspaper Izvestiya in 1987 that the Soviet Navy would in future be concentrating on quality, not quantity, in their nuclear submarine programme.

Nevertheless, despite Admiral Chernavin's optimistic statement, the continuing dissatisfaction with submarine design and build quality was reiterated by the Soviet Defence Minister, General Dmitri Yazov, during an interview with the journal Jane's Defence Weekly in September 1989, a statement prompted by the most dramatic and tragic loss of one of the Russian Navy's most modern nuclear-powered submarines, together with a large proportion of her crew.

The sole Project 685 (NATO designation 'Mike'-class) submarine was a prototype, probably intended as a refined version of the fast, but noisy, Project 705K ('Alfa'-class) boats and built to test various concepts in construction and weapon systems. The titanium-hulled boat had been launched at Severodvinsk in June

1983 and handed over to the Northern Fleet on 20 October of that year, but had been manned by a trials crew until just before her fateful voyage, her first as an operational vessel of the Soviet Navy. The boat departed from her home port for a patrol at the beginning of March 1989 with not only a new commanding officer and crew, but also a new name - *Komsomolets*.

On the morning of 7 April 1989, *Komsomolets*, with a crew of 66 and three staff observers aboard, was running at a depth of 50 metres, 120 miles southwest of Bear Island. At just after 1100, the serenity of her covert mission was shattered by the sound of klaxons, followed swiftly by reports of a major fire in the after-most 7th compartment, the electrical propulsion and steering compartment. Attempts to contact the crewman on watch in the compartment received no response and so the Commanding Officer, Captain First Rank Yevgeniy Vanin, ordered the operation of the fixed fire-suppression system and that the submarine be surfaced. Compartment seven had

already been sealed and, on receipt of the order to operate the LOKh system - containing a form of Freon gas - a Warrant Officer in the adjacent 6th compartment, the turbo-generator room, opened the valve to inject the gas into the space.

However, a high-pressure air pipe had apparently ruptured, feeding the fire with a fresh supply of oxygen and, before the LOKh could take effect, a deafening explosion was heard from within the electrical propulsion room. As the temperature within the compartment soared, the Warrant Officer informed the control room that the bulkhead was already starting to glow and that smoke was seeping through melting bulkheads glands. Oil was also spurting from beneath the starboard turbo-generator and immediately igniting, necessitating it's shutting down. A few minutes later, the second turbo-generator suddenly tripped, followed almost immediately by an explosion in the turbo-generator room that killed the sole occupant.

Without electrical power, the reactor was also shut down and so, his boat with-

*Forty-two crewmen perished when the Soviet Project 685 submarine Komsomolets sank in the Norwegian Sea on 7 April 1989 following a fire.*

*(G. Demin)*

out propulsive power, Captain Vanin ordered the blowing of all ballast tanks with high-pressure air to take her to the surface. *Komsomolets* was also fitted with a powder-gas generator system, whereby the mixture of the two ingredients would result in the formation of a high-pressure which, when injected into the ballast tanks, would displace the water, but this system was not used on this occasion.

Evidence that the original explosion had been the result of a short circuit within the submarine's electrical distribution system was soon manifesting itself throughout the boat in the form of a power surge, with consoles, panels and cables smouldering and bursting into flames as the boat made its ascent towards the surface. The cooling-water pump for the diesel generator was lost and the engine had to be shut down, followed soon after by the steering console catching fire.

The thick, toxic smoke that was rapidly filling the boat poured from the hatches as they were thrown open immediately the *Komsomolets* reached the surface at 1116. Captain Vanin ordered the transmission of distress signals, but it was another 25 minutes before the first of these were received in Severomorsk. The identity and position of the crippled boat was not immediately evident and so it was another thirty minutes or so before a rescue task force, including the nuclear-powered Project 1144 battle-cruiser *Kirov*, was despatched to the area. However, even at maximum speed, it would take some thirteen hours for *Kirov* to reach the *Komsomolets*.

Meanwhile, the situation aboard the submarine was rapidly deteriorating. The fire had spread forward, engulfing the 5th an 4th compartments - the engine room and the passage above the nuclear reactor compartment respectively. As the crew worked furiously to isolate systems and fight the numerous fires, the choking smoke forced them to don emergency breathing masks, attached by hoses to the boat's compressed breathing air system. It was only when several men began keeling over that the medical officer realised that the air system had become contaminated with lethal concentrations of carbon monoxide and ordered all crewmen to remove their masks.

Deprived of their primary air source, the fire-fighting teams donned portable breathing apparatus and prepared to re-enter the 4th Compartment. Although they found no fires, two men wearing personal breathing masks were evacuated from the smoke-filled passage. The damage-control party then moved into the engine room at about 1300, where they discovered seven casualties, all suffering from burns and asphyxiation. Five injured men were evacuated, but two others had died after inhaling air from the contaminated breathing air system.

Progress was stalled on reaching the engine room/turbo-generator room bulkhead, as smoke could still be seen emitting from a test cock, so it was decided that the fixed fire-suppression system in the turbo-generator room should be activated. However, the fire continued to rage unabated in the electrical propulsion room, leaving them little choice but to let it burn itself out. Then, at 1624, a series of massive explosions, probably originating from the oxygen-regeneration tanks, shattered the after section, breathing new life into the inferno. It soon became evident that the watertight integrity of the two after compartments had been compromised and *Komsomolets* began settling by the stern as water flooded into the hull.

Captain Vanin was left with little choice but to order his boat to be abandoned. As the Engineer Officer left the reactor compartment, he noted that, since the insertion of the final rods nearly three hours earlier, the temperature of the primary loop had been reduced to a safe 35°C and that the coolant pumps were still running, this system being autonomous and being operable even after the ship's main electrical distribution system had failed.

The first Soviet aircraft, an Il-38 'May', arrived on the scene at about 1440, nearly $3\frac{1}{2}$ hours after the initial distress signals had been transmitted, but there was little that this sole aircraft could do but relay messages and drop a few additional small life rafts. Snow flurries were partially obscuring the scene, but the submarine was still visible, shrouded in smoke, with force 3 winds causing waves to wash over the casing. At 1642, crewmen were seen to be inflating two large life rafts, but a vicious gust of wind tore one of the rafts away from the boat, whilst the other was overturned, leaving the survivors little choice but to jump into the freezing water and scramble for whatever buoyancy aids they could reach. The air-dropped life rafts simply drifted away, empty, the crewmen too exhausted to swim after them.

Captain Vanin looked with dismay at the events unfolding on the submarine's casing from his vantage point on the bridge, noticing also that the submarine's rubber anechoic coating was bubbling and peeling off of the hull in the vicinity of the after compartments. Nevertheless, his main concern lay with the evacuation of all personnel from his foundering submarine, several of whom were still within the boat gathering classified documents. As he descended the ladder back into the submarine, the crippled craft lurched under the influence of several heavy swells striking the hull and began to sink. Realising the inevitability that the submarine was about to plunge below the surface, the last man on the bridge, Warrant Officer Alexander Kopeyko, slammed the hatch shut and dived into the sea. Moments later, at 1708, *Komsomolets* sank stern-first, in position 73°43'17"N, 13°15'51"E.

*Komsomolets*, like many other Soviet submarines, was equipped with a 40-foot VSK escape capsule, built into the bridge structure, which could accommodate the crew and be released from its parent vessel to float to the surface. As the submarine plunged towards the sea floor 1,858-metres below, Captain Vanin gathered the last survivors into the escape capsule. As they sealed the lower hatch behind them, they heard the frantic knocking of another survivor, but before they could re-open the hatch, the hull of the submarine could be heard collapsing with an ear-rending crack and the knocking ceased.

As the needle of the depth gauge crept past 400-metres, the five occupants fought in vain to free the capsule using the special wrench. So desperate were their efforts that they bent the heavy steel wrench but, just at they thought their end was nigh, the capsule broke free of the submarine and shot towards the surface.

The speed of the capsule's ascent was such that a massive pressure built up within it and, on reaching the surface, the upper hatch - which had probably not been properly secured - burst open, the sudden depressurisation sucking one warrant officer from within and catapulting him into the air and, having struck his head as he was expelled from the chamber, he later drowned. A second man was also sucked out, but the velocity of his ejection was slowed as one of his legs snagged on the hatch and he managed to crawl free - the only survivor amongst the capsule's five occupants, as the remaining three drowned as the capsule flooded and sank.

Survivors were now clinging desperately to the upturned life raft, whilst others merely struggled to stay afloat, the silence broken only by the howling of the wind and the voices of men calling to their comrades. Survival in these freezing waters, even when wearing special survival suits, was estimated at only about 20 minutes and men were soon losing their grip and slipping free from the single life raft, never to be seen again.

At 1820, a little over an hour after *Komsomolets* had slipped below the surface, the fish-factory ship *Aleksey*

*Hlobystov* arrived on the scene and, lowering her boats, plucked thirty survivors, as well as several bodies, from the water. Three of the survivors died soon afterwards, the remainder later being transferred to the *Kirov*, which was equipped with extensive sickbay facilities. The battle-cruiser then raced back towards Severomorsk at full speed. Of the 69 men who had sailed with the *Komsomolets* on her fateful voyage, 42 perished. Only nineteen bodies were recovered.

Despite their lust for secrecy in the initial stages of the incident, the Soviets soon exhibited some extraordinary signs of 'Glasnost' and released extensive details of the tragedy to the Soviet Press, via the official news agency TASS. As well as extensive news articles in the newspapers 'Pravda' and 'Izvestya', the Navy also allowed the publication of extracts from the official inquiries in military journals such as 'Krasnaya Zvezda' (Red Star), whilst several high-ranking officers gave revealing interviews regarding the tragedy and the conditions aboard the Soviet Navy's nuclear-powered submarines. Other prominent Soviet naval officers wrote articles which were extremely scathing of the design and build quality of their ships, submarines and equipment.

Such criticisms, especially from serving military officers, would have been unheard of prior to the death of Leonid Breshnev in 1982, as the Soviet press was, until then, constrained in what it was allowed to report by the official publication 'Index Of Infor mation Not To Be Published In The Open Press', which effectively prevented news of military accidents from being publicised. Even the death of Soviet leaders was treated with secrecy. Under Gorbachev, this policy slowly changed, as he promised to open up Soviet society, to release the Soviet economy from the shackles of the Stalinist industrial system, and to reduce the power of the politically-selected Communist regime.

In the 1980s, the Soviet media reported in unprecedented detail on a number of disasters including the sinking of the cruise ship *Mikhail Lermontov* off the cost of New Zealand in March 1986, the Black Sea loss of the liner *Admiral Nakhimov* with the loss of 400 lives in August 1986, and even the loss of the Project 667A ('Yankee'-class) SSBN *K-219* in October of the same year, with television coverage of the kind never before seen in the Soviet Union. Nevertheless, the delay in alerting the world, and even the local inhabitants, of the Chernobyl nuclear reactor fire in April 1986 proved that there is still a long way to go before the level of 'openness' reaches that normally found in Western nations.

There were initial fears of massive contamination of the area, not only from *Komsomolets*' nuclear reactor, but also from two nuclear-tipped torpedoes carried by the boat, but due to the fact that the reactor had been safely shut down before the *Komsomolets* sank, together with experience gained from the loss of previous nuclear weapons, the risk of such an environmental disaster was judged as negligible and these fears were to prove unfounded. Nevertheless, the Soviets decided to mount an operation to raise the submarine and, in May 1989, assembled a task force of six ships - including the research ship *Akademik Mstislav Keldysh* and two Project 1135 ('Krivak'-class) missile frigates - to search for the wreck.

As the position of the wreck could be estimated with some accuracy, it was not long before it was located and photographed by one of *Akademik Keldysh*'s two *Mir* submersibles, revealing that the boat was evidently still in one piece and lying upright with no major structural damage. However, examination of the boat's interior revealed extensive damage, but most worrying of all were reports that the plates covering the warheads of the two nuclear-tipped torpedoes had broken loose, exposing them to corrosion and presenting an eventual danger that the 15kg of plutonium may leak out. Such leakage would result in the contamination of a massive area, with a danger that the plutonium may ultimately enter the food chain.

Following analysis of thousands of photographs, the contract for the recovery of the wreck was awarded to a Dutch firm - Netherlands Deep Sea Operations Consortium (NODC) - who won the work amidst stiff competition from American, Finnish, It alian and Norwegian salvage firms and who would work closely with the Leningrad-based naval-engineering agency Rubin. However, the cost of such a project, which required the building of a special salvage barge capable of lifting the 7,810-tonne submarine, was estimated at around US$250-million and consequently the project was delayed until mid-1993 at the earliest.

In late-1992, reports that high levels of radioactivity had been detected in the area were dismissed by the Norwegian's as "sensationalist" and led to suspicions that the Russians were attempting to raise concerns over pollution in an effort to raise the necessary funds to recover the Komsomolets, as the operation was further delayed by budget constraints.

The findings of the investigations into the loss of the Komsomolets were studied fervently, not only in Russia, but also in all other submarine-operating nations, particularly those of the west, and many of the lessons have since been incorporated into damage-control training syllabuses. Reasons for the alarming speed with which the fire spread throughout the boat can be attributed to two main factors: the ineffectual bulkhead integrity from the engine room aft in way of poor shaft seals and oil system bulkhead glands; and the apparent lack of suitable over-current protection of electrical equipment and systems.

Once established, the fires were fed by the failure of fuel and oil systems, whilst attempts to blow high-pressure air into the main ballast tanks probably resulted in air being injected into the after compartments due to the melting of seals in the pipework, thus negating the decision to allow the fire to burn itself out. The crew lacked suitable fire-fighting clothing, such as fearnought suits, which may have allowed them to attempt a re-entry into the burning electrical propulsion room.

Finally, the choice of fixed fire-suppression system was not a wise one. LOKh gas is known to be ineffective as a fire-suppression medium as it burns itself at around 580°C to produce poisonous phosgene gas. Royal Navy submarines use AFFF as the main fixed fire-fighting medium, although Halon systems, or derivatives, are being considered for future submarine classes. Nuclear submarines also have the added availability of steam with which to drench a compartment and suffocate a fire - a system that, if fitted, may have changed the outcome of Komsomolets' blaze.

The cause of the flooding that led ultimately to the sinking of the submarine has not been positively established, although it is likely that either flexible sea water pipework melted or that system pipework may have been fractured by the explosions. As water flooded into the electrical propulsion room, it would have seeped into the turbo-generator room and thence the engine room through the shaft seals and various bulkhead glands, so flooding more than the two compartments that the submarine was designed to sustain.

However, the most tragic aspect of this accident was the unnecessary loss of life after the submarine was evacuated. Only four men were killed as a direct result of the explosions and fires, with another five fatalities during the bungled capsule escape bid. The majority of the fatalities were due to hypothermia and drowning, as exhausted men, some of whom were injured, clung to the totally inadequate flotation aids available to them. Survivors also had difficulties in operating the additional life rafts dropped by the Soviet aircraft, as they were designed for use by the crew of downed aircraft.

Although President Gorbachev was relatively swift to alert US President George Bush, British Prime Minister Margaret Thatcher, and Norwegian Prime Minister Gro Harlem Brundland of the disaster, this did not occur until some nine hours after the fire had broken out. An earlier call for assistance would have resulted in the Norwegians despatching aircraft, helicopters and rescue ships to the area. The Norwegians stated that they could have had helicopters overhead within two hours of a request for assistance, meaning that had they been alerted shortly after noon, they would have been on station before the *Komsomolets* sank. These helicopters would have plucked some survivors from the sea whilst providing better survival equipment, such as inflatable enclosed life rafts - actions that would undoubtedly have cut the hypothermia fatality toll considerably.

It was later revealed that the Norwegians did offer the services of their Sea King helicopters, based 370 miles from the scene of the disaster, but the offer was declined. Such an attitude had been typical of the Soviet Navy, as in the case of the Project 57M ('Kanin'-class) destroyer that refused assistance from the aircraft carrier *HMS Hermes* (R12) after suffering a major explosion and fire off Norway in 1974, but it was surprising in the post-'Cold War' climate. Such a reluctance to accept assistance still exists in the Russian Navy, as was to be illustrated following the tragic loss of the Project 949 submarine *Kursk* in August 2000 (see Chapter 7).

Soviet/Russian nuclear submarines are known to be manned by a high proportion of officers and warrant officers. *Komsomolets*' complement at the time of her loss was revealed as 33 officers, 21 warrant officers and 15 seamen, of which

18 officers and 12 warrant officers were lost, whilst only three seamen survived. This could be explained by the inexperience on the part of the younger seamen, whose short-term conscriptions resulted in them being less prepared for the unexpected disaster than their professional, longer-serving, superiors. No such distinctions were made though when each and every crewman of the ill-fated boat was awarded the Order of the Red Banner.

Electrical faults are the main source of fires aboard submarines, although the professionalism of the average submariner - every one of which is generally conversant with all of their boat's main systems - results in most being extinguished quickly. However, major blazes do occur from time to time, such as the switchboard fire aboard the British nuclear-powered submarine *HMS Turbulent* (S110), whilst berthed at Devonport in February 1992, injuring twenty-three crewmen. The fire necessitated the rapid shutting down of the boat's reactor in an adjacent compartment. Although damage to the boat was not serious, the incident was later officially described "potentially lethal". A few months later, on 29 May, a Russian nuclear-powered submarine was damaged at the Northern Fleet's submarine base at Severomorsk when an electrical compressor exploded during routine maintenance, killing on officer and injuring five other crewmen. *TK-17* - one of the Russian navy's six colossal Project 941 (Typhoon-class) SSBNs - is also reported to have sustained major fire damage during the same year, the extent of which almost resulted in the vessel being scrapped.

As in surface ships, special fixed fire-fighting systems, in addition to the normal portable fire-fighting equipment, are essential, especially in battery compartments and weapon stowage areas. Various systems are available using either an inert gas or water as the extinguishing medium. Salt or fresh water spray systems are more effective at cooling the area of the fire on activation, especially important in weapon stowage areas, but the activation of water-spray systems in a submarine could upset the boat's trim and thereby add to an already perilous situation. This consideration has lead to the development of watermist systems, using an atomised spray to cover larger areas for a given volume of water, so reducing the amount of water required. Such an installation would also have obvious benefits aboard surface ships, where its adoption would reduce the danger of stability problems caused by fire-fighting water.

Improved ship design and the provision of effective fire-fighting systems and equipments are only part of the damage-control equation. Without a well-trained crew, able to operate these systems and equipments whilst taking into consideration the wider implications of their actions, the benefits of such equipments, provided at considerable expense, will be negated.

The Royal Navy has, for many years, been regarded as one of the leaders in fire-fighting training, much of which has been developed as a result of lessons painfully learnt, or re-learnt, during the many post-war conflicts with which it has become embroiled. A requirement for a dedicated damage-control school was recognised soon after the end of the Second World War, with the opening of *HMS Phoenix* at Portsmouth in 1949. Subsequently, dedicated fire-fighting training units were established at Portsmouth, Plymouth and Rosyth, where special three-decked, multi-compartment steel structures were built to replicate the construction of a typical ship. Although these units were completely devoid of furnishings and equipment, they gave Royal Navy personnel the opportunity to tackle live fires in fairly realistic surroundings, complete with intense heat and copious quantities of thick black smoke. Individual personnel or entire ships' teams could be given first-hand experience in the use of fire-fighting

equipments such as high pressure hoses, foam generators and portable extinguishers, as well as the wearing of fearnought suits and breathing apparatus, whilst fighting live fires or searching for casualties in smoke-filled compartments.

These antiquated units were, however, limited in their capacity to simulate various types of fire, as well as being expensive to operate and being environmentally unsound, due to the clouds of thick black acrid smoke produced during training serials. They have now been replaced with new fire-fighting training units at Portsmouth, consisting of a number of twelve-compartment multi-decked modules, not unlike those they replaced. However, each unit has been more realistically fitted out to represent the compartments of a typical modern warship, whilst flames are produced by computer-controlled propane gas burners, instead of the wood or oil-burning hearths of the old units. Artificial smoke is used to add realism, whilst hot air at up to 200°C is ducted into compartments to provide the intense heat that would be experienced in a real blaze. The flame, heat and smoke ingredients of each fire scenario are computer-controlled to react to the actions of the students, whilst providing a wide variety of fire simulations, from a simple wastepaper bin fire to fierce oil-based blazes in machinery compartment bilges. Personnel can therefore be trained to adopt a flexible approach to individual shipboard fire situations.

Students leave these units, after typical courses lasting between one and three days, with a sound basic theoretical and practical understanding of fire-fighting methods and procedures, as well as an awareness of the dangers created by a shipboard fire. Every Royal Navy officer and rating undergoes basic fire-fighting training as a new recruit and must undertake refresher training prior to each occasion of joining a seagoing ship.

The provision of such training facilities

are, however, meant to complement, not replace, shipboard fire drills. Fire exercises should take place on a regular - almost daily - basis on all seagoing vessels, training the crew in all aspects of fire-fighting, such as command and control, fire-fighting procedure and methods, isolation of ship's systems, operation of fixed and portable fire-fighting systems and equipments, smoke clearance, casualty evacuation and, last but not least, general ship knowledge. Exercises should cover all types of fire, utilising all damage-control equipments, with added realism provided by the use of smoke generators. No drill could possibly prepare anyone fully for the terrifying experience of a real shipboard fire, but if the initial, instinctive fire-fighting actions of personnel are borne of experience gained from comprehensive fire-fighting training, their

chances of extinguishing a blaze and so saving not only equipment, but also lives, will be immeasurably increased.

As a final point, it should be remembered that fires normally start as a result of human carelessness. The inquiry in to the fire aboard the Soviet Navy's first nuclear submarine, the Project 627 ('November'-class) *Leninskiy Komsomol* (ex-*K-3*), that killed 39 crewmen on 8 September 1967, determined that the fire had been started by a crewman smoking in the torpedo compartment. Furthermore, the destruction of the Libyan Polnochny 'C'-class landing ship *Ibn Al Qis* (113) in September 1978, caused by a crewman smoking at a refuelling point during a landing exercise, serves to illustrate that even the most obvious safety precautions, when forgotten, can lead to disaster.

# Chapter Three

# GROUNDINGS

The effects on a vessel's hull of a grounding incident range from minor damage to underwater fitting such as propellers, rudders, stabilisers and sonar domes, to the complete loss of the craft when the hull plating is ripped out or the vessel's back is broken. The extent of the damage inflicted will be dependant on a number of factors, such as the type of vessel involved, the terrain on which the grounding occurred, the speed at which the vessel was running when the incident occurred and the weather conditions prevailing at the time.

Although many groundings are a direct result of the influence of storm-swept seas - which were covered in Chapter One - the most common cause of such incidents is navigational error. The reasons for these navigational mishaps are numerous, but the prime ingredient in the majority of cases is that of human error.

Countries all around the world were still rejoicing at the newfound peace after World War Two when the first warship loss due to grounding was reported.

The 252-tonne whaler *Kos XIV* was one of several ships of the class requisitioned by the Norwegian Navy in 1940 and converted to minesweepers, being renamed *Mandal*. Although the ship survived the war, her peacetime career was to be short-lived.

*HMNS Mandal* was west of Lista, en route back home to Norway from the Firth of Forth in Scotland on Monday, 17 September 1945 when, at about 1730, a lookout aboard the ship spotted a drifting mine. During the hour that it took to dispose of the hazard by gunfire, a thick bank of fog had descended on the area, but the ship returned to her former heading towards Lista Lighthouse. In an attempt to make up for the time expended in the mine disposal task and to maintain her original ETA, the Commanding Officer ordered full speed, about 12 knots.

It is probable that, during the mine destruction operation, the ship had drifted away from her estimated position, the fog preventing an accurate fix to be made. The ship's Type 252 radar failed to alert the crew to the proximity of land and, at about 2300, *Mandal* grounded at Steinodden on Lista. The ship's hull was badly holed in the vicinity of the engine and boiler compartments, which quickly flooded, along with the orlop deck. Whilst attempts were made to control the flooding, radio contact was gained with the Oslo-based merchant ship *Lerka*, which arrived on the scene in the early hours of the morning. Most of the 26-man crew were evacuated to the *Lerka*, while four men remained aboard *Mandal* to carry on the damage-control effort, but these too abandoned ship at 0330.

Salvage operations began later that day, with key members of the crew returning to their ship to retrieve valuable items of equipment and classified material. A survey of the damage to the hull by divers revealed a large gash along the starboard side, which, it was hoped, could be patched to allow the ship to be re-floated. However, over the next few days, the weather deteriorated, with a strong force 6-7 wind blasting in from the southwest, forcing suspension of the work on Friday the 21st. The work resumed the following month, but bad weather again disrupted the salvage attempt and the hopeless task was finally abandoned on 1 November. The rusting wreck was finally sold to a shipbreaker in Drammen in May 1947.

The loss of submarines due to grounding is a relatively rare occurrence, but it was only two days after the loss of the *Mandal* that such an incident resulted in the French Navy's first post-war casualty.

The Standard Almirante-class submarine FS *Minerve* (P26), laid down as *Q185*, was commissioned into the French Navy in September 1936, serving initially with the 2nd Submarine Flotilla of the Atlantic Fleet. In the summer of 1939, with war clouds gathering over Europe, the 12th Division of submarines was transferred to the Mediterranean, based at Oran. From 30 November 1939 the Division transferred to the Moroccan Navy and carried out operational patrols in the defence of the Canaries.

On 14 January 1940 *Minerve* left Casablanca to undergo a refit at Cherbourg. When the Germans broke through at Sedan on 19 May 1940 the boat was hurriedly repaired to allow her to sail in order to prevent her capture by the Germans, only to be subsequently seized on 3 July by the British at Plymouth, along with *Junon*, where their crews were treated as prisoners. Both vessels were transferred to the Free French Navy, *Minerve* re-commissioning on 31st January 1941 under the command of Lt. de Sonnerville, and participated in many hazardous operations in the Norwegian Sea and Arctic Ocean during the war years. On 10 October that year *Minerve* had a frighteningly close encounter when she was mistakenly attacked by RAF aircraft, but escaped without serious damage.

Unfortunately, like the *Mandal*, the *Minerve* never reached home after her wartime service. Whilst under tow from Britain to France on 19 September 1945, the boat was wrecked by running aground on Portland Bill in bad weather as a result of a navigational error and was removed from the French Navy lists in February the following year.

Only a month after the loss of the *Minerve*, the Japanese submarine *Yu3002* was en route back to Japan to join the other remnants of the former Imperial Navy when the boat ran aground in the Sozan Sea, south of Inchon. Tragically, *Yu3002* quickly capsized and sank, taking half of her crew with her to a watery grave.

The combination of fog and human navigational error was soon to claim another Scandinavian minesweeper, just at the time when these vessels were most

*On 29 January 1946, after drifting off course in fog, the Danish minesweeper ME1016 ran aground and was wrecked on the Jernhatten, off the east coast of Djursland.*

*(Kommandørkaptajn Holm, Marinens Bibliotek )*

The Danish patrol cutter HDMS Skarven (Y382) was declared a constructive total loss after grounding off Mjovanes, in the Faeroe Islands, on 7 May 1966. (Kommandørkaptajn Holm, Marinens Bibliotek )

desperately required in the operations to clear the extensive wartime minefields.

*MMS1016* was one of several vessels of the class lent to the Danish Navy by Britain towards the end of the war, being transferred on 7 August 1945. Only five months later, on 29 January 1946, *ME1016* - as she was now known - was en route from an anchorage in Hjelm Dyb to participate in a minesweeping operation in the Kattegat, when she encountered a thick bank of fog. Somehow, the vessel drifted off course with the result that she ran aground on the Jernhatten, off the east coast of Djursland, Jylland. The ship took the ground with such force that her hull was torn open and she was later declared a total wreck. The subsequent enquiry attributed the accident entirely to human navigational error.

This was not to be the only Danish Navy vessel to suffer the indignity of grounding due to navigational errors, with two such losses occurring in the 1960s. On 10 January 1961 the ex-German inshore minesweeper *HDMS Eganaes* (MR157) was stranded east of Odden Havn on the northern coast of Sjælland and was sold as a constructive total loss six days later. Then, on 7 May 1966, whilst transiting from Thorshavn to Klaksvig in calm seas, the patrol cutter *HDMS Skarven* (Y382) ran aground off Mjovanes in the Faeroe Islands. An SOS was transmitted, which was intercepted by a nearby Hvidbjornen-class patrol ship and a merchant ship, but neither vessel was able to reach the area in time and the *Skarven* sank in 20 metres of water, five hours after the grounding.

Even more recently, the Danish survey vessel *SKA11* was conducting survey

On 10 January 1961, the ex-German inshore minesweeper HDMS Eganaes was stranded on the coast of Sjaelland and was declared a total loss. (Kommandørkaptajn Holm, Marinens Bibliotek )

*The Danish Navy survey vessel SKA11 foundering on 3 May 2006 after striking rocks in Arsuk Fjord, Greenland.*

*(Island Command Greenland, courtesy of www.navalhistory.dk).*

operations off Naval Station Gronnedal in the Arsuk Fjord in Greenland on April 27 2006, when she struck a submerged rock. As the craft quickly flooded, the crew abandoned the vessel and were rescued by her sister ship, *SKA12*, operating nearby. Salvage efforts were hampered by gale force winds and snow and, despite the assistance of a tug from Nuuk, attempts to extract *SKA11* from the rocks proved futile. Damage sustained to the hull over the next few days sealed the craft's fate and, as she was hauled from the rocks on 3 May 2006, she sank in 300 metres of water.

Problems with navigational equipment can lead to vessels being unwittingly piloted off-course. Compensatory calculations can sometimes allow defective equipment to be used to give useable navigational data if the extent of the equipment's inaccuracies is known. However, such calculations can sometimes be misinterpreted by the crew, with disastrous results.

The Canadian Algerine-class fleet minesweeper HMCS *Middlesex* (J328)

was commissioned on 8 June 1944 and, following a brief war service on convoy escort duties in the North Atlantic the ship was refitted at Halifax and used as a tender to the New Entry Training Establishment, HMCS *Cornwallis*, in the Bay of Fundy. In February 1946 the ship was returned to service at Halifax, employed in the task of disposal of surplus ammunition from Bedford Basin and as the Halifax Station emergency ship.

Moored at Halifax in the early hours of Monday, 2 December 1946, the ship received a priority signal from the Commanding Officer Atlantic Coast (COAC) to sail immediately and to render assistance to the 90-foot Boston-based fishing vessel *Ohio*, which was in distress after losing her propeller in mountainous seas in position 44°30'N, 60°50'W, halfway between Sable Island and the coast of Nova Scotia. Although only six officers and 41 ratings of her crew were on board when the orders were received, the urgency of the task did not allow time to recall the rest of the crew and it was decided that there were sufficient men aboard to handle the ship. Twenty minutes later, at 0135, *Middlesex* sailed on her mercy mission, with an estimated time of arrival at the rescue position of 0930 that morning.

The ship's antiquated Sperry gyro compass was running, but the Electrical Artificer was having problems getting it to settle as it kept 'tilting', and so the Commanding Officer, Lt. Eric Fisher, RCN(R), piloted his vessel out of the harbour using the magnetic steering compass, located in a binnacle on the bridge. At 0225 *Middlesex* passed the inner Automatic Whistle Buoy and a few minutes later altered course to 068° magnetic and increased speed from 11 knots to 15.5 knots. With the error on the magnetic compass, determined during the last compass swing in March of that year, known to be 22-degrees west, a course of

068° was ordered by Lt. Fisher in order to achieve the desired course of 090° 'true' required to achieve the rendezvous with the *Ohio*. Unfortunately, the magnetic compass error should have been added to the required 'true' course, giving a magnetic course of 112°. The simple mathematical error was further compounded by the acceptance of the ordered course, without question, by the Officer of the Watch, who also happened to be the ship's Navigating Officer and who should have spotted the mistake and enlightened the Commanding Officer.

Yet another factor was to add to the tragic string of events. As there was a shortage of watch-keeping personnel aboard due to the ship's hurried departure from Halifax, the radar was shut down after testing of ranges against known points. A force 3 northeasterly wind was getting up and causing a short swell, which was further exacerbating the Electrical Artificer's attempts to settle the gyrocompass. Nevertheless, despite the darkness of the night, visibility was judged as 'good', with objects being visible for distances of two-three cables and lights at ten miles.

After satisfying himself that his ship was apparently proceeding on the correct course and that there were no other vessels in the vicinity, Lt. Fisher went below to check on the Electrical Artificer's progress, ordering the Officer of the Watch, Lieutenant A.O. Grav, to maintain the ship's present course and speed.

Lt. Fisher was still in the Gyro Room at 0315 when a watch-keeper on the bridge spotted a white light ahead, but Lt. Grav took this to be another vessel, although he did not inform his Commanding Officer of this observation. Five minutes later, a lookout spotted land and breakers directly ahead of the ship and Lt. Grav immediately ordered engines 'Full Astern'. The sudden change in engine revolutions did not go unnoticed by Lt. Fisher who, on returning to the bridge, was informed that the engine were at full astern and a "slight bump" had been felt. After ordering the engines to be stopped Lt. Fisher checked his bearings and noted

*The Canadian fleet minesweeper HMCS Halifax ran aground on 2 December 1946 after an incorrect course was plotted due to gyro compass errors.*

*(BGM Photo Centre)*

a flashing white light on the starboard quarter and a white light astern, which he assumed to be the Outer Automatic Flashing White Whistle Buoy and Chebucto Head respectively.

Having supposedly fixed his position, he then ordered engines half ahead and for the original course to be resumed. A few minutes later, land and breakers were again sighted, this time to starboard. Lieutenant Fisher ordered 20-degrees of port rudder and that the echo sounder be switched on, but before these orders could have any effect, the ship grounded. He immediately ordered "Stop starboard, full astern port" in a desperate attempt to extricate his vessel, but both propellers were now firmly jammed on the rocks. The time was now 0330.

An immediate check of all underwater compartments revealed no serious hull damage, but the ship was stuck fast and was being buffeted by the waves. Both boilers were ordered to be shut down and the ship's diesel generator was started to provide lighting and emergency power. Fortunately, no casualties had been sustained amongst the crew, despite the tremendous force with which the ship had struck the rocks.

After transmitting a grounding incident report to COAC and requesting the immediate assistance of a tug, the Commanding Officer ordered all non-essential members of his crew to abandon ship. With the temperature dropping rapidly and light snow falling, the ship's whaler was lowered into the water but was torn away from the ship by the surf breaking over the rocks and, although recovered, was soon smashed against the ship's side and wrecked in the increasingly heavy swell.

*Middlesex*'s position was 44°38'N, 63°19'W, to the seaward side of Shut In Island, off Laurencetown, some 20 miles east of Halifax. Land could be seen a short distance away, illuminated by one of the ship's searchlights. A Carley float was lowered and, with a lifeline attached, was manoeuvred to the shore only 20 yards away by two ratings. By attaching another line to the shore the Carley float was passed to and from the shore, ferrying 27 of the crew to safety, where they took shelter in nearby farmhouses. The other five officers and fifteen crewmen remained aboard to prepare their stranded vessel for receiving a towline.

At first light, *HMC Tug Riverton* (ATA-528) arrived on the scene and, anchoring 150 yards from *Middlesex*, passed a line to her. This line was then used to pass the main towing line. *Middlesex* had grounded less than two hours after high tide, so it was hoped that she could be re-floated at the next high tide at around 1100. However, despite being pulled aft a distance of some 20 feet, it proved impossible to re-float the stranded ship. *Middlesex* was now being severely buffeted by the waves as the weather deteriorated, smashing the hull repeatedly against the rocks. A fresh examination of the ship's watertight compartments and tanks revealed considerable damage, but although the hull was showing some signs of leakage, there was no evidence of major holing as of yet.

Meanwhile, the drifting *Ohio*, with her seventeen-man crew, was being towed through snow flurries and heavy seas towards Halifax by the RCMP cutter *French*, where she arrived safely on 4 December.

For the next two days *Riverton*, together with the Glen-class tugs *Glenevis* (YTB-502) and *Glendyne* (YTB-503), continued attempts to haul *Middlesex* from the rocks, but the operation had to be temporarily suspended on the morning of Wednesday, 4 December, due to the deteriorating weather conditions. By midnight the situation had not improved and the rest of the crew were evacuated. Savagely cold westerly winds and a heavy surf were now causing the ship to rock back and forth and become further embedded on the rocks, making salvage an increasingly difficult proposition as each hour passed.

Salvage operations continued the following morning. Although the diesel generator was still running and No.2 boiler had been flashed and banked, damage to the minesweeper's hull was now extensive. Water was flooding into her magazines, the forward messdeck and No.1 boiler room through the large splits that were opening up along her starboard side. Many valuable items of equipment and the crews' personal effects were already being removed from the ship using a series of minca barges, transported back and forth to Halifax by *Glendyne*, *Glenevis* and the harbour tug *Greenwood* (YMT-551), and to the shore via the four breaches buoys that had by now been rigged. By Saturday night the boiler and generator were shut down and the machinery was being dismantled.

Over the next few weeks as much equipment as possible was salvaged from the *Middlesex*, as all chances of re-floating her had now faded. An armed guard had to be placed aboard the ship to prevent scavengers from removing any valuable or attractive items and the ship was subsequently declared a constructive total loss and paid off on 31 December 1946. To add insult to injury, a fire broke out aboard the hulk during salvage of valuable equipment on 15 January 1947, caused by careless use of oxyacetylene cutting equipment.

During the Board of Inquiry into the accident, held at the shore base *HMCS Scotian* on 10 December 1946, it was established that the incorrect magnetic compass error calculation had resulted in *Middlesex* being 44-degrees off course when she ran aground. The Commanding Officer, Lt. Eric G.T. Fisher, RCN(R), was held to blame for the stranding of his ship, in that he ordered an incorrect course be steered after passing the Inner Automatic Whistle Buoy and that, after returning to

the bridge, he ordered speed and course to be resumed without positively determining his ship's position. The Navigating Officer, Lt. Arthur Owen Grav, RCN, was also held to blame in that he failed to check the course ordered, failed to accurately fix the ship's position as Officer of the Watch, and neglected to call the Commanding Officer when a light was sighted ahead.

Both officers faced a court-martial on 19 December. Lt. Fisher was convicted of negligently endangering and stranding his ship, his first command. He was severely reprimanded and lost one year's seniority in the Royal Canadian Naval Reserve. Lt. Grav was also convicted on the same charges, for which he was dismissed from the service.

The transit of a river or waterway may appear to be a relatively straightforward operation in daylight with unimpeded visibility, but a night transit can be an infinitely more difficult undertaking. Even an experienced mariner may find that a route which he has successfully navigated safely innumerable times before in daylight will contain hazards hidden from the human eye by the veil of darkness. In such circumstances, all available navigational aids should be fully employed to ensure that the ship's position is known at all times and in pilotage waters an echo-sounder should not only be running, but it must be monitored by a well-trained and well-briefed operator to ensure that the invaluable information is promptly reported and acted upon.

The Swedish Sprängaren-class patrol vessel *HMS Sökaren* (V47), built in 1917, was relegated post-war to open sea target towing duties. On the night of 3 October 1953 she set sail from Saltsjöbaden, southeast of Stockholm, to ferry around fifty troops to a group of ships waiting offshore. Although *Sökaren*'s Commanding Officer had taken his ship along this route several times in daylight,

*Although the Commanding Officer reduced speed and used the searchlight to pick out navigational hazards, he failed to prevent HMS Sökaren running aground and sinking near Inägarolandet.*

*(Sjöhistoriska Museet)*

he had not transited the area at night before. The fairway was not marked with light buoys and as the ship approached the tiny island of Saltsäcken, near Inagärolandet, the Commanding Officer ordered speed to be reduced and the searchlight to be used to search for a navigational fix.

Minutes later the ship shuddered to a halt as she struck the bottom. With skilful use of main engines and steering gear, the crew managed to re-float their ship fairly swiftly, but it grounded again almost immediately and water began pouring into the vessel through breaches in the hull. As the vessel began to settle deeper in the water, it became obvious that any attempts to save the ship were doomed to failure and the order was given to abandon ship. Utilising *Sökaren*'s own two lifeboats and several small boats berthed nearby, all of the crew and passengers were ferried safely to shore, only 150 metres away, whilst damage-control efforts continued in vain. As the final crewmen left their ship, *Sökaren* quietly sank to the bottom of the channel 40 metres below.

Divers surveyed the wreck over the following days but, due to the extent of the damage to the hull and the age of the vessel, it was decided that *Sökaren* would not be salvaged.

Darkness can provide a dense veil, hiding dangers from the unwary mariner that would normally be seen and avoided in daylight. However, when darkness is mixed with a sprinkling of inexperience and a dash of complacency, an unstable cocktail is formed which all too often explodes in the face of carelessness.

A unit of Naval Reserve Mine Division 21, based at Portsmouth, New Hampshire, the old YMS-136-class minesweeper *USS Grouse* (MSC(O)-15) was manned by a nucleus US Navy crew, supplemented by US Naval Reserve personnel of the First Naval District.

On Friday, 20 September 1963, *USS Grouse* was ordered to proceed to Cape Cod to take part in manoeuvres with other US Naval Reserve vessels off Provincetown, Massachusetts. As the little ship slipped from her berth shortly after 2130 on that night and headed out of

Portsmouth Harbour, Commander Naval Reserve Mine Division 21 (Commander R.C. Dalton, USNR), the ship's Commanding Officer (Lt.Cdr. A.E. McCarthy, Jr., USNR), and the Executive/Navigating Officer (Lieutenant Per T. Saverstrom, USNR), were all on the bridge. Shortly after *Grouse* had safely cleared the harbour, Cdr. Dalton and Lt.Cdr. McCarthy left the bridge, leaving Lt. Saverstrom as Officer of the Deck (OOD).

The weather was calm and visibility good, with only intermittent rain showers. As a projected course for the night had not been plotted in advance, the navigator delegated the task to the quartermaster, QM2 R.W. Bow, USNR. The ship's position at this time was calculated as 43°01.45'N, 70°41.85'W, and QM2 Bow laid out on the chart a projected course line that he determined to be 165° true. However, he had failed to secure the chart to the chart table before plotting the course and, although the protractor he used had been aligned with the edge of the chart, a slight movement of the chart resulted in a small error being built into his calculations, the actual course required being 163°.

Although Lt. Saverstrom ordered Bow to secure the chart and check the plotted course, the miscalculation went unnoticed and the error was further compounded by the navigator, who checked and agreed with the quartermaster's calculation. Furthermore, Lt. Saverstrom failed to appreciate the fact that the plotted course intersected the shoal water between Dry Salvages and Little Salvages and would take the ship within 950 yards to the east of shoal water off Cape Ann, all of which was clearly marked on the chart.

At 2215 Lt. Saverstrom was relieved as OOD by Lieutenant S.H. Domeij, USNR. Apparently contented with the course he was steering, it was over an hour before Lt. Domeij took a navigational fix, at which time he calculated the ship to be about 600 yards to the west of the projected course. Despite this fact, Lt. Domeij decided not to adjust his course to the east. Curiously, a further fix a half-hour later, at 2347, showed the ship to be back on track. A few minutes later he was in turn relieved as OOD by Lieutenant (JG) E.W. Petterson and QM2 Bow by QM3 L.L. Blake. Before going off watch, Bow instructed Blake to call him when a flashing bell buoy '1' was sighted off Cape Ann, if visibility was reduced, or if the ship approached within three miles of land.

At 0030, QM3 Blake took a two-bearing narrow-angle fix but, a little confused by his inability to identify the visible navigational lights, he attempted, unsuccessfully, to obtain another. Unsure of his findings, he alerted the OOD and suggested he call QM2 Bow, but Lt. Petterson shrugged off this suggestion as unnecessary. At about 0050 a single navigational light could be seen off *Grouse*'s port bow, whilst two further lights were visible on the starboard bow and another on the starboard quarter. These lights should have permitted the ship's position to be estimated fairly accurately, had they been identified. Although *Grouse* was equipped with sufficient navigational aids, including charts, gyrocompass, LORAN, fathometer and radar, the fathometer was not used by the OOD as an indication as to the depth of water beneath the hull to give him an additional positioning aid.

An unclear radar presentation hampered attempts to obtain radar ranges but, when the presentation cleared at about 0100, the OOD calculated range to the nearest land to be 4,950 yards. However, a couple of minutes later Lt. Petterson sighted 'white water' ahead, but failed to take any action to take way off the ship or alter course and, at 0105, the ship ran aground on Little Salvages Reef, off the coast of Cape Ann, Massachusetts, in position 42°40.14'N, 70°34.17'W.

The Commanding Officer and the navigator were quickly on the bridge. Receiving reports that his ship appeared undamaged, Lt.Cdr. McCarthy attempted to re-float his stranded vessel by reversing main engines. When this proved unsuccessful, he ordered that an anchor be dropped off the starboard quarter in order to attempt to extract the ship from the reef by using the anchor windlass to haul in on the anchor cable. At the time of the grounding the tide had been flooding and, as the hours passed the ship was left high and dry until, by 0400, there was insufficient depth of water beneath the hull to cover the seawater inlets and the generator had to be shut down through lack of cooling water.

At 0120, a message was received at Portsmouth stating that the *Grouse* had grounded and requesting assistance. By daylight, a thirty-foot Coast Guard lifeboat was on the scene, followed shortly afterwards by the tug *USNS Keywadin* (ATA-213) and a smaller yard tug. While the lifeboat stood by, the two tugs secured a bridle, made up from the minesweeper's anchor chain, to bitts on *Grouse's* stern and attempted to pull her from her perch, but this only resulted in the bridle parting and the bitts being wrenched from the ship.

In order to lighten their ship prior to any further attempts to re-float her, the crew began jettisoning fuel oil and water. Meanwhile, salvage assistance had been requested from Commander Service Force, US Atlantic Fleet, which resulted in the formation of Task Unit 48.4.4, comprising the tugs *USNS Keywadin* and *USNS Mosopelea* (ATF-158), the submarine rescue ship *USNS Tringa* (ASR-16) and the salvage vessel *USNS Opportune* (ARS-41), plus various harbour craft.

Lack of light foiled a further attempt to free *Grouse* at 0200 on Sunday, 22 September, and by noon that day the weather began to deteriorate rapidly, with strong winds developing waves of up to ten feet in height. Nevertheless, the Task Unit managed four further salvage attempts between the 24th and the 28th. However, the effect of the waves battering the ship against the reef's rocks eventually took their toll and by the morning of the 24th a large hole had been smashed in the minesweepers hull on the starboard side which, together with the parting of hull planking, resulted in extensive flooding throughout the ship.

On 28 September it was decided that further salvage attempts were futile and the decision was taken to strip the stricken vessel of all valuable equipment and then destroy the hulk by fire to prevent her becoming a hazard to navigation.

The subsequent Court of Inquiry convened at the Headquarters of the First Naval District in Boston, Massachusetts, found Lt.Cdr. McCarthy and Lt. Saverstrom guilty of negligence and both were reduced to the Standby Reserve status. Both officers were later ordered to undertake further training at one of the Naval Reserve Officers' Schools to improve their level of training.

Although Lt.Cdr. McCarthy had instructed in his Standing Night Orders that the ship's course and position be verified frequently, he had failed to enforce this order, or to make himself aware of the projected course that was to be steered through the night. Lt. Saverstorm had also been negligent by not accurately checking the course set by QM2 Bow and by allowing a course to be plotted that would take the ship dangerously close to known navigational hazards. Both officers should also have been present on the bridge during the transit between the shoals.

Lt. Petterson was found negligent in that he failed to call his superiors when he became unsure as to the ship's position. Also, although Lt. Petterson had been qualified as an Officer of the Deck four months earlier by Lt.Cdr. McCarthy, the grounding of *USS Grouse* had occurred during his first independent watch at night. It was considered that Lt. Petterson had insufficient watch-keeping experience to have been so qualified, but the Court recognised that it was the Commanding Officer's prerogative as to this judgement.

The Court of Inquiry also recommended that the training of commanding officers of US Naval Reserve crews be standardised and that uniform procedures be followed by these officers when qualifying their Officers of the Deck underway. Also, the Commandant, First Naval District, was instructed to initiate a programme to have the effectiveness of commanding officers of Reserve ships periodically assessed by the Selected Reserve Division Commander.

The grounding of *USS Grouse* had been due to a large element of complacency on the part of the ships officers, combined with the inexperience of the OOD in piloting a ship during a night passage, resulting in the entirely avoidable loss of a valuable US Navy minesweeping asset. Some elementary rules of navigation had been ignored. The worst-case scenario must always be considered, especially during night transits, as complacency has led to many vessels foundering in waters that are well navigated. The ship's track should be planned carefully, using all aids available. If a certain light has not been sighted by the expected time then the ship's position must be held in doubt. If doubt or uncertainty exists as to the position of a vessel, the only safe action is to take way off until the ship's position has been positively ascertained by a 3-bearing fix. An alteration in course could prove disastrous, especially in confined water.

Even experienced officers can fall foul when transiting at night areas that they are familiar with in daylight.

The small Greek Nasty-class vessel *HS Iniochos* (P22) was the duty boat at the Torpedo Boats Command in Amphiali base during the afternoon of 19 October 1968, with most of her crew standing by so that the boat may react promptly to any emergency. The Duty Commanding Officer was the commanding officer of one of *Iniochos'* sister vessels, *Toxotis*, and was an experienced Lieutenant widely regarded as one of the best torpedo-boat captains serving with the TB Command at the time.

Late that afternoon, a distress call was received from a fishing boat in the area of Fleves Island, off the southwest coast of southern Attica in the Saronikos Gulf. The weather was extremely foul. A gale warning had been issued and civilian passenger craft and vessels were warned not to put to sea unless absolutely necessary.

In response, a search and rescue mission was ordered at about 1730 and the crew of the *Iniochos* were scrambled, the hurried departure necessitating the vessel's sailing minus her executive officer, Chief engineer and a couple of ratings.

*Iniochos'* departure was noticed by the Commander Torpedo-Boats, who at the time was dining with C-in-C Fleet, whose house commanded a clear view of Salamis channel. Concerned that one of his ships was putting to sea in such terrible weather conditions, he contacted the Operations Room at the naval base. However, when he learned the identity of the boat's commanding officer he went back to his meal, content that the operation was in good hands.

As *Iniochos* cleared the Salamis channel and the approaches to Piraeus harbour the weather conditions worsened still further, with the wave height and the heavy rain combining to reduce visibility to less than a mile. Wind force was varying between near gale to gale and the boat's maximum attainable speed - normally up to 40 knots - was restricted to a mere 16 knots. *Iniochos* kept Amphiali informed of the deteriorating conditions via SSB/HF radiotelephone as they proceeded to search for the missing fishing boat.

When nothing could be found, it was decided that the torpedo-boat should herself seek shelter, either under the lee of Anghistri Island or heading gingerly towards Salamis against the wind. The Commanding Officer decided to take a route for home that would subject his vessel to the minimum of pounding by the now mountainous seas. He first set a course towards the south-west and, with a second turn to starboard, planned to pass to the south of the Aegina-Anghistri island group and then between the Methana peninsula and Anghistri Island before turning north.

At about 0200 *Iniochos*, having left the Methana peninsula well to port, turned to the north in order to pass to the west of Anghistri, the south-western tip of which is formed by the small islet of Doroussa islet. Between this islet and the larger island is a rather narrow channel running roughly north-south. In calm weather mariners familiar with the area can safely negotiate this channel, although, in order to avoid the small islet of Doraki, lying on the north-east side of the northern exit, it is necessary to turn the helm sharply to port.

The Commanding Officer, familiar with the area, nevertheless intended to pass to the west of Douroussa, but the sea, the rain and the flying spray were rendering the torpedo-boat's radar almost useless and in the darkness none of the bridge crew realised that they were actually within the small channel. Consequently, *Iniochos* smashed onto the rocky islet of Doraki, wrenching a gash in the boat's hull along almost her entire length.

Having ordered main engines stopped, the Commanding Officer descended the small ladder from the bridge, only to find the weather deck already awash. He had no choice but to order his crew into one of the life rafts that, fortunately, had been automatically inflated as the torpedo-boat started sinking. Minutes later *Iniochos* sank out of sight, leaving the raft to drift southwards under the influence of wind and tide, whilst the crew let off flares at regular intervals.

At first light the raft beached on the northern coast of the Methana peninsular and the cold and weary crewmen climbed up the nearby cliff. On reaching the top they simply caught a town bus, which took them to the local Coast Guard office, from where they telephoned Athens to report that they were all safe and well.

Meanwhile, shortly after midnight, *Iniochos'* normal Commanding Officer, having learned that his boat was missing, drove to the Naval Base, where he requested permission to take another of the torpedo-boats to sea to search for her. Although receiving verbal permission to do so, he was ordered to await written confirmation. Impatient to get on with the mission, he selected a craft with sufficient crew aboard and quickly put to sea. However, soon after the vessel had cleared the Salamis channel he was notified that the verbal permission was cancelled due to the inclement weather and was ordered back to base.

Ironically, it was discovered later that day that the missing fisherman had found refuge in a protected cove and had been safely ashore for most of the night.

Although, in the ensuing court-martial, the Commanding Officer was acquitted of the charge of the negligent loss of his vessel, he was later punished by an internal Board of Enquiry to four months temporary dismissal due to "*failing to fulfil obligations emanating from the application of Navy Rules and Regulations.*" Two years later he resigned his commission.

In his mitigation, although an experienced officer, the Lieutenant had been commanding a boat with a crew with which he was not used to working. It is also likely that, due to heavy spray, the anti-clutter switch of the boat's radar was turned full on and, when the boat entered the relatively protected waters of the

Anghistri-Doroussa area, the operator failed to reset it to its normal position with the result that there was no echo from the low-lying coastline.

It must also be pointed out that the Lieutenant was a victim of his own experience and confidence, in that a less experienced officer would have been afraid to risk his boat and his crew under such terrifying weather conditions to undertake such a daring rescue mission. Nevertheless, any blame for the loss of the craft must be shared by the Navy General Staff on duty that night, whose decision to send such a small craft as the *Iniochos* - which was only 24.5 metres in length - on a rescue mission in gale force conditions must be brought into question, resulting as it did in an "institutional accident".

Even in calm weather and clear visibility, the misinterpretation of navigational fixes can lead to tragedy.

On the night of 21 August 1958, three Aggressive-class minesweepers *USSs Pivot* (MSO-463), *Pluck* (MSO-464) and *Prestige* (MSO-465) were en route from Yokosuka to Kure. Engine defects on the *Pivot* had put the squadron behind schedule and so the ships were ordered to alter course and take a more direct route through the Naruto Straits.

The ships entered the strait just after midnight on 23 August but the bridge crew mis-identified navigation lights in the 800-yard wide channel, with the result that the Executive Officer ordered a turn 100-yards early. At 0135, *Prestige* ran aground in Naka Se, in position 34°39.1'N, 134°39.4'E. Attempts to manoeuvre the ship off of the rocks proved futile. Attempts by *Pivot* to tow the stranded ship free resulted in her too running aground and losing her sonar, but *Pivot* was able to use main engines to extricate herself.

Further damage to *Prestige*'s hull throughout the day caused extensive flooding and, at 2345, fearing that the ship was in danger of capsizing, the Commanding Officer gave the order to abandon ship.

Over the following weeks the ship was lightened by the removal of upper deck equipment, but the ship's fate was sealed on the night of 25-26 August when Typhoon Flossie drove her further onto the rocks and removed all hope of salvage. The ship was destroyed by demolition charges and fire ten days later.

That other consumer of visibility, fog, has similarly been a major contributor in the grounding of countless vessels. The inability of an Officer of the Watch/Deck to obtain accurate visual fixes can result in total disorientation, with tragic results. One such victim was a sister-ship of *USS Prestige.*

Entering Charleston harbour during the afternoon of 19 March 1970, dense fog forced *USS Sagacity* (MSO-469) to reduce speed. However, as the ship slowed to around 3-knots, steerage way was lost and the ship was driven by the current onto the seaward side of the south jetty. The Commanding Officer immediately ordered full astern, but was forced to emergency stop both engines when the propellers struck rocks. There was no other alternative but for anchors to be dropped and assistance requested. By the time a US Navy tug arrived to render assistance an hour or so later, at about 1800, further damage had been caused to

*USS Prestige (MSO-465) hard aground in August 1958.*

*(E. Shea)*

*Hsuen Yang was one of several Taiwanese destroyers that were written off following grounding incidents between 1957 and 1977. The ship was wrecked in 1970.*

*(M.D.J. Lennon)*

the ship's hull and underwater fittings, with minor flooding in the after engine room. The starboard engine was re-started and, with the tug's assistance, *Sagacity* was manoeuvred free of the rocks and escorted to her berth.

Subsequent surveys revealed extensive damage to the shaft lines, rudders, sonar and hull and the ship was declared beyond economical repair, decommissioned and scrapped.

The combination of fog, strong currents and narrow channels is a dangerous cocktail that has claimed several larger warships.

Having been sunk by Nationalist aircraft at Gijón, in northern Spain, on 21 October 1937 during the Spanish Civil War, the Churruca-class destroyer *Ciscar* was salvaged by the nationalists and repaired from 1938 to 1939. This ill-fated vessel later suffered an even more undignified fate however, when, on 17 October 1957 she ran aground in fog off Ferrol. With the combination of the extensive hull damage sustained during the grounding and the subsequent relentless battering by waves over the

following days, the destroyer's keel finally snapped and she broke in two. She was later declared a constructive total loss and the 2,175-ton hulk was discarded and scrapped the following year.

A similar fate befell another Spanish destroyer less than a decade later. On 25 February 1966 the five year old *SNS Ariete* (D36) - English translation 'battering ram' - apparently attempted to live up to her name when she ran aground on rocks at the entrance to the Ria de Muros y Noya waterway, on the Spanish Galician coast. The stranded vessel was subsequently declared a constructive total loss and was scrapped.

Clearly, the loss of such a major fighting unit as a destroyer is a crippling blow to any navy, but several such vessels have been lost due to navigational errors in the post-war years.

*IJS Kamikaze* was one of the few Japanese destroyers surrendered at Singapore in August 1945 in a seaworthy condition, with the result that she was employed on repatriation duties. On 6 June 1946 *Kamikaze* became stranded near Cape Omaezaki whilst taking part in a salvage attempt on the repatriation ship *Kunashiri* and was later declared a constructive total loss. She was broken up where she lay by November 1947.

In 1957 the Tiawanese destroyer *Hui Yang* was wrecked by running aground and in May 1970 this navy was to suffer another destroyer casualty when the *Hsuen Yang* (16) was critically damaged in a similar incident. Subsequently, two sister vessels, ex-US Gleaves-class destroyers, were transferred from Japanese naval service in August 1970 for spares to repair *Hsuen Yang*, but it was found that the damage was irreparable and so the ex-*Hatakaze* (Ex-*USS Macomb*, DD-458) was commissioned in her place, taking both her name and pennant number, whilst the original *Hsuen Yang* (Ex-*USS Rodman*, DD-456) was scrapped.

Incidentally, the Taiwanese Navy appears to have a particularly poor record for losing vessels by grounding, with known losses including several destroyers, a tanker and three tank landing ships. The Gearing FRAM I destroyer *Lao Yang* (D930) was the only one of twelve sister ships excluded from the *Wu Chin* modification programme after receiving extensive damage in a grounding incident, although she was later repaired and remained in service until the late-1990s. Also lost was one of several 173-ft *PC-461* class submarine chasers lent to Taiwan by the USA in the 1950s. *Han Kiang* (PC-124, ex-*PC-1175*) was stricken on 15 June 1969 after being seriously damaged in a grounding incident. The USA later sold the wreck to the Taiwanese government for scrapping.

Another destroyer loss due to grounding during 1970 was that of the A.M. Sumner-class *USS Soley* (DD-707), which was serving as Naval Reserve Training Ship. The badly damaged ship was decommissioned on 13 February and, on 18 Sept 1970, was stricken and sunk at sea as a target.

Although the T-53-class destroyer *FS Duperre* (D633), the French Atlantic Fleet Flagship, was seriously damaged by grounding on 13 April 1978, her value dictated that she be repaired, at great cost, using components cannibalised from her inactivated sisters *La Bourdonnais* (D634) and *Jauréguiberry* (D637). It was almost two years before *Duperre* returned to service following these expensive repairs.

The damage-control skills of her crew and the close proximity of rescue services armed with specialist salvage equipment were paramount in preventing the sinking of one of the Royal Navy's Island-class patrol ships. The consequent flooding and salvage presented a rare example of a ship which was flooded almost to the point of loss, but which remained balanced on rocks in a steady state.

Visibility was limited to only a few hundred yards by thick fog as the 1,210-ton fishery protection vessel *HMS Guernsey* (P297) was approaching Aberdeen harbour on Friday, 17 April 1987. At about 1245 the vessel was proceeding at a leisurely 3 knots past the Girdlestone rocks when the close proximity of the shore was detected on radar. Although the ship's engines were set to full astern, *Guernsey* yawed on to the rocks off her port side and rapidly took in water through several large gashes in the hull, flooding the engine-room, shaft tunnel and generator room. Main engines were shut down immediately as they rapidly became submerged by the rising water level. By 1300, fast flooding of the vessel stopped as *Guernsey* was sat firmly on the rocks.

As luck would have it, the local Grampian Fire Brigade had in the previous nine months been reviewing its routines for dealing with major incidents, including how to deal with ship fires. A volunteer team were in the final stages of training at Stonehaven, involving helicopters, rescue boats and divers. This undoubtedly helped them to instigate a speedy and effective rescue mission. Within an hour three pumping units had been transported to the *Guernsey* and were removing 240 tonnes of water per hour from the vessel, whilst harbour tugs ferried large quantities of additional equipment to the stricken ship, including portable pumps and breathing apparatus.

Water was flooding into the ship through the punctured steel hull at the rate of around 2,000 tonnes/hour. This far exceeded the capacity of the ship's three 50-tonnes/hour general service pumps, two of which had been rendered useless when the engine room and the shaft tunnel were flooded shortly after grounding. Slow flooding of the generator room via an unpacked cable gland in the engine room/generator room bulkhead eventually resulted in all power being lost at about 1400, due to the flooding of the ship's main generators, all three of which are in one compartment, so denying the use of the vessel's own salvage pumps. The small 50kw emergency generator, located on the starboard side of the engine room, had also been quickly lost in the initial flooding.

By the time assistance arrived from shore, an RNLI lifeboat was already in attendance and the crew were making preparations to abandon ship. The rising tide was causing the ship to flood to a greater depth, floodwater by this time having entered the engineers workshop on 3-deck, above the shaft tunnel. Water was also present in the after end of 2-deck. Stability wise, the ship was in a very precarious position as the vessel teetered atop the rocky pinnacle. Pumps provided by tugs were soon removing over 500 tonnes/hour of water from *Guernsey* and the leak-stopping actions of the crew had reduced the ingress of water into the generator room and 2-deck to an extent where the pumps were just holding their own. There was nothing that could be done for the engine room and shaft tunnel, which had free-flooded to the depth of the new waterline.

High tide was at 1621 and, at 1630, *Guernsey* was successfully towed off of the rocks by two tugs that were then secured either side of their charge as the flooded ship was gingerly guided into the harbour. Within 30 minutes of arriving alongside the quay, commercial pumps were removing over 600 tonnes/hour of water from the ship and the vessel was successfully dry-docked at 1800 the

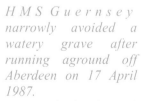

*HMS Guernsey narrowly avoided a watery grave after running aground off Aberdeen on 17 April 1987.*

*(Walter Sartori)*

following day. It was only then that the full damage could be appreciated. Calculations revealed that another 60 tonnes of water per hour, equivalent to a split $1\frac{1}{2}$-inches long by $\frac{1}{2}$-inch wide, would have been sufficient to capsize the vessel. The judgement of the crew and fire brigade in handling the flooding and preventing free-surface water had undoubtedly saved the vessel from a watery grave.

Hall Russell shipyard, who had, incidentally, built the ship a decade earlier, was contracted to repair the vessel, which was returned to service about five months later.

The design of the Island-class includes no watertight decks that would have limited the extent of flooding from a hole beneath the waterline. The failure of non-return valves on vents passing through 2- and 3-decks allowed secondary flooding to an unprecedented extent and breaching of the watertight boundary of the engine room by an unpacked cable gland was also responsible for secondary flooding of the generator room. That said, the Island-class do have watertight bulkheads reaching to just below one deck, an improvement on the original design, that of the *Jura*. Furthermore, the wisdom of siting the emergency generator within the main machinery spaces must be questioned.

In the Hunt-class MCMVs for example, the emergency generator is located in a separate compartment high up in the superstructure. Nevertheless, the saving of *HMS Guernsey* remains a credit to the training and efficiency of her crew and of the rescue services involved in the incident.

Often though, fog and darkness cannot be used as mitigation for a grounding accident, the blame resting firmly and squarely with the navigational actions of the vessel's officers. Every navy, without exception, suffers its share of grounding incidents, although most of these accidents are of a minor nature and usually result in the matter being dealt with by a formal Board of Enquiry. Occasionally though, the incident results in the sinking, destruction, or disposal of the vessel.

One such incident befell the Latvian Navy on 2 November 2000. The patrol craft *Spulga* (KA02) was en route to Karlskrona when it ran aground 15 miles from the city. The ship's punctured hull quickly began taking on water and the crew were soon evacuated by Swedish armed forces helicopter and rescue craft.

The craft's single propeller had been destroyed in the grounding and the forward sections of the ship were severely damaged. Over the next few days, preparations for the vessel's salvage proceeded, with the removal of stores and weaponry to lighten it. However, with the prospect of deteriorating weather conditions, the salvage effort was accelerated during the early hours of 6 November. The Swedish Coast Guard tug *KBV-181* finally managed to haul the *Spulga* free of the rocks at 0700 and began the slow tow towards Karlskrona. Unfortunately, the water flooding into the vessel's shattered hull could not be stemmed and at 0849, 2.5 miles from where she had grounded, the *Spulga* capsized and sank.

The Latvian National Armed Forces Navy commander, Captain Ilmars Lesinskis, received a reprimand and was instructed to review the navigation training given to ships' commanders and helmsmen.

Some obstacles, even in broad daylight, remain invisible to the human eye and to the detection of radar. This in itself though is not an excuse for a grounding incident when the hazard is clearly marked on charts. Reefs pose a particularly potent danger to the unwary mariner, especially at high tide when they may by completely submerged and obscured from view.

Normally though, they are visible to a vigilant lookout in the form of a line of seething white surf. Unfortunately, even this telltale indication of the proximity of such a hazard sometimes goes unseen until it is too late.

Several vessels of the once proud Imperial Japanese Navy were lost after striking reefs in the immediate post-war years, whilst employed on repatriation duties with the Allies. The former submarine chaser *Cha.81* was captured in August 1945 and employed by the Minesweeping Service until, on 18 April of the following year, she ran aground on a reef off Matsushima. Attempts to salvage the stricken vessel failed and, on 21 February 1947, the final deathblow was dealt when she caught fire and the entire fore end of the ship was destroyed.

Little more than six weeks were to pass before the next Japanese vessel employed on repatriation duties was to become the victim of a reef. On 4 June 1946, the former Type A escort vessel *Kunashiri* was wrecked off Omae-Zaki, Suruga Wan, in position 34°35'N, 138°15'E. Although the ship's upperworks remained above the water's surface, her hull plating had been ripped open along its entire length, resulting in extensive flooding of compartments and equipment. *Kunashiri* was subsequently declared a constructive total loss.

Several other vessels were to fall foul of reefs in similar circumstances before repatriation duties were concluded in 1948, when many former warships were handed back to Japan to form the nucleus of the newly formed Japanese Maritime Safety Agency. This fledgling force was soon to suffer a double blow when, in October 1950, two minesweepers were wrecked within days of each other. On the 27th, the former Pa.No.1-class patrol vessel *MS30* was stranded on a reef near Koriyama. Then, only three days later, her sister-ship *MS28* struck another reef off Suzaki in Shizuoka Prefecture.

Over the past fifty years, hundreds of vessels - both military and civilian - have fallen victim of the great reefs of the Pacific Ocean and it is therefore inevitable that the largest of the Pacific Rim navies should have also have suffered the indignity of such incidents.

The Mission-class tanker *USS Mission San Miguel* (T-AO-129) was lost after grounding on 8 October 1957 on Maro Reef in the Hawaiian Islands, in position 25°25'N, 170°35W. The ship, en route from Guam to Seattle, was in ballast and running at full speed when she struck the reef at 15 knots, ripping a series of massive gashes in her hull. Despite the close proximity of the reef, the darkness of the night, and the 8-foot waves, the Commanding Officer of the US Navy landing ship *LST-664* skilfully and daringly manoeuvred his vessel close enough to affect the rescue of the entire crew of the tanker as it silently began to settle by the stern. The *Mission San Miguel* was stricken from the US Navy list on 20 December and the hulk was simply abandoned. The wreck was never recovered, although it was later used as a bombing target by US Navy and Air Force aircraft.

This was not to be the only US Navy tanker to be lost by grounding. The *USS Cowanesque* (AO-79) ran aground at Kin Bay, Okinawa, on 23 Apr 1972. She was deemed beyond economical repair and was subsequently sold in her damaged condition to Great China Steel Enterprise Company, arriving at Kaohsuing, Taiwan, for scrapping in September of that year.

*HMS Cook* (A307) had been laid down as the Loch-class frigate *Loch Mochram* in November 1944, but whilst under build the design of the vessel was modified and she became instead the Bay class frigate *Pegwell Bay* (K638). The ship was launched on 24 September 1945, but fitting-out work was halted shortly afterwards as the post-war strength of the Royal Navy was rapidly reduced.

However, it was soon decided that some warships that were in an advanced stage of construction should be employed on other duties and, to this end, four Bay-class vessels were modified and completed as survey ships from 1948. *Pegwell Bay* was taken in hand by HM Dockyard, Devonport, and was commissioning as *HMS Cook* in July 1950.

From 1957, *HMS Cook* was employed in the Far East and, following a refit in Singapore in the summer of 1962 she was re-commissioned for survey operations in the South West Pacific, under the command of Commander F.W. Hunt, MBE.

In 1963 the ship's main surveying assignment was that of Bligh Water, the large expanse of ocean, much of it reef-filled, between the two main Fijian islands of Viti Levu and Vanua Levu. Having completed the survey of the central area of Bligh Water, the ship spent the months of July and August in the area of the Gilberts (now Kiribati) and then provided officials and support for the first South Pacific Games at Suva at the beginning of September.

On 1 October, *HMS Cook* departed Suva to resume the Bligh Water survey, which was now to be concentrated on the Vatu Ira Channel at the eastern end of Viti Levu. Commander Hunt had planned to make the passage through the fringing reef off the island of Vatu Ira in the early afternoon, so that the high midday sun would highlight any coral. The ship would then anchor before dispatching the launches to begin plotting triangulations in preparation for the commencement of the new survey the following morning. However, delays in taking aboard fresh provisions at Suva delayed departure and the ship eventually arrived off Vatu Ira at about 1700, with the sun declining into the west ahead of the course into the anchorage.

To ensure a safe passage through the reef, one of the ship's boats was lowered and sent in ahead to guide the *Cook* and detect any dangers. As *Cook* edged slowly through the reef on a course of roughly west-north-west, the crew of the boat reported coral dead ahead but, as the ship was altering course to avoid this danger, her bow struck a second coral to starboard of the first.

Echo sounding indicated a water depth of about twelve fathoms all around the ship, tailing off rapidly to a depth of some 300 fathoms less than a cable astern. In a futile attempt to break free, the main engines were ordered full astern, but by 1815 the falling tide was leaving her firmly embedded on the reef.

Although damage-control reports initially revealed no breaches of the hull plating, the waves developed by the moderate south-easterly force 4 to 5 breeze soon drove her more firmly onto the coral head and leaks began to appear. A kedge anchor was laid out, but it dropped over the edge of the shelf into deep water and so could not gain a purchase sufficient to haul the vessel from her perch.

For the next seven hours the port engine was kept at about $^3/_4$ power astern, except for very brief intervals to cool the bearings. Even so, the ship was gradually pushed further onto the coral head and successive compartments were breached. Initially the lower deck held but, with the continual rocking of the ship on the reef, the sounding tubes of the fuel and water tanks below were punched up through the decks, breaching their watertight integrity.

As each successive compartment began flooding the crew worked feverishly to shore the buckled decks and bulkheads. So much shoring was required that the ship's stock of damage-control timber was soon exhausted and even oars and survey beacon poles had to be utilised for this purpose.

By about 0200 the dents and rents in the bottom were reaching the forward bulkhead of the forward boiler room. As it was feared that the forward boiler room might also be flooded, consideration was given to using the remaining steam to drive the ship firmly onto the coral to prevent her foundering. Fortunately, the rising tide, the kedge anchor and the faithful port engine allowed the ship to float free of the reef at about 0330. The kedge was recovered and the ship steamed slowly back to Suva, escorted by the New Zealand Navy frigate *HMNZS Taranaki* (F148), which had arrived on the scene shortly after 0400.

Back in Suva, the ship's divers examined the hull and reported that it was badly dented and split for a length of 50 feet from about 15 feet aft of the stem. Emergency, if not permanent, repairs were required before *Cook* could proceed safely anywhere, but the nearest dry dock was in Auckland. Suva's slipway, operated by the Public Works Department, was only rated for 1,000 tons, although it could handle ships of up to 1,300 tons displacement and a length of 198 feet - *HMS Cook* was 307 feet long and, with the additional 380 tons of floodwater, her damaged displacement was calculated at 2,500 tons. Nevertheless, the risk of steaming her to New Zealand, especially in the hurricane season, was unacceptable and so, somehow, the Suva slipway had to be used.

In order to lighten the ship sufficiently for her to be winched up the slipway, she had to be practically stripped of every fitting that could be removed or unbolted and every lorry available from the local Public Works Department was utilised. By the 12th the ship had been lightened to a calculated 1,560 tons, and the following day she was hauled bow-first up the slip, her stern remaining in the water with some 360 tons being waterborne at low tide. A false bottom was built over the damaged plating, returning the vessel's watertight integrity, and the ship was re-floated on 27 October. The dismantling process was now reversed, the only items not replaced back on board being the four 3-pdr saluting guns, which had been cut off and which were presented to the Fijian Military Forces for their new barracks.

By 22 November, *Cook* was ready to proceed to sea, although with no echo sounders, sonar or refrigeration machinery, she could not be considered a functioning survey unit and so was ordered to return to the United Kingdom, where she arrived on 24 February 1964.

This was the time at which the 'new look' surveying flotilla of commercially design ships - the Hecla and Bulldog classes - were being laid down to replace the Dampier-class vessels. *Cook* had been earmarked as the last to be disposed of, since before her accident she was in the best material state of the four ships. In the event, after reaching Devonport without incident she was deemed beyond economical repair, decommissioned and was sold for scrap a few years later.

At a court martial in Singapore, Commander Hunt was found guilty of hazarding his ship and his command was relinquished. There can be no doubt, however, that Cdr. Hunt had taken what he considered to be prudent precautions against grounding by using one of his ship's launches to scout ahead for signs of danger, although, in hindsight, the wisdom of attempting the transit through the reef with the setting sun dead ahead of his ship must be questioned. Radar and echo-sounders are of little use in detecting the proximity of reefs, which can rise steeply from the sea floor to just below the water's surface. A low-lying sun, whether it be rising or setting, can effectively render ships' lookouts 'blind' to low-lying land or reefs, as the crew of the US Navy cargo ship *USNS Sgt. Jack J. Pendleton* (T-AK-276) were to discover to their cost almost a decade later.

*Pendleton*, heavily laden with a cargo that included large quantities of ammunition, was en route eastwards from

*USNS Jack J. Pendleton sits perched on a reef near Triton Island on 1 November 1973, having run aground five weeks earlier. Her rudder has been ripped from its seating by heavy seas.*

*(R. Melman)*

Da Nang on the morning of 25 September 1973, when she struck a small reef near Triton Island in the Paracel Islands. Lookouts on the ship's bridge had not spotted the reef, protruding less than ten feet above the water's surface, as the vessel headed towards the bright rising sun. Furthermore, the low-lying obstacle would have produced a poor radar reflection. The jagged corals ripped open the ship's hull and the forward holds were flooded almost immediately.

Despite desperate attempts to re-float her, the ship remained embedded on the rocky pinnacle, leaving the Commanding Officer no choice but to order the transmission of a distress signal. Several vessels from the US 7th Fleet were despatched to the area over the next few days to render assistance to the stranded ship, including *USNS Beaufort* (ATS-2), *USNS Reclaimer* (ARS-42), *USNS Hitchiti* (ATF-103), *USS Tioga County* (T-LST-1158) and the civilian tugs *Saigon 240* and *Viking*. The first vessels on the scene found *Pendleton* lying serenely atop the reef in the bright sunshine, with her bow raised out of the water and her stern drawing approximately six feet more than her normal deep waterline.

The salvage operation, centred on the salvage-and-rescue ship *USNS Beaufort*, was able to begin almost immediately in the calm weather conditions. Salvage experts and divers examining the stranded vessel discovered that she was wedged firmly atop the pinnacle with a large gash in her hull. The extremely deep water surrounding the reef rendered the laying of salvage anchors impracticable. The ship had therefore to be lightened as much as possible before she could be hauled from her perch and the *Tioga County* began pumping fuel from *Pendleton*'s tanks.

On the evening of 2 October a tow wire was passed to the stranded ship from *Beaufort*, whilst *Reclaimer* attached her's to *Beaufort* and *Hitchiti* in turn passed another wire to *Reclaimer*. As the latter was a single screw vessel, the tug *Saigon 240* pressed her bow against *Hitchiti*'s starboard side amidships in order to prevent her from slewing off course when the strain was taken on the tow. The chain of vessels began to haul together on the tow wires but as *Pendleton* remained stuck fast and the strain on the wires increased, *Reclaimer*'s tow wire parted with a deafening crack, forcing the crew on her deck to dive for cover. Any further attempts to haul the ship free in the following days were thwarted as the weather began to deteriorate and it became increasingly apparent that the re-floating of *Pendleton* was an impossible task with the rescue vessels in attendance.

*Pendleton* had to be de-stored in order to lighten her still further and, to this end, *Hitchiti* was despatched to the Subic Bay Naval Base to collect a large barge, while the tug *Saigon 240* was sent to Saigon to

assist in the towing of a large floating crane to the scene. This crane was to be used to remove all movable equipment from the stranded ship to the barge, including two large portable generators which were located atop the hatch of No.2 hold, while the ammunition ship *USS Mount Hood* (AE-29) used her helicopters to remove the explosive ordnance from the *Pendleton*'s holds. The urgency of the task was increased by the imminent approach of a typhoon, which struck the area in the third week of October, forcing the rescue fleet to head for shelter in Subic Bay.

When the salvage fleet returned to the scene a few days later, on 23 October, they found that *Pendleton* had been forced broadside onto the reef. Her rudder had been ripped from it's seating and her hull was further gashed by the rocks. This additional damage resulted in the ship

being declared a constructive total loss and further salvage work was confined to the removal of the remaining ammunition and stores - including the portable generators - from her, the activities now being monitored by the South Vietnamese destroyer-escort *Tran Khanh Du* (HQ-40).

The de-storing task was completed over the following couple of weeks and the *Sgt. Jack J. Pendleton* was abandoned to the forces of the sea.

The subsequent enquiries into the loss of the ship revealed that she had strayed from her intended track before she grounded on the reef. A likely explanation for this was that the atmospheric conditions at the time might have resulted in propagation that affected the ship's Loran navigation system and therefore resulted in a failure of the ship's watch-keeper's to accurately fix their position.

Reefs are not the only hidden hazards lurking silently to rip open the hull of passing vessels. The 8,189-ton Wave-class tanker *RFA Wave King* (A264) was stranded after striking a submerged rock in position 01°04'S, 44°32'W, north of São Luis de Maranho, Brazil, on 9 September 1956. Although the vessel was successfully re-floated and returned safely to the United Kingdom, examination of the hull after the ship was dry-docked in South Shields revealed extensive damage and she was subsequently written off as beyond economical repair and sold for scrapping.

The ship was apparently off-course when she struck the rock, the presence of which the crew were apparently oblivious. However, even vessels operating in familiar waters near their home ports fall foul of underwater obstacles that are clearly marked on local charts. On 12 November 1945, the Isles class anti-submarine trawler *HMS Eriskay*, on loan to the Portuguese Navy as *P8*, became a total loss after striking rocks off Manadas Point, Sao Jorge, in the Azores. The crew of approximately 40 men evacuated the ship safely and were accommodated in Hesperides. This vessel's loss left the Royal Navy without a trawler available for air-sea rescue duties in the area, as the other trawler in the area - the Dance-class vessel *HMS Mazurka* (T30) - was out of action due to a burst boiler tube. Over the next two months the Portuguese Coast Guard maintained a watch over the stricken *P8* to prevent her being stripped of anything of value by opportunists, but the wreck was finally abandoned at the end of January 1946.

Built for the Chilean Navy in the late-1930s as a harbour tug, the 320-ton *Contramaestre Brito* was used on a wide variety of auxiliary duties at the Valparaíso Naval Base. On 22 October 1952, the *Brito* was ferrying personnel from Papudo to Valparaíso - a duty on which she had been employed many times before. Tragically, the tug never reached her destination as, at about 2210, she struck rocks to the north-west of Quintero, a well known hazard marked on local charts. The tug's hull was ripped open and the engine and boiler rooms rapidly flooded. As the water level reached the boiler it exploded with such devastating force that, within three minutes, *Brito* had slipped beneath the waves. Fortunately, her Commanding Officer, Sub-Lieutenant Ramiro Frías Fernández, had ordered the transmission of a distress signal immediately after the grounding and, although only half of this message was transmitted before the ship sank, it was sufficient to alert the Naval Command at Valparaíso.

As the SOS had not included the tug's position, the frigates *Covadonga* and *Baquedano* were immediately despatched to search along her most probable route. By 2300 there was still no trace of the tug and so the cruiser *O'Higgins* (02) was ordered to sail to assist in the search. Within an hour the cruiser was using her powerful searchlights to search the coastline near Quintero, but rising seas

and the formation of fog hampered the search by significantly reducing visibility. Nevertheless, by pure chance, one of the cruiser's crew heard through the mist the shouts of survivors and, at about 0200, four men - including the Commanding Officer and a US navy enlisted man on loan service to the Chilean Navy - were spotted in the freezing cold water, clinging to a large wooden door. Although about half of the 27 men aboard the *Brito* had jumped overboard before she sank, these were the only survivors and, despite an extensive search by warships and aircraft, only six bodies were recovered. The wreck of the *Contramaestre Brito* was never recovered.

One morning in April 1963, the Algerian minesweeper *Djebel Aures* slipped from her berth at Algiers and headed out of the harbour for another routine patrol operation. However, as the ship sailed out of the harbour mouth and turned to port towards the open sea, the prevailing wind and tide caused her to drift off course to port, with the result that she struck the defensive bar that extended across the entrance to the harbour. Desperate manoeuvres to free the ship only resulted in her being blown onto the jetty by the force 4-5 north-easterly wind. Her wooden hull gouged open, the ship quickly flooded and sank. This accident was probably the result of inexperience on the part of the officer-of-the-watch, who was unaware of the intensity of the wind and tidal forces and the effect they could have on a ship manoeuvring out of the harbour mouth.

The thousands of shipwrecks that littered the world's waterways at the end of the war also constituted a hazard that, inevitably, claimed further victims. The Japanese former escort vessel *CD59* was used on repatriation duties post-war. Whilst employed in the salvage operation on the battleship *Hyuga* in Kure harbour during a storm on 30 July 1946, *CD59* struck the submerged wreck and quickly sank as a result of the damage sustained. The ship was later raised and scrapped.

In a stark reminder that no ship is unsinkable, the vulnerability of vessels to damage by ice was graphically illustrated to the world when the liner *ss Titanic* sank after striking an iceberg in 1912. Thankfully, the loss of warships or naval auxiliaries after striking icebergs is a rare occurrence. Nevertheless, when the hull of a ship comes into contact with heavy pack ice, the damage inflicted on the unfortunate vessel can be serious.

*USS Whitewood* (AN-63) was launched in April 1944 as a 1,175-ton net layer, but post-war she was re-designated as an auxiliary, receiving the new pennant number AG-129. Her employment in this guise was, however, to be short-lived as the vessel's steel hull was badly holed by heavy pack ice on 6 December 1948 and she had to be beached to prevent her sinking. The hull was patched sufficiently to permit the *Whitewood* to safely make slow passage to Boston, where she arrived a month later. There, the damage to the hull of the vessel was surveyed but was

found to be so severe that she was declared a constructive total loss and was subsequently decommissioned on 1 April 1949 and the stripped hulk sold for scrapping the following year.

Not all navigational hazards marked on charts are physical in nature. In certain areas, magnetic anomalies exist which can interfere with a vessel's compasses. When more intricate navigational equipment is not carried aboard a vessel, such a phenomenon can be the catalyst for a tragic series of events to be set in motion.

After assisting in the rescue of the submarine *HMS Taciturn* (S34), which had dragged her anchor and run aground on a beach in Campbeltown Loch on the west coast of Scotland, the Bar-class boom defence vessel *Barcombe* (P216) herself grounded at the entrance to Loch Buie, Isle of Mull. On passage through the Firth of Lorne in fog in the closing hours of the night of 13 January 1958, the crew of the vessel were unaware that their vessel was several miles off course. It is probable that the ship's magnetic

*Her lower hull plating almost completely torn away, the British boom defence vessel, HMS Barcombe, lies amid rocks beneath Ton Tyre cliff on the Isle of Mull. (The Herald, Evening Times)*

compass, the only one fitted aboard, was disrupted by a magnetic anomaly, one of many indicated on charts of waters off the west coast of Scotland. The crew of the *Barcombe* were rudely awaked as their vessel crashed without warning onto the rocks. An SOS signal was transmitted immediately. Following receipt of this faint distress signal by the Naval Headquarters at Pitreavie, Fife, and by the Admiralty tug *Saucy* (A386), a massive search, involving aircraft, naval vessels, fishing boats and lifeboats was instigated. For 20 hours, nothing more was heard from the stranded vessel.

Following the initial grounding, the ship was continually pounded by the heavy seas and was being slowly pushed further and further onto the rocks. Water was cascading into the vessel through the gaping holes that had been ripped in her hull. Realising that their ship was in imminent danger of sinking, the Commanding Officer, Lieutenant-Commander Derek Godfrey, RN, gave the order to abandon ship. A young Able Seaman Diver bravely volunteered to swim through the cold, tempestuous seas in the pitch darkness to the shore, with a line. This was then used to pull a larger rope ashore, which was secured around a rock and along which the rest of the 33-man crew made their escape.

However, once ashore, their hopes of salvation were dashed as they were confronted with an impenetrable 500-foot cliff-face. They were now stranded, soaking wet and extremely cold in the biting wind, some with no footwear, clinging to the rocks with no prospects in sight of an early rescue. Despite this, morale was kept at a high level as they struck up a sing-song whilst huddled together beneath an overhang. It soon became clear that their chances of survival would be higher if they were to return to the shelter and warmth of their stranded and flooded vessel, and so two crew members made their way back to the ship

to lower the small ship's boat from the port derricks. Using this boat, and the lifeline already rigged, the rest of the crew were ferried back aboard.

The initial signal transmitted by *Barcombe* at 2116 had been vague and very weak. Due to the disruption of her magnetic compass, the position given in the distress signal had led the searchers to believe *Barcombe*'s position to be many miles south of her actual position. The search, made more difficult by the heavy seas, thick fog and low cloud ceiling of 200 feet, was initially concentrated around the islands of Colonsay and Oronsay. Having thoroughly investigated the coastlines of these islands, the search was later widened to the north-west and north-east to encompass the Torran Rocks and the small Garvelloch Islands, enthusiastically assisted by the islands' inhabitants.

Fortunately, fate was finally to lend a hand in favour of the crew of the missing ship. The skipper of the seine netter *Rosebud*, heading back towards Oban from the Tiree Strait, had decided to hug the south coast of Mull for safety. Noticing a series of white flares as his vessel rounded Ardlanish Point, the skipper decided to investigate the source and, at around 1800 on 14 January, stumbled across the badly holed *Barcombe* and immediately reported the sighting by radio. The submarine rescue ship *HMS Kingfisher* and the Islay lifeboat were soon on the scene, closely followed by the *Saucy*. Three of the *Barcombe*'s crew, one of whom was seriously ill, were transferred to *Saucy* and transported to hospital at Oban, whilst *Kingfisher* landed the rest of the crew at Faslane early the following morning.

Salvage work on the stranded ship was initially confined to the removal of portable equipment and the crew's personal belongings. The 750-ton vessel was severely damaged, with her lower hull plating almost completely torn away and most of her compartments flooded up to the level of the weather deck. Following further detailed surveys, it was not considered viable to salvage her and, in October of the same year, the cliff above the ship was blown up to cover the wreckage. Portions of the vessel can still be seen protruding from the rocks beneath the Ton Tyre cliff.

The delay and waste of resources incurred in the early stages of the operation were clearly due to two factors. The first of these was the disruption to *Barcombe*'s magnetic compass, leading the crew to transmit an inaccurate position report as part of their SOS signal. The second important factor was the complete breakdown in communications following the transmission of the distress signal, due to the failure of *Barcombe*'s radio, so preventing the further transmission of SOS or Mayday distress calls. Following the receipt of the initial distress signal, rescue organisations would have been monitoring the relevant VHF channels, notably 500kHz for SOS Morse signals and 2182kHz voice frequency for Mayday calls. Even though *Barcombe* had given an incorrect position, rescue forces would have been able to home in on the stricken vessel's distress signals using Direction Finding equipment.

Techniques for tracking of ships in distress are being constantly updated, notably with the development and deployment of satellite systems, in particular the US SARSAT (Search & Rescue Satellite) and the Russian COPSA systems. The 1990s also saw the introduction into service of the Gl obal Maritime Distress and Safety System (GMDSS), which has been widely adopted as the most far-reaching development in maritime emergency assistance. These and similar systems constantly monitor the airways for distress signals. Once detected, these are passed to the nearest Rescue Co-ordination Centres, for further onward transmission to Coastguard, Lifeboat, Naval or Air stations.

Also, the majority of vessels of all sizes are now equipped with some form of satellite navigation system which can give the crew an accurate fix of their vessel's position to within a few metres, so decreasing their reliance on the common magnetic compass. Although the design and reliability of gyro-compasses has also improved, the provision of automatic plotting tables has made foolproof navigation more readily available, together with aids such as NAVSAT, Loran C and OMEGA. The NavSTAR Global Positioning System is replacing the older Transit system in modern ships, whilst in submarines, radar and improved periscopes allow navigation whilst submerged. In well charted areas it is also possible to use bottom-contour navigation methods. Nuclear submarines are usually additionally equipped with SINS - Ship Inertial Navigation System. The combined use of more than one of the above can provide accurate checks of a ship's or submarine's position.

Most areas of the world's continental shelves have been well surveyed over the years and most countries operate hydrographic survey ships specifically designed for this task. Nevertheless, charts of some areas have not been updated since the early years of the 20th century, or even earlier, leaving seafarers oblivious to hidden danger to their vessels.

The Royal Fleet Auxiliary ship *RFA Ennerdale* (A213) was a 47,470-dead-weight ton tanker on charter to the Ministry of Defence (RN) from Naess-Denholm of London since July 1967. Together with her sisters *Derwentdale* and *Dewdale*, she was modified to provide limited Replenishment at Sea (RAS) facilities for service east of Suez. With the imminent closure of the British base of Aden these ships, manned by the RFA, were used to supply Royal Navy ships in

*RFA Ennerdale before her loss in 1970.*
*(J. Maber)*

*Probably the largest naval vessel lost by accident since the end of World War Two, the Royal Fleet Auxiliary tanker RFA Ennerdale (A213) sank after striking a submerged pinnacle in the Indian Ocean on 1 June 1970. This view shows the stricken ship before the wreck was destroyed by explosive charges.*
*(Royal Navy Historical Branch)*

the Indian Ocean with fuel and basic stores. Whilst operating in this area on 1 June 1970, *Ennerdale* struck a submerged object and sank, fortunately without loss of life.

Proceeding to sea from Mahe in the Seychelles just after 0700, in fine weather, *Ennerdale* passed over a patch of water charted as nine fathoms. The chart being used for navigation was based on a survey of 1890 and the actual depth of water over the patch was far less than that indicated, in the form of two granite pinnacles. It would have been easy to navigate around the patch, but the master of the tanker did not consider this area as potentially dangerous, as the maximum draught of his vessel, loaded with 12,000-tons of fuel oil, was just under 39 feet, giving an apparent safety margin of over 15 feet. The vessel was using her echo-sounder, but even this couldn't have given sufficient warning of the impending danger.

At 0724, the ship's master ordered Full Ahead, but at 0737, whilst travelling at 12½ knots, a terrific rumble, persisting for about 45 seconds, was heard coming from right forward. It was at first thought that the starboard anchor cable had broken free and was running out, so the master ordered that the ship's engine be stopped.

It was only then that it was realised that the ship had struck something, ripping open the hull plating along the starboard side for almost the entire length of the vessel. After attempts to manoeuvre the ship astern, the engine died and the ship began listing heavily to starboard. The extent of the damage inflicted on the hull was such that the master quickly realised that no amount of damage-control could possibly save his crippled ship, leaving

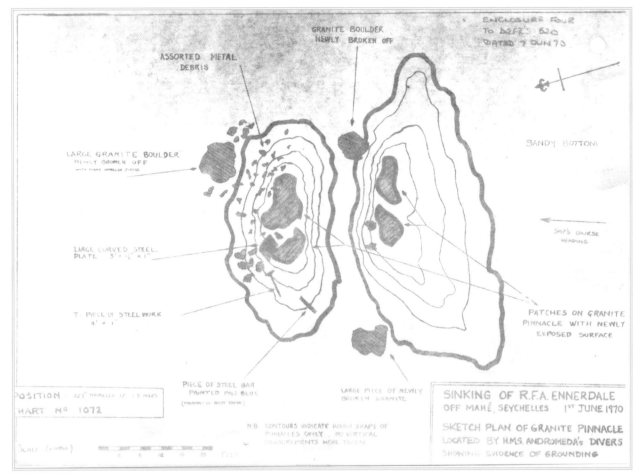

ENCLOSURE FOUR
TO D2FL's 520
DATED 7 JUN 70

GRANITE BOULDER
NEWLY BROKEN OFF

ASSORTED METAL
DEBRIS

SANDY BOTTOM

LARGE GRANITE BOULDER
NEWLY BROKEN OFF
WITH MANY SMALLER PIECES

SHIP'S COURSE
HEADING

LARGE CURVED STEEL
PLATE   3' x 1½' x 1"

T- PIECE OF STEEL WORK
4' x 1'

PATCHES ON GRANITE
PINNACLE WITH NEWLY
EXPOSED SURFACE

PIECE OF STEEL BAR
PAINTED PALE BLUE
(PROBABLY A BOAT DAVIT)

LARGE PIECE OF NEWLY
BROKEN GRANITE

POSITION   225° MAMELLE LT  1.5 MILES

CHART  No 1072

N.B. CONTOURS INDICATE ROUGH SHAPE OF
PINNACLES ONLY, NO VERTICAL
MEASUREMENTS WERE TAKEN

SINKING OF R.F.A. ENNERDALE
OFF MAHÉ, SEYCHELLES  1ST JUNE 1970

SKETCH PLAN OF GRANITE PINNACLE
LOCATED BY H.M.S. ANDROMEDA's DIVERS
SHOWING EVIDENCE OF GROUNDING

SCALE (APPROX)       0    4    8    12    16    20       FEET

*Diagram depicting the rocky pinnacles struck by RFA Ennerdale on 1 June 1970.*
*(Royal Navy Historical Branch)*

him little choice but to order 'abandon ship' at around 0800. The entire crew of 60 men managed to board the ship's life boats and rafts and clear their vessel before she sank.

Although the sunken vessel was not totally submerged, salvage proved impossible, and the hulk was later destroyed by mortar bombs and torpedo warheads lowered from a Wessex helicopter from the stores ship *RFA Stromness* (A344). At 710-feet long, *Ennerdale* was probably the biggest naval vessel lost by accident.

The loss of such a major asset as the *Ennerdale* illustrates the value of constantly updating charts, especially in coastal areas. Although the number of hydrographic survey vessels in service has been severely cut back in recent years due

to financial stringencies, this reduction has been counter-balanced to a certain extent by the use of advanced technology, such as more efficient sonar and satellites. In peacetime, a nation's mine-countermeasures assets can be gainfully employed by using their advanced sonar systems and mine-search vehicles to constantly update the bottom contour maps of rivers and estuaries, noting the position of the smallest obstacle that may represent a hazard to shipping. Maintaining such detailed data, particularly in harbour approaches, will also provide a means of rapidly clearing channels of mines in times of conflict, as previously identified anomalies on the sea floor can be instantly eliminated from further time consuming investigations.

Bottom contour charts have been built up

over many years from a large number of sources, some of which were of questionable accuracy in terms of both soundings and navigation. Accurate and up-to-date charts of the sea floor are probably even more vital to submarines to ensure safe submerged navigation and many submarines have sustained quite serious hull damage after striking the bottom of the sea. Although the reasons for several submarine losses are still unexplained, it is not thought that any submarines have been sunk as a direct result of such an incident. Nevertheless, the consequences to a submerged submarine and her crew, should the pressure hull be breached during a submerged grounding are only too obvious.

*HMS Alaric* (S41) sustained minor damage when she collided with a submerged reef in Church Bay off Rathlin Island, Northern Ireland, in May 1953, whilst on 3 October 1960, the bow of her sister boat *HMS Anchorite* (S64) was damaged by striking an uncharted rock whilst submerged at a depth of 110 feet in Hauraki Gulf, off North Island, New Zealand. Both boats returned to harbour safely for repairs.

Far more serious damage was sustained by the Polish M-class submarine *ORP Kurp* (306) when she grounded in 1958. Although the boat was later repaired during a lengthy refit, the Polish Navy saw fit to rename the vessel *ORP Mazowsze*.

Several US Navy nuclear-powered submarines have also come to grief after striking the sea bed. *USS Skate* (SSN-578), whilst on patrol in 1959, was slightly damaged when she hit the sea bed at a speed of 7-knots. This occurred after the boat's Executive Officer, without informing the Captain or the Navigating Officer, ordered the boat to dive to 700 feet. Unfortunately, he did not consult the charts, which would have told him that the depth of water in the area was only 500 feet!

In 1968 *USS Theodore Roosevelt* (SSBN-600) was extensively damaged when she struck the sea bottom in the Londonderry Operating Areas whilst transiting at a depth of 200 feet. The boat was repaired and continued in service until 1981. Investigations revealed that the bottom in this area reached to within 138 feet of the surface. Charts used by *Roosevelt* at the time had indicated a depth of 300-360 feet in the area of the grounding. Concern for this type of hazard had been expressed to the Chief of Naval Operations by the Submarine Safety Centre in 1966, stressing the increased danger to the newer nuclear-powered submarines with their greatly increased depth and speed capabilities.

It was recommended that extensive surveys be carried out of all submarine operating areas and that updated charts be produced. Commander Submarines Atlantic (ComSubLant) had submitted an urgent request for updated bottom contour charts to the Defence Intelligence Agency in November 1965. However, at that time the US Navy had only four ships capable of carrying out such surveys - *Bowditch*, *Dutton*, *Michaelson* and *Compass Island* - and so it was to be many years before these surveys could be completed.

Despite such efforts, accidents continue to occur. On 13 March 1986, the Lafayette-class submarine *USS Nathaniel Greene* (SSBN-636) ran aground whilst submerged in the Irish Sea. There were no personnel injuries amongst the crew and damage was confined externally to ballast tanks and the rudder. The boat freed herself from the bottom and steamed into the Holy Loch under her own power and subsequently proceeded to Charleston, South Carolina, where detailed surveys revealed the true extent of the damage. *Nathaniel Greene* was subsequently retired on 15 December instead of her sister-boat *USS Alexander Hamilton* (SSBN-617) .

Even more recently, on 8 January 2005,

the Los Angeles-class submarine *USS San Francisco* (SSN-711) was transiting submerged en route to Australia at flank (maximum) speed, approximately 360 nautical miles southeast of G uam, when the boat struck an underwater seamount. The immense force of the impact propelled crew and equipment around the boat with tremendous force, causing various degrees of injury to 98 of the 138 crewmen, one fatally. Miraculously, the pressure hull was not breached and crew were able to execute an emergency blow of all ballast tanks, bringing the boat safely to the surface from a depth of 525 feet, despite the boat's bow-down attitude.

The boat was then able to proceed under her own power, escorted by the US Coast Guard cutter *USCG Galveston Island* (WPB-1349) and *USNS Kiska* (AE-35) and *Stockham* (T-AKR-299).

On arrival at her home port of Guam, the boat was immediately docked and surveys of the damage revealed how close the boat had come to being lost. The forward port side ballast tanks had been ripped open, the bow dome completely destroyed and all four torpedo tube door baldy damaged. Fortunately, it appears that the bow dome and ballast tanks, which were full of water at the time of the collision, may have absorbed much of the force of the impact.

The subsequent investigations found that the boat's officers had failed to identify a series of danger signs before the collision and that they had not checked the depth of the seabed with sufficient frequency whilst travelling at a submerged speed in excess of 30-knots. It was revealed that the last depth sounding had been taken at 1130, some 13 minutes before the crash, indicating a water depth of nearly 6,600 feet. Although the seamount was not marked on the chart in use at the time, it was considered that other hazards that were indicated on the other charts of the area held on board should have prompted greater caution. Recent satellite images had shown that the mountain rose to within 100 feet of the surface, but the main chart in use aboard

*The Los Angeles-class submarine USS San Francisco (SSN-711) in dry dock at Guam. The nuclear-powered boat sustained immense damage when it struck an underwater seamount at flank speed on 8 January 2005. Miraculously, the pressure hull was not breached and crew were able to bring the boat safely to the surface from a depth of 525 feet. The boat was under repair throughout 2005. (U.S. Navy)*

the *San Francisco* at the time of the collision had not yet been updated. Routine inspections during the previous year had identified shortcomings in procedures used by the boat's navigation department, including failure to properly operate the fathometer warning system and the electronic Voyage Management System (VMS), as well as deficiencies in their chart review process.

The boat's Commanding Officer, Commander Kevin Mooney USN, was subsequently relieved of his command and reprimanded. The US Navy later issued advice to it's submarine commanders to treat underwater charts with "a sceptical attitude" and to be vigilant to other clues, such as sonar soundings that do not match those indicated on charts.

Initial fears that the *San Francisco* would be scrapped proved unfounded, despite the extent of the damage and the age of the vessel, which was first commissioned in 1981. The boat had only completed a two year, $200 million overhaul and reactor refuel in 2002 and so the decision was made to repair her. Temporary repairs at Guam included cutting away the damaged section and welding in place a 20 metre diameter steel dome, after which the boat sailed for Puget Sound Naval Shipyard, Washington, for permanent repairs. The entire forward section of the boat was replaced with that taken from her sister boat *USS Honolulu* (SSN-718), decommissioned in early 2007. By the time *USS San Francisco* returns to service in 2008, repairs will have cost an estimated $79 million. In comparison, to overhaul the Honolulu and refuel her nuclear reactor would have cost around $170 million.

Damage sustained by the Norwegian submarine *KNM Stadt* (S307) on 30 March 1987 was, however, not considered uneconomical to repair. The boat was carrying out routine submerged manoeuvres in Korsfjorden, south south-west of Bergen, in 80 metres of water when, at 1445, she struck rocks on the sea bed, slightly injuring four crewmen. The depth of water beneath the hull was thought to be much greater, but evidently the boat was some way off of her intended track. It is not known why the boat's sonar or echo sounder did not detect the anomaly, but it is apparent that they were either not in operation or were not being efficiently monitored.

Unlike the *Nathaniel Greene*, however, *Stadt* had been destined for further service, being one of three boats of the Kobben-class intended for transfer to the Danish Navy from 1989 as the class was being replaced in Norwegian service by the new Ula-class boats. Although damage to the submarine was claimed by the Norwegian authorities to be 'slight', *Stadt* was removed from the Danish program, being replaced by a sister boat, *KNM Kya* (S317). Laid up at the naval base at Hakonsvern, from where she was paid off on 12 May, the hulk was heavily cannibalised of equipment for the other boats of the class before being sold to Brdr. Anda shipbreakers at Stavangar in the summer of 1990 for scrapping.

Incidentally, another of the Norwegian Kobben-class submarines transferred to Denmark took rather longer than intended to reach her new owners. *KNM Uthaug* (S304), renamed *HDMS Saelen* (S323), was under tow of the new patrol vessel *HDMS Havkatten* (P552) from Copenhagen to Århus on 5 December 1990, when she flooded and foundered north of Sjaelland. No crew were aboard the boat at the time and she was later raised and repaired over the next two years, utilising spares from another Norwegian boat of the class sold to Denmark specifically for that purpose.

A distinct danger regarding the bow-on collision of a submarine with an underwater obstacle is damage to the weapons within the boat's torpedo tubes.

Whilst operating submerged on clandestine operations between the Falkland Islands at the time off the conflict in May 1982, the Oberon-class submarine *HMS Onyx* (S21) struck an uncharted rock, the force of the head-on collision stopping the boat dead in her tracks. Luckily, the pressure hull was not pierced, but two warshot torpedoes were damaged inside the lower tubes in her badly dented bow. The boat was able to continue operations in the war-zone, which included the sad duty of torpedoing the landing ship *RFA Sir Galahad* (L3005), devastated by an Argentine air attack on 8 June, as a war grave. *Onyx* then headed home to Portsmouth, where the damage was successfully repaired.

Charts of the area in which *Onyx* came to grief were produced by Captain Cook in the late 1700s, and were thus both out of date and of insufficient detail necessary for the safe operation of submerged submarines.

Submarines, by design, are a clandestine weapon. When used as intelligence gatherers in waters in which they have no lawful business, it is perhaps ironic when a boat involved in such a mission comes to grief. On 28 October 1981, the Soviet Project 613 ('Whiskey V' class) diesel-electric submarine *S363* ran aground off the Swedish Naval Base of Karlskrona, causing a diplomatic incident. As the tide receded, the submarine was left high and dry on the beach. The widespread news coverage given to the incident caused extreme embarrassment to the Soviet government, who for many years had rigorously denied having any part in the alien submarine incursions into Swedish territorial waters.

Following the end of the Cold War the numbers of intrusions reduced significantly, especially after September 1991, but Sweden reported another increase in the occurrence of such incidents after May 1992. In 1992, the red-faced officer who had commanded the submarine *S363*, Captain Anatoly Gushin, stated in an interview on Swedish television that the grounding of his boat had been the result of a failure of navigational equipment. He also admitted that torpedoes carried aboard his boat at the time had been armed with nuclear warheads.

South Korea has also been plagued by foreign submarine incursions and was provided with physical proof of their suspicions when, shortly after midnight on 18 September 1996, a taxi driver spotted a stranded submarine on fire off An-in Beach, 9km south of Kangnung. South Korean Army units quickly descended on the site and found a badly damaged North Korean Sang-O-class submarine.

The boat had entered South Korean waters on the night of 15 September to land a reconnaissance team to spy on military facilities in the Kangnung area. Having retired to deeper water, the boat had made an unsuccessful attempt to retrieve the 3-man team the following night. During a second attempt 24 hours later, the boat was crippled when it ran aground and the Captain, Lt Col Chong, was forced to order his crew to abandon the boat. Shallow water prevented the crew from scuttling the submarine and so they were to set it alight.

A huge military search ensued for the infiltrators, with the first being captured later that afternoon. Soon afterwards, 11 more crewmen were found dead and are believed to have committed suicide to avoid capture. Thirteen others were killed in firefights with ROK forces, whilst one man escaped capture.

The 275-ton submarine, believed to have been one of four of the class modified for clandestine duties, was salvaged on 22 September and towed to Tonghae by *Chang Won* (ARS-26) and *Gum I* (ARS-27), where it was dismantled and examined by US and ROK intelligence teams.

This was not the first North Korean submarine to have been captured in South Korean waters. On 5 July 1965 a crude 5.7-meter long North Korean midget submarine was found abandoned on a mudflat at the juncture of the Imjin and Han Rivers.

Whatever the reasons for the grounding of a vessel, the damage to the craft's hull can be magnified in direct proportion to the speed at which it was operating at the time. Many small fast attack craft and patrol boats have been written off or sunk in incidents which may have proved minor had they been operating at slower speeds.

In the 1960s the US Navy embarked on a programme to investigate the feasibility of several hydrofoil designs, which they hoped would be useful in the fast gunboat role. The design eventually evolved into the Pegasus (PHM-1) class vessels that, unfortunately, have never been found a permanent role in the US Navy Order of Battle beyond that of drug interdiction patrols. One of the prototype vessels was

the 58-ton *USS Tucumcari* (PGH-2), commissioned on 7 March 1968. Her career was short-lived as, on 16 November 1972, the craft ran aground in shoal water, two miles north-west of Punta Mulas, Vieques Island, in the Virgin Islands.

*Tucumcari* had been taking part in exercise Escort Tiger XIII - an amphibious landing exercise under the overall command of Commander Amphibious Squadron Ten - which had begun three days earlier off the east coast of Puerto Rico. *Tucumcari*'s role in the exercise was to prevent small 'hostile' craft from entering the area around the island of Vieques, pursuing and 'destroying' any such craft. Her patrol area stretched in an arc from the south-west of the island to Mosquito Piers on the north side. However, by the third day, the 13-man crew of the hydrofoil were extremely tired, as each crewman had to perform several tasks that on a larger ship would have been undertaken by a number of different personnel. Even in the fine

*USS Tucumcari*
*(The Boeing Company)*

weather conditions prevailing at the time, the fatigue effect of being constantly buffeted around within the tiny 80-foot craft had also taken its toll.

At about 0100, the on-watch navigator reported two contacts on the surface radar display, but stated that neither of them was identified on the charts, therefore suggesting that they may be 'hostile' craft. In fact, the small scale chart of the area - C&GS 904 - was in use at the time, rather than the larger scale, smaller area chart C&GS 940, as use of the latter would have necessitated frequent changes of chart as the craft transited at high speed around her patrol area. Nevertheless, visibility was good at over seven miles and so, by taking a series of fixes, the OOD determined that one of the contacts was a radar buoy. *Tucumcari* increased speed to over forty knots and turned towards the second contact - believed to be a small craft lying dead in the water - but as she drew closer the radar contact split in two, seemingly imitating a tactic which had been used by the opposing force previously in the exercise, whereby two small PTF craft would lie close together until spotted, after which they would 'scatter' to avoid interception.

Soon afterwards, a shoal was spotted dead ahead, but too late for the Commanding Officer - who was in the pilot house - to order the hydrofoil to turn or slow down before she struck Caballo Blanco, a small, low, grassy island ringed by shoals, situated in position 65°28'W, 18°10'45"N. It appears that the second radar contact had in fact been Caballo Blanco and possibly the red sector warning light, both of which were marked on chart C&GS 940 and were described in Coastal Pilot and Sailing Directions.

*Tucumcari*'s foils were ripped off by the force of the impact with the shoal. Other vessels were quickly on the scene and, by 0430, all crewmen were evacuated - seven of who required hospitalisation for their injuries. During the next few days,

*Tucumcari*'s badly dented and torn hull was patched, following which she was re-floated and towed to the Naval Station at Roosevelt Roads, Puerto Rico, where she arrived at 0100 on 22 November. Detailed surveys revealed extensive damage to the craft's hull and, consequently, she was paid off and the hulk scrapped.

Hull-borne, *Tucumcari* was capable of speeds of up to six knots whilst propelled by her diesel engines, or up to 13 knots on her gas turbine, whilst at higher speeds - up to 50 knots - she was propelled on her canard foils by water expelled beneath her hull by her gas turbine-driven water pumps. The vessel carried several navigation aids, including surface search radar, gyro-compass, magnetic compass and DE-721A fathometer. Unfortunately, the latter was only of use whilst the craft was hull-borne and no foil-borne variant of this equipment was fitted, although, at the time of her grounding, the fathometer was inoperative anyway. Navigation aboard the craft at the time of the grounding was by seaman's eye - comparing the radar picture with the charts - but the poor lighting within the pilot house made reading of the charts difficult, whilst also causing a glare on the structure's plastic windows and making it difficult to see out of them at night.

The investigation into the circumstances surrounding the grounding of *Tucumcari* determined that the incident had resulted from the mistaken identification of Caballo Blanco as a small craft of the opposing force and that the glare of the lights within the pilot house may have prevented the crew from spotting the red sector warning light. It was also found that the vessel's navigators were clearly unqualified for such an important task, mainly due to the fact that each crewman was required to fulfil a number of tasks for which he was not adequately trained. Furthermore, the high speed operation of a craft such as *Tucumcari* was one of which few within the US Navy had much experience, especially with regards to navigation. The complex task of obtaining accurate navigational fixes at one minute intervals in confined waters was one that would tax even the most experience navigating officer, as at a speed of 45 knots the craft would cover a distance of 1,500 yards in a minute. *Tucumcari*'s senior navigator was a petty officer second class inexperienced in this task. Whilst it would have been possible to navigate safely at 45 knots on a predetermined route, navigating whilst manoeuvring violently in confined waters at such a high speed is clearly far more difficult. Taking these points into account, together with the fact that the craft's navigators were inexperienced and ill-equipped for the task, it was decided that no disciplinary action be taken against the on-watch navigator.

*Tucumcari*'s Commanding Officer had been under great pressure from his superiors to operate his craft aggressively and at high speed during the exercise and, although he had officially stated that he deemed such manoeuvres unsafe in such confined waters, his operational commander had commended him for the handling of his craft during the exercise. Nevertheless it was decided that the craft had operated safely within the area for sufficient time prior to the incident for the existence of navigational hazards to be observed and so the Commanding Officer was awarded a punitive letter of reprimand.

It was recommended that an improved, automatic, navigation system be developed for such high speed craft and that they be restricted to more conventional speeds until such time as this system was available. Furthermore, the conning officer and helmsman should be provided with a clear, unrestricted view, where their night vision would be unimpeded by the glare of lights.

Due to the country's rugged and serrated coastline, with its hundreds of fjords and islands, the Norwegian Navy has evolved around a nucleus of small submarines and fast attack craft, the latter armed with surface-to-surface missiles or torpedoes, or a combination of both. The backbone of the Norwegian Navy's missile-boat force since the 1960s had been the Storm-class vessels. The class prototype had been completed in 1963, but was scrapped following extensive modifications and development work only two years later. The first of the series boats of the Storm-class, *KNM Blink* (P961), was commissioned in December 1965, followed closely by her nineteen sisters over the next three years, one of which took the name of the prototype. Unfortunately, two of these boats have been involved in serious grounding incidents during high speed exercises.

*KNM Pil* (P976) was condemned as a result of extensive damage sustained in a high speed grounding in 1980. The craft was stripped and laid up ashore for use as a training hulk for fire-fighting at the navy's damage-control school at Hakonsvern Naval Base, Bergen, being renamed *KNM Arken*.

A few years later, on 6 October 1983, *KNM Storm* (P960) was participating in an exercise with other units of the 22 MTB Squadron in Raftsund, near Svolvær, when, at about 2300, she ran aground at a speed of 29 knots. Visibility at the time was good, except for a light rain shower. The other boats of the squadron quickly closed the crippled *Storm* which, following evacuation of all crewmen, was towed to Svolvær. Close inspection revealed serious damage to the bow and a large gash amidships on the port side.

Following temporary repairs, the vessel was towed to Håkonsvern, Bergen, where she was condemned and laid up. However, she was later re-designated as an auxiliary vessel and renamed *VSD11*, to be utilised as an experimental craft to trial Hedemora diesel and water-jet propulsion being

Two views of the Royal Navy SRN6 hovercraft XV617, taken before and after its demise. The craft was driven on to a rock off Hong Kong on the night of 19 January 1982 whilst in fast pursuit of smugglers. The extensive damage caused to the front of the craft can be seen in the image below. The wreck was recovered and stripped of all usable components.

(Hovercraft Museum Trust)

developed for the planned replacement for the Storm-class. Incidentally, another of the class was involved in a grounding incident in 1983, although damage to the *Trygg* (P964) was of a minor nature and was quickly repaired.

Like the US Navy, the Royal Navy has shown little interest in coastal forces in the post-war years. In 1970, three Scimitar-class training craft were completed for the purpose of training surface and air units in anti-fast patrol boat tactics. Three crewmen were injured when, on 25 July 1980, one of these boats, *HMS Sabre* (P275), ran into a breakwater at Alderney and lost 15 feet of her bow. The damage was never fully repaired, the damaged bow section being merely plated over. Although the Royal Navy have

ventured into the field of hovercraft and hydrofoil designs, none of these have been exploited to their full potential.

In the 1970s, the Royal Naval Hovercraft Trials Unit was set up at Lee-on-Solent, near Portsmouth, to examine the employment of hovercraft in several roles, such as mine-countermeasures, fishery protection and logistic support. However, despite many years of trials and research, only a few craft entered operational service at that time, with two 10-ton Winchester SR.N6 craft being employed as high-speed pursuit craft by the Royal Marines in Hong Kong. Unfortunately, one of these craft, *XV 617* (P237), suffered severe damage after striking rocks on 19 January 1982 whilst in hot pursuit of a speedboat off the province and was subsequently written off as a constructive total loss.

The Omani Navy is another of those that have been built around small, heavily-armed fast attack craft. A requirement for a 'quick-reaction boat' resulted in the selection of the Tyler Vortex design from Cheverton Boats, two of which entered service in 1981. However, one of the 12.1 metre craft, *QRB1*, was critically damaged in 1986 after it ran aground off Muscat in the Gulf of Oman. The vessel was later seen mounted on stocks within the Omani naval base with severe damage to her hull and was subsequently scrapped as beyond economical repair.

More recently, the South African Navy air-sea rescue patrol craft *P1552* was departing Saldanha on 7 October 1988, to act as safety vessel during weapons exercises by the South African Air Force, when she struck a submerged obstacle at high speed. The 70-ton craft was left dead in the water with a large gash in her hull and, although an attempt was made to tow her back to port, *P1552* sank in 47 metres of water in Saldanhabaai. Fortunately, there were no casualties amongst the crew, but the vessel was assessed as unsalvageable.

Investigations revealed that *P1552* had struck Cap Rock, a submerged hazard clearly marked on charts of the area. Underwater photographs taken by divers revealed fresh paint scuffs on the rock, which were determined to have come from the hull of *P1552*. Blame for the navigational error that led to the loss of the craft rested firmly with the vessel's Commanding Officer.

While high speed manoeuvres have been the root cause of many groundings, the lack of propulsive power may also prevent the crew of a ship from avoiding such an incident. The crew of a drifting vessel may be powerless to do little else but prepare damage-control measures and await the inevitable crunch or rumble that tells them they have run out of seaway.

The Norwegian Oslo-class frigate *KNM Oslo* (F300) departed from her Bergen naval base on the afternoon of 24 January 1994 to participate in an anti-submarine exercise with one of the Norwegian Navy's small diesel-powered boats. For the previous 24 hours a violent storm had been wreaking havoc in the area, with local residents reporting widespread damage to their properties. Although the storm was now slowly abating, a force 6-7 wind was still blowing. The Oslo-class ships are, however, noted for their seaworthiness and so there were no reservations from the Naval Command about continuing with the planned manoeuvres.

At about 1755, the *Oslo* was passing the Marstein lighthouse, south-east of Bergen, when her propulsion plant suffered an unexpected fuel pump failure. As the flame in the boiler extinguished, steam pressure was lost and the turbine ground to a halt. Without propulsive power, *Oslo* was at the mercy of the wind and waves and was carried by the heavy swell towards the rocky shoreline. Loss of steam pressure also resulted in the failure of the turbo alternators, necessitating the starting of the ship's two diesel

generators, but difficulties were also experienced in the starting of these machines. The lack of electrical power prevented use of the standby boiler fuel supply pump, thereby hampering the engineering crew's feverish attempts to restore propulsive power. Meanwhile, a nearby fishing boat attempted to pass a tow to the drifting frigate but, tragically, two of *Oslo's* crewmen were swept overboard during this operation, one of whom drowned. Shortly afterwards, at 1822, the ship was driven hard aground, almost directly beneath the lighthouse, injuring a further nine crewmen.

Although electrical power had been briefly restored, the force of the grounding put the only serviceable diesel generator out of action, leaving the vessel with no electrical power with which to tackle the heavy damage inflicted on the stranded vessel's hull, which had been ripped open by the jagged rocks. As the ice-cold sea flooded into several underwater compartments and the vessel began to settle deeper in the water, the Commanding Officer made the painful decision to order his ship to be abandoned. By 2100, all crewmen were safely evacuated and, in accordance with tradition and protocol, the Commanding Officer was the last to leave his ship.

Despite a confusing distress signal,

*The South African air-sea rescue patrol craft P1552 sank after striking the submerged Cap Rock on 7 October 1988.*

*(South African Navy)*

*KNM Oslo being raised after the frigate sank following her grounding on 24 January 1994.*
*(Norwegian Naval Museum)*

rescue vessels from the nearby naval base were quickly on the scene and a tow secured to the stranded frigate. The intention was to tow her to harbour or to beach her on a sandbank in a suitable sheltered bay, but the pounding of the waves against the ship over several hours as she lay helpless on the rocks had resulted in severe damage to the hull plating and further uncontrolled flooding. As Coast Guard vessels and tugs stood by overnight, the engine room crew struggled to stem the flow of flooding in waist-deep water as the ship settled deeper, her decks almost awash. *Oslo* was eventually hauled free of the rocks, but, as the frigate settled deeper in the water, it became clear that she would not reach the harbour safely and the tow was abandoned. Shortly afterwards, *Oslo* slipped silently beneath the waters of the Bakkasund at about 1050, coming to rest on the bottom of the channel 20 metres below, her mast just below the water's surface.

After recovering from their harrowing ordeal, the commander and crew of the sunken *Oslo* were transferred to her sister ship *KNM Stavanger* (F303), whilst *Stavanger*'s crew were in turn transferred to the *KNM Bergen* (F301), which had lain in inactive reserve for some time due to financial stringencies.

Two investigative commissions into the accident were immediately ordered by the Royal Norwegian Navy. Meanwhile, a salvage operation was set in motion and over the following weeks all ammunition, fuel and oil was removed from the sunken vessel. The *Oslo* was finally raised on 23 April and towed into Hockelswein naval base aboard a barge. Damage to the ship was so extensive that she was stripped of spares to keep her ageing sisters operational and the hulk was then sold for scrapping.

In early 1995, the report of the investigative commissions was published, criticising the crew for their failure in preventing the tragedy. It was determined that the cause of the initial fuel pump failure had been contamination of the fuel storage tanks by a concentration of 30% salt water. Although this had been discovered before the ship sailed from Bergen, the mechanic responsible for draining the water from the fuel tanks had been prevented from completing the task by being re-assigned to other duties and by the instigation of a damage-control exercise immediately after sailing. The contaminated fuel also prevented the running of one of the two diesel generators, so further hampering attempts to light up the standby boiler. Without electrical power, *Oslo* had been helpless and the crew could not prevent her being driven aground. The ship's officers were, however, condemned for their failure to utilise the anchors to prevent the grounding and for failing to shut all watertight doors to prevent the spread of flooding. Nevertheless, the crew were praised for their calmness and professionalism in the face of heavy seas and darkness, both during the damage-control efforts and the subsequent evacuation of their vessel. Consequently, no legal or disciplinary actions were taken, although procedures regarding damage control and ship's watertight integrity were revised to incorporate the lessons learnt during the most serious loss of a Norwegian Navy vessel in several decades.

The five frigates of the Oslo-class, partly funded by the United States, were commissioned during 1966 and 1967 and were a modified version of the US Navy's Dealey-class destroyer escorts, with high freeboard forward for better sea-keeping qualities. Although she was the first of the class to be built, *Oslo* was the last of the five to undergo an extensive modification, which was completed in February 1991, extending her planned life until the turn of the century. Replacements for the class, long overdue, are now being built in the form of the five advanced *Fridtjold Nansen* (F310) class, the first of which commissioned in April 2006. The Oslo-class were reportedly noted for their vulnerability to total power failures from their propulsion plant, which comprises two Babcock & Wilcox boilers feeding a single De Laval Ljungstrom double reduction geared turbine, producing 20,000shp to a single propeller shaft. This single-shaft propulsion system makes them particularly vulnerable to the spectre of a total propulsion loss, especially as the normal cruising mode for these ships is to have one boiler 'flashed', with the second in a standby state. Although bad weather contributed to the damage inflicted on *Oslo*'s hull during the grounding, the

*KNM Oslo following her salvage on 23 April 1994. The extensive damage to the vessel's hull can be clearly seen.*

*(Norwegian Naval Museum)*

unavailability of an emergency means of propulsion was undoubtedly the primary factor that determined the vessel's fate.

The advantages of multiple-shaft machinery installations over the single shaft configuration are largely self evident, providing as they do greater manoeuvrability and a certain level of redundancy should breakdown or damage occur. The majority of warships designs incorporate twin propulsion systems that are entirely independent of each other, with port and starboard shafts being driven by their own engines. In larger vessels, port and starboard machinery plants may also be 'staggered' in separate machinery spaces, providing an insurance against the total loss of propulsive power should a single compartment be flooded. Nevertheless, single-shaft propulsion systems have the dubious merits of being cheaper and offering a substantial saving in machinery weight. It is primarily for these reasons that the US Navy have selected the single-shaft option for almost all of their destroyer-escort and frigate designs since the Second World War, namely the Dealey, Bronstein, Brooke, Garcia, Knox and Oliver Hazard Perry classes - a decision which has caused considerable controversy and received much criticism over the years.

A further consideration in its adoption in the Dealey class, the US Navy's first post-war destroyer-escorts, was that the design would lend itself to any future requirement for mass construction. However, the realisation of the requirement for an emergency propulsion system in such high-value vessels resulted in the incorporation of two 360shp retractable propulsors into the Oliver Hazard Perry (FFG-7) design. These electrical propulsion pods, mounted well forward, provide the ship with a 6-knot 'get-me-home' facility should damage or a serious defect result in failure of the main power plant.

Vessels cast adrift whilst under tow as a result of the parting of the towing hawser are in an even more precarious position, in that there is usually few - if any - crewmen aboard the vessel to attempt to restart engines or to carry out damage-control actions should she run aground or collide with another craft. Invariably, the vessel under tow will be unable to utilise her own machinery to aid her cause, as she may either have suffered some mechanical breakdown or be in transit from one port to another for the purpose of transfer to a refitting yard or to new owners. Much has already been said on this subject in Chapter One, although it should be borne in mind that the cause of parting towlines is not totally confined to the additional stresses imposed upon them by the effects of adverse weather conditions. However, it is usually an immeasurably easier and safer task to recover the tow of a vessel in calm weather conditions and any damage caused by a grounding incident will normally be less extensive.

A further factor that will determine the extent of additional damage imposed upon a vessel following her stranding will be the speed with which a salvage operation can be effected. Much will depend upon the proximity of tugs or suitable salvage craft, but the speed of reaction to the incident by the authorities responsible for the vessel will play a major part in the limitation of damage.

The Mexican frigate *California* (B3) had been commissioned in the final months of World War Two as *USS Belet* (APD-109, ex-DE-599), one of a number of destroyer-escorts of the Rudderow-class converted during build to high-speed troop transports. The war ended just as the ship was undergoing pre-commissioning trials and so, soon afterwards, she was laid up in reserve at Jacksonville, Florida. In December 1963, together with five of her sisters, she was sold to the Mexican Navy. Based at Acapulco, the *California* was employed in the task of training cadets of the Vera Cruz Naval Academy.

On the morning of Sunday, 16 January 1972, the ship was on one of her routine training cruises off the west coast of the Baja California peninsula, cruising slowly south towards Ensenada. Weather was calm, but thick fog had appreciably reduced visibility. Somehow, the ship had drifted slightly off course and, at 0810, she struck a gently-sloping sandbank 200 yards off the beach off Punta San Miguel, about nine miles north of Ensenada. Before the OOD could take any actions, the ship had broached and was soon lying with her port side parallel with the beach. Attempts to free the ship using main engines proved futile as she quickly became firmly entrenched in the soft sand and began to list to port.

A request for assistance was radioed to the Ensenada Naval Station, who promised that tugs would be despatched immediately to assist the stranded vessel. Meanwhile, the ship was enduring a constant beating from the waves that were thrashing against her starboard side, driving her progressively nearer the beach. Her crew of eighty men, plus eighteen naval cadets, were helpless to do anything but constantly monitor the hull of the ship for any damage or leakage. The hours dragged on and, as night fell, there was still no sign of any assistance.

As daylight broke the following morning, the ship could be seen lying helplessly offshore and throughout the day a growing crowd of sightseers gathered on the nearby cliffs. By early afternoon the ship had been driven across the sandy shoal to within a hundred yards of the beach, assisted by the passing of several tides. Her stern was now clear of the water and the constant rocking of the vessel was taking its toll, with an ever increasing number of minor leaks appearing in her hull. Sufficient electrical power was being maintained to pump out any floodwater, but the crew were becoming increasingly bewildered as to the lack of any rescue attempt. The Commanding Officer finally ordered that

*Lack of urgency in initialising a salvage operation sealed the fate of the Mexican frigate California after the ship ran aground on 16 Janaury 1972. The California was later declared a constructive total loss.*

*(K. Bonner)*

*The Brazilian survey ship Barreto de Menezes grounded on marshy ground near the mouth of the River Parnaiba on 4 October 1954 and was later abandoned.*
*(Ministerio de Marinha)*

a line should be passed to the beach so that a limited 'ferry' service could be established with one of the ship's rubber rafts. As night again descended on the scene, still no tugs had arrived.

About 48 hours after *California* had become stranded, help finally materialised, in the form of two small tugs from Ensenada. Two US Navy vessels - the fleet tug *USNS Molala* (ATF-106) and the salvage ship *USNS Gear* (ARS-34) - had also arrived on the scene, now shrouded with fog, but were unable to render assistance unless formally requested to do so. The two Mexican tugs tried in vain to pass a line to the *California* but, due to the huge breakers now crashing over the ship, assistance had to be limited to the transfer of additional pumps to help cope with the now serious flooding of several spaces, including the engine room.

The Mexican Government finally swallowed their pride and, on the afternoon of Wednesday, 19 January, requested assistance from the US Navy. Divers from the *Gear* promptly carried out a survey of *California*'s outer hull and confirmed that the ship was now lying on a jagged rocky ledge. Most of her lower compartments were flooding through ever-larger holes that were being ripped in the outer plating and damage-control efforts were rapidly being overwhelmed.

Although a line was attached to the ship from the *Gear*, the surf breaking across the ship dashed any hopes of dragging her free.

The crew were finally forced to evacuate their ship on Thursday afternoon as the rising water level reached her boilers, causing them to explode. At low tide they waded ashore, carrying their personal belongings above their heads. Fortunately, apart from being thoroughly exhausted after their four-day ordeal, none of the crew or the cadets suffered any serious injury.

Over the next couple of days the *California* was further battered by the waves and could be seen settling deeper in the water as her hull was torn apart by the rocks. Throughout 1972 the ship was dismantled where she lay, watched over by armed guards to prevent the removal of any valuable items of equipment, including ammunition, by souvenir hunters or looters.

Charts of the western coast of the Baja California peninsula clearly indicate the presence of rapid shoaling from a depth of 200 fathoms to about 35 fathoms at a distance of 1,000-1,500 yards from the beach and so the frigate's crew should have been able to detect the presence of this natural hazard by the use of her radar and echo-sounder. Nevertheless, although the cause of the ship's grounding could be attributed to a simple navigational error in reduced visibility due to fog, her ultimate loss was undoubtedly avoidable. The Mexican Navy has not satisfactorily explained why tugs were not despatched from nearby Ensenada more urgently. Nor has their failure to request assistance from the US Navy, who could have despatched specialist salvage ships to the scene within hours from the major US naval station at San Diego, a little over a hundred miles to the north.

This apparent apathy and lack of urgency to set in motion an effective salvage operation effectively left a once-proud warship to suffer a slow and agonising death. Furthermore, the evident lack of concern for the safety of the ship's crew can only be regarded with an air of disbelief. Serious damage to the ship did not occur until she had been aground on the sandy shoal for about two days and it is obvious that, had suitable rescue vessels been made available to haul her free in the first 24 hours, little harm would have come to her.

Nevertheless, certain circumstances can render even the most expeditious rescue operation unavailing. On 4 October 1954, shortly after being deployed to the north coast, the Brazilian Navy survey ship/lighthouse tender *Barreto de Menezes* ran aground off Barra de Tutóia, near the mouth of the River Parnaíba. The terrain of the area is predominantly marshy and the ship was soon in the death-grip of quicksand. Her crew of 67 men were safely rescued, but all attempts to salvage the 680-tonne ex-trawler were finally abandoned on 17 October.

Similarly, it is immeasurably more difficult to salvage a grounded vessel once she has capsized. On 28 January 1989 the Argentine Antarctic supply ship *ARA Bahia Paraiso* (Q6) had just visited the US research base Palmer Station, near Torgersen. Two miles off the Antarctica coast, the ship struck an underwater rock, ripping a 30-foot gash in her hull. All 150

crew were rescued before the *Bahia Paraiso* capsized and sank in shallow water five days later, taking with her two Sea King helicopters. The 9,200-ton ship, which had landed troops for the invasion of South Georgia and later served as a hospital ship during the Falklands conflict of 1982, was subsequently declared unsalvageable and written off as a constructive total loss. The wreck was still leaking diesel fuel and oil in 1996 and was blamed for decimating local bird populations.

This was not the first Argentine naval vessel lost by grounding. On 22 September 1949 the patrol ship *Fournier* sank after striking an uncharted rock at the entrance to the San Gabriel Channel. Despite an extensive search, no survivors were found from her 79-man crew.

On 10 January 1976, the Cherokee-class patrol ship *ARA Comandante General Zapiola* (A2) was carrying out hydrographic research in the Morton Strait, Antarctica, when she ran aground on rocks at the north-east end of Isla Nevada (Snow Island on Chilean charts) in the South Shetland Islands. The Chilean Navy quickly responded to the ship's distress call and at 1430 that afternoon, the hydrographic ship *Yelcho* (AGS64) - a former sister-ship of the *Zapiola* - was despatched to assist the stricken ship, arriving on the scene at 0500 the following morning. Later that day, the *Yelcho* was joined by the Chilean Navy transport ship *Piloto Pardo* (AP-45) and oiler *Beagle* (AOG54) and the Argentine Navy transport ship *ARA Bahia Aguirre* (Q2).

During the rescue attempt, the *Yelcho* also struck rocks 350 yards to the east of the *Zapiola*, tearing a 17-inch hole in her hull, but was able to refloat herself and control the minor flooding. Despite the best efforts of the rescue flotilla, the *Zapiola* continued to flood through massive holes in her shattered hull as the next high tide approached and the *Piloto*

*Pardo* was forced to evacuate the foundering vessel's crew. The *Zapiola* was abandoned at position 62°43'04"S, 61°10'01"W and later capsized and sank and was never salvaged.

The Commanding Officer of the *Yelcho* was exonerated of any blame for the grounding of his ship, as the Chilean Navy did not, at that time, have detailed charts of the Morton Strait.

The susceptibility of a stranded vessel, once abandoned, to plundering by looters, pirates, or simply souvenir hunters, and its prevention by the employment of guards stationed on or near the stranded vessel, has been touched upon many times already in this chapter. Whilst in most cases theft from an abandoned ship will be limited to attractive items such as ship's bells, compass binnacles and small brass fittings, the more extensive stripping of a ship constitutes an act of piracy. Although this term conjures up images of swashbuckling seafarers scouring the trade routes for prey in their wooden sailing ships with a skull and crossbones flag flying from the mainmast, modern-day pirates are still a major headache in certain areas of the world.

In the waters of the Indian Ocean, Sunda Shelf and South China Sea, and even in the seemingly idyllic waters of the Caribbean, pirates using fast speedboats prey on defenceless merchant ships or private yachts, robbing and murdering their crews or, in some cases, even seizing the entire vessel and its valuable cargo. These nautical highwaymen are particularly prevalent in the narrow channels and straits around the islands of Indonesia and Malaysia, presenting a major problem to the local naval forces and coast guards. Clearly, a helpless stranded naval vessel presents a tempting target, with the prospective bonus to the scavengers of possibly acquiring illicit weapons with which to further ply their evil trade.

The lengths to which pirates will go to plunder a stranded vessel was illustrated by their negotiation of a deadly reef to reach the wreck of *HMS Aire* in December 1946, the loss of which was covered in Chapter One. The salvage of another British vessel was rendered uneconomical only a few months earlier after she ran aground off India.

The Alligator-class tug *Crocodile* (W88) had been operated for the British Admiralty by a Ceylonese crew at

Colombo until April 1946. Earmarked for further duties in the Rosyth Naval Base in Scotland, she began the first part of her journey to Aden under tow of the civilian tug *Assistance* , from where she was to proceed under her own power back to the UK. However, on 3 May she broke her tow and ran aground off the Sind coast, south-west India (now Pakistan) in position 23°54'N, 67°34'E. All of her crew were safely evacuated and plans were drawn up for the salvage of the vessel.

*Crocodile* was officially paid off on 23 May, although specialist equipment and stores had already been sent to Karachi in preparation for her salvage. By 21 June the hull and machinery was still salvageable, but many of the more valuable fittings, such as propeller blades, compass and telegraphs had been stripped by pirates. The salvage operation was cancelled and she lay in this state until 29 April the following year, when she was put up for sale for scrapping on site.

Many warships and naval auxiliaries stricken from the active list following grounding incidents in which their hulls or machinery are irreparably damaged, are subsequently utilised in a non-seagoing role in support of the operational fleet. Although the requirement for accommodation ships is much diminished with today's generally smaller naval forces, several grounding-damaged vessels have been used in this role in the past. Two critically damaged French Navy vessels were so employed following groundings in the early-1950s.

The coastal escort *FS Le Volontaire* (ex-PC-543) was one of a large number of PC-461 class submarine chasers transferred to the French Navy from the USA in 1944. In 1952 the ship suffered grave structural damage in a grounding incident. Her engines and machinery were irreparably damaged, as were her gearboxes and shaft lines. In 1953, following makeshift repairs to her hull, the now immobile hulk

of *Le Volontaire* was towed to Toulon where it was employed as a static barracks ship for the locally-based minesweeper squadron. The hulk was condemned in March 1964, due to the poor condition of her hull, and scrapped.

The landing ship *FS Adour* (L9007, ex-LST-860) was another ex-US Navy vessel to suffer a similar fate. On 19 May 1951 the *Adour* exploded and sank after running aground. The wreck was later raised written off as uneconomical to repair, but continued in service for some years after as an accommodation hulk. The ship had been one of eight of the class transferred between 1949 and 1951, the rest of which paid off between 1958 and 1970 as new French-built vessels replaced them.

A similar fate befell the Chilean landing ship *Comandante Toro* (R88) after she grounded on the beach at Carolina, Isla San Félix, on 24 January 1977. Dry-docked at Talcahuano on 7 April, it was discovered that the ship had sustained major structural damage, which rendered her totally unseaworthy. Although the ship had only been transferred from the USA to the Chilean Navy in February 1973, the cost of repairing the damage was deemed to be far in excess of her commercial value and she was removed from service. After being stripped to provide spares for her sister ships, the hulk was utilised as a barracks ship until scrapped a few years later.

Many other vessels have ended their unfortunate active careers as test-beds for various machinery systems, as training hulks, or sunk at sea as weapons targets.

Most types of amphibious landing ships are designed to beach on hostile shorelines to discharge their cargo. However, only a very small proportion of beaches are suitable for such operations, as they must be of a gentle sloping profile and consist of soft sand or shingle in order for the vessels to beach without damage. The success of such missions will rely on

*The Republic of Korea LST Munsan, broached and was abandoned north of P'ohang on 15 September 1950.*

*(US Navy)*

accurate charts of the assault area and detailed reconnaissance. It is therefore not surprising that several landing ships have come to grief when carrying out such operations.

Following World War Two, the US Navy utilised a large number of landing ships on occupational duties in the Far East, moving equipment and stores around and repatriating personnel. It was not long before the first of these vessels were lost.

*USS LST-1136* was converted to a repair ship during build, commissioning towards the end of the war as *USS Bellona* (ARL-32), but became a total loss after grounding on 1 December 1945 on Kama Rocks near Iwo Jima. The hulk was destroyed the following May. Only a few weeks later, on 30 December 1945, *LST-814* was severely damaged during a beaching operation off Sasebo, Japan. Decommissioned on 16 April 1946, the hulk was scuttled on 12 August 1946. Less than four months after *LST-814*'s grounding, on 6 April 1946, *LST-1005* was de-commissioned after sustaining severe hull damage during beaching operations. After removal of all salvageable equipment the hulk was destroyed where it lay.

On 11 January 1947, *LSM-432* ran aground on the east coast of Babuyan

Island in the Philippines and was subsequently abandoned as unsalvageable. The following March, *LST-1130* was also declared beyond economical repair and abandoned after sustaining severe damage during a grounding incident at Yap. Then, on 6 July 1948, *LSM-5* ran aground at Saipan and was decommissioned two days later.

A large number of landing ships were transferred to other countries after in the post-war years, one of which was to be lost during assault operations during the Korean War. *LST-120* was transferred to the Military G overnment of Korea in February 1947. Re-named *ROK Munsan*, the ship was used in the Changsadong Raid in September 1950. Whilst part of a task force attempting to insert South Korean guerrillas behind enemy lines north of P'ohang on the 15th, the ship broached and ended up broadside on to the beach. The badly damaged and flooded ship was subsequently abandoned.

Another ship stranded and abandoned behind enemy lines during the Korean War was the Thai frigate *Prasae*. The ship ran aground in a snowstrom on the Korean coast on 7 January 1953. Despite a massive salvage effort by the US Navy, damage inflicted on the ship's hull resulted in the *Prasae* being abandoned and the wreck destroyed.

The Philippine Navy has lost several landing ships after grounding incidents. In June 1971, the ex-US LSM-1 class medium landing ship *RPS Batanes* (LP65) ran aground and was declared a total loss. A similar fate befell the ex-US LST-511 class ship *RPS Aurora* (LT518), which was written off after grounding in June 1988, whilst a sister-ship caused an international incident in 1999 after running aground in the Spratly Islands. This island group, situated in the South China Sea, has been the subject of a dispute for many years, being claimed wholly or partly by China, Taiwan,

Vietnam, Malaysia, Brunei and the Philippines. On 9 May 1999, the *RPS Sierra Madre* (LT57) ran aground on a reef near Second Thomas Shoal. The ship's outer hull was cracked open, flooding the ship's auxiliary engine room. Six days later it was alleged that two Chinese 'minesweeping frigates' had approached the stricken vessel and trained their guns on her. This incident incensed Filipino naval officials, who requested the filing of a diplomatic protest against China after considering the behaviour a "hostile act", a charge vehemently denied by the Chinese. Relations were further strained when, on 23 May the Philippine Navy patrol ship *BRP Rizal* (PS-74) collided with one of three Chinese fishing boats it was chasing away from the Scarborough Shoals. All 11 Chinese fishermen on that boat survived, but their craft sank. Six months later Beijing were still insisting that the stranded ship be removed from the disputed shoal, whilst the Philippines maintains that the shoal is well-within its 200-mile exclusive economic zone as defined by the UN Convention on the Law of the Sea. Unsalvageable, the *Sierra Madre* has since been used as a base and continues to be guarded by Philippine troops.

The largest landing ship to be written off following a grounding incident was the 8750-ton Newport-class Landing Ship Tank *USS La Moure County* (LST-1194). On 12 September 2000, the ship was participating in an annual UNITAS amphibious exercise with Chilean forces in Caleta Cifuncho Bay, about 100 miles south of Antofagasta. Just before 0500, the ship made it's approach to the beach when it stuck a reef. Despite attempts to back her off of the rocks using full available engine power she remained stuck fast. Several large compartments were opened to the sea and free-flooded and the ship sank some six feet by the bow, whilst damage repair teams attempted to stem the flooding in others.

*The Thai frigate Prasae abandoned on a Korean Beach after grounding on 7 January 1953.*
*(US Navy Archives)*

Over the next 14 hours, efforts were concentrated in three major compartments, where fuel tanks had ruptured, adding a severe fire danger to the ship's already precarious position. Teams worked waist-deep in fuel to plug holes and shore up decks and bulkheads.

Once the situation was stabilised, divers conducted a survey of the damage, revealing that a 70-foot section of the hull had been torn open, with over thirty splits of various sizes up to 20-feet long. Internally, the ship's propulsion systems were flooded and inoperable. Evidently, it was only the damage-control skills and determination of the crew that saved their ship from foundering. Fortunately, despite the extensive damage suffered by the ship, there were no injuries amongst her 270 crew.

The ship was later hauled from the rocks by the Chilean *LST Valvadia* (93), a sister-ship that had been transferred to Chile in 1995, and anchored in Cifuncho Bay to further evaluate the damage. After over six weeks of emergency repairs to make *La Moure County* seaworthy, she began the 700 mile journey, under tow of the Chilean icebreaker *Oscar Viel Toro*, arriving at the Chilean Naval Base at Talcahuano on the 31 October. Damage to the ship, which had commissioned in 1971, was deemed beyond economical repair and the *USS La Moure County* was de-commissioned eight weeks after her grounding at Talcahuano. Stripped of all valuable equipment, the hulk was sunk as a target by US, Chilean and British warships on 10 July 2001 during the naval exercise UNITAS 2001, at location 32°49'82"N, 74°17'92"W, in 1841 fathoms of water.

Even the largest vessels have groundings, although the loss of major warships such as battleships or aircraft carriers to this cause have not occurred

*The destroyer HMS Nottingham, severly damaged and flooding after striking a rock off Lord Howe Island on 7 July 2002.*
*(Royal Australian Navy)*

since World War Two, save en route to the breakers. There are many reasons for this, not least of which is the relatively small, and decreasing, number of such vessels in existence. The extensive use of compartmentalisation and double bottoms in such ships, together with the abundance of highly-trained crew available to deal with any damage resulting from grounding, increases their chance of surviving such an incident. The high operational value of these units will also

justify their repair at great monetary cost, whereas smaller, less valuable, vessels may well be scrapped after sustaining less extensive damage as 'beyond economical repair'.

The Iowa-class battleship *USS Missouri* (BB-63) suffered severe damage to her starboard keelson and the major starboard strength beam when she ran aground on 17 January 1950, resulting in misalignment of the engine seatings. The ship remained aground for almost two weeks after being driven several hundred yards up a sand bank when her new Captain allegedly ignored numerous warnings from his subordinates. Although the damage was repaired by the end of February at the Norfolk Navy Yard, a bent keelson is virtually impossible to repair, especially when engine misalignment is involved. This damage resulted in the *Missouri* having a 5-knot slower speed than her three sisters, which could be propelled at up to $32\frac{1}{2}$ knots by their 212,000shp propulsion plant. However, this speed loss was considered insignificant when considering the speed at which she would have been expected to operate as part of a battle group.

Aircraft carriers, destroyers and nuclear submarines have replaced battleships and cruisers as the capital ships of the major navies in the post-WWII era. Coupled with the smaller number of these high-value assets in modern navies, it is inevitable that considerable resources may be expended in the repair of damage to these ships that, in by-gone years, would have resulted in the vessel being scrapped.

On the evening of 7 July 2002, the Royal Navy Type 42 destroyer *HMS Nottingham* (D91) was manoeuvring to recover her Lynx helicopter, with the ship's Commanding Officer aboard, when she ran aground on a large charted rock near Lord Howe Island, off the coast of Eastern Australia. The hull of the ship was torn open through over 100 feet of its length from the bow to the forward engine

*HMS Nottingham, loaded aboard the Dutch-registered heavy lifting vessel MV Swan prior to her return to the UK for repairs. (Royal Australian Navy)*

room and the sonar dome was ripped off. The 4.5-inch gun and Sea Dart missile magazines, as well as several other sections, were free-flooded and the hatches had to be shored shut to control flooding, whilst the forward engine room was flooded to within a few feet of the deckhead through the gaping hole in the hull where the starboard forward stabiliser had been shorn off. The ship came perilously close to sinking, but the Marine Engineering Officer convinced his Commanding Officer that the damage-control teams could save her. All through the night, the crew battled valiantly to shore up hatches and bulkheads, control flooding and pump out other compartments to restore some of the vessels lost buoyancy. Australian and New Zealand warships were quickly on hand to render assistance, whilst military aircraft ferried essential pumps and shoring timber to Lord Howe Island for onward transfer to the *Nottingham*, now anchored offshore.

Over the next few weeks the vessel was made seaworthy with emergency repairs, whilst huge girders were welded across the flight deck in preparation for towing.

On 6 August, the tug *Pacific Chieftain* began towing the crippled warship stern-first to Newcastle, with the tug *Yam-O* acting as a sea anchor and the *Austral Salvor* standing by. On arrival at the Australian port a few days later, a delicate operation began to remove the Sea Dart missiles and 4.5-inch shells, some badly crushed, from the ship's magazines. The destroyer was later transported back to her homeport of Portsmouth aboard the Dutch-registered heavy lifting vessel *MV Swan*, in the same way that her sister-ship *HMS Southampton* (D92) had been after a collision in the Persian Gulf 14 years earlier.

The *Nottingham* had only completed an expensive refit a little over a year before her grounding. Despite the extensive damage, the Royal Navy therefore decided that she should be repaired. After repairs totalling £26m, including replacement of over 100-tonnes of steelwork, 15 miles of cabling and much of her machinery, *HMS Nottingham* finally returned to the Fleet in 2004, almost 2 years to the day after she had nearly foundered.

The pinnacle that so almost claimed the

ship, Wolf Rock, was well charted, but it appears that the bridge crew were using larger scale charts at the time of the grounding and failed to maintain a safe distance from the hazard. Four of the ship's officers later faced courts martial for endangering their ship: the Commanding Officer accepted his failure to delegate the responsibility of command properly and received a reprimand; the Executive Officer and the Officer-of-the-Watch were both dismissed from their current ships after pleading guilty to negligence; and the Navigating Officer was sentenced to a severe reprimand. Several other members of the crew received commendations for their efforts in saving their ship, once again illustrating that there is no substitute for extensive damage-control training.

It is clear that there are many reasons for the grounding of vessels of all sizes, but it remains a fact that the most common cause of such accidents is navigational error. To prevent such incidents it is imperative that the perishable skills of seamanship and navigation must be constantly cultivated, despite the availability of ever more accurate navigational aids such as satellites, radar and sonar. However, the constant reductions in military budgets, combined with the continued operational requirements for such valuable national assets as naval vessels, can only result in a reduction in time available for training commitments. Often, it is not considered economically viable to have the operational availability of these assets 'unnecessarily' curtailed to further such an 'invisible' commodity as the skill of the crew.

Simulators are now easing this burden, with their increasing use for the training of personnel in a wide variety of skills, including the operation of weapons and electronic warfare systems, the operation of machinery plant, damage-control and fire-fighting and, more recently, seamanship and ship handling. Ship handling simulators, in use for many years with the merchant marine, are now being integrated into naval service. For example, the Royal Australian Navy and the German Navy are using versions supplied by Krupp Atlas Electronik, incorporating a full-size bridge layout replica with panoramic screens in place of bridge windows. The system also has an instructor's panel, workstation and recording facilities for debriefing.

Latest systems also offer simulated pitch and roll movement, like those used in submarine and flight simulators, for added realism. Systems like these will undoubtedly improve training in bridge handling skills at an affordable cost, without tying up valuable front-line warships for training duties.

# Chapter Four

# COLLISIONS

Collisions occur for any number of reasons, but it has to be said that, in almost every case, negligence or complacency are the primary ingredients of the accident, whilst a sprinkling of inexperience will only add to the deadliness of the cocktail. Ultimately, blame for any collision rests with the Commanding Officer of the vessel at fault, as he is responsible for all that happens in, or to, his ship. As the commanding officer cannot expect to be on the bridge all of the time to oversee every manoeuvre, he must have ultimate faith in his chain of command. To this end, he must ensure that his qualified officers-of-the-watch/deck (OOW/OOD) have sufficient training to handle any unforeseen event, exercising control of these watch-keepers by the issue of concise, detailed and unambiguous orders, which must include situational criteria by which it is mandatory that the commanding officer be summoned to the bridge. Nevertheless, this control should not be overly constraining to the degree that his subordinates' confidence and initiative are unduly stifled.

Most collisions occur when the ship is transiting narrow and busy channels or is engaged in active manoeuvres, during which times the commanding officer's presence should be felt either on the bridge or in the ship's Control Room/CIC. Unfortunately, this is not always the case and the commanding officer is often only involved in the final moments of a dangerous incident, too late to take an active role in preventing the collision. Conversely, the commanding officer's belated intervention has, on occasions, only added to the confusion on the bridge and thereby exacerbated the situation. Like grounding incidents, collisions are seldom the result of a single incorrect order or decision, but are more commonly due to an accumulative series of minor events or miscalculations.

It is the responsibility of the Commanding Officer to ensure that his bridge watch-keepers are able to recognise these events as they unfold and to ensure that they learn to use all of their experience and initiative to extricate their vessel from a developing situation. The strict adherence of the crew to established standardised procedures, utilising an efficient chain of command is paramount in the safe operation of any ship.

The level of awareness of the bridge crew should be matched to the prevailing situation. An open ocean transit permits a certain amount of relaxation and may allow the ship to be in the hands of a more junior qualified officer, whilst operating in shipping lanes or as part of a task group requires a much higher level of experience and vigilance. In order to prevent a collision situation developing, a combination of criteria must be constantly monitored, including ship's course, speed and position, depth of water beneath the keel and relative positions and tracks of other vessels. All of these factors must be borne out by comparison with charts, visual sightings and radar scanning. When any of these criteria are in doubt, it is time for the commanding officer to be informed and for him to take action to retrieve the situation.

When these basic principles are ignored or neglected by a vessel's on-watch personnel, it is to tempt fate and thereby put at risk not only their vessel, but also the lives of all on board.

Major collisions within harbours are a relatively rare occurrence, probably due to the high level of awareness on the bridge of any vessel within these constrained areas, together with the availability of tugs for awkward manoeuvres.

Nevertheless, collisions within these areas do occur from time to time.

On 18 September 1945, the destroyer-escort *USS Jordan* (DE-204) was seriously damaged in a collision at Miami with the merchant *ss John Sherman*. Following a survey of the damage, she was declared a constructive total loss and, after being laid up at Charleston, was scrapped two years later.

One of the large number of landing vessels given to the Royal Navy during the war, the LST(2) class tank landing ship *LST405* was preparing for her participation in the Malayan campaign with the 12th India Flotilla in October 1945, when she was involved in a collision with a troopship in Colombo Harbour. Damage to the 1,625-ton landing ship was so extensive that she was considered a constructive total loss and, with US approval, was written off on 12 March 1946 and scuttled at sea.

Four months later, on 8 January 1946, the small US Navy tug *Achigan* (YTB-218) was sunk in a collision with the amphibious transport ship *General J.C. Breckenridge* (AP-176) at Philadelphia. *Achigan* was salvaged and returned to service the following year, serving until 1957. Less than three weeks later, on 27 January, one of *Achigan's* sister craft - *Tamaroa* (YTB-136) - was involved in a similar incident in San Francisco harbour with the cargo ship *USNS Jupiter* (AVS-8). Although later raised from a depth of 42 feet, *Tamaroa* was discarded as a total loss.

Other tugs sunk in collisions include the Italian naval tug *Atlante* (A5317), sunk in January 1948 in a collision in Genoa harbour, and the US Navy's *Palatka* (YTB-801), which was rammed and sunk by the amphibious assault ship *USS Nashville* (LPD-13) on 17 January 1972. Both of these craft were subsequently salvaged and returned to service.

A more recent warship casualty was the Bluebird-class minesweeper *USS*

*The Italian naval tug Atlante (A5317) was one of many such vessels sunk in collisions with larger warships or merchantmen. However, the ship was raised from the bottom of Genoa harbour in 1948 and returned to service.*
*(Ufficio Storico Della Marina Militaire)*

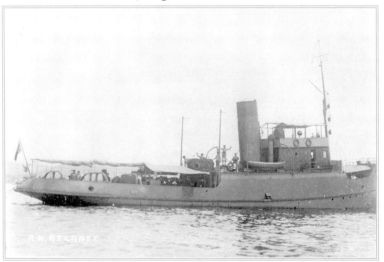

*Kingbird* (MSC-194), which was seriously damaged in a collision with a merchant ship at Pensacola, Florida, on 21 May 1971 and, following a survey of the damage, was declared a constructive total loss.

Occasionally, naval vessels can be mere victims of collisions between civilian ships. On 21 September 2003, the Panamanian-flagged *mv Eagle Strength* swerved to port to avoid a small craft and collided with the container ship *mv Banglar Biraj* . Out of control, the *Eagle Strength* careered into a group of Bangladeshi Navy ships moored at their jetties. The patrol boat *BNS Jamuna* (P212) was badly damaged, seven other warships received minor damage and 20 sailors were injured. It is believed all of the naval vessels were subsequently repaired.

The sinking of any vessel within a busy waterway or river can cause immense disruption to the free passage of other vessels and, for this reason, the expeditious removal of such wreckage is of paramount importance. A simple precautionary regulation enforced in most busy maritime highways to prevent these collisions occurring is the establishment of channels, or traffic separation schemes, for vessels proceeding in each direction, separated in most cases by a narrow 'no-go' area which may only be utilised by vessels crossing the waterway. Such measures are often supplemented by the attendance of local pilots, who are not only familiar with the navigational hazards of the area, but who will also be aware of any local additions to the laid down international navigational regulations. Nevertheless, even when these channels are clearly marked on charts and when local pilots are embarked, the misinterpretation of the intended actions of another vessel can lead to tragedy.

In August 1946, the tug *Beaverton*, a Canadian naval auxiliary vessel owned and controlled by the Saint Lawrence River King's Harbour Master and operated by a civilian crew, was employed in the task of towing ammunition lighters, under escort, out to sea, where the explosives could then be jettisoned. Having just completed one such mission, she was ordered to proceed to Montreal to render routine assistance to the aircraft carrier *HMCS Warrior* (CVL-31).

Proceeding up the Saint Lawrence River towards Montreal at around 0420 on the morning of 27 August 1946, *Beaverton* was sighted near Cap aux Oies (Goose Cape) by the ex-merchant aircraft carrier *Empire MacAlpine*, five miles away on her starboard bow at a bearing of 010°. With fair weather and good visibility, the *Empire MacAlpine* was herself sighted a few minutes later by the tug's lookout, off her starboard bow in the North Channel. The 8,000-ton *mv Empire MacAlpine*, still outwardly resembling an aircraft carrier, had sailed from Montreal at noon the previous day with a cargo of wheat, bound for the United Kingdom. Both vessels had licensed pilots aboard for the river passage, and both were proceeding at a speed of about 12 knots. The river at this point had a navigable width of some six or seven miles, so allowing more than enough space for the vessels to pass each other safely. However, off Cap aux Oies, the separate north and south-bound channels merged for a distance of about ten miles, separating again off the north-west corner of Ile aux Coudres.

When abeam of Cap aux Oies, the *Empire MacAlpine* changed course from 170° to 040° to assume the next leg of the river transit, but her pilot, Edmond Baquet, was puzzled to see *Beaverton's* red port navigation light, indicating that the tug had changed course to starboard. *Empire MacAlpine* made a signal of two blasts on the ship's siren. Although not an authorised signal to assist vessels with an end-on or nearly end-on aspect in the avoidance of a collision, this was a generally accepted signal used by St. Lawrence River pilots to indicate a wish to pass starboard to starboard. Unfortunately, due to the noise of her engines, and the lookout being positioned inside the wheelhouse, this signal was not heard aboard *Beaverton*. *Beaverton*'s green starboard light was then seen momentarily by *Empire MacAlpine*, who believed their signal had been heard and that the tug was complying, but *Beaverton*'s red navigation light once again came into view and the tug continued to change course erratically and unexpectedly.

A now anxious Baquet ordered the two-blast signal repeated, but *Beaverton* continued to alter course erratically. It suddenly became apparent that the tug was attempting to cross *Empire MacAlpine*'s bow and, in an effort to avoid the smaller vessel, Baquet ordered full astern and helm hard-a-port, thus turning his ship to starboard. Unfortunately, these actions were instigated too late to avoid the inevitable collision and, at about 0437, the 260-ton *Beaverton* was struck by *Empire MacAlpine* port side amidships. Her hull gouged open by the bows of the large grain carrier, *Beaverton* sank about one mile off Corneille Point on the river's north shore in just a few minutes.

*Empire MacAlpine* immediately reversed course and returned to the scene of the collision, whereupon a number of survivors were spotted clinging to one of the tug's upturned lifeboats and to a single Carley float, while several others could be seen floundering around in the water. A lifeboat was lowered and seventeen men were rescued, but an extensive search failed to find two missing crewmen - her master, Captain H. C. Richard, who had been a wartime Lieutenant-Commander in the Royal Canadian Navy, and an oiler, R.G. Vibert. At 0620, *Empire MacAlpine* gave up the search and set course for Quebec, where the survivors were all admitted to hospital, mostly suffering from shock.

An enquiry was held by the Department of Transport, in the presence of a Naval Observer from Halifax the following day, followed in late-September/early-October by a Naval Court of Inquiry in Montreal. Blame for the accident was placed wholly with *Beaverton*'s pilot, Hermenegilde Lachance, for attempting to cross *Empire MacAlpine*'s head when there was no need to do so. *Empire MacAlpine*, whose maintenance of a steady course should have made her intentions perfectly obvious, was judged to have been piloted in a proper and seamanlike manner. *Beaverton* on the other hand, made no signals and her erratic course changes would have made her intentions almost impossible for those on the *Empire MacAlpine* to comprehend.

Outward bound vessels had the choice of two channels, with the North Channel or the South Traverse. It appears that the pilot of *Beaverton* considered that he had the right of way, but, had this been the case, he should have maintained his course - which he did not do - and had he done so the collision almost certainly would not have occurred. Lachance had seemed determined to pass the larger ship port to port, in accordance with the 'International Rules of the Road'. However, these regulations also stated at that time that: "Every vessel which is directed by these rules to keep out of the way of another vessel shall, if the circumstances admit, avoid crossing ahead of the other." Nevertheless, *Beaverton* continually attempted to cross ahead of *Empire MacAlpine*. Furthermore, had the lookout or pilot aboard *Beaverton* heard either of the larger vessel's two-blast signals, they should have realised *Empire MacAlpine*'s intentions to pass 'green to green'.

This overwhelming urge of some mariners to always pass another vessel port-to-port, despite the risk of collision, was later to result in the destruction of a patrol craft of the Hellenic Navy. At about 0405 on the morning of 24 August 1977, the patrol boat *HS Antipoploiarchos Pezopoulos* (P70), on a routine operational patrol from Rhodes to Leros island, entered the eastern end of the Pserimos Channel between the islands of Cos and Pserimos in the south-east Aegean. As the ship altered course slightly to starboard to a new heading of 268°, the Roussa light and the silhouette of the south-eastern tip of Pserimos could be clearly seen a little over half a mile to the north, such was the brightness of the full moon. Steaming at a speed of 11 knots on an oily calm sea, the Executive Officer on the bridge of the 440-ton patrol craft was having a peaceful watch, the serenity of the scene broken only by the occasional routine reports from the radar operator in the ship's CIC.

Shortly afterwards, the radar operator reported a contact about four miles away on an approximate bearing of 15° off the starboard bow, travelling on a roughly east-south-easterly heading. Although the other vessel was hidden from visual contact by the island, the low-lying coast had allowed the radar to detect it in good time. The vessel, brightly lit by all of her accommodation lights, was sighted by the OOW a few minutes later and was quickly identified as a ferry, travelling at high speed down the channel. It soon became apparent that both vessels would safely pass each other starboard-to-starboard and so the patrol boat maintained her course and speed. Then, when about 50-60° to starboard of *Pezopoulos* and at a distance of about 1,200 yards, the ferry suddenly turned sharply to starboard, her green and red navigation lights becoming clearly visible from the patrol craft. Inexplicably, the ferry continued to turn to starboard and, despite the westerly course of *Pezopoulos*, her bow continued to follow the patrol craft.

*Pezopoulos'* OOW immediately ordered a turn to port and the sounding of two short blasts on the horn. Alerted by these actions and the sounding of the general alarm, the Commanding Officer appeared on the bridge moments later, just as the OOW ordered full speed ahead. However, the unexpected actions of the ferry, the *Athens Express*, had left the patrol craft little opportunity to avoid the collision and, at 0415, the ferry slammed into the starboard side of the *Pezopoulos* at a speed of 18½ knots, pushing her sideways for a short distance. Although the patrol craft's turn to port had reduced the angle of the impact somewhat, the bow of the *Athens Express* gouged into the hull, opening up a large gash in the engine room and wrecking the starboard engine.

Despite the water flooding into the compartment, the two shaken engineers managed to keep the port engine running and, with the rudder at hard to starboard, the craft was kept clear of the shallows of Pserimos Island. However, water cascading through the open watertight door between the engine and generator rooms soon led to the failure of the generators and all power was lost.

At 0445, the *Athens Express* approached the now drifting *Pezopoulos* and evacuated all crewmen except for the officers and petty officers. A towline was quickly passed and secured and the ferry towed the crippled patrol craft towards Cos harbour, where the tow was passed to local caiques and secured alongside.

The construction of the *Pezopoulos* had clearly prevented any major casualties amongst her crew, as the heavy steel hull and the armoured bridge - meant to withstand small arms fire - protected them from flying debris as the bow of the ferry smashed into their ship. Nevertheless, damage to the ship, which had been in service with the Hellenic Navy since 1947, was so extensive that she was declared a constructive total loss and was scrapped.

The subsequent Naval Court of Inquiry

*Lack of vigilance when transiting busy channels resulted in the loss of the Chinese corvette Fu Po, in a collision with a merchantman in the Formosa Strait on 19 March 1947.*
*(Maritime Photo Library)*

acquitted the Commanding and Executive Officers of the *Pezopoulos* of any blame for the accident. Evidence given by the watch on the bridge of the ferry maintained that, although they had seen the *Pezopoulos*, they had thought that the lights shown by the patrol craft belonged to a fishing boat and that they were unsure of the craft's movements. Although inexplicable - especially given the clearness of the night - it appears that the officer on watch, 'unsure' of the other craft's movements attempted to take the 'safe' course of action and pass her port-to-port. A civilian court later convicted the master of the *Athens Express* of negligence and awarded him a short custodial sentence but, following an appeal, this sentence was later rescinded.

Whilst the loss of the *Beaverton* and the *Pezopoulos* were clearly the result of the misinterpretation of 'International Rules of the Road' regulations, vessels being in the wrong channel due to navigational errors cause many other river collisions. Such was the case when the tanker *USS Mission San Francisco* (T-AO-123) was involved in a collision with the Liberian merchantman *ss Elna II* whilst transiting the Delaware River, near New Castle, on 7 March 1957. Rupturing of the *Mission San Francisco*'s fuel storage tanks caused a fire to break out, followed by a tremendous explosion that ripped the ship in two. Ten crewmen, including the ship's master, Captain William Allen, were killed and the US Navy later declared the burnt out wreck unsalvageable.

Similar navigational errors resulted in the loss of two minesweepers in the 1960s. On 30 September 1962, the East German motor-minesweeper *Sternberg* (422) was sunk in a collision with a

lightship near Verstoss after straying into the north-bound channel. Although later raised, the craft was declared a constructive total loss and decommissioned on 1 February of the following year. Then, on 14 January 1967, the US Navy minesweeping boat *MSB-14* was sunk in a collision with the 1,340-ton Norwegian freighter *Mui Finn* in the Long Tau River, 30 miles south-east of Saigon, with the loss of three of her crew.

Lack of vigilance when transiting confined channels that are subject to a high volume of traffic has also resulted in the tragic loss of many smaller warships. The Chinese Flower-class corvette *Fu Po* was sunk following a collision with the merchantman *Hai Ming* in the Formosa Strait on 19 March 1947.

Then, on the night of 16/17 May 1953, the Egyptian frigate *ENS Misr* was run down south of Suez by a Norwegian merchantman. This ship, believed also to be an ex-Royal Navy Flower-class corvette, was later discovered and examined by British divers during Operation Rheostat - the 1974 mine clearance operation of the Suez Canal.

The Danish torpedo boat *HDMS Tranen* (P567), under the command of Lt Cdr Kaj Thygesen, sank after a collision with a Norwegian fishing cutter *Trygg* in Stavanger Fjord on the night of 27 March 1963. Fortunately, all of the boat's crew were rescued. As the weather at the time of the collision was clear, with a brisk force 2-3 south-south-easterly wind blowing, the cause of the loss was attributed to human navigational error. The wreck was raised the following month and sold to a shipbreaker. Then, during the night of 31 August 1968 the East German torpedo boat *Willi Bäntsch* (844) was involved in a collision with the Swedish ferry-boat *Drottningen* and sank with the loss of seven of her crew.

The Dutch Navy's only peacetime accidental destruction of a major warship

Following a collision with a merchantship in the Westerschelde on 9 January 1974, the Dutch destroyer HrMS Noord Brabant was towed into port and was later declared a constructive total loss.
(Afdeling Maritieme Historie van de Marinstaf)

occurred in the early hours of 9 January 1974. The Holland-class destroyer *HrMS Noord Brabant* (D810) was entering the Westerchelde, in position 51°25'N, 03°32'E, when she was struck on the port side by the 16,700-ton British bulk carrier *mv Tacoma City*. The *Noord Brabant*, which had been heading for Flushing Roads, was badly holed in the vicinity of the after boiler room, rapidly flooding the compartment and killing two crewmen. The *Tacoma City*, on the other hand, suffered only minor damage and shortly afterwards continued her journey outbound from Antwerp to the North Sea.

The crippled destroyer was eventually towed back to her home port where, partly due to the extent of the damage and partly due to the fact that she had been in service since 1955, she was declared a constructive total loss. Removed from the active list on 28 May 1974, she was sold for scrap to a Belgian firm in Gent.

A similar fate befell the French Sirius-class minesweeper *FS Capella* (M755) after she was seriously damaged in a collision with a Guatemalan merchant ship off Zeebrugge on 28 February 1987. Such was the force of the collision, that the minesweeper's hull was completely

severed aft of the engine room bulkhead. The crippled vessel was assisted into Zeebrugge by her sister ship *Capricorne* (M737), which was secured to her port side, the assistance effort being taken over by the tug *Fighter* once within the harbour. Although originally commissioned in 1956, *Capella* had been almost immediately laid up in reserve until March 1962, and was again reduced to normal reserve at Brest from 1965 until 1973. Therefore, although she was over thirty years old at the time of the collision, she had only been in active service for

With her aft section torn off, the French Navy minesweeper FS Capella is assisted into port following collision with a merchantship off Zeebrugge on 28 February 1987.
(L van Ginderen)

about half of that period. Nevertheless, due to the severe structural damage inflicted on her in the collision, together with the commissioning of the new Tripartite minehunters, *Capella* was considered beyond economical repair and was scrapped.

In October 1985, the Turkish Kartal-class missile boat *TCG Meltem* (P325) was involved in a fatal collision in the Bosporus with the 8,500-ton Soviet Navy Project 887 Smol'ny-class training ship *Khasan*. The craft was later salvaged but was found to be completely beyond repair. In February 1988, the Soviet Government announced the payment of US$250,000 compensation to the families of the five Turkish seamen killed in the accident.

A simple but fatal error of judgement led to the worst accident in the Singapore Navy's proud history since it's founding in 1975.

At about 2320 on the night of 3 January 2003, the Fearless-class patrol ship *RSS Courageous* (P96) was transiting the north-east-bound channel of the Singapore Straits Traffic Separation Scheme (TSS) at a speed of about 9 knots. A few miles astern of her in the same channel was the 52,000-ton Dutch container ship *ANL Indonesia*, travelling at 23 knots and quickly gaining on the *Courageous*. The naval ship was maintaining a patrol in the area of the Horsborough Lighthouse and, at 2325 made a 180° turn to port to a course of 235°, remaining within the eastbound TSS but travelling against the flow of traffic. In the calm weather conditions and visibility of about 10km, this manoeuvre did not go unnoticed or cause any alarm amongst the bridge crew aboard the *Indonesia* as the relative courses of the two vessels would still allow them to pass each other safely port-port. However, a further 20° turn to port by the *Courageous* five minutes later put the two vessels on a collision course, with the 3km distance between them closing rapidly.

Suddenly realising the impending danger this course change had caused, the *Courageous* made two further changes of course to port and increased speed to avoid the larger container ship. Rule 14(a) of the *International Regulations for Preventing Collisions at Sea*, 1972, states that "When two power-driven vessels are meeting on reciprocal or nearly reciprocal courses so as to involve risk of collision each shall alter her course to starboard so that each shall pass on the port side of the other." Accordingly, the *Indonesia* altered course to starboard and sounded a warning to the smaller vessel on her sirens.

However, the change of course was too late to avoid the inevitable collision and, just after 2335 the *Indonesia* struck the starboard after quarter of the 452-ton *Courageous*, shearing off the after two sections of the warship and crushing much of her superstructure. As the *Courageous* scraped along the starboard side of the *Indonesia*, the patrol ship's compartment 3 was flooded and a fire broke out on deck. As the *Indonesia* stopped to render assistance and raise the alarm with the Maritime and Port Authority of Singapore, damage control measures were being taken to prevent the *Courageous* from sinking and to extinguish the fire. Shortly afterwards, a head count revealed that four female personnel who had been in their sleeping quarters in the severed stern section were missing and another eight members of the 44 crew had sustained minor injuries. Damage to the *Indonesia*'s bow was minor and there were no injuries to any of her crew.

Rescue services were immediately despatched to the scene and, a little over an hour later, the Police coastal patrol craft *Hammerhead Shark* evacuated the crew of the *Courageous*. Despite intensive search operations, only three bodies were recovered - the fourth was never found.

The *Courageous* was taken in tow to

Changi Naval Base and hoisted onto the slipway on the morning of 4 January, where she remained in the damaged state for over a year before undergoing repairs.

The findings of the Maritime and Port Authority of Singapore's inquiry into the collision, published three months later, concluded that no material or manning shortcomings had contributed to the accident, but rather it had arisen from an error of judgement on the part of the *Courageous*' OOW. At the time of the accident, the ship had been under the control of a trainee OOW, supervised by a qualified officer. Whilst the *Indonesia* had correctly turned to starboard to avoid the collision, the *Courageous* had contravened local and international regulations by continuing to turn to port across the bows of the container ship. The OOW had failed to correctly supervise the trainee in his charge and was held responsible for the tragic events of that night.

When warships are involved in naval exercises they often display few, if any, lights. At night, this can render the vessel almost invisible, especially if other shipping is not using all available navigational aids. On 4 November 1996, the Greek La Combattante IIIB–class missile boat *Antipoploiarchos Kostakos* (P25) was taking part in the naval exercise Parmenion, hiding in wait less that half a mile off Vathi, Samos island. At about 1830 the craft was struck by the 3,800-tonne Greek ferry *Samaina*, outbound from Vathi en route to Karlovasi, ripping a huge hole in the starboard after end of the warship. The engine room was immediately flooded, claiming the lives of the four engineers in the compartment. The *Kostakos* sank at 1845 in 168 meters of water. Another Greek missile boat, operating less than a mile away, was quickly on the scene and rescued the 34 survivors, but an intensive search operation throughout the night failed to recover the four missing sailors.

Although the ferry was badly damaged, there were no injuries amongst the *Samaina*'s 122 passengers and crew.

The ensuing investigation determined that the *Kostakos* had been lying close off shore without any lights visible. The OOW had visual contact with the ferry before the collision, but had mistakenly believed that he had sufficient time to cross in front of her. The ferry's bridge crew had been navigating by visual fixes on lights ashore and was not using their navigational radar. Consequently, the *Kostakos* was virtually invisible and went unseen by the ferry's bridge crew until it was too late to avoid the collision.

The Board of Inquiry found *Kostakos*' OOW, Ensign Mihail Dimoulkas, guilty of the negligent loss of his ship and also charged him with four counts of negligent manslaughter. Having sighted the ferry and located her on the craft's electronic surveillance systems, he had failed to inform his Commanding Officer, in violation of his superior's standing orders.

The ship's Commanding Officer, Lieutenant Commander Konstantinos Lazaris, was also held responsible for the tragedy. However, witnesses also claimed that the ferry had suddenly changed course to port immediately prior to the collision. Consequently, the ferry's captain, Mathios Pnevmatikakis, was also charged with negligence and four counts of involuntary manslaughter and was also cited for not effectively using navigational equipment and for sailing at excessive speed. The Greek Navy claimed that all authorities were informed that the exercise was taking place in the area.

The *Kostakos* was raised on 15 March 1997 and the bodies of the three missing sailors recovered. After being examined at the Salamis naval yard, the ship was scrapped.

The majority of the cases mentioned so far occurred during the hours of darkness, when some mitigation for the collisions may be placed with a failure to correctly interpret the navigation lights of other vessels, or to confusion arising from the presence of background lights along the shoreline. However, even in broad daylight, when visibility is completely unimpeded and the movements of other vessels can be easily tracked and anticipated, complacency and a complete disregard for the safety of other vessels in the vicinity can result in the entirely avoidable sinking of a ship and heavy loss of life.

At about 1342 on the afternoon of 15 November 1972, the 210,000-dwt supertanker *World Hero* departed from the Skaramanga shipyard, west of Athens, bound for the Persian Gulf. This huge tanker was riding high in the water, her bunkers containing a mere 65,000 tons of fuel and water ballast. Shortly afterwards, at 1400, the Hellenic Navy landing ship *HS Ypoploiarchos Merlin* (L166), under the command of Lieutenant G Beyietis HN, slipped from her moorings at the Salamis Naval Dockyard, on the western bank of the Salamis Channel. The 1,100-ton ship, with a crew of six officers and 51 ratings aboard, together with a civilian fork-lift truck driver, was loaded with Naval equipment intended for delivery to one of the many garrisons in the Aegean Sea islands.

As the *World Hero* steamed through the Salamis Channel, the *Merlin* slipped into her wake, approximate 500 yards astern. Then, while the tanker continued eastwards through the eastern Psyttalia Island passage (Thermistocles Strait), the landing ship turned to starboard and headed instead through the Aeginites Strait to the west of Psyttalia Island - the normal route for naval vessels departing from Salamis - increasing speed from 5 to 8 knots. At 1447, the tanker slowed to three knots just outside the entrance to Piraeus harbour, in order to disembark the local pilot and two owner and shipyard representatives who were aboard. Three minutes later, the officer on watch on the

bridge of *World Hero* ordered 'Full Ahead', followed at 1500 by 'Full Away'.

As the tanker settled on her intended course of 160° at a speed of 14 knots, the autopilot was engaged and her bridge crew relaxed.

Meanwhile, *Merlin* had increased speed to 10 knots and, on clearing the strait between the islets of Psyttalia and Atalanta at about 1450, dispersed the 'special sea dutymen' (additional men closed up for safety during the channel transit) and set a new course of 147°. At 1457, Lieutenant Beyietis left the bridge, leaving control of the ship in the hands of the OOW - a Naval Reserve Sub-Lieutenant who also happened to be the ship's Navigating Officer - with orders that he was to be notified immediately should there be any cause for concern. Also on the bridge was the ship's Marine Engineer Officer and five lookouts, whilst in the steering platform, beneath the bridge, three other ratings were on duty.

The presence of the tanker was noted at a distance of 1,500-2,000 yards, bearing down on *Merlin* from a heading of approximately 150-160° to port. When, at 1508, the distance had closed to 500 yards, the Commanding Officer was alerted and the landing ship's horn was sounded in an effort to alert the tanker of her presence. As the huge mass of the tanker bore down on them, the OOW ordered the helm hard to port and then, almost immediately, hard to starboard, this last order being endorsed by the Commanding Officer as he reached the bridge, adding the order 'flank speed'. This second order was never executed, as the massive bulbous bow of the tanker smashed into the LSM's port quarter. As Lieutenant Beyietis ordered abandon ship, the momentum of the first collision propelled the landing ship forward so that the tanker's bow smashed into her again almost amidships and capsized her to starboard. *Merlin* floated upside down for only a few minutes before slipping beneath the surface.

It was only the slight sensation of a 'bump' felt aboard the tanker that alerted the crew to the terrible realisation that they had hit another vessel. Although engines were immediately ordered to stop, the huge vessel drifted on for several thousand yards. Of the 58 men aboard *Merlin*, only fifteen managed to scramble free before she sank, only to be sucked into the depths by the vacuum caused by their ship plunging to the bottom some 90 metres below. Miraculously, fourteen of these men survived, including Lieutenant Beyietis, the Engineer Officer and the relief OOW, who had just arrived on the bridge at the time of the collision. Of the eleven ratings that survived, five had been on the bridge and three at the steering platform. All of the survivors were plucked from the water by the Dutch merchantman *Swindlegt* and the Greek fishing vessel *Aghios Nikolaos* .

Through the night, a flotilla of warships, coastguard craft and tugs searched for further survivors, whilst helicopters hovered overhead and dropped flares and life buoys. The only body recovered was that of a young Lieutenant - the ship's Executive Officer - who had been sucked beneath the water's surface as his ship sank. Due to the depth of water and the lack of suitable salvage equipment, the ship was never recovered.

The ensuing Court of Inquiry concluded that the bridge crew of the *World Hero* were negligent, in that their actions in ordering full speed and the engagement of autopilot in a congested sea lane was not conducive to the safe passage of their ship or of other vessels transiting the area. Lookouts aboard the tanker had either not paid any attention to, or had simply not seen the landing ship. Some crewmen aboard the leviathan reported sensing a small shock, but it appears that lookouts only realised that they had struck something when they noticed men floating in the water and gesticulating wildly to them. Consequently, the master of the *World Hero* was convicted of negligence and sentenced to 37 months imprisonment, a sentence that was later reduced to 33 months by the Court of Appeal.

The over-reliance on autopilot appears to have been a major contributing factor in another tragic collision between a merchant vessel and a warship. At 0345 on the morning of Sunday 6 August 2000, the Uruguayan Navy Kondor II-class minesweeper *Valiente* (32) was patrolling about 11 miles south of Cabo Polonio in thick fog, when she was run down by the 24,000-ton Panamanian-flagged freighter *mv Skyros*. The 400-ton minesweeper was cut in two and sank ten minutes later. Eight of the 24-man crew were killed in the collision, whilst thirteen survivors were rescued and later taken to La Paloma where they were treated for hypothermia. A massive search throughout Sunday failed to find the remaining three crewmen, who were all believed to have been in the minesweeper's engine-room.

The Uruguayan Navy later claimed that the *Skyros* had been cruising on automatic pilot and had failed to answer radio calls from the minesweeper just before the impact. Like the loss of the *World Hero*, the failure of the crew of the *Skyros* to maintain a sufficient watch on radar or radio had resulted in the loss of a warship and many of her crew.

Vigilant lookouts or radar operators should easily be able to spot other surface vessels and, if the OOW is alerted, should ensure that a collision is averted. On the other hand, a submarine running on the surface presents a poor radar return and, even in calm weather, may go unseen from the bridge of a surface vessel. At night, the red and green navigation lights on the boat's fin is augmented only with a small Grimes yellow flasher. It is therefore hardly surprising that several submarines have been lost in nighttime collisions with surface vessels.

On the night of 12 January 1950, the

Royal Navy T-class submarine *HMS Truculent* (P315) sank after a collision in the Ouze Deep, eight miles east of Sheerness, in the Thames Estuary. *Truculent* had been carrying out sea trials following a refit at Chatham Dockyard and was returning on the surface to Sheerness. Besides her normal complement of 61 men she had a team of 18 civilian dockyard workers aboard. It was just after 1700 and the 643-ton Swedish motor tanker *Divina* was transiting down the Thames from Purfleet at a speed of 7½ knots, bound for Ipswich with a cargo of paraffin. Under Port of London Authority local regulations for ships carrying dangerous cargoes, *Divina* was displaying an additional red light. All vessels transiting the Thames, including the *Truculent*, should have been aware of such local rules.

At about 1900, the submarine's Commanding Officer, Lieutenant C. P. Bowers, was called to the bridge, as the OOW was confused by the sighting of two red and one green navigation lights, which he had interpreted as being those of a stationary vessel a mile or two away in the north of the channel. Seemingly agreeing with his subordinate's hypothesis, Lt. Bowers judged that it would not be possible to pass to the right of the contact for fear of grounding and so ordered a turn to port. Unbeknown to them, the lights were really those of the *Divina* and no sooner had *Truculent* begun her turn to port than the tanker's bows loomed out of the night. Realising his terrible mistake, Lt. Bowers ordered full astern and hard-a-starboard, but it was too late and, at 1904, the reinforced ice-breaking bows of the tanker smashed into *Truculent*'s starboard side in the vicinity of the forward torpedo compartment.

The force of the collision ripped off the submarine's starboard hydroplane and split the pressure hull from its apex down to about six feet from the keel. Five men on the submarine's bridge were swept into the river and the submarine sank rapidly by the bow, disappearing below surface in about a minute. Of the seventy-four men still trapped within the stricken submarine as it sank to the sea bed 66 feet below the surface, ten drowned in the immediate flooding, as water pouring into the boat prevented the closure of several watertight doors. In only a few minutes, all the compartments forward of the engine room were flooded. Securing the engine room forward bulkhead watertight door behind them, the survivors huddled together and began to formulate a plan for their escape.

The master of the *Divina* was under the impression that he had collided with a small trawler and that the Dutch vessel *Almdyk*, inbound for Gravesend, had rescued the majority of the craft's crew. In fact, the men that *Almdyk* had plucked from the water about an hour after the collision had been the five crewmen swept from the *Truculent*'s bridge in the collision. A lifeboat had been lowered by the *Divina* to search for further survivors, but when none were spotted the boat was recovered and *Divina* prepared to proceed on her way. About an hour later several men were spotted in the water and *Divina*'s lifeboat was again launched to pick up a further ten survivors.

However, these men were in such a state of shock that they were unable to communicate to their rescuers the fact that a large number of their shipmates were still trapped on the bottom of the estuary. *Divina* continued on her way with what was believed to be the entire crew of the vessel with which they had collided. No distress signal was therefore sent. When the rescued men had recovered enough to explain the true facts of the tragedy, *Divina*'s radio was found to be malfunctioning and so a further delay resulted before the alarm could be raised.

Meanwhile, the survivors had divided themselves into two groups. One group, under the command of Lieutenant F.J.

Hindes, proceeded to the junior rating's messdeck in the after end, whilst the second, under CERA Sam Hine prepared for an escape from the engine room. The sound of propellers overhead led the trapped men to believe that help was at hand, but in reality, none of the vessels that passed over the scene were aware of the tragic events which had just taken place. The twill trunk was prepared, and by 2020 the first men were ready to escape.

Over the next hour or so, they executed an efficient and orderly escape from *Truculent* using DSEA sets or free ascent, but on reaching the surface they found no vessels in sight. It was an extremely dark night and the estuary's strong ebb tide proceeded to sweep them out to sea.

Having picked up the first few survivors, the crew of *Almdyk* had made no immediate calls for assistance as they assumed that *Divina*, as the first ship on the scene had already done so. The alarm was eventually raised by the *Almdyk* at 2045, when the true horror of the situation was realised. On receipt of *Almdyk*'s signal, the Admiralty set a full scale 'Subsmash' operation in motion. Several ships and craft, including the Hunt-class frigates *HM Ships Bicester* (F134) and *Cowdray* (F152), the Algerine-class minesweeper *HMS Cadmus* (M230), the Naval tug *Adherent* (W18), two wreck dispersal ships and two lifeboats, quickly assembled in the vicinity of the accident, marked by *Truculent*'s rescue marker buoy, which in the pitch darkness took some time to find.

The destroyer *HMS Finisterre* (D55) was also despatched from Portsmouth, carrying recompression gear and, as dawn broke, further ships and Fleet Air Arm aircraft joined the search for survivors. However, by the time the first vessels arrived on the scene, most of *Truculent*'s escapees had already been swept away, the vast majority of whom subsequently drowned or died of exposure or shock. In hindsight, they should have waited until they were contacted by rescuers before beginning their escape, or at least waited until dawn, when they would have been more easily spotted on the surface. Only fifteen survivors were picked up - ten by *Divina* and five, including *Truculent*'s Commanding Officer, by the *Almdyk*. Sixty-four men, including 16 civilians, perished.

The *Truculent* had sunk in a busy shipping lane and salvage operations began immediately, in order to prevent surface shipping colliding with the wreck. Divers from the Navy's specialist diving vessel, *HMS Reclaim* (A231), dived on the sunken boat and tapped on the hull in an effort to make contact with further survivors. No response was forthcoming from within *Truculent*. Hand grenades were also dropped in the vicinity to let any survivors know that help was at hand, but by late on 13 January, all hope of any crew still being alive within the boat was abandoned.

A further incident was to add to the tragedy. During the search operations an RAF Lancaster aircraft, on its way to transport divers from Rosyth to Manston Airport in Kent, crashed near Kinloss, killing the five-man crew.

As the salvage effort got under way, two ex-German heavy-lift vessels, *Energie* and *Ausdauer* - the only vessels then available for the task - were manoeuvred into position above the wreck. Progress was hindered by the severe tidal conditions and bad weather, with wind gusting up to force 10 at times. Working mainly by touch in the murky waters, divers assisted in the passing several 9-inch thick steel hawsers around the boat. These were then passed to the stern gantries of the two lifting craft and, on 14 March, the 1,570-ton *Truculent* was lifted from her watery grave. The lifting operation was suspended for a short time due to the wreck being bow-heavy. Water in the submarine's forward compartments

*HMS Truculent being raised from the Thames Estuary after being sunk in collision with the merchantship Divina on 12 January 1950.*
*(Royal Navy Submarine Museum)*

was ejected using compressed air and the lift recommenced. With the submarine suspended beneath the gantries of the lifting vessels the formation was slowly manoeuvred upstream the following day and beached at Cheney Spit sandbank three miles from Sheerness.

Two days later, the wreck was moved 1,000 yards inshore, half a mile from the coast, off Sheppey. There, she was pumped out and the bodies of ten drowned crewmen were recovered. Over the next week, a great deal of top-weight was removed from the boat, including the gun mounting, in order to improve the wreck's stability and, following temporary patching of her crushed hull, she was re-floated and towed into Sheerness Dockyard on 23 March by the tug *Typhoon* (W87) and the coastal salvage vessel *Swin*. After being dry-docked, further examination of the damage resulted in the conclusion that *Truculent*

was beyond economical repair and she was sold on 8 May for scrapping at Grays Shipbreakers on the Thames.

A Board of Enquiry, convened by the Commander-in-Chief, the Nore, at the Royal Navy Barracks, Chatham on 14 January, attributed 75% of the blame to the *Truculent* and 25% to the *Divina*. It was shown that, apart from the misinterpretation of *Divina*'s lights by *Truculent*, no sound signals were given by the submarine to inform other shipping of her intended manoeuvre to port. Lieutenant C.P. Bowers was court-martialled and found not guilty of negligently or by default losing his ship, but was found guilty of 'negligently or by default hazarding his ship' by altering course across *Divina*'s bows and, in view of his excellent record, received a severe reprimand.

His Majesty, King George VI, sent a message of condolence to the victims' families, and a memorial service was held in Porchester Church in the presence of the First Lord and the First Sea Lord. The King also approved the award of posthumous Albert Medals to two members of *HMS Truculent*'s crew, namely the boat's First Lieutenant, Lt. F.J. Hindes, and CERA F.W. Hine, DSM, for the way in which they calmly organised escape from the stricken vessel and ensured that the escape sets available were allotted to the weakest swimmers, briefing each man on the correct drill to be observed. The number of Davis escape sets however proved totally inadequate, as extra sets had not been embarked to cover the additional personnel carried on board at the time.

As a result of this disaster, submarine crews were later issued with immersion suits, with a white light fitted in the shoulder, although it was several years before their issue throughout the Submarine Service was complete. The provision of life jackets fitted with lights had recently been authorised by the Admiralty and their issue was also accelerated. As *Truculent* was not yet fully operational following her Chatham refit, the ship's crew were still to be provided with the modified life jackets. The provision of these two items of equipment would undoubtedly have helped the escapees to survive in the freezing water and resulted in more of them being spotted and rescued on that cold January night.

A further outcome of the inquiry was the fitting of an additional steaming light to submarines to improve their visibility at night from surface ships. Flashing lights were also fitted to the indicator buoy released by sunken submarines.

It is not known whether all of the lessons of *Truculent*'s loss filtered through to other navies in the succeeding years, but whilst *Truculent*'s crew had perhaps been premature in their escape from their sunken craft, the same could not be said of the crew of another boat sunk in a collision only three years later.

The loss of the ex-US Balao-class submarine *TCG Dumlupinar* (S339) was only Turkey's second submarine disaster. Whilst en route from Çanakkale to Instanbul in the early hours of the morning of 3 April 1953, she was rammed by the Swedish freighter *Naboland*, off Nagara Point, three miles north of Çanakkale, in the Dardanelles. *Dumlupinar*, transiting on the surface, sank 15 minutes later at 0215. The five crewmen on the bridge at the time of the collision, including her Commanding Officer, Commander Sabri Tchelebioglu, managed to jump clear before the boat went down with rest of her 86 personnel. At 0640, an indicator buoy released by the boat's trapped crew was spotted by a searching Turkish Navy launch.

Whilst in US service, the boat's escape hatches had been modified to accept the McCann Rescue Chamber, an item of equipment already in service with the Turkish Navy aboard another ex-US Navy vessel, the Bluebird-class submarine-rescue ship *Kurtaran* (A584). The *Kurtaran* arrived on the scene later that morning and moored above the stricken boat, lying on the bottom 276 feet below. Attempts were made to attach the haul-down cables, necessary for the operation of the McCann Chamber, but were hampered by the strong and treacherous currents sweeping through the narrow Dardanelles channel from the Sea of Marmara, sweeping divers from the submarine's casing and so prevented them attaching any salvage wires or haul-down cables. In the late afternoon, despite the possibility that some of *Dumlupinar*'s crew may still have been alive, the rescue attempt was abandoned. *Dumlupinar* was never salvaged. The crew of the *Naboland* were held to blame for the accident and their vessel was impounded until compensation could be agreed and paid.

Why the crew did not attempt to escape themselves is not clear, but it may have been because they were insufficiently trained in escape techniques from this depth of water, or that the ice-breaking bow of the 4,000-tonne *Naboland* caused such severe damage to the boat that she was flooded throughout almost immediately, killing or drowning all aboard.

Incidentally, the *Dumlupinar*'s namesake - the GUPPY IA modified boat *USS Caiman* (SS-323), transferred to Turkey as *TCG Dumlupinar* (S339) in 1972 - was herself involved in a serious collision in the Dardanelles with the Russian freighter *Szik Vovilov* on 1 September 1976. Having been beached to avoid foundering, the boat was eventually repaired and returned to service, until scrapped in the mid-1980s.

Although collisions involving submarines have never again reached the magnitude of those involving the *Truculent* or the *Dumlupinar*, several other lesser incidents have nevertheless resulted in either the scrapping or sinking of boats.

An ex-German Type VIIC submarine launched in May 1943 at Wilhelmshaven, *U766* was surrendered to the French when found at Pallice in 1945. In 1947 she was incorporated into the French Navy as the *Laubie* (S610) and, following repairs and a refit that included the removal of the guns and the addition of a snorkel, entered service in October 1948. By 1960, most of the war-built submarines had been replaced by the Narval- and Arethuse-class boats, whilst the first of the new Daphne-class was nearing completion. So, when *Laubie* suffered severe collision damage on 17 October 1961, she was not considered worthy of repair and was declared a constructive total loss. Placed in Special Category B Reserve in her damaged state for a short time under her new title of *Q335*, she was finally stricken on 11 March 1963 and scrapped.

One of several Soviet Navy submarines lost as a result of collisions with merchant ships, a Project 641 ('Foxtrot'-class) boat was scrapped following a collision with a Soviet vessel in the Mediterranean in January 1971, losing a 30 foot long section of its bow.

Then, on 13 June 1973, the Project 675 ('Echo-II'-class) SSGN *K-56* was involved in a collision with the research vessel *Akademik Berg*. The nuclear-powered submarine was rounding Cape Rotary in Peter the Great Bay shortly after 0100 when the research ship was first detected on radar, but it was several minutes more before it's navigation lights were spotted by lookouts on the submarine's bridge. Last-minute attempts to manoeuvre out of the research vessel's track were taken too late to avoid the inevitable collision and the *Academik Berg* smashed into the starboard side of *K-56* at a speed of 9-knots. The impact tore a four-metre gash in the submarine's hull between the 1st and 2nd compartments, flooding the 2nd compartment within minutes and killing 27 men. The crew, including the 22 men trapped in the 1st compartment, fought valiantly to stem the flooding of the adjacent compartments, whilst the Commanding Officer steered towards shallower water and ran his boat aground.

Over the following days salvage pontoons were secured around the crippled boat and she was towed in to a dry dock in Leningrad. Due to the extensive damage, the boat was subsequently paid off and scrapped.

Eight years later, on 21 October 1981, the Project 613V ('Whiskey I'-class) *S-178* sank after a collision off Vladivostok.

The diesel-powered boat was heading back to port after a short training cruise, travelling on the surface at a speed of about 9-knots. Visibility was good, with a slight 2 foot swell running.

In order to advance the boat's ETA, permission was given to alter course through Golden Horn Bay. However, the maritime authorities ashore had also directed the merchant ship *Refrigerator-13* through this same channel. At 1930, the crew of the *Refrigerator-13* spotted what was thought to be the lights of a trawler against the background illuminations ashore. On board *S-178*, the bridge lookout reported the sighting of the merchantman but assumed that the submarine had right of way. At the last minute the Commanding Officer, Captain 3rd Rank V.A. Marango, ordered hard-a-starboard, but too late to avoid the collision. At 1945 the *Refrigerator-13* struck the *S-178*'s port side in the vicinity of the 6th compartment and rolled her over to starboard, throwing the eleven personnel on the bridge into the sea. For ease of access, most of the boat's watertight doors had been left open and so she rapidly flooded, sinking in about 40 seconds to the bottom 31-metres below. Eighteen crewmen were killed as the 6th, 5th and 4th compartments flooded, whilst four more trapped in the 7th compartment drowned when their efforts to evacuate through the escape hatch or the torpedo tubes failed. As water continued to flood into the 3rd compartment - the control room - the 26 other survivors mustered in the two forward compartments.

Meanwhile, having rescued seven submariners from the freezing water, *Refrigerator-13* raised the alarm and a massive rescue operation was soon launched. By 2200 the first rescue vessels were on scene. At 0845 the following morning the Project 940 ('India'-class) rescue submarine *BS-486 Komsomolets Uhzbekistana* began the first of several deployments of her special Deep Submergence Rescue Vehicles (DSRVs), but due to the sunken boat's heavy list to starboard, attempts to dock failed. In the early hours of 23 October, divers began efforts to rescue the trapped men, but by that evening, the conditions within *S-178* were becoming intolerable and the

survivors decided to carry out a free-ascent escape to the surface using ISP-60 sets. Although they all successfully evacuated by 2030, three were swept away in the darkness, whilst another two died later, bringing the death toll to 31.

Work to salvage the boat and recover bodies continued over the following weeks and the submarine was finally raised on 15 November, towed to a dry dock and later scrapped. The subsequent inquiry found both Captain Marango and the master of the *Refrigerator-13* guilty of negligent manslaughter.

In a collision that mirrored that involved by the *Truculent* and the *Divina*, the Peruvian submarine *BAP Pacocha* (S48) was sunk after being struck by a Japanese fishing vessel four miles west of Callao on Friday, 26 August 1988.

The *Pacocha* was returning to Callao after a torpedo exercise, but when the *Kiowa Maru* was first sighted her brightly lit structure made it difficult for *Pacocha*'s lookout to determine the fishing boat's course. Believing that they had the right of way, the submarine maintained her course and speed. However, it is evident that the crew of the 412-ton tuna boat did not see the submarine and, despite last-minute manoeuvres by the *Pacocha*, the *Kiowa Maru*'s ice-breaking bow slammed into her at 1850, puncturing the boat's pressure hull port side aft. Unaware of what she had hit, the *Kiowa Maru* initially stopped, but when nothing was spotted, continued on to port.

As the *Pacocha* began to sink, water flooded into the boat through the breached hull, bridge, forward and after escape hatches and then the main induction valve. Within about five minutes the boat sank, but not before 23 crewmen had managed to scramble out of the open hatches. A further three had been killed in the collision, whilst the Commanding Officer, Commander Daniel Nieva Rodriguez, had died whilst attempting the close the bridge hatch.

Within the sinking boat, the survivors

gathered in the forward torpedo room, where luckily the senior officer present, Lieutenant Cotrina, managed to close the forward torpedo room escape hatch.

*Pacocha*'s 1900 ETA at Callao passed without any great concern, until reports were received that the *Kiowa Maru* may have hit another vessel. At 2000 a full-scale search was instigated. Within an hour of the alarm being raised, the tug *Jennifer II* and a flotilla of small boats had arrived on the scene three miles from the port and spotted a red distress flare fired from the stricken boat. Another flare released from *Pacocha* at 2120 illuminated the boat's emergency buoy, which had been released by the trapped men 140 feet below. By 2240, twenty survivors and three bodies had been recovered from the cold water.

During the night, divers located the sunken submarine and established communications with the trapped men by tapping on the hull. Later notes were passed to divers through the boat's signal ejector. As the Peruvian Navy possessed no effective submarine rescue capabilities, urgent assistance was requested from the U.S. Navy, who immediately despatched rescue and medical teams and a McCann rescue system.

Within the boat, Lt Cotrina knew that any chance of rescue would depend on the speed with which the U.S. Navy could provide assistance and so he arranged training in the use of the Steinke Hood in preparation for escape. Investigations into the flooding boundaries revealed that the boat was flooded as far forward as the main control room.

Despite constant re-generation of the air within the boat using lithium hydroxide canisters, by mid-morning on Saturday the atmosphere was affecting the survivors, pressure was rising and there was only a failing battle lantern for light. Lt. Cotrina therefore decided to organise his men for a buoyant escape to the surface. Although an air connection was attached to the boat and began pumping fresh air in, the decision was made to go ahead with the escape, the first group entering the escape trunk at 1130. By 1800, all 22 men had reached the surface, but poor training in the use of the Steinke Hood and in escape from such a depth resulted in twenty of them suffering from cerebral embolisms and requiring recompression treatment ashore. One of the escapees ultimately died, bringing the death toll to eight, whilst another was left with severe brain damage. The prompt arrival of rescue forces (albeit ill-equipped to deal with such an incident) and the decision to escape from the stricken submarine before the condition of the survivors deteriorated to a point where they would be too weak to escape, where all factors which kept the death toll to a minimum. However, whether waiting another 24 hours or so for the arrival of the U.S. Navy rescue chamber would have reduced the casualty toll further will never be known. Nevertheless, the incident forced the Peruvian Navy to review their submarine escape training.

The wreck of the *Pacocha* was later salvaged and was subsequently cannibalised for spares to keep her sister, the 44-year-old ex-US GUPPY-IA boat *BAP La Pedrera* (S49), operational.

The formation of fog clouds along rivers and coastal areas can constitute a significant additional hazard to mariners by reducing visibility to a level whereby other vessels and static obstacles may not be seen until it is too late to avoid a grounding incident or a collision. Fog is formed by the passing of warm, moist air over a cold surface - such as water - causing the air to cool to the point where the moisture held in suspension in the air is allowed to condense. The tiny water droplets released form a cloud of mist near ground level. These fog clouds are graded by weathermen by the distance to which visibility is restricted: 'fog' reducing visibility to less than one kilometre; 'thick fog' to under 200 metres; and 'dense fog' to below 50 metres.

When vessels find themselves engulfed in a fog cloud, or bank, the crew have several options to ensure the safety of their vessel. Firstly, the vessel's speed should be reduced to that which would permit it to stop within a safe distance in order to avoid a collision, whilst maintaining standby engines in a condition whereby they may be started immediately to provide additional propulsive power at short notice.

Additional lookouts may have to be closed up to supplement fitted navigational aids such as radar, so that any hazards may be detected in ample time to allow early alterations of course or speed to avoid them. Finally, each vessel should use their fog horns, and listen out for those of other vessels, in accordance with '*The International Regulations For Preventing Collisions At Sea*'. If these simple rules are obeyed, then there is little additional danger of collision, but when ignored, disaster may befall not only the perpetrator, but often the crew of an innocent vessel.

Canada's worst peacetime naval disaster - in terms of loss of life - occurred on 16 July 1947, when the recently commissioned Tribal-class destroyer *HMCS Micmac* (R10) was involved in a collision in fog with the merchantman *ss Yarmouth County* near Halifax, Nova Scotia. The destroyer's forward section was almost entirely wrecked as far aft as 'B' gun and bent over to starboard at an obscene angle, whilst 'A' turret was completely uprooted and reduced to a mangled mass of twisted metal. Several crewmen, who had been in the forward messdeck at the time of the collision were killed outright and many others were badly injured.

Just before the collision, *Micmac* had been proceeding at full power, but had slowed considerably on entering a bank of thick fog. The 10,000-ton *Yarmouth County*, which had not been detected because of the forward blind spot of the Type 293 radar, suddenly loomed out of the fog shortly afterwards, too late for *Micmac*'s OOW to avoid the collision.

Despite very extensive damage, *Micmac* underwent a prolonged repair period, during which she was partially converted to a destroyer-escort, returning to service almost three years later. She went on to serve until 1963, when she was paid off, finally being broken up at Faslane, Scotland, from October 1964.

Far more tragic, however, was the loss of a US Navy hospital ship a few years later. The six-year-old 11,800-ton steamship *Benevolence* was one of a number of merchant vessels converted to hospital ships for service with the US War Department in the late-1940s. On 25 August 1950, *USNS Benevolence* (AH-13) was carrying out post-conversion acceptance trials San Francisco Bay, prior to assignment to the Military Sea Transportation Service. As the ship was transiting near Golden Gate Bridge, she was involved in a collision with the steamship *Mary Luckenback*. The hospital ship sank in a matter of minutes with the loss of 23 lives as the fog, which had reduced visibility at the time of the collision, hampered rescue attempts.

Even when a local pilot is embarked, the convergence of shipping channels where a river or estuary narrows, coupled with the incapacitating effects of fog, can result in a dangerous situation developing should the vessel be even marginally off course.

Henry Robb Ltd. of Leith had completed the naval tug *Reward* in October 1945 as one of four Bustler-class vessels. In 1975 she was taken out of reserve and refitted at Chatham. Rearmed with a 40mm gun forward, *HMS Reward* (A264) re-commissioned in July 1976 as a North Sea oil rig patrol vessel. In her short Naval career she was well-loved by those who served in her, until, on the night of Monday, 10 August 1976, she was involved in a collision in the Firth of Forth and sank.

On the morning of the accident, *Reward* had sailed from Rosyth with a Royal Navy film crew on board. She returned up the Forth that evening in dense fog and as she passed below the railway bridge the crew could hear the starlings chirping away beneath the bridge structure. Seamen on the fo'c'sle were making ready to break the anchor in preparation to secure to No.10 buoy, close to Rosyth Naval Base. When a lookout on the starboard bridge wing suddenly spotted a large shadow through the fog, he assumed that it was the bridge's north pillar, but he was horrified when, a few seconds later, the bow of a ship loomed out of the mist.

On the bridge, the Commanding Officer, Lieutenant Commander R. J. Sandford, ordered engines to be stopped, immediately followed by full ahead and wheel hard to starboard. Too late, the German container ship *Plainsman*, outward bound from Grangemouth, struck the patrol ship in the starboard side amidships in the vicinity of the engine room. The time was approximately 1912.

The response of the German ship, with a local pilot on board, was to order full astern. Lucky, Lt.Cdr. Sandford managed to contact the bridge crew of the *Plainsman* by portable stornophone on Channel 16, telling them to maintain headway forward. This undoubtedly saved many lives on *Reward*, as had the container ship gone astern and thereby ceased to plug the gaping hole in the patrol ship's side with her bows, *Reward* would have sank immediately.

Within minutes, the water level was lapping over the tow deck and *Reward* had begun to heel, so the order was given to abandon ship. Headropes from *Plainsman* were passed over the bow and these, together with aluminium ladders from *Reward*, allowed the crew of four officers, 36 ratings and two passengers to safely evacuate the sinking vessel, the last two to leave being the Bosun and the Navigating Officer. During this evacuation, a young steward went into automatic mode, running fire-fighting hoses along the upper deck - despite the fact that there was no fire! Nevertheless,

*The patrol ship HMS Reward during salvage operations. The ship had sunk following a collision in the Firth of Forth on 8 August 1976. A huge gash in Reward's hull can be clearly seen.*
*(B. Brearley)*

as the vessel had no internal tannoy system, he would have had no way of knowing this, and had just acted on his own instinct and naval training.

As soon as the two vessels parted, *Reward* began to sink as the engine room and the large after hold rapidly flooded. Within ten minutes she had disappeared stern first beneath the surface, bows rising at an acute angle as she sank in 30 metres of water at position 56°02'N, 03°24'W.

The minehunter *HMS Nurton* (M1166), following *Reward* up the Forth estuary, noticed that she had disappeared from radar. On reaching the scene of the disaster she located the wreck of *Reward* with her sonar and laid a short scope danbuoy to mark the spot, then anchored nearby. The fog was so dense that even *Nurton*'s 10-inch signal lantern failed to penetrate it for any distance. Immediately afterwards, that area of the Firth of Forth was closed to all shipping.

*Plainsman* anchored off nearby Inchkeith Island, whilst the duty tug, *RMAS Cairn* (A126), was despatched from Rosyth to evacuate the crew of the *Reward* to the shore base *HMS Cochrane*. During the entire ordeal, the Royal Navy crew had reacted calmly and professionally and the only casualty was one stoker with a burnt wrist. In fact, the only personnel to even get their feet wet were the last ones to leave the sinking vessel's rapidly flooding engine room.

The German ship sustained only slight damage, and at around 0145 the following morning quietly slipped anchor and continued her voyage to Rotterdam, where she arrived safely at 0800 on 12 August. A survey of her damage later revealed the forecastle plating to be heavily buckled and two large gashes 2-3 metres in length in the shell plating in way of the forepeak tank, damage that was later repaired at the Rotterdam and Schiedam shipyard.

Before the collision, the 7,000-ton *Plainsman* had been heading out of the Forth with a 690-tonne cargo, 70% of which consisted of whisky. It appears she had been slightly off course and unaware of her true position and had been heading down the Rosyth Naval Base 'fairway'. It is probable that, had she not struck *HMS Reward*, she would have eventually run aground at South Queensferry - with the prospect of the local inhabitants being the subject of another 'Whisky Galore' type scenario!

The subsequent Court of Inquiry resulted in a court martial, in which the Commanding Officer of *HMS Reward*, Lt.Cdr. R.J. Sandford, RN, was totally cleared of any charges of negligence.

As a direct result of this incident, no more than one vessel is now allowed in the channel between the Forth road and railway bridges at a time, outbound traffic having the right of way. The maximum speed allowed is 10 knots to the west of the bridges and 12 knots to the east, whilst the flow of shipping is controlled by Forth Navigation, whom it is compulsory to contact on radio Channel 71 on nearing the bridges from either direction.

As the wreck of the *Reward* was blocking a major commercial shipping channel, a salvage operation had to be undertaken with some urgency. The following morning, a diving survey revealed that *Reward* was lying upright with a slight list to starboard, with a large hole in her starboard side and the stern settled some 12 feet into the mud. Preparations proceeded at a feverish pace over the next two weeks until, on 28 August, the 1,600-ton wreck was raised by the floating heavy lift shear-legs *R.B. Brunel* - named after the famous engineer - with assistance from the salvage vessels *RMASs Goosander* (A164) and *Layburn* (P191), and beached nearby off St. David's harbour the following morning. Following a structural survey and patching of the gaping wound in her hull, *Reward* was paid off for disposal and towed for scrapping to the nearby shipbreakers James White & Co. Ltd, St. David's Harbour.

Collisions in open waters between warships and merchant vessels are, more often then not, the result of the different attitudes regarding ship navigation of naval and civilian mariners. Merchantmen plying their trade normally proceed between two points in a direct line, at a constant speed - often with the

*The stern section of the French destroyer FS Surcouf at Cartagena. The ship's forward section sank after a collision with a Russian tanker on 6 June 1971.*

*(Service Historique de la Defense/Departement Marine)*

assistance of autopilot - observing the '*International Rules of the Road*' to maintain their distance from other vessels.

Warships on the other hand, use the transit times between points to exercise their crews in battle scenarios, whilst time on station is spent patrolling a designated area and investigating other vessels, for whatever reason.

When a collision occurs between vessels of these two different breeds, fault is usually with either the merchant vessel for sticking staunchly to the regulations - despite the risk of collision - or with the naval vessel for manoeuvring across the track of a large lumbering merchantman, or in some cases, a combination of the two. A naval escort that gets in the way of

one of these mercantile leviathans will inevitably bare the brunt of the damage - and the casualties.

On 14 November 1952, five crewmen were killed and a further 29 injured aboard the amphibious transport ship *USS Ruchamkin* (APD-89) when she was rammed by the tanker *Washington* in the Atlantic. Seven embarked troops were also killed and a huge 20-foot hole was ripped in the transport's side in the collision 60 miles east of Cape Henry. Despite the extensive damage, *Ruchamkin* was later repaired and returned to service.

Another vessel that strayed across the path of a tanker fared even worse. The French Type T47 destroyer *FS Surcouf* (D621), had been built by the Lorient Naval Dockyard between 1951 and 1954, with a superstructure constructed largely of aluminium and other light alloys, and her hull entirely welded. Following her commissioning on 1 November 1955 she served initially in the Mediterranean, transferring to Brest after her refit in 1959. A second refit, completing in 1964, saw her forward twin 57mm gun mounting moved to 'A' position and her superstructure extended forward, providing space for additional communications compartments for the ship's new role as a command ship. It was in this guise that, after her third refit in 1969, the *Surcouf* once again served in the western Mediterranean as flagship of Admiral Daille.

Her new role was to be short-lived as, on 6 June 1971, *Surcouf* was involved in a terrible collision with the Russian tanker *General Boukharov*, which struck the destroyer in the vicinity of the forward boiler room. Soon afterwards, the destroyer snapped in two and the entire section forward of frame 62 rapidly sank, taking with it ten of *Surcouf*'s crew. The after section stayed afloat and was later towed to the Spanish naval base at Cartegena, 60 miles away, by the French destroyer *FS Tartu* (D636). After temporary repairs to make the stern section watertight, it was towed to Toulon, where it was utilised to provide spares for other ships of the class, the wreck being officially paid off on 1 August 1971.

A subsequent Court of Enquiry determined that blame for the collision rested with the crew of the *Surcouf*, who had placed their vessel in extremis by cutting across the tanker's bow in an area of heavy shipping traffic. The tanker had right of way at the time and so her crew were exonerated.

A similar act by the crew of a destroyer resulted in the Royal Navy's worst accident of the 1980s. On 4 September 1988, the Type 42 destroyer *HMS Southampton* (D90) was operating as part of the Royal Navy's Armilla Patrol, escorting merchant ships through the Straits of Hormuz in to the Gulf to ensure their safe passage from marauding Iranian gunboats. At about 2100 that night, whilst patrolling an area 70km north of the east coast of the United Arab Emirates, the *Southampton* was involved in a collision

with the British container ship *Tor Bay*. The destroyer had attempted to cut across the track of the container ship, but the bridge staff had misjudged the distances and the speed of the merchant ship.

The 33,000-ton *Tor Bay* struck the destroyer's port side, between the Sea Dart missile launcher and the bridge, the port side of the bridge being crushed as the container ship's bulbous bow penetrated the hull as far as the keel. Several compartments were immediately flooded through the cavernous hole - extending from the main weather deck to below the waterline - including the magazines containing ammunition for the 4.5-inch gun and Sea Dart missiles. Miraculously, no-one was killed or seriously injured in the collision and the damage control parties, acting on their own initiatives due to the loss of communications throughout the ship, quickly contained the flooding. Furthermore, in comparison to the 1987 *USS Stark* incident (see Chapter 8), the high pressure salt water system was

*The badly damaged Royal Navy destroyer HMS Southampton returns to Portsmouth aboard the heavy lift ship Mighty Servant I.*
*(Source??)*

quickly isolated, preventing this water from adding serious stability problems to the already precarious position.

The badly damaged ship, down by the bow and listing heavily to port, was later towed to the port of Fujairah, where emergency repairs were carried out, including plating over of the gaping wound, the removal of the 4.5-inch gun mount and the Sea Dart launcher, and disembarkation of the crushed contents of the main magazines. Three months later, *Southampton* was returned to Portsmouth aboard the Dutch heavy lift vessel (HLV) *Mighty Servant I*, where the HLV was partially submerged in the Solent to allow the destroyer to re-float and tugs towed her into the naval base.

Detailed surveys of the vessel's damage were then carried out before her fate could be decided, an option which was speculated to include scrapping as a constructive total loss. The ship had been scheduled to begin a major refit in August 1989 and so it was decided that this work would be advanced to incorporate the necessary structural repairs. Repair and refit work, costing an estimated £45 million, was carried out at the Swan Hunter shipyard from August 1989 till May 1991, although it was another year before she rejoined the active fleet, having completed all weapons updates and trials.

Following a prolonged Court of Inquiry, a court-martial was held and the Commanding Officer, Captain Stephen Taylor, was reprimanded for hazarding his ship by negligence. It was claimed that the Captain had been in his cabin at the time of the collision and had left an inexperienced officer, who had never carried out a night rendezvous with a ship, in charge of the bridge. The OOW at the time of the collision was also severely reprimanded. The Portsmouth court martial was also informed that this was Captain Taylor's second reprimand for hazarding a ship. In 1971, the minesweeper he commanded, *HMS*

*Belton*, was scrapped after it was stranded at Loch Maddy in the Western Isles.

Immediate, energetic and efficient damage control actions by the ship's crew undoubtedly saved *Southampton* and can only serve to re-enforce the value of realistic damage control training, such as that carried out regularly by the crews of all Royal Navy ships at the Damage Repair Instruction Units at Portsmouth and Plymouth, together with a complementary and comprehensive series of sea-based training exercises.

Several other escorts have suffered damage, of the extent of that inflicted on *HMS Southampton*, in recent years. These include: the Brazilian destroyer *Sergipe* (D35), which required eight months of repairs following a collision with a merchant ship in November 1984; the ill-starred Nigerian MEKO 360-H frigate *NNS Aradu* (F89), which suffered serious damage in two groundings and a major collision in 1987; and the new Bangladeshi frigate *BNS Osman* (F18), seriously damaged in a collision with a merchant ship in August 1991 and subsequently under repair throughout 1992 and 1993. Fortunately though, none of these incidents have been as catastrophic as the destruction of the *Surcouf*. That said, naval vessels do not always come off worst in such incidents. For example, on 21 June 1979, the German merchant tanker *Tarpanbek* sank off the Isle of Wight after a collision with the British landing ship *RFA Sir Geraint* (L3037).

Nearly two years later, on 9 April 1981, the ballistic-missile armed submarine *USS George Washington* (SSBN-598) was operating at shallow depth in the East China Sea, 100 miles south-west of Sasebo, Japan, when she collided with the 2,350-ton Japanese merchantman *Nisho Maru*. Although the ship had been detected a few minutes earlier, it was too late to avoid the ensuing catastrophe. When the submarine surfaced to render assistance, the *Nisho Maru* was nowhere to be seen. Visibility was poor due to fog and driving rain, and the submarine later resumed her patrol, having radioed a report of the incident ashore and requesting a search aircraft. The crew of the *George Washington* were unaware that the *Nisho Maru* had sunk, with the loss of two of her 15-man crew. A Japanese destroyer rescued the survivors 18 hours later. Damage to the submarine was superficial, a small area of the conning tower suffering some grazing and denting.

The resultant enquiry by the US Navy found the Captain of *USS George Washington* to blame for the incident due to lack of command supervision and sound judgement, and duly relieved him of his command. An apology was extended to Japan.

One of the more emotive issues of recent years - which deserves a brief mention here - is that regarding the few highly-publicised instances of fishing boat sinkings by submerged submarines. On 23 July 1988, the Japanese Yuushio-class submarine *Nadashio* (SS577) collided with a fishing boat, which quickly sank with the loss of the thirty souls aboard. The incident brought widespread condemnation on the operation of submarines in coastal waters and the ensuing row led to the resignation of the Director-General of the Japanese Defence Agency. In response, the Japanese Maritime Self Defence Force stated that, along with the instigation of safer operating practices in areas where fishing craft were suspected of operating, all Japanese submarines and minesweepers would, in future, be equipped with portable telephone systems which will enable two-way communication between ships and shore and thereby allow closer liaison between fishing vessels and submarines.

The Royal Navy was also forced to review its submarine operations following an accident in the Firth of Clyde on Thursday, 22 November 1990. The nuclear submarine *HMS Trenchant* (S91) was exercising off Arran when she became entangled in the nets of the Carradale-based fishing vessel *Antares*, which was then dragged beneath the waves by the submarine, along with her four-man crew. The sinking sparked a storm which intensified when it was revealed that the submarine had been in the command of a trainee commanding officer and a subsequent enquiry resulted in a 'reprimand' for the OOW at the time of the collision. The Royal Navy later raised the *Antares* from her watery grave on the seabed, 400 feet down.

Following public outcry at this incident the Royal Navy agreed to a package of safety measures, including a reduction of 30% in submarine operations in the Clyde area. In mid-1992 a contract was awarded to Graseby Dynamics to provide 100 acoustic transducers for issue to fishermen. In an 18-month trial beginning in early 1993, these items were fitted to trawler nets to alert submarines of their presence. The Royal Navy also agreed to issue twice daily briefs to local shipping authorities concerning the movements of submarines in the Clyde area.

Further incidents have continued to occur. On 11 February 1998, *USS La Jolla* (SSN-701) collided with and sank the South Korean fishing boat *Yong Chang* 11km off the coast of the republic. The nuclear-powered submarine was not damaged and all five of the fishing vessel's crew were rescued. A more serious accident involving one of *La Jolla*'s sister-boats occurred on the afternoon of 9 February 2001. *USS Greeneville* (SSN-772) was hosting a sea day for distinguished visitors and was conducting a demonstration emergency main ballast tank blow exercise, during which a submarine shoots to the surface. As the submarine broke surface, her rudder struck the Japanese fishing training vessel *Ehime Maru*, which sank 10 minutes later with the loss of 9 men and teenage boys of the 35 aboard. Widespread condemnation of the incident was intensified when it was revealed that a civilian was at the controls of the submarine during the emergency surface evolution. At the subsequent Court of Inquiry, *Greeneville's* Commanding Officer, Commander Scott Waddle, was found guilty of dereliction of duty and hazarding a vessel and was forced to retire from the US Navy.

These are probably the most serious incidents of their kind in recent years, but cases of submerged submarines being caught within the nets of fishing craft is not a new phenomenon, with probably hundreds of recorded incidents world-wide over the past fifty years. Whilst the *Nadashio*, the *Trenchant* and the *Greeneville* were clearly at fault in their individual cases, the masters of fishing craft have also been known to cast their nets in areas specifically designated on charts as naval exercise areas. Others fail to monitor their VHF radios or respond to radio or signals, and some are poorly maintained with inadequate sea survival equipment. Whilst a submarine commander may utilise all of his boat's sensors and take the utmost care to avoid a trawler, its nets - being hauled several hundred yards astern of the craft - may ultimately go unnoticed until the heart-wrenching sound of scraping wire along the boat's hull is heard. By then of course, it is too late to avoid a dangerous incident and so, whilst such occurrences are regrettable, they are nonetheless inevitable as long as these two types of craft wish to use the same stretches of water.

Whilst there can be some mitigation for collisions in confined or congested waters, collisions between naval vessels in transit on the open sea can only be attributed to negligence on the part of the bridge crews of the ships involved. Such occurrences have resulted in several escort vessels being written off as constructive total losses.

On 19 July 1960, the Fletcher-class destroyer *USS Ammen* (DD-527) was in transit from Seal Beach to San Diego for decommissioning when she was rammed by *USS Collett* (DD-730). A large hole was opened up in *Ammen*'s port side, resulting in extensive flooding of her engine room. Eleven of *Ammen*'s crew were killed and a further 20 injured in the collision. The badly listing *Ammen* was towed to Long Beach and later to San Diego, where she was decommissioned on 15 September and sold for scrapping on 20 April 1961 to National Metal and Steel Corporation. *Collett*'s badly damaged bow was later replaced with that of the partially completed *USS Seaman* (DD-791) at Long Beach, California.

The Crosley-class amphibious transport ship *USS Walter B. Cobb* (APD-106) was transferred, along with her near-sister *USS Gantner* (APD-42), to the Taiwanese Navy in 1966. However, the ex-*USS Cobb* never reached her new owners as, during the delivery voyage, she was involved in a collision with the ex-*Gantner* off Point Sur, California. Despite desperate attempts to keep her afloat, she finally foundered four days later, on 21 April 1966. Ex-*USS Gantner* reached Taiwan safely and became *Wen Shan* (834), serving until the early 1990s.

A high proportion of collisions involving warships occur during naval exercises. During these periods, ships are routinely required to manoeuvre in close formations, normally at high speed and often at night with ships blacked out with few, if any, lights showing. Such high-speed manoeuvres will inevitably reduce the time available to react to a dangerous situation and will therefore increase the risk of collision, whilst the damage resulting from such an incident may be infinitely more extensive because of the higher speeds involved.

Such naval exercises are, however,

imperative if a navy is to be able to perform efficiently and effectively in a combat situation, but the advantages of highly trained crews and the use of sophisticated radar equipment reduces the risk of collision during close formation manoeuvres to a minimum. Nevertheless, as with any high-risk scenario, safety is directly proportional to those personnel participating in it. When concentration or diligence wanes, it is inevitable that, sooner or later, a catastrophe will occur.

One of the most hazardous tasks that have to be performed routinely by destroyers is that of plane guard to an aircraft carrier, especially at night. Tragically, since the Second World War, three destroyers have been lost by collision, with horrific loss of life, whilst performing this duty.

During night exercises 700 north-west of the Azores on 26 April 1952, the Bristol-class destroyer *USS Hobson* (DMS-26) was involved in a collision with the 38,000-ton aircraft carrier *USS Wasp* (CV-18) and sank with the loss of 176 of her crew, making this the worst US naval accident since the war.

En-route to the Mediterranean to join the US Sixth Fleet, the *Wasp*, with the two destroyer-minesweepers *US Ships Hobson* and *Rodman* (DMS-21) acting as her plane guards, was carrying out flying operations against the rest of Task Group 88.1, situated about fifty miles to the south. All three ships were operating in 'Lighting Measure Green', a darkened state, for the duration of the exercise, with only two red aircraft warning lights at the mastheads. These lights were clearly visible to all ships despite the lack of moonlight, as the night was clear, with visibility of about ten miles. Winds were light, 7-10 knots, and the sea was calm.

At just after 2000 on that fateful evening, *Wasp* launched a flight of ten aircraft for a night attack against the task group and from then until 2210 the trio of ships steamed at 25 knots on a parallel course of 102°. From the *Hobson's* position on plane guard station number two, the carrier could be seen off the destroyer's port side at a distance of 3,000 yards, on a bearing of 065° true.

*Rodman* was positioned 1,200 yards off the carrier's port bow in plane guard station number one. The commanding officer of the *Wasp*, Captain Burnham C. McCaffree, USN, ordered the following message to be signalled to the destroyers: "FOX CORPEN 265 BACKLINE FOX SPEED 27", which instructed them to prepare to turn into the wind to an aircraft recovery course of 265° and to increase speed to 27 knots, a message which was acknowledged by both escorts. This manoeuvre required a simple change of course to starboard for *Wasp* and *Rodman*, but *Hobson* was also to change her position relative to the carrier to night plane guard recovery station two, on the *Wasp's* port beam on a bearing of 270-280° true, 1,000 yards from her.

On the bridge of the *Hobson*, the OOD, Lieutenant William A. Hoefer, Jr., USNR, discussed the manoeuvre with the Commanding Officer, Lieutenant-Commander William J. Tierney, USN. The OOD suggested a simple turn to starboard and a reduction in speed to 15 knots to fall into position. However, he was overridden by Lt.Cdr. Tierney, who recommended a course change to 130° and, when *Wasp* bore about 010° true, turn to port to take up the recovery position. When the OOD expressed his misgivings as to the safety of such a manoeuvre, the Commanding Officer took over the 'conn' of the ship. Consequently, when the signal "TURN 260 TACKLINE SPEED 27" - ordering the ships to execute a course change to 260° (instead of the previously ordered 265°) - was passed by the carrier at 2221, *Hobson* altered course to 130°, whilst *Wasp* began her long wide turn to starboard, using 'standard rudder', at an average speed of 22.5 knots.

Two minutes later, Lt.Cdr. Tierney

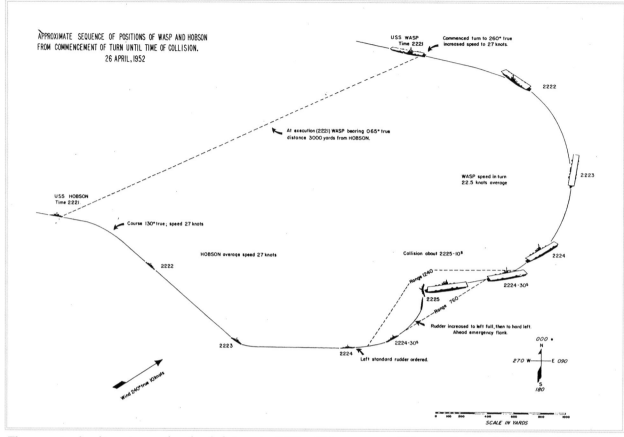

APPROXIMATE SEQUENCE OF POSITIONS OF WASP AND HOBSON
FROM COMMENCEMENT OF TURN UNTIL TIME OF COLLISION.
26 APRIL, 1952

*The events leading to the collision between USS Wasp and USS Hobson on 26 April 1952.*

*(US Naval Institute)*

ordered a left turn to 090°. This course was maintained until, about a minute later and well before the carrier bore 010°, he ordered "*left standard rudder*". At the time of this inexplicable turn, range between the two ships was only about 1,240 yards. The turn was viewed with concern by the CIC officer on watch, who called to the bridge through the voice pipe "*What the hell is going on?*", to which the OOD answered that the Captain had the 'conn'. As the range reduced to 700 yards it became obvious aboard *Hobson* that they were crossing the bow of the carrier, and, in an attempt to extricate his ship from an extremely dangerous position, the Commanding Officer ordered the rudder angle increased to "*left full*", followed by "*hard left, all engines ahead emergency flank*". The Commanding Officer of *Wasp* had just ordered a course change to 250° when the OOD noted the left turn of the

*Hobson*. Captain McCaffree immediately assumed the 'conn' and ordered all engines "*back emergency full*". As the seconds ticked away, *Wasp's* speed reduced slightly to about 22 knots, but not enough to avoid the inevitable collision, and at 2225 her bow crashed into the destroyer's starboard side, just aft of amidships at about frame 123, pushing the smaller ship sideways for several hundred yards until both vessels ground to a halt.

The impact was such that *Wasp's* bow penetrated two-thirds of the way into the destroyer's 36 feet beam and snapped her in two. *Hobson's* stern section sank immediately, while the forward section swung round against the starboard side of *Wasp's* bow as the ships came to a stop. Searchlights were switched on immediately aboard the carrier and several life rafts, life jackets and other flotation gear, as well as eight of *Wasp's* water. Four minutes after the impact, *Hobson*'s forward section also disappeared stern-first beneath the water's surface, sinking to the seabed 2,700 fathoms below. A large section of the carrier's bow had disappeared, from about 3-4 metres above the waterline.

*Rodman* closed the scene expeditiously and another three destroyers - *US Ships Corry* (DD-817), *Stribling* (DD-867) and *O'Hare* (DD-889) - were despatched from the task group, arriving at 0015. At this point *Wasp*, *Rodman* and *Corry* were temporarily released from the rescue operation in order that the carrier could recover her aircraft, which were now very low on fuel. All five ships continued their intensive search until 0730 the following morning, by which time any chance of finding any further survivors was considered negligible. Despite the speed and intensity of the rescue operation, only 61 of *Hobson*'s crew of 237 survived, forty of who required hospitalisation. Her Commanding Officer, who had been seen jumping from *Hobson*'s port bridge wing after the collision, was among those lost. Only one body, that of a young enlisted man, was recovered, the rest of the crew going down with their ship in position 42°21'N, 44°15'W.

At daylight, the destroyer's propeller shaft could be seen protruding obscenely from the mangled wreckage of the carrier's bow. Swift damage-control action aboard *Wasp* had limited flooding to a relatively few sections and she safely reached Gravesend Bay, New Jersey, on 6 May. Repair of her damaged bow cost a little over US$1 million.

The Court of Inquiry into the incident found that sole blame for the tragic loss of *USS Hobson* was deemed to have lain with Lt.Cdr. Tierney, whose dereliction of duty was the sole cause of the collision. Although the opinion of the Court of Inquiry was that Captain McCaffree and the *Wasp*'s OOD, Lieutenant R.B. Herbst, were themselves negligent in that they

failed to avoid the collision, this was later overruled by the President of the Court, Rear Admiral O.B. Hardison, USN, who judged that both officers had taken prompt action as soon as possible after *Hobson*'s inexplicable left turn was realised and that *Hobson*'s final turn was detected and the danger recognised by them promptly and as soon as could be expected. In fact, Captain McCaffree was later praised for his seamanship in the execution of the search and rescue operation, in his actions to recover his aircraft safely in low wind conditions with his ship's mangled bow and later bringing his damaged ship safely into port.

There were three possible explanations for Lt.Cdr. Tierney's fatal left turn order. Firstly, he may have become confused as to the overall tactical picture, mistakenly believing that there was room for the manoeuvre. Secondly, he may have ordered "*left rudder*" when he meant instead to have ordered "*right rudder*", only becoming aware of his mistake when his ship swung to port, and that he instead decided to attempt to accelerate out of danger. Finally, he may have mistakenly judged his position to be on the carrier's

*A single propeller shaft protruding from the bow of USS Wasp was all that remained of USS Hobson, following their collision on 26 April 1952.*

*(US Naval Institute)*

judged his position to be on the carrier's starboard bow, when he was in fact on the port bow, and turned left to avoid crossing ahead of the carrier. Lt. Hoefer testified that, in the minutes before the collision, radar ranges between the two ships were regularly passed to the bridge by the CIC and that the Lt.Cdr. Tierney took frequent visual bearing on the *Wasp*.

It was estimated that, had *Hobson* not made that fatal turn, then the closest point of approach of the two vessels would have been about 800 yards. The alternative manoeuvre suggested before the evolution by the OOD would have been the safer course, especially as *Hobson*, with two boilers on line had a maximum available speed of 28.5 knots, leaving a very small reserve of speed. However, as Lt.Cdr. Tierney was not among the survivors and Lt. Hoefer could not explain his Commanding Officer's actions, the true reason for that fatal final manoeuvre will never be known.

In the opinion of the Court, Lt.Cdr. Tierney had been in violation of several articles of the '*International Rules of the Road*', as well as US Navy Regulations, two articles of which were especially pertinent. Article 924 of the publication 'USF 4' directed that "*station units required to perform an evolution within a formation, or when changing from one formation to another in obedience to a manoeuvring signal will avoid courses which cross ahead of other ships,*" and states that "*turns should be made away rather than towards other ships.*"

Furthermore Article 478 of 'USF 2' directed that "*smaller more manoeuvrable ships shall avoid hampering the movements of large ships within a formation, and that particularly they should not attempt to cross the bow of a*

*HMAS Voyager was sliced in two by HMAS Melbourne during night exercises on 10 February 1964.
(Navy Photographic Unit - Sydney)*

*large ship unless ample sea room is available, the manoeuvre is required and is obviously safe for all concerned; that, if any doubt exists, it is incumbent upon the smaller vessel to cross astern; that a clear situation should not be changed into an awkward one, either through a lack of timely indication to others of the smaller ship's intent, or from an impatient haste in accomplishing the movement."*

The aforementioned aside, Lt.Cdr. Tierney had only been in command of *Hobson* for about five weeks, of which only seven days had been spent at sea. Although the manoeuvre was a standard evolution, his inexperience regarding carrier plane guard operations may have been a contributing factor. In view of this, the Court recommended that the experience and competence of the crews of ships in company be taken into account before Operational Commanders order high-speed manoeuvres, particularly during night operations. Where time permits, plane guards should also be positioned in advance of turning to the launching or recovery course, rather than during the manoeuvre. The various Fleet publications directing the movement of ships in company were also revised and aligned with each other, particularly with regard to movement orders and execution signals and renewed emphasis was to be placed on thorough familiarity of officers with these tactical publications and with the 'International Rules of the Road' prior to their qualification as OOD underway.

These final points are all the more relevant today, as more and more operations involve ships of many countries forming numerous coalitions, each with their own differing procedures, orders and experience levels, not to mention languages.

Despite the lessons of the *Hobson* tragedy, two further catastrophes, almost identical in both cause and outcome, occurred in the 1960s. Ironically, both incidents involved the same aircraft carrier - *HMAS Melbourne* (R21) - although in neither case was the crew of the 20,000-ton carrier to blame.

At the beginning of 1964, Australia's armed forces began working up in preparation for a conflict in Indonesia, which was expected to erupt by the end of the year. It was anticipated that Australia's prime contribution would consist of a task group, formed around the Navy's only aircraft carrier - *HMAS Melbourne*. *Melbourne* completed a refit in January 1964, as did the Daring-class destroyer *HMAS Voyager* (D04), which was intended to be her escort during the forthcoming operation. *Voyager's* refit had been a very rushed affair, partly due to cost and partly due to the requirement to have her ready for duties with the Strategic Reserve by early 1964. *Melbourne's* refit, on the other hand, was awarded a much higher priority and much additional work was undertaken by the Garden Island dockyard to bring her up to the required standards. Both vessels spent the month of January engaged in post-refit trials, with *Voyager* under the command of the newly-promoted Captain H. Stevens, RAN.

Captain Stevens was regarded as a highly experienced destroyer captain who was thoroughly familiar with manoeuvring in company with aircraft carriers. Both vessels had seen a major turnover amongst their officers and ratings during their refits, including a large number of new recruits, many of which had never been to sea before. This high proportion of new faces amongst the crews added considerably to the training element of the work-up periods of both ships.

*Melbourne* and *Voyager* sailed independently from Sydney on the morning of Thursday, 6 February to conduct further post-refit work-up exercises and operated together briefly the following day before anchoring overnight in Jervis Bay. Shortly after midnight,

*Voyager* was ordered to weigh anchor and proceed to sea to attempt to retrieve a drifting battle practice target and was later assisted by *Melbourne* . After the target was taken in tow by the research vessel *HMAS Kimbla* (AGOR-314), both ships again anchored in Jervis Bay on Sunday morning.

Sailing early on the morning of Monday, 10 February, *Voyager* and *Melbourne* exercised anti-aircraft operations together during the forenoon, whilst in the afternoon *Voyager* conducted an anti-submarine exercise with the British submarine *HMS Tabard* (S42).

Early evening found the two ships about 20 miles south-east of Jervis Bay, as *Melbourne* prepared to conduct a series of night flying exercises, with *Voyager* acting as her plane guard ship. It was a clear, moonless night, with visibility of about 20 miles. Sea conditions were smooth, with a slight south-easterly swell running, although the light variable winds would necessitate the carrier carrying out her flying programme at high speed and on varying courses to launch her aircraft into the wind.

Both ships were darkened, with only the minimal operational lighting showing, including port and starboard sidelights, a white stern light and mastheads lights. *Melbourne* also had her flight deck floodlit, but this would only be visible from her port side, whilst her sidelights were dimmed so that they were not visible beyond a distance of a mile. This was the first time since her refit that *Melbourne*'s flight deck was floodlit, but checks to ensure that none of the red lighting would be visible from starboard had been carried out the previous weekend by the navigator and another officer, in order to ensure that it could not be mistaken for the port side light.

At 1929, *Melbourne* signalled to Voyager: "FOXTROT CORPEN 180 TACK 20. STATION X-RAY 14 TACK 1. MIKE CORPEN 000 TACK 10", meaning "Execute to follow. Estimated course for impending aircraft operation is 180 (speed 20 knots). Take planeguard station No.1. My course is 000 (my speed is 10 knots)." This was followed at 1930 by "Stand by - Execute." On receipt of these orders, *Voyager* closed *Melbourne* from her position five miles ahead of the carrier, to assume her designated plane guard station, 20° on the port quarter of the carrier at a distance of 1,000 to 1,500 yards. The destroyer would be required to maintain this relative position on *Melbourne*'s port quarter whenever the carrier turned to a new flying course, in order to be in a position to rescue crewmen from any aircraft which may be unfortunate enough to have to ditch.

At 1950, *Melbourne* signalled to *Voyager* that they were turning to port into the wind and that speed was being increased to 25 knots. Both ships turned together to their new heading and, shortly afterwards, flying operations began on course 175° and a speed of 22 knots. The light variable wind would necessitate further minor course and speed corrections in order to provide sufficient wind over the deck for flying operations.

During the 'first' watch (2000-2359), those on *Melbourne*'s bridge consisted of: the Commanding Officer, Captain John Robertson; the Navigating Officer, Commander James Kelly; and the OOW, Sub-Lieutenant Alex Bate. This was S/Lt. Bate's first night watch as OOW on *Melbourne*, although he had gained considerable experience on his previous ship, the minesweeper *HMAS Gull* (M1185). Aboard *Voyager*, five officers were on the bridge, including Lt. David Price, RN, as OOW, the Commanding Officer, Executive Officer, Navigation Officer, and a young Acting Sub-Lieutenant, J.S. Davies. This was also Lt. Price's first experience of service aboard an Australian ship, his previous experience being aboard the minelayer *HMS Plover* (M26) and the minesweeper *HMS Fiskerton* (M1206) .

At 2030, course was altered to 190°, just as Carrier Air Group's Sea Venom aircraft arrived over the ship from Nowra Naval Air Station, ready to conduct a series of 'touch and go' exercises that entailed the aircraft making landing approaches until their wheels just touched the carrier's flight deck before accelerating away for another cycle. However, there was at this time insufficient wind over the deck to permit such operations and so, whilst *Melbourne* found a more suitable course, the exercise was delayed for ten minutes.

At 2041, *Melbourne* passed the signal "TURN 020", instructing *Voyager* that both vessels were to turn together to starboard to a new course of 020°, followed a minute later by the 'Execute' order. *Voyager* acknowledged both signals. This turn resulted in *Voyager* assuming a new position ahead and 30° to port of *Melbourne*, but as the turn was completing, Captain Robertson decided to compare the wind available on a course 060° and so, at 2047 signalled "TURN 060", meaning "Immediate execute - Turn together to 060, ships turning to starboard. I say again turn together to 060, ships turning to starboard. Stand by - Execute". However, on assuming the new course, it was decided that the wind had been more favourable on the 020° track.

Consequently, at 2053, *Melbourne* instructed *Voyage* "020 TURN", followed a minute later by the instruction "FOXTROT CORPEN 020 TACK 22" - "Estimated course for impending aircraft operations 020 (speed 22 knots). Time 2054". This was to be *Melbourne*'s final signal to *Voyager*. Darkness had enveloped the scene during the previous few minutes and all that could now be seen of *Voyager* from the bridge of the carrier were her navigation and masthead lights.

*Melbourne*'s slow turn to port changed *Voyager*'s relative bearing to a position 48° to starboard and 1,275 yards ahead of the carrier. *Melbourne*'s intention to assume flying operations meant that *Voyager* would have to resume plane guard station No.1. *Voyager* was sufficiently far ahead of the carrier to be able to turn immediately to port across her track at a safe distance, then slow into her station, but the most logical, and safest, course for *Voyager* to take would have been a long slow turn to starboard, crossing astern of *Melbourne* and edging into her required position 20° off of the carrier's port quarter.

From the bridge of the carrier, Captain Robertson and Cdr. Kelly could plainly see the destroyer turning to starboard, as expected. Then, for some unknown reason, *Voyager* began a turn to port, leading to an assumption aboard *Melbourne* that the destroyer was executing a 'fishtail' manoeuvre. This manoeuvre would entail the destroyer reducing speed and allowing the carrier to overhaul her, whereby she would slip to port across the carrier's wake, into her required position. Meanwhile, aboard the *Voyager*, Captain Stevens and the Navigating Officer had retired to consult the chart table, positioned on a platform beneath the main bridge.

By 2055, with *Voyager* continuing her slow turn to port without slowing, it became apparent to Cdr. Kelly that the destroyer was rapidly closing the carrier and that an extremely dangerous situation was developing. Thirty seconds later, with *Voyager* only about 600 yards from *Melbourne*, he ordered "*half astern both engines*", followed a few seconds later by the order "*full astern both engines*" from Captain Robertson.

On *Voyager*'s bridge, the port lookout shouted a warning to Lt. Price, a call which also alerted Captain Stevens at the chart table who, on realising the bearing of his ship to the carrier ordered "*Full ahead both engines. Hard-a-starboard*", quickly followed by an order to pipe 'Collision Stations'. It was by now too late to avoid the imminent collision and,

*The damaged bow of HMAS Melbourne following the aircraft carrier's collision with HMAS Voyager.*
*(T. Ferrers-Walker Collection)*

although the carrier had slowed slightly to 20 knots, the impact was tremendous. *Melbourne*'s bow smashed into *Voyager*'s port side amidships, crushing her superstructure, mast and funnel and pushing her right over onto her starboard side. All those on *Voyager*'s bridge were killed instantly. As the destroyer began to right itself, it snapped in two, the forward section capsizing completely as it scraped down *Melbourne*'s port side, whilst the after section sprang upright. Ten minutes later, the forward section sank to the bottom of the Pacific, 600 feet below, taking with it many of the crew.

The crew of a circling Gannet aircraft later reported seeing a massive fireball as the two ships collided.

At the time of the collision the majority of *Voyager*'s crew were below decks, with about seventy of them playing tombola in the messdeck, whilst others were asleep in their bunks. As the forward section capsized and rapidly flooded, the men trapped in the forward messdeck could be heard screaming as the water level rose - few of these men escaped. Survivors began emerging on to the upper deck soon after the impact. One petty officer finding

his way barred by an escape hatch whose opening mechanism had been snapped by the impact, wrenched open the hatch with a mop handle. Then, balancing himself on the hatch coaming, he helped haul ten men to safety before he was forced to jump into the sea as the forward section began to sink.

The forward boiler and engine rooms were immediately flooded, but quick actions by the crew in closing doors and hatches saved the after compartments. Attempts were made to re-supply electrical power to the forward section of the ship, the damage-control team aft being unaware that the forward half of their ship had gone. It was only after the main circuit breakers had tripped several times that they were informed of the ship's predicament.

As the carrier ground to a standstill, *Voyager*'s after section was secured to her starboard side. Over the next three hours, all crewmen were evacuated from the sinking stern section, which, despite feverish shoring efforts, itself sank at 0017 after a main watertight bulkhead collapsed, its propellers rising into the air as it plunged beneath the surface.

When the first, confused, report of the collision reached Sydney at 2113, warships and helicopters were immediately despatched to the scene. It was only after a further two clarifying signals were sent by *Melbourne* at 2128 and 2140, that the full extent of the disaster was realised. Within about an hour of the collision, eight Wessex helicopters from Nowra Naval Air Station arrived over the scene and, following initial attempts to winch men from the water, it was found that they could best assist the rescue operation by illuminating the scene with their powerful searchlights. Soon afterwards two rescue craft arrived and, guided by the helicopters, immediately began plucking survivors from the oil-smothered water. Having picked up about seventy survivors, these craft transported them to Jervis Bay, where they were taken to hospital suffering from shock and the effects of swallowing thick fuel oil.

Reports of the disaster were first released by the Co-ordinator of Navy Public Relations, Mr. Tony Eggleton, at 2330, followed in the early hours of the 11th by a confirmation that there were heavy casualties amongst the destroyer's crew. It would, however, be some time before the extent of the casualties would be realised. Later that morning, the Prime Minister, Sir Robert Menzies, made an announcement expressing sympathy to the bereaved families of those killed and stating that there would be a prompt and thorough investigation into the tragedy which, in difference to normal naval investigations, would be a public affair conducted by a judge.

There were 232 survivors, nineteen of which required hospitalisation. Captain Stevens, thirteen other officers, 67 ratings and one civilian dockyard technician had lost their lives. There were no casualties aboard *Melbourne*, but she did suffer extensive damage to her bow, extending aft for about 36 feet, together with scoring down both sides of her hull, caused by the two sections of the destroyer scraping along it.

*Melbourne*'s search for survivors continued until shortly after dawn, when she eventually began her journey back to Sydney, with engine revolutions for eight knots giving her a speed of advance of a laborious 4½ knots. *HMAS Stuart* (F48) remained at the scene to continue the search until about 1800 and on Wednesday the minesweepers *HMA Ships Curlew* (M1121), *Hawk* (M1139), *Ibis* (M1183), *Snipe* (M1102) and *Teal* (M1152) made a final sweep of the area, but all that was found was a large quantity of wreckage. In all, during these extensive search operations, only three bodies were recovered.

Later that year, *HMS Duchess* (D154) was supplied by the Royal Navy on loan to Australia to replace *Voyager*. After eight years service with the Australian Navy she was purchased in 1972 at scrap value for conversion into a harbour training ship to replace the Battle class destroyer *HMAS Anzac* (D59).

Neither of the two Royal Commissions that investigated the accident could ascertain why *Voyager* had turned first to starboard and then to port, as all of the destroyer's bridge crew had been killed. However, it is possible that, as she was slightly out of station on *Melbourne*'s starboard bow, the OOW had initially begun a turn to starboard and that, perhaps Captain Stevens had overruled this course and ordered a manoeuvre to port instead, but the time lost in the initial turn had allowed the carrier to catch up with the destroyer, with the result that *Voyager* was struck port-side amidships as she crossed the larger ship's bow. The Commissions could only find that the collision, Australia's worst peacetime naval disaster, had been the result of an error of judgement on the part of *Voyager*'s bridge crew. Captain Robertson was completely absolved of any blame for the accident.

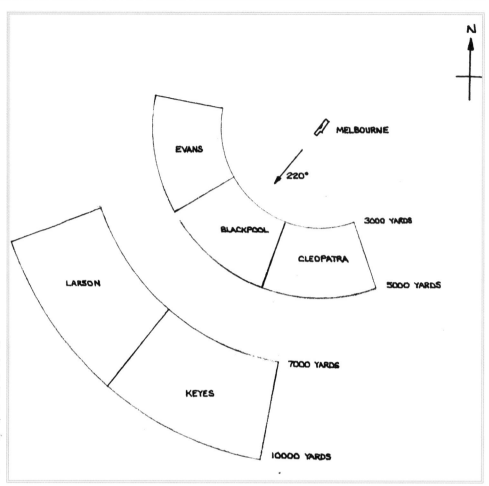

EVANS

BLACKPOOL

CLEOPATRA

LARSON

KEYES

N

MELBOURNE

220°

3000 YARDS

5000 YARDS

7000 YARDS

10000 YARDS

*From 2236 on the night of 2 June 1969, during Exercise Sea Spirit in the South China Sea, HMAS Melbourne's five escorts were assigned to ASW screen sectors ahead of the carrier.*

*(Author)*

This tragedy reinforced doubts as to professional standards within the navy, raised following a series of other serious accidents that had plagued the Australian Navy in the years since 1958.

*Voyager* had been the first destroyer built in an Australian shipyard with extensive use of electric arc welding and also represented a major improvement on previous designs, in terms of weapons and electronic systems, as well as incorporating significant improvements for crew comfort. However, flaws in the design included a poorly designed and laid out wheelhouse and bridge, elements which had been criticised many times by officers and naval architects. The problem on the bridge was primarily caused by the multi-levelled bridge deck,

with its non-functional layout that meant that it was necessary for personnel to move around considerably during the course of their watch-keeping tasks. This shortcoming was eventually eradicated in the surviving ships by the modification of the bridge layout into a single level during their 1969-73 refits.

Controversy surrounding the disaster continued for many years and, ten years afterwards, Mr. Evan Whitton, of '*The National Times*', approached the Whitlam Government to have files on the tragedy made available. The Government refused. Nevertheless, Tom Frame later used these files in his book '*Where Fate Calls*', published in 1992 - 28 years after the incident - but doubt still exists as to the true cause of the accident.

Only five years after the loss of *HMAS Voyager*, the unfortunate *HMAS Melbourne* was involved in a second fatal collision with a destroyer.

On 2 June 1969, whilst involved in the SEATO exercise Sea Spirit in the South China Sea, the A.M. Sumner FRAM II-class ship *USS Frank E. Evans* (DD-754) was operating with *Melbourne* as part of Task Group 472.1 and Task Unit 472.1.0, along with the destroyers *USS James E. Keyes* (DD-787) and *USS Everett F. Larson* (DD-830) and the frigates *HMNZS Blackpool* (F77) and *HMS Cleopatra* (F28). Tactical command of the Task Group rested with the Commanding Officer of *HMAS Melbourne*, Captain John P. Stevenson, RAN. USS *Evans*, commanded by Commander Albert S. McLemore, USN, had, from around 1800, been assigned as rescue (plane guard) destroyer for *Melbourne*'s flying operations.

From 2236 on 2 June, the escorts were formed around the carrier on the following relative bearings:

ASW Screen (symmetrical about a bearing of 220°) - *Cleopatra*, *Blackpool*, and *Evans* in adjacent 40° sectors from 160° to 280° between 3,000 and 5,000 yards distant;

*Keyes* and *Larson* in adjacent 30° sectors from 190° - 250° between 7,000 and 10,000 yards from *Melbourne*.

*Evans* was assigned a sector with outer bearings 240° to 280°, as the right flank escort of the inner sector screen. Ships were to patrol their own sectors, but keeping clear of adjacent sectors by at least 500 yards. As rescue destroyer, *Evans* had been ordered to alternate between her 'screening', 'rescue destroyer' and 'form column' stations several times during the evening.

At 2308, *Melbourne* was instructed by Commander Task Unit (CTU) 472.1.0 to zigzag on a base course of 220° at a speed of 18 knots. This manoeuvre was continued until 0206, and again form 0215 to 0246. A further "Execute to follow" signal from CTU to *Melbourne* to resume the previous zigzag manoeuvre was sent at 0253. At 0307 *Melbourne* changed course to 260° in accordance with the zigzag plan. The next scheduled zigzag turn was at 0313, to a course of 240°.

The Task Group was steaming in 'darkened ship' conditions except as required for flight operations, at which time *Melbourne*'s moonlighting (in three sections, forward centre and aft) would be turned on. These lights, sited on the mast, would not themselves be visible from other ships, although the objects on the flight deck illuminated by them could be clearly seen from a considerable distance away. From 0130, the centre - and possibly the aft - groups of moonlighting were switched on. *Melbourne*'s red masthead lights, mast flying lights and three red vertical droplights on the stern were turned off after the launch of a helicopter at 0304, but visibility was unrestricted in the bright moonlight and the sea was glassy calm.

At 0309, CTU signalled "Execute to follow" to *Melbourne* and *Evans*, followed a minute later by "Form Column" and "Execute" signals. These signals, received, understood and receipted by *Evans*, ordered the two ships to form column at a standard distance of 1,000 yards, with the escort astern of the carrier prior to taking up its rescue destroyer station. At this time *Melbourne* was on course 260° at a speed of 18 knots, with her navigation lights turned on at full brilliance. *Evans'* was in her patrolling station about 3,700 yards from the carrier at a bearing from her of 234° and a speed of 22 knots. On the bridge of the destroyer, the Junior Officer of the Deck (JOOD), Lt. (JG) James A. Hopson, was aware of his ship's correct speed, but the OOD, Lt. (JG) Ronald C. Ramsey, believed *Evans* speed to be only 20 knots.

Further differences of opinion ensued. Lt. Hopson mistakenly believed the base course of the formation to be 185°, speed 16 knots, and that *Melbourne* would be turning to 205° and continuing the zigzag manoeuvre. Lt. Ramsey, however, knew that the carrier's course and speed, in accordance with the zigzag plan, was 260° at 18 knots at the time of the "Form Column" signal. This difference of opinion did not come to the attention of the two officers during the course of their duties, and neither consulted the crew on watch in the CIC. Before commencing the manoeuvre, Lt. Hopson reportedly took a radar bearing of *Melbourne* and determined that she bore 084°, a supposition that was not checked by a visual bearing. This bearing was incorrect as it - together with his disbelief that the carrier's course was 185° - would have placed *Evans'* position well to the right of the carrier's track.

At 0311, following receipt of the "Form Column" signal, Lt. Hopson, who had the 'conn', ordered 10-degrees right rudder. This action turned the destroyer towards *Melbourne*, a fact which caused some concern on the carrier's bridge, resulting in Captain Stevenson, who had arrived on the carrier's bridge a few minutes earlier, ordering the transmission of the signal "*Evans* this is Task Unit Commander, My course is 260 time 2012" (GMT). This signal was sent in code, in the form "JULIET SEVEN THIS IS MIKE TWO CORPEN SHACKLE ZULU UNIFORM UNIFORM LIMA UNSHACKLE TIME TWO ZERO ONE TWO" and was received and receipted by *Evans*. However, Lt. Ramsey interpreted the message incorrectly to read the course as 160° instead of 260°, and so believed that the carrier would be turning to starboard when she would in fact be turning to port to 240°. It is not known why he should have mistaken the code "ZUUL" (Zulu Uniform Uniform Lima) as 160°, as the

code for this course was "NVUL".

As *Evans'* heading passed 030°, Lt. Ramsey observed from a visual sighting that he was on the carrier's port bow. When, at 0313, her heading reached 040°, range was about 2,600 yards on a bearing of 245° from *Melbourne*. The destroyer settled on a course of 050° - a collision or near collision course with the carrier, which was still on course 260°. At this time Lt. Hopson noted by a visual bearing that the carrier bore 070°, a fact which confused him as its bearing had moved to the left instead of right as he expected. These had been his first visual bearings of the manoeuvre. Range was now 2,200 yards, and a now anxious Captain Stevenson ordered the transmission of the signal "You are on a collision course", which was repeated when an acknowledgement was not immediately received from *Evans*.

Lt. Hopson, either on his own initiative or under direction of the OOD, ordered left 5-degrees rudder. He believed at this time that he was on *Melbourne*'s starboard bow, when in fact he was on her port bow. Neither officer noticed the carrier's port navigation light, even though it was illuminated at full brilliance. About 15-20 seconds after the signal was heard by Lt. Ramsey, he ordered "*Right full rudder*" and transmitted the message "*Roger my rudder is right full over*". At almost the same time, Captain Stevenson ordered "*Port 30 - Port 35*" and the transmission of the signal "*I am going hard left*", which was heard on *Evans'* bridge loudspeakers 10-15 seconds later, together with the sound of two short blasts from the carrier's siren.

*Evans* now bore 247° at a range of only 1,200 yards from *Melbourne*. When it was suddenly realised aboard the carrier that a collision was imminent, the OOW ordered "*Stop both engines*", an order which was received by the engine room, followed by "*full astern both engines*", whilst aboard the destroyer, Lt. Hopson

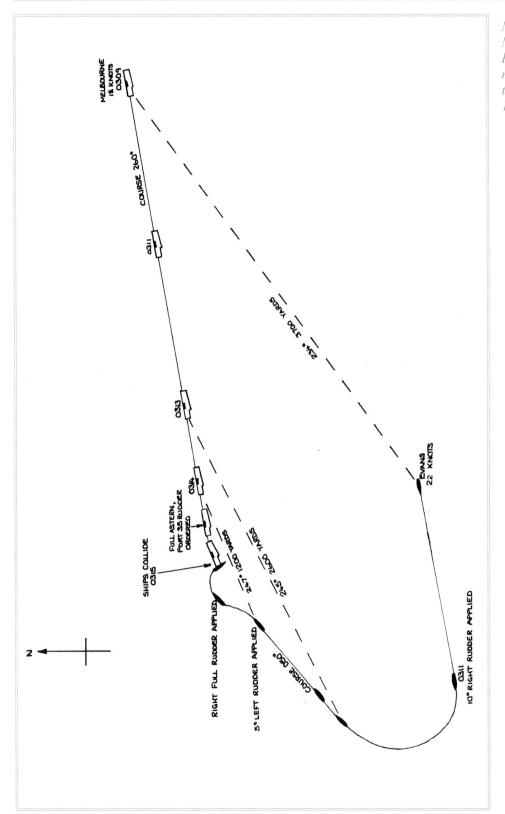

*Movements of HMAS Melbourne and USS Frank E Evans in the minutes leading up to their collision on 3 June 1969.*

*(Author)*

ordered "*All back full*". These orders came too late to prevent the inevitable, and at 0315 the two vessels collided.

In a tragic replay of the earlier *Voyager* collision, *Melbourne* struck *Evans*' port side at almost right angles, rolling her right over onto her starboard side. The destroyer split in two in the vicinity of the expansion joint at frame 92 and, whilst the after section righted itself, the forward section remained at a large angle of list, caused by the inrush of water through open doors and hatches. As the bow section drifted down the port side of the carrier, its angle of heel increased and it finally capsized and slowly settled towards its after end. Four officers and 33 enlisted men escaped, most of who had been thrown from their bunks by the force of the collision. Suddenly finding themselves standing or lying on the vessel's starboard side, they had to climb or swim through darkened compartments to escape. The ship's commanding and

*The abandoned stern section of USS Frank E Evans on the morning of 2 June 1969. The forward section had sunk with the loss of 74 lives.*

*(US Naval Institute)*

executive officers both called out to survivors to get clear of the hull before they themselves entered the water.

Nine minutes after the collision, the bow rose into the air and the section slipped beneath the surface, taking 73 of the men to the seabed 1,100 fathoms below. Another man, a seaman apprentice stationed at the forward lookout station above the pilot house, drowned when he became entangled in the cord of his headset. His body was later recovered from the water by one of *Melbourne*'s motor cutters.

The after section of the stricken ship drifted down the carrier's starboard side. Some power had been immediately restored by the automatic starting of the after diesel generator. The forward engine room flooded rapidly to within a few feet of the deckhead, whilst fractured steam pipes had caused all but one of the six men on watch in the compartment to suffer first and second degree burns. All

were lucky to escape with their lives. The after engine room was evacuated by the five watch-keepers stationed there as this compartment also flooded. In the steering compartment right aft, the seaman apprentice on watch had been thrown against the starboard side of the ship, but quickly recovered his bearing, engaged the local steering controls and endeavoured to contact the bridge, unaware that is was no longer attached to the section of the ship he was in.

When it was realised that the forward half of their ship had disappeared, the survivors began mustering on the fantail, where they were organised by the Operations Officer into search parties. They were then despatched throughout what remained of their ship to ensure all compartments were clear of personnel and to set damage control condition Zebra by closing all watertight doors and hatches. The Engineer Officer entered the after engine room and fire room to ensure that the propulsion plant had been safely shut down and that there were no fires. He noted that the forward bulkhead of the after fire room was visibly 'panting' with the force of water on the other side of it and the level of water in the bilge was rising slowly. Proceeding back to the fantail, he informed the Operations Officer of the vessel's critical state and recommended that the crew be evacuated. Life jackets were mustered from various storages and life rafts were launched, while lines were prepared in readiness for securing the crippled hulk to the starboard quarter of *Melbourne*, where it was ultimately secured at 0325, 10 minutes after the collision.

Immediately following the collision, Captain Stevenson had ordered 'Emergency Stations', causing all members of her crew to close up at their emergency positions from where they could best be utilised to deal with the incident. Ladders, scrambling nets and even helicopter cargo nets were passed

between the two ships and injured personnel were evacuated to the carrier's sick bay, which by now was fully manned and awaiting to treat the first of the casualties. By 0400, all 162 men who had been in the after section of *Evans* before the collision had been transferred to *Melbourne*.

The engineer officers of both vessels, armed with information from numerous sources, concurred in the view that the stern section of *Evans* was now settling by the head and that it's foundering was imminent. With the danger of the carrier's starboard propeller being damaged when the section sank, it was decided by Captain Stevenson that the hulk should be cast off, but only after *Evans*' Executive Officer had carried out another thorough search of his ship for survivors. This done, the lines joining the two vessels were cast off at 0407 and, with a touch ahead on *Melbourne*'s port engine, *Evans*' stern section drifted clear. Responsibility for the abandoned section was now passed to *USS Larson*.

Meanwhile, Exercise Sea Spirit had been terminated and all ships of the Task Unit were ordered to close *Melbourne* and assist in the rescue of *Evans*' survivors. An international distress signal was not transmitted, as it was considered that sufficient units were in the area.

Two of *Melbourne*'s helicopters, joined shortly after by helicopters from *USS Kearsarge* (CVS-33), forty miles away, joined in the rescue operation, winching men from the water and using their landing lamps to pick out swimmers, directing boats and rafts to them. At 0340, one of *Melbourne*'s helicopters lowered his Search and Rescue diver into the water to rescue an exhausted swimmer, the last of *Evans*' crew to reach the safety of the carrier. In total, 199 of *Evans*' 273 crew were rescued all of whom were transferred to *USS Kearsarge* later that morning.

The search, utilising up to eight

helicopters at a time and all ships in the Task Unit, continued until around 1900 that evening, covering an area of some 100 square miles. Every item of floating wreckage was recovered in order that no survivors would be overlooked. At dawn, a salvage crew, headed by *Evans'* Engineer Officer, returned to the hulk and found that it had settled by about 12-inches at the forward end since being cut adrift from *Melbourne*. The after engine room and fire room were still flooding and first aid damage control measures, including the rigging of portable pumps, were taken to reduce the entry of water.

Following these actions the vessel was secured alongside *USS Larson* and further pumps and emergency lighting rigged. Items of equipment on the upper deck were cut free to lighten the vessel and, combined with the removal of free-surface floodwater, a comfortable margin of stability was restored. A towing bridle was rigged and, just before noon, *USNS Tawasa* (ATF-92) arrived to take *Evans* in tow. The following afternoon the two vessels began the long haul to Subic Bay, where they arrived on the morning of the 9th. It was decided that the surviving section of the destroyer be decommissioned on 1 July 1969, finally to be expended as a target on 10 October. The forward section of the ship was never recovered.

There were no casualties on *Melbourne*, but she suffered extensive bow damage both above and below the waterline, flooding No.1 and 2 trim tanks and necessitating shoring of number 16 bulkhead from 5-deck to the keel. She was later able to proceed at 15 knots to Singapore, where she entered King George VI dock on the 9th. Following emergency repairs she returned to Sydney where, between 17 July and 11 October, a new bow section was fitted.

A combined Royal Australian Navy - United States Navy Board of Investigation was convened over twenty days during June and July 1969. Their findings were that primary responsibility for the collision rested with *USS Evans*, in that she had a duty to keep clear of the carrier. Lt. Hopson, who had the 'conn' as JOOD, was responsible for the orders that led to the collision. As the OOD, Lt. Ramsey was directly responsible for the actions of his subordinate in ensuring the safety of his ship. Both officers had shown a casual approach to their watch-keeping duties and communication between the pair, and CIC, was poor, in that their differing interpretations of *Melbourne*'s movements was not discovered.

The lack of visual checks, cross referenced by radar bearings, by the JOOD and the lack of supervision by the OOD, allowed these mistakes to go unnoticed until the situation had developed into one of grave danger. Visual bearings, with the carrier's moonlighting and navigational lights on, should have quickly alerted them to the true situation. Furthermore, both officers failed to call the Captain when unsure of the situation, despite the fact that both Standing Night Orders and Night Orders were clear on this point.

*USS Evans'* Commanding Officer, Commander Albert S. McLemore, in as much as he was responsible for the overall safety of his ship, inevitably shouldered some of the blame for the accident. These responsibilities were judged to have been effectively carried out in that a qualified and trained watch was posted and detailed and comprehensive Standing Night Orders had been issued - signed by all officers standing bridge or CIC watches to state that they had read and understood their content. However, whilst these orders included inter alia instructions for calling him, they did not necessitate the calling of the Commanding or Navigation Officers for changes of course and speed solely for the purpose of patrolling a screen assignment, nor did Night Orders call for the Commanding Officer to be called in connection with *Melbourne*'s flying operations scheduled for 0300-0330. It had been Commander McLemore's practice to decide whether or not to be on the bridge after taking account of several considerations, such as time, difficulty of manoeuvre, darken ship routines and the experience of the OOD. Changing station at night did not necessarily dictate that he should be on the bridge.

As Task Group Commander, Captain Stevenson also bore a portion of the responsibility in that he was responsible for the safe operation of all ships in the Task Unit. The fact that *Evans*' navigation lights were not on during the early part of the manoeuvre had not hindered the bridge crew of *Melbourne* from determining the destroyer's position and movements, although it had not been noticed that, in the hours leading up to the collision, *Evans* had been out of station at least twice and had ventured into *Blackpool*'s sector. The carrier's lighting in use for flying operations had apparently confused the JOOD of *Evans*, and it was recommended that this aspect should command closer attention by carrier escorts in future operations.

The confusion in the mind of Lt. Hopson as to *Melbourne*'s base course was not completely explained. Although the zigzag course was laid down as 220°, it is possible that, following a signal at 0253 instructing "Turn together, Left to 185", followed two minutes later by "Resume previous zigzag", he assumed this to be a new zigzag course. This assumption was wrong, as it was well understood throughout the Task Group that base course for zigzag during this phase of the exercise was 220°. Tactical doctrine applicable to manoeuvres and evolutions in the exercise were promulgated in Maritime Operating Procedures (MOP), while further guidance for the escorts was promulgated in the *HMAS Melbourne* Escort Handout.

Zigzag plans were contained in FOCAF order 1/69, as it was uncertain whether all vessels taking part were in possession of ATP-3(A), the recently updated orders ATP-3, in which details of such aspects as zigzag plans differed widely, although neither publications were authorised for use in this exercise.

Lt. Ramsey's incorrect decoding of *Melbourne*'s signal "My course is 260" to read a course of 160°, was also a major source of confusion, which could have been avoided had the course signal been passed uncoded, but a visual sighting of the carrier's movements would have alerted him to this error. The board could not determine why the watch in CIC apparently made no effort to provide the bridge watch with information, as both officers in CIC were lost with the forward section of the ship.

The action of both Commanding Officers in ordering full astern was correct. Nevertheless, had this action been taken when the rudder orders were given it may have reduced the force of the impact, although it is likely that the collision would still have occurred.

In view of the difficulties encountered by crewmen attempting to escape from the ship in pitch darkness, it was also recommended that the fitting of relay actuated battle lanterns for emergency lighting be rationalised - the number and location of these lights had previously been at the discretion of ship's Commanding Officers. A greater number in *Evans* would have helped some of the crew in the forward section of *Evans* to gain their orientation and assist their escape effort.

There are several similarities between these three catastrophic carrier-destroyer collisions which should be noted. All occurred at night whilst the destroyer was attempting to take up its station as plane guard and was caused by the OOW/OOD placing his ship in extremis by attempting to manoeuvre across the bow of the

carrier, instead of adopting the safer option of passing astern. An element of complacency on the part of the OOW/OOD, combined with a lack of communication between the bridge and the Operations Room/CIC, caused them to become disorientated and to lose track of the changing tactical situation. A further contributory factor in the *Melbourne/Evans* collision was the over-reliance by the OOD on navigational aids and radar, instead of good old-fashioned visual fixing.

Confusion regarding the lights of a carrier was later to be one of the main contributory factors of the collision, on 22 November 1975, between the cruiser *USS Belknap* (CG-26) and the aircraft carrier *USS John F. Kennedy* (CV-67). The incident occurred whilst the two vessels were involved in night flying exercises near Sicily. Just prior to the collision, the carrier had begun a turn to port to recover aircraft when the *Belknap*'s OOD, confused by the large number of lights on the bigger ship, decided to make a slow turn to starboard. The two ships collided port-port, the *Belknap* catching under the

carrier's overhang, rupturing fuel tanks on the carrier and sending fuel cascading down onto the cruiser. Ignition of the fuel resulted in a fire which almost totally destroyed her largely alloy superstructure. Six men were killed on the *Belknap* and another on the *John F. Kennedy*. The official enquiry resulted in *Belknap*'s OOD being court-martialled and the Commanding Officer being reprimanded. The cruiser was later towed back to the USA and repaired, returning to service in 1980.

Less that a year later, the *John F. Kennedy* was involved with a collision with another escort ship whilst participating in the NATO Exercise Teamwork 76 in the North Sea, 100 miles north of Scotland. The destroyer *Bordelon* (DD-881) was re-fuelling from the carrier during the evening of 14 September 1976 when a steering gear failure caused her to slew to port and smash against the starboard side of the 83,000-ton leviathan. The impact with the carrier's overhang completely flattened the destroyer's masts, funnels and much of the superstructure and injured six crewmen, whilst the *John F. Kennedy* suffered only minor damage. *Bordelon*'s forward 5-inch gun was also knocked off of it's mounting and flooding forward resulted in her sitting very low in the water.

The *Bordelon* withdrew from the exercise and, escorted by *USS Brumby* (FF-1044), limped into Devonport, England, for repairs. Eleven days later, *Bordelon* sailed under her own power to Charleston, South Carolina, escorted by the destroyer *USS Luce* (DDG-38) and the replenishment ship *USS Kalamazoo* (AOR-6), where she was declared beyond economical repair and de-commissioned. The ship was later stripped for spares and sold to Iran for further stripping, where boiler spares were removed before the hulk was finally sunk as a target.

The subsequent Court of Inquiry cleared *Bordelon*'s Commanding Officer, Commander George Pierce, of any blame for the collision. Ironically, the *Bordelon* had been one of the ships that had aided the crippled *Belknap* following her collision the previous year and had towed the cruiser to Augusta Bay, Sicily for repairs.

Although these reports are some of the most disastrous cases of collisions between naval vessels during night exercises, they are by no means unique and several other escorts have been lost or critically damaged whilst operating with larger ships.

In the summer of 1959, the Battle-class destroyer *HMS Hogue* (D74) was involved in a near collision with the aircraft carrier *HMS Centaur* (R06) in the Bay of Biscay during a refuelling exercise with the tanker *RFA Wave Victor*. Whilst serving with the First Destroyer Squadron later that year, on 29 August, her luck ran out when she was struck by the Indian cruiser *INS Mysore* (C60 - formerly *HMS Nigeria*) off Ceylon. One crewman was killed and a further three were injured. *Hogue* was extensively damaged and,

after being towed to Singapore, was laid up and declared as 'damaged beyond repair', finally being sold for scrap on 7 March 1962.

The *Mysore* was involved in another collision with an escort ship in 1972, when she struck the Indian frigate *INS Beas* (F37), although luckily neither ship suffered serious damage.

At least two Soviet destroyers have received serious damage in collisions with cruisers during naval exercises. Following a collision with the *Chapayev* on 23 March 1957, the Project 30 ('Skoryy'-class) ship *Ostvetstvennyi* was reclassified as the auxiliary *PKZ-48*, finally being scrapped in 1963. On 16 May 1986, the bow of the Project 61 ship *Strogiy* was badly damaged in a scrape with the Project 1134-B cruiser *Nikolayev* in the Soya Straits. Both ships were subsequently repaired, but the Commanding Officers of *Strogiy* and *Nikolayev* - Captain Third Rank V. Fadeyev and Captain Second Rank V. Ionov respectively - were both dismissed from their ships.

On 15 February 1982, units of the South African Navy began what was intended to be a two-week exercise period in an area

*Her bow bent and twisted, the destroyer HMS Hogue lies alongside a depot ship at Singapore following a collision with the Indian cruiser INS Mysore on 29 ugust 1959.*

*(A.H. Standish)*

south-west of Cape Town. In preparation for an anti-submarine exercise with the submarine *SAS Emily Hobhouse* (S98) on the night of the 17th, the frigates *SAS President Kruger* (F150) and *SAS President Pretorius* (F145) took up station on either bow of the 27,000-ton replenishment ship *SAS Tafelberg* (A243) to form an anti-submarine screen, with *Kruger* to port and *Pretorius* to starboard. Although there was a large swell running, whipped up by a strong south-easterly wind, visibility was good and the OOW on each of the three surface ships had no trouble tracking the others.

The exercise scenario necessitated a course reversal, programmed to take place at 0350, with the frigates turning first to take up their stations prior to *Tafelberg* executing her part of the manoeuvre. Both frigates were to turn to starboard, with the completed manoeuvre resulting in *Kruger* taking station on *Tafelberg*'s starboard bow and *Pretorius* on her port. Although the turn to starboard would result in *Kruger* turning towards

*Tafelberg*, there was judged to be sufficient room for the manoeuvre to be undertaken safely, provided the turn was executed with a large angle of rudder. Unfortunately, the OOW ordered only 10-degrees of rudder applied, resulting in a wider turn by the frigate.

Although the Principal Warfare Officer (PWO) on watch in the ship's Operations Room pointed out to the OOW that he was using an insufficient rudder angle, this only served to confuse him. Shortly afterwards, *Tafelberg* was lost in clutter on the PWO's radar screen. A few minutes later, the Executive Officer arrived on the bridge to take over the watch, just as *Kruger* was completing her 180° turn, but looking towards the *Tafelberg* he noticed with alarm that they were heading directly towards each other. His order to turn hard to starboard had only just begun to take effect when the replenishment ship smashed into the frigate's port side in the vicinity of the boiler room, her massive bow embedding itself into the frigate's 41ft beam by about 15 feet.

The collision ruptured a main watertight bulkhead and also completely demolished the chief and petty officer's mess, killing fourteen men within and thereby denying the ship of most of its experienced damage-control personnel. Nevertheless, there was little that could be done to save the ship, such was the magnitude of the damage and the speed with which the water level - mixed with fuel and oil from ruptured tanks - rose within the vessel. The Commanding Officer was left with little choice but to order all non-essential personnel to take to the life rafts whilst others feverishly tried to stem the flooding. Soon afterwards, as the ship heeled over to port to an angle of 50°, these personnel were also forced to abandon ship. Tragically, two crewmen drowned during the evacuation process, one of whom left the ship on his own, whilst the other was trapped in a raft when it strayed under the plunging ship as it sank to the seabed 3,000 metres below, in position 34°59.8'S, 17°07.5'E.

Immediately following the collision, *Tafelberg* withdrew to carry out emergency damage-control operations on her damaged bow, but quickly returned to the scene to assist the *Pretorius* in the rescue of *Kruger*'s 177 survivors. At first light, aircraft continued the search for the sixteen missing crewmen, assisted by the *Emily Hobhouse* and several other naval and civilian vessels. The search operation was finally abandoned the following day in the face of worsening weather conditions.

The conclusions of the Board of Inquiry and the public inquest were that the Commanding Officer and the PWO did negligently endanger their ship and that their actions amounted to culpable homicide. The Commanding Officer was forced to retire and the PWO received a serious reprimand. The Navy was forced to review its standing orders and OOW training programme, particularly with regards to the authority of the OOW and

his relationship with the Warfare Officer in the Operations Room.

This incident was slightly reminiscent of one of the worst disasters in British naval history - the 1893 collision between the battleships *HMS Victoria* and *HMS Camperdown*. The two battleships were part of a large Royal Navy squadron undertaking manoeuvres off Tripoli, under the command of Vice-Admiral Sir George Tryon. The squadron was steaming in two columns, six cables (1,200 yards) apart and the Admiral intended that they were to reverse course by turning inwards. Despite protests from

*A diagramatic view of the maneouvre that led to the collision between SAS President Kruger and SAS Tafelberg.*
*(Lt D. Loosely, RN)*

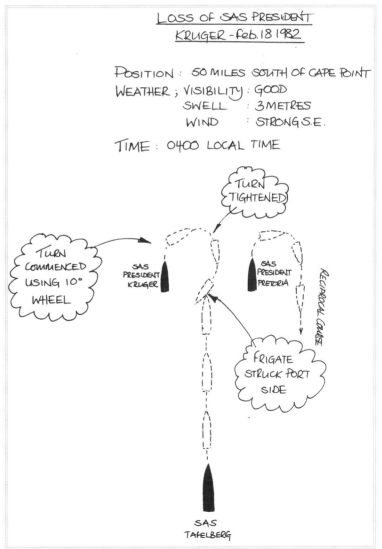

LOSS OF SAS PRESIDENT KRUGER - Feb. 18 1982

POSITION : 50 MILES SOUTH OF CAPE POINT
WEATHER ; VISIBILITY : GOOD
SWELL : 3 METRES
WIND : STRONG S.E.

TIME : 0400 LOCAL TIME

TURN TIGHTENED

TURN COMMENCED USING 10° WHEEL

SAS PRESIDENT KRUGER

SAS PRESIDENT PRETORIA

RECIPROCAL COURSE

FRIGATE STRUCK PORT SIDE

SAS TAFELBERG

his Captains that the minimum safe distance between the columns for such a manoeuvre should be eight cables, he stubbornly stuck by his order. Consequently, the two lead ships turned inwards and collided, the *Victoria* capsizing and sinking almost immediately with the loss of 358 officers and men, including Admiral Tryon. Apart from the obvious seamanship lessons, this disaster illustrated the need for watertight bulkheads to be unpierced by doors, valves, etc., a requirement largely fulfilled by the time *HMS Dreadnought* was completed in 1906.

Although the *Kruger* had had sufficient room for her turn towards *Tafelberg*, the looseness of the frigate's turn had caused her to reverse course directly into the larger ship's path.

An encounter between two similarly sized escorts resulted in the Royal Navy's second post-war collision-related destroyer disaster when, during anti-

submarine exercises with the submarine *HMS Sealion* (S07) in the Firth of Clyde soon after midnight on Thursday, 2 August 1962, the frigate *HMS Ursa* (F200) collided with the Weapon-class destroyer *HMS Battleaxe* (D118). Both vessels were operating a 'darken ship' routine whilst carrying out high speed manoeuvres, at about 17 knots, when they collided south of Garroch Head, Bute, about $2\frac{1}{2}$ miles east of Arran. The bow of *Ursa* sliced into the port bow of the *Battleaxe*, splitting the destroyer's hull vertically down from the weather deck to the keel. *Ursa*'s stem was bent back around her bow by the collision.

Seven of *Battleaxe*'s crew were injured by the impact, three of them seriously, when the forward messdeck was crushed, throwing the sleeping men from their beds. One rating, a mechanic, narrowly escaped death as the hammock he had occupied only a few minutes earlier was almost cut in two. Fortunately, the timing

*The badly damaged destroyer HMS Battleaxe arrived at Greenock to tie up alongside the frigate HMS Ursa following their collision on 2 August 1962.*

*(The Herald, Evening Times)*

of the collision meant that many men were at that time either taking over, or coming off, watch. But for this - and with the fact that the forward messdeck of *Ursa* had been altered into a paint store when the ship was converted to an anti-submarine frigate in 1955 - the casualty toll would almost certainly have been much higher.

After the vessels disengaged, the injured ratings were transferred to *Ursa*, which then made its way up-river at 10 knots, the maximum safe speed with her mangled bows. As the damaged ship steamed northwards past the Cumbraes at about 0130, a civilian doctor was transferred to her by launch to care for the injured. Soon after, *Ursa* docked at the Deep Water Berth, Princess Pier, Greenock, when the three most seriously injured ratings were transferred to hospital by ambulance.

Meanwhile, *Battleaxe*, taking in water and listing badly, was eased slowly up-river with the assistance of the civilian tug *Brigadier*. The crippled ship, a gaping wound in her side, reached Greenock later that morning and was secured alongside *Ursa*.

Both vessels later made their way to Portsmouth, where *Battleaxe* was laid up. Although a survey found the damage not to be excessive, she was paid off as 'uneconomical to repair'. At the time the 2,935-ton destroyer, attached to the 5th Destroyer Squadron, had seen some 15 years service, having been commissioned in 1947 and modernised and converted to a fleet radar-picket in 1958-59 at a cost of £1,000,000. She was approved for scrapping in 1963 and later used by the Naval Construction Research Establishment (NCRE) at Rosyth for trials. The hulk arrived at Blyth 20 October 1964 to be broken up.

*Ursa* later underwent repairs and a refit at Devonport before being returned to service.

Five officers and one petty officer were subsequently court-martialled and reprimanded, including the Commanding

Officers of both ships. The unusual action of court-martialling a rating after a collision at sea resulted from the fact that it had been the responsibility of the local operations plot officer to track the movements of his own ship, as well as those of others operating nearby, on radar.

The petty officer had been *Ursa*'s on-watch local operations plot officer at the time of the collision, and as such was deemed to have been negligent in his duty.

It was said that another contributory factor in this incident was the lack of astern power in the Weapon-class destroyers, due to modifications in the propulsion machinery. All four ships of the class had been plagued with turbine troubles when they first entered service, mainly due to faults in the design and casting of the casings. The astern turbine casing caused problems and these were remedied by blanking off the steam feed to the lower half of the casing, which consequently reduced astern power. The Weapon-class ships were something of an aberration in British destroyer design and were often criticised as being under-armed and difficult to handle.

Many smaller warships have also been

*MTB1030, which sank off the Hook of Holland on 28 March 1952 after a collision with her sister-boat MTB1032.*
*(Maritime Photo Library)*

sunk in collisions during naval exercises. The first of these occurred only days after the cessation of hostilities when, on 11 September 1945, the US PC-461-class submarine chaser *PC-815* was rammed and cut in two by the destroyer *USS Laffey* (DD-724) in thick fog in San Francisco Bay. The destroyer stopped and rescued all but one of the sunken patrol ship's crewmen.

On 28 March 1952 the two British Vosper 73ft motor torpedo-boats *MTB1030* and *MTB1032* were in collision with each other 30 miles off the Hook of Holland. *MTB1030* sank and *MTB1032* was badly damaged. Although some sailors were injured, thankfully there were no fatalities in the accident and *MTB1032* was later repaired and returned to service.

The Danish Navy suffered two such losses in the 1950s, the first of which took place on 26 January 1951 during naval exercises off the Shipwash Sands, Felixstowe, when *T59* (ex-*S197*), one of eighteen ex-German Schnellbootes in service with the Danish Navy at that time, was struck by the British torpedo-boat *MTB5518*. *MTB5518*, her bow badly damaged, took *T59* in tow but flooding

could not be contained and she sank soon afterwards. The boat was raised a couple of months later and repaired in Lurssens Dockyard in Vegesack, Germany, during which her bow was modified to the same design as the Danish-built MTBs of the Flyvefisken-class. All boats of the class were renamed in 1951, *T59* becoming *HDMS Raagen* (P559), under which name she served until 1957.

Whilst *T59* had proved repairable after salvage, one of her sister-craft was not so fortunate. During naval exercises in the Store Baelt, between Fyn and Sjælland, in the early hours of the morning of 4 September 1957 the Gribben-class MTB *HDMS Høgen* (P555, ex-German *S206*) was struck by the new MTB *HDMS Flyvefisken* (P500). *Høgen* immediately began sinking and navigation lights were turned on to prevent further collisions, while *Flyvefisken* transmitted a distress signal. At 0321 - fourteen minutes after the collision - the frigate *HDMS Rolf Krake* (F342) arrived at the scene to find the forward section of *Flyvefisken* still embedded on top of *Høgen*'s port side aft, just forward of the 40mm gun mounting. *Rolf Krake* picked up survivors from

*Høgen*, which sank immediately afterwards at 0325 in 17 metres of water. One of the crew, an engine room rating, was missing and later assumed to have been killed.

Attentions were then turned to the badly holed *Flyvefisken*, which was taking in water and slowly settling by the bow. Thankfully, the weather was calm with a gently north-westerly breeze blowing and the MTB was secured starboard side to alongside *Rolf Krake*, her bow in line with the frigate's stern. Portable pumps from both vessels were rigged aboard the MTB and first-aid damage control actions were carried out to stem the ingress of water. By 0430 both ships were moving at five knots towards Korsør, Sjælland, where they arrived just after 0700.

Over the next five days emergency repairs were carried out to the damaged *Flyvefisken* before she was transferred to a Naval dockyard for a refit, following which she continued to serve for many years.

*Høgen* was later raised from her watery resting-place but the hull and machinery were beyond repair and she was sold to ship-breakers on 23 September.

The South Korean Navy also suffered two serious collisions during the 1950s that resulted in the ex-US Navy craft being written-off as constructive total losses. First of these was the frigate *ROKN Apnok* (PF-62), critically damaged on 21 May 1952 when she was struck by the ammunition ship *USS Mount Baker* (AE-4) off South Korea and subsequently returned to America for scrapping. Then, in October 1955, the YMS minesweeper *ROKN Kosung* (MSC-518) was also written-off following a collision.

The navies of China, Vietnam, North Korea and the Soviet Union have undoubtedly incurred the loss of dozens of small patrol and attack craft as a result collisions in the post-war years. However, the low value of these craft within these navies, together with the uncertainty of

the true numbers of such craft actually built, means that details of such incidents are very hard to come by - if they exist at all. Many such countries regard an attrition rate of several such craft annually - by whatever means - as perfectly normal and acceptable.

There have been at least three fatal collisions between submarines and destroyers during naval exercises in post-war years. On 27 June 1946, the Spanish Navy lost its first submarine since it first entered this specialisation in 1888, when *C4* was rammed and sunk by the Churruca-class destroyer *SNS Lepanto* off the Balearic Islands. The badly holed submarine sank in minutes with her entire crew of 46 men.

Commissioning in 1943, *M200 Myest* was the prototype of a Soviet Navy submarine class that went into series production after the war. On the evening of 21 November 1956, the Project 96 boat was returning to Tallinn, in the Gulf of Finland, after a short training cruise when the navigation lights of the Project 30-bis (Skory-class) destroyer *Statnyi* were seen at a distance of about 5 miles. As the destroyer closed on the submarine, she altered course slightly to starboard to pass her on the port side. Inexplicably, as the distance between the vessels closed to less then 800-yards, the *Myest*'s Commanding Officer, Captain Third Rank Shumanin, ordered a sharp turn to port, across the destroyers bow. At 1953, unable to avoid the inevitable collision, the *Statnyi* struck the starboard side of the 350-ton submarine in the region of the 5th and 6th compartments, killing six men instantly. The *Myest* quickly settled by the stern and sank less than ten minutes later, taking with her 28 original survivors. Only eight were able to escape, but two of these men drowned before they could be rescued.

Rescue services were quickly on the scene and at 2105 found the sunken boat's emergency buoy and established communications with the trapped

*The bow of the destroyer-escort USS Silverstein lies firmly embedded in the hull of USS Stickleback on 29 May 1958. All crew were evacuated safely before the submarine sank.*

*(US Navy)*

survivors, but many of them had already perished as the 3rd and 4th compartments flooded. Attempts to connect an air hose to the boat failed and, by the early hours of the following morning, the remaining survivors began preparations to escape by free ascent. However, by the evening of 22 November, none of them had left the boat.

The deteriorating weather forced a cessation of the rescue and salvage effort at 1800 and the cable securing the emergency buoy was parted by rising seas. In the early hours of 23 November, divers finally managed to reach the boat, but on opening the outer escape hatch

found a seaman trapped inside the chamber, effectively preventing any escape. There were no survivors.

The *Myest* was raised on 29 November by the salvage ship *Kommuna* and towed to Tallinn, where she was scrapped. The subsequent inquiry into the loss of the *Myest* found that both Shumanin and the *Statnyi*'s Commanding Officer, Captain Third Rank Savchuk, were equally to blame for the accident.

The US Navy suffered its only collision-related submarine loss in the late-1950s. Taking part in anti-submarine exercises in the Pacific 20 miles south-west of Pearl Harbour on 29 May 1958, the Balao-class submarine *USS Stickleback* (SS-415) carried out a crash dive manoeuvre to avoid a simulated depth-charge attack by the destroyer-escort *USS Silverstein* (DE-534). An error in the operation of the propulsion system resulted in a loss of control and the Commanding Officer, Lt. Cdr. Quinley R. Schulz, ordered his boat to surface immediately by blowing all ballast. Unfortunately, the submarine surfaced directly ahead of the escort and, still without power, was unable to avoid the inevitable collision.

*Silverstein* struck the submarine on the port side between the forward battery compartment and the control room, breaching the boat's pressure hull. Luckily, *Silverstein*'s Commanding Officer, Commander Charles S. Swift, USN, had the presence of mind to maintain just enough headway to keep the destroyer's bow embedded in the submarine's hull, so slowing the rate of flooding. This action provided valuable time for the entire crew of eight officers and 87 enlisted men to abandon the submarine, to be rescued soon after by *Silverstein* and other warships involved in the exercise. Attempts were made to take *Stickleback* in tow, but the boat sank at 1857 in water 1,800 fathoms deep, in position 21°05'45"N, 158°17'46"W.

The subsequent Court of Inquiry determined that the cause of *Stickleback*'s loss of control had been the unexpected tripping of the battery main circuit breakers just as the controllermen were shifting from parallel to series operation of the batteries. This was an operation that was new to the GUPPY conversions, of which *Stickleback* was one. Previous submarines had operated their batteries entirely in parallel, whereas the GUPPYs could change to series operation to provide twice the voltage and current to the propulsion motors, so increasing their submerged speed over short distances.

Lt. Cdr. Schulz had ordered the change to parallel operation to give him the necessary speed to evade the destroyer's sensors. As the submarine built up to the maximum speed available with the batteries in parallel and maximum field current in the motors, preparations were being made to shift to series control. At this moment the supervising electrician noticed that the trainee port controllerman was turning the rheostat controlling the motor field current in the wrong direction, but was too late to take corrective actions. Lowering of the motor field current caused a surge of current from the batteries to the motor armature which tripped the main battery circuit breakers.

The phenomenon of the main battery breaker tripping was known to the US Navy's design authority, BuShips (Bureau of Ships). During trials of the early GUPPY conversions, boats had experienced tripping of the breakers, forcing the crew to blow all ballast, the submarine often broaching on surfacing. It was discovered that the breakers fitted tripped at too low a current to allow for the surge caused during the transfer from parallel to series operation of the batteries. The operating characteristics of the breaker over-current relays were therefore altered to rectify this discrepancy.

The resultant isolation of electrical power had plunged *Stickleback* into darkness and all manoeuvring control was lost. To avoid an uncontrollable dive - a very real danger if the planes are in the down position at the moment of power loss - the Commanding Officer had no choice but to order the blowing of all ballast tanks. Blowing of the ballast tanks requires no electrical power, high-pressure air being injected into the tanks via an air manifold, blowing the bow buoyancy tank first to bring the bow of the submarine up. There would be insufficient time to vent the tanks to regulate the rate of ascent and so the boat rose uncontrollably to the surface. Without electrical power there would have only been enough reserve power in the hydraulic accumulator to cycle the vents once. Once the hydraulic pressure was exhausted, there would be no way to close the vents, which may result in the boat sinking again. Although the Commanding Officer had ordered the operation of the vents by hand, there would have been insufficient time in the circumstances for this action to have any real effect.

That the submarine happened to broach immediately in front of the destroyer can only be described as tragically unfortunate. The Court of Inquiry cleared Lt. Cdr. Schulz of all blame for the loss, deciding that he had taken the correct actions in the circumstances, as laid down in the SubPac Standard Operating Procedures book, and that there had been nothing more he could have done to prevent his boat from broaching.

The cause of the loss was attributed to operator error. However, the court decided that the trainee controllerman had been properly trained and briefed in his duties and that he had been adequately supervised. No members of the crew were therefore court-martialled.

Whilst steaming at high speed in close company in the English Channel in June 1954, the Daring-class destroyer *HMS Diamond* (D35) collided with the frigate *HMS Salisbury* (F32). The collision, which caused minor damage to both ships, was caused by the two ships being drawn together by the vacuum effect of their hulls during the manoeuvre - a phenomenon known as 'interaction'.

A ship moving through the water creates areas of varying pressure around her hull, increased pressure being created at the bow and stern and a reduced pressure over the midships section. When two ships are steaming in close proximity, such as during a replenishment-at-sea (RAS) operation, these variations in pressure create areas of interaction and repulsion forces. Water flowing between the ships will first be subject to increased pressure as their bows deflect the flow of water, with a tendency to force their stems outwards. As the water passes between the hulls, a converging tunnel effect is experienced with a resultant increase in velocity and, with the reduced area, a reduction in pressure, causing suction forces between the hulls.

On approaching the sterns of the ships, the water flow decelerates and an increase in pressure is experienced. The effects of these forces are more pronounced in water shallower than about 40 metres or with increased speed and should not be underestimated. This phenomenon has resulted in numerous collisions between ships, including the Royal Navy's worst peacetime disaster since the 1951 loss of the submarine *HMS Affray*.

The NATO exercise Teamwork 76 had already been dogged by disaster, with the collision between the *USS John F.*

*HMS Mermaid's unique shortened forecastle was a critical factor in the frigate's collision with the minesweeper HMS Fittleton on 20 September 1976.*
*(Navy News)*

*Kennedy* and the *USS Bordelon*. A few days later the *John F. Kennedy* suffered another accident when an F-14 Tomcat aircraft was lost overboard from her flight deck, whilst the Dutch Navy support ship *HrMS Poolster* (A835) was also involved in a minor collision with the Canadian replenishment oiler *HMCS Protectuer* (AOR-509). Worse was to follow.

Weather conditions on 20 September were fine, with a light 15-knot wind and good visibility. At about 1500 on that afternoon, 80 miles from the Dutch coast, the frigate *HMS Mermaid* (F76) - with Admiral Commanding Reserves embarked - rendezvoused with a group of six mine-countermeasure vessels, in order to distribute mail by heaving line transfer.

This manoeuvre was one frequently practised between minesweepers, but seldom between minesweepers and frigates.

The unique design of *HMS Mermaid* was a factor that would greatly influence the events to follow. Launched by Yarrows in December 1966 for President Nkrumah of Ghana, she was never delivered, but was instead laid up until taken over by the Royal Navy in April 1972. Although her hull-form was based on that of the Salisbury-class, she did not possess their raised forecastle and her superstructure was carried well forward. Her very short forecastle meant that her RAS position was much further forward than that on other frigates.

Following the rendezvous, the minesweepers were ordered to form a line-ahead formation astern of the frigate, on a course of 100° and a speed of 11 knots, in preparation for carrying out the planned manoeuvre, with *HMS Fittleton* (M1136) immediately astern of *Mermaid* at a distance of 250 yards. Rather than remain as guide ship, *Mermaid* delegated this task to *Fittleton*, while the frigate took up a position about 500 yards to starboard of the line of minesweepers, before issuing the order for them to close one at

a time to carry out the transfer. Shortly before 1530, *Fittleton* increased speed to 13 knots and turned hard to starboard towards *Mermaid*. Having reversed course by 180° and passed between the frigate and the line of minesweepers, *Fittleton* then reversed course again by making a sharp turn to port and closed *Mermaid* from astern.

As *Fittleton* closed to within 50 feet of the frigate, the increasing water pressure between the hulls of the two vessels caused her to drop about 45 feet astern into a position which, although stable and close enough to *Mermaid*, made it impossible to conduct the transfer at the normal RAS position. It was therefore necessary for *Fittleton* to make a second attempt.

Having increased speed and pulled away, *Fittleton* again closed *Mermaid*. As before, she manoeuvred to within about 100 feet on the port side of *Mermaid* before altering course slightly to starboard and closing to an intended 40 feet. However, on meeting the suction zone along *Mermaid*'s flank, the minesweeper found herself being drawn rapidly towards the frigate. *Fittleton's* Commanding Officer ordered port rudder to be applied and, as his ship appeared to be drawing slowly ahead of the frigate, ordered a reduction in engine revolutions. These actions were to no avail and *Fittleton* continued to be drawn further forward and towards *Mermaid* until the two ships collided bridge-to-bridge. As *Fittleton* bounced off of the frigate her stern was still dangerously close to the *Mermaid* and a reduction in rudder angle paralleled the vessels. Nevertheless, despite further decreases in engine revolutions, *Fittleton* continued to be drawn ahead under the flare of *Mermaid*'s bow. Because of the ship's forward movement down the resistance barrier between the suction and pressure zones at 3 knots faster than the engine shaft revolutions would normally produce, the Commanding Officer decided not to stop engines and so run the risk of damage and possible injury to the guard-rails and fo'c'sle party. He instead tried to utilise the minesweeper's noted acceleration from its two Napier Deltic main engines to drive it out of further trouble.

At first, with the rudder hard to port and both engines at full ahead it was thought that she would break away safely, but the pressure of *Mermaid*'s bow waves acting on the underside of *Fittleton*'s hull aft forced her stern to port, with the result that her bow swung to starboard and *Fittleton* was driven across the path of the frigate. Despite a 'full astern' order on the bridge of the frigate, *Mermaid*'s bow struck *Fittleton*'s starboard side in the region of the minesweeping store and rolled her over, capsizing her completely in just a few seconds.

Those of *Fittleton*'s crew who had been on the upper deck were thrown clear as their ship capsized, but most of them were trapped in the upturned vessel. *HMS Mermaid* and an accompanying minesweeper, *HMS Crofton* (M1216),

stopped immediately, dropping life rafts and shutting down their engines to prevent the men in the water, many of whom were emerging from beneath the minesweeper, from being sucked into the propellers. One rating managed to swim underwater, along his vessel's now submerged upperworks, and upwards to scramble onto the keel via the now stationary propeller shafts.

An officer from the frigate was landed onto the upturned hull, from where tapping could be heard emanating from inside the ship in the vicinity of the engine room. Considerations were given to blowing a hole in the hull to rescue the men, but this was considered too dangerous, not just because of the danger to the trapped men, but also due to the risk of the ship sinking rapidly. Divers worked frantically to rescue the trapped men as two accompanying minesweepers attempted to keep the ship afloat until specialist salvage ships could arrive by passing strops around her propeller shafts. Unfortunately, the strops parted and, at 1945, *Fittleton* sank stern first in 160 feet

*The wrecked minesweeper HMS Fittleton being towed into Chatham following her salvage after being sunk in a collision on 20 September 1976.*
*(T. Ferrers-Walker Collection)*

of water with ten crewmen still aboard.

Ships of the British, Dutch and German navies, as well as several helicopters, took part in the rescue operation and 32 survivors, along with two bodies, were taken to Har wich aboard *Mermaid*, six being detained at the Royal Military Hospital at Colchester suffering from the effects of swallowing oil and sea water.

One of *Fittleton*'s sister ships, *HMS Nurton* (M1166), which had earlier been despatched to Portsmouth with a sonar defect, was ordered to return to the scene to act as navigation guard, until relieved next day by *HMS Bronington* (M1115). Command of the salvage operation was later passed to the frigate *HMS Achilles* (F12) and, following accurate location of the wreck by the Dutch minesweeper *HrMS Roermond* (M806), diving operations began at first light. When no evidence of any further survivors could be heard from inside the hull, marker buoys were attached in preparation for the salvage operation. Royal Navy divers working from the German salvage tug *Taurus* later attached steel hawsers to the hull. The wreck of *Fittleton* was raised by the 1,060-ton floating crane *Magnus I* and towed the 80 miles to Den Helder on 4 October and beached, following which the bodies of the ten entombed crewmen were removed from the vessel and flown back to Britain for burial.

The ship's upper-works had been smashed and her wooden decks were warped and twisted. After being re-floated on the 9th of that month, the hull of the minesweeper was patched up and she was towed to Chatham by naval the tug *RMAS Roysterer* (A361), arriving there on 11 October. The vessel was subsequently declared beyond repair and scrapped the following year. A memorial plaque in memory of the twelve men killed in the tragedy can be found at St. Martins-in-the-field, London.

The Board of Inquiry into the incident found that there had been many errors leading up to the accident, beginning with the far from ideal station of the frigate, to starboard of the minesweepers, prior to the manoeuvre. Ideally, *Mermaid* should have remained in her station at the head of the line of ships. It was also found that the minesweeper had closed too near and at too sharp an angle to *Mermaid* in her approach, instead of maintaining the statutory 75-feet minimum distance between the ships.

A critical factor in the accident was the unique design of *Mermaid*, with her short fo'c'sle, which meant that the position of the transfer placed the smaller ship in the convergence area of the pressure and suction zones emanated by *Mermaid*'s hull. Forward of the frigate's RAS point, the minesweeper would have experienced a pressure area, requiring substantially more power than normal to keep pace with the larger vessel, whereas aft of this point, as was so tragically discovered, a strong suction force was experienced. It was also felt that instead of ordering full ahead and hard-a-port in an attempt to disengage, *Fittleton*'s Commanding Officer should have accepted the risk of a further minor collision and ordered a sharp decrease in speed, together with the rudder movements necessary to allow his ship to draw clear astern of the frigate. At a court-martial on 25 February 1977, he was initially found guilty of negligence, but this charge was later quashed. *HMS Mermaid* was sold to Malaysia in May 1977, being renamed *Hang Tuah* (76) , and remains in service as of 2008.

There is no doubt that the loss of *HMS Fittleton* was the result of human error and non-compliance with the safety regulations laid down for this routine operational procedure. The effects of interaction should be fully understood by the officers in command of the ships involved in any RAS or transfer operation. One of the most critical parts of the operation occurs during the approach phase, when the suction zone of the delivering ship will coincide with the pressure zone of the receiving ship. A similar situation occurs during the breakaway phase as the receiving ship tries to overcome the suction forces between the hulls. In both cases the situation is complicated by the effects of the turning moments created by the attraction and repulsion forces, a situation further complicated when these turning moments reverse as the ships draw level with each other, or as they disengage from the operation and the individual pressure and suction zones created by the ships overlap. These turning moments will require alterations of rudder angle to compensate for their effect.

As shown during the *Fittleton* tragedy, another effect felt by the approaching ship as it approaches the delivering ship will be a reduction in resistance, which will manifest itself in the form of a sudden surge of speed. The opposite effect will be felt as the receiving ship draws level with or attempts to draw ahead of the delivering ship and the pressure zones emanating from the bows of the vessels cause an increase in resistance, with a resultant drop in speed. When the two ships involved in the operation are of different sizes the effects of interaction will be felt more acutely by the smaller vessel.

It can be seen that the effects of interaction require extreme vigilance during the RAS operation, particularly during the approach and disengaging phases. Both vessels should observe extra precautions such as the immediate availability of standby engines and steering systems, together with an increased state of watertight integrity. It is of the utmost importance that common procedures be observed and fully understood by the OOWs of both ships in the event of any emergency affecting the safety of the operation.

A form of interaction was also a contributory factor in the loss of a US Navy tug. On the afternoon of 22 March 1986, the *Secota* (YTM-415) approached the ballistic-missile submarine *USS Georgia* (SSBN-729), three miles south of the Midway channel sea buoy, in order to ferry one of the submarine's crewmen ashore. Although owned by the US Navy, *Secota* was contractor-operated and manned by foreign nationals.

As *Secota* approached, *Georgia* slowed to 3 knots and altered course to 180° to provide a lee for the tug. As the submarine steadied on her course, *Secota* manoeuvred alongside her starboard quarter, just aft of the sail, on a parallel course. At 1544, the personnel transfer completed, *Secota* began backing away from the submarine, using engine and rudder orders to move her stern 30° to starboard. At this point, the tug's port engine stopped, thereby reducing the power available to the craft's two electric propulsion motors and so slowing her single shaft. Realising his craft was in danger of bumping into the submarine, the tugmaster requested that *Georgia* apply right full rudder, in order to swing the submarine's stern away from the tug. This request was not in order with standard procedures for personnel transfers, which dictated that the submarine should maintain course and speed. Nevertheless, when the tugmaster repeated his request, *Georgia*'s Commanding Officer duly complied, while also ordering an increase in engine speed to 'ahead standard', which would have the effect of tripling the submarine's turning rate.

During the next minute, *Georgia*'s speed increased to 6.7 knots, whilst *Secota*'s heading swung to the right, returning her to a course almost parallel to that of the submarine. Consequently, when power was regained and *Secota* again began backing away, she was moving directly down the side of the submarine, rather than away from her as the tugmaster had intended. As the submarine continued moving ahead, the suction effect created along her flank kept the tug almost alongside, until it impacted with the SSBN's stern plane.

Meanwhile, *Georgia*'s Commanding Officer had ordered the submarine's shaft to be stopped, in order to prevent the propeller from slashing the tug's hull or injuring any personnel who might fall into the water. As *Georgia* slowed, *Secota* became impaled on her stern plane, with her bow resting on the submarine's turtle-back. The tugmaster continued to back his craft's motors in an attempt to break free, but she immediately began flooding through her ruptured hull and was soon settling deeper in the water, her stern gunwale almost submerged. Twenty seconds later, the tug rolled to port, settled by the stern and quickly sank, her demise being hastened by the craft's poor watertight integrity.

*Georgia* immediately manoeuvred to rescue survivors and, during the next hour, ten of the tug's crewmen were plucked from the water, together with the recently transferred submariner. An intensive search by the submarine and two harbour craft continued until after sunset, but tragically failed to locate the tug's chief engineer and a deck hand.

As the other Midway tug, *Winamac* (YTM-394) , was not fitted with the necessary fendering which would permit her to safely come alongside a submarine, *Georgia* then submerged and headed for Pearl H arbour with the survivors. The following morning, a further search was carried out by a flotilla of small craft and several aircraft, but there was no trace of the two missing crewmen.

The water's depth at the position where *Secota* sank - 28°07'N, 177°21'W - is about 900 fathoms and so salvage was deemed impracticable. *USS Georgia* suffered minor damage to her starboard stern plane vertical stabiliser and the loss of her AN/BQQ-9 towed sonar array.

Several factors had contributed to this incident, the primary one being the failure of one of *Secota*'s engines, both of which were notoriously unreliable and had failed on several occasions, despite a recent overhaul. The subsequent investigation revealed that the Midway Base Operations Support contractor had not been fulfilling its contractual responsibilities with regards to maintenance of the tugs in its charge.

The tug master's dubious decision to back away from the submarine was also a major contributory factor, as was the continued backing of his engines after the tug had lost propulsive power and had slewed around parallel with the submarine. This was a grave error of judgement by the tugmaster, as the accepted doctrine for clearing the side of a submarine is for the submarine to slow to dead in the water and then for the tug to ease ahead slowly until clear. Alternatively, with the submarine moving slowly ahead, the tug should move ahead, sliding forward, utilising the bow cushion created by the submarine and small angles of rudder to ease clear.

A retired naval man, the tugmaster had gained three years previous experience operating tugs at Pearl Harbour prior to moving to Midway, although he had never before undertaken a personnel transfer with an underway submarine at sea. Although he was aware of the submarine's protrusions aft, such as her fairwater and stern planes, he erroneously continued backing his craft until it struck the submarine's stern planes.

Finally, the tug's dangerous predicament was further aggravated by the hull suction forces caused by the submarine's forward movement which, despite the Commanding Officer's actions in applying right full rudder, drew the tug towards her.

During the 'Cold War', the practice of NATO and Warsaw Pact warships shadowing the others' naval exercises resulted in many minor collisions and such occurrences were regarded as an accepted hazard of the intelligence-gathering 'game'. Such 'accidents' were commonly attributed to errors of judgement on the part of one ship for cutting across the bow of the other or for getting too close in an effort to acquire clearer pictures of the adversary. However, in reality they were generally the result of aggressive navigation, whereby one vessel would intentionally 'nudge' another in order to dissuade them from getting too close to sensitive naval manoeuvres.

Dozens - or maybe even hundreds - of minor scrapes between surface vessels have occurred, the May 1967 collision between the Soviet Project 56 ('Kotlin'-class) destroyer *Besslednyi* and *USS Walker* (DD-517) being typical. The Soviet vessel had been shadowing US Naval forces in the north-west Pacific when the two destroyers were involved in a side-scrape, causing some minor denting of hull plating and guard-rail damage on both ships.

One of *Besslednyi's* sister ships was involved in a more serious collision with a British aircraft carrier $3\frac{1}{2}$ years later. On the night of 9 November 1970, the *Bravyi* was observing night flying exercises by *HMS Ark Royal* (R09) in the Mediterranean. Despite the carrier displaying lights in accordance with the 1965 international law - to which the Soviets were a signatory - to indicate that she was carrying out flying operations, the destroyer was steaming in extremely close company. For some unknown reason the *Bravyi* turned sharply across the carrier's bows and was only saved from the same fate as *HMAS Voyager* and *USS Frank E. Evans* by the swift actions of the *Ark Royal's* Commanding Officer, Captain Ray Lygo, who ordered full astern at the critical moment.

The inevitable collision caused extensive damage to the Soviet vessel's superstructure and buckling to her hull plating amidships, whilst two members of her crew were lost overboard. *Ark Royal*, which carried out an intensive search for the lost Soviet sailors, was holed in the bow. Both vessels were able to conclude their respective operations before retiring for repairs. A formal protest was later lodged by the Foreign Office through the British Embassy in Moscow, but the Soviets claimed that it had been the British ship that had unexpectedly altered course.

Submarines are ideally suited to intelligence-gathering missions. Their characteristics have always permitted stealthy and sometimes close observation of ships, submarines, coastlines and harbours. There have been numerous reported incidences of minor collisions between the warships and submarines of the super-powers, many of which have been of an aggravated nature and may have resulted in international incidents had not the most serious of them been regarded as closely guarded secrets for many years.

Just how many of these incidents actually took place may never be known, but a 1976 Congressional Report stated that US submarines had collided with nine Soviet vessels in or near Soviet waters between 1965 and 1975, whilst a more recent statement by the Chief Navigator of the Russian Navy, Vice Admiral Valery Aleksin, highlighted at least seven collisions between Soviet and US Navy submarines between 1968 and 1987. He even suggested that such collisions could have been responsible for the loss of the Project 629A SSB *K-129* in 1968 and the Project 667A SSBN *K-219* in 1986.

Assuming such a theory to be without substance, probably one of the most serious incidents occurred in June 1970, when *USS Tautog* (SSN-639) was closely shadowing the Soviet Project 675 ('Echo-II'-class) nuclear-powered cruise missile submarine *K-108* in the northern Pacific. So close was she shadowing that *Tautog's* crew were taken by surprise when the

Soviet boat abruptly changed course - possibly undertaking a manoeuvre known in the West as a 'Crazy Ivan' - and were unable to avoid a collision. The force of the impact as *K-108*'s propellers struck *Tautog*'s sail holed the Soviet boat and bent her starboard propeller shaft and resulted in a short uncontrolled dive before control was regained. *Tautog* suffered damage to her sail and periscopes. As the US boat headed to Pearl Harbor for repairs, it was unknown whether or not the Soviet boat had survived the incident, but she too returned safely to port. This incident was mentioned in several American newspaper articles in the mid-1970s, which reported on a secret US Navy submarine intelligence operation code-named Holystone, in which specially equipped Sturgeon-class submarines were used to gather intelligence on Soviet fleet activities in the 1960s and 1970s.

Whether the Soviet boat was aware of *Tautog*'s presence and intentionally attempted to shake off her shadower by ramming her, or whether this was an entirely accidental collision, will probably never be known. However, that Soviet submarine commanders were prepared to ram submarines that got too close was shown in the early 1960s, after the Project 658 ('Hotel'-class) SSBN *K-19* narrowly avoided a collision with the US Navy's first nuclear submarine, *USS Nautilus* (SSN-571). *Nautilus*, which had been shadowing *K-19*, had suddenly found herself cutting across in front of the Soviet boat. It was later revealed that Admiral Gorshkov criticised *K-19*'s Commanding Officer, Captain Nikolai Zateyev, for not having rammed the *Nautilus*. *K-19* was later involved in another collision incident with the Permit-class attack submarine *USS Gato* (SSN-615), whilst submerged at a depth of 60 metres in the Barents Sea on 15 November 1969. Both submarines suffered minor damage and returned to harbour safely.

Other examples included the near-fatal collision on 3 November 1974 between *USS James Madison* (SSBN-627) and a Soviet Project 671 ('Victor I'-class) nuclear attack boat in the North Sea. Nine years later, on 31 October 1983, a Project 671RTM ('Victor III'-class) boat fouled the towed array sonar array of the frigate *USS McCloy* (FF-1038) in the Atlantic, suffering such damage that she had to be towed into Cuba for repairs. In March 1984, another Project 671 boat collided with the aircraft carrier *USS Kitty Hawk* (CV-63) in the Sea of Japan. These are just a few of the 'unfortunate' incidents between Soviet and NATO vessels during the 'Cold War', as each side tried to keep track of the others naval vessels, particularly their ballistic-missile submarines. However, despite the demise of the Berlin Wall, there have been several further scrapes between American and Russian submarines.

US and Russian news reports differed regarding the collision, on 11 February 1992, between the Los Angeles-class boat *USS Baton Rouge* (SSN-689) and the Russian Project 945 ('Sierra-I'-class) nuclear attack submarine *Kostroma* (K-276). The main variance was in the reported location of the incident, which the US Navy claimed occurred in position 69°39'N, 33°49'E, whilst the Russians reported it to have taken place slightly further west in position 69°38.7'N, 33°46.9'E, bringing into dispute whether or not the incident took place within Russian territorial waters.

*Baton Rouge* was operating submerged at a depth of 18 metres and was on a south-south-westerly heading when the collision occurred. It was claimed that sonar acoustic conditions at the time were severely degraded by rough seas and the Russian boat was not detected until it was too late. Both vessels suffered minor damage and the US Navy later reported that the Commanding Officer of the American boat was informally cautioned.

*The French boat FS Galatée being salvaged following a collision with the South African submarine SAS Maria van Riebeeck on 20 August 1970.*

*(Marius Bar)*

crew began passing out through lack of air and six crewmen drowned after falling unconscious into the water flooding the after torpedo room. The diesel engine finally stopped through air starvation and fresh air was sucked into the boat through the open conning tower voice tube. As the crew began coming round, the Commanding Officer, Lt. Cdr. Lauga, decided to run his boat aground to avoid her sinking.

Damage to the *Maria van Riebeeck* turned out to be minor, but the *Galatée* required significant structural repairs to her damaged pressure hull and propeller shafting. Both submarines were returned to service after repairs. However, had the *Galatée's* crew not come round from their unconscious state, the submarine may well have become the third vessel of her class to be lost, following the disappearance of her sister boats *FS Minerve* (S647) on 27 January 1968 and *FS Eurydice* (S644) on 4 March 1970, both in the Western Mediterranean near Toulon (see Chapter 9).

Various disputes regarding fishing rights have resulted in a number of incidents, epitomised by the clashes between Royal Navy warships protecting British fishing fleets from harassment by Icelandic 'gunboats'. During the 'Cod War' in May 1959 the destroyer *HMS Chaplet* (D52) collided with the Icelandic fisheries-protection ship *Odinn* in what was claimed by the Admiralty to be a navigational error. The Icelanders claimed that the destroyer had deliberately tried to ram the *Odinn*.

This was one of a large number of similar incidents between Icelandic gunboats and Royal Navy warships escorting British fishing vessels. In two further 'Cod Wars' in 1973 and 1976, at least ten British frigates suffered damage ranging from bent guard-rails to minor flooding through split hull plating, after clashes with the Icelandic fisheries-protection ships *Odinn, Aegir, Thor,*

This incident was followed, in March 1993, by a further clash in the Barents Sea between *USS Grayling* (SSN-646) and a Project 677BDR ('Delta III'-class) ballistic-missile submarine.

Serious collisions between submarines of allied navies are rare, but one such incident between two boats of the same class came close to resulting in the loss of an entire crew.

The new South African Daphné-class submarine *SAS Maria Van Riebeeck* (S97) was returning to Toulon from a day of trials on the evening of 20 August 1970 when the French boat *FS Galatée* (S646) was spotted on the surface a short distance away leaving the harbour. As the *Galatée* passed ahead of the *Maria van Riebeeck* she suddenly altered course to starboard towards the South African boat. Despite the Commanding Officer ordering emergency astern, the *Maria van Riebeeck* was unable to avoid the collision and struck the *Galatée's* port quarter, damaging the French boat's propeller.

The impact caused the *Galatée* to begin flooding through the shaft stern seal. As the diesel engine air intake valve became submerged, the engine began sucking air from inside the boat. Soon afterwards, the

*Baldur* and *Tyr*. On several occasions, the ice-strengthened 'gunboats' were filmed apparently attempting to ram the frigates or cut through the nets of British fishing vessels.

Occasionally, confrontations arise out of territorial disputes. In July 1969, during one of the many disagreements over the sovereignty of Gibraltar, *HMS Arlingham* (M2603) was rammed by a 90-ton Spanish customs launch, which was attempting to cut under the British inshore minesweeper's stern.

As stated at the beginning of this chapter, one of the major factors in many collision incidents is inexperience on the part of the bridge crews of the ships involved. Naval exercises, whilst improving the standard of crew training in an operational environment, also expose ships to increased risk of collision, which is why navies that actively participate in regular exercises are more prone to such incidents. The training of OOW/OODs in the skills of ship handling is an expensive and time-consuming evolution, requiring the commitment of a high proportion of a navy's precious resources.

It is imperative that the training of junior officers in the art of ship handling is built upon a firm foundation of theory and practical experience, both ashore and at sea. It has been proven time and again that, when training standards are allowed to lapse, so the number of accidents will increase, even in the most professional of navies.

A spate of naval accidents, culminating in the tragic loss of *HMAS Voyager* in 1964, shocked the Australian Navy into the realisation that their professional standards had fallen to an unacceptable level. In the same time frame, the Royal Navy had also suffered a similar series of disasters, notably the scrapping of the destroyers *Hogue* and *Battleaxe* following their collisions in 1959 and 1962 respectively, whilst during exercises in the Mediterranean in 1959 the cruiser *HMS*

*Birmingham* (C19) was involved in a collision with the destroyer *HMS Delight* (D08). Two of the cruiser's crew later died after becoming overcome by fumes whilst inspecting for damage below the waterline. It was suggested that this and several other accidents that year were attributable to the lack of sea-time available for training due to monetary constraints, with cruisers limited to only 60 days sea time and destroyers and frigates 70-90 days, during that financial year.

Meanwhile, manpower shortages were indirectly blamed for the collision two years later between the Type 12 frigate *HMS Falmouth* (F113) and a Royal Fleet Auxiliary tanker. The frigate, involved in sea trials before her entry into service with the Royal Navy, was carrying only five officers of her normal complement of fifteen, resulting in some of them spending as much as 14 hours on watch at a time, a fact which was taken into account at the subsequent courts-martial. At this time, the brunt of the Royal Navy's manpower shortages was borne by the Home Fleet ships.

More recently, on 14 November 1989, the U.S. Navy Secretary, H. Lawrence Garrett III, and the Chief of Naval Operations, Carlisle A.H. Trost, ordered a "safety stand-down", during which the mighty US Navy were to cease all operational activities for a period of 48 hours whilst safety procedures were reviewed throughout the fleet. This extraordinary move followed a spate of major accidents that year which had resulted in the death of over sixty sailors. It was further revealed that, in the previous six years alone, US Navy submarines had been involved in at least 42 collisions. A year later, the US Navy outlined proposals for lowering the accident rate, including raising the standard of theoretical training and practical skills of personnel, the introduction of computer-based trainers, and closer monitoring of naval vessel building and repair.

Professional, all-volunteer, navies have the benefit of a certain amount of consistency in their training load, in that the trained manpower is not overly diluted by the constant influx of large numbers of inexperienced conscripts who may have had little incentive to give their best in a career which is not of their choosing. The Soviet Navy has always consisted of a high proportion of conscripted manpower within its ranks, necessitating a higher proportion of the crews of their warships being of officer or warrant officer status. In January 1991, the period of conscription was decreased from three to two years. However, this latter move resulted in conscript sailors, who form 75% of the Navy's strength, having insufficient time in service to become trained as valued members of a ship's company, particularly with regards to the ever-increasing complexity of weapons and machinery in their newer nuclear submarines. Consequently, the numbers of conscripted servicemen in these boats are low, with a high proportion of their crews being senior michmen (warrant officers), carrying out tasks which in western navies would be carried out by more junior ratings.

Conscription deferments for university students have also been reintroduced, denying the Russian armed forces of the higher educated recruits. This can only result in a further drop in the quality of ship's crews. In an attempt to counter this, pay scales of career servicemen have been increased to a level equivalent to up to 35 times that of a conscript, providing an incentive for more conscripts to 'sign on' for further service. In the long term, this may result in an increasing proportion of Russian warship crewmen being volunteers, thereby increasing the standard of operation to match the increases in quality and complexity of the hardware. However, training within the Russian fleet has suffered a severe setback due to the financial crisis in which the country finds itself and, until recently, even the most modern units of the fleet have been tied up at their berths, insufficient funds being available to fully crew or fuel them. Their problems are further compounded by the fact that there are around 120 different languages spoken within the former-Soviet Union, as well as several religions - with the resultant deep-rooted rivalries inherent.

The problems of the Russian fleet - namely the use of large numbers of poorly-educated conscripts, coupled with insufficient funds to support training needs - are suffered by a large number of navies, a fact painfully evident in the poor material state of their naval vessels. In many countries, such an 'invisible' commodity as training comes a poor second to the procurement of complex weapon systems with which to arm their craft. This is obviously a false economy when the cost of repairs to vessels - or their complete replacement - is taken into account. An increasing number of navies are now realising that simulators can ease the burden of training crews in a variety of skills, not least that of ship handling. A wide range of bridge simulators are now available and are being procured by several navies, thereby reducing the training bill by carrying out training ashore, at an affordable cost, without tying up valuable front line warships for such duties.

As a footnote to this chapter, it is not just collisions with other ships that have resulted in the loss of naval vessels. During 'Exercise Bluebird' on 5 June 1952, two Netherlands Air Force F-84E Thunderjet aircraft were tasked with carrying out mock attacks on a small Royal Navy flotilla operating off Den Helder. The first two attack runs by the aircraft went without incident, but on the third run at 0615, the lead aircraft approached too low and flew into the British Fairmile 'B' Harbour Defence Motor Launch *ML2582*.

The small 73-ton craft was engulfed in a huge explosion and quickly sank. Two sister vessels, *ML2221* and *ML2586*, were quickly on the scene, but only one wounded survivor was found amongst the wreckage. The aircraft's pilot and the other fourteen member of *ML2582*'s crew were all killed. Tragically, the sole survivor, William James Johnson, died at home whilst on sick leave recovering from his injuries the following week.

Even more bizarre was the loss of the US minesweeping boat *MSB-43*. The 17.45 metre-long wooden-hulled craft sank on 20 January 1967 after colliding with a dolphin at Charleston, South Carolina. The vessel was later re-floated, but was written-off as a constructive total loss on 1 February. A similar incident occurred in late-1974, when the experimental hydrofoil patrol craft *USS Flagstaff* (WPGH-1) was badly damaged in collision with a whale, although she was later repaired.

More recently, the West German submarine *U27* (S176) collided with a North Sea oil rig on 6 March 1988. The boat was submerged at a depth of about 30 metres when she first stuck the anchoring cable of the hotel platform *Polyconfidence*, before becoming ensnared in the underwater structure of the main Oseberg Bravo platform, west of Bergen. While the 300-man crew of the platform was evacuated, believing that an earthquake had struck the area, it was over an hour before the startled submariners could free their boat and bring her safely to the surface. *U27* was later escorted home and her minor damage repaired, whilst her Commanding Officer was reprimanded for failing to steer clear of the platform, which was noted on her charts, by the statutory distance of 500 metres.

These incidents clearly illustrate that disaster can strike from totally unexpected angles and that crews should be prepared for any eventuality.

# Chapter Five

# MATERIAL AND STRUCTURAL FAILURES

'Material or structural failure' is a wide-ranging term that can be used to account for almost any naval accident. For instance, many fires result from the material failure of fuel pipes or the breakdown of electrical insulation, whilst the grounding of a vessel can often be attributed to engine or steering gear defects resulting from failures of components within the machinery. Nonetheless, such material failures can often only be regarded as the catalyst that began a chain reaction of incidents that eventually led to the crippling, or loss, of a vessel. This chapter, therefore, is primarily concerned with the loss of vessels solely due the failure of hull structures, fittings or appendages, resulting in the flooding - and possibly sinking - of the vessel. Such failures can usually be attributed to one of two factors: the degradation of a structure due to neglect or to inadequate maintenance procedures; or unforeseen metallurgical imperfections built into the hull or its fittings.

Vessels built during the Second World War suffered from many shortfalls in their construction. In order to support the war effort, vast shipbuilding programmes were initiated and had to be sustained throughout the conflict to both replace sunken vessels and to satisfy the requirement for an ever-increasing number of warships, landing craft, auxiliary vessels and merchant tonnage. Such programmes required a constant supply of materials, far in excess of the quantities that the industries would normally have been able to provide. Steel furnaces worked flat out to match the demand, whilst the wood mills devoured forests to provide timber. Coupled with this, the armaments industries required massive quantities of high-grade steels with which to manufacture the weapons to arm the vessels. To match these demands, the acceptable quality of steel used in shipbuilding had to be lowered; whilst younger timber had to be used as the supplies of older trees were exhausted.

This massive expansion of the ship- and boat-building industries meant that yards had to take on labour from wherever they could find it, as millions of men were called to arms. Previously unskilled workers had to quickly pick up the threads of their new jobs without the benefit of apprenticeships or protracted training periods. Neither could they afford to take the time in learning their new trades, as the urgent requirement for ships meant that construction times, and trial programmes, had to be considerably reduced, necessitating the adoption of newly developed mass-production building methods.

The most important of these mass-production techniques was undoubtedly the use of electric arc welding instead of the more time consuming riveting of joints. Electric arc welding had previously been used for the manufacture of lesser structures which were not subject to high stress, but the undisputed saving in weight and construction time offered by welding led to its use in the assembly of main strength members and hull plating. Construction times were further reduced by the adoption of modular building techniques, whereby complete sections of hull and superstructure would be assembled, sometimes in separate shipyards, before being brought together to form the completed vessel. Furthermore, refinements in design such as curved and shaped steel, gave way to sharp corners, which required less time to manufacture, but also formed high stress points that had a tendency to crack. All of these shipbuilding methods had to be undertaken by relatively unskilled welders who, although they quickly learned their trades under a baptism of fire, were compelled to work long hours and were ever being pushed to improve productivity.

Finally, standards of quality assurance inspection, so rigorously applied in peacetime, had to be reduced. It should be remembered, however, that most vessels were built to perform a purely functional, 'hostilities only' task, be it engaging the enemy or transporting supplies and equipment - they were not intended, in most cases, to have long service careers.

Given these overriding constraints under which the shipyards were forced to operate, it is hardly surprising that there were many reports of hull plating welds cracking or splitting, causing flooding of compartments and often the foundering of the vessel.

Following the cessation of hostilities in the Pacific in September 1945, the battered and ill-maintained vessels of the decimated Imperial Japanese Navy lay in ports and anchorages around the Japanese islands. Many of these vessels had received almost no maintenance in the closing months of the war, and most had been damaged in some way by the overwhelming onslaught of the Allied bombing campaign. Others lay incomplete at their fitting out berths. Although the imperial Japanese Navy effectively ceased to exist following their surrender, all available seaworthy surface ships, particularly minesweepers and escort vessels, were commandeered for service with the allied operations to clear the harbours, anchorages and estuaries of the continuing serious threat of the mine.

It was inevitable therefore that several of these vessels would founder at their berths as they lay neglected by their demoralised crews. During the remaining months of 1945, dozens of vessels simply developed leaks in their hulls and sank. Many more were lost in the same typhoons that caused such destruction to the US Navy occupational fleet at Okinawa, as the storm raged across the Japanese islands. The vast majority of these vessels were never repaired, there being a huge world surplus of most types of war-built naval vessels, and most of them were simply raised and scrapped. Similar fates befell vessels laid up all around the world, as their crews were demobilised and returned to their peacetime occupations.

A large number of war-built vessels continued to serve for many years after the cessation of hostilities, despite their poor material state. The Japanese Type D Escort *CD62* was launched in 1945, but was surrendered incomplete to the Allies at Mukaijima, Ohanichi. At the end of the year, the ship was towed to Kure, where she was completed for repatriation duties. However, before she could perform any useful tasks, *CD62* sank on 14 January 1946 after flooding through leaking hull plating. Likewise, the naval tug *Eisen 1651* - an ex-submarine chaser - had been taken over by the allies after her capture at Aruga in August 1945, but a year later, leaks in the vessel's poorly maintained hull caused her to sink. Both of these vessels were later raised and scrapped.

Many war-built wooden craft, such as minesweepers, had also been constructed using poor quality materials, with boatyards being forced to use green, unseasoned timber, which had a tendency to warp and crack. In many cases, this merely resulted in alignment problems with a vessel's main engines and shafting as the settling of the hull caused its shape to deform slightly. However, it was common for such vessels to leak badly in areas of weakness such as the stern glands, particularly in rough weather, whilst bilges generally contained a certain amount of seawater that had seeped into the vessel via leaking hull planking.

So it was that the Royal Navy motor minesweeper *MMS288 (M1788)* - which had been involved in the search for the submarine *HMS Affray* in April 1951 - was herself lost on 21 October of the following year. The vessel foundered off Winterton Ness after the engine room flooded whilst on passage from Harwich to Rosyth. Fortunately, there were no casualties amongst the vessel's crew, as they were picked up by nearby vessels.

During the Second World War, the Australian Government ordered a large number of wooden harbour tugs. Subsequently, small coastal shipyards throughout Australia built over sixty of these 45-feet long towboats. Although many of these craft gave faithful service well into the 1960s, by the mid-1950s many of them were in very poor condition and were rapidly being disposed of, necessitating some redistribution of the remaining craft to provide adequate support to naval ships at a number of bases. However, because of the small size of these craft and the undue wear put on their engines by lengthy sea transits, the safest means of transporting them was

either as deck cargo or under tow. During such towing operations, two of these 21-ton towboats were lost, primarily due to the poor condition of their copper-sheathed hulls.

Whilst under tow from Manus, on Manus Island on the Bismarck Archipelago, to Sydney by the fleet tug *HMAS Sprightly (W103)* on 28 March 1956, *TB-6* began taking on water and later foundered. The subsequent Board of Inquiry, whilst unable to attribute blame for the loss of the craft to any particular person, determined that the pumping facilities available in the boat had been totally inadequate, making it impossible to contain flooding through leaking hull planking. It had not been possible to overhaul the hull of the tug prior to her journey, as a suitable dock was not available. Nevertheless, when the decision was taken in July 1956 to tow *TB-11* from Fremantle to Manus, lessons learnt from the loss of *TB-6* were considered, but it was soon apparent that the lack of suitable pumping arrangements aboard these craft had not been remedied.

During the first leg of the journey, under tow of the minesweeper *HMAS Wagga (M183)*, on 10 December, the two vessels were forced to heave to off Capedon, as water was entering the engine room of the tug faster than her pumps could eject it. After putting a steaming party aboard to pump out *TB-11,* it was discovered that water was seeping into the craft through most of the seams in the hull. It appeared that, with the weight of the towing cable depressing the tug's bows, water was entering through seems which would normally have been above the water line. Also, additional stresses imposed on the hull by the tow also opened up seams in the deck and allowed rainwater to pour in.

Nevertheless, with a contingent from *Wagga's* crew aboard the tug to keep the pumps running, the tow was continued and Darwin was reached safely two days later. Here, a survey of the craft revealed that, even when stationary, the vessel was continually flooding through her hull seams and that her machinery was in a poor state of repair. It was surmised that the 1,100-mile tow from Fremantle had put excessive strain on the craft's wooden hull and, as a result, it was recommended that *TB-11* would not be fit to continue her voyage to Manus until she received a refit to make her seaworthy.

Following a period of repair, including re-caulking of hull seams, *TB-11* was prepared for continuation of her journey, under tow of the minesweeper *HMAS Junee* (M362), but adverse weather conditions caused her departure to be delayed and the towing task transferred to the research vessel *HMAS Kimbla* (AGOR-314). Meanwhile prolonged unserviceability of *TB-5* at Manus added an element of urgency to the operation, whilst a minor berthing collision between *Kimbla* and *TB-11* further delayed departure until 1200 on Thursday, 20 June 1957.

A small transit crew, consisting of three ratings from *Kimbla*, had been put aboard *TB-11*, with orders to start the tug's engines at least twice a day in order to run the engine-driven bilge pump and to keep the engine starting battery fully charged. The vessel's small auxiliary generator was inoperable. They were further instructed that, in the event of the tow parting, the tug's engines were to be started and they were to steam in company with *Kimbla*. During this second-leg transit, no difficulties were encountered with the engines and water ingress through the tug's hull seams was no more than had been expected. The two vessels arrived safely at Port Moresby, Papua New Guinea, a week later.

*Kimbla* and *TB-11* departed Port Moresby at 1115 on Monday, 1 July under ideal weather conditions. A mild breeze was blowing from the south-south-east and a slight swell was running. This swell increased slightly as the pair cleared the Basilisk Passage, whilst the wind increased to force 4, but these conditions gave the towing party no real cause for concern. Nevertheless, *Kimbla* was forced to reduce the speed of the tow from 6 knots to 5 knots, as the research ship's large bow tended to slam into the troughs. Speed was further reduced to 4 knots at 1900, as the swell had increased slightly to 6 feet. *TB-11* meanwhile, was riding the swell with relative ease and with only minor spray being cast over her bow. No undue strain had so far been put on the towing cable and three-quarters of its 100-fathom length was constantly submerged.

Shortly afterwards, the sound of the tug's engines running was heard aboard *Kimbla*, giving the impression that all was well aboard the little craft. It had been arranged that the transit crew aboard *TB-11* would flash the letters 'O.K.' in Morse to *Kimbla* once an hour and these reports were received up until just after 2300. When no such report was received at midnight, it did not give cause for concern, as it was known that only one of the ratings aboard the tug was in possession of a watch. In any case, the weather conditions had improved a little and as people could be seen moving around the tug, *TB-11* was not considered to be in any difficulties.

This illusion was shattered at 0020, when a red flare was fired from *TB-11*, indicating in a pre-planned code to *Kimbla* "I am making water rapidly and require assistance." As the alarm was raised, the Commanding Officer, Lieutenant Commander A.R. Pearson, RANVR, arrived on the bridge, whilst the First Lieutenant and the Chief Engine Room Artificer headed to the quarter-deck to investigate the cause of the tug's distress signal. *Kimbla*'s speed was reduced, whilst the winch was started and the towing cable hauled in to bring the tug to short stay. As *TB-11* was drawn to within 100 feet of *Kimbla*, one of the transit crew shouted that, although the tug's engines were running, suction on the bilge pump could not be maintained, despite a depth of water in the engine room of 36 inches. In fact, the transit crew had not been able to obtain suction at 1930 and they had been struggling with the pump since the engines were restarted at about 2300.

Although the mechanic had checked the pump strainer and tightened the drive belt by removing a couple of linkages, suction was still not obtained. To assist in the diagnosis of the defect, the Chief ERA ordered that the engines be shut down and sent a senior ERA across to the tug. On arrival aboard *TB-11*, the artificer attempted to locate the cause of the pump's defect, but, unable to do so, he asked for advice from the Chief ERA, who ordered that the engines be restarted in order to conduct further trials. However, by this time the rising water level had reached the engine starting batteries, thereby flooding them and making it impossible to restart the engines.

No portable pumps were available aboard *Kimbla* for transfer to the tug and, with the water level continuing to rise at an increasing rate, the four men aboard the tug resorted to bailing out the craft using a small semi-rotary hand pump and buckets. At 0130, Lt.Cdr. Pearson ordered a course be set for a return to Port Moresby at a speed of 8 knots.

The situation now deteriorated rapidly, especially as the following swell was making the tug unmanageable and causing her to sheer wildly at the end of the 100-fathom tow line and eventually resulted in the towing cable parting close to the swivel piece on the tow end. Lt.Cdr. Pearson manoeuvred his ship towards *TB-11* and ordered that preparations be made for re-establishing the tow. This was successfully achieved on the second attempt, but by then it could be seen that *TB-11* was rapidly settling by the bow and developing a heavy list to port. Fearing

that the tug was in danger of foundering, Lt.Cdr. Pearson ordered that the transit crew be evacuated. At 0315, having manoeuvred *Kimbla* close alongside *TB-11* so that they could jump aboard, the cable was veered out to 120 fathoms and the tow recommenced in the direction of Port Moresby at a painfully slow speed of 2 knots. It was intended to head for Hood Bay, some twenty miles away, where a motorboat would be lowered to tow *TB-11* onto the beach. Inevitably, the little craft continued to sink lower in the water and, at 0416, the tow was severed and *TB-11* finally foundered, bow first, in 1,300 fathoms of water in position 10°24.5'S, 147°45'E. After retrieving minor items of flotsam, *Kimbla* resumed her course for Manus.

A Board of Inquiry was convened at *HMAS Tarangua* on Monday, 8 July to investigate the circumstances attending the foundering. It was considered that, whilst *TB-11* had been certified as seaworthy prior to her departure from Darwin, this condition was dependent on the efficiency of her pumping arrangements; such was the leakage through her hull planking. Attempts had been made by Lt.Cdr. Pearson to obtain a spare portable pump from Port Moresby as an added precaution, but a unit had not been available for issue. The Board considered that HMAS *Kimbla* had undertaken the tow of *TB-11* in a professional and seamanlike manner but that, had the transit crew reported difficulties with the engine-driven pump when recognised at 1930, it may have been possible to take actions to save the craft.

Nevertheless, no-one was considered culpably negligent in the course of his duty and the loss was determined to have been due to the poor state of the vessel's hull and to the inability of her pumping arrangements to contain the sea water entering through parted hull seams. It was further recommended that, in view of the loss of both *TB-6* and *TB-11*, similar craft should not in future be steamed or towed on long ocean passages.

The 1960s saw a large number of war-built vessels being towed off to the scrapyard, their hull plating by then badly corroded and rotted through, partly due to the inconsistency of the quality of wartime steel. Nevertheless, it is surprising that so many war-vintage ships, mostly of US origin, are still in service with navies around the world, albeit in rapidly decreasing numbers. Apart from those that foundered in the immediate post-war years due to the neglect of being laid up without preservation, and losses of less well-maintained examples in some third-world navies, those vessels that have remained in constant operation have given good service. Such vessels were acquired in large numbers, at minimum cost, to rebuild the decimated naval forces of previously occupied countries. Favoured for their simple, robust designs and uncomplicated power plants, many of these ships have been extensively rebuilt many times and some, such as the Taiwanese ex-Gearing-class destroyers, bore little resemblance to their original appearance by the time they were being paid off in the late-1990s. However, when not adequately maintained, such elderly vessels can quickly deteriorate to a state whereby they are no longer seaworthy or structurally sound.

The majority of the vessels belonging to the major navies of the world receive effective maintenance, interspersed with regular docking periods, during which the hull plating and fittings in particular are subjected to a thorough inspection for any signs of deterioration or damage. However, this is not always the case in some of the smaller navies, many of which are comprised purely of foreign-built vessels. Often these countries have little or no shipbuilding or ship-repair facilities or experience and their naval personnel are poorly trained in the art of

ship-husbandry, relying to a large degree on the services of contractors from the countries supplying their vessels to undertake detailed maintenance and refits on their behalf. The seaworthiness of their vessels is often of a low priority compared to the procurement of increasingly sophisticated weapons with which to arm them.

The Algerine-class ocean minesweeper *HMS Hare* (M389) was sold to Nigeria on 21 July 1959 and renamed *NNS Nigeria*, being employed as an escort vessel. However, during a survey at Chatham Naval Dockyard only three years later, it was discovered that the ship's boilers were in such a poor state that the vessel was deemed to be beyond economical repair. The ship was consequently scrapped in October 1962. Other vessels of the Nigerian Navy were to suffer from such similar neglect.

In 1972 the Nigerian Navy took delivery of two Mk.3 corvettes from Vosper-Thornycroft's Southampton shipyard, subsequently named *NN Ships Dorina* (F81) and *Otobo* (F82). By April 1987, both vessels were in an extremely poor state of repair, having been inoperative for several years following damage during fumigation and heavy cannibalisation of useful materials. The vessels were taken to Snake Island in Lagos harbour for repairs and overhaul by the Dutch/Polish consortium Nigerdock, where it was discovered that their hulls were badly corroded due to the lack of maintenance of their sacrificial anodes, and were condemned. Had either of the corvettes put to sea in their dilapidated condition, there would have been a good chance that they may never have returned to harbour.

Both ships received some minor repairs to their weakened hulls and were handed back to the Nigerian Navy. However, the repairs were only intended as a temporary measure, as both vessels required much of their hull plating replaced completely.

*The corvette NNS Otobo (F82) was one of two sister ships built by Vosper-Thornycroft for Nigeria in 1972. By 1987, both vessels were in an extremely poor state of repair. On 18 May 1987, sister-ship NNS Dorina (F81) sank at her moorings, whilst Otobo, berthed alongside her, narrowly escaped the same fate. The Otobo was repaired, but Dorina was raised and declared a total loss.*
*(Vosper Thornycroft (UK) Ltd)*

Within days the hulls were leaking badly and pumps were required to be run 24 hours a day to keep them afloat. For some unexplained reason, the pumps were switched off when the crews went on leave and both ships began taking on water. Damage-control actions succeeded in saving the *Otobo*, but the *Dorina* sank at her moorings, with only her mast protruding above the water's surface.

*Dorina* was raised on 18 May 1987, but the extensive damage to her hull and equipment rendered her a constructive total loss, although the hulk remained in existence for many years after. *Otobo*, a pitiful sight with her dilapidated, rust-covered hull and superstructure, was taken in hand for a two-year repair period at the Oran yard in Genoa from 21 April 1988. The ship had to be transported there on the heavy lift ship *Condock 1*, since her hull was unlikely to have survived the journey. The refit cost the Nigerian Navy US$24.2 million and included a complete overhaul of her severely corroded hull plating, replacement of the main engines and an armament update to prepare her for

her new role as an offshore patrol vessel. The forward twin Mk.19 4-inch gun mount was replaced by one of her after 40mm guns.

Other minor navies have suffered similar losses in recent years. For example, in 1991, the Chinese-built Shanghai II-class patrol ship *P101* belonging to the navy of Zaire sank at its moorings on the Congo River. The vessel was later raised and scrapped. Such occurrences are not uncommon with naval vessels of third-world countries, particularly with small, low-value craft. This form of attrition provides a constant market for replacement craft of an identical type, thereby camouflaging the extent of the problem.

Larger, higher value units have also suffered such undignified ends. By the late 1980s, the six Project 641 ('Foxtrot'-class) submarines - completed by the Soviets for the Libyan Navy between 1976 and 1983 - were in such a poor state of repair that their diving depth was seriously restricted. Although the true circumstances of the incident have not been released, it is probable that the poor material state of the hull was the cause of the sinking of one of these boats at her berth in the summer of 1993. *Al Khyber* (S315) was later raised and, after lengthy repairs, was back in service five years later.

Further examples of such neglect can be seen today in most ex-Soviet naval bases, where ships of all types, from auxiliary vessels to major fighting units, can be seen in a dilapidated and sometimes sunken state. It is not only de-commissioned vessels that succumb to such neglect, as evidenced by the foundering of the Russian Project 61 ('Kashin'-class) destroyer *Skoryy*, alongside her berth in Sevastopol in November 1997. Although the last of her class then in commission, she was replaced in Baltic Fleet service by one of her previously laid up sisters, *Smetlivyy*. The *Skoryy* was raised and scrapped the following year.

The occurrence of such incidents illustrates the importance of regular hull surveys and the replacement of sacrificial anodes. The dissimilar metals used in the construction of the hulls of most ships, such as the steel of the hull and the alloys of the propellers, rudders, cooling water inlets and other hull fittings, will result in a small electrical charge passing from one metal - the anode - to another - the cathode. The seawater in which the hull is immersed forms a most effective electrolyte. As the small electrical current flows through the electrolyte from one material to the other, the anodic material, the one possessing the smallest electrical potential, will be slowly 'eaten' away and corrode. To prevent this occurring, small lumps of material of an even smaller electrical potential are fixed to the vessels hull at carefully chosen positions, so that these will be slowly 'eaten' away in preference to the ship's hull. Zinc is a common material used for such sacrificial anodes. To remain effective however,

these anodes have to be renewed at regular intervals; otherwise certain areas of the hull will again become anodic and begin to corrode.

In most modern warships, sacrificial anodes are fitted to supplement a more effective form of corrosion control. A cathodic protection system uses reference electrodes to measure the small electrical current flowing between hull components and, through a control panel, provides an output current of the opposite potential to a series of anodes situated at strategic points around the ship's underwater area to cancel out the residual current. Increasing or decreasing the voltage to the anodes, usually in the region of 500-800mV, controls the current.

These systems are further supplemented by coating the hull with an anti-fouling paint scheme. These coatings, which have improved vastly over the years, not only serve to prevent corrosion of the hull, but also prevent the formation of marine growth, with the result that vessels require fewer dockings for the purpose of bottom cleans.

Approximately 80% of all structural defects involve cracking, itself a product of poor ship design or construction quality control. The inclusion of sharp corners in the structure of a vessel will serve as a means of reducing the building costs, but in the long term it may prove to be counter-productive, as these joints will form high stress points, with a tendency to crack, whilst also providing havens for the formation of corrosion, which may take some time to reveal itself. These in-built stress points are likely to cause problems throughout the life of the ship, particularly in the first few months or after a docking period. When subjected to the stresses of heavy seas, particularly in sub-zero temperatures, a small brittle fracture may result in a crack that will propagate at a rate of a mile per second.

Such a brittle fracture was to result in the dramatic loss of an ex-US Navy replenishment ship in 1947. The 3 year old 22,380-ton Suamico-class tanker USS *Ponaganset* (AO-86) was stricken from the US Navy 23 Apr 1947 and returned to the Maritime Commission for disposal. On the night of 9 December that year, the ship was lying empty at a wharf in Boston, Massachusetts, when the hull of the ship literally snapped in two. The hulk was later raised and scrapped. . Investigations determined that the fracture had emanated from a fillet weld that joined a chock on the deck. The high stress point at the crack, combined with the low ambient temperature of 35˚F that night, caused the crack to propagate with terrifying velocity around the hull and ultimately sealed the ship's fate.

It is a common feature of many modern vessels that minimal corrosion allowances, in the form of additional material thickness, are built into the design, reliance being placed instead on the control of corrosion by the application of advanced preservation methods and coatings, but some of these methods, although effective, may also prove to be extremely expensive.

Fatigue affects a hull by the continuous flex encountered due to the passage of waves, and is cumulative, with larger waves taking a bigger toll than smaller ones. To this end, a vessel working continuously in the North Atlantic will approach its fatigue limit some 3-4 times faster than one serving world-wide, due to the higher average wave heights and lengths in this ocean. Also, the increased pressures put on navies to cover the same operational commitments with fewer ships means that each vessel will spend more time at sea, and so reach its fatigue limit at an earlier age. This situation is often further exacerbated by cuts in defence procurement budgets, which result in vessels being kept in service much longer than originally intended when they were designed and built, in turn making them even more susceptible to

loss when receiving accidental damage, such as in a collision or grounding.

To counter the effects of all of these factors, it is imperative that the material condition of a ship's structure be continuously monitored and recorded, both by ships' staffs and by dockyards, in order that likely weak points are discovered before they become critical. In the Royal Navy, the Chief Naval Architect has responsibility for ensuring that its warships maintain a high standard of structural safety, as well as overseeing naval architectural and material standards, culminating in the issue of a Certificate of Safety, Structural Strength (CSSS). He has the power to issue safety certificates, detailing any areas of concern that will require close monitoring, whilst periodic surveys are carried out to ensure that high standards are maintained in the condition of hulls and fittings. Statements of Stability are also issued for the guidance of the ship's staff, both in the day-to-day operation of the vessel and in damage situations.

It is not only the structure and primary hull fittings that must be monitored and maintained. Occasionally, the failure of a single component may result in the loss of a vessel, particularly those affecting the watertight integrity of small craft.

At about 1314 on the afternoon of 15 December 1960, the newly completed Finnish utility landing craft *Kave 5* was taken in tow off Turku by the coastal minelayer *Keihässalmi* (05). The small landing craft, only 18 metres in length and with a standard displacement of 27 tonnes, had been designed for only short coastal journeys, and so, even in the calm sea and slight force 3 easterly wind then prevailing, had insufficient range to travel the sixty or so miles to Hanko under her own power.

At 1753 that evening, as the two vessels neared the port of Hanko, at the entrance to the Gulf of Finland, the mechanism holding shut the bow door of *Kave 5* suddenly failed and the door dropped open with a splash. Water cascaded into the open cargo bay, forcing the bow to submerge with the forward motion of the craft. Fearing that his vessel was about to plunge beneath the waves, one of the three crewmen aboard apparently panicked and jumped overboard. Tragically, the rating drowned before he could be rescued.

Meanwhile, *Kave 5* was taking in water via vents and openings in the cargo bay and it soon became apparent that she was indeed in danger of foundering. The crew of the minelayer managed to draw the landing craft alongside, but their efforts to stem the flow of water into the craft were futile and the remaining crewmen were evacuated. Minutes later, at 1817, *Kave 5* sank, four miles from J ussaro light in position 59°43.5'N, 23°30.5'E. Initial searches failed to locate the wreck and the craft was never recovered.

As a result of the accident, the bow door mechanisms of the other four vessels of the class, as well as those of the Finnish Navy's other minor landing craft, were immediately inspected and later modified.

A similar failure almost claimed a US landing ship some years earlier. *USNS T-LSU-1362* was under tow in September 1951 when the vessel's bow ramp fell off in rough seas. Fortunately, the craft was towed stern first into harbour and repaired. Likewise, one of twelve ex-East German Frosch-I-class landing ships, the *Teluk Lampung* (540), suffered serious damage and began flooding through her bows doors during her transfer journey after her sale to the Indonesian Navy in June 1994, but made port safely and was repaired.

Instances of a surface vessel sinking as the result of the failure of a single component are rare, and in any case, seldom result in major loss of life. With a submarine, however, the effect on the boat's equilibrium should failure of a single fitting or component compromise the watertight integrity can, unless the crew promptly takes action, prove disastrous.

On Tuesday, 17 April 1951 the submarine *HMS Affray* (S20) mysteriously disappeared. She had sailed from her base at Fort Blockhouse, Gosport, at 1615 the day before with 75 men aboard, including twenty trainees of the Officers' Submarine Course and a detachment of four Royal Marines who were to be involved in an exercise in the West Country. At 2116 that night, the submarine signalled that she was diving in position 50°10'N, 01°45'W, about 30 miles south-south-west of the Isle of Wight. Nothing more was heard from the submarine and she failed to surface and report as expected, 20 miles south east of Start Point, the next morning between 0800 and 0900.

An hour after the submarine's expected report became overdue a 'Subsmash' search was set in motion Several ships, including the destroyer *HMS Agincourt* (D86), the frigates *HM Ships Flint Castle* (F383), *Hedingham Castle* (F386), *Tintagel Castle* (F399) and *Helmsdale* (F253) and *HM Submarines Sea Devil* (S44), *Scorcher* (S58) and *Sirdar* (S76), all from Portland, as well as the radar training ship *HMS Boxer,* rushed to the area to begin a search for the boat. Eighteen other naval vessels, including two US destroyers, a Belgian frigate and three French patrol craft, as well as a large number of Royal Navy and RAF aircraft, were also activated. Meanwhile, the wireless transmission station at Rugby transmitted a message every 15 minutes, to which it was hoped *Affray* would respond. Control of the massive search operation was exercised by Flag Officer, Submarines, from the headquarters of the Commander-in-Chief at Portsmouth.

The area of the search was necessarily vast as *Affray* was, as part of Exercise Training Spring, to simulate a war patrol for a period of three days and so her movements would have been at the

discretion of her Commanding Officer, Lieutenant Jo hn Blackburn, DSC. However, the initial search operations were concentrated in the English Channel between St. Aldhelm's Head and Start Point, as it was assumed that the most likely time for the submarine to encounter difficulties would have been soon after diving. Hopes were raised and dashed by many false alarms. A reported Asdic contact at about midnight on 17-18 April by HM Submarines *Sea Devil* and *Trespasser* (S12) resulted in the congregation of several vessels in the area at daybreak, in preparation for a rescue operation. After many hours of searching and of dropping small explosive signal charges, it became evident that *Affray* was nowhere near and the search moved on.

A large patch of oil was investigated the following day near the Casquets, a group of rocky islands 8 miles northwest of Alderney in the Channel Islands, but a search of the area failed to find any evidence of *Affray*. It was calculated that, if *Affray* was lying on the seabed in an undamaged condition, her crew would be able to survive for a maximum of three days and so, by the evening of the 19th - 69 hours after *Affray*'s last report - all hope of finding survivors was abandoned and the search scaled down, releasing all foreign vessels from the task.

The primary aim of the search then became one of salvage rather than rescue, to which end a large number of salvage vessels were activated and the two ex-German heavy-lift craft *Energie* and *Ausdauer* - which had been involved in the salvage of *HMS Truculent* the year before - were prepared for use. As well as further searches by aircraft, surface ships and submarines, a number of Royal Navy minesweepers - *HM Ships Wave* (M385), *Pluto* (M46), *Welfare* (M356), *Marvel* (M443) and *MMS1788* (herself to be lost the following year) - dragged chains along the seabed in the hope of finding *Affray*, while another craft marked the searched area with danbuoys. Divers were despatched to investigate whenever the chains snagged a large object. Needless to

*HMS Affray disappeared during a naval exercise on 17 April 1951, leading to the most intensive search operation undertaken by the Royal Navy in post-war years. (Royal Navy Submarine Museum)*

*The diving support ship HMS Reclaim. A camera lowered by this ship finally located the wreck of HMS Affray on 15 June 1951, nearly two months after the boat's disappearance.*

*(E. Mulliner)*

say, this method did not bear fruit, but many other innovations were used in the search, including a new experimental aircraft, *Hermes II*, which it was hoped would be able to pick up the distortion in the earth's magnetic field caused by the presence of the submarine.

On 21 April the fifteen other A-class boats in Royal Navy service were ordered by the Admiralty not to sail until the cause of *Affray*'s disappearance could be determined, whilst all other submarines were banned from snorting - except for *HMS Taciturn*, which had just re-commissioned after being fitted with separate induction and exhaust masts. It thus appears that the Admiralty already had its suspicions as to the cause of *Affray*'s disappearance.

The search operation was now centred on the new diving support ship *HMS Reclaim* (A231), with sonar assistance provided by several frigates. The search area extended over an area of 1,500 square miles, an area throughout which wrecks of hundreds of years were scattered, each of which had to be investigated and discounted, the task being further complicated by Channel tides and poor weather conditions. Over the following weeks around 150 contacts were investigated. To speed up the search process, sonar equipment on *Reclaim*, together with a newly-developed underwater television camera operated by a team from the Admiralty Research Laboratory, were utilised from the end of May, thus eliminating the necessity to despatch divers to investigate each contact.

The camera proved to be a most valuable asset, as it could remain in the search area for several hours, whereas a diver's maximum time submerged at a depth of 200 feet was about 45 minutes. Divers would then only need to be used to investigate a small number of unidentified submarine wrecks which were suspected as possibly being that of the missing boat.

Following an Asdic contact on the evening of 13 June, *Reclaim* anchored nearby and preparations made for the investigation of the latest site the next morning. At about noon on the 14th, the camera was lowered and, soon afterwards, pictures relayed back to a monitor aboard

*Reclaim* revealed first a conning tower guard-rail, then the unmistakable letters of the boat's name plate. *Affray* had been found and positively identified, almost two months after her disappearance, lying in 48 fathoms of water at the edge of the Hurd Deep in the English Channel, some 30 miles north of Guernsey and 37 miles south-west of her last reported position.

This point near the Casquets, at position 49°49.9'N, 02°34.2'W, was not far from the position in which the oil patch had been spotted early in the initial search operation, in an area which had been used as a dumping site for thousands of tons of German ammunition and arms after the Second World War. The boat was on an almost even keel, listing slightly to port, with all hatches closed and with her marker buoys still in position. Her navigation radar aerial and periscope were extended, whilst her hydroplanes were in the maximum rise position and her bridge telegraphs indicated 'Stop'. It was evident from a nearby 'trench' that she had struck the bottom with considerable force and had bounced.

Early examinations of the wreck revealed a clean break at the base of the snort induction tube, approximately three feet above deck level, the tube hanging over the boat's port side permitting visual confirmation that the hull valve was still open. The snort induction tube was later retrieved and delivered to Portsmouth on Monday, 2 July, where it was subjected to a detailed examination. No signs of damage from an external source, such as a collision, were found, but laboratory tests determined that a combination of brittleness of the metal and poor welding had almost certainly been responsible for the mast's fracturing. Examinations of the snort induction tubes aboard two other A-class submarines revealed similar sub-standard conditions. Subsequently, a modified and strengthened form of snort induction mast was fitted to A-class submarines following exhaustive and successful testing.

The snort induction tube, manufactured by Stewarts and Lloyds and fitted to *Affray* during a post-war refit, consisted of a galvanised steel tube, 28 feet long and streamlined in section. An internal strengthening plate, perforated for lightness, divided the mast along its entire length. The head valve and guide pipe were fitted at the top, whilst the base was machined and welded into a hollow steel forging about which the mast pivoted and was known as the mast trunnion bearing. The mast was hydraulically raised and lowered and, when raised to its full elevation, was secured to the after end of the conning tower by a locking plate and bolt, which was secured from inside the submarine. At its upper end was a float valve that would automatically close should the top of the mast become submerged. A quick-acting power-operated valve was fitted where the tube entered the pressure hull, activated by a lever in the engine room.

However, if the snort mast had been the cause of *Affray*'s loss, then it was believed that she would have sunk by the stern as the engine room flooded through the 10-inch hole, but there was no sign of damage to suggest that the boat had hit the seabed stern-first. The pressure of water entering the hull at the rate of around $^1/_2$-ton per second would have flooded the engine room in only 4 minutes and, unless watertight hatches were closed immediately, flooding would have spread rapidly to other compartments.

The fact that the rescue buoys were not released and that there were no external signs of an attempted escape, also indicated that the crew would have been incapacitated, although the position of the diving planes and the telegraphs suggest a desperate attempt to bring the submarine to the surface. The disablement of the crew could have come about in a number of ways, one of the most plausible being a battery explosion. The gases given off by lead/sulphuric acid batteries contain an explosive mixture of oxygen and hydrogen that, if ignited by a spark, can produce an extremely violent explosion, spreading poisonous gases quickly throughout the boat. It could also have resulted in the rupturing of the pressure trunking amidships between the hull and the casing. This would have caused the boat to sink on an even keel. An explosion of this type may also have caused propagation of a crack in the snort induction tube and it's ultimate failure as she struck the seabed, but no external damage was found in *Affray*'s after section to indicate that such an explosion had occurred.

Another theory was that the diesel engine could have sucked all the air out of the boat, causing a vacuum and very quickly rendering the crew helpless. However, this is considered highly improbable as the position of *Affray*'s bow planes and engine telegraphs indicate that the crew took initial actions to save themselves and would therefore have shut the engine down. Nevertheless, such an incident did occur in 1970 aboard the French submarine *FS Galatée* and was a possible cause of the deaths of the crew of the Chinese submarine *No.361* in 2003. One of twenty Ming-class diesel-electric submarines in service, *No.361* had been missing for ten days when she was found wallowing at periscope depth near the Neichangshan Islands in the Yellow Sea. Divers managed to enter the boat and found all crewmen dead at their posts. There was no sign of any panic and the boat was intact. After being brought to the surface, *No.361* was towed to Dalian, where the bodies were recovered and investigations initiated. In an unprecedented act of openness, the Chinese released details of the accident on 2 May and televised the visit of President Hu J intao and his predecessor, Jiang Zemin, to the boat. It was the first time the Communist Chinese regime had admitted any of their submarine accidents,

although the reports would only disclose that the submarine had suffered "mechanical problems".

The crew are thought to have died of asphyxiation at their posts on 16 April. Although the cause was not revealed, it was probably due to one of two incidents: either salt water had entered the battery compartments and released chlorine gas; or as in the case of the *Galatée*, the inadvertent closure of an exhaust valve inside the boat caused the snorkelling diesel engine to suck all of the oxygen from the boat. Whatever the cause, all 70 men aboard *No.361* are thought to have died in the space of two minutes.

Other theories as to the cause of the loss of *Affray* included striking a mine and collision. However, the fact that no external damage was found on the boat to indicate such events, and the lack, despite extensive enquiries made early in the search operations, of any ship having reported being in collision with an unknown vessel, these possibilities were discounted.

On 15 November 1951 Mr J.P.L. Thomas, the new First Lord of the Admiralty, announced in the House of Commons that no further operations would be carried out in connection with the loss of *Affray* and that there was insufficient evidence to positively determine the cause. It is possible that the tragedy was the result of several smaller incidents that, occurring together, served to compound their effect. Nonetheless, fracture of the snort induction mast remains the most likely explanation and the Admiralty subsequently ordered all submarines to cease using their snort masts until further notice.

Salvage of the submarine was considered, but due to the depth of water, the dangerous tides, the fact that work could only be undertaken during the five summer months, the high degree of risk and the inordinately high costs of such an operation, the Admiralty decided that salvage was not feasible and that *Affray* should be left in peace in her final resting place. Although positive identification of the cause of the loss may never be known, it was not considered that salvage of the boat would provide any further evidence in this respect.

An added tragic twist of fate was that one of those lost aboard *Affray*, Sub-Lieutenant Anthony Frew, had been one of the five survivors of *HMS Truculent* picked up by the *Almdyk*, only 15 months earlier.

On 9 August 1990, whilst working on the Casquets Traffic Separation Scheme, a team of Naval hydrographers on board the motor ship *British Enterprise IV* came across the wreck of the *Affray*. Images of the wreck, located using sidescan sonar, revealed her to be still in good condition and lying almost upright on the seabed close to the position recorded in the Hydrographic Office, about 16 miles west-north-west of Alderney.

Although the Dutch had experimented with an air induction tube in the late-1930s, the concept of the schnorchel was really developed by the Germans as a means to allow their submarines to remain submerged whilst charging their batteries, thereby making them less vulnerable to detection by Allied anti-submarine forces.

After the surrender of Germany, this equipment was viewed with great interest and submarines of the British, US and Russian navies were quickly fitted with their own interpretations of the schnorchel, the first British boat so fitted being *HMS Truant* (N68) in May 1945. After a brief series of successful trials, snorkels - or 'snorts' in British parlance - were fitted to most of the T- and A-class boats.

This initial snort mast incorporated twin pipes for air induction and engine exhaust, the induction pipe being fitted with a float operated head valve which would automatically close off the pipe should it become submerged and so prevent ingestion of water into the engines. An additional seal was provided where the mast penetrated the pressure hull, in the form of a hydraulically-operated induction valve. A further isolating valve was fitted in the exhaust line, with high pressure air being used to eject water from the exhaust tube on initial starting of the engines, thereafter the engine exhaust pressure inhibiting water entry.

Since these early designs, the snort mast has been continually developed, particularly with modifications of the induction and exhaust valves. The problem of air starvation of the diesel engines when the induction valve closes has been tackled in a number of ways. Many navies allow the engines to draw air from inside the boat in such situations - a method hardly conducive to crew comfort - whilst Dutch boats utilised air storage bottles to temporarily supply combustion air. Modern IKL-designed submarines have sensors fitted in the snorkel that automatically shut down the diesels when water closes the air intake, preventing air being drawn from inside the boat.

The snorkel, or snort mast, is now regarded as an essential element of diesel-powered submarine design, although the advent of air-independent propulsion systems may ultimately result in its demise.

A snorkel malfunction is also believed to have resulted in the loss of a Soviet submarine in 1961.

Commissioned in 1951 as a standard Project 613 ('Whiskey'-class) diesel-electric submarine, *S-80* was one of several boats of the class extensively modified under Project 644 ('Whiskey Twin Cylinder') to carry two P-6 (SS-N-3A 'Shaddock') cruise missiles. Whilst on patrol in the Barents Sea on 27 January 1961, the boat disappeared without trace. Despite an extensive search, it was to be another seven years before the wreck of the *S-80* was found, in water 196 metres deep in position 70°01'23"N,

36°35'22"E, about 100 miles north-east of Severomorsk. Like the *Affray*, poor seasonal weather conditions hampered salvage attempts and it was to be another 13 months before the boat was finally recovered, on 24 July 1969. It was only then that a detailed examination of the boat revealed vital clues to allow the mystery of her loss to be pieced together.

It appears that *S-80* had been heading back to base in the early hours of 27 January 1961, operating at periscope depth and snorkelling to recharge her batteries. It is known that the weather on that morning was poor, with rough seas, bitterly cold Arctic winds and sub-zero temperatures. It is believed that the float valve at the top of the snorkel iced up after heating to the valve had been switched off and that the valve failed to shut. As the snorkel head became submerged, water cascaded into the boat's engine room, the

5th compartment. For whatever reason, the hull valve was not closed quickly enough and the engine-room quickly flooded. As the boat plunged stern-first towards the seabed, the pressure successively breached the bulkheads to flood the 4th, 3rd and 2nd compartments. Twenty-four crewmen remained trapped in the torpedo room, but at a depth of 600-feet, escape was impossible. All 68 crewmen perished in the tragedy.

Undoubtedly the worse submarine disaster of post-war years was the loss of *USS Thresher* (SSN-593) in 1963. It was also to be the first loss of a nuclear-powered submarine. *Thresher* had been ordered from Portsmouth Naval Shipyard on 15 January 1958 as the first of a new breed of nuclear submarine, the hunter-killer. Previous nuclear-powered submarines had a primary mission against surface vessels, whereas *Thresher*'s

*The nuclear-powered attack submarine USS Thresher undergoing sea trials prior to commissioning. The boat's loss on 10 April 1963, with 129 souls on board, was attributed to the failure of a silver-brazed joint in her sea water system.*

*(US Navy)*

primary task was anti-submarine warfare, being designed to seek out and destroy the new Soviet ballistic-missile armed submarines. Commissioning on 3 August 1961, she then underwent an extensive trials programme.

However, she was dogged by technical problems and spent two-thirds of her 20-month commissioned life alongside in a series of maintenance periods, the last of which was an overhaul at Portsmouth from 16 July 1962 until 8 April 1963. This refit, the work content of which had been increased from 35,000 to over 100,000 man-days because of an initial underestimation of the defect rectification work required, culminated in a series of test dives. During one of these test dives, an auxiliary sea water system leak occurred which took damage control personnel 20 minutes to isolate. Further minor leaks developed during sea acceptance trials, but these were all successfully rectified. During this refit period, several key ship and dockyard personnel were replaced, including the Commanding Officer, Executive Officer, the ship's superintendent (representing the shipyard and responsible for liaison between the shipyard and the boat's officers during the sea trials) and his assistant.

*Thresher* left her berth at Pier 11 in Portsmouth Naval Shipyard, New Hampshire, at 0800 on Tuesday 9 April to begin sea trials 200 miles off the coast of New England, as part of Submarine Development Group 2 (SubDevGru 2). As well as her crew of 12 officers, including her Commanding Officer, Lieutenant Commander John W. Harvey, and 96 enlisted men, she carried 21 observers. These included 13 civilians from Portsmouth Naval Shipyard, four civilian contractors and an officer from Deputy Commander, Submarine Force, U.S. Atlantic Fleet. Such was the overcrowding in the boat that temporary bunks had to be assembled in the Torpedo

Room, no weapons being required for the trials.

After rendezvousing with the Penguin-class submarine rescue ship *Skylark* (ASR-20) east of Boston later that morning, she carried out a series of successful trials. *Thresher* had been assigned the code-name 'War Club', whilst *Skylark* was to be 'Dipper Sierra'. By noon the two vessels were 30 miles south-east of Portsmouth. *Thresher* then carried out a successful shallow dive, the first since her overhaul, undertaken in water shallow enough to permit a salvage operation should things go drastically wrong. Later, a dive to 400 feet revealed only some very minor leaks of glands, which were either tightened up there and then, or noted for rectification on return to Portsmouth on the 11th.

The next trial, the 'Crash Back', tested the boat's ability to manoeuvre from full ahead to full astern instantly. This being successful, a series of tight turns were executed, proving the hydraulic systems of the diving planes and rudder. The first days trials satisfactorily completed, *Thresher* arranged a new rendezvous with *Skylark* for 1200Z (0700 local time) the following day, in position 41°46'N, 65°03'W. Minor trials continued during the overnight passage, which was undertaken partly submerged and partly on the surface, at various speeds and courses.

The following day, Wednesday 10 April, with *Skylark* in attendance as escort, *Thresher* began a further series of diving trials, the culmination of which was to be a dive to a test depth of 1,000 feet. Visibility was good at about 10 miles, and there was a moderate swell. All had gone fairly well up to this point, the only unknown factor being the main ballast tank high-pressure air reducer valves, used to expel water to de-ballast. *Thresher* had until now tended to dive with minimum negative buoyancy, being driven under at a shallow trim using the forward and aft trim tanks. Surfacing had been achieved by using the planes and the power of the 18,000 shaft horsepower steam turbine. This was a different method to that normally used by diesel submarines, which rely on the ballasting and de-ballasting of the main ballast tanks for diving and surfacing. However, *Thresher* had a small and inadequate capacity to blow her main ballast tanks, and de-ballasting had not yet been attempted at test depth.

*Thresher* began her serial of trials at about 0745 that morning, intending to descend in a large clockwise spiral so as to avoid straying too far from her escort. A few minutes later *Skylark* requested that a Gertrude - underwater telephone - check be made every 15 minutes. The only communications common to both vessels was the underwater telephone and a pulse-code (Morse) radio system. By 0752, *Thresher* was at a depth of 400 feet and reported only minor leaks, well within the capability of her pumps to cope with. Leaks of up to 7-gallons/hour could be expected in any submarine from such sources as shaft seals, periscope glands, salt water piping systems etc.

At 0808 *Thresher* informed *Skylark* that she was nearing half test depth, and at 0835 she was at 600 feet and "*Proceeding to test depth*". Eight minutes later, the last segment of the first circle in her downward spiral completed, *Thresher* passed over the edge of the continental shelf. *Skylark* was again informed at 0853 that the submarine was "*Proceeding to test depth*". At 0902 *Thresher* reported that she was on course 090° at a depth of 800 feet, although for some unexplained reason it took *Thresher* eight minutes to reply, but two minutes later she requested a Gertrude check to re-establish communications.

At 0913, as *Thresher* approached her test depth, *Skylark* received a garbled message from the submarine on acoustic telephone, stating that she was

"*Experiencing minor difficulties. Have positive up angle. Am attempting to blow. Will keep you informed.*" Immediately afterwards, the sound of the submarine attempting to blow ballast tanks was heard. Unknown to *Skylark* at that time, the submarine's Commanding Officer was attempting an emergency surface. A minute later *Skylark* relayed that there were no contacts in the area, and requested *Thresher*'s range and bearing, hoping that the submarine would pop to the surface at any moment.

Receiving no reply *Skylark* enquired "*Are you in control?*" At 0917 an unexplained message was received "*900N*" (presumably informing *Skylark* that she was at 900 feet and was not in control) followed by "*Exceeding test depth*", a message that was barely intelligible aboard the surface vessel. Immediately after, *Skylark* detected a dull muted sound as *Thresher*'s hull imploded under the immense water pressure as the submarine sank to the bottom of the Atlantic 8,400 feet below the surface, taking with her all 129 souls aboard.

Despite all of *Skylark*'s attempts to raise contact with the stricken submarine over the next eight hours, including dropping hand grenades overboard from 1040 onwards - a signal that the submarine should 'surface immediately' - nothing more was heard. Using sonar, *Skylark* commenced an expanding search pattern and then, at 1104, her Commanding Officer, Lieutenant Commander Stanley Hecker, ordered that New London be informed by radio that *Thresher* was missing, but due to technical difficulties, this message was not received until 1245. This message stated: "*Unable to communicate with Thresher since 0917R. Have been calling by UQC voice and CW QHB every minute explosive signals every 10 mins with no success. Last transmission recd was garbled. Indicated Thresher was approaching test depth. My present position 41°43.'N, 64°57.'W.*

*Conducting expanding search.*" A 'Submiss' operation was immediately initiated.

The 205ft long *Skylark*, one of only a handful of submarine rescue ships in service with the US Navy at that time, was not equipped to render any effective assistance to the stricken vessel - even if rescue was a possibility - being equipped only with a simple McCann rescue chamber, which although useful on the Atlantic continental shelf down to a depth of 850 feet, was totally unsuited to a rescue operation at almost ten times that depth. In fact, use of the McCann chamber would only be possible in around 16% of the world's ocean areas. It was, however, the best equipment available until the first of the new Deep Submergence Rescue Vehicles (DSRVs) came into service a few years later.

During the massive search subsequently undertaken by US Navy ships and aircraft, there was little *Skylark* could do but relay messages to Radio New London or to Portsmouth Naval Yard. She was joined later that afternoon by the repair ship *Recovery* (ARS-43), which, at about 1730, sighted an oil slick about seven miles south-east of the position *Skylark* had occupied when contact with *Thresher* had been lost. Samples of the oil slick - as well as several pieces of floating plastic debris - were retrieved and the following day further debris, including several rubber gloves, were fished from the sea. Analysis of these items by the laboratory at Portsmouth Naval Shipyard could only conclude that they may have come from *Thresher*, but none of them could be positively identified as having belonged to the missing submarine.

On arrival in the search area, the new research ship *Atlantis II* began taking bottom samples, but no traces of radioactivity beyond normal background levels could be detected. Later, *USS Dupont* (DD-941) was employed as the command ship for the search operations,

whilst the oceanographic research ship *Mizar* (T-AGOR-11) - which later assisted in the searches for *USS Scorpion* and the French submarine *Eurydice*, as well as in the recovery of an H-bomb lost at sea off Palomares, Spain - also participated.

In an effort to plot *Thresher*'s resting place, the US Navy prepared the submarine *Toro* (SS-422), which had been decommissioned the month before, for a trial in which she was to be intentionally sunk to assess the way in which a boat would sink when out of control. For this purpose she was to be fitted with a sonar reflector to assist tracking of her as she sank. Due to have been carried out at the end of May, this trial was later called off and the *Toro* was scrapped instead.

Hopes were raised on May 30 when the research ship *Robert Conrad* (AGOR-3) produced photographs thought to be of *Thresher*, but these later proved to be part of the camera itself!

On 23 June the deep-diving bathyscaphe *Trieste* arrived in the area under tow of *USNS Preserver* (ARS-8) and the following morning began the first of ten dives. The descent to the ocean floor took over an hour, but nothing was found on that first day. On the third, fourth and fifth dives some small pieces of wreckage were found. *Trieste* then returned to Boston for an overhaul, returning to the search area six weeks later to complete a second series of dives.

On the eighth dive, on August 28, a pipe from *Thresher*'s galley was retrieved from amidst a large area of wreckage. The scattered remains of *Thresher* had been found only a short distance from her last known position, at a point 41°45'N and 64°56'W, approximately 250 miles east of Cape Cod. However, even the thousands of photographs taken of the submarine's partial remains could not positively reveal the cause of the accident, although it was ascertained that it had not been due to a nuclear plant accident, nor had she hit a sea mount.

Nevertheless, the photographic evidence of the wreckage did suggest that the implosion may have been followed by an explosion in the vicinity of the engine room, possibly as a result of diesel oil - which ignites at 460psi - being subjected to a pressure of at least 800psi. Given the boat's history of problems with her auxiliary salt water system piping, it is probable that a high-pressure water leak, an extremely dangerous event at depth, necessitated the isolation of the system. This act would have cut off the supply of cooling water to the reactor and forced the main turbine to be stopped to prevent a reactor scram - if this hadn't already occurred. (A 'scram' is an unexpected or premature shutdown of the reactor.) Main steam stop valves would have had to be shut to prevent over-cooling of the reactor, thus also starving the turbo-generators of steam. From this point, seven minutes would be required to get the reactor

critical again, the boat being reliant in the meantime on her batteries, which could provide a speed of 3-knots. However, even with the planes in the full-rise position, this would not have been enough to drive the boat towards the surface. She would then have started to slide backwards into the depths.

De-ballasting of her seven main ballast tanks and two trim tanks were not enough to allow *Thresher* to rise, as she could only expel 1/7th of the water she displaced at maximum blow. This problem would be exacerbated by the fact that her weight was increasing with greater depth due to the pressure of seawater on her hull. The only source of further power now would be to use the 'heat sink' steam in the reactor and risk the damage it would cause to the reactor envelope. All efforts to halt the downward slide failed and *Thresher* probably imploded at a depth of about

*The starboard side of the USS Thresher sail with part of the hull number '593' visible. The image was taken in 1964 from a deep-sea vehicle deployed from USNS Mizar (T-AGOR-11)*
*(US Navy)*

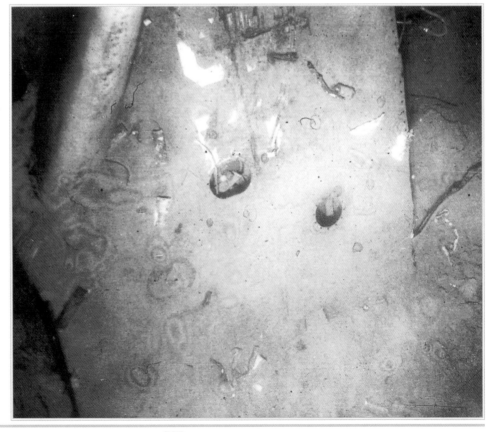

1,800 feet. All personnel would have perished instantly as the pressure rose from 14 to 800psi with the collapse of the vessel's pressure hull. The shattered hull was scattered over an area of 140,000 square yards, with some of the heaviest pieces of the wreckage striking the sea floor at a great velocity. The reactor compartment is probably buried deep in the silt.

The US Navy was quick to act on the loss of the *Thresher*. On the afternoon of *Thresher*'s sinking, Admiral Robert L. Dennison, Commander-in-Chief, US Atlantic Fleet, ordered a Court of Inquiry into the incident. The Court first met at 0825 the following morning and, over the succeeding weeks, dozens of high-ranking officers and other experts were summoned to testify, including: Vice-Admiral Hyman G. Rickover, Bureau of Ships; Vice-Admiral Elton W. Grenfell, Commander Submarine Force, US Atlantic Fleet; Rear Admiral Ralph K. James , Special Assistant to the Secretary of the Navy; Rear Admiral Charles J. Palmer, Commander, Portsmouth Naval Shipyard; and Commander Dean L. Axene, the former Commanding Officer of *Thresher*.

This inquiry revealed several problems with the design and construction of the latest SSNs, including inadequate stored air pressure for blowing dry ballast tanks for emergency surfacing and that, up until that point, no submarine in the US Navy had had its de-ballasting system tested against a simulated pressure of a deep dive, a procedure which was quickly instigated as part of every submarine's harbour acceptance trials before being accepted from the builders or shipyard.

De-ballasting trials aboard *Thresher*'s sister boat *USS Tinosa* (SSN-606) shortly before her completion at the Portsmouth Naval Shipyard the following year revealed that ice forming in the high pressure air pipework quickly blocked the air flow to the main ballast tanks before even half of the water had been expelled.

Later submarines of this (subsequently known as the Permit (SSN-594) class) and successive classes were delayed because of safety programme (Subsafe) modifications, increased quality control of submarine construction, and specific problems at the New York Shipbuilding Corporation and the Portsmouth Naval Shipyard. *Thresher*'s previous captain, Commander Axene, had also expressed concern over the amount of decorative bulkhead and deckhead coverings that concealed vital mechanisms such as valves, switches and pipework.

During building of *Thresher*, Admiral Rickover - often referred to as the 'father' of the US submarine nuclear reactor - who had repeatedly criticised the quality of workmanship in the shipyards, ordered that all silver-brazed joints on the reactor cooling pipe flanges be re-welded. Silver-brazed joints and flexible hose connections were used extensively in vital piping systems aboard the boat, in accordance with the build specifications provided by the Bureau of Ships, but these instructions were deficient in not adequately stating the quality assurance checks of welds or joints, or fully defining the amount of twist which would be acceptable in flexible pipes. Following the discovery of several over-twisted flexible pipes, all were inspected and subsequently, a comprehensive list of all flexible pipes fitted in the boat was compiled and maintained.

*Thresher* continued to have problems with her sea water system, including a jammed main inlet valve, misalignment of piping, and unreliable joints. Another SSN, the Skipjack-class *USS Snook* (SSN-592), which was commissioned only ten weeks after *Thresher*, also suffered several failures of silver-brazed joints in her sea water system, one of which burst while she was submerged. This particular fault was at first blamed on stainless steel being used instead of Monel, a corrosion resistant nickel-copper alloy, but was later attributed to defective joints. This had not been an isolated incident, as the diesel-powered submarine *Barbel* (SS-580) narrowly escaped a tragedy when, not long after she was commissioned in 1959, a salt water system pipe joint burst whilst the boat was submerged. As a result of this incident, all silver-brazed joints aboard *Thresher* were subjected to a programme of visual examinations, mallet tests, chemical material re-identification tests, hydrostatic tests and hydraulic pressure cycling tests, but there was no extensive retrofit of silver-brazed joints in the vessel.

Following the loss of *Thresher*, ultrasonic testing of all silver-brazed piping joints became a priority in deep-diving nuclear submarines. This form of testing had been initiated the previous year, but had only been carried out on a small percentage of *Thresher*'s pipes. Of those tested, 14% had been found to be unacceptable. The remainder of the silver-brazed pipes had been subjected only to a pressure test of $1^1/_2$-times the maximum working pressure. All reactor pipes are now checked with radiographs, these records being retained for at least seven years.

It was the opinion of the Court of Inquiry that quality assurance procedures at the Portsmouth Naval Shipyard should undergo a further radical review. The shipyard had already instigated a major expansion of its quality assurance organisation, including an increase in the number of personnel employed in the programme from 152 to 243. Nevertheless, inspection processes and the recording and reporting of all defects to the Shipyard Commander, via the Quality Assurance Division, were some of the areas where, it was felt, improvements should be immediately instigated. Coupled with this, the design and construction of vital submarine systems were to be reviewed, as was the training of nuclear submarine crews in order to improve their damage-control capabilities under casualty conditions, such as uncontrolled flooding. It was also the opinion of the Court of Inquiry that "*The substantially contemporaneous transfer of Thresher's commanding officer, executive officer, Ship's Superintendent and Assistant Ship's Superintendent in the final portion of her post shakedown availability was not conducive to optimum completion of the work undertaken.*"

Another deficiency in the boat's design was the lack of any recording device, such as the 'black box' carried in airliners, which may have provided further clues as to the cause of the disaster. All US submarines now carry tape recorders for this purpose.

In an effort to keep the weight of the submarine down and still maintain an acceptable reserve of buoyancy - which on *Thresher* amounted to only 579 tons - the thickness of the pressure hull plating had to be kept to a minimum necessary for strength. *Thresher*'s design was the first to use the new HY80 high yield steel in her construction, which has the ability to withstand pressures of 80,000lbs/in (56kg/mm) - reportedly giving her a diving depth of 1,300 feet. (In high-yield steels - HY80, HY100 and HY130 etc. - the number indicates the yield stress in 1,000lb/in2).

However, any steel is only as strong as the welds that join the hull sections together and *Thresher* experienced a series of defective welds. It was discovered that, when welded, this hard steel had a tendency to become brittle, resulting in cracking, which in turn necessitated expensive radiographs to be taken of every weld. Following the tragedy, *USS Tinosa*, launched 17 months after *Thresher*, was forced to remain in Portsmouth Naval Shipyard after the radiographs of her hull mysteriously 'disappeared'. This was not the first time, nor was it to be the last, that such important documentation 'went missing'.

Later US submarines of the Los Angeles-class have been constructed using the even stronger HY100 steel, the use of which permits deeper diving depths, which in turn makes it even more important that welds are of a high quality. However, in the light of the welding problems discovered in the new boat *Seawolf* (SSN-21) during 1991, the recently commissioned Los Angeles-class boats *Topeka* (SSN-754) and *Albany* (SSN-753) had to be re-examined. The problem, discovered when the *Seawolf*'s hull was 15% complete, led to her having to be restarted. Over-high carbon welding rods led to brittleness and cracking of the welds in the HY100 steel.

Welding quality problems are not a new phenomenon. Some welders in German building yards during World War Two, ever pressed to put more and more U-boats to sea, are reported to have been executed for laying welding rods in welds and welding over the top of them to speed up their task - not exactly a comfort to those having to sail in them! Many years later, the use of new inspection techniques, such as ultrasonic testing, revealed cracks in the internal bulkheads of the British SSN *HMS Dreadnought* (S101) in 1965, resulting in her forthcoming refit, planned for the following year, being brought forward. Subsequently, similar minor hairline cracks were discovered in the SSBN *HMS Resolution* (S22) at the time of her launch in September 1966. British submarine builders at this time were using HY80 high-tensile steel imported from America as the British steel industry was unable to produce a suitable alternative.

Further problems were experienced in *Dreadnought* in 1967 while returning from a visit to the USA, when leaks were discovered in a number of brazed pipe joints, allowing water to be sprayed over reactor control instruments. In the light of the then recent loss of *USS Thresher*, coupled with the fact that this first British SSN had been built to a largely US design, fabrication and fitting out practices for later British nuclear submarines were later revised. A couple of years later, water dripping from a pressure gauge in *Dreadnought* revealed that when coming into contact with lagging it produced an extremely corrosive compound. All Royal Navy nuclear submarines were later modified with new piping and lagging.

Construction quality problems have been reported periodically in the press over the years and have also affected the first of the US Navy's latest class of SSBNs, *USS Ohio* (SSBN-726). In November 1978, whilst the boat was under construction at the General Dynamics Groton Yard, an alert tradesman noticed that the steel was incorrectly coded and should not have been used for submarine building. A year later, it was discovered that 2,772 of her 36,000 welds had no inspection records. On re-inspection of these welds, a third were found to be of an unacceptable standard and had to be re-welded.

As a result of disputes between the US Navy and General Dynamics over these quality control failings, the contract for the construction of *USS Tennessee* (SSBN-734) was instead awarded to Newport News shipyard. Similar problems were later discovered in the Los Angeles-class boat *USS Bremerton* (SSN-698), when it was found that inspection documentation for 45% of her 17,800 welds were not available. A total of 2,802 (27%) had to be re-welded after inspection.

Welding quality has improved over the years as better techniques, together with improved examination and quality control processes, have been introduced, whilst almost all submarine construction work now takes place in covered building yards. Despite the problems highlighted above, it is not thought that any Western submarine has been seriously endangered by such defects. To put the problem into

perspective, it should be remembered that, such is the effectiveness of examination and survey techniques, these defects have usually been detected long before any serious cracking would have occurred.

Following the discovery of the wreck of another submarine in 1999, 31 years after her disappearance, the cause of the loss of *INS Dakar* was finally attributed to the failure of a critical system or structure. In November 1964, it was announced that the T-class submarines *HM Submarines Turpin* (S54), *Totem* (S52) and *Truncheon* (S53) were to be sold to the Israeli Navy. Following extensive refits by Vickers and at HM Dockyard, Portsmouth - which included streamlining of the hull and fitting of a five-man escape chamber in the modified fin - the boats were renamed *IN Submarines Leviathan* (75), *Dakar* (77) and *Dolphin* (79) and commissioned into the Israeli Navy on 19 May 1967, 10 November 1967 and 9 January 1968 respectively.

The unarmed *Dakar* set sail from Portsmouth on 9 January 1968, under the command of Lieutenant Commander Ya'acov Ra'anan, passing up the chance of a thorough work-up with the Royal Navy as her presence was urgently required by the Israelis in their war with the Egyptians. The first leg of the journey was undertaken on the surface, ending with a brief refuelling stop at Gibraltar on the 15th. Departing from Gibraltar, the boat's submerged transit through the Mediterranean, snorting to recharge her batteries at night, was to take her via the channel south of Crete, to arrive at the Israeli port of Haifa on 2 February. *Dakar* was to transit the Mediterranean submerged and Ra'anan was to report the boat's position to Haifa every six hours, with each 0600 radio report including her location, fuel and battery status and planned programme for the following 24 hours.

Good progress was made during the transit and so Lt Cdr Ra'anan signalled Haifa requesting permission to enter port early and was granted permission to arrive on 29 January. On 21 January, he requested a further advance to the boat's arrival time, but his request was denied and he was ordered to proceed as previously ordered. *Dakar*'s last report was transmitted at 0002 (Israeli time) on 25 Januar y, giving her position as 360 miles west of Haifa.

When *Dakar* failed to send her next scheduled report, attempts were made to contact her on all naval and international frequencies. Around 1600 a full-scale 'Subsmash' routine was set in motion, involving the Royal Navy destroyer *HMS Diana* (D126), and the Dartmouth Training Squadron frigates *HM Ships Eastbourne* (F73), *Scarborough* (F63) and *Tenby* (F65), as well as ships from the US, Greek, Turkish and Lebanese navies, several vessels from the Israeli navy and numerous aircraft, the search being controlled from RAF Akrotiri in Cyprus. No trace of the *Dakar* and her crew of 69 men was found, although a monitoring station near Nicosia reportedly received an SOS message from a submarine distress buoy the following day from a position estimated as being southeast of Cyprus. The unsuccessful search was finally called off on 4 February.

A Committee of Inquiry under General Tal, appointed by the Chief of Staff Bar Lev, and an official investigation - eventually compiled into the Harel Report - undertook to determine the effectiveness of the initial search operation and carry out detailed analysis into the possible location of *Dakar*. The submarine's material state, crew training status and her pre-sailing preparations were examined in detail for any clue as to the cause of the disappearance. No blatant anomalies were uncovered. It was finally surmised that the boat had been lost in the eastern Mediterranean basin, possibly as a result of a collision with the sea bottom or with another vessel, although no such collision was reported by any other ship. A former Egyptian official once claimed that the Egyptian Navy had sunk the boat, a claim

vigorously disputed by the Israelis.

A strange quirk of fate surrounds the boat as, during her service as *HMS Totem*, a totem pole was presented to her crew by a North American Indian tribe in Canada. The pole was meant to bring good fortune to the boat and her crew, but it was said that if ever the submarine sailed without its totem it would never return. The totem was left behind when the boat was sold to Israel and is now displayed at the Royal Navy Submarine Museum at *HMS Dolphin*, Gosport, near Portsmouth. *Dakar*'s sister boats *Leviathan* and *Dolphin* served on until 1974 and 1977 respectively.

On 9 February 1969, the Israeli Navy announced that an Arab fisherman had found a distress buoy from the lost submarine on a beach four miles north of Khan Yunis in the Gaza Strip. The stern marker buoy carried the words in English "*S.O.S. H.M. SUBMARINE DAKAR S.O.S. FINDER INFORM NAVY, COASTGUARD OR POLICE. DO NOT SECURE TO OR TOUCH*".

Examinations of this buoy revealed many clues as to *Dakar*'s resting place. The collapsed state of the buoy's flotation bottles and transmitter indicated that they had been subjected to a pressure equivalent to that found at a depth of about 325 metres, whilst the transmitter's antenna showed signs of having been cut by a sharp blow or explosion, rendering the transmitter inoperative.

It was not possible to deduce positively whether such an explosion had occurred before of after the boat was lost, but the buoy's cable was bent in such a way as to suggest that it had been partially severed by a sharp blow and had remained attached to *Dakar* for about a year before the few remaining strands corroded through and were broken by tidal motion, allowing the buoy to break free. Seaweed deposits also rendered many clues, leading to an assumption that the buoy had been at a minimum depth of 60 metres

*The bow and sonar dome of the Israeli submarine Dakar, 2900 metres beneath the surface. The plaque, laid by divers from the Nauticos Corportion in 1999, reads, "To the men of the INS Dakar - never forgotten"*

*(Nauticos LLC)*

before drifting for around three weeks. Examinations of charts lead to a conclusion that *Dakar* was to be found in the area to the north of Alexandria.

In 1982 an Egyptian salvage vessel, with Egyptian officers aboard, carried out the first of three unsuccessful searches for the *Dakar*. Then, in September 1986, the civilian research vessel *Gulf Fleet 51*, hired by the US Navy and with the involvement of Egyptian officials, carried out a search in Egyptian territorial waters at depths of up to 550 metres, but failed to find any trace of the submarine.

A new Israeli committee was appointed in 1987 to re-examine all the evidence acquired to date. New scientific research methods were employed to examine the distress buoy, a seashell attached to it and the various environmental factors such as wind, currents and mineral deposits. The assumption that the buoy had remained attached to *Dakar* for about a year was reaffirmed. However, further examination of the seaweed revealed that the buoy

could have drifted for around six weeks instead of the previously assumed three. This obviously vastly expanded the area that had to be searched.

A theory was reached that the *Dakar* could be lying in the eastern part of the Aegean Sea around the Greek islands of Crete or Rhodes. It was assumed possible that, having surplus time to fill, the submarine's commander had diverted his boat to this area - a favoured training ground for submarines - to carry out further training serials and that the boat struck a reef in the island chain.

Following resumption of diplomatic relations between Israel and Greece in 1990, the Greeks gave permission for a search to be carried out in the area between Crete and Rhodes. A new report was produced under US supervision with contributions from Israeli, Turkish, Greek, and Italian authorities and a search of the area between Rhodes and Crete was begun in 1992 by the Israeli research vessel *Tonir*, with two Greek oceanographers and a Greek naval officer aboard, the Greeks requesting that certain details of the search not be publicised in the interests of security in their territorial waters.

An area of approximately 100 by 20 nautical miles, covering depths of between 60 and 350 metres, was to be searched using side-scan sonar and magnetometer, both linked to a systems integrating computer. A Global Positioning System was utilised to ensure precise locations could be obtained for any contacts found. On detection of any metallic objects the ship anchored and lowered an underwater vessel that incorporated a camera, transmitting pictures of the object back to the ship for analysis. Still no trace was found of *Dakar*.

The Israelis refused to give up and a new search committee was set up under the command of Rear Admiral Gideon Raz. US Navy experts were consulted and provided classified satellite data on Mediterranean currents. In 1999 it was decided to instigate yet another search, the 26th, this time along *Dakar*'s intended route to Haifa. This area had not been searched before due to the misleading evidence found on the boat's marker buoy and the earlier lack of technology to search the depths in the eastern Mediterranean.

The American Nauticos Corporation were contracted to conduct the search, using two Cypriot research vessels - the *Flying Enterprise* and the *Argonaut*. The *Flying Enterprise* would search the seabed using an advanced AMS-60 towed sonar, whilst the *Argonaut* would interrogate any contacts using a Remote Operated Vehicle (ROV). The ships arrived in the area on 9 May 1999 and proceeded to conduct the slow survey of the designated 60-mile search lanes. On the evening of 24 May, the sonar detected a large contact 2900-metres below on the seabed, surrounded by a number of smaller contacts, but poor weather conditions prevented an immediate examination using the ROV. Finally, at 0700 on 28 May, the ROV was launched and a few hours later began transmitted pictures of the wreck back to the Argonaut - the *Dakar* had at last been found, 270 nautical miles from her original intended destination of Haifa. It was now evident that the original conclusions had been wrong and that *Dakar* had never detoured from her programmed route. It also appears that the emergency buoy had become detached from the boat immediately after her sinking and it is possible that the monitoring station near Nicosia may have indeed detected an SOS message on 27 January 1968.

Over the next 17 months, a detailed examination of the wreck was conducted. *Dakar* was lying upright, her bow facing southeast. A gyrocompass recovered from the site indicated that the boat had been on course 120° when disaster struck. Her stern and conning tower had been ripped off and were lying alongside the hull. It has now been determined that disaster befell *Dakar* during the early hours of 25 January 1968, whilst the boat was submerged, snorkelling near the surface to

*The forward section of Dakar's conning tower was raised from the sea bed in October 2000 and inaugurated on 30 May 2003 at the Naval Museum at Haifa as a permanent memorial to the 69 crewmen who perished.*

*(U.D. Bochner)*

recharge her batteries. Although the exact cause of the accident could still not be determined, collision with a surface ship and a grounding incident could both now be ruled out. It is probable that there was a major flooding incident in the forward section of the boat, possibly due to fractured pipework, upsetting the submarine's trim and sending her into an uncontrolled forward dive. The rapidity of the dive prevented the diesel engines from being shut down and the electric motors being connected to the shafts before the boat reached its crush depth some 30 seconds or so later and the submarine's hull imploded. The force of the implosion broke off the bridge section at the forward end of the conning tower and released the stern emergency buoy, but also fractured its pulley mounting, with the result that the pulley and the 600-metre long cable acted as a sea anchor to the buoy, preventing it floating on the surface and affecting the route that the currents would take it. Several minutes later, *Dakar* struck the seabed with such an impact that the rest of the conning tower was detached from the hull and the stern section was snapped off at the bulkhead between the engine-room and the stern compartment. The fact that the boat's bow section is almost completely intact suggests that the forward compartments were flooded before the boat reached crush depth.

In October 2000, the forward part of the *Dakar*'s conning tower was raised from the seabed and, on 30 May 2003, was inaugurated at the Naval Museum at Haifa as a permanent memorial to the 69 crewmen who perished. The museum also displays *Dakar*'s emergency buoy.

Pipe weld failures still constitute one of the most serious hazards to submariners, a fact all too tragically illustrated by a more recent accident aboard a French nuclear-powered submarine. Ten of the 66 crewmen aboard the Rubis-class SSN *FS Émeraude* (S604) were killed when a steam pipe fractured whilst the boat was submerged in the Mediterranean, off Toulon, on 30 March 1994. The resultant fire did not affect the vessel's CAS 48 pressurised water nuclear reactor and the *Émeraude* reached Toulon safely, on the surface, later that night. Three other boats of the class were recalled from patrols for 'urgent examination', along with the other two boats that were alongside at their home port at the time of the incident.

How many of the numerous Soviet submarine losses have been due to the failure of hull or system welds may never be known, even with the more recent releases of details and openess regarding many such incidents. Even the Soviets themselves have often openly criticised the quality of their submarines, which have been constructed in vast numbers by the state-owned shipyards. Particularly disturbing has been the numerous reported incidents of radiation leakage aboard their nuclear-powered boats, including the Soviet Navy's first nuclear ballistic-missile armed submarine, the Project 658 ('Hotel'-class) boat *K-19*. Whilst on transit to a missile test range off Greenland on 4 July 1961, *K-19* suffered a radiation leak from one of its two nuclear reactors after a coolant pipe failure. Amazingly, in their hurry to get their new nuclear submarines to sea as quickly as possible, the Soviet designers had not incorporated a back-up coolant system to the reactors and so, in order to carry out a repair, several crewmen had to enter the reactor compartment. As the reactor temperature continued to rise towards meltdown, *K-19* surfaced and attempted to radio for assistance, but water had leaked into the long-range antenna and rendered it inoperative.

Several crewmen volunteered to enter the reactor compartment and rigged a rubber hose to an emergency coolant pump, but this failed almost immediately, causing further damage to the reactor. After three hours, the engineers managed to weld a new pipe in place and restored the coolant supply to the pressurised water reactor, thereby preventing a nuclear disaster. However, all eight men of the damage control teams had received massive doses of radiation and died horrible deaths over the next few hours.

Radiation levels within the rest of the boat were also rising and the Commanding Officer, Captain Nikolai Zatayev, decided to head south-east whilst continually transmitting an S.O.S. message. Captain Zatayev considered scuttling the heavily contaminated boat, but after rendezvousing with other Soviet submarines early the next morning, the remaining crew were evacuated and *K-19* was then towed back to the North Banner Fleet's submarine base at Polyarny. In total, fourteen of *K-19*'s 139 crew died in the accident, whilst several suffered the effects of radiation sickness for many years. This incident was recently dramatised in a major movie starring Harrison Ford as *K-19*'s Commanding Officer (*"K-19 The Widowmaker"* - Paramount pictures 2002). *K-19* was rebuilt over the next three years and fitted with a new reactor, the damaged one being dumped off Novaya Zemlya.

All future Soviet nuclear submarines were fitted with back-up coolant systems, but further incidents occurred with frightening regularity, including the laying up of the Project 645 ('November'-class) submarine *K-27* following a reactor accident in May 1968 which killed nine crewmen (this boat subsequently being scuttled off the east coast of Novaya Zemlya in 1983). The unreliability of the reactors of the first-generation classes of nuclear-powered boats led to the de-commissioning of most of them in the early 1990s.

Other notable incidents include reactor meltdowns aboard the ice-breaker *Lenin* in the 1960s, whilst in 1970 a Project 705 ('Alfa'-class) SSN, *K-377*, had to be towed back to port after suffering a reactor meltdown. The boat was later photographed by a US reconnaissance satellite, having been cut in two prior to being scrapped.

The unreliability of these early reactors was a direct result of their accelerated development, as the Soviets strove to build a nuclear submarine force to rival that of the US Navy. This technological inertia, coupled with the desire to get their boats into service as quickly as possible,

*A Project 705 (Alfa-class) SSN of the Soviet Navy. One of this class, K-377, had to be towed back to port after suffering a reactor meltdown in 1970 and was subsequently scrapped.*

*(US Navy)*

also resulted in the retention of double-hulled construction for nuclear submarines, as post-war reconstruction of Soviet shipyards had barely been completed, so it was hardly a time for the introduction of any radical changes in building techniques. Externally framed hulls are easier and cheaper to build, as well as being inherently stronger and requiring less advanced steels, whilst allowing more space for internal equipment, or a smaller pressure hull.

The advent of nuclear power in submarines meant that external fuel saddle tanks were no longer required and so led to western navies adopting single hulls in their nuclear submarines. The pressure hull therefore forms the major part of the external surface of the boat, with buoyancy tanks being relegated to the fore and aft extremes, rounding off the hull. Additionally, this reduces the size of the submarine, resulting in less drag and so higher speeds, whilst the lack of free flood holes makes the boat quieter. Displacements of single-hulled boats are also correspondingly lower. For example, US Lafayette-class SSBNs reportedly had a submerged displaced of around 8,250 tons, compared with 9,300 tons for the similar Soviet Project 667 boats.

However, the Soviets managed to keep the size of some of their attack boats down by the adoption of high strength materials such as titanium, as well as by sacrificing crew comfort. Plans by some Soviet designers to adopt the single-hull were vehemently opposed, due to concern that the smaller internal ballast tanks would result in a major reduction in reserve buoyancy. It was argued that large ballast tanks distributed along the sides of the boat were also less susceptible to damage in collisions than the smaller fore and aft tanks, whilst additionally providing a 'buffer' zone against damage by torpedoes. Such simplicity of design should, theoretically, have resulted in an increased safety margin and a lower susceptibility to damage. However, the poor safety record of Soviet/Russian submarines suggests not only a lower standard of training amongst their crews, but is also evidence of the poor quality of their construction and equipment, particularly their early nuclear power plants.

The Soviet shipbuilding industry expended considerable resources and employed experienced and highly skilled personnel to build its submarines at a rapid pace. Tremendous pressure was put on the chairman of the State Committee for Approval from the whole hierarchy of the Ministry of Shipping and Industry, as well as the Chief Commander of the Navy, to deliver a quota of boats by the end of each year, regardless of their state. This led to boats being handed over with numerous structural and material defects and not having completed all necessary builder's trials. Serious accidents were inevitable. This pressure to provide operational submarines also extended to the ship-repair industry, with lax quality control and poor attention to detail. Such pressures were undoubtedly instrumental in the loss of at least one nuclear submarine.

The Project 670 ('Charlie I'-class) cruise missile submarine *K-429* was in a desperately needed maintenance and repair period in June 1983 when her Commanding Officer, Captain 1st Rank Nikolay Suvorov, was ordered to put to sea immediately for exercises. His crew had all been sent on leave and so a crew was assembled from various other boats and insufficient time was given to properly reassemble systems under repair. Captain Suvorov's protests that such a makeshift crew could not safely operate the boat and that the *K-429* was not prepared for sea were over-ruled.

*K-429* sailed on 23 June and headed for the exercise area in Savannaya Bay in the Bering Sea. On arriving in the area late on the following evening, Captain Suvorov decided to carry out a test dive, but shortly after submerging, water began flooding into the 4th compartment through an open tank vent valve. The systems had been under repair before the boat sailed and had probably been incorrectly re-assembled in the haste to get the boat to sea, so that the valve position indications were incorrect. The fourteen men within the 4th compartment managed to shut down the reactor, but all were trapped and were drowned. Without power, *K-429* sank to the seabed 50 metres below the surface.

Trapped within the boat, the crew attempted to release the emergency buoy, but found that it's securing mechanism had been welded to prevent the buoy being lost at sea. The escape capsule, which would have taken those trapped in the first three compartments safely to the surface, was similarly secured. The crewmen had no choice but to wait for rescue.

Ashore, the authorities did not realise that *K-429* was missing until noon the following day. By this time, Suvorov had decided to allow two men to don survival suits and carry out a free ascent to the surface via one of the forward torpedo tubes, where they were spotted and rescued by the Project 1124 ('Grisha'-class) patrol ship *MPK-122*. Other rescue vessels were soon on the scene and the rest of the crew escaped via the torpedo tubes and the after escape hatch. Unfortunately, two of them drowned, bringing the death toll to 16 men.

Primarily a poorly trained crew, an endemic problem within the Soviet Navy, had caused the sinking of *K-429* at the time. However, the incorrect alignment of a crucial system during maintenance had ultimately been a major factor in the incorrect operation of the system that led to the boat's loss. Furthermore, the Soviet hierarchy's disregard of the Commanding Officer's concerns about proceeding to sea with an ill prepared, ad-hoc crew provided the additional catalyst for the

disaster to occur. The subsequent Court of Inquiry found Captain Suvorov guilty of the negligent loss of his boat and sentenced him to three years imprisonment.

*K-429* was raised six weeks later and towed to port for repair. Unfortunately, the boat sank alongside the pier on 13 September 1985 and was subsequently de-commissioned.

Russian shipyards are now tightening up on their quality control processes in the light of several serious incidents in recent years, such as the loss of the *Komsomolets* in April 1989. Their stated intention to improve the status of their fleet, not only in terms of build quality, but also by the introduction into service of smaller numbers of newer vessels and the disposal of large numbers of obsolete and ill-maintained craft, is only hampered by the economic turmoil within the country, brought about by their quest to stay a step ahead in the arms race of the 'Cold War' years.

An uncontrolled dive is probably one of the most terrifying incidents that a submariner can experience in peacetime. Such a phenomenon can be caused by flooding within the boat, as in the case of *HMS Affray* or *INS Dakar*; or by equipment failure, as in the case of *USS Thresher*. A simple equipment failure ultimately also led to an uncontrolled dive that resulted in the disposal of a US submarine.

On the afternoon of 11 February 1969, the destroyer *USS Hawkins* (DD-873) was conducting an anti-submarine exercise against the Gato-class submarine *USS Chopper* (SS-342) near Cuba. The submarine was operating at a depth of 150-feet at her maximum underwater speed of about 8-knots when one of her two on-line AC motor-generators tripped. The resultant power surge tripped the second motor-generator, depriving the control room of all communication systems and indication, including the

*The US Navy submarine USS Chopper (SS-342) was condemned after damage sustained during an uncontrolled dive off Cuba on 11 February 1969.*

*(J. Hummel)*

motors halted the boat's descent and the submarine started making way astern towards the surface. Meanwhile, the forward dive planes were being moved by hand power to the rise position.

But the crew's ordeal was not yet over. As the submarine began to level out, the Commanding Officer, who had managed to fight his way to the control room, ordered 'Full ahead'. The boat then began rising at an increasing angle towards the surface. As the planesman once again attempted to level the diving planes to halt the rise angle, the Commanding Officer ordered the forward ballast tank vents to be closed and blowing of the after tanks. About 60 seconds later, the boat reached the surface with an up-angle of over 80° and sprung out of the water, before once again sliding stern-first beneath the surface. After submerging about 200-feet, the submarine rose to the surface at an angle of 40° and this time remained there.

The whole ordeal had lasted only 2½ minutes.

The inside of the boat was total carnage, with all loose items, including machinery, equipment and deck plates having been thrown first forwards and then aft. Miraculously, there were no serious injuries amongst the crew and shortly afterwards *Chopper* got under way and limped back to Guantanamo Bay on the surface. There, a structural survey was carried out to ensure the boat was seaworthy for a transit back to Key West, on the surface and under escort. More detailed surveys revealed major structural damage to the hull, which had been severely stressed and twisted during the dive to 2½-times the normal operating depth. Condemned, *Chopper* was decommissioned in September 1969 and, following several years as a training hulk, finally sank off Florida in 1976 while being prepared for use as a target.

The subsequent investigations into the incident resulted in modifications to the AC systems to prevent the total loss of

position of dive planes and rudders. At that moment, the stern planes were in the down position, sending the boat into a dive with an increasing down-angle. The OOD immediately ordered 'Ahead ⅓' but, with no communications or telegraphs, this order never reached the engine-room. As the bow-down angle passed 45° and the depth passed 400-feet, the OOD ordered 'All stop' and then 'All back full' and the blowing of all bow buoyancy. Fortunately, the controllerman in the engine-room took the initiative and put the electric motors to full astern. After about a minute, the boat's down-angle had increased to over 80° and the depth forward passed 1000-feet, well below the submarine's normal operating depth of about 400-feet. All loose equipment within the boat was thrown against the forward bulkheads and personnel struggled to maintain their footing. Mercifully, the effects of blowing the forward ballast tanks and full astern on the power to vital systems due to power surges. It also recommended improved crew training in emergency breakdown procedures.

Mechanical and structural failures will continue to occur, but the *Chopper* and *K-429* incidents clearly indicate that the effects of such failures can be limited by effective crew training in not only emergency operating procedures, but also in damage control. Advances in all areas of ship construction, from computer-aided design, to better quality materials, improved assembly techniques and the latest non-destructive testing processes, serve to reduce the occurrences of vessel loss through material failure to an almost negligible rate, especially when compared to that of bygone years. The susceptibility of early 20th century vessels to loss by such causes can perhaps be most graphically illustrated by the foundering on 26 September 1904 of the C-class destroyer *HMS Chamois*. The 355-ton vessel was exercising with other ships in the Gulf of Patras when a blade on one of her two propellers shattered, the large shard acting like a projectile and piercing the vessel's hull aft of the 'A' bracket. Flooding quickly spread forward through successive compartments until *Chamois* finally sank.

# Chapter Six

# SHIPYARD AND DOCKYARD ACCIDENTS

Vessels under construction or in dockyard hands for refit or major overhaul are vulnerable to damage from a variety of sources, such as fire, flooding or, in some cases, sabotage. The latter does not come within the scope of this book and so will not be covered here. However, although vessels under construction cannot strictly be classified as naval ships until their completion and acceptance into service, it is felt that such instances of the destruction of vessels under construction for naval forces is relevant as they may already have been designated naval names, and so such cases are discussed in this chapter.

By far the most serious, and most common, danger to vessels in shipyard or dockyard environments is the risk of fire. Although the dangers and consequences of fire on board ships have been examined in some detail in Chapter Two, this chapter will cover those vessels that have received critical damage whilst still in the relatively 'safe' haven of the shipyard or dockyard.

On the building slip, all of the materials and components required to construct the hull and superstructure and install major machinery items of a vessel are brought together and assembled. In the case of steel or aluminium vessels, and to a lesser degree in wooden or GRP construction, the assembly of such materials is dependent on the use of a great deal of welding, cutting and grinding, to be undertaken both on and within the hull. Such heat will, given sufficient time, tend to dissipate safely throughout the immediate structure after the heat source has been removed. However, when carelessness allows this heat to be conducted to combustible materials, which may be incorporated in the structure or stored in large quantities in the vicinity of the work, the risk of fire is significantly increased.

The careless discarding of combustible materials or of cigarettes is also a major cause of fires in such circumstances. A fire may not ignite until several hours after the heat source has been removed, smouldering unseen until it suddenly bursts into flames, sometimes with devastating effects. Such fires occur with unnerving regularity, often resulting in a serious delay in the completion of the vessel and the spiralling of the building costs, or in other cases resulting in the incomplete vessel being broken up or scrapped, being more economical to restart the construction from scratch.

Whilst under construction for the US Navy on 2 February 1955, the hull of the US Navy's first glass reinforced plastic minesweeper was destroyed by fire. Although the 39-ton *MSB-23* was rebuilt, she was never used operationally, and was delivered to the Naval Ship Research and Development Laboratory at Panama City, Florida, in August 1956 for use as an experimental GRP hull.

The Type 42 destroyer *HMS Sheffield* (D80) also suffered a fire whilst in build at the Vickers' Barrow shipyard. To regain some of the lost construction time, the ship's fire-damaged stern section was replaced with that of the Argentinean ship *ARA Hercules*, also under construction at the yard. Tragically, and perhaps ironically, the ill-fated *Sheffield* was later to become the first Royal Navy casualty of the Falklands conflict after the ship was devastated by an Argentine Exocet missile on 4 May 1982.

A far more devastating fire occurred on 14 August 1986 at the Rotterdam Dry Dock shipyard aboard the new Netherlands submarine *HrMS Walrus* (S801). The fire, which began at about 1100 that morning, was only brought under control and extinguished five hours later after using copious quantities of water as a last resort in an attempt to save the expensive electronic equipment already installed. The cause of the fire, which had started in the battery room and devastated the midships upper deck, was attributed to a short-circuit in temporary lighting used by dock workers, although it could equally have been caused by welding on the deck below, or by a discarded cigarette.

It was initially speculated that the boat might have to be scrapped because of the extensive damage to an entire section of the hull due to fire-fighting water, which had resulted in the steel plating of the boat being impregnated with hydrochloric acid. The submarine's completion was delayed by two years, making the sister boat *Zeeleeuw* (S803) the first boat of the class to commission in April 1990. Frame 54 of *Walrus'* structure had to be replaced, but luckily the hull damage was largely repairable. A major proportion of the boat's hydraulic and electronic equipment and cabling was destroyed and had to be replaced, adding over 30% to her overall cost, and resulting in one of the largest insurance claims ever submitted from a shipbuilder being sent to Lloyds of London, the cost of the damage being estimated at around NLG225 million (US$112.5 million).

Often, a serious fire aboard a ship in build will require that a major section of the hull be completely rebuilt. Such was the case following a cable fire aboard the Brazilian Oberon-class submarine *Tonelero* (S21) in 1975, under construction at the Vickers shipyard in Barrow, which required a 60-feet long section of the hull be replaced. Not only was this boat's birth marred by an accident - another was to hasten her demise from active service when she later sank alongside her berth at Rio de Janeiro in 2000.

Fires are not always tackled, however, before the damage inflicted renders rebuilding sections of the vessel uneconomical. A major fire at the Tacoma Boat Yard in August 1968 totally destroyed the almost complete Ashville-class patrol boat *USS Benicia* (PG-96) as well as a significant amount of assembled materials for sister-vessels *Grand Rapids* (PG-98) and *Douglas* (PG-100). The burnt-out hulk of *Benicia* had to be scrapped and construction of all three vessels restarted the following year, eventually completing in 1970.

A similar fire at the Marcelo Yard in Manila destroyed fourteen new hulls of the De Havilland 9209-Type patrol craft and effectively halted production of the class. By the time of the fire in late 1976, twenty-five out of the original eighty boats ordered in August 1975 had been delivered to the Philippine Navy.

Vessels undergoing refit or repair in dockyards are also subject to an increased risk of damage from fire or explosion. The reduced number of personnel living aboard, coupled with the large amount of welding work which is usually undertaken during such maintenance periods, means that a small fire, which may have been smouldering away unnoticed for a considerable period of time, may have grown out of control before any alarm is raised. The removal of much of the vessel's fire detection and fire-fighting equipment and systems for repair or overhaul may also result in a delay in the tackling of any blaze, which may be further fuelled by accumulations of flammable material around the ship.

It may only be possible for personnel in the vicinity to attempt to contain the blaze, by the use of portable appliances or hoses supplied from emergency fire pumps, until the arrival on the scene of the local area fire services. Additional precautions, such as the careful checking of areas of any welding undertaken 30-60 minutes after the work has ended, and the removal

of oxygen-acetylene gas bottles and any accumulations of combustible materials from internal compartments, should be observed.

The Australian tank landing ship *HMAS Tarakan* (L3017) was one of six Royal Navy LST(3)-class vessels transferred to the Australian Navy soon after the war. In 1949 *Tarakan* was taken in hand for a short overhaul period at the Garden Island Naval Dockyard at Sydney. During the closing stages of this refit, on the morning of 25 January 1950, the vessel was lying alongside at her berth when a huge explosion ripped through the after sections. One of the twenty-five crewmen aboard the ship at the time of the explosion was killed instantly by the blast and the resultant fireball that tore through the nearby messdecks seriously injured a further twenty. A number of fierce fires broke out and the entire after section of

*Whilst in the closing stages of a refit period at the Garden Island Naval Dockyard on 25 January 1950, the Australian tank landing ship, HMAS Tarakan, was ripped apart by a major explosion.*

*(Navy Photographic Unit - Sydney)*

the ship was filled with acrid black smoke, made even more deadly by the burning of refrigerant gas from a shattered pipe in the refrigeration machinery compartment, which added highly toxic methyl chloride fumes into the air.

At the time of the blast, shortly before 0800, most of the crewmen were located in the messdecks aft, having just finished breakfast. The men, some of them badly burned, were trapped in the compartments, their escape routes blocked by the inferno. As all electrical power was immediately lost and light fittings were shattered by the blast, the shocked crewmen were plunged into pitch darkness.

Rescue services, in the form of the local fire brigade and personnel from the frigate *HMAS Murchison* (F442), were quickly on the scene and, having donned breathing apparatus, fire-fighters boarded the ship to tackle the fires, which were quickly extinguished. The priority now shifted to the evacuation of the trapped men, some of whom could be seen gesticulating wildly from the portholes aft. A courageous dockyard worker with gas cutting equipment quickly set to work cutting holes in the port side of the ship to allow the rescue services to reach the trapped men, some of whom were already dead or dying from the poisonous fumes. So feverish were the welder's activities that he collapsed, unconscious, soon after cutting the second hole that permitted most of those trapped to escape or be rescued within 45 minutes of the blast.

Over the next four hours, civilian and naval personnel worked together to tear a path through the carnage of twisted metal and shattered equipment to search for further dead or injured men, many of whom had been trapped by the debris strewn around by the explosion. Some of the injured men died later from severe burns or asphyxiation, either in the ambulances or in hospital over the next three days, bringing the final death toll to eight.

Most of *Tarakan*'s after compartments were completely wrecked by the explosion and the vessel could be seen to be settling slightly by the stern, partly due to the massive quantities of water that had been poured into the smouldering vessel to quench the flames. The damage to the ship was surveyed over the following weeks. The explosion damage was mainly confined to the petrol compartment, petrol lobby and the after messdecks, where decks were blown upwards and split and several adjacent bulkheads destroyed or buckled, but the hull structure throughout the after part of the ship was severely distorted. It was therefore decided that she was beyond economical repair. The vessel, which had only been completed in June 1945 and transferred to the Australian Navy in July 1946, was laid up in her damaged state of Garden Island until it was sold for scrap four years later.

A Naval Court of Enquiry was immediately set up to investigate the cause of the disaster. It was determined that, on the afternoon before the accident, Commander (E) Parker, an engineer officer serving with the refitting authorities ashore, had ordered that the lid of the disused petrol storage tank be readied for removal by the following morning in preparation for the dockyard to undertake work in the vicinity. Engine Room Artificer Second Class W.L. Hoy duly arranged for the tank lid to be removed and for a portable fan to be set up to blow fresh air into the tank, for the purpose of venting it of any flammable gases. The fan was connected to an electrical switch located within the petrol control room. For the next 14 hours, the fan blew air into the tank, forcing the explosive gases upwards through the open tank lid, only to accumulate in the petrol control room above and thence out into the lobby.

The following morning, a young stoker mechanic was told to disconnect the fan and return it to the dockyard. However, the cover of the switch was not correctly secured and so, when the rating operated the switch to stop the fan at 0757, the inevitable spark was not contained within the switch's casing. This tiny spark was sufficient to ignite the lingering petrol vapour, the resultant explosion hurling the rating out of the compartment and into the lobby, killing him instantly.

Since the last time that the tank had been used for the storage of petrol, originally carried to supply the vehicles the ship was designed to transport, some three years previously, it had been partially filled with water. Nevertheless, an appreciable amount of petrol had been left floating on the surface of the water, evidence of which was a persistent smell of petrol fumes in the after sections of the ship in the vicinity of the tank over a considerable period of time. Despite this, the tank had never been properly cleaned during the three-year period to remove the potential danger of petrol fumes, a requirement clearly laid down in the publication *BR175 - Regulations for the Storage and Handling of Petrol*.

In this respect, primary responsibility for the explosion was laid with Engine Room Artificer Hoy, who was himself one of the tragedy's fatalities. However, in mitigation, it was noted that he had only been in charge of the engine room department for about a month prior to the explosion. Also, his actions in prematurely removing the tank lid without previously flooding the tank three times with water, in accordance with regulations, was probably the result of his misinterpretation of the instruction by Commander Parker to have the lid removed, ready for the tank's inspection by the dockyard by 0900 on the 25th.

The ship's duty Commanding Officer, Lieutenant J. Ferguson, was also found to be blameworthy, in that he did not make himself aware of ERA Hoy's actions, with respect to the safety of the ship. Together with *Tarakan*'s Commanding Officer, Lt.Cdr. C.J. Cochran, Lt. Ferguson was court-martialled, but both officers were later acquitted.

The Court of Enquiry also recommended that methyl chloride be replaced by the less toxic Freon refrigerant gas and that escape scuttles be fitted to permit an alternative escape route from compartments in the event of a fire.

The dangers from the accumulation of poisonous or explosive gases within enclosed spaces, such as tanks or void spaces, should not be underestimated. Such spaces are likely to be completely devoid of oxygen and may instead contain an unusually high concentration of carbon monoxide gas or fuel vapour, both of which are highly toxic and flammable. On initial opening of any compartment or space that has been sealed from the atmosphere for an extended period of time, the area must be adequately ventilated of such gases and vapours. These areas must in turn be exhausted to the open air and the necessary precautions against ignition, such as the prohibition of smoking or welding in the vicinity, strictly enforced. The casing of all electrical equipment in the area must also be effectively sealed to prevent the ignition of vapours by electrical sparks.

Despite the lessons learnt from this incident, an electrical spark was also responsible for the destruction of the US Navy Aggressive-class minesweeper *USS Stalwart* (MSO-493) at San Juan, Puerto Rico, in 1966. At about 0330 on the morning of 25 June, an explosion and fire wracked the engine room. For almost nine hours, the crew fought feverishly to extinguish the fire, but the volume of water entering the ship was not controlled and *Stalwart* capsized onto her starboard side and sank at 1210 in 30 feet of water. Fortunately there were no casualties amongst the ship's crew.

The burnt out ship was re-floated the following month, when the true extent of the damage was surveyed. The main deck and much of the superstructure was totally gutted and the hulk was de-commissioned before finally being sunk as an artificial reef off Florida.

Three years later, one of *Stalwart*'s sister ships succumbed to a fire whilst in dry-dock at Baltimore, although under totally different circumstances.

*USS Avenge* (MSO-423), together with three of sister ships, arrived at Bethlehem Steel Corporation Shipyard in Baltimore, Maryland, in August 1968, in order to undergo extensive modernisation. Custody of the ships was transferred to Bethlehem Steel Corporation, who thereafter was responsible for the safety and security of the vessels. Together with *USS Exultant* (MSO-441), *Avenge* was later docked in dry-dock No.5 in the Fort McHenry shipyard, where all ship's systems were isolated, including electrical power, all lighting and fire-fighting water supplies being provided from temporary installations supplied from shore-side mains. *Avenge*'s reduced ship's company of two officers and ten enlisted men were not accommodated aboard and the ship was unmanned outside of normal dockyard working hours.

The modernisation work was over 50% complete and the ship almost ready to undock when, on 6 October 1969, a fire broke out in the after machinery room. At the time, none of the crew were aboard the ship, but dockyard workers had just downed tools for their lunch break, several of them remaining aboard to eat their packed lunches. During the forenoon, brazing work had been carried out in several compartments, whilst brazing and manual inert gas (MIG) aluminium welding had been ongoing in the after machinery room, where the main engine mounting systems were being modified to accommodate the installation of new Waukesha diesel engines. The yard fireman had inspected the safety of this work at about 1045, but MIG welding

work was still in progress and no such inspection had been undertaken after this time. A few minutes after the sounding of the 1130 lunch whistle, workers noticed smoke rising from the after machinery room. The local fire alarms were activated and, soon after, the fire station was alerted.

Bethlehem Steel's fire truck arrived on the scene a few minutes later, but heavy smoke obscuring the central casualty control station on the main deck, starboard side, where fire-fighting equipment was stowed, hampered their attempts to tackle the fire. It quickly became apparent that the blaze would require further assistance from the Baltimore City Fire Department, who were duly alerted, but by the time the first of their fire tenders arrived shortly after 1150, the blaze had gained a firm hold.

For the next hour, the blaze continued to spread with terrifying speed forward and upwards through the hull and through the superstructure as far as the pilothouse, as the combined team of fire-fighters struggled to bring it under control. The fire was finally extinguished at 1310.

Examination of the damage revealed that a total of fifteen compartments and passageways had been completely gutted by the blaze, with extensive smoke damage evident right forward. In the after machinery room, there was extensive charring of the wooden hull planking on the starboard side at the turn of the bilge in the vicinity of frames 54 and 55, mushrooming upwards across the deckhead and thence forwards and upwards. The lowest position of the charring indicated that the fire had originated directly beneath the starboard forward engine mounting and that it was probably caused by the smouldering of molten metal arising from welding operations, eventually igniting the oil impregnated wood.

In fact, the last person to leave the compartment, at about 1120, later stated that there were welding fumes emanating from the starboard side of the space when he left. However, he did not notice any flash that would have indicated the use of the MIG welding set. Scrutiny of each workman's testimony regarding his time of departure from the compartment suggested that the welder had already left and so it is probable that the fire had already started at this time. Damage to the ship was estimated at between $2.5 million and $3.75 million, an amount that far exceeded the vessel's operational value. USS Avenge was stricken from the navy list on 1 February 1970 and was later scrapped

The contract specification for the modernisation of the minesweepers included a requirement for a fire protection plan to be produced by the refitting shipyard. Bethlehem Steel's plan provided for the posting of firemen in work areas and the provision of sufficient portable and dockside fire-fighting equipment to deal with any shipboard fires that could be expected to arise. To this end, portable fire extinguishers, together with charged salt water hose connections and a chemical air mask were positioned at the central casualty control station on Avenge's main deck, whilst four salt water fire points were located on the dockside.

The maintenance of this equipment and the monitoring of fire hazards was the responsibility of a single fireman assigned to the two ships during the working day. However, the inquiry revealed several deficiencies in the yard's fire plan, which had been approved by the Resident Supervisor of Shipbuilding, Construction and Repair (ResSupShip), Baltimore, in that there was no requirement for the assigned fireman to be informed of hot work being performed within the ships. Nevertheless, even had he been so informed, it would not have been possible for him to oversee all hot work taking place on both ships at any one time - each ship should have been assigned its own fireman.

There was also no provision within the plan for the fitting of an automatic fire alarm system, connected to the fire station, relying instead on a telephone call to raise the alarm, whilst few of the dockyard's employees had been properly briefed on the actions to take in the event of a fire. Furthermore, the requirement within the contract that "fire resistant coverings shall be secured in place prior to hot work to protect piping and equipment" was one of several requirements not fully complied with in the fire plan. This latter point is particularly relevant, as no such coverings had been in place in the after machinery room to protect the oil impregnated wooden structure from splatters emanating from the brazing and welding work taking place. Had the bilge area been so protected, it is unlikely that the fire would have occurred.

The opinion of the Court of Inquiry was that neither the Bethlehem Steel Corporation's fire plan, nor it's fire-fighting capabilities, had been adequate to cope with the fire, further stating that the assistance of the Baltimore City Fire Department should have been requested earlier. Therefore, the opinion of the Court was that responsibility for the fire aboard USS Avenge should rest with the Bethlehem Steel Corporation. It was further recommended that fire plans be revised to account for the aforementioned deficiencies and that the central casualty control station should be located in a more accessible position adjacent to a terminus of access to the vessel.

Another vessel which was damaged beyond repair was the Danish minesweeper HDMS Graadyb (M568), which was virtually destroyed by an explosion whilst under repair in the Copenhagen Naval Dockyard on 14 October 1955.

During periods of protracted peace,

*HDMS Kløryb (ex-ML2), a sister-ship to HDMS Graadyb, which was virtually destroyed by an explosion whilst under repair in the Copenhagen Naval Base on 14 October 1955. The burnt-out wreck was condemned on 4 February 1956.*

*(Kommandørkaptajn Holm, Marinens Bibliotek)*

large numbers of warships and naval auxiliaries are often laid up in reserve in order to balance the annual defence budget, with the intention that sufficient ships would then be available at a reduced state of operational readiness should they be required in times of increased tension. During the early 1950s, the Royal Navy embarked on a major minesweeper construction programme. These ships, the Ton-class coastal minesweepers and the Ham and Ley-class inshore vessels, were constructed with wooden hulls and aluminium superstructures to reduce their magnetic signatures to a minimum. Many of these ships were not immediately commissioned, but were laid up after trials at various sites around the UK. Some ships were kept in large hangar-like sheds and others, like those maintained at *HMS Hornet*, Haslar Creek, Gosport, had their superstructures covered in a wooden weatherproof structure, with only their masts protruding.

Shortly after 1600 on Friday, 28 September 1956, a fire broke out on one of the vessels berthed at Haslar Creek. The dry wooden protective structure of *HMS Broadley* (M2006) quickly ignited, the fire raging out of control and spreading to the minesweeper berthed alongside her. Both ships broke adrift from their moorings and collided with those berthed forward of them, spreading the inferno to one of these vessels as well.

Local Fire Brigades from Gosport and Fareham, together with naval personnel from *HMS Hornet* and *HMS Dolphin*, were quickly on the scene, some arriving via MTBs and dockyard craft from nearby Portsmouth Naval Base. The fire on the three minesweepers was now raging out of control and the other reserve vessels were towed through the dense smoke cloud by harbour craft and tugs into the centre of the harbour and placed alongside the submarines *HM Ships Talent* (S37) and *Thule* (S25), to prevent them too catching alight. For the next hour, firefighters fought to bring the situation under control, by which time the *Broadley* had sustained serious damage and the Ham-class vessels *HM Ships Bisham* (M2607) and *Edlingham* (M2623) were completely burnt out. Another Ham-class vessel, *Etchingham* (M2625), was also slightly damaged in the fire. It was only the prompt action of naval and civilian fire-fighting teams that had rushed to tackle the blaze that prevented the fire spreading to even more vessels. The total cost of the damage caused by the fire was estimated at around £600,000.

A Court of Inquiry into the incident was convened on 2 October 1956 at *HMS Hornet*, with Captain John Grant, RN, of *HMS Vernon* presiding. The cause of the fire was thought to have originated from a discarded cigarette, which ignited the dry timbers of *HMS Broadley* (M2006). The three fire-damaged minesweepers were docked in the floating dock *AFD11* between 8 October 1956 and 14 June 1957, but all were subsequently written of as constructive total losses. They were sold on 8 August 1957 to Harry Pound Shipbreakers, Portsmouth, for scrapping. However, following initial dismantling, the three blackened hulks lay at Tipnor until May 1979, when work began on breaking up the wooden hulls, a task completed in January the following year.

Vessels in dry dock, in refitting sheds, or on synchrolift complexes, are subjected to

additional handicaps, in that the distance over which suitable quantities of water may have to be pumped in order to tackle a blaze may be quite considerable. The addition of large quantities of water into a hull during fire-fighting operations may also lead to areas of the vessel's structure being subjected to excessive stresses due to the weight of the water, and may even result in the vessel toppling from her position atop her dock blocks or cradle, causing further serious damage.

A more recent incident was the near loss of a vessel on charter to the Royal Navy whilst undergoing a refit at a west coast shipyard in 1991. The Royal Aerospace Establishment's research vessel *Colonel Templer* was in dry dock when a fire broke out aboard her. The fire was so fierce that the ship had to be scuttled to extinguish the flames. The forward section of the ship suffered severe structural damage and was completely burnt out, whilst the engine room and main electrical systems were completely flooded. It was at first thought that the ship was beyond repair, but at the end of March that year the tug *RMAS Rollicker* (A502) towed her into Portsmouth Harbour where she underwent

extensive repairs and rebuild by the Royal Navy's Fleet Maintenance and Repair Organisation (FMRO), completing in July 1992.

This was not the first time that the desperate measure of sinking a vessel in order to extinguish a serious fire has been taken. Whilst alongside at the US Navy Submarine Base at Pearl Harbour in 1960 the Skate-class nuclear attack submarine *USS Sargo* (SSN-583) was seriously damaged by a fire, resulting from the rupturing of a charging line whilst the submarine was charging it's banks with oxygen. The accident necessitated submerging the boat at the dock in order to flood the after torpedo room, the area most affected by the fire. The boat was later raised and repaired and served well into the 1980s.

However, fire is not the only danger for a vessel whilst undergoing major maintenance. Very often, the simplest of safety precautions is overlooked, and lessons already learnt at great cost have to be re-learnt. Such was the case when, on the evening of Thursday, 1 July 1971, the A-class submarine *HMS Artemis* (S49) sank alongside the jetty at Fort

*The research vessel Colonel Templer under tow into Portsmouth Naval Base in March 1991 to undergo major fire damage repairs.*
*(Walter Sartori)*

The raising of the submarine HMS Artemis, which flooded and sank at her berth at Fort Blockhouse in July 1971. The boat was subsequently written off as beyond economical repair.

(Royal Navy Submarine Museum)

Blockhouse, Gosport, in 30 feet of water.

The boat had been moved from the Admiralty Floating Dock *AFD26* in Portsmouth Harbour to her berth at the submarine base by tug earlier in the day. To achieve a suitable trim of the boat prior to undocking, No.5 main ballast tank (MBT) aft had been flooded to the proposed waterline, even though the submarine was already heavier than when she had docked four days earlier due to No.4 MBT being in a partially filled state.

Thus, a tragic series of miscalculations and errors was already in progress.

Following her arrival at her berth at *HMS Dolphin*, the process of 'first filling', or 'comping', the external fuel tanks prior to fuelling was begun. The forward tanks, with a capacity of 53 tons, were filled first. In hindsight, this left only Nos. 1, 2 and 3 MBTs forward, and the external fuel tanks aft, supporting the weight of the boat. Comping up of the after fuel tanks was commenced at around 1700. As the after tanks were filled, the extra weight of compensating water, totalling 178 tons, increased the draught aft to such a state that water began flooding into the submarine through the after escape hatch. The subsequent flooding of the after end increased the draught still further until the water level reached the open after torpedo loading hatch and began flooding into the boat at a torrential rate.

On discovering this, a rating descended through the engine room hatch to attempt to close the watertight door in the motor room/after ends bulkhead, but was unable to reach it. Wading through knee-deep water, he tried in vain to close the engine room hatch, due to the fact that electrical shore supply cables had been passed through it. The same cables prevented the watertight door between the engine and control rooms being closed. The stern of *Artemis* was now sinking fast and, at 1907 she slid stern first beneath the surface, coming to rest at a slight angle of list with only a small portion of the fin protruding from the water.

Twelve crewmen and three Sea Cadets being shown around the submarine, managed to scramble to safety but three ratings were trapped as the boat sank. Closing the watertight door between the control room and the accommodation spaces against the water cascading through the boat, they made their way forward to the forward torpedo stowage compartment and slammed the watertight door behind them. Fortunately for them, the forward torpedo loading hatch had been shut from the outside by a quick thinking rating. The three men were now trapped in the torpedo stowage compartment as the boat sank.

Immediately it was noticed aboard the submarine *HMS Ocelot* (S17), alongside *Artemis*, that *Artemis* was sinking, the alarm was raised and personnel from the *Ocelot* and her sister boat *HMS Otus* (S18), berthed nearby, rushed to the aid of vessel. A full rescue operation was quickly instigated by the transmission of a 'Subsunk' signal.

Throughout the night, contact was kept with the men trapped in *Artemis* by radio-telephone from *HMS Ocelot*, which was held in place by a tug to prevent *Artemis* from listing further. The trapped men could have been rescued at any time but, due to *Artemis'* slight list to starboard, her forward escape hatch was sited just below *Ocelot's* ballast tanks. A cable was passed around the bow of the stricken boat and she was dragged to a more upright position. With the assistance of divers to guide them, the trapped men escaped to the surface through the forward escape hatch at 0500 the next morning. None of them were seriously hurt, although all were visibly shaken by their ordeal.

The Board of Enquiry into the incident resulted in the boat's duty officer and Marine Engineer Officer being reprimanded, and the dis-rating of the duty technical Senior Rate to Petty

*The rusting hulk of ex-HMS Artemis lies forgotten in the corner of a scrapyard in December 1989, eighteen years after sinking at Fort Blockhouse.*

*(R.Scott)*

Officer, all having been found guilty of negligence. The Board found that, due to the undocking being brought forward at short notice - resulting in the Commanding Officer being unavailable - and the coincidence of the First Lieutenant - and many other key personnel - being on leave, charge of this exacting operation was left in the hands of inexperienced junior officers. These officers had been oblivious to the danger signs accumulating rapidly, from the ship's tank state on undocking, the number of upper-deck hatches negligently left open, the running of shore power supply cables through the engine room hatch instead of the conning tower hatch, and the consequences of further depleting the already minimal reserve of buoyancy by comping up.

The lack of adherence to well established safety procedures laid down in numerous orders, including Ship's Standing Orders, was also severely criticised, and resulted in a tightening up of safety procedures throughout the Royal Navy's submarine fleet.

The 1,120-ton *Artemis* was raised five days later by the salvage vessels *RMA Ships Goldeneye* (P195) and *Kinloss* using heavy lift cables, the boat having been pumped full of compressed air to expel most of the water within her. During her salvage, the boat sprang out of control to the surface, damaging a yard craft, *YC484*. *Artemis* was subsequently paid off and was sold to H.J. Pounds, Portsmouth in 1972 to be broken up, where her hull could still be seen well into the 1990s.

The *Artemis* incident was an almost exact replay of the sinking of the submarine *H29* in 1926, so emphasising that 'too many people had forgotten the basic principles of submarine safety and ship stability'.

However, yet another strikingly similar accident claimed a Brazilian submarine many years later. The Oberon-class submarine *Tonelero* (S21) was two months into a 2½-month overhaul period at the Arsenal de Marinha do Rio de Janeiro Naval Shipyard when, at around 2300 on the night of 24 December 2000, she sank alongside the pier. All nine men on watch aboard at the time managed to escape before the boat sank, coming to rest on the harbour floor 9-metres below with a list to starboard. The submarine was raised on 3 January 2001 but, having been used on training duties during the previous few years and been programmed for retirement in 2002, the *Tonelero* was deemed beyond economical repair, de-commissioned on 13 June 2001 and was scrapped.

The subsequent Board of Inquiry determined that the sinking had been due to incorrect filling of the boat's after ballast tanks. Rather than filling one tank at a time, three were filled in quick succession, causing the boat to trim by the stern until the aft hatch became submerged. Efforts to close the hatch failed due to the routing of external ventilation tubes through it and the boat quickly flooded by the stern and sank.

An incident involving the Sturgeon-class nuclear-powered attack submarine *USS Guitarro* (SSN-665) was another example of wholly avoidable damage to a submarine fitting out when she sank in 35 feet of water in San Francisco Bay Shipyard, Mare Island, on 15 May 1969. On that afternoon, two separate teams were working on the boat: a civilian nuclear construction team were carrying out calibration of instruments in the after tanks, whilst a non-nuclear team were attempting to trim the boat. The work entailed the nuclear team gradually filling aft tanks with five tons of water whilst the non-nuclear team were to add water to tanks forward to reduce the 2-degree aft trim. Unfortunately, neither team was aware of the other's work. Consequently, as the nuclear team added water to aft tanks, the non-nuclear team added an increasing amount of water to the forward trim and ballast tanks in an attempt to

correct the trim. The boat's loss of freeboard over the next four hours went unnoticed, until the wash from passing boats caused water to cascade into *Guitarro* through an open sonar dome access manhole. Shortly after, as the teams were leaving the boat for a meal break, water was noticed flooding through hatches into the forward sections. Attempts to stem the flooding by closing doors were thwarted by the routing of cables through them and *Guitarro* sank bow first at 2055.

The boat was raised three days later. Fortunately, the reactor had not yet been installed, but damage to electrical and electronic gear amounting to US$25million delayed *Guitarro*'s completion until September 1972, some 28 months late. The official enquiry

*Completion of the nuclear attack submarine USS Guitarro was delayed by 28 months due to extensive damage caused when the boat sank in 35 feet of water whilst under construction in San Francisco Bay Shipyard on 15 May 1969.*

*(US Navy)*

found the immediate cause of the sinking was the culpable negligence of certain shipyard employees and held the shipyard accountable for all repair costs. The lack of co-ordination between the nuclear and non-nuclear groups had been the major cause of the series of events leading to the boat's sinking. Amongst the enquiry's recommendations were that one single person should be responsible for co-ordinating the work of all groups and that cables passing throughout vessels under construction should be provided with suitable connections that could be quickly broken in an emergency.

In comparing the above two cases, it should be noted that the damage inflicted on USS Guitarro was far greater than that suffered by HMS Artemis. The decisions to repair Guitarro, but to scrap Artemis, were taken on a purely economic basis, it being judged as uneconomical to repair the boat for only an estimated twelve months further service whereas Guitarro was a new boat and much of the boat's equipment had yet to be fitted.

The regularity with which basic lessons have to be relearned was illustrated more recently, when the Sturgeon-class SSN USS Archerfish (SSN-678) almost sank whilst berthed at La Maddalena, Sardinia, in April 1994, after her ballast tanks were flooded in error. Only swift action by her crew prevented another embarrassing accident on the scale of the Guitarro incident.

A further example of a simple oversight resulting in extensive damage to a ship was the sinking of the French cruiser FS De Grasse (C610) . Construction of the cruiser had originally begun in November 1938 and continued post-war, followed by her launching on 11 August 1946. As the ship neared completion in 1954, she was re-docked for routine hull maintenance. However, her completion was to be delayed even further as a result of the vessel's sinking in June 1954 after she had been floated out of dry dock with her sea-cocks open. De Grasse was eventually completed on 3 September 1956 and served until 1973.

Other major navies have occasionally suffered the indignity of vessels foundering alongside their berths. For instance, the Australian replenishment tanker HMAS Supply (AOR-195) sank at her berth at Garden Island, Sydney, one night in January 1964 after flooding of her engine room went unnoticed. The ship, resting on the bottom of the harbour with only her main deck and superstructure remaining above water, was raised and repaired. The Marine Engineer Officer of the ship was summoned to the subsequent enquiry, but no disciplinary action was taken.

Similarly, the French submarine Siréne (S651), a boat of the ill-fated Daphne-class, sank at her berth at Keroman, Lorient on 11 October 1972 after flooding through one of her torpedo tubes. Raised eleven days later, the boat was repaired and continued to serve into the 1990s.

From time to time, disaster strikes from a totally un-foreseeable direction, causing extensive damage to ships lying at their berths. In December 1979 the Royal Navy Leander-class frigate HMS Minerva (F45) suffered extensive damage when a 200-feet tall crane crashed onto her superstructure at Devonport during a gale. However, a more bizarre incident was to occur only 18 months later.

Whilst moored at Aberdeen's Regent Quay at around noon on 9 June 1981, the Aberdeen University Naval Unit's training ship, the inshore minesweeper HMS Thornham (M2793), was seriously damaged by a 45-ton mobile crane that crashed onto her deck. Four crewmen were below decks when the accident happened and were lucky to scramble from the listing vessel unhurt.

The runaway crane, owned by the Aberdeen Harbour Board, had careered 100 yards along the jetty before toppling onto the minesweeper, crushing upper

deck fittings and piercing the deck into the engine room. The jib of the crane embedded itself in the harbour floor. Luckily, the vessel's watertight integrity was not breached. It took two heavy lift cranes and a number of welders over five hours to cut the crane free from the wreckage and place it back onto the dockside, the jib being extracted from the harbour later.

*HMS Thornham* was dry-docked two days later, whereupon a survey revealed extensive damage to the vessel's hull, main engines and shafting. Consequently the minesweeper, one of the last Ham-class ships in Royal Navy service, was paid off as beyond economical repair, partly due to the fact that her service career had been scheduled to end within a year anyway. The ship had been programmed to begin a European and Scandinavian deployment when the accident occurred and a civilian vessel, the 170ft offshore support vessel *Harlaw*, had to be chartered for the summer training cruise.

Outside of the Western navies, whose safety standards are rigorously controlled, the possibility of serious nuclear accidents occurring during refit, refuelling or decommissioning cannot be discounted. The rapidly increasing number of decommissioned nuclear-powered boats laid up at various locations, mainly by the Super Powers - totalling well over 200 already - is creating a major headache as each country ponders over how to dispose of the radioactive elements of each boat's

*The inshore minesweeper HMS Thornham with a mobile crane embedded in her upper deck at Aberdeen on 9 June 1981. Thornham was later paid off as beuond economical repair.*

*(Aberdeen Press and Journal)*

propulsion systems. Although the number of nuclear-powered submarines in commission is presently reducing, the future procurement plans of several other navies, such as those of China, Brazil and India, can only exacerbate the future disposal problem. The safety record amongst the Soviet Union's vast submarine fleet is not reassuring.

Apart from the well-documented disasters at the Three Mile Island and Chernobyl power stations, one of the most serious nuclear accidents to date was that which occurred on 10 August 1985 at the Soviet Pacific Fleet base at Chazhma Bay, near Vladivostok. During a reactor refuelling operation aboard the Soviet Project 675 ('Echo II'-class) SSGN *K-431*, a violent thermal explosion wracked the boat's reactor, rupturing the boat's pressure hull and starting a blaze that took four hours to extinguish. Few details of the disaster are available, but according to a report published by the Bellona Foundation in August 2003 (*www.bellona.no/en/international/russia/envirorights*), the explosion hurled the freshly fuelled nuclear reactor core some 80 meters. It was also claimed that the radioactivity released by the blast was around one seventh of the total released in the Chernobyl disaster, or seven times that released by the Hiroshima bomb in 1945. Ten people were killed instantly and another 49 suffered various levels of radiation sickness. The boat was not repaired and was still lying at Vladivostok 20 years later, awaiting scrapping.

According to information obtained from open sources by the Environmental Rights Centre Bellona, at least 15 then-Soviet submarines suffered nuclear reactor accidents at an average of more than one accident every two years.

It has also recently been revealed that the Soviets have scuttled at least seventeen surplus nuclear reactors - seven of which contained radioactive fuel - along with vast quantities of nuclear waste, near Novaya Zemlya in the Arctic Ocean since the 1960s. The reactors dumped include two contained in the discarded mid-ships section of the nuclear-powered icebreaker *Lenin*, which suffered a reactor meltdown in 1966. The economic turmoil suffered by the former Soviet Union means that the Russians possess neither the finances nor the technical expertise required to dispose of the large number of decommissioned nuclear submarines stored at sites such as those near Murmansk and at Pavlosk, without a great deal of financial and technical assistance from the USA, the UK and Japan. Urgent assistance has also been provided to carry out a major clean-up operation of Russian nuclear shipbuilding and repair facilities, which have a deplorable radiation cleanliness record.

The final category of accident that will be briefly covered in this chapter is that of berthing accidents. Virtually every vessel afloat will, at some time, be involved in a minor berthing incident, from striking jetties to collisions with other ships and tugs. Fortunately, such mishaps seldom result in more than slight denting or rupturing of the vessel's hull, damage to ship's fittings, or a minor setback for the career of the ship's officers. Nevertheless, hull damage is extremely costly to repair and is a major drain on increasingly scarce resources, not only in the form of financial penalties, but also in lost operational availability of the vessel.

The captain of a vessel attempting to leave or approach a berth, particularly in adverse weather conditions or where strong or unpredictable tidal conditions prevail, should consider his situation carefully before disregarding the advice of a local pilot or refusing the assistance of a tug. He should also ensure that at least one of his ship's anchors has been prepared for immediate release in case the need should arise to stop his ship quickly.

Where tugs are employed in the

assistance of larger vessels, it is important that their captains are aware of the dangers of girding of attendant tugs. Girding is caused when a tug's towing hawser is hauled laterally to the craft to port or starboard, thereby causing her to roll over and capsize. Failure to appreciate such a danger can have dire consequences, particularly for the crew of the smaller vessel.

Whilst assisting the Canadian aircraft carrier *HMCS Magnificent* (CVL-21) to berth at Halifax on 15 February 1957, the 97-ton naval tug *Glendyne* (YTB-503) was girded when the carrier manoeuvred unexpectedly. The tug capsized and sank with the loss of two of her seven crewmen - a cook trapped in the galley and a deckhand who was caught beneath the vessel as it rolled on top of him.

*Glendyne* was raised from 80 feet of water four days later by the crane barge *Foundation Scarboro* and was refitted for further service, finally being decommissioned in 1975 and scuttled in Halifax Harbour as a diver-training site.

Another victim of girding was the RMAS tug *TID 97*, completed in September 1944, which had been in the service of the Captain of the Dockyard at Chatham since November 1945. On 29 December 1962 *TID 97* was one of four small tugs attempting to manoeuvre the Royal Fleet Auxiliary store ship *Hebe* (A406) in Chatham's No.3 Basin. With a blustery wind acting against the slab-sided hull of the lightly loaded ship, the small harbour tugs were struggling to maintain control of their charge.

In an effort to assist the tugs accomplish their task and to prevent his ship from striking a lighter berthed near his stern, *Hebe*'s master ordered that his ship's main engines be manoeuvred ahead slightly. Their vessel secured to the store ship's starboard quarter, out of sight of the larger ship's bridge, the crew of *TID 97* was attempting to prevent *Hebe*'s stern from swinging to port. Unfortunately, due to *Hebe*'s ahead manoeuvre, the tug's towing cable was hauled at right angles to the centre line. Before the cable could be slipped, the 54-ton vessel was girded and, at 1533, *TID 97* capsized to port and quickly sank. The tug's master and two of engine room crew were drowned. *TID 97* was subsequently salvaged on 4 January 1963 and sold for scrap in October the same year.

Despite the presence of a basin pilot on the bridge of *Hebe*, responsibility for the ship was still with the vessel's master, who should have avoided operation of his engines to the point where his ship gathered headway. By doing so, he had caused the angle of the towing hawser to increase away from the tug's centre line. The high power to displacement ratio of the tug's engines, coupled with the strength of the deck fittings and of the towing hawser, resulted in the tug being hauled laterally by the larger ship, with tragic consequences. As a result of this accident, Admiralty tugs have since been fitted with the Clyde Towing Arm that permits the towing hawser to be slipped instantly in an emergency by remote control from the wheelhouse.

Had it been fitted, such a device may have saved the 130-tonne Hellenic Navy tug *Romaleos* (A418) from capsizing and sinking on 9 January 1985.

At about noon on that fateful day, the *Romaleos* - together with the similarly sized naval tug *Aias* (A412) - was assisting an 18,000-ton naval auxiliary, preparing to sail from pier K9 of Suda Bay Naval Base, Crete. The assistance of the tugs was required due to prevailing force 4 south-westerly winds, which was in effect holding the auxiliary against the jetty.

*Romaleos* made fast to the auxiliary's bow at a relative angle of 40° to starboard and *Aias* at right angles to the stern, in order to pull the ship ahead and away from the pier. Although the auxiliary's Commanding Officer was in charge of his

*On 27 June 1990, the Brazilian Navy tug Commandante Didier was girded and sunk whilst maneouvring a larger vessel at the Rio de Janiero Naval Base. (Ministerio da Marinha)*

ship, the operation was under the supervision of a local pilot, stationed on the bridge. At 1205, the auxiliary's Commanding Officer ordered engines 'Ahead $^1/_3$' and 30° left rudder. As the stern of the big ship moved clear of the pier, the *Aias* cast off. Seeing this however, the Commanding Officer perceived that the wind was pushing the stern of his ship back towards the pier and so ordered his engines 'Ahead $^1/_3$', quickly followed by 'Ahead $^2/_3$'.

As the ship gathered headway, the pilot was alarmed to see the mast of the *Romaleos* moving rapidly down the auxiliary's starboard side and, dashing across the bridge, noticed the ship's engine order telegraph at 'Ahead $^2/_3$'. No sooner had the pilot ordered 'Stop engines', than *Romaleos* was heard transmitting an urgent request for the auxiliary to reduce speed, while sounding

her whistle. On the starboard bridge wing, the Commanding Officer had suddenly realised his error and ordered 'Stop engines' and then 'Back $^1/_3$'.

The hawser had been attached to the tug without the benefit of a tripping hook and, at the other end, was wrapped around one of the larger ship's bollards in a multiple figure-of-eight manner, so rendering as futile all attempts to release it. As the auxiliary, which was still moving ahead, pulled the tug stern-first water began to flood over her quarter-deck. Attempts by the master of the *Romaleos* to use the tug's engines to manoeuvre only increased the strain on the hawser until it eventually parted. The moment that had been created about the tug's longitudinal axis caused her to roll over to port so rapidly that she capsized. As the *Romaleos* sank, her nine-man crew jumped overboard and were promptly picked up by the *Aias*.

Powerless to do anything but watch the tragic events, the auxiliary anchored and waited for the investigating officers to arrive. A brief lapse of concentration had, in the space of a very few minutes, sent another vessel to a watery grave.

The *Romaleos* was an elderly craft, having been completed by the Missouri Valley Steel Inc. in Leavenworth, Kansas, in 1952 and transferred to the Hellenic Navy ten years later, and so was not fitted with the latest safety equipment which may have prevented such an incident. However, even more modern tugs succumb to similar incidents. Built at the Turn-Ship shipyard of Coden, Alabama in 1981, the 115-tonne Brazilian Navy tug *Comandante Didier* (R16) was girded and sunk at about 0845 on the morning of 27 June 1990, whilst manoeuvring a larger vessel between Piers II and III at the Rio de Janeiro Naval Base. The *Didier* had no facility to slip the towing hawser as the angle of the tow became hazardous. Fortunately, her crew of two officers and six ratings were all rescued and, with the assistance of the floating crane *Atlas*, the vessel was raised on 24 July. Following extensive repairs in the base's No.2 dock, including the complete rebuild of her main engines, *Comandante Didier* was returned to service on 3 February 1992.

Such accidents will undoubtedly continue to occur, especially as more of the service duties previously undertaken by naval or auxiliary service-manned craft are passed to private contractors. In the face of the present economic climates and the reducing defence budgets of most nations, it can only be hoped that such contractors be willing to expend precious financial resources on such safety aspects and appropriate training.

# Chapter Seven

# AMMUNITION AND WEAPONS ACCIDENTS

Weapons and their ammunition, by their nature, are inherently dangerous, especially when not handled with the respect and caution they demand. Strict safety precautions and comprehensive procedures are dictated by all armed forces for the operation of weapons and the handling of ammunition. However, when these precautions and procedures are ignored or are compromised due to complacency, disaster is inevitable, the spectre of death waiting to pounce at the slightest invitation. The level of danger is further heightened when faulty or ill-designed materials or components are involved. Accidents involving ammunition very often have devastating effects, causing death and destruction on a tragic scale.

At the end of World War Two, massive stocks of ammunition were held in dumps around the world and in the following years thousands of tons of surplus and obsolete ordnance were disposed of, either in controlled explosions or in designated dumping sites at sea.

The Italian Navy lighthouse tender *Panigaglia* was one of the first casualties whilst employed on such duties on 1 July 1947. Whilst offloading munitions at Santo Stefano, Sardinia, the ship was wracked by a massive explosion that totally destroyed her and killed 68 men.

Just before Christmas 1948, the British armament carrier *Enfield* was dumping ammunition off May Island when part of her cargo exploded, blowing a large hole in the side of the vessel. First aid damage control actions ensured that the gaping wound was temporarily patched, allowing the ship to make port safely, where she was later repaired for further service. The vessel could so easily have foundered, a fate that was to befall a similar vessel some twelve years later.

The 300-ton armament stores carrier *AV1356* was completed for the Australian Army in November 1945 and named *Ashburton*, but was transferred to the Navy at Melbourne two months later and commissioned as *HMAS Woomera* on 20 February. Much of her service life was

*One of two Italian vessels destroyed by fire in 1947, the lighthouse tender Paningaglia exploded in Stefano harbour on 1 July.*
*(Ufficio Storico Della Marina Militaire)*

*The Australian Navy armaments carrier HMAS Woomera was totally destroyed and sank following an explosion caused by the ignition of a parachute flare, off Sydney on 11 October 1960.*

*(Australian War Memorial, Negative No.301752)*

spent disposing of surplus war-stock ammunition in special coastal dumping grounds between Melbourne and Darwin and in the New Guinea area.

*Woomera*'s career came to an abrupt end on 11 October 1960, 23 miles off Sydney. At about 0920, whilst in the process of jettisoning 140 tons of obsolete ammunition comprising mostly of old 6-inch shells, she was wracked by a massive internal explosion which killed two of her 27-man crew. The initial blast caused other flares, and then some of the remaining 6-inch shells to explode, blowing a huge hole in the side of the wooden-hulled ship and hurling some of the crew into the water.

The explosion was thought to have been the result of the ignition of a parachute flare after the parachute somehow became detached from it's casing. An SOS distress signal was transmitted as the crew fought valiantly to control the fierce fires that raged through the ship. The fire-fighting efforts were complicated however by the phosphorus contained within the flares, on which water had little effect. As the blaze grew out of control the Commanding Officer, Lt.Cdr. D.A. Marshall, RAN, gave the order to abandon ship.

The ship was now ablaze from bow to stern and her engines were still turning at 'slow ahead'. As the survivors floundered in the water and clung for over an hour to a few tattered rafts and other scraps of wreckage they were subjected to a series of vicious attacks by a circling flock of albatrosses, which they fought off by swinging lumps of wood above their heads.

Unbeknown to them at the time, a large shark was circling nearby, no doubt waiting its turn to add to the sailors' distress. However, all of the survivors were safely rescued by the destroyer *HMS Cavendish* (D15) and the frigate *HMAS Quickmatch* (F04), which had been taking part in naval exercises nearby.

Attempts by the crew of the *Cavendish* to extinguish the fires by playing fire hoses on the blazing vessel were of no avail. As the *Quickmatch* was rescuing them, the survivors witnessed their ship's final agonising moments as it sank in 300 fathoms of water in a cloud of steam and acrid black smoke at 1112. Both rescue ships continued to search for a few hours for the two missing crewmen, who were never found, before *Quickmatch* headed for Sydney to land the *Woomera*'s survivors at Garden Island, where some of them were admitted to hospital suffering from burns.

Two courts-martial followed the official investigations into the incident, but both resulted in the acquittal of Lt.Cdr Marshall and his First Lieutenant of charges of negligence and of endangering their vessel, although the Lt.Cdr Marshall later incurred the 'displeasure of the Naval Board'.

The movement and handling of large stocks of ordnance is a essential duty, undertaken to ensure that warships' magazines are kept topped up with suitable quantities of the shells, missiles, torpedoes and depth charges which may be required for any mission that the vessel may be called upon to undertake. Most sizeable navies have specially built armaments carriers and ammunition ships for the purpose of keeping their naval bases and ships of deployed task forces replenished with ammunition. Overseas naval bases need to have their ammunition stocks replenished on a regular basis, the cheapest and safest means of undertaking such a task being the use of specially designed ships.

The British Naval armaments carrier *NAV Bedenham* departed from Devonport on 20 April 1951 with a cargo of stores and ammunition for transport to the Royal Navy bases at Gibraltar and Malta. At about 1000 on 27 April, the *Bedenham* was berthed alongside Ordnance Wharf, Gibraltar, when a fire broke out on the lighter into with the ship was discharging some of her cargo. The fire quickly grew out of control and spread to the *Bedenham*, detonating the ammunition in a massive explosion that was heard all across the rock. The blast wrenched open

*A massive explosion of her cargo completely destroyed the British Naval armaments carrier NAV Bedenham, whilst berthed at Gibraltar on 27 April 1951.*

*(World Ship Photo Library)*

the hull and superstructure of the 1,192-ton vessel and she quickly sank. The Assurance-class tug *RFA Cautious* (A385), berthed nearby, was seriously damaged and widespread destruction was caused to buildings in the immediate dockyard area, with hundreds of windows shattered over a more extensive area. Thirteen people on the dockside were killed and several others injured.

A team of Naval ordnance experts immediately flew to Gibraltar from the UK to investigate the incident, but no findings were ever made public, although it is suspected that the blast was caused by the detonation of a defective torpex-filled depth charge.

The mangled wreck of *Bedenham* was raised and declared a constructive total loss. It was later sold for scrapping and arrived at Clayton & Davie's Dunston breakers yard on 31 May 1952. The damaged upperworks of the tug *Cautious* were repaired and she continued in service with the RFA until October 1964.

*Bedenham*'s destruction had been the worst disaster involving a British ammunition ship since 14 April 1944, when the stores ship *Fort Stikine* exploded in Bombay docks, causing widespread damage to the area and damaging several ships in the harbour, including the total destruction of three landing ships and craft. However, neither incident matched the destruction caused by the explosion, on 23 August 1949, of the 3,300-ton Chinese merchant steamship *China Victor* whilst unloading her cargo of ammunition at Kaohsiung, Formosa. The port area suffered widespread damage and over 500 people were either killed or injured by the blast.

The most recent disaster of this type occurred on 30 April 1997, when the French naval netlayer *La Fidele* (Y751) exploded and sank in the English Channel, five miles off the coast of Cherbourg. The 600-ton vessel was sailing out into the Atlantic to dump her cargo of ammunition, including 1,400 hand-grenades. As personnel were priming grenades prior to jettisoning, one of them detonated, sparking off by two massive explosions. A Royal Navy sail-training vessel, the *Sea Harrier*, was only a short distance away from *La Fidele* at the time and was soon joined by several French naval vessels in a huge rescue operation. However, despite the speed of the rescue effort, two of *La Fidele*'s crewmembers had been killed and three were still missing out of her complement of sixteen French naval personnel and six civilian ordnance experts. Four others were seriously injured.

Since explosives were first carried aboard men-of-war, hundreds of ships have been destroyed or lost through the accidental detonation of the ammunition in their storerooms, or magazines. The Royal Navy, in particular, suffered more devastation from magazine explosions aboard their battle fleet during the Battle of Jutland in May 1916, than from enemy gunfire. The battleship *HMS Invincible* was struck by a shell from the German battleship *Derflinger* that blew off the roof of 'Q' turret, setting fire to the cordite propellant. The flash quickly reached the magazine and *Invincible* was blown in two by a massive explosion. All but three of her crew were lost, including Rear-Admiral the Honourable Horace Hood.

The further loss that fateful day of the battle-cruisers *HMS Indefatigable* and *HMS Queen Mary* highlighted the poor quality of British cordite and the fact that the lack of flash-tight doors made it all too easy for damage in the turret, barbette or working chamber to generate a flash which could detonate the contents of the magazine. The armoured cruiser *HMS Defence* was also sunk by German gunfire as a result of cordite charges catching fire in the ammunition passages, with the loss of her entire crew of 893 men. The battle-cruiser *HMS Lion* was only saved from a similar fate after being hit by thirteen 12-

inch shells from the German battle-cruiser *Lutzow* by a mortally wounded Royal Marines officer who gallantly ordered the magazine of 'Q' turret to be flooded.

Nevertheless, the British were not alone in having problems. On 1 September 1917 the Japanese armoured cruiser *Tsukuba* sank at Yokosuka after a huge explosion in one of her magazines, caused by the decomposition of the propellant stored within.

The Royal Navy took immediate action to address the causes of the tragic magazine explosions which had cost the lives of thousands of British sailors, including improved quality control measures, limiting service life of volatile nitro-cellulose charges, the provision of fearnought screens and dedicated explosion venting arrangements in magazines and the replacement of flash doors. Flash doors were already fitted to most ships to contain any explosion, but these were often left open, or removed in action in an effort to increase the rate of fire of the ships' main armament.

The effectiveness of flash doors was proven with the explosion in No.2 16-inch gun turret of the battleship *USS Iowa* (BB-61) on April 1989. Although 47 crewmen were killed, the blast failed to reach the magazine and was confined to the turret, so preventing an even more tragic disaster. The possibility that the blast had been caused by unstable propellant charges, premature detonation of the ventaxial detonator or premature explosion of the shell itself inside the gun were quickly discounted and investigation focused on the possibility of sabotage by one of the turret's crew who had died. However, following a two-year investigation costing US$25 million, the US Navy announced that it could not positively determine the cause of the explosion and apologised to the family of Gunner's Mate Second Class Clayton Hartwig, the man who had formerly been blamed for the accident.

The frequent tragedies amongst the ships of the British fleet before and during the First World War were due almost entirely to the volatility and instability of the nitro-cellulose in their cordite charges. Cordite was the term used for most types of solid propellant apart from gunpowder. Any impurities in the raw materials used to manufacture the nitro-cellulose could result in spontaneous combustion and explosion with devastating consequences. Massive stocks of cordite were quickly withdrawn and replaced with propellants manufactured in a modified and improved manner, but not before the further tragic loss of the battleship *HMS Vanguard* at Scapa Flow in July 1917.

Following these disasters, investigative trials carried out on the old battleship *Prince of Wales* also revealed that charges could be ignited during a fire by molten lead from electric cable insulation dripping onto them and this type of cable was quickly removed from magazines.

Many lessons regarding the storage and handling of ammunition were learnt from these, and other, tragedies. The magazines of modern warships incorporate elaborate safety features to prevent the detonation of ammunition by any cause, such as fire, stray electric or electromagnetic fields, or penetration of foreign bodies. Such compartments are carefully shielded from stray electric fields and electrical components within them, such as lighting switches, are designed to contain inevitable sparks within their casings. Fire protection

*A photo taken from the bridge captures the explosion of the No. 2 16-inch gun turret aboard the battleship USS IOWA (BB-61). 47 sailors were killed by the blast, which occurred as the ship conducted a routine gunnery exercise 330 miles northeast of Puerto Rico.*

*(Lt Thomas Jarrell/ US Navy)*

usually includes automatic alarm and fresh water sprinkler systems, backed up by high-pressure salt water systems, which will continue the fire extinguishing and cooling effort once the fresh water supply has been exhausted. Ship hull plating is often thicker in the vicinity of the magazines, with the US Navy in particular utilising Kevlar armour to protect vital compartments in their newer combatants.

However, such disasters involving the detonation of ammunition within ships' magazines have not been restricted to wartime, and peacetime catastrophes, although now relatively rare, from time to time hit the headlines.

Whilst unloading ammunition at Earle Ammunition Depot, Leonardo, New Jersey, on 30 April 1946, a massive explosion ripped through the Buckley-class destroyer-escort *USS Solar* (DE-221). One officer and six ratings were killed and a further 56 crewmen were wounded.

*Solar*, a unit of the Operational Development Force, Atlantic Fleet, had arrived at the depot at 0830 that morning, berthing at berth NB-2 of the Barge Pier, for the purpose of de-ammunitioning prior to being taken in hand for an overhaul at the New York Naval Shipyard.

Two hours into the evolution, at about 1133, the first of three blasts erupted on the forecastle, followed by another explosion two minutes later and a third a minute after that. The force of these blasts completely destroyed the entire forward section of the ship, propelling her 300 feet aft - a full ship's length - to a position in line with berth NB-4, until she came to rest with the forecastle completely submerged and with her bow resting on the seabed. The bottom and sides of the ship had been blown completely out and the forward superstructure was blown upwards and backwards, reducing the whole of the vessel forward of the forward engine room bulkhead to a mass of burning, mangled wreckage. The blast also caused severe damage to a large section of the pier, hurling a loaded freight car into the water and completely demolishing the signal tower at the seaward end of the pier. Several ammunition lighters were also damaged.

*Fires aboard the shattered hulk of the destroyer-escort USS Solar are doused from a pier and from tugs following an ammunition explosion aboard the ship at Earle Ammunition Depot, New Jersey, on 30 April 1946.*
*(US Naval Institute)*

The base's Fire and Disaster Plan was initiated immediately following the first blast and within minutes all but one craft, the lighter *YF-416*, were moved from their berths at Barge Pier 1 to buoys away from the danger area, including several tugs and ammunitions lighters and the landing ship *LST-28*. A feverish effort was also made to remove as many railroad cars, some of them containing explosive ordnance, from the pier. The ammunition ship *USS Great Sitkin* (AE-17) and the destroyer *USS Ishbell* (DD-778) were also moved from the nearby Pier 2 to safe anchorages.

The two station fire boats and the tugs *YTB-277* and *YTB-215* were quickly on the scene, directing streams of water onto the burning wreck and the damaged pier and railway freight carriages, assisted soon after by emergency fire trucks and ambulances, which evacuated the wounded away from the disaster area.

Damage to the pier was so severe that, following a two-month clearance operation by a Mine and Bomb Disposal Unit, a 130-ft section of it had to be demolished.

*Solar* was declared a constructive total loss and decommissioned three weeks after the explosion. Stricken from the US Navy on 5 June 1946, the hulk was towed out to sea and scuttled four days later.

A Court of Inquiry, convened by Commander Destroyers, U.S. Atlantic Fleet (ComDesLant), was set up at the Headquarters of the Third Naval District to investigate the cause of the disaster and, in the course of these investigations, several scenarios were put forward by the various bureaux and agencies who's input was requested. In January 1947, a report from the Chief of the Bureau of Ordnance suggested that the initial explosion had been caused by "*a low-order detonation of a 7.2-inch torpex-loaded projectile for the projector Mark 10 [Hedgehog], probably caused by inadvertently bumping or dropping it against some projection with sufficient force to dent the thin-walled case of the projectile.*" Burning torpex or flames then probably passed through an open hatch to the magazine, setting off the other explosions that caused such destruction to the vessel and the surrounding area.

Another theory was that the mass detonation of the ordnance in the 7.2-inch projector magazine might have been initiated by the burning of inflammable liquids or gases in the adjacent paint store, which then leaked into the magazine through a ruptured bulkhead between the two compartments. However, the accepted chain of events, recommended by the Bureau of Ships, was that the initial detonation of a Hedgehog charge within the forward 3-inch gun shield, probably as a result of it being accidentally dropped resulted in the burning of other charges in the area, which then caused the second explosion. These explosions ruptured the forecastle deck, propelling flames and other projectiles into the bowels of the ship through the deck and through the open door in bulkhead 23 and the open hatch leading to the magazine at location A-305-M. The hedgehog charges within this magazine then exploded, resulting in the mass detonation that destroyed the forward section of the ship.

The Bureau of Ships criticised the failure of a rating to close the magazine hatch and operate the sprinkler system on abandoning the magazines, suggesting that this failure contributed materially to the destruction of the *USS Solar*.

As a result of the Court of Inquiry, all safety precautions regarding the safe handling of such thin-walled high explosive containers were revised and thereafter all personnel involved in the movement of such ordnance were to be fully briefed on these precautions prior to the commencement of every such evolution. Furthermore, ComDesLant recommended that all torpex-loaded ammunition be removed from service as soon as practicable and that the programme for their replacement by HBX-filled ammunition be accelerated.

The cause of some ship losses have been shrouded in doubt, particularly during times of conflict when the vessel is claimed sunk by the actions of an enemy. The Tench-class submarine *USS Diablo* (SS-479) had been transferred to the Pakistani Navy on 1 June 1964 and renamed *PNS Ghazi* (S130). During one of the fierce conflicts between India and Pakistan in the early 1970s, *Ghazi*, under the command of Commander Zafar Mohammad Khan, operated off the Indian coast in the hope of getting an opportunity to attack some of the Indian Navy's larger warships, in particular the aircraft carrier *INS Vikrant* (R11). The submarine failed to return from one of these patrols in December 1971 and the Indian Navy later claimed to have sunk her in the Bay of Bengal near Vishakhapatnam. None of *Ghazi*'s 83 crewmen survived and the boat was never recovered.

The Pakistani Navy have stated that *Ghazi* was lost on 4 December as a result of an internal explosion, probably as a result of the detonation of one of her own mines, suggesting that the boat was on an offensive mining mission at the time of her loss. An event that adds credence to this theory as to the cause of *Ghazi*'s disappearance was the sound of a massive explosion heard at Vishakhapatnam late on that night, the force of which was powerful enough to overturn several wooden chocks around an Egyptian Project 640-U ('Whiskey'-class) submarine undergoing refit in a drydock at the base.

The Indian Navy later produced evidence that they had located the *Ghazi* in 150-feet of water near the entrance to their naval base at Vishakhapatnam in position 17°41'00"N, 83°21'05"E, and claimed that the forward section of the boat had been blown outwards. They also claimed that they had lured the *Ghazi* there by the release of false intelligence that the *Vikrant* was in port, when the carrier was in fact in the Andaman Islands at the time, and that the destroyer *INS Rajput* (D141) had launched two depth charges at the submarine at 0015 on 4 December. These depth charges, they claimed, had set off the chain of events that had resulted in an internal explosion that sank the *Ghazi*.

The United States and the Soviet Union both offered to raise the boat, but the Indian Government refused permission. There appears little doubt that an internal explosion occurred, possibly of a mine being prepared for laying from one of the submarine's torpedo tubes, but whether *Ghazi* was sunk by the Indians or was the victim of an accident will probably never been known for certain and we are left to draw our own conclusions.

Although there is little information available yet to highlight many recent problems the Soviet Union may have experienced with their more complex surface warship designs and weapon systems, it would be surprising indeed if they were to have come through the 30 years of Gorshkov's reign without any hitches. The complacency with which the Russians handled weapons and ammunition was graphically demonstrated on 10 February 1949, when the ex-Royal Navy battleship *HMS Royal Sovereign* was returned to Britain.

The ship had been transferred to the Russian Navy on 30 May 1944 and commissioned as the *Arkhangelsk*. When grudgingly handed back, it was found that every gun on board was loaded with live ammunition, from the 15-inch main armament down to the 2-pdr. anti-aircraft guns. As a further sign of neglect, or perhaps simply as a statement of contempt at having to return the ship, the mess decks were covered in human excrement. Members of the Royal Navy were also surprised to find that they were not allowed to mix with any of the Russian crew, who only a few years previously had been their allies in the fight against the Germans.

In fact, the Soviets' record with regards to weapon safety has continued to be poor, and there have been several reports in Western newspapers over the years of serious explosions aboard Soviet surface ships and submarines, the stricken vessels often refusing offers of assistance from NATO warships. Nevertheless, the severity of some of the reported incidents have undoubtedly been blown out of all proportion by the media in the constant effort to gain propaganda points during the era of the 'Cold War'.

There is no doubt however of the consequences of one more recent incident, although claims of the number of lives lost were sensationally exaggerated by the western press at the time.

Whilst taking part in routine manoeuvres with other units of the Black Sea Flotilla off the Crimean Peninsular on 30 August 1974, the Project 61 ('Kashin'-class) guided-missile destroyer *Otvazhnyy* suffered an internal explosion and fire which reduced the after end of the ship to a burnt out mass of twisted metal before she sank.

The *Otvazhnyy* was, at the time of her loss, one of the Soviet Navy's most sophisticated warships, having been built by the 61 Kommunar shipyard at Nikolayev and commissioned into service on 31 December 1965 as one of a class of twenty ships which claimed the status of being the first class of major surface warships to be propelled purely by gas-turbines. The ship had a 'double-ended' weapon system layout, with twin 76mm gun turrets and twin ZiF-101 launchers for Volna M-1 ('SA-N-1') surface-to-air missiles forward and aft.

Just after 1000 on that fateful morning, a missile sustainer motor in the after Volna M-1 magazine of the ship caught fire, probably whilst the weapon was being prepared for an exercise firing, an operation which would include the application of power to the missile's supply circuits. The fierce blaze burned for nearly half an hour before at least one other missile exploded with such force that the after superstructure was blown apart, as if ripped open by a giant can opener.

Twenty-four men, many of whom had been involved in fighting the original fire,

*Schematic diagram of the sequence of events leading up to the loss of the Soviet destroyer Otvazhnyy following a booster motor explosion in the aft Volna M-1 (SAN-1) missile magazine on 30 August 1974.*

*(Warship International)*

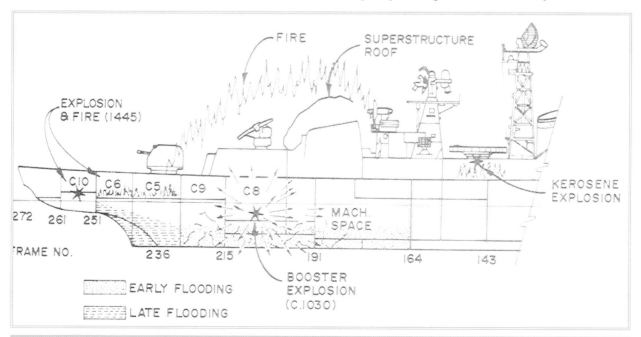

were killed in the blast and the ship received severe damage to the hull and to watertight bulkheads in the area. In particular, all those personnel in the galley were killed instantly as that compartment was completely destroyed by the initial blast. Several compartments began flooding and *Otvazhnyy* soon began to list to starboard.

Damage-control efforts were severely hampered by the spread of smoke and heat throughout the after end of the ship and smaller fires were soon breaking out well away from the main seat of the explosion. The situation was to get far worse when, a couple of hours after the initial fire, helicopter fuel ignited below the helicopter landing platform, causing a further massive explosion.

Other ships involved in the exercise, including *Otvazhnyy*'s sister ship *Komsomolets Ukrainy*, the Project 56 ('SAM Kotlin'-class) destroyer *Soznatel'nyi* and the Project 56U ('Kildin'-class) destroyer *Bedovyy*, closed the stricken ship to render fire-fighting assistance, providing additional fire parties and equipment and playing their own fire-hoses on the ship's blistering external surfaces. Shortly before 1100, *Soznatel'nyi* managed to attach a hawser to the burning vessel for almost an hour before being forced to slip the line.

By 1245 the heat radiating from the ship was so extreme that all vessels moved away in case of further explosions. It was decided to once again take the now heavily listing ship in tow towards nearby Sevastopol, a task which was successfully undertaken for a few hours by the *Bedovyy*, until at 1447 a further explosion ripped through the vessel's stern in the 10th compartment, killing several more men. *Otvazhnyy*'s Commanding Officer, Captain 3rd Rank Ivan Petrovich Vinnik, now had no choice but to order his ship to be abandoned, some five hours after the fire had first broken out in the magazine.

The ship could now be seen to be listing 30° to starboard settling by the stern and, just before 1600, she sank in position 44°44.4'N, 33°01.5'E. In a final act of defiance and a demonstration of the excellent watertight integrity of the forward compartments, the vessel's bow protruded vertically from the water for a length over 150 feet before she finally slid quietly beneath the waves. Thirty-one of her crew of around 270 had perished in the disaster, significantly less then the "over 200" reported by the western media at the time! Weapons and other items from the destroyer were later salvaged in an operation including the salvage vessels *Karpati* (Project 530) and *SB-15* (Project 733) .

That the magazine's automatic spray system had not activated following the initial explosion was the direct result of a series of previous flooding accidents involving the system. Several ships had had the expensive contents of their magazines irreparably damaged by accidental flooding of the compartments due to faulty fire detector heads, with the result that Admiral Gorshkov ordered that the systems be isolated. Manual operation had proved impossible in the circumstances of the explosion and fire aboard the *Otvazhnyy*. In fact, tests aboard *Otvazhnyy*'s sister ship *Komsomolets Ukrainy* indicated that it could take up to twenty minutes to operate the system.

This was not to be the last Soviet vessel to be lost as a result of the explosion of the highly combustible propellants used in missile booster motors. A more recent casualty was the much-publicised loss of the Project 667A ('Yankee'-class) ballistic-missile submarine *K-219* on 6 October 1986, whilst on routine patrol off the east coast of the United States.

At 2238 on the night of 3 October, *K-219* was submerged 500 miles east of Bermuda when leaking liquid propellant from one of the vessel's sixteen RSM-25 (SS-N-6 'Serb') ballistic missiles ignited, causing a massive explosion. The blast wrenched open the hatch from the third missile silo on the port side, silo No.6, causing the silo to flood and sending the submarine into a steep dive. The Commanding Officer, Captain Igor Britanov, ordered his boat to surface. Later photographs of the dive planes on the boat's sail in the full up position provided evidence of the urgency of this action.

Once on the surface, the crew attempted to vent the deadly toxic gases and pressure build-up from the fuel and water mixture

ship *SB-406* from the Faeroe Island area and the salvage ship *Agatan* from Cuba. These fleet movements did not go unnoticed by the Americans and caused considerable alarm, especially as it was only a few days before Presidents Reagan and G orbachev were due to attend the Reykjavik Peace Summit on 11 October.

On board *K-219*, the situation was getting worse. The fire was out of control and, preparing for the worse possible scenario, should one of the missiles explode, Captain Britanov decided to take his boat north-eastwards to deeper water.

*A port view of the Soviet Yankee class nuclear-powered ballistic missile submarine, K-219, that was damaged by an internal liquid missile propellant explosion. Three days later the submarine sank in 18,000 feet of water.*

*(US Navy)*

in the missile section in the 4th compartment. A survey of the boat's casing revealed that No.6 silo hatch was missing, with further damage to the hatches of adjacent silos. A second explosion then wracked the boat, as the fuel in the missile compartment ignited. The Commanding Officer ordered that Moscow be informed of the boat's predicament and the Soviet Navy immediately despatched all available ships to *K-219*'s aid, including the nuclear-powered cruiser *Kirov* from the Northern Fleet, the Project 712 salvage

Attempts to extinguish the blaze by using the fixed LOH fire suppression system were unsuccessful and only resulted in further contamination of the boat with poisonous freon gas through fractured pipes. Deadly smoke and fumes were spreading aft to the 5th and 6th compartments and all personnel in these sections had to don breathing apparatus, but supplies of breathing air bottles were critically low. The fire had also damaged the reactor controls, the temperatures in the reactors rising with the loss of the coolant pumps. Engineering teams had to enter the reactor compartments in protective gear and lower the reactor rods by hand to shut them down. By late afternoon, the reactors had been made safe, but one man had been killed in the effort when his air supply ran out.

In a desperate act, Captain Britanov decided to temporarily dive and partly flood the missile section in order to extinguish the fire. The gamble paid off and the boat re-surfaced, the fires finally out. However, damage to the boat's hull meant that slow flooding could not be controlled.

Overnight, several merchant ships arrived on the scene. *K-219*'s crew continued to try to save their boat whilst continuing their passage north-eastwards. On the morning of 5 October, the steam ship *Krasnygvardensk* took *K-219* in tow. The speed of the tow was painfully slow, as the men aboard the submarine fought constantly to stem the flow of water into the boat. The vessels' progress was monitored fervently by NATO ships and aircraft and by a veritable swarm of aircraft chartered by the world's media. Despite the best efforts of the damage-control parties, the vessels had travelled only 80 miles since the explosion when there were difficulties with the tow and the submarine was seen to be settling deeper in the water. Around 2300, the tow parted and efforts to re-establish it were unsuccessful as *K-219*'s flooding continued to spread to further compartments. Realising that their feverish battle had been lost, Captain Britanov reluctantly gave the order to abandon the boat and, at 0403 on 6 October, *K-219* sank some 600 miles east of Bermuda.

Four crewmen had been lost in the disaster, whilst another two died of their injuries. The survivors were taken to Cuba and then flown to Moscow, where Captain Britanov was held responsible for the loss of his boat and was dismissed from the Soviet Navy.

In a rare press release, the Soviet Government stated that three crewmen had died in the explosion but that all survivors, some apparently injured, were evacuated before the submarine sank. The site of the wreck has been monitored almost constantly since 1986 by the Soviet/Russian Navy, probably more to ensure that NATO forces, which could reach her with mini-submersibles, do not try to retrieve sections of the boat than to monitor levels of contamination. Because *K-219* was flooded before sinking the boat is likely to be largely intact, apart from the explosion damage and damage from the impact with the sea floor, which may have partially buried the wreck. It may, therefore, be feasible to retrieve the hull almost intact, together with her valuable payload, although the operations would be extremely costly and politically provocative. For example, the cost of Operation Jenifer, the mission to recover the Project 629A ('Golf II'-class) boat in the Pacific in 1973, was reportedly over US$350-million.

As in the case of several other disasters, there were initially claims that the accident had resulted from a collision with a western submarine, in this case the Los Angeles class boat *USS Augusta* (SSN-710), an accusation fervently denied by the US Navy. However, this was most likely an attempt to deflect criticism away from the Soviet hierarchy, as photographs show no sign of collision damage to *K-219*'s hull. Nevertheless, the theory was perpetuated in yet another disaster movie ("*Hostile Waters*" – World Productions 1997).

It is unlikely that the reactor in *K-219* is going to cause the ecological disaster at first feared, even though at 18,000ft below the surface a pressure of 3.6-tons-per-square-inch is exerted on it. Reactor pressure vessels are constructed of non-ferrous materials, the primary circuit generally being of stainless steel, and are designed to sustain very high pressures, both internally and externally.

Monitoring of the area of this accident, and also those of *USS Scorpion* and *USS Thresher* and of the Soviet Project 627 ('November'-class) nuclear-powered submarine *K-8* lost off Cape Finisterre in April 1970, have revealed no unusual levels of radioactivity. This is not something even the secrecy fanatics in the Kremlin would have been able to hide, as independent monitoring of all these disaster sites is regularly carried out - Greenpeace being a notable siren to ecological dangers. It is also unlikely that there is any danger from the nuclear warheads of the R-21 missiles which went to the bottom in *K-129* or the RSM-25 missiles of *K-219*, or from those weapons in any of the other sunken nuclear-powered boats, although the Russians announced in 1993 that they were to seal two corroding nuclear torpedoes lost when the nuclear-powered submarine *Komsomolets* sank in 1989. It is unknown if the *K-219* was carrying its full complement of missiles when it sank.

Project 667A class SSBNs, rapidly phased out of service with the Russian Navy or converted to attack boats during the late-1980s/early-1990s, carried sixteen missiles, of either the 1,300-mile range RSM-25 (SS-N-6) Mod.1 or 1,600-mile Mod.2 or 3 types, all of which used liquid fuel as a propellant. The later RSM-40 (SS-N-8 'Sawfly), carried on Project 677B ('Delta I'-class) and Project 677BD ('Delta II'-class) boats, and RSM-50 (SS-N-18 'Stingray') missiles carried aboard Project 677BDR ('Delta III'-class) SSBNs, are also liquid-fuelled. However, with the lone Project 667AM ('Yankee II'-class) boat the Soviets changed to solid fuel to propel its twelve RSM-45 (SS-N-17 'Snipe') missiles, a trend which was continued with the Project 941's RSM-52 (SS-N-20 'Sturgeon') weapons and the latest RSM-54 (SS-N-23 'Skiff') missiles in the Project 677BDRM ('Delta IV'-class) boats. In contrast, the Western navies have always relied on solid fuel for its production SLBMs and have enjoyed a much better safety record.

Just how close the explosion and fire aboard the *K-219* came to endangering the nuclear warhead of the RSM-25 weapon in the silo will probably never be known. To date, as far as we know there have been no major naval disasters involving nuclear warheads, certainly not on the scale of the Chernobyl or Three Mile Island nuclear power station accidents. However, there have been several occasions when nuclear weapons have been lost at sea.

In December 1965 an A4-E aircraft carrying a thermonuclear weapon was lost overboard from the aircraft carrier *USS Ticonderoga* (CV-14) in 4,800 metres of water 130 kilometres from the coast of southern Japan. The weapon was never recovered, but the Japanese Science and Technology Agency has undertaken detailed surveys since and noted no unusual levels of radioactive contamination in the area. Only weeks later, on 17 January 1966, another incident occurred near Palomares, Spain, after a USAF B-52 bomber collided with a KC-153 refuelling aircraft, killing 8 of the aircrafts' 11 crewmen. The B-52's load of four hydrogen bombs were dropped as the bomber crashed to the ground; two rupturing over nearby farms; a third landing intact near Palomares and the fourth falling into the sea 12 miles from the coast. The submerged bomb was successfully recovered three months later from the slope of the continental shelf at a depth of 870 metres by the Deep Submergence Vessel (DSV) *Alvin*.

Although the number of nuclear warheads carried aboard ships at sea has been significantly reduced since the ending of the 'Cold War', the terrifying possibility of future accidents involving these awesome weapons is increasing. With the break-up of the Soviet Union, their control of their massive nuclear arsenal has loosened. The temptation for scientists and technicians to work for anyone offering a large enough salary, and the sale of components and materials to the highest bidders is all too real, with some governments willing to pay practically any price to acquire the necessary technology to manufacture their own weapons of mass destruction with which to hold their enemies to ransom.

In the 1990s, the Swedish Navy and Coast Guard intercepted several radioactive items being smuggled into their ports from former Soviet states across the Baltic. Tight controls on the export of any components or materials that may be utilised in the construction of such weapons of mass destruction have to be strictly enforced by all governments. The post-9/11 war against terrorism and the 2003 liberation of Iraq has highlighted the fact that present controls are not stringent enough to prevent them falling into the hands of ruthless dictatorships or fanatics.

Drones are frequently used to provide ships' weapons crews with realistic targets to track and destroy, so providing valuable experience in the operation of increasingly sophisticated equipment. Some of these drones accurately simulate anti-ship missiles, being of similar size and taking up appropriate flight paths at realistic speeds. Although not incorporating a warhead, the striking of a vessel by such an object can have grave consequences. Whilst taking part in a naval exercise in the Pacific on 16 April 1987, the Soviet Project 1234.1 ('Nanuchka-III'-class) missile corvette *Musson* was struck by such a target drone. The resultant explosion was followed by a fire that quickly grew out of control and the vessel sank a short time later with the loss of 39 of her crew. This was the second such incident in only a few years. The Project 205 ('Osa'-class) missile boat *R-82* was destroyed by a fire after being struck by a dummy missile during exercises with the Northern Fleet on 23 March 1983.

Whilst operating in the Aegean, 80 miles west of Izmir, as part of the annual NATO naval exercise 'Display Determination 92' a few minutes after midnight on Friday, 2 October 1992, the Turkish destroyer *TCG Mauvenet* (DM357) was struck by at least one of two Sea Sparrow missiles fired accidentally from one of the Mk.29 launchers on the US 6th Fleet aircraft carrier *USS Saratoga* (CV-60). The 48 year-old destroyer was not equipped to evade such a sophisticated weapon, fired from a range of only three miles, and was hit in the area of the bridge, killing the Commanding Officer, a junior officer, a non-commissioned officer and two ratings. A further thirteen men were injured.

The fierce fire that broke out was brought under control within ten minutes with the assistance of other warships that had rushed to the stricken ship's aid, but it quickly re-ignited. Two helicopters from *Saratoga* flew the bodies of the five men, as well as five of the most seriously injured crewmen, to the port of Izmir. *Mauvenet* was later taken in tow to the Turkish Naval Base of Gölcük, where she arrived on the following Monday.

NATO's top Commander in Europe, General John Shalikashvili, was quick to apologise for the tragic accident and promised a full Court of Inquiry. An immediate restriction was placed on the operational readiness of Sea Sparrow missiles on all US warships, by removing the 'safe to operate' plugs from launchers to a centrally controlled position. This would prevent the firing sequence of the missiles being completed. The Turkish authorities made it clear that they would not make waves diplomatically with the United States over what had clearly been a tragic accident. No live missile firing had been planned as part of the exercise. The fact that two missiles were launched is not surprising, as it is general practice for anti-aircraft missiles to be launched in pairs to increase the chances of a kill.

In late-November 1992 the US Navy stated that the Captain and seven crewmen aboard *USS Saratoga* were to face disciplinary charges in connection with the incident. The Court of Inquiry revealed that an officer aboard *Saratoga* had called a surprise drill, dragging ratings from their bunks to take part. The officer failed to stress that the procedure was a drill and did not realise that the operators, who showed a lack of familiarity with laid down procedures, were preparing for a live firing.

Although damage to the *Mauvenet* was largely confined to the bridge and forward superstructure screen, the elderly vessel was judged to be beyond economical repair and was consequently paid off. The US Navy later offered the Turkish Navy the Knox-class frigate *Elmer Mongomery* (FF-1082) as a replacement for the destroyer on a grant basis under the Foreign Assistance Act. This vessel was subsequently used to provide spare parts for the other eight Knox-class vessels transferred during 1993-94, one of which - ex-*USS Capodanno* (FF-1093) - was commissioned into the Turkish Navy as the new *TCG Mauvenet* (F250).

Some ships have also been badly damaged when firing their own weapons. On 7 December 1967, the frigate *HMAS Queensborough* (F02) suffered significant hull and machinery damage after firing her own 4-inch guns, but managed to return to Sydney under her own power. More recently, the Indian Navy Project 1241PE ('Pauk'-class) corvette *INS Agray* (P36) was badly damaged during an exercise on 5 February 2004. The *Agray* was taking part in an anti-submarine exercise 120 miles from Mumbai when an RBU anti-submarine rocket fired by the ship, misfired and fell into the water close to the hull before exploding. The blast wrenched open a hole in the vessel's hull, resulting in flooding of the engine room. The ship was towed back to the Naval Dockyard in Mumbai and repaired. Fortunately, there were no casualties amongst the ships' crews in either of these cases.

During the Second World War, the Allies lost several warships to accidents involving their torpedo armament. One of the worst accidents occurred at Greenock on the afternoon of 30 April 1940. During a maintenance operation aboard the Free French destroyer *Maillé Brézé*, which entailed raising the ship's torpedo tubes, a live torpedo slipped from the mounting and plunged onto the vessel's deck, exploding on impact. Several crewmen, both above and below decks, were killed instantly and the death toll rose to twenty-eight in the fierce blaze which ensued and which resulted in the ship sinking at it's berth.

Only a few days later, on 5 May, the Royal Navy destroyer *HMS Khartoum* had to be beached and abandoned off Perim, near the southern entrance to the Red Sea, after an air vessel on the starboard torpedo mounting exploded causing an uncontrollable fire. On 29 March 1942 the cruiser *HMS Trinidad* was seriously damaged and 18 of her crew killed when a torpedo she had just fired at a German destroyer suffered a gyro malfunction, ran wild and struck her, exploding on impact. Despite these, and a series of less serious accidents, British war-built torpedoes enjoyed a reputation of excellence and reliability, compared to those manufactured by other countries. After the war, several navies began experimenting with alternative forms of propulsion in their quest for faster and deeper diving torpedoes to counter the newer submarines entering service. The US Navy had attempted to develop a hydrogen peroxide propulsion system for installation in their anti-submarine torpedoes in the 1930s and later successfully developed their Navol (hydrogen peroxide) powered Mk.16, which remained in service until 1975.

The British, however, suffered a series of production disasters, with 90% of the twenty or so designs developed proving to be dismal failures before they even entered production. Hopes were high with the High Test Peroxide (HTP)-fuelled Mk12 torpedo, code-named 'Fancy'. HTP ($H_2O_2$) is a colourless and odourless liquid, derived from adding an extra oxygen atom to water ($H_2O$) and is mixed within the engine with fuel to produce a violent chemical reaction to propel the weapon. The Mk.12 was driven by what was basically a Mk.8 burner-cycle propulsor modified to run on HTP and had been developed from the German pre-war 'Steinbut' HTP weapon. The Mk.12 also had its problems, which were to lead to a series of tragic accidents in the 1950s, the worst of which resulted in the loss of one of His Majesty's submarines.

The S-class submarine *HMS Sidon* (S59) had been one of the boats involved in the search for *HMS Affray* in April 1951. On the morning of Thursday, 16 June 1955, *Sidon* was one of five submarines berthed alongside the depot ship *HMS Maidstone* (A185) in Portland Harbour. Most of the boats were preparing to sail on exercises to trial the new Mk.12 'Fancy SR' ('Silent-Running') torpedo, two of which were embarked aboard *Sidon*. The weapons were trial prototypes and as such were not fitted with warheads.

The boat alongside *Sidon*, her sister ship *HMS Springer* (S64), slipped at 0820 and proceeded out of the harbour. The 58 men aboard Sidon, including crew, trainees and trials personnel, were closed up at their stations and were carrying out pre-sailing checks. All hatches, except the conning tower hatch, were shut, but watertight doors throughout the boat were open for ease of access. Unnoticed by anyone, fuel leaking from one of the Mk.12 torpedoes was causing an immense pressure build-up within *Sidon*'s No.3 torpedo tube.

A few minutes later a violent explosion, equivalent to around 150lb of TNT, burst from the tube, blowing open the bow cap and blowing off the inner tube door. A massive fireball erupted through the submarine as far as the control room, venting itself in an uprush of hot air and smoke through the conning tower, killing six men in its path instantaneously and injuring several others. A large and dense cloud of toxic fumes, including deadly carbon monoxide, closely followed the blast. As water poured into the boat via the open torpedo tube and she began to list and settle by the bow, some of the crew were already scrambling from her hatches.

Immediately following the explosion, *Sidon*'s Commanding Officer, Lieutenant-Commander H.T. Verry, summoned assistance from the depot ship and ordered the two after hatches to be opened. He then ordered the First-Lieutenant and the engineer officer to don breathing apparatus and return below to assess the damage and rescue trapped crewmen. Everyone in the after sections were escaping in an orderly disciplined manner, but access forward of the conning tower was blocked by debris from the explosion. Some doors were shut in an attempt to contain the fires and fumes but others were blocked by the carnage within the forward compartments.

Soon after, Lt.Cdr. Verry donned a DSEA breathing set and went below to see for himself how damage-control efforts were proceeding. Finding his way forward of the control room blocked, he returned to the bridge. *Sidon* was quickly settling by the bow, the smoke emitting from her conning tower growing thicker all the time as more men were hauled, blackened and choking, from the boat. Under orders from the Commander Submarines aboard the depot ship, Lt.Cdr. Verry reluctantly gave the command to abandon ship and was the last man to leave the vessel. An attempt was made to

*HMS Sidon following her salvage in June 1955. The submarine had sunk alongside a depot ship at Portland after the detonation of a Mk12 Fancy-SR torpedo within one of the boat's torpedo tubes.*
*(Royal Navy Submarine Museum)*

close the after hatch but was not successful due to the immense pressure now building up inside the boat.

The crew of the Danish submarine *HDMS Saelen* (S323), berthed on *Sidon*'s port side alongside *Maidstone*, closed all watertight doors and mustered on deck, following which their boat was towed out of harms way. At 0850, twenty-five minutes after the explosion, *Sidon* slipped bow-first beneath the surface, coming to rest with a 25° list to starboard in about 36 feet of water.

The depot ship immediately transmitted a 'Subsunk' signal and personnel and equipment were soon being mustered to assist in the rescue operations. The mooring vessel *Moordale* had manoeuvred alongside *Sidon* and attached a wire around her stern, but the weight of the sinking submarine was too much for her and the line was slipped. Divers aboard *Maidstone* quickly donned diving gear and slipped into the murky water. On descending to the submarine they tapped in Morse code on the hull in the hope of a reply from the dozen or so crewmen thought to be still aboard her when she

sank. No such response was forthcoming. This activity continued into the afternoon, by which time all hope of there being any further survivors was abandoned.

Many acts of gallantry followed the explosion, notably that of Surgeon Lieutenant Charles Rhodes who, although not a submariner and being unfamiliar with the boat's layout, donned DSEA, even though he was not proficient in its use, and entered the boat by the conning tower hatch to rescue injured and trapped men. His valiant efforts saved the lives of at least three crewmen, but sadly, following his second re-entry into the submarine, Lieutenant Rhodes himself succumbed to the smoke and died of asphyxiation. When his body was recovered it was found that the mouthpiece cock of his DSEA was shut, indicating that he had not been using the set correctly. For his bravery Lt. Rhodes was posthumously awarded the Albert Medal.

Evidence submitted to the subsequent Board of Inquiry showed that the torpedo that had exploded with such tragic consequences had initially been incorrectly loaded into the torpedo tube. During the loading routine, the safety chocks from the flap of the blowing-head mechanism, the air lever and the propeller had been removed from the weapon. Unfortunately, the stop valve, which prevented the weapon's compressed air charge from mixing with the HTP fuel, had been left shut, so preventing the torpedo's propulsion system from operating once ejected from the tube.

Ten minutes before the explosion, one of the torpedo party left the submarine with the safety chocks. When a Petty Officer checked the compartment a couple of minutes later he noted that the torpedo's stop valve was still shut. Another Petty Officer visited the compartment two minutes before the explosion and noticed nothing untoward, as did a Leading Seaman a minute later. However, when sections of the torpedo were recovered after the boat was salvaged, the weapon's stop valve was found to be open.

It was therefore concluded that, sometime between 0816 and 0823, an unknown person had withdrawn the torpedo from the tube and opened the stop valve. Unfortunately, as the safety chocks had already left the boat, removal of the torpedo from the tube would have allowed the air safety lever to operate so allowing the compressed air and HTP fuel to mix. When the weapon was loaded back into the tube, there would have been no outward signs that the systems were pressurised. It now only took a slight leak in the torpedo's fuel system to result in a violent reaction, which vented itself in the devastating explosion a few minutes later, blowing the forward components of the torpedo into the sea through the bow cap and ejecting the after section into the submarine with immense destructive force.

Lieutenant-Commander Verry was cleared of any blame for the incident, and it was accepted that all personnel involved had done their utmost to prevent the loss of their boat. Similarly, it was determined that the crew of *HMS Maidstone* had taken all possible steps to attempt to prevent the submarine sinking. The rescue operation had been carried out heroically, but was for the major part judged to have been uncoordinated. It was found, however, that the ratings who had responsibility for the torpedo had been inexperienced in the maintenance and operation of the weapon and that personnel of the Torpedo Experimental Establishment had shown a lack of appreciation of the dangers of HTP fuel fires. The board recommended that further detailed investigations be carried out to improve the safety of this weapon.

Nevertheless, following another accident with a Mk.12 torpedo soon after the *Sidon* incident, in which one of the weapons exploded at the torpedo test range at Arrochar, Scotland, the Royal Navy dropped research into this form of propellant. The Mk.12 torpedoes had been converted from the readily available Mk.8s as a cheaper option to developing and building them from scratch. Unfortunately, the materials from which the Mk.8 torpedo was constructed were incompatible with the HTP fuel, causing a volatile reaction, particularly in contact with materials other than synthetic rubber or porcelain. In 1970 a serious fault was found in the Royal Navy's Mk.8 torpedoes, in that because of age and corrosion of the detonators, there was the possibility that they could explode prematurely. The weapons, including those in service in the Australian and Canadian navies, were hastily modified to alleviate the problem.

Salvage of *Sidon* began two days after her loss. An attempt to raise the boat by pumping her full of high-pressure air failed due to the large number of air leaks. Four pontoons, or camels, were rigged around her hull, two on each beam by the salvage vessels *Kinbrace*, *Swin* and

*Barcross*. As the large buoyancy cylinders were slowly filled with air to expel the water ballast in them, the 990-ton *Sidon* began rising to the surface. First her stern and then her conning tower rose slowly from the water, but the boat was seen to be listing heavily to port. She was lowered beneath the surface again whilst efforts were made to correct the list.

A week after her sinking, in the early hours of 23 June, the scene eerily illuminated by spotlights, *Sidon* was again raised and successfully secured alongside *Maidstone*. The following day, aided by two salvage vessels and two motor fishing vessels, the submarine was towed to Chesil Beach and beached near the main Weymouth-Portland road, where the task of removing the other Mk.12 torpedo from No.4 tube was undertaken. The bodies of the three officers - including Lt. Rhodes - and ten ratings were recovered from their boat two days later. Most of them had been killed by the initial blast from the explosion. In a poignant ceremony, the tragic victims were buried in a small cliff edge naval cemetery overlooking Portland Harbour and Weymouth Bay on 28 June.

*Sidon* was paid off on 2 July 1955 and, re-floated, she was secured alongside the coaling pier. On 14 June 1957 the hulk was quietly towed out to sea and sunk as an Asdic target on the seabed off Portland in 20 fathoms of water.

Other unsuccessful British torpedo designs followed, such as the wire-guided Mk.23, which was already obsolescent when it entered service in 1971, having been designed nearly 20 years earlier. The development of later torpedoes was transferred from the Admiralty Underwater Weapon Establishment to private enterprise companies such as Marconi Space and Defence Systems. The newer Tigerfish and Stingray weapons are powered by electric motors, whilst the latest Spearfish torpedo uses a Sundstrand gas turbine that burns Otto fuel, in itself a very flammable liquid. This necessitates the submarine's magazine to be fitted with a water-based fire-fighting system designed to remove all oxygen from the compartment within seconds.

Russian wartime torpedoes had proved unreliable, and so a new type was developed, known in the west as the Type 53-VA, entering service with the Project 613 ('Whiskey'-class) submarines in 1951. This was a steam-propelled 533mm diameter heavyweight torpedo similar to the British Mk.8 and the US Mk.14 weapons. The successor to this torpedo, an HTP-propelled type, was to be the cause of the worst disaster to hit the Russian Navy, early in the new century.

The Project 949A Anteiy (NATO Oscar-II) class boat *Kursk* (K-141) was one of the most modern and powerful submarines in the fleet. Having commissioned only five years earlier on 20 January 1995, she displaced some 18,000-tonnes and was armed with 24 P-700 Granit (SS-N-19 'Shipwreck') anti-ship cruise missiles and up to 28 torpedoes.

On the morning of 10 August 2000, the *Kursk* slipped quietly from Pier 8 at the secret submarine base of Vidyaevo and headed out into the Barents Sea to take part in the biggest Northern Fleet exercise for a decade. Three other nuclear-powered submarines and up to 32 warships and auxiliaries were involved in the exercise, the culmination of which was to be a series of submarine strikes on a surface fleet, headed by the massive Project 1144.2 cruiser *Pyotr Velikiy*.

For the exercise, *Kursk* had earlier embarked a load of 22 Granit cruise missiles and 18 torpedoes. Amongst the latter were included a number of 81-R Viyuga (SS-N-15) and 86-R (SS-N-16) anti-submarine missiles and a training torpedo. This was an old, much re-cycled and modified Type 65-76 weapon, the designation meaning that it had a 650mm diameter and that the type was first introduced into service in 1976. Whilst the Royal Navy had abandoned High Test Peroxide-fuelled torpedoes following the loss of *HMS Sidon*, the Soviet Navy were seduced by the superior speed of such weapons and developed first the 53-57 and then the 65-76, which became the Russian submarine fleet's standard anti-ship torpedo. HTP is mixed within the engine with kerosene to produce the chemical reaction to propel the 11m-long, 5-tonne weapon at up to 50 knots, with a range of around 27 miles.

At 0851 on 12 August, *Kursk* transmitted her last signal, indicating that the submarine was ready to conduct a pre-planned torpedo-firing attack run against the *Pyotr Velikiy*. The Project 677BDR (Delta-III) SSBN *Borisoglebsk* (K-496) and the Project 671RTMK (Victor-III) SSN *Danil Moskovsky* (B-414) carried out their runs, but no such attack came from the *Kursk*. It was not until much later that clues began to emerge as to the fate of the boat.

The fourth boat taking part in the exercise was the Project 667BDRM (Delta-IV-class) SSBN *Karelia* (K-18). The boat was at periscope depth 32 miles away preparing for a planned launch of one of her ballistic missiles (SLBM) when, at 1128 they were rocked by a massive shock wave, followed by a second, much larger one some two minutes later. However, the boat's captain was forbidden to make any signals reporting the blasts, as this would betray his position to any lurking western boats. The Los Angeles class attack boat *USS Memphis* (SSN-691) had been lurking in the area for several days with her two acoustic arrays deployed, monitoring the exercise, hoping to track one of the Northern Fleet SSBNs, and also detected the shock waves. Her Commanding Officer, Commander Mark Breor, immediately ordered his boat westward away from the scene, fearing that his boat would be discovered or even attacked.

The shock wave from the first blast, detected by the Arctic Experimental Seismic Station (ARCESS) at Karasjok, Northern Norway, measured 1.5 on the Richter scale. The readings were relayed to the Norwegian Seismic Array (NORSAR) Headquarters near Oslo, where they were analysed to determine their source. The second shock wave, estimated to be about 250 times the intensity of the first and measuring 3.5 on the Richter scale, was detected as far away as Scotland, Alaska and the Central African Republic. US/UK surveillance systems and satellites scanned the Barents Sea for any clues as to the source, but detected no unusual activities and no increase in the movements of the Russian Northern Fleet.

Meanwhile, the failure of *Kursk* to conduct her attack run on the *Pyotr Velikiy* or to signal her position at 1100 went largely unquestioned. It was not until 1700 that concerns began to be raised aboard the flagship and the Commander of the Northern Fleet, Admiral Vyacheslav Popov, was alerted. All attempts to contact the boat were unsuccessful, but then communications problems were not uncommon in the poorly funded post-Soviet Northern Fleet. However, the shock waves had also been detected aboard the *Pyotr Velikiy* and Rear-Admiral Gennady Verich, the head of the Northern Fleet's Rescue Services, was alerted and Ilyshin Il-38 'May' maritime patrol aircraft scrambled to conduct a search.

At 1740, the Project 05360 submarine rescue ship *Mikhail Rudnitsky* was put on standby to sail. This 20-year old vessel was all that was left of the Northern Fleet's formerly well-equipped submarine rescue service, which had been almost completely starved of funds since the collapse of the Soviet Union. Struggling to maintain all but the key combat units, the fleet's support infrastructure was neglected, including the specialist rescue submersibles. The Northern Fleet no longer had any serviceable decompression chambers. *Rudnitsky* was not equipped with any of the special positioning systems fitted to western rescue vessels, and her two salvage submersibles were totally unsuited to any operations in anything more that a State 3 seaway.

The Il-38 aircraft failed to find any signs of the *Kursk* and returned to Severomorsk just after 2000. Shortly afterwards, the Northern Fleet's HQ contacted the *Karelia* and were informed of the shock waves that had been detected at around 1130 that morning. All data held by *Karelia* was passed to try to pinpoint the locality of the blasts, but it was now evident that something terrible had happened to the *Kursk*. At 2330, Admiral Popov released a statement that the *Kursk* was missing and that a search-and-rescue mission had been launched.

The *Rudnitsky* had sailed at 2000 on Saturday evening. Aboard was the *AS-32*, a search submersible with manipulator arms, and the *Priz*, a 50-tonne rescue submersible with the ability to mate with a stricken submarine's escape hatch and evacuate up to 18 survivors at a time. However, a major deficiency of *Priz* was her poor battery capacity, providing only a short duration on task before having to return to the mother ship to carry out a 12-hour battery re-charging operation. As the Arctic dawn broke over the Barents Sea at about 0030 on Sunday 13 August, the search was under way for any sign of the *Kursk*, her rescue chamber, or emergency buoys.

President Vladimir Putin had only been in office for a few months and was on holiday at his official dacha on the Black Sea coast. At 0700 that morning, he was informed that the *Kursk* was missing, but it appears the severity of the incident and the detection of the blasts by the *Karelia* was either not relayed or was played down. Over the coming days, Putin would receive regular updates on the search and rescue mission, but he remained on holiday.

The *Rudnitsky* reached the area of the Murmansk Banka at around 0900 and joined the Project 1452 rescue tug *Altay*. The *Pyotr Velikiy* had apparently detected an acoustic anomaly in the area.

By Monday morning, western analysts were beginning to suspect that one of the Northern Fleet's submarines was in trouble, having detected the activities of the search-and-rescue ships. The Norwegians despatched a P-3 Orion maritime patrol aircraft from Andøy to investigate and the commander of Norway's northern forces, Rear-Admiral Einar Skorgen, telephoned the Northern Fleet's HQ at Severomorsk and his offer of assistance was relayed to Admiral Popov aboard the *Pyotr Velikiy*. Popov insisted that the situation was under control and that no assistance was required.

It was evident to the Russians that news of the accident was out and, shortly after 1100 on Monday morning, the Northern Fleet's press service released a report that the *Kursk* had suffered a malfunction, but that the crew were alive and communications had been maintained with them. This was followed shortly afterwards by a television report that the *Kursk* was lying on the seabed. However, these initial reports suggested that the accident had happened on Sunday, giving the impression of quick response to the accident by the Northern Fleet, whereas the *Kursk* had now been on the seabed for almost 48 hours. The old Soviet trait of disinformation and secrecy was clearly alive and well.

The Norwegians by now suspected that the seismic signals detected at 1130 on Saturday morning were connected with the incident. Further offers of assistance from the British and the Norwegians were dismissed, perhaps because the Russians did not want the West anywhere near one of their newest submarines. However, at the Royal Navy's operational headquarters at Northwood, near London, plans were already underway to prepare the United Kingdom Submarine Rescue Service's (UKSRS) submersible *LR5* for deployment. The Royal Navy had been preparing for a submarine rescue exercise in the Mediterranean and equipment was in various stages of deployment, but it was all recalled and an Antonov heavy-lift cargo aircraft chartered to fly *LR5* to northern Norway.

Later that evening, the Commander-In-Chief of the Russian Navy, Admiral Vladimir Kuroyedov, released a statement that the *Kursk* had been involved in a collision. Although he did not specify what she had collided with, rumours were circulated of a second wreck on the seabed and detection of a foreign SOS signal from the Barents Sea. Admiral Popov also voiced this accusation to Admiral Skorgen and the Russians despatched Il-38 aircraft to search the Norwegian coast for any signs of a damaged US or British SSN. When *USS Memphis* berthed at the Norwegian Naval Base at Haakonsvern several days later to unload equipment, the Russians requested, and were refused, permission to inspect the boat for damage. The British, US and Norwegian navies vehemently denied that any western submarine had been involved.

By Tuesday 15 August, the Russian free press began to publish interviews with wives of the *Kursk*'s crew, complaining at the lack of information being released. At a press conference later that evening the Russian Navy suggested that the surviving crew could last for 5 or 6 days and that two-way tapping communications were being maintained.

A large fleet of vessels, including the Russian Navy's sole aircraft carrier, *Admiral Kuznetsov*, and a number of other large warships, were now on the scene.

As well as the *Rudnitsky* and the *Altay*, the Project 714 tug *SB-523* and a Project 141 engineering support vessel were now moored near the stricken sub, but the weather had taken a turn for the worst and, without dynamic positioning systems, the *Rudnitsky* was finding it impossible to maintain a position over the *Kursk*. Amid dwindling hope and frustration with the poor equipment, the rescue operation was suspended, but another submersible, the *Bester*, was ordered to the scene, together with the crane ship *PK-7500*. No further knocking had been heard from the *Kursk* and it is probable that initial reports of tapping by *Pyotr Velikiy* were really chains banging against *Rudnitsky*'s hull.

The *Priz* finally reached the *Kursk* on Wednesday 16 August. Soon after, the first pictures of *Kursk*'s shattered bow and of debris scattered over a wide area of the seabed were relayed back to the rescue flotilla. The fact that *Kursk*'s after sections appeared intact provided some hope of survivors. The *Priz* managed to mate with the hatch several times, but each time an attempt was made to equalise the pressure in the connecting tunnel, the *Kursk*'s hatch began to open, breaking the submersible's seal with the hull. Later investigations revealed that the hatch had been left in an idle state, held shut only by external water pressure. Any attempt to open the hatch would require the assistance of the trapped crew, from whom nothing had been heard. It was also claimed that the poor visibility, strong currents and *Kursk*'s heavy list hampered the attempted docking operations.

Within the Russian Ministry of Defence in Moscow, there were conflicting views over whether or not to accept offers of help from Norway and Britain. The debate was further confused by conflicting information from the Northern Fleet. Eventually, Putin gave permission for the British Naval Attaché in Moscow to be contacted and for the assistance of *LR5* to be requested. He was told that the

*Kursk*'s forward end was destroyed, but that she was lying almost upright, with good visibility for diving - all of which contradicted earlier reports. At 2030 that evening, the Russian foreign Ministry officially requested assistance from Norway and the UK. A few hours earlier, Admiral Kuroyedov released a statement that there was enough oxygen within the stricken boat to last until 25 August, keeping alive the hope that there were still survivors to be rescued. The western rescue operation immediately slipped into top gear.

Few navies maintain a permanent saturation diving capability, so Norway chartered the company Stolt Offshore, a multi-national support company for the oil and gas industry with headquarters in Aberdeen and Stavanger, to provide diving services. The company's diving support vessel *Seaway Eagle* was ordered to suspend her operations in the Asgard Field and head for Tromso, 385 miles away, to pick up divers and equipment. Meanwhile, Britain's *LR5* was deployed to Trondheim aboard a chartered Antonov An-124 heavy-lift aircraft, where she would be embarked aboard the mother ship *Normand Pioneer II*. The *Seaway Eagle* would be responsible for providing the divers to survey the wreck and prepare the after escape hatch for the arrival of *LR5*. The Russians had also agreed to provide detailed specifications for the design and operation of *Kursk*'s after escape hatch. Recently modified with the latest systems, *LR5* had the ability to mate with almost any submarine and, as well as her 3 crew, had the capacity for evacuating 15 survivors. Her battery power was sufficient to make up to eight dives before her requiring re-charging, giving her the ability to evacuate all of *Kursk*'s 118 crew, if they were alive.

On Friday morning, the *Seaway Eagle* reached Tromso and loaded all of the necessary equipment to support the embarked eight British and four Norwegian saturation divers, sailing again at noon for the final leg of her trip.

In Vidyaevo, Admiral Kuroyedov and the Russian Deputy Prime Minister, Ilya Klebanov, arrived for a meeting with the families of the *Kursk* crewmen in the base's Officer's Club. The emotional scenes at the meeting were televised worldwide. One distraught woman, Nadezhda Tylik, the mother of one of the submarine's officers, angrily raged at Mr Klebanov and the world was stunned to see her being restrained by a Naval officer, forcibly injected with a sedative by a nurse and dragged from the hall.

The British and Norwegian rescue teams arrived at the scene on Saturday and a high level meeting of the rescue teams and the Russian Navy was held aboard *Seaway Eagle*. Frustratingly, the Russians insisted on being given another 24 hours before allowing the western teams to dive on the submarine. It was evident at this stage that the Russians believed that the boat was completely flooded. Despite requests to allow divers to immediately begin surveying the area of the wreck for obstacles, weapons and radiation, the *Seaway Eagle* and the *Normand Pioneer* were ordered to anchor several miles away. Aboard the *Seaway Eagle*, preparations continued through the night to launch the robot Remote Operated Vehicle (ROV) *SCV006* and the camera ROV *Sea O wl*. After much debate, permission for operations to begin was finally given early the following morning, but with the caveat that the teams were to remain aft of the emergency buoy position, located between Compartments 7 and 8.

On Sunday morning, *Seaway Eagle* positioned herself just aft of *Kursk*'s location and lowered *SCV006*. There was little current to hinder the tiny ROV and, in good visibility, *Kursk* was found at 69°36'59"N, 39°34'26"E, about 85 miles off Severomorsk, heading approximately 285°, almost upright but about 8° bow down. At 1055, a diving bell was lowered into the water and, a little over 10 minutes later the first of the three divers left the bell and dropped onto *Kursk*'s casing, his way lit by *Sea Owl*'s lights. After checking for a zero reading on his Geiger counter, he began tapping on the hull of the submarine with a hammer, stopping between each attempt to listen for any signs of life from within. Although no reply came, it was not inconclusive proof that there were no survivors and so the escape hatch was examined and an attempt made to open the equalising valve. Milk was used in the water to show any flow into the valve, which would indicate that the escape tower was not flooded. Despite earlier promises, the technical details on the after hatch were slow to materialise. The hand-drawn sketches eventually provided were useless. The Russians had informed the divers that the valve opened by rotating it anti-clockwise, but the diver was only able to move it fractionally before it apparently seized solid. When questioned, the Russians insisted that the valve opened anti-clockwise. After trying the valve again, the diver decided to try turning the valve the other way and found that it indeed opened in a clockwise direction! Only a tiny flow of water was seen to enter the valve, so it was evident that the escape tower was flooded. Despite the pressures being equalised each side of the upper hatch, it refused to open, even when flotation bags were attached. The divers returned to the diving bell and were recovered to the *Seaway Eagle*.

That afternoon, Admiral Popov visited the *Seaway Eagle* and agreed to allow two of the divers to visit one of *Kursk*'s sister boats to examine the hatch mechanism and shortly after they were flown ashore to board the *Orel* (K-266) in a floating dry-dock at Severomorsk. Here the divers were able to examine the hatch mechanisms and were told about the boats leaking stern glands.

Back aboard the *Seaway Eagle*, Admiral Verich wanted to rip the *Kursk*'s upper hatch off with a crane, but Admiral Popov disagreed to such a drastic action and finally gave permission for the launching of *LR5*. However, nature was to intervene and, at dawn the following morning, *Kursk*'s upper hatch suddenly opened. The ebbing tide had marginally reduced the water pressure on top of the hatch, allowing the flotation bag to overcome the resistance of the hatch to open. Luckily no divers were in the vicinity at the time. On inspection, the escape tower was found to be empty, with the lower hatch shut, but gas bubbles were seen leaking from the hatch, suggesting that the 9th Compartment (motor room) was flooded. It was deemed too dangerous to get a diver to open the lower hatch and so a tool was quickly manufactured to allow *SCV006* to open the hatch remotely. At 1030 on Monday 21 August, the lower hatch was opened and a large volume of gas was exhaled from the boat. The evidence was now irrefutable - all of the crew had perished.

The western rescue mission was over and the Russians took over what was now a recovery operation. The western divers were not permitted to enter the boat, but they did lower a camera into the 9th Compartment, where they viewed charred bulkheads - evidence of a flash fire. One corpse in blue overalls was spotted floating in the debris. A sample of trapped gas was taken and analysed and was found to contain 23% carbon monoxide and only 6% oxygen - the carbon monoxide more evidence of a fire and the oxygen level incapable of supporting life.

The following day, President Putin finally arrived in Vidyaevo to speak to the families of the lost sailors. During yet another heated meeting in the Officers' Mess, Putin promised the families compensation and that the *Kursk* would be raised. But the families wanted to know why Putin had not broken off his holiday and why the Northern Fleet rescue services had failed to enter the *Kursk* in over a week, when the western divers had succeeded so quickly after arriving on the scene?

In October 2000, the giant offshore platform *Regalia* was towed into position and used as a base for divers employed in the recovery operation. The American commercial firm Halliburton was employed and British and Norwegian divers used to cut a series of holes into the hull to permit the entry of Russian military divers into individual sections of the boat. No bodies were discovered in the 7th and 8th Compartments (turbine rooms), but six were recovered from the 9th Compartment. The Russian divers moved forward to the crew's quarters in the 4th Compartment, where they retrieved classified documents, but the 3rd Compartment was impenetrable.

The first two bodies were brought aboard the *Regalia* on 25 October 2000, both of which were burned on the upper parts of their bodies. In the breast pocket of one of them was found three notes in a waterproof wrapping. This was the body of Captain-Lieutenant Dmitri Kolesnikov. Another note was later found on the body of Captain-Lieutenant Rashid Ariapov. With the evidence provided in these notes, examination of the bodies and the inside of the submarine itself, it is possible to piece together what happened on that fateful morning of Saturday 12 August 2000.

Having signalled the flagship that they were ready to commence the final stages of the exercise, *Kursk* would have been stalking the fleet at periscope depth, about 18 metres. As the practice torpedo was being manoeuvred into tube No.1, it is probable that a leak within the weapon's casing resulted in HTP coming into contact with copper or brass components, resulting in a violent chemical reaction. At exactly 1128:27, the instantaneous combustion of the highly volatile HTP caused a blast equivalent to 100kg of TNT. All seven men in the boat's 1st Compartment would have been killed instantly and the destructive power of the blast would have been amplified by the rupturing of several high pressure hydraulic and air systems. Although regulations require that the door between the Torpedo Room and the Control Room (2nd Compartment) should be shut during loading evolutions, it appears that it was normal practice for it to be left open during torpedo firing drills. Within the Control room, most of the 36 men, including the commanding officer, Captian1st Rank Gennady Lyachin, would have been killed or incapacitated by the impact, whiplash and noise. The crew were powerless to prevent the boat plunging towards the seabed, or to order the sending of a distress signal from the radio room in the 3rd Compartment. All Russian submarines carry an emergency buoy that is operated automatically when a fire, flood or high internal pressure is detected, or it can be manually released. However, either the force of the initial explosion destroyed the operating mechanism or, as some reports have claimed, the buoy locking restraints had mistakenly been left fitted.

The temperature within the 1st Compartment quickly rose to many thousand degrees Centigrade, melting systems and weapon casings. At 1130:42, 135 seconds after the first explosion, several other warheads within the 1st Compartment detonated in a second, much larger explosion that completely destroyed the forward section of the boat. All internal bulkheads as far back as the 4th Compartment were ruptured, killing all within these sections instantly and flooding the forward four sections of the boat in seconds. Luckily, the bulkhead at the fwd end of the 5th Compartment buckled but remained intact, preventing the blast from reaching the boat's two OK-650B nuclear reactors in the 5th and 5-bis Compartments and averting a major nuclear disaster. Both reactors instantly scrammed, but, with the fwd batteries destroyed, the boat was left without power. Equally fortunately, although some of the forward Granit missile tubes were flooded, none of the warheads detonated.

The *Kursk* had sailed with a total of 118 men aboard, including a few from *Kursk*'s sister ship *Voronezh* (K-119), five Captains from the 7th Submarine Division observing the exercise, and one civilian torpedo design engineer. Only 38 survived the explosions. The rafting arrangement of the machinery sections would have partially insulated the survivors in the after compartments from the intense shock waves. The 15 men in the reactor compartments sealed themselves in by closing the hatches forward and aft and stayed at their posts to ensure the safety of the reactors in their charge. They probably succumbed soon afterwards to toxic gases or nitrogen narcosis. With the 6th Compartment already slowly flooding, the survivors from the 6th, 7th and 8th Compartment machinery spaces moved into the 9th Compartment, which contained the electric propulsion motors and the after escape hatch that offered their only chance of escape. The VSK escape chamber in the conning tower was unreachable. Trapped in their stricken boat, with no power, they were faced with only two choices. They could escape, one at a time, through the escape tower - this would entail each crewman entering the tower, closing the bottom hatch behind him and opening the equalising valve to flood the tower until the pressure equalised, allowing the top hatch to be opened and escape to the surface. However, they had never been trained in the 'free ascent' method of escape and knew that this would be an extremely dangerous evolution from a depth of over 100 metres and would almost certainly result in them suffering from the 'bends'.

Also, they would not have known whether rescue vessels were in attendance, so there was the added danger of them reaching the surface, only to succumb to the freezing waters. The Russian Navy did not use the 'rush escape' method practised by Western Navies, where each man connects his facemask to the Built-In-Breathing-System (BIBS) whilst the entire compartment is flooded and all survivors then evacuate the boat together.

Their preferred alternative was therefore to await rescue. After all, they were only a short distance from their base and their commanders would surely have already activated the Northern Fleet's submarine rescue services? The main dangers now facing the survivors were the lack of oxygen and the build up of carbon dioxide, along with the cold and the rising pressure within the hull. To counter these, each man had a personal emergency air bottle with a duration of 15 minutes and thick green thermal clothing, stored within each compartment – a lesson drawn from the loss of the *Komsomolets* eleven years earlier. Exercising to keep warm was out of the question, as they would have been ordered to keep movement to a minimum to conserve oxygen. To refresh the oxygen, they loaded air-regeneration cartridges into a blower or hung them up. These cartridges contain superoxides that react with moisture in the air, absorb $CO_2$ and emit oxygen.

As the hours dragged on, Captain-Lieutenant Dmitri Kolesnikov decided to start compiling a diary of events. Tearing a page from a logbook, he calmly listed the names of each of his 22 fellow survivors and finally signed and dated it. The time was now 1358 on the 12 August 2000. Evidently, at this point some emergency lanterns and torches were still functioning.

Although apparently possessing all they required for survival, the design of the Project 949 submarines was to introduce another danger. The stern seals of the boats' two propeller shafts leak when the shafts are stationary; a problem negated when alongside in port by the fitting of special clamps. As the after section of the boat slowly flooded, the pressure of the reducing volume of air in the compartment would have been increasing. Kolesnikov wrote his second note on the reverse side of the first, stating that it was now dark and that the pressure was increasing. Finally, at 1545, he wrote a final note to his wife, Olga.

Compounding the dangers in the cold and the dark was the chance that someone would drop one of the air-regeneration cartridges into the oil-contaminated water, which would result in a violent chemical reaction and a fire. That such a blaze happened is evidenced by a clear tidemark, above which the paintwork was severely scorched. The survivors were still alive at this point, as post-mortems showed severe burns above the waistlines of several of the bodies. Furthermore, their lower limbs were pink, a symptom of oxygen starvation. All of them died from carbon monoxide poisoning from the combustion products of burnt paint and oil.

How long they survived will never be known. Some sources originally estimated their final moments as some time on Thursday 17 August, around the time that the *Priz* made it's last aborted attempt to reach them, but post-mortem examinations suggested that they died at about the time that the *Rudnitsky* sailed from Severomorsk at 2000 on Saturday evening, 12 August.

A total of twelve bodies were recovered from the wreck before the recovery operation was suspended for the winter on 7 November 2000.

The Dutch Companies Mammoet and Smit International were contracted to raise the *Kursk* the following summer in an operation estimated to cost around $65 million. On 15 July, a team of Russian,

Dutch, Norwegian and British divers arrived on site aboard the diving ship *DSND Mayo*. Admiral Verich commanded the operation from his Headquarters ship, the Project 1155-bis destroyer *Severomorsk*. Using remote-controlled cable saws, the team first cut away the forward 18 metres of the *Kursk*'s shattered bow and then 13 holes were cut along each side of the hull. In late-September, the 24,000-ton, 122-metre barge *Giant-4* was towed into position above the wreck and 26 lifting cables, each with a capacity of 900-tonnes were secured to the holes along the *Kursk*'s flanks. *Giant-4*'s hydraulic winches then lifted the *Kursk*, together with 22 Granit cruise missiles and the rest of her crew, from the seabed, securing the boat in a cradle beneath the barge. As the weather closed in, the barge, escorted by the *Pyotr Velikiy*, was towed to Roslyako, arriving two days later on 10 October 2001. Once secured in a dry dock, the *Giant-4* was removed and the dock slowly drained. It was only then that the true destructive power of the blasts that had ripped the giant submarine apart could be seen. Almost 100 bodies were recovered, the last being that of Captain Gennady Lyachin. Twelve bodies were never found. The last of the funerals was held in January 2002. Lyachin was posthumously honoured with the rank of Hero of the Russian Federation, whilst all 117 crewmen were awarded the Courage Order.

Following removal of all weapons and evidence, the wreck was towed to Nerpa and scrapped. The *Mikhail Rudnitsky* and an RTM-500 unmanned submersible removed the final sections of the bow and all other wreckage from the seabed during the summer of 2002.

Naturally, a great deal of fist wringing followed such a national disaster. In-house jostling, political wrangling, a Soviet 'Cold War' mentality and a reluctance to accept help from well-equipped western navies had resulted in the complete failure to save any of the *Kursk*'s crew. Ultimately, at a Board of Inquiry held on 30 November 2001, Prosecutor-General Ustinov declared that Putin had been deceived by his senior staff and ordered the dismissal or demotion of 14 senior naval officers, especially those who had initially tried to blame the disaster on a collision. Admiral Popov and Vice-Admiral Motsak were demoted. Those dismissed included Rear-Admiral Verich, Vice-Admiral Burtsev (Commander of the 1st Submarine Flotilla), Rear-Admiral Kuznetsov (Commander of the 7th Submarine Division) and Captain Teslenko (in charge of operations on the *Rudnitsky*). Following an appeal Admirals Kuznetsov and Burtsev were re-instated.

On 18 February 2002, the Prosecutor-General overruled any further speculation as to the cause of the disaster and the Navy was forced to admit that the explosion of a hydrogen-peroxide-fuelled torpedo sank the *Kursk*. Admiral Kuroyedov ordered that the weapon be removed from all submarines.

Several fundamental lessons have been painfully learnt from this tragedy, not least that it is at imprudent to scrimp on training and safety equipment. That the submarine's emergency systems were ineffectual and the crew ill-trained to operate them were symptomatic of a Navy which had neglected the basic safety infrastructure and principles that should be of primary concern to a major submarine-operating nation.

That a defective torpedo caused this accident is bad enough, but the lengths to which the Russian military went to cover up the true cause by using Soviet-era style disinformation and the extent to which they went to blame the accident on a collision with a western submarine is almost unbelievable. Unforgivable though, was the false hope given to the families of the crew by repeated claims of communications with survivors for up to five days after the sinking, the reluctance of the Russians to accept that their Northern Fleet submarine rescue services were utterly useless and the failure to accept genuine offers of help from so many nations well-equipped in this area. Although President Putin was desperate to portray himself as open and dispel any image the west may have of him as an ex-KGB head, the actions of his Naval Staff showed that the Russians had learned little since the loss of the *Komsomolets* eleven years before.

The utilisation of HTP has not been totally abandoned however - the Swedish Navy's 60-knot Tp 61 torpedo utilises a thermal propulsion system using a mixture of hydrogen peroxide, alcohol and water. In 1991 the Swedish Navy awarded a SEK200million contract to Swedish Ordnance for the final development of their heavyweight Torpedo 2000, a wire-guided weapon that uses an HTP-based thermal pump-jet propulsion system, giving a speed of over 55 knots and a range in excess of 45 kilometres.

Meanwhile, the British firm Dowty Fuel Systems has been undertaking research into a closed-cycle thermal propulsion system driven by steam generated by injecting gaseous sulphur hexoflouride into molten lithium. Honeywell has also pursued a similar system combining sulphur hexoflouride with lithium to produce steam in a closed cycle system for their Mk.50 lightweight torpedo for the US Navy. However, the high cost of this weapon has lead to the development of the new Mk.54 torpedo, which combines the Mk.50's search and homing systems with the Mk.46 torpedo's Otto-II fuelled two-speed reciprocating external combustion engine.

The protracted development programmes of modern weapon systems ensures that weapons are no longer rushed into service before all of the safety equipment and factors have been designed and produced in parallel with them and have been successfully tested and proven. Nevertheless, the quest for propulsion systems which can propel torpedoes at increased speeds and to greater depths to counter the ever faster and deeper diving submarines necessitates that research into more efficient, innovative propulsors and fuels continues unabated.

The accidental detonation of torpedo warheads is relatively rare, but the loss of the *Kursk* showed that the results of such an incident are devastating. A lesser-known incident that rivalled the *Kursk* disaster in terms of the high death toll occurred nearly thirty years earlier.

On 11 January 1962, the Project 641 ('Foxtrot'-class) submarine *B-37* was berthed outboard of the Project 633 ('Romeo'-class) boat *S-350* at their Northern Fleet base. Aboard *B-37*, the crew were carrying out maintenance when a fire broke out in the 1st compartment, the forward torpedo room. The intense blaze quickly grew out of control and a few minutes later the warheads in the compartment exploded, completely destroying the 1st and 2nd compartments and sending a fireball through the boat that killed most of the crew. All of the other men aboard the boat were either trapped or succumbed to the deadly heat and fumes that quickly spread throughout *B-37*. There were no survivors as the boat sank in minutes.

The force of the blast aboard *B-37* also engulfed *S-350* and killed several men on the jetty. The hull of *S-350* was torn open and she too quickly sank bow first with heavy loss of life. Such was the total destruction of *B-37*, that the true cause of the initial fire may never be known, but it is believed to have been started by a crewman using a welding torch in the vicinity of live torpedoes. The failure to observe even basic safety precautions when carrying out hot work in the vicinity of explosives had not only claimed 122 lives, but also destroyed two of the Northern Fleets newest submarines, both of which had only been commissioned in the previous two years or so.

The circumstances surrounding the second loss of a US Navy nuclear-powered submarine were shrouded in a

*USS Scorpion alongside USS Tallahatchie at Naples. This is believed to be one of the last photographs of Scorpion before she was lost, with all hands in May 1968.*
*(US Navy)*

veil of secrecy for many years. However, in recent years, the declassification of documents relating to the 1968 loss of the Skipjack-class submarine *USS Scorpion* (SSN-589), as well as that of the earlier disappearance of *USS Thresher* (SSN-593), have revealed that the Scorpion was, in all probability, sunk by one of her own torpedoes. Certain documents supporting this theory were declassified after a request was made in 1984 by "*The Virginia-Pilot/Ledger-Star*" newspapers under the Freedom of Information Act. Further partially declassified reports were released by the US Navy Office of information in 1993, 25 years after the submarine's tragic loss.

*USS Scorpion* had sailed from her home port of Norfolk, Virginia, on 15 February 1968 for a 3-month deployment in the Mediterranean, where she visited the Italian ports of Taranto, Augusta and Naples and took part in two NATO exercises and manoeuvres with the US Sixth Fleet. During this period, the submarine had operated throughout her authorised depth and speed limitations.

On the night of 16-17 May 1968, *Scorpion* carried out a boat transfer of personnel off Rota, Spain, before beginning her return journey home to Norfolk, Virginia, coming under the command of ComSubLant at this time. Weather along her planned track was good, with only moderate swells.

During her Atlantic transit, *Scorpion* was maintaining electronic radio silence, except for emergency messages and routine position reports. The boat was detoured on the 20th to monitor a group of Soviet warships operating in the vicinity of the Canary Islands. This mission had apparently been completed when a message, despatched by *Scorpion* at 2354Z (GMT) on 21 May and received at the US Naval Communications Station in Greece, stated that she was 27 miles off course and 40 miles behind schedule and that her estimated time of arrival (ETA) at

Norfolk was 1700Z (1300 local time) on 27 May. This was the last communication received from the boat.

Between this message and the last reported ETA at Norfolk, nine messages were transmitted on the submarine broadcast to *Scorpion*, three of which, on 23, 24 and 25 May, directly requested replies from her. However, her failure to reply would have been justified under her operation order specifying electronic silence. Nevertheless, concern was now being voiced in Norfolk and in Washington, and ComSubLant, Vice Admiral A.F. Schade, ordered an intensive communications check at 1640Z on 27 May. No replies were received and a few hours later, at 1515, a 'Submiss' was declared, setting in motion a huge air, surface and sub-surface search.

This initial search, involving twelve submarines and dozens of surface ships, as well as up to 27 long-range patrol aircraft flights per day, was divided into three general areas along *Scorpion*'s estimated track and twenty miles either side, expanding to forty miles either side west of 60°W. These areas encompassed *Scorpion*'s last reported position in the eastern Atlantic, the western Atlantic Shelf and the broad area of ocean in between, with priority being given to those areas where a rescue operation would be possible should she be found.

The western Atlantic search, involving ten submarines and nineteen surface ships was so intensive that a previously uncharted submarine wreck, believed to be that of a World War Two German U-boat, was discovered. The mid-ocean area was covered by five surface ships and five submarines in separate waves over two tracks, the submarines following 135 miles behind the surface ships so that either the surface or sub-surface search along the missing boat's presumed track would be conducted in daylight hours. The search was further intensified by the participation of over a dozen vessels diverted from normal transits. Probabilities of finding *Scorpion*, either on the surface or on the ocean floor, were estimated at 94-100%.

The area of Cruiser Sea Mount and Hyeres bank was searched initially by several submarines and submarine rescue ships. *Scorpion's* prescribed track south of the Azores passed within eight miles of the charted 13-fathom sounding in the vicinity of Cruiser Sea Mount. *USS Compass Island* (AG-153) later carried out a detailed bathymetric survey of the area but failed to find any trace of *Scorpion*.

On 27 May *USS Scorpion* was listed as overdue and presumed lost with her entire crew of 99 men, and was officially declared lost on 5 June 1968.

On 12 June *USNS Mizar* (AGOR-11) began her search using a towed sled-mounted magnetometer, ocean bottom scanning sonar (OBSS) and camera. A little over two weeks later, on 27 June, a shiny, uncorroded piece of metal about two feet long was photographed by *Mizar* on the ocean floor 10,000 feet beneath the surface about 400 miles south-west of the Azores and was judged to have come from the missing submarine. Nevertheless, it was not until 29 October that the rest of the *Scorpion*'s remains were photographed by *Mizar*'s cameras.

Early the following year, *USNS White Sands* (ARD-20) was towed to the Azores to support investigation of the remains of *Scorpion*. On board was *Trieste-II*, the same bathyscaphe research vessel that had been involved in the search for *Thresher*, but renamed in 1964 following a major rebuild that gave her a diving capacity of 20,000 feet. Between May and October 1969, *Trieste-II* carried out a total of nine dives on the site, taking thousands of photographs of the wreckage.

*Scorpion* was found with her hull snapped in two amidships and her sail completely torn off. The forward section was lying in a shallow trench, whilst the aft section of the boat, including the nuclear reactor compartment and engine room, was lying in a deeper trench that had been formed by the impact of the vessel with the ocean floor. Although wreckage was strewn over a large area, there was no sign of any debris from the operations compartment.

Examination of the thousands of photographs taken of the boat's remains eventually led to only one possible conclusion, that she had been sunk by the detonation of one of her own torpedoes, a conclusion given further credence by extensive computer analysis during the weeks following the disaster of acoustic data recorded at the time of *Scorpion*'s disappearance from hydrophone pick-up stations on the Canary Islands and in Argentia, Newfoundland.

One of these recordings, timed at 1859 GMT on 22 May, revealed a series of noises, lasting for a period of over three minutes, which could only be attributed to a large explosion and possibly the sounds of a submarine imploding and breaking up as it sank. These hydrophone recordings had also aided the US Navy in pinpointing the position of the boat.

Occurring as it did only five years after that of the *Thresher*, the loss of the Scorpion sparked the longest and most far-reaching Court of Inquiry in the history of the US Navy. Every possible cause for the tragedy was investigated, much of which deserves some mention here.

The Court heard that, following her Restricted Availability period, in which the boat was docked and refuelled in February to October 1967 at Norfolk Naval Shipyard, her crew carried out extensive refresher training that resulted in the boat being judged as ready in all respects to join the operational fleet. The Engineering aspects of the inspections in particular were judged as "excellent". Later, during exercises in the Mediterranean in March 1968, the

Operations Officer on the staff at ComSubLant 8 stated that he considered *Scorpion* to be a well-trained, well-run submarine.

A Nuclear safety inspection also carried out in the Mediterranean found no major defects in the condition or operation of the boat's propulsion plant. The Atomic Energy Commission reported to the Court of Inquiry that nuclear submarine reactors are so designed as to minimise environmental damage in the event of a submarine accident and that it was physically impossible for a reactor core to explode. In fact, the reactor's protective cladding on the fuel elements, which are extremely corrosion resistant, meant that the reactor core could remain submerged for decades without releasing any fission products into the surrounding ocean area. Even once the corrosion, at the rate of a few millionths of an inch per year, penetrated the protective cladding, the release rate of the radioactivity would be negligible. There is also little risk that the reactor pressure vessel would have ruptured as the boat sank, as the pressure of sea water inside and outside the pressure vessel would have equalised, either through small bore piping or seal welds.

It was also reported that the work carried out by the Charleston Naval Shipyard during *Scorpion*'s overhaul in 1963-64 incorporated many of the SubSafe modifications recommended by NavShips as a direct result of the loss of *USS Thresher*, including the ultrasonic testing of all sea-water pipe joints and valves, the certification of all silver-brazed joints on the emergency main ballast system, inspection of all flexible connections in critical piping systems, radiographic inspection of all cast fittings 4-inches and larger, inspection of all valve bonnets subject to sea pressure and torpedo muzzle and breach doors, and the visual and acid-spot inspection of all hull and back up valve bolts and studs and verification that they were manufactured from non-ferrous materials or monel metal.

Also included was a 150% hydrostatic test of the stern diving hydraulic system. The SubSafe certification criteria was directed to four principal areas, namely establishing piping system and hull boundary integrity, improving emergency recoverability, increasing stern plane reliability and providing a system of recording proof of certification. *Scorpion*'s main ballast tank blow system actually exceeded the criteria laid down in the SubSafe recommendations and the boat had not experienced any problems with this system in service, including the icing up of air systems encountered on earlier US Navy submarines.

*Scorpion*'s main batteries had been tested to 106% in January 1968, with no adverse problems with hydrogen generation. Such releases are monitored and controlled aboard submarines by hydrogen detectors, battery ventilation air flow meters, atmosphere analysers and CO-$H_2$ burners. The likelihood of a hydrogen explosion aboard *Scorpion* was judged as very low, and would probably not have resulted in catastrophic hull damage.

The possibility of *Scorpion* being the victim of a collision was deemed highly unlikely, as no vessel having transited her estimated route reported any such incident. Even if a surface ship had collided with *Scorpion* and then herself sank, the surface ship would almost certainly have been reported overdue by her owners. There would also have been some evidence of the collision in the form of survivors or floating debris.

An investigation of Soviet Block ships in the vicinity of the submarine's track revealed that only two Soviet and one Cuban cargo ship had crossed *Scorpion*'s track during the period 22-27 May. However, none of these was thought to have come within 50 miles of her estimated position. Two Soviet hydrographic survey vessels, a submarine rescue ship and two Project 675 ('Echo II'-class) submarines had been involved in hydro-acoustic survey operations south-west of the Canary Islands. A further two Soviet ships - a Project 57B ('Krupnyi'-class) destroyer and a tanker - had left Algiers on 18 May to join this operation, but none of these vessels came within 200 miles of *Scorpion*'s position.

A collision with a sea mount was also considered unlikely. Navigational charts held on board *Scorpion* had been inspected in November 1967 and found to be the latest editions, although during the search for the lost boat it was found that these charts did not show all sea mounts, and that some others indicated on the charts could not be located. However, none of these previously uncharted pinnacles should have affected *Scorpion* at her restricted transit depth of less than 300 feet. During the search of the Cruiser Sea Mount area, the minimum depth sounding recorded was 128 fathoms (768 feet). It had been standard practice for the Chief of the Watch on *Scorpion* to take a sounding every 30 minutes, and when these did not agree with those on the chart the Navigator would take continuous soundings. *Scorpion* had been suffering some problems with her 'Loran C' navigation system during her transit to the Mediterranean in March, but it had been promptly recalibrated by the support ship *Canopus* (AS-34).

The possibility of foul play was considered, particularly in view of the unexplained loss in January of that year of the French *Minerve* and the Israeli *Dakar*, both in areas of the Mediterranean where *Scorpion* had been operating during her deployment. However, taking into consideration the security provisions in nuclear submarines, the time lapse between leaving her last port of call and her loss, and the skill required to sabotage such a sophisticated vessel, this

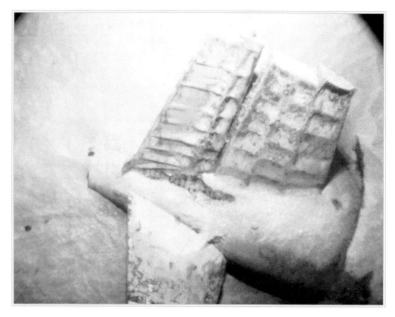

possibility was considered very low. An irrational act by one of *Scorpion*'s crew was also discounted as there had been no evidence of any psychiatric illness among any of the 12 officers and 87 men aboard the boat on her final voyage.

The probability of flooding of the boat due to structural failure or personnel error was also investigated. *Scorpion*'s hull was constructed of HY-80 steel, which had been proven in extensive tests to be a tough material, even under extremely

*Atlantic Ocean, August 1986 - Two views of USS Scorpion lying in 10,000 feet of water. The upper image shows the stern, with the upper part of the rudder and port stern plane in view. The lower image shows the remains of the sail.*

*(US Navy Naval Historical Centre)*

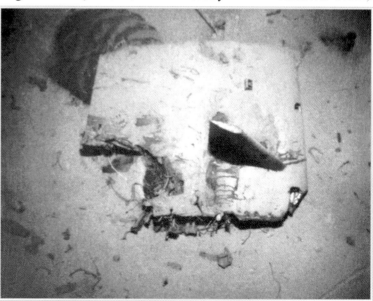

cold conditions. Any cracks would not be subject to rapid propagation or catastrophic failure. Areas of highest stress in Skipjack-class submarines were monitored to assure structural soundness by the HY-80 Hull Surveillance Program, which had been established by NavShips in 1960.

Although the US Navy later admitted that *Scorpion* had deployed to the Mediterranean with several minor technical problems, including a rusty whip antenna and a leak on the propeller shaft, as well as a minor hull crack found by hull surveillance inspection by *USS Orion* (AS-18), these defects were not considered a danger to the vessel's safety and were programmed for repair in the next Restricted Availability Period. The fact that the boat would have been operating at a depth of less than 300 feet and that she had been operating throughout her speed and depth envelopes during the previous months makes this an unlikely scenario.

Loss of ship control was considered a feasible scenario. The standard cruising state of the boat had allowed watertight doors to be left open, including the periods during which torpedoes were being handled and when the boat was approaching periscope depth. It had been standard practice at speeds above 15 knots to control the boat's depth within ten feet of the required depth using the fairwater planes, with the stern planes in emergency mode at zero angle. Duplication of electrical and hydraulic power supplies ensured that the total loss of a single source of supply would not cause the loss of hydraulic power to the ship control systems. However, a hydraulic oil sample taken in February 1968, showed massive salt water contamination of the system. Although the system was subsequently flushed and the oil renewed, no record of post-flush oil sample results could be found. Salt water contamination has been found to result in stress corrosion cracking

of aluminium alloy hydraulic control components, but this defect had not resulted in total loss of plane or rudder control on any submarine, although it is known that *Scorpion* suffered a steering failure en route to the Mediterranean when her rudder jammed hard left. A program to replace aluminium alloy hydraulic control valves with titanium components, as well as further improvements to stern diving plane reliability had been instigated by NavShips. These included the establishment of independent steering and diving system power plants, fitting of a stored energy accumulator for stern planes and dual stern plane rams.

US Navy Predicted Safe Operating Limits and Emergency Recovery Capabilities for Skipjack-class submarines judged that the boats had the capability to recover safely from a stern plane jam on hard dive, and *Scorpion*'s crew were well practised in drills simulating this breakdown. In fact *Scorpion* had, in 1960, twice recovered from such a situation whilst operating at 20 knots at a depth of 200 feet, by emergency backing of her propulsion plant, putting fairwater planes on hard rise and blowing main ballast tanks, without exceeding design test depth. Further precautions against such incidents had been incorporated into *Scorpion*'s operating orders by her Commanding Officer, such that the boat was to at all times operate within a safety envelope which took account of the depth of water, bottom contours, boat's speed and the presence of other vessels.

Studies into the effect of stern plane jamming showed that the crew would have about twenty seconds to respond to the situation before the boat achieved an angle of decent from which it would be difficult to recover. In general, a well-trained crew such as that on *Scorpion* would react in under ten seconds. At *Scorpion*'s estimated depth of under 300 feet and speed of around 18-20 knots, even the situation of a stern plane jam on full dive would have been easily retrievable.

In 1964 the US Navy issued a Statement of Operational Requirements for a Submarine Emergency Alerting and Locating Device (SEAL). This would be installed in the existing messenger buoy space and tethered to the submarine, and on release would transmit a call signal on multiple emergency frequencies. Whilst such a device would not have saved either *Thresher* of *Scorpion*, it would have served to alert the Command authorities immediately of the boats' predicaments and so saved the extensive search operations for the stricken submarines.

Although, the investigation failed to ascertain the certain cause of *Scorpion's* loss, it's opinion was that, apart from an improbable gas explosion, the only other single source of explosion present within the ship with the energy to rupture the pressure hull was that of a torpedo warhead detonation. It is probable that, by 22 May, preparations were in hand in the torpedo room for the off-loading of the weapons on return to Norfolk Navy Yard. A total of 21 conventional torpedoes, including seven Mk.14 and fourteen Mk.37 variants, were carried on board at the time of loss.

There are several ways in which a detonation of a torpedo warhead could have occurred. During unloading preparatory work on the torpedoes the weapons would have to be disarmed, including the removal of the exploder mechanism and booster. Although detonation of the booster should not be possible under normal circumstances, age could have resulted in increased sensitivity of the component, especially if dropped and could have caused detonation of one or more warheads. This may have caused the rupture of the Torpedo Room after bulkhead, the pressure hull or the torpedo tubes, which even at a shallow

depth of around 200 feet may have resulted in an uncontrolled dive to the ocean's floor. Warhead detonation could also be initiated by an uncontrollable fire in the Torpedo Room, such as the blaze that resulted in the loss of the Soviet submarine *Komsomolets* in April 1989.

The fuel for the Mk.14 torpedoes, ethyl alcohol, was highly inflammable, with a flash point of 48-52°F. Any spillage of this fuel could be easily ignited in any number of ways. Numerous other fire hazards exist aboard a nuclear submarine, including high pressure lubricating oil, diesel oil and hydraulic oil, as well as combustible gases such as oxygen, hydrogen, carbon monoxide, propane and methane. *Scorpion's* 3000-psi oxygen system, which had a capacity of 500 gallons, had been recharged from the depot ship *Orion* in February 1968. In concentrations of over 26%, oxygen can cause spontaneous ignition of combustible materials, although it will not by itself burn or explode.

Between 1951 and 1968 there had been eight fires and explosions aboard US Navy SSNs, including fires on *USS Sargo* (SSN-583) and *USS Shark* (SSN-591) caused by oxygen charging line failure. A leak of ethyl alcohol, combined with an oxygen leak would have resulted in a fierce eruption of flame, which could quickly have become uncontrollable.

In November 1967, a Mk.45 torpedo had been inadvertently empulsed out of one of *Scorpion's* torpedo tubes rather than being allowed to swim out. The following month, a Mk.37 torpedo was lost after an inadvertent activation. Despite these mishaps, *Scorpion's* torpedo crew were considered an experienced 'gang'.

Early versions of the Mk.37 torpedo had a tendency to arm themselves while still in the tube, and the standard procedure in this situation was to flood the tube to keep the weapon cool, shut down the torpedo's motor, drain the tube, open the inner tube door, install the propeller lock and jettison the weapon, whilst the boat initiated a 180° turn, which would trigger a safety device to shut down the torpedo. However, if there was insufficient time to install the propeller lock, the weapon may have circled and struck the *Scorpion*, causing her hull to implode. This theory has been endorsed by several experts in recent years, among them Admiral Bernard Claray, who was Vice Chief of Naval Operations in 1968, and John P. Craven, a University of Hawaii professor who was in charge of the US Navy's Deep Submergence Systems Project in 1968/9 and who was a leading figure in the investigation into the loss of *USS Scorpion*.

In an interview with *"The Virginia Pilot/Ledger-Star"* newspaper in December 1984, Professor Craven said that the torpedo warhead explosion theory *"is the one scenario that, in my opinion, fits all the evidence."* He went on to say; *"You always have that problem in [torpedo] tests, in that you don't really test something until you get pretty close to actuating it"*, and also stated that the US Navy had redesigned test equipment used with these weapons since the accident.

Reports that, when found, the remains of *Scorpion* were pointed in a easterly direction, would tend to bear out the theory that she was engaged in a U-turn when she was struck by a jettisoned torpedo, the detonation of which tore off the boat's sail and broke her in two. This would not have been the first time such an incident has been suspected. On 24 October 1944, *USS Tang* was sunk by one of her own torpedoes which circled back and struck the boat during a night attack on a Japanese convoy. Only 15 days later, another US submarine was sunk in similar circumstances. The 'official' cause of the loss of *USS Growler* (SS-215) on 8 November 1944 was that she was sunk off Mindoro by the Japanese destroyer *Shigure* and escorts *Chiburi* and *No.19*.

However, the Japanese, who were notorious for their exaggerated claims of submarine sinkings, registered no such claim. In fact, the crews of the Japanese warships stated that they only dropped a few depth charges, with no visible results. On the other hand, two other US submarines patrolling nearby - *US Submarines Hake* (SS-256) and *Hardhead* (SS-365) - reported hearing the sound of three depth charge explosions, followed by a single torpedo explosion. Could it be that *USS Growler* was the victim of one of her own torpedoes, fired at the attacking Japanese ships, but which instead either detonated prematurely or circled back on her? It is known that at least two other US submarines limped home for repairs following premature explosions of their torpedoes. The truth however, may never be known.

As with any accident, it is important that any deficiencies in design, operation or procedure highlighted by the investigation are addressed and action taken to remedy the imperfections. The Court of Inquiry into the loss of *USS Scorpion* made several recommendations, including that satellite navigation be fitted to all nuclear submarines, that stern plane reliability be continually improved, that routines for maintenance of hydraulic system cleanliness be tightened, and that investigations be made into the effects of explosions inside submarines. They also highlighted the requirement for a recoverable data-recording device, similar to an aircraft's 'black box', so that the circumstances of accidents may be documented and lessons learnt, and the need as a matter of priority for detailed bathymetric surveys and production of updated bottom contour charts for submarines.

Although the Mk.37 torpedo entered service as long ago as 1957, it has been produced in huge quantities. Being launch- and fire-control compatible with many newer boats, including the German

Type 206 boats, the later NT 37E has remained in service into the 21st century with over a dozen navies.

Nevertheless, despite the US Navy's steadfast claim that *Scorpion* was the victim of a torpedo explosion, the mystery surrounding the boat's tragic loss lingers on, fuelled by recent claims that the submarine had been involved in a secret confrontation with a Soviet nuclear-powered attack submarine.

It has been claimed by an ex-US Navy submariner, Jerry Hall, who worked as an aide to Vice Admiral Schade in 1968, that the submarine had been diverted from her planned track in order to assist a US Navy SSBN to 'shake off' a Soviet SSN that was trailing her. Such a mission would have required aggressive actions and manoeuvres by the *Scorpion* to interfere with the Soviet boat's sonar equipment and allow the 'boomer' to escape.

Such aggressive manoeuvres are known to have resulted in several high-speed collisions over the years, although the US Navy has always maintained that the adversary has never tracked any of its strategic missile submarines. We already know that *Scorpion* was diverted on 20 May to monitor a group of Soviet warships operating near the Canary Islands - could this have been a story released to conceal the boat's true mission? If the *Scorpion* had indeed been involved in such a mission, it would add credence to the further claims that a secret search for the *Scorpion* began on 23 May 1968 and that the US Navy knew exactly where to search for the missing boat, its location being recorded by the escaping SSBN.

The US Navy has always maintained that they were able to pinpoint the *Scorpion*'s resting place after detailed analysis of hydrophone recordings taken at the time of the loss, including additional soundings recorded by a third 'secret' hydrophone array. However, the declassified Wagner Associates report revealed in 1984 that such detailed data had not been available until mid-July 1968 and therefore could not have been utilised prior to the initial debris find on 27 June.

Coupled to this theory was the fact that, when found, *Scorpion*'s wreckage appeared to exhibit no signs of 'classic' torpedo damage to the submarine's hull. Also, the boat's outer torpedo tube doors were found to be shut, although it is not inconceivable that they were quickly closed after the torpedo was jettisoned.

A further twist to the mystery was the fact that the Soviets appeared remarkably well informed regarding the details of *Scorpion*'s loss and published such material in a 1975 edition of the Soviet military journal *"Morskoi Sbornik"*. However, the Soviets are thought to have gained details of the search for the boat from the spy John Walker, who had been a communications supervisor at the Norfolk headquarters of ComSubLant at the time of the boat's loss and who fed secrets concerning submarine operations to the KGB until he was finally arrested in 1985. However, it is almost inconceivable that the Russians would still keep secret details of any supposed encounter between one of their own SSNs and *USS Scorpion*, especially when they have in recent years been releasing detailed accounts of the loss of their own boats during the 'Cold War' era.

The US Navy still stands by its 'official' view that the *Scorpion* was sunk by the detonation of one of her own torpedoes and it is considered unlikely that any material to substantiate claims of alternative causes of her loss will surface in the near future, as part of the Court of Inquiry report remains 'Top Secret' to this day, almost 40 years after the accident. However, as long as such documents remain classified, conjecture and speculation as to the cause of *Scorpion*'s loss is certain to continue.

One of the most persistent legacies of

the Second World War has been the extensive minefields, both defensive and offensive in nature, laid by almost all of the countries which played a part in the conflict. These minefields present a deadly unseen peril to both merchant and naval ships alike. If the world's channels, estuaries and rivers, particularly in the continental shelf areas, were to once again be considered safe for the passage of shipping, a series of major mine clearance operations had to be conducted.

Hundreds of thousands of mines were laid in extensive minefields during the Second World War. Immediately following the cessation of hostilities the first priority was the clearance of the fields located on the major shipping lanes and approaches to harbours and estuaries. The position of many of these minefields had gone unrecorded, and so for many years following the war, new fields were being discovered throughout the world. Even today, it is not uncommon for trawlers fishing on the European continental shelf to find sixty-year-old mines snagged in their nets. In fact, as recently as 19 December 2003, a World War Two German mine was trawled up in the nets of a fishing vessel off North Berwick and had to be destroyed by an Army bomb disposal team.

There were two main types of mine sown in large numbers during the war, namely the contact and influence types, both of which still exist in huge quantities in the arsenals of the world's major, and minor, naval powers. The first of these, the contact mine, is the simplest and most common type and consists of two main components: the familiar horned mine which encloses the explosives and it's detonating mechanisms, and the sinker. A cable, the length of which is determined by the depth of water in which it is sown, links these components. These mines generally contain around 500lbs of explosive and are activated by the striking of one of its fragile horns, in which are

glass tubes containing acid. Breakage of the tube will allow the acid to generate an electrical charge within a small battery, which then triggers the explosive charge.

It is International Law that these mines incorporate a safety device to deactivate the mine should it become detached from its sinker. They are generally swept by minesweepers using their 'A' and Oropesa sweeps, cutting their anchoring cables so that they float to the surface, where they can be detonated by gunfire.

The second type, the influence mine is by far the more difficult to counter and modern versions can be activated by a number of influences. However, in the immediate post-war period the main type was the magnetic mine, which had been invented by the Germans during the early stages of the war. The mine was activated by the deflection of a delicate magnetic needle within the weapon by the approach of a large magnetic metal mass, such as the hull of a ship, so activating an electrical firing mechanism, completing an electrical circuit to detonate the mine. Special mine-sweeping methods had to be hurriedly devised by the Allies following the discovery of one of these weapons washed up on a muddy beach off Shoeburyness, in the Thames Estuary, on 20 November 1939, after it had been laid by a German aircraft the night before. The mine was defused by a valiant naval team from *HMS Vernon* and it's secrets laid bare.

These then were the pestilent and deadly weapons lurking clandestinely in the world's waterways, waiting for their chance to shatter the newly found peace of vessels going about their business after six years of conflict.

The war in Europe effectively ended with the surrender of Hitler's Germany on 7 May 1945. The following month, the Berlin Declaration charged Germany with the task of clearing all minefields. The German Mine Sweeping Administration (GMSA) was formed in July, at the British

Admiralty's initiative and under British control, with a force of 755 vessels, including 440 ex-Kriegsmarine minesweepers manned by 16,000 German seamen. A further 513 British minesweepers later assisted in this task. Over the next couple of years, this large force swept a total of 581,000 mines, 126,000 of which were German.

By December 1947 the GMSA had been disbanded and replaced by the German Minesweeping Unit of the Customs Inspection, Cuxhaven. This subordinate arm of the British Frontier Inspection Service was supervised by the Royal Navy in the last of the mine clearance and was disbanded in June 1951. The last area to be cleared was the stretch of the Denmark Straits between Kiel and Korsør to permit a ferry service to be restarted which, rather ironically, was undertaken by two converted car ferries, re-designated as *M607* and *M608*.

Up until the end of 1951, a total of seventeen vessels involved in the north European mine-clearance operations had been lost and a further twelve had been damaged, whilst over 250,000 square-miles of water had been cleared. Some of these losses occurred whilst the war was still raging in the Far East against Japan.

The first vessel to be lost was the German-manned minesweeping trawler *V5311* on 18 June 1945, whilst operating as a dan-buoy layer, laying buoys to mark minesweeping channels near Floro on the west coast of Norway. Only two of her 25-man crew were saved. A week later the British minesweeper *MMS168* was mined and sunk whilst clearing Genoa harbour. The following month, on 18 July, *MRS25* was sunk, also in Norwegian waters. On 9 August, the minesweeper *R228* sank in the Kattegat in position 57°27.6'N, 11°24.8'E, after an explosion of ammunition on her upper deck which killed two of her crew. Only five days later, the old German steamer *Berlef*, which was being used as an armaments

carrier to dump stocks of obsolete ammunition at sea, sank in the Kattegat.

Further losses were to follow. The 20-year-old German minesweeping trawler *V6507* sank during mine-clearance operations in the Kattegat in position 56°01'08"N, 11°03'03"E on 3 October with the loss of six of her crew. On 13 February 1946 the 690-ton mine transport *Inn* (DW35) was lost after striking a mine near the Elbe River in position 53°58.4'N, 0°12.7'E. A much more serious disaster was to follow on 24 February, when the steamer *Lichtwark* - which had been commandeered by the Naval War Office to transport 150 GMSA soldiers to Cuxhaven - was sunk by a mine in the Elbe with the loss of 97 lives, including three of the vessel's four-man crew. The Elbe was to claim a further victim when, on 25 March, the lightship *DB30* - formerly the 325-ton trawler *Schwarsburg* - was sunk by a mine in position 54°01'N, 08°07'E.

Although the vast majority of the war-laid mines had been swept by 1951, mine clearance operations were still necessary by all of the north European navies for many years afterwards, as further mines were discovered, either in previously uncharted fields or drifting mines which had broken free from their moorings as their cables rusted through. Ten years after the end of the war, over a dozen vessels a year were still being sunk by mines in the areas around the coasts of the north-west European countries. Even as late as March 1964, new fields were being discovered, such as the coastal mine barrier found off the island of Sylt, near the German-Denmark border.

It was not only vessels involved in the minesweeping effort which became the victims of the silent, unseen enemy lurking in the shipping lanes, rivers and estuaries, in areas all around the coasts of the European continental shelf. The German Type VIIC submarine *U345* had survived damage by bombs from US aircraft at Kiel, only to be sunk by a mine on 27 December 1945 near Warnemunden, in position 54°19'N, 12°01'E, whilst on passage to surrender. Dozens of civilian vessels were struck by uncharted or drifting mines, with fishing vessels being particularly prone to dragging the lethal weapons from their resting places in their nets. Many naval vessels going about their normal peacetime business were also lost.

The 274-ton Empire-class tug *Oriana* (ex-*Empire Frieda*) was completed in January 1946 and was later based at Chatham. At about 1320 on 19 January 1948, whilst towing the motor minesweeper *D366* to Brightlingsee, she struck a mine and sank in the River Blackwater off Knoll Buoy, Clacton, Essex. Her entire sixteen-man crew perished. *Oriana*'s charge was rescued by the tug *Empire Lucy*. In June of the following year the German naval ferry *No.212* (ex-*F212*) was sunk by a mine near Bremerhaven.

Even vessels lying serenely at their anchorages in areas that had been swept clear and where the threat of the mine had long since been considered eliminated were not free from this deadly legacy of the war.

In September 1946 the major western powers had agreed to each provide a series of weather ships to monitor weather conditions in the North Atlantic. Each country was allocated one or more of 13 fixed positions, designated 'A' to 'M', at which a vessel would be kept constantly on station. In general, each ship would carry out a tour of duty of approximately three weeks before being relieved by a sister ship. *Laplace* (F13, ex-*USS Lorain*) was one of four Tacoma-class patrol frigates bought from the USA in March 1947 and converted to meteorological frigates. Conversion of the 1,400-ton ship at Brest between July and December 1947 included the removal of her armament and the fitting of further radar suites.

Following this conversion, the ship left for her first watch on station 'L' on 14 December, returning to her home port of Brest in January 1948. Over the next couple of years *Laplace* took turns with her sister ships to maintain a watch at this station, transmitting constant weather reports to Paris.

On 14 September 1950, *Laplace* finished another tour of duty at position 'K' (45°N, 16°W) and set course for St. Malo, where her Commanding Officer, Captaine de Frégate Remusat, was to represent Monsieur Andre Monteil, Secretary of State for the Navy, at the inauguration ceremony of the Great Lock. She arrived in Frenaye Bay on the afternoon of Friday, 15 September and anchored for the night.

Just before 0030 the following morning, a massive explosion rocked the ship, the force of which 'tripped' the ship's generators and plunged her into complete darkness. Water began flooding into her shattered hull and she soon developed a heavy list to starboard. It quickly became obvious that it was impossible for the crew to save their vessel and the order was given to abandon ship. Tragically, most of the lifeboats had been smashed to pieces by the force of the explosion and the crewmen were forced to jump into the oily water. About ten minutes after the explosion, *Laplace* capsized, taking many of her crew with her to the bottom of the bay fifteen metres below. Although the ship was less than a kilometre from the shore, many of the men who had evacuated the ship perished in the water, bringing the death toll to 52 dead or missing, including three civilians. Many of the 40 survivors were seriously injured.

The French Navy ordered an immediate inquiry into the catastrophe. Divers examining *Laplace*'s hull determined that she had been struck by a stray German magnetic mine. A major minesweeping operation was undertaken to ensure no further mines were still lurking in the area.

The funeral for those killed in the accident was held at St. Cast on Tuesday, 19 September 1950.

The enclosed waters of the Mediterranean and Black Seas were also riddled with mines, and these too were to claim their share of victims after the war. The Royal Navy harbour defence launch *HDML1226* was mined and sunk on 4 October 1945, while employed on minesweeping duties in the approaches to Alexandroupolis, Turkey, north of the Dardanelles. Later that month, the Greek Navy was to suffer its first post-war loss.

The Norwegian yacht *Busen 11* had been requisitioned by the Royal Navy in 1940 and, following conversion to a minesweeper, was renamed *Snowdrift* (FY1842). On 1 January 1943, the vessel was transferred to the Royal Norwegian Navy, but on 18 July was given to the Royal Hellenic Navy and renamed *HS Pinios*. For the rest of the war the ship operated with the 168th Auxiliary Minesweeping Group, based at Levant, Alexandria. After the war, a Greek minesweeping flotilla was tasked with clearing the extensive minefield to the south of Corfu. This task completed, the flotilla, which consisted of *Pinios*, four YMS type minesweepers, four Fairmile 'B' minesweeping motor launches and a fleet tender, were ordered to carry out a mine clearance operation in the approaches to Prévesa, on the Greek Ionian Sea coast.

The flotilla used a standard procedure for the task. Firstly, the little APC tender marked a narrow channel with dan buoys, followed closely by the four MLs, which cleared a narrow path using their Oropesa sweep gear. These were in turn followed by the larger YMSs, which widened the channel still further using a 'G' formation sweep. This method entailed the four minesweepers proceeding in diagonal line ahead with the starboard sweep of the first vessel trawling ahead of the second vessel in line, and the second in turn covering the

third, and so on. As the sweeps' cutters severed the mines' cables and they bobbed to the surface, they were detonated by gunfire from the minesweepers. Meanwhile, the tender was marking the new right hand limit of the cleared channel with further dan buoys. *Pinios* was acting as mine destructor vessel, following the minesweepers through the swept channel and destroying by gunfire any mines that had escaped the guns of the YMSs.

The operation was proceeding well when, at about 1049 on the morning of 24 October 1945, a lookout on *Pinios'* forecastle alerted the bridge that a mine had been spotted in the water dead ahead of the ship. As the bridge ordered engines 'full astern' and the ship slowed, a second mine struck her stern. From the other vessels of the flotilla, a muffled explosion was heard and a huge tower of water enveloped *Pinios*. Seconds later another, much louder, explosion was heard and the ship seemed to disintegrate in a cloud of thick black smoke, which quickly cleared to reveal the shattered hull of *Pinios* slipping beneath the water's surface. This second explosion was probably caused by the 'bursting' of the ship's coal fired boilers, ripping a huge hole in the vessel's hull so that she sank in seconds.

Two of the motor launches closed the scene at full speed, apparently oblivious to the danger of further mines. Tragically, there was only one survivor from the ship's crew of 23 men - the forecastle lookout, who had suffered a broken leg when he was thrown overboard by the force of the blasts.

It was soon realised that *Pinios* had somehow drifted into the minefield, either due to a steering error or due to one or more incorrectly laid dan buoys. The laying of dan buoys is a delicate operation, not least because the laying craft has first to mark a channel in an unswept area ahead of the minesweepers. It is critical that the dan buoys are laid in precisely the correct location and that the anchoring ropes are of the correct length. If the anchor rope is too long, the accuracy of the buoy's laid position will be negated, the buoy's position instead being determined by the currents prevailing, whilst a short rope will either allow the sinker to submerge the buoy or the buoy will drift, rendering it useless.

Despite exhaustive mine clearance operations in the Black Sea, stray mines were still being discovered for many years after 1945.

The Italian battleship *Giulio Cesare* had been ceded to the Russians as part of her share of war reparations in 1948 and commissioned into the Soviet Navy as the *Novorossisk*. Whilst anchored in Sevastopol harbour at about 0130 on 29 October 1955, the battleship was lifted bodily from the water by a massive explosion that blew a huge hole in the ship's hull and killed dozens of her crewmen. Despite desperate damage-control actions, with assistance from several other ships in the harbour, thousands of tons of water continued to flood into the forward compartments of *Novorossisk* through the cavernous hole in her starboard side, and she could be seen to be settling quickly by the bow.

The decision was made to tow the ship out of the harbour, for fear of her foundering and causing a severe navigational hazard to other shipping. Further crewmen lost their lives in the feverish damage-control effort, but they were fighting a losing battle and, at 0415, the battleship suddenly rolled over and sank, taking with her a large number of her 1,600-man crew. Although a major rescue operation was quickly set in motion by a number of vessels in the vicinity, many more men drowned before they could be spotted and pulled from the freezing water, such was the darkness of the night. A total of 608 men were killed, including crewmen from several other ships who were assisting in the damage-

control effort, making this the worst peacetime naval accident of the post-war period.

The unusually high death toll was due in part to the rapid capsizing of the vessel and the failure of the command to give the order to abandon ship when it became obvious that their vessel could not be saved. Also, the ship's Commanding Officer at the time, Vice-Admiral Victor Parkhomenko, decided not to beach the ship to prevent her sinking, incorrectly believing that the water was too shallow for the wide ship to be in danger of capsizing. Both he and the Navy Commander-in-Chief, Admiral Nikolai Gerasimovich Kuznetsov, were later dismissed from their posts.

Although the area had been declared clear of mines and the anchorage had been in use for many years by warships of the Soviet Navy, a further search of the area after the loss of *Novorossisk* revealed several more German influence mines on the seabed, where they had lain undiscovered for over ten years.

The reason for the ship's rapid sinking was due mainly to the extent of the damage caused by the mine blast, which extended over the entire starboard section of the hull forward of the foremost 12.6-inch gun turret. It may also be significant to note that the ship had been extensively rebuilt during the inter-war years, raising her displacement by some 6,000-tons to over 29,000-tons, and that she had been further modified post-war by the Russians with new weapons and radar suites. *Novorossisk* was raised in March 1956 and her upturned hull towed to Kazach Bay, where it was broken up over the following 18 months.

There has been renewed interest in this incident with the recent claims by the Russian writer Boris Karzhavin in his book Taina Gibeli Linkore '*Novorossisk*' ("*The secret of the loss of the Novorossisk*"), that *Novorossisk* was the victim of an attack by Italian special forces. Another Russian book by Aleksandr Shirokorad has recently attributed the battleship's demise to a sneak attack by British midget submarines ("*Ships and Cutters of the USSR Navy, 1939 – 1945*", 2002, Minsk). Nevertheless, these claims remain largely unsubstantiated by any official report or investigation into the loss of the ship.

The cessation of hostilities in the Pacific, with the formal surrender of the Japanese on 2 September 1945, necessitated a similar mine clearance initiative to that which was already well underway in Europe. As in the European theatre, hundreds of thousands of mines had been laid in estuaries, rivers and coastal areas all along the western Pacific rim. During the latter stages of the Second World War the Japanese laid thousands of mainly moored mines around their island empire in an attempt to prevent the invasion of their home waters by the rapidly advancing enemy. A large number of influence mines were also laid around these islands by US aircraft to deny the use of these waters to Japanese shipping. Unfortunately, the war-ravaged Japanese Navy had very few mine-countermeasure vessels of a seaworthy nature with which to undertake such a mine clearance task, and so much of the initial operation fell to the victors of the conflict to undertake.

The mine clearance operations in Japanese waters began on 28 August, under the command of the Commander Minesweeping Craft Pacific, Rear-Admiral A.D. Struble, US Navy. The first priority was the clearance of the main sea lanes around the Japanese islands to allow the safe passage of the Allied occupational forces. For this task, the US Navy had converted dozens of destroyers into destroyer-minesweepers (DMSs), which could undertake fast minesweeping runs at speeds in excess of 15 knots, far faster than could be accomplished by the purpose-built minesweepers. The first

area cleared by these ships was the approaches to Tokyo Bay, including the important harbours of Yokohama and Yokosuka, followed in the first two weeks of September by the areas around Sendai, Kagoshima, Sasebo and Nagasaki.

The mine clearance effort suffered a severe setback on 16 September when typhoon Louis struck the US fleet at Okinawa, sinking four minesweepers and damaging several others. A second swipe at the US fleet by the typhoon the following month accounted for another ten minesweepers and two DMSs. Nevertheless, the task continued almost unabated, with the first of several hundred Japanese-manned vessels, mostly modified escort ships and naval auxiliaries, joining the growing fleet of ships employed in the operation towards the end of September. Several Japanese and US ships were used as mine destructor vessels, or 'Guinea Pigs', being filled with buoyancy material and driven over suspected minefields to intentionally detonate mines.

One major minesweeping operation, designated 'Operation Rickshaw', was designed to sweep the extensive field of moored mines sown between the southern tip of Korea and the island of Saishu-To (now Cheju-do), some seventy-five miles away. This operation succeeded in sweeping a total of 517 mines by November 1945. During this mission, the Japanese Momi-class Destroyer *Kuri* sank off Pusan after striking a mine on 8 October. Then, at about 1100 on 16 November, the Ukuru-class escort *Daito* hit a floating mine in the Eastern Sound of the Tsushima Strait, sinking rapidly with heavy loss of life.

These were not the only casualties in those first months of the mine clearance efforts. The Hirishima-class minelayer *Niizaki* had been captured in August 1945 and pressed into service with the Allied Minesweeping Service. Her new career was short-lived as, on 4 October, she was severely damaged by a mine off Muroran and was subsequently laid-up inoperative at the port until scrapped in 1947.

It was only to be a matter of time before the US Navy suffered their first disaster of the mine clearance operation. In late-December 1945, a small minesweeping flotilla was employed in the clearance of a field of moored mines in the Tsushima Straits between the island of Shimono Shima and the mainland island of Kyushu. The flotilla, under the tactical command of Captain T.W. Davidson, USN, comprised the destroyer-minesweeper *USS Earle* (DMS-42) - operating as flagship - the Raven class minesweepers *USS Minivet* (AM-371) and *USS Redstart* (AM-378), four Japanese-manned minesweepers and a number of small Japanese mine disposal vessels. The two American minesweepers were responsible for the laying and retrieving of the dan buoys used to mark the terminus of each pass of the Japanese minesweepers, whilst the mine-disposal vessels would follow astern of the formation to detonate the swept mines as they bobbed to the surface of the water with rifle or machine-gun fire.

On the morning of 29 December, *Minivet* was acting in her capacity as a dan buoy tender, and so was assumed to be manoeuvring in swept waters, when she was suddenly wracked by a devastating explosion slightly abaft amidships. The after third of the ship was practically disintegrated by the blast and *Minivet* immediately capsized onto her port side. The ship quickly began sinking by the stern and within a minute of the explosion only about thirty feet of her bow was left protruding vertically from the water. About ten minutes later, *Minivet* finally slipped beneath the water's surface.

The Japanese vessels of the flotilla, seemingly oblivious to the dangers of further mines lurking unseen in the area, quickly rushed to the aid of the men floundering in the water and pulled as many men and bodies - some of them barely recognisable - as possible from the calm but chilly winter sea. The recent conflict was seemingly forgotten as the Japanese sailors now risked their own lives in an effort to save fellow seafarers - their former enemies - from a watery grave. The Japanese sailors even gave up their valuable and almost irreplaceable foul-weather clothing to wrap around the shivering US sailors. All of the survivors and bodies were transferred to *USS Earle*, which then departed for Sasebo at a speed of 33 knots. Nineteen of *Minivet*'s crew of around 85 were killed in the accident, at least one of which died aboard *USS Earle* after being plucked from the water.

A Court of Inquiry convened in Sasebo by Commander Minecraft Pacific, failed to determine the precise cause of the loss and no blame was apportioned. A probable explanation is that the ship struck a mine that was floating just beneath the water's surface. It was known that Japanese chemical horned mines were subject to corrosion that could cause them to leak and become waterlogged and so lose some of their buoyancy. It is possible that one such mine, perhaps cut free on a previous pass of the minesweepers, went undetected by the mine-disposal vessels and that *Minivet* struck the weapon with devastating results. The fact that mines floating on the calm surface of the water would have been visible for several hundred yards on that fateful morning would seem to add credence to this theory.

January 1946 saw the loss of the former Japanese submarine chaser *Cha.248* after she struck a mine in Iki Sound. However, as in the UK/German operations, it was not just ships involved in the mine clearance task that succumbed to the mines. Apart from the growing toll of civilian vessels sunk or damaged after being mined, several naval vessels found themselves the victims of this deadly prey.

On 26 September 1945, the Bathurst-class minesweeper *HMAS Strahan* (J363) struck a mine off China and had to be towed into Hong Kong. Following repairs, the ship returned to Australia under her own power and eventually paid off into Reserve on 25 January 1946.

Three days after the *Strahan* was damaged, the Cannon-class destroyer-escort *USS Roche* (DE-197) was extensively damaged by a mine whilst en route to Japan. Three of her crew were killed and the ship's stern was totally wrecked by the explosion. She was later towed to Tokyo by the naval tug *ATR-35*, where the damage was surveyed by the Board of Inspection and Survey on 18 October, following which she was declared a constructive total loss and cannibalised for spares before being scuttled off Yokosuka on 11 March 1946.

A Japanese submarine, *I363*, on passage to Sasebo to surrender on 29 October sank after striking a mine.

These incidents were quickly overshadowed however when, on 22 January 1946, the Japanese merchantman *Enoshima Maru* struck a mine 30 miles from the mouth of the Yangtze River. The ship was employed in the repatriation of Japanese personnel and, of the 4,300 people aboard at the time, around 600 perished when it sank.

The LST(2)-class tank landing ship *LST199*, launched on 7 March 1943 at the Chicago Bridge and Iron Company, Seneca, was one of several of the class provided to the Royal Navy during the war. Following an active wartime career - which included participation in landings in the Mediterranean and at Normandy on 'D' Day in June 1944 and later in the Far East - the vessel took part in the Malayan campaign with the 4th LST Flotilla late in 1945.

On 5 November, *LST199* embarked several hundred Indian troops, accompanied by British officers, at Surabaya, Java. There were so many personnel aboard that the troop spaces

were full and a large number of men were accommodated in the tank deck. As *LST199* set sail at about 1730, many of the soldiers and crew were relaxing on the upper deck. Just after 1800, a massive explosion shattered their peaceful 'cruise' as a mine detonated under the landing ship's hull. With so many personnel crammed aboard the ship there was initial bedlam and it was some minutes before the crew gathered their wits and undertook a detailed search for damage and casualties. Both of the ship's engines, whilst still idling, were pumping fuel, oil and water into the engine room through shattered pipework and engine casings and they were quickly shut down for fear of a violent secondary explosion. Almost all machinery and mess-deck fittings had been ripped from their mountings. Luckily, two of the vessel's diesel generators were still running, so electrical power was available for those pumps that had not been torn from their bedplates. Amazingly, there was only one minor casualty, a radio operator who had been struck on the head by a dislodged item of radio equipment.

Damage-control teams from the cruiser *HMS Sussex*, anchored nearby, were quickly despatched to the crippled ship to render assistance, but there was little for them to do, as there were no major leaks in the hull and, miraculously, no fires had broken out. Nevertheless, some of the troops were evacuated to the cruiser and thence to shore. Her engines out of action, *LST199* anchored for the night off Surabaya, close to the *Sussex*.

The following day, the remaining troops were disembarked and senior naval personnel carried out a detailed survey of the ship. There was extensive damage to her hull plating and the engines were declared as beyond repair. For the next few months *LST199* was maintained alongside at Surabaya with a skeleton crew, being utilised by the Dutch authorities as a refrigeration ship, her

*Listing heavily to starboard, HMAS Warnambool is settling by the bow after striking a mine during mine-clearance operations off the Queensland coast on 13 September 1947.*
*(Navy Photographic Unit - Sydney)*

refrigeration machinery being one of the few items of equipment escaping serious damage in the mine explosion. All valuable and useful equipment having been stripped from the ship, she was finally 'struck off' of the Navy List on 25 March 1946 and was later towed out to sea and sunk.

Being part of the Netherlands East Indies, a Dutch minesweeping force had been despatched to the area in early October 1945. This small force, comprising mainly of ex-RN MMS type vessels, was largely successful in sweeping a large number of mines from the extensive minefields laid by the Japanese during the war. Tragically, whilst undertaking a sweep of one of these fields in the Makassar Strait, off Balikpapan, on 19 November 1946, the minesweeper *HNlMS Walcheren* (MV18) struck a mine and quickly sank. Of the vessel's crew of nineteen men, three were killed and a further eleven wounded.

The Empire-class tug *Empire Christopher*, completed in August 1944, spent most of her active service in support of the British Far East Fleet at Singapore. Her short career ended however, on 21 April 1946, when she struck a drifting mine and sank in just five minutes in position 14° 09'N, 98°03'E, off Maungmagon Bay, Gulf of Martaban, Burma. Seventeen of her crew were killed and another nine injured.

As the Allied minesweeping operation was wound down in 1948, the task of clearing any new fields found was delegated to the newly formed Japanese Self Defence Force (JSDF). This force consisted of mainly ex-Imperial Japanese Navy coastal ships, repaired and suitably converted for their peacetime employment as patrol and mine-countermeasures vessels. The JSDF suffered its first minesweeping loss the following year, when *MS27*, the former patrol vessel *Pa.No.154*, was mined at 1347 on 23 May 1949 near Manju Island, at the exit of the Straits of Shimonoseki. Four of her crew were killed and the critically damaged ship was laid up until scrapped in 1955.

Having seen service as part of the Allied Minesweeping Service, the former submarine chaser *No.202* was re-commissioned with the JSDF in 1948 as the minesweeper *MS14*. The ship sank on 10 October 1950 after striking a mine in Yong Hung Bay, near Wonsan, in position 39°20'N, 127°30'E. What the ship was doing off North Korea is not clear.

The Australian Navy's post-war mine clearance operations were first concentrated on the extensive mine fields off the southern Australian coast, a task that took them almost a year. Following the sinking of a fishing vessel off Palm Island in November 1946, with the loss of three of her crew, the Australian Navy decided to intensify its minesweeping effort off the north-east coast along the Great Barrier Reef, where 18,000 mines had been laid during the war by *HMAS Bungaree* as part of Australia's defence plan.

A 300-mile stretch of coast north of Cairns was closed to shipping whilst the area was swept of mines. A number of these weapons, some which had been laid over five years earlier, were by this time popping to the surface as the mooring cables rusted and parted, to be carried freely by the tide. A RAAF launch was later stationed in the area to destroy by gunfire any floating mines that were spotted. The 20th Mine Sweeping Flotilla was despatched to the area in January 1947 and soon cleared the area between Cairns and Townsville. Their attention then moved to the areas to the north of Cairns, where further defensive minefields had been laid during the war. After destroying over 700 mines, the Flotilla retired to Sydney for maintenance in June, returning to continue the minesweeping task two months later.

The flotilla consisted of seven minesweepers (the Grimsby-class sloop *HMAS Swan* (U74) and the Bathurst-class vessels *HMA Ships Warrnambool* (J202), *Katoomba* (J204), *Lithgow* (J206), *Mildura* (J207), *Deloraine* (J232) and *Echuca* (J252)), four harbour defence launches (*HDMLs 1323, 1326, 1328* and *1329*) and the stores lighter MSL706. On the afternoon of Saturday, 13 September 1947, they were engaged in one such sweeping operation off the Queensland coast when, at about 1555 the flotilla leader, *Swan*, lost one of her paravanes and had to pull out of No.1 position. As *Warrnambool* swung behind the sloop to take up her new position in the formation she was struck by a contact mine on the starboard side, just aft of the bridge. A huge plume of water and spray enveloped the ship. Two of her crew were killed instantly by the blast and whiplash seriously injured several others, including the Commanding Officer, Commander A.J. Travis, who was thrown from his seat on the bridge into the ship's steering wheel.

Damage aboard the vessel was widespread, with the bridge completely devastated and the mainmast lying at an absurd angle across the superstructure.

*A motor launch maneouvres alongside the sinking minesweeper HMAS Warnambool to help evacuate survivors. The ship sank less than two hours after striking a mine on 13 September 1947.*

*(Commonwealth of Australia)*

An explosion in the boiler room was only averted by the swift action of the stokers on watch in isolating fuel supplies and shutting down the boilers. The ship's condensers and turbines were wrecked by the blast of the mine and her steering gear was jammed, causing the ship to slew out of control, leading to fears that she may detonate further mines. The hatch to the magazine, in which a large quantity of ammunition was stowed, was also blown from its coaming.

As *Warrnambool* listed heavily to starboard, life rafts were thrown into the now slimy, oil-blackened water. *Mildura*'s whaler was lowered to rescue survivors from the ship, but as it neared *Warrnambool* she rolled over and crushed the small craft, its five crew narrowly escaping serious injury by jumping into the water. Although all watertight doors aboard the 780-ton *Warrnambool* - classed as a corvette by the Australian Navy - were closed at the time of the explosion, the damage caused by the blast was such that there was little chance of saving the ship. Attempts to pass a towline, with a view to hauling her to a beaching site, failed, partly due to the mine danger to the other ships of the flotilla. The crippled vessel finally sank at 1745, off Cockburn Reef, near Cape Grenville, 300 miles north of Cairns in position 11°45.5'S, 140°14.2'E. Despite a search by vessels of the flotilla the body of one of *Warrnambool*'s signalmen was not found and he was declared missing, presumed dead.

The 26 injured crewmen were transferred to *HMAS Swan*, which arrived at Cairns at 0600 on Monday, 15 September. Most of the injuries had been sustained as a result of the concussion of the blast that had thrown their bodies like rag-dolls against bulkheads, machinery and fittings. Others suffered serious burns from escaping steam and hot oil from fractured pipes. One of the injured men died four days after the explosion, bringing the death toll to four. The survivors were later flown to Sydney by a RAAF Dakota aircraft.

There were immediate calls by the Navy Minister, Mr Roirdan, for restoration of special payments to the crews of ships involved in the hazardous task of clearing the minefields around Australia's coasts, a benefit which had been discontinued in the recent pay review only a few months earlier. However, the minesweeping task was now in the closing phases and all but completed by the end of that year.

*HMAS Swan*, together with a boom defence vessel, returned to the area in May 1948 with a team of Navy divers aboard. They found *Warrnambool* lying on her starboard side in nine fathoms of water and over the following days they removed valuable and classified items from the ship. A plan was formulated to raise *Warrnambool* and refit her as a diving tender, but the Navy Board rejected this. Surprisingly, following application by a Sydney salvage firm, the wreck was sold by public tender to the Southern Cross Diving and Salvage company on 3 July 1972 for A$1,100 and was later raised and broken up. A condition of the sale was that a secret cryptographic machine and any classified documents found in the ship, as well as her nameplate and any items of historical interest, would be returned to the Royal Australian Navy.

The mine-countermeasures mission is, necessarily, one of most technologically advanced sciences in modern naval warfare. Apart from the more effective methods of minesweeping that have been devised since 1945, many methods of countering the magnetic mine have also been developed, such as 'wiping', 'deperming' and 'degausing', to reduce a ship's magnetic signature. However, modern mines incorporate a number of new innovations. These include acoustic fuses, which may be programmed to react to only a certain type of vessel, or even to a specific ship. They, like many other types of mine, may also include counters that allow a number of vessels, or sweeps, to cross over them before activation, making sweeping operations long and tedious.

Other new types include Underwater Electric Potential mines (UEPs), which react to the small electric currents emanating from a vessel's hull. Some ground mines even have the ability to rock and bury themselves in the seabed, such as the new Intelligent Self-Burying Hunter Mine (ISBHM), being developed in the UK. Combined with GRP construction or anechoic coatings, this can render the mine almost undetectable, even using the latest sonar and Unmanned Underwater Vehicles (UUVs).

This continuing evolution of the mines means that the mine-countermeasures necessary to neutralise this most clandestine of weapons much be constantly improved. It has been proven time and again since the mine was first used that a country ignores this threat at its peril. No longer can the unglamorous task of mine-countermeasures be relegated to a low position on a country's list of naval requirements. At the outbreak of hostilities in September 1939 the Royal Navy, then the world's most powerful, found itself woefully lacking in vessels capable of undertaking even the most basic mine-sweeping operations. Throughout the war, a massive building programme was necessary to provide the vessels, and technology, to enable the mine threat to be contained. The threat

*The amphibious assault ship USS Tripoli (LPH-10) in dry dock for repairs to a hole in its starboard bow caused by an Iraqi mine. The ship struck the mine on February 18 while serving as a mine-clearing platform in the northern Persian Gulf during Operation Desert Storm. (US Navy)*

*The destructive power of a sea mine. Repair crews inspect the hold that was ripped open in the hull of the USS Tripoli (LPH-10) when the ship struck an Iraqi mine during Operation Desert Storm.*

*(US Navy)*

mine threat. It should not be forgotten that mining remains a relatively cheap and effective method of waging war and it requires an effort to neutralise it that is out of all proportion to the effort expended in laying it. It is for this reason that almost every conflict since 1945 has resulted in the use of this clandestine weapon to some degree. There have also been many cases of indiscriminate mining, a notable example being the terrorist act of mining the Suez Canal by the Libyan Ro-Ro vessel *Ghat* in 1984, which effectively blocked the passage to shipping until a major mine clearance effort could be activated.

Even during the 1991 Gulf War for the liberation of Kuwait, the almost insignificant Iraqi Navy managed to inflict some considerable damage to US navy ships by the use of the mine, namely the mining of the cruiser *USS Princeton* (CG-59) and of the amphibious landing ship *USS Tripoli* (LPH-10), not to mention the April 1988 mining of the frigate *USS Samuel B. Roberts* (FFG-58) . The US Navy appears to have learnt it's lesson and in recent years revitalised it's mine-countermeasures fleet with new vessels and mine-countermeasures helicopters.

History has shown though, that such lessons are quickly forgotten in the face of peacetime financial stringency and policies such as the so-called 'peace-dividend'. The major reductions forced upon the Royal Navy's mine-countermeasures forces - once the envy of the world - has been sanctioned at a time of world instability, when the direction from which the next threat will appear is almost totally unpredictable, especially considering increasing terrorist activity.

posed by the mine, even more than that posed by Germany's ubiquitous U-boat fleet, came so close to bringing Great Britain to it's knees during the dark days of 1939 and 1940.

Despite these lessons, learnt at such a high cost, the majority of modern navies possess insufficient mine-countermeasures forces to ensure that their sea lines of communication can remain clear in the face of even a token

# Chapter Eight

# MISTAKEN IDENTITY AND FRIENDLY FIRE

Although the scope of this book does not include vessels sunk or crippled by enemy action, vessels attacked in error as a result of mistaken identity during times of conflict or during naval exercises can be classified as accidental losses. This chapter is dedicated to such cases.

The reasons for such attacks on friendly forces are numerous, but are almost always due to human error, either because of mistaken visual identification, incorrect intelligence information, or unexpected actions of the unit that leads to its classification as that of a 'hostile' vessel.

There have been several cases in the post-World War Two period whereby vessels have been badly damaged or sunk by friendly forces during the many conflicts which have erupted in this period. Almost every conflict has its incidents of 'accidental fire' due to the confusion of the fog of war, a fact much publicised during the 1991 Desert Storm operation for the liberation of Kuwait from its Iraqi invaders. Apart from the nine British soldiers killed when a USAF A-10 Thunderbolt aircraft attacked their armoured vehicle, there were several lesser incidents. Five US M1A1 tanks were reportedly destroyed by allied tanks of the same type and two US Perry-class frigates - *USS Nicholas* (FFG-47) and *USS Jarrett* (FFG-33) - were attacked by 'friendly' aircraft firing HARM missiles, although thankfully the weapons did not hit their targets.

Humans are not infallible, and when confronted with a situation in which the decision whether or not to open fire has to be made within seconds, it is inevitable that mistakes will be made. Often, these attacks are terminated before any serious damage is done, but the accuracy and destructive capability of many modern weapons is such that, once fired, the fate of the unit fired upon is sealed.

In November 1956, at the height of the Anglo-French operation to regain control of the Suez Canal, Operation Musketeer, the Royal Navy had two close encounters with 'friendly' forces within days of each other, either of which could have had very tragic consequences. At the beginning of the month the Black Swan-class frigate *HMS Crane* (F123) was ordered into the Gulf of Aqaba in search of the Egyptian frigate *Rasheed* (43), thought to be operating in the area. *ENS Rasheed* was an ex-Royal Navy River-class frigate (ex-*HMS Spey*) transferred to Egypt in 1948, and was of similar size and of not dissimilar appearance to the British ship sent to intercept on.

On 3 November, *HMS Crane* edged north through the narrow channel between the Sinai Peninsula and the island of Tiran, effectively bottling the Egyptian frigate in the Gulf of Aqaba, should she still be there. A fierce battle was raging between Israeli and Egyptian forces to the west. During the afternoon, one of *HMS Crane*'s lookouts spotted what was thought to be five Egyptian MiGs, but as they approached they were identified as 'friendly' Israeli Air Force Dassault Mystere fighter-bombers. Unfortunately, these aircraft was not as positive with their identification of the ship below them and turned to attack, diving from 6,000-feet.

With the realisation that they were under attack, *Crane*'s gunners opened fire, damaging one of the Mysteres, but the ship was hit by several rockets and sustained damage to the quarterdeck. The aircraft then circled for a second attack, strafing the ship and dropping several bombs, which luckily all missed. Another of the aircraft was hit and crashed into the sea ahead of the ship. As the aircraft headed for home, *Crane* reversed course and fled to the south. Although the damage to her hull was widespread, it was not serious and none of the crewmen were badly injured.

Later that same month, the French submarine *La Creole* (S606) was on patrol off the Egyptian coast when she detected a submerged contact, which she took to be a Soviet submarine (the Egyptians having no submarines at this time). *La Creole* manoeuvred into a firing position, reporting her contact to the Task Force Commander, who ordered her only to fire in self-defence. Luckily, the attack was aborted when the contact was positively identified as the British submarine *HMS Tudor* (S126) that, due to a navigational error, was off course and operating in the wrong sector.

Thankfully, neither of the above incidents resulted in severe damage or serious casualties, and similar episodes have been documented during almost every conflict since World War Two. Unfortunately, another ship caught up in a later Arab-Israeli war was not so lucky.

During the Six-Day War between Israel and several Arab nations in June 1967, the US Navy Belmont-class technical research ship *USS Liberty* (AGTR-5) was patrolling in international waters in the eastern Mediterranean, 1.3 miles off the coast of Al Arish on the Sinai peninsular, monitoring communications and electronic transmissions from the warring factions. During the morning of 8 June, the ship was 'buzzed' by numerous Israeli aircraft and her radio frequencies jammed. Just after 1400, the *Liberty* was attacked without warning by several Israeli aircraft, the aircraft attacking with guns, rockets and bombs. One bomb struck the ship port side amidships and started several major fires. Thirty minutes later the ship was attacked by three Israeli motor torpedo boats which launched three torpedoes, one of which struck the *Liberty* and blew a hole forty-feet wide in her starboard side. The persistent attacks lasted over two hours and left 34 US sailors dead and 172 injured.

The hull and superstructure of the badly damaged ship was riddled with over 800 rocket and shell holes. Determined to finish the ship off, Israeli helicopters attacked and machine-gunned her. In an attempt to save his ship from sinking the Commanding Officer, Commander W. L. McGonagle, USN, steered his ship towards shallow water. The attacks only ended when aircraft from the US Sixth Fleet arrived on the scene.

The Israeli government quickly apologised for the attack. Despite the fact that the *Liberty* was flying the US flag and her hull numbers were clearly visible, the Israelis claimed that they had mistaken the vessel for a much smaller Egyptian Navy ship. As late as October 2003, there were calls by the Joint Chiefs of Staff Chairman for a full investigation into the incident, with claims that evidence from the *Liberty*'s crew that may have been deemed harmful to Israel had not been heard at the earlier Court of Inquiry. Accusations of a cover-up continue.

The *Liberty* was escorted to Valletta, Malta, by the aircraft carrier *USS America* (CVA-66), the cruiser *USS Little Rock* (CLG-4), the destroyer *USS Davis* (DD-937), and the tug *Papago* (ATF-160), arriving on 14 June. After initial repairs, the ship sailed for Norfolk and paid off into the Atlantic Reserve Fleet on 28 June 1968.

There is sometimes doubt as to whether a supposed case of mistaken identity is in reality a cover for a more sinister motive. It is often more acceptable for an aggressor to pass off an indiscriminate attack as that of an accident, allowing the perpetrator to flex their military muscle in what they claim to be territorial waters and at the same time retain some political credibility.

Whilst undertaking a routine patrol near the Ragged Island Range on Saturday, 10 May 1980, the Bahamas Defence Force patrol craft *HMBS Flamingo* (P02) sighted two Cuban vessels fishing illegally within Bahamian territorial waters. The poachers immediately took flight, but after several shots were fired across their bows the vessels were eventually stopped and boarded, one-and-a-half miles south of Cay Santo Domingo, at around 1845. The vessels had just been taken in tow when a military helicopter and MiG-21 fighter aircraft appeared over the scene.

The Cuban jets fired several rockets at *Flamingo*, hitting the ship and starting fierce fires. Several more attacking waves with rockets and cannon reduced the 103ft Vosper Thornycroft-built *Flamingo* to a burning, sinking wreck. Fifteen of the nineteen-man crew, three of which were injured, abandoned their ship and took over the captured fishing vessels. With the eight illegal fishermen aboard, the two Cuban boats were piloted to Duncan Town, Ragged Island, arriving at 0130 the following morning.

However, the hostile actions by the Republic of Cuba's Air Force was to continue throughout Sunday, military aircraft 'buzzing' Duncan Town. Bahamian and US Coast Guard vessels searching for the four missing marines were also harassed.

A strong protest was lodged with the Cuban Government of Dr. Castro, and the acting Prime Minister of the Bahamas, Arthur Dion Hanna, called an emergency meeting of the National Security Council and stated that presentation of their case to the United Nations Security Council was being considered in the event of an unsatisfactory response from the Cubans.

The incident gained worldwide news coverage, especially in Britain, where the Bahamian Prime Minister, Lynden Pindling, was making a state visit. The Cubans immediately responded by claiming that their fighters had "misidentified" the vessel, having believed that *Flamingo* was a pirate ship attacking innocent fishermen, a claim widely broadcast by the official Cuban News Service, Prensa, which described the incident as "worrisome".

The Bahamians fiercely disputed the Cuban misidentification claim. The attack had happened in daylight and *Flamingo* was painted naval grey with her pennant

*Her pennant number P02 clearly emblazoned on her grey hull, HMBS Flamingo was 'mistakenly' attacked and sunk by Cuban aircraft on 10 May 1980.*

*(The Nassau Guardian)*

number 'P02' emblazoned on her hull. She had been flying the Bahamian flag, supplemented with further identifying flags, on approach of the Cuban aircraft. Furthermore, *Flamingo*'s gun-covers had been replaced immediately prior to the attack and so gunfire was not returned.

The Cubans later suggested that the two boats, described as Cuban fishing boats *No.165* and *No.54*, were attacked in international waters, and claimed that the whole incident had been orchestrated by the "Yankee CIA" to draw the two island neighbours into conflict. However, a seven-man Cuban delegation to the Bahamas communicated deep regret for the incident, admitting that *Flamingo* had indeed been in Bahamian waters and stated that the airmen involved would face disciplinary action.

On Tuesday, 13 May, following two days of intense diplomatic wrangling, Cuba offered compensation for the loss of the patrol boat and the dead crewmen. Reparations of US$5 million for *Flamingo* - which had cost US$4.5 million new two years earlier - and US$100,000 for each of the dead marines were made by Cuba. The marines killed in the incident were later honoured by having four of the six patrol craft transferred from the US Coast Guard in 1989 named after them - namely *HMB Ships Fenrick Sturrup* (P06), *David Tucker* (P07), *Austin Smith* (P08) and *Edward Williams* (P09).

The motives for the 'trigger-happiness' of the Cuban pilots are still not clear, but interrogation of a Cuban sailor, who defected to Miami on 13 May 1980, led to speculation that it was linked to attempts to keep secret the presence of two Soviet submarine bases in the extreme north-east of the island state. The Cubans still claim that it was a case of mistaken identity.

The armed forces of some of the more aggressive nations patrol international waters near their coast with a 'shoot first, ask questions later' attitude. In April

1989, two Soviet naval auxiliaries - a Nyryat-class diving tender being towed by the Goryn-class naval tug *SB-524* - were mistakenly attacked by a Syrian Mi-25 'Hind-E' helicopter off the Syrian coast. Several anti-tank missiles struck the diving tender, badly damaging the vessel and injuring seven of its crew. The injured men were later transferred to the Soviet Project 1123 (Moskva-class) helicopter cruiser *Leningrad* that, along with the Project 61 ('Kashin'-class) destroyer *Krazny-Krim*, had rushed to the area to render assistance.

The Syrian government later apologised for the attack, claiming that their aircraft had mistakenly identified the vessels, although they did not elaborate on their classification of them. However, it is possible that the attack was a botched attempt to interfere with a French Naval squadron, including the hospital ship *La Rance* and the tanker *Penhors*, which was attempting to evacuate civilian casualties from the port of Juniyah, north of Beirut.

In times of conflict, mistaken identity can result in vessels being subjected to 'friendly fire' often with tragic consequences, as was the case on several occasions during the prolonged period of the Vietnam War. An attack by USAF aircraft on the US Coast Guard cutter *Point Welcome* (WPB-82329) off the Vietnamese De-Militarised Zone (DMZ) in the early hours of 11 August 1966 killed one crewman, and injured five others, one of whom, the Commanding Officer, Lt JG David C Brostrum, USCG, died later. The cutter, badly damaged and on fire, was beached and abandoned two miles south of the Cua Tung River, but was later re-floated and repaired at Da Nang. Following this incident, aircraft were required to gain clearance from the Coastal Clearance Center in Danang before attacking any targets detected in the area. Despite the lessons learnt from this incident, worse was to follow.

Whilst operating just south of the DMZ,

near Cau Viet, just after midnight on 16 June 1968, USAF F-4 Phantom aircraft attacked the US Swift-class patrol craft *PCF-19*, after mistakenly identifiying the small craft as a low flying helicopter. *PCF-19* was bombed and exploded and sank in position 16°159'22"N, 107°09'55"E, killing four of the six-man crew and injuring the other two. A sister-boat, *PCF-12*, patrolling nearby, sped to the scene to render assistance and arrived as the US Coast Guard cutter *Point Dume* (WPB-82325) was pulling the two seriously wounded survivors from the water. Shortly afterwards, *PCF-12* also came under cannon fire from two aircraft, which continued to chase the boat as it fled. Initial reports that rockets fired from a hostile helicopter had sunk *PCF-19* were to lead to further tragedy the following morning.

At 0330 on 17 June, the 'look-down' radar of a patrolling USAF Phantom jet operating north of the DMZ near Tiger Island mistakenly classified two further vessels as low flying 'enemy' helicopters. The vessels were in fact the cruiser *USS Boston* (CAG-1) and the Australian destroyer *HMAS Hobart* (D39). As *Hobart*'s Identification Friend or Foe (IFF) system identified the aircraft as 'friendly', the aircraft launched a Sparrow air-to-air missile that struck the destroyer on the starboard side amidships. A few minutes later, the aircraft fired two more missiles, both of which struck the *Hobart*.

Two crewmen were killed and another seven injured in the attack. The wounded men were airlifted to Da Nang and the Hobart retired to Subic Bay for repairs.

Later that morning other USAF aircraft attacked the destroyer *USS Edson* (DD-946) when it too was mistaken for an enemy helicopter. Fortunately, the *Edson* avoided damage or casualties.

The subsequent Board of Inquiry found that shortcomings in the Phantom's radar system were partly to blame for the incidents. The radar had a cut-off

mechanism to prevent large targets flooding the radarscope, resulting in returns from warships and slow moving low-flying helicopters appearing similar on-screen.

Later in the protracted conflict, the cruiser *USS Worden* (DLG-18), operating in the Gulf of Tonkin in support of a major strike against Hai Phong harbour on 15 April 1972, was the victim of the detonation of two AGM-45 Shrike missiles, inadvertently fired by USAF aircraft. The anti-radiation air-to-surface weapons homed in on the ship's radar transmissions and exploded 80-100 feet above the ship. Although they only contained 50lbs of explosive, the detonation of the weapons sprayed the cruiser with fragments, putting her completely out of action, with no power or communications, for 30 minutes. One crewman was killed and a further nine were injured. The damage sustained in this accident had reduced the cruise's fighting effectiveness by some 60% and necessitated a lengthy spell in dockyard hands at Subic Bay before the ship was again fully operational.

The most tragic case of mistaken identity in the period covered by this book was undoubtedly the sinking of the Turkish destroyer *TCG Kocatepe* (D354) on 22 July 1974 by the Turkish Air Force.

The events leading up to this tragic incident began three days earlier, with the sailing of the Hellenic Navy LST *HS Lesbos* (L172) from Famagusta, eastern Cyprus, at about 1800 on 19 July. *Lesbos* had delivered a relief force of soldiers of Eldyk (Greek Force-Cyprus) and was to return to Greece. This was part of a routine turnover of the Greek garrison on the island that took place every few months, the relieving troops taking over the arms of their predecessors.

Overnight, *Lesbos* headed slowly westwards along the south Cypriot coast, on a course of 260°, at a steady ten knots. As the sun rose the following morning she was to the south of Lemessos. The tranquil atmosphere aboard the ship was to be shattered however when the Commanding Officer, Commander El. Handrinos HN, heard the distressing news that Turkish forces were at that moment invading northern Cyprus. On hearing this news he rushed to the bridge and ordered the ship's course to be changed to 220°, away form the coast, as he had no wish for Turkish aircraft to catch his lightly armed vessel alone on open sea.

In Athens, the Naval General Staff decided that the troops aboard the *Lesbos*, although practically unarmed, were needed for the defence of the island and, at 0900, the ship was ordered to proceed to Larnax, a port on the south-east coast. These orders were to change again soon afterwards however, as *Lesbos* was directed to disembark the troops instead at Paphos, the westernmost port of the island.

Arriving at the port shortly after noon, *Lesbos* anchored about 500 yards from the pier and proceeded to disembark the troops using three of the ship's four LCVPs. Whilst this task was in hand, Commander Handrinos received a request from the colonel in charge of the local Greek army garrison for some fire-support from the ship, in order to assist his small force of local guardsmen in their effort to remove a group of Turkish partisans from the castle of Paphos who were firing on the town. *Lesbos* was armed only with three twin 40mm Bofors guns on her forecastle, but after considering the possible ramifications his actions may have, Cdr. Handrinos ordered the forward starboard twin 40mm mounting to open fire on the fort. After some 900 to 950 rounds were fired at the fort, the Turks surrendered at about 1700, following which *Lesbos* ceased firing and immediately set sail to the south.

*Lesbos* maintained her southerly course until midnight, by which time she was about 60 miles to the south of Paphos,

before changing course to the west. At 0330, Cdr Handrinos was forced to break radio silence in order to report the death, by heart attack, of the civilian forklift truck driver who had sailed with the ship from Salamis. By 1500 on the afternoon of 21 July, the LST was some 160 miles to the west-south-west of Paphos. The ship continued on that course until about 0530 on the 22nd, when she changed course to the north and, following a short stop at Ayios Nikólaos, Crete, to disembark the body of the unlucky yard employee, arrived at Salamis Naval Base and lowered her ramp as darkness fell.

In the meantime, the disembarkation of troops and the firing on the fort by the landing ship had been reported to Ankara.

This news, which was grossly exaggerated, appeared to reaffirm reports that had been received from Turkish reconnaissance aircraft that a Greek convoy, escorted by several warships, had been sighted in the area. Believing that the port was the subject of a major amphibious landing by the Hellenic Navy, the Turkish Air Force despatched a squadron of aircraft to bomb the town. In fact, the only Hellenic Navy ship in the area had been the *Lesbos*, but each subsequent report further inflated the composition of this 'phantom' convoy.

The Turks approached the Americans, who were acting in the capacity of mediators, demanding that the Greek convoy reverse course and return to Greece, to which Athens replied that there were no Greek ships in the area and if the Turks found them they were welcome to sink them. The Turkish authorities refused to be convinced.

In the early hours of Sunday, 21 July, the Turkish Gearing-class destroyers *Kocatepe*, *Maresal Fevzi Cakmak* (D351) and *Adatepe* (D353) , were engaged in the bombardment of shore positions and escorting the amphibious force ships off Kyrenia, on the north coast of Cyprus. At 1000 that morning the three destroyers, under the overall command of Captain Irfan Tinaz, aboard *Adatepe*, were released from this task and ordered by the General Staff in Ankara to proceed to the west and intercept and attack a Greek convoy. This convoy was now believed to consist of eight or nine transports escorted by several warships. As the destroyers proceeded along the north coast of Cyprus, their rules of engagement were modified to allow them to engage any Cypriot or Greek-flagged ships found within the Turkish declared 'prohibited area'.

Reconnaissance reports on the 'phantom' convoy were being constantly updated and by 1218 it was reported to consist of eleven amphibious vessels escorted by five warships. By this time the destroyers had reached Cape Arvanitis, the westernmost point of the north Cyprus coast, and turned south, the force commander fully expecting to obtain a visual sighting of the 'enemy' convoy soon after. However, by mid afternoon the only ships sighted were three merchantmen, two of which were heading peacefully towards Paphos and the third towards Libya. The General Staff were insistent that the ships heading for Paphos must be the 'Greek convoy' and so ordered Captain Tinaz to give them an ultimatum, turn around or be engaged and sunk! Nevertheless, Captain Tinaz was not convinced and requested the assistance of a reconnaissance aircraft in the identity of the ships. A few minutes later the aircraft arrived on the scene and quickly confirmed that the ships were in fact merchantmen, one of which was named *Line Messina*. No other vessels were sighted in the area.

Despite this, the Turkish command in Ankara were convinced of the existence of the Greek convoy and so ordered the destroyers to back off and allow the Turkish Air Force to carry out the first strike, but that they should stand by to form a follow-up attack. The 'Greek convoy' continued their easterly course, oblivious that their presence was the subject of so much interest. The destroyers maintained a patrol to the north-west of Paphos at a distance of about 25 to 30 miles from the 'convoy'. During this period, Captain Tinaz transferred his command from *Adatepe*, hoisting his pennant instead on the *Cakmak*.

At about 1415, a total of 48 F-100D and F-104G aircraft, armed with rockets and bombs, took off from three Turkish Air Force bases and approximately 45 minutes later arrived over the area. Sighting the three Turkish destroyers and mistakenly believing that they were the 'phantom' Greek convoy, the aircraft dived towards the warships and attacked with rockets. The destroyers replied with a barrage of anti-aircraft fire.

Lookouts on the *Adatepe* spotted Turkish markings on the aircraft, diving on them at over 700-km per hour, and alerted their Captain Tinaz, but not before *Kocatepe* was struck by a rocket that destroyed her Combat Information Centre. Commander Rizah Nur Ontzu, *Adatepe*'s Commanding Officer, quickly alerted Ankara that they were under attack by Turkish aircraft. However, the Turkish pilots were adamant that the Turkish flags flying prominently at the mastheads of the destroyers were simply a ploy by the enemy and that they weren't fooled.

Astonishingly, Captain Tinaz ordered that *Adatepe* and *Cakmak* close formation and turn to the north, while firing on the still attacking aircraft, leaving the unfortunate *Kocatepe* to the mercy of the unending onslaught of attack. The ship, unable to co-ordinate her fire power due to the fire in her CIC, was quickly hit by four more rockets, which destroyed her radar and communications, as well as putting a boiler-room and an engine room out of action and destroying her main electrical distribution board. Within minutes, *Kocatepe* was dead in the water, without electrical power to run fire-fighting pumps and with her forward twin 5-inch gun mount disabled. Even though *Kocatepe* was clearly helpless, with fires burning from stem to stern, the majority of the aircraft continued to attack her relentlessly, instead of attacking the other two ships, which, incidentally, were still putting up a barrage of anti-aircraft fire. Nevertheless, both ships did suffer some minor superstructure damage and *Adatepe*'s radar was put out of action.

The crew of the *Kocatepe* fought valiantly to save their crippled ship but, under continued attack and with further fires breaking out throughout the ship, the Commanding Officer, Commander Giuven Erkayai, was finally forced to order 'abandon ship' at 1615. Seeing this, the aircraft finally ceased their attack on the ship, which continued to burn for several hours until she finally sank at about 2200 that night, some ten nautical miles west of Paphos.

Ironically, this large force of modern aircraft could easily have overpowered all three of the elderly destroyers, all of which had originally been built for the US Navy in the latter stages of World War Two. By concentrating their attention on *Kocatepe*, the Turkish pilots had spared *Cakmak* and *Adatepe* from a similar fate.

As the aircraft returned to their bases, their pilots jubilantly reported to the Airforce General Staff in Ankara that *"The Turkish Airforce attacked the ships fetching reinforcements to Paphos and sank one of them"*. Even the Turkish Prime Minster was overjoyed that the 'enemy' invasion convoy had been stopped! In Ankara, the Public Relations and Press Office of the (National Defence) General Staff issued the following statement: *"Despite all friendly warnings which kept being issued up to this afternoon, a large Greek landing convoy, escorted by Greek military aircraft, managed to penetrate the area which had been declared as 'prohibited'*

*since the evening of 20 July and to arrive, by 1500 hrs off Paphos. The convoy replied with heavy fire to the warning of our Airforce and Navy and commenced landing troops at Paphos. The landing was aborted after Turkish Airforce attacks on the port of Paphos. Our Airforce attacks caused very heavy casualties to the warships and the landing ships of the convoy."*

This mood was soon to change to one of disbelief and sadness when the full facts of the tragedy came to light a few hours later. As the survivors of *Kocatepe*'s 270 crewmen were transported home aboard *Cakmak* and *Adatepe*, the death toll was put at thirteen officers and 51 ratings.

A sister ship to *Kocatepe*, ex-*USS Norris* (DD-859), which had been purchased on 7 July 1974 to provide spares for the other ships of the class, was quickly refitted, renamed *TCG Kocatepe* (D354), and commissioned into the Turkish navy on 24 July 1975.

Two major factors contributed to this tragedy. Firstly, neither the destroyers nor the aircraft had their Identification Friend or Foe (IFF) systems switched on. This was strictly against regulation but in the case of the pilots, the fear that an enemy might use the transmissions to guide an anti-aircraft missile onto his aircraft made the use of IFF undesirable. The Turkish forces may also have been reluctant to use the system's NATO frequencies, which would also have been known to the Greeks. Nevertheless, the almost hysterical way in which the Turkish forces pursued the 'phantom' Greek convoy raises doubts as to whether the use of IFF would have deterred the Turkish pilots in their quest for a 'kill'.

Secondly, the armed forces of both Turkey and Greece were equipped with very similar weapons systems. The aircraft that had attacked the Turkish destroyers were of an identical type to that in service with the Hellenic Air Force. *Kocatepe* (Ex-*USS Harwood*, DD-861) was one of five ex-US modified Gearing-class destroyers in service with the Turkish Navy, almost identical to four vessels of the same class then in service with the Hellenic Navy. Even today (2008), these two NATO navies are made up of a large number of ex-US Navy minesweepers, landing craft and naval auxiliaries of the same classes, whilst some of their newer vessels are also of similar design. For instance, Greece has eight German-built Type 209 submarines in service whilst Turkey has fourteen similar boats in service or under construction in local shipyards, and both countries have built German-designed MEKO 200 frigates.

Although a state of hostilities no longer exists between these two countries, there were frequent confrontations during the 1980s and 1990s between their military forces over sovereignty of islands in the Aegean Sea, such as the 1987 incident in the area between their naval forces that stopped just short of shots being fired. The possibility of a repeat of that tragic accident in July 1974, although extremely unlikely, is nevertheless a remote possibility.

However, it is not just opposing forces that are at risk from 'friendly' fire during conflicts. Often, innocent bystanders going about their normal business find themselves unexpectedly under attack. During the long and bloody Iran-Iraq war, warships of many nations were despatched to the Persian Gulf and Gulf of Oman to protect merchant shipping that were being subjected to indiscriminate attacks by the warring factions. Whilst undertaking these duties in the Persian Gulf at around 2112 local time on 17 May 1987, the Perry-class frigate *USS Stark* (FFG-31) was struck by two AM-39 Exocet missiles fired from an Iraqi Air Force Mirage F1 in a totally unprovoked attack.

The first missile struck the *Stark* on the port side under the bridge, 8 feet above the waterline, but the warhead failed to explode. However, being fired from only twelve miles away, excess fuel and oxidiser resulted in several fires that burnt to 3,500°F and instantly ignited all combustible materials and melted the structure. About 30 seconds later the second missile struck a few feet forward of the first, detonating with devastating effect, killing 37 of the vessel's crewmen and injuring 26 others. The explosion sent a destructive heat pulse through the accommodation area and ruptured the fire-main forward. The frigate's crew fought valiantly to contain the fire to three sections of the ship, even when the flames threatened the ship's Standard missile magazine. The lack of fire-main and the loss of the magazine sprinkler system exacerbated this dangerous situation. Fortunately the crew managed to fight their way over the superstructure above the fire to flood the magazine via hoses. Meanwhile, the inferno had spread upwards through the RICER space and engulfed the CIC.

Soon after midnight the salvage tug *Smit Rangoon* arrived and proceeded to assist in boundary cooling of the magazine area. Due to the ruptured fire-main and water from the fire-fighting effort, the ship had developed a 16° list to port, causing fears for the vessel's stability. The ship's metacentric height was reduced to as low as six-inches and stability had to be re-stored by counter-flooding. In this condition, it was fortunate that the sea was flat calm - had the ship been in more tempestuous conditions, such as those found in the Atlantic, it is possible that she may have foundered. Despite her precarious position, *Stark* was able to proceed at slow speed, under tow by the destroyer *USS Conyngham* (DDG-17), towards Bahrain, whilst the crew continued to struggle to save their crippled vessel. Assistance was also provided by the command ship *USS La Salle* (AGF-3), destroyer *USS Waddell*

*A view of damage to the port side bridge area sustained by the guided missile frigate USS Stark (FFG-31) when it was hit by two Iraqi-launched Exocet missiles while on patrol in the Persian Gulf.*

*(US Navy)*

However, when the aircraft climbed from its low-level approach and illuminated the ship with its target-acquisition radar, which was detected on the ship's AN/SLQ-32(V)2 radar warning receiver, *Stark* sent out two ship-identification messages in English, neither of which were acknowledged. Twelve miles from the ship the aircraft fired the first of it's two Exocet SSMs. At this range, *Stark* had little time to take evasive action or to switch the ship's Phalanx close-in weapon system to automatic. The missiles struck the frigate on the port side below the bridge, 30 seconds apart.

The Iraqi President, Saddam Hussein, quickly made a "fulsome apology" for the attack, saying that *Stark* had been mistakenly identified as an Iranian warship. The United States claimed that the frigate had been the victim of an indiscriminate attack, and demanded full compensation for the ship and her casualties.

On 23 June 1987 Captain Glenn Brindel was relieved of his command of *USS Stark* and faced court-martial action, along with some of his senior officers. It was claimed that command errors resulted in the failure of the frigate to warn the Iraqi pilot of the ship's identity. It was also claimed that the ship should have turned away from the imminent strike and so presented a smaller target, and given the Phalanx CIWS a better field of fire against the incoming missiles.

(DDG-24) and frigate *USS Reid* (FFG-30). It was not until 1900 on the 18th that the last of the fires were extinguished.

The attack on *Stark* occurred some 400 miles from the Iraqi coast at a point 70 miles north-east of Qatar. Although a Saudi-Arabian Air Force E-3A AWACS aircraft had warned the frigate and her five consorts in the US task force of the presence of the Iraqi aircraft, which *Stark* had detected on her primary surveillance radar at a range of 200 miles, they had taken little action as the aircraft was identified as 'friendly'.

After some intense repair work, *Stark* left Bahrain on 5 July 1987 and proceeded under her own power towards Mayport, Florida, where she arrived a month later. Repair of the ship, from November 1987 until August 1988, was estimated to cost US$142million. The Ingalls yard used modular methods in the repair, removing the damaged sections of the ship and installing newly constructed ship modules, one of which weighed 65 tons.

The majority of the incidents mentioned could have been avoided by the effective use of a simple device, known as Identification Friend or Foe (IFF). All modern warships and most merchant vessels, as well as all military aircraft and civilian airliners, now carry an IFF transponder. Most medium and large warships and warplanes also carry on IFF Interrogator. This takes the form of a small transmitter that emits a coded signal to any contact detected by the vessel's or aircraft's surveillance systems. This signal will trigger an automatic response from a transponder on the interrogated vessel or aircraft, in the form of a binary coded signal that will then be received aboard the interrogating unit and compared against identification codes of known friendly ships or aircraft in the area and classified by a computer.

To prevent misuse of the system these codes are changed on a regular basis. Therefore, for this system to be effective, the ship's or aircraft's computers need to be constantly updated with the necessary data to identify friendly units. An additional benefit of the system is that the IFF transmitter can also be used to emit MAYDAY or other distress codes. Modern IFF interrogators and transponders are so compact that they can be easily accommodated aboard all vessels of fast patrol craft or minesweeper size or larger.

Unfortunately, even when IFF equipment is utilised, mistakes can still be made, especially when tensions are running high and an attack is expected from an unpredictable aggressor. Such an unfortunate incident occurred in 1987 with the downing of an Iranian A300 Airbus in mistaken identity for an F-14 fighter by the cruiser *USS Vincennes* (CG-49). The immediate Iranian and US accounts of the incident differed enormously, the US Department of Defence maintaining that the airliner was transmitting a military code, a claim that is fiercely denied by the Iranians.

The *Vincennes* reported that the airliner was descending from 9,000ft to 7,000ft and that it was not replying to radio signals, while the Iranians claim it was climbing and that no communications were received. However, it was later conceded by the Pentagon that the aircraft was not out of position. It is possible that either an F-14's transmissions were mistaken for that of the Airbus, or that the Airbus may have been screening an F-14, or even that the Airbus had been fitted with a military transponder.

Several factors contributed to this disaster: the direction from which the aircraft was tracked by *Vincennes*, that of Bandar Abbas airport, has both military and civilian airfields; the transmissions detected by the ship reportedly indicated a military target; the recent attack on the *USS Stark* in May of that year meant that nerves were already strained; and the fact that at the time of the incident, *USS Vincennes* was engaged in a surface action against Iranian Boghammer craft. These factors probably resulted in the crew of *Vincennes'* CIC suffering from a condition known by psychologists as 'scenario fulfilment'. Also, the date was 4 July, US Independence Day, which would have been an ideal date for the Iranians to carry out a revenge attack against their "Western aggressors".

In July 1992, a sister ship of the *Vincennes*, *USS Cowpens* (CG-63), whilst taking part in a naval exercise in the Pacific, threatened to shoot down an Australian airliner with 300 passengers aboard unless it changed course. The US Navy later apologised for the incident.

To maintain weapons and crews at a high state of readiness for time of conflict, procedures and equipment have to be exercised frequently. Such exercises inevitably include the firing of weapons, often involving the use of live ammunition against simulated targets. There will always be an element of risk involved when carrying out such exercises, although strict adherence to safety precautions and regulations will minimise the occurrence and effects of accidents. There have been several accidents where weapons have been fired against the wrong targets, resulting in loss of ships and the lives of their crews.

On 25 August 1946, the Royal Navy-manned tug *Buccaneer* (W49) was designated to tow a battle practise target, in support of a gun calibration firing exercise with the destroyer *HMS St. James* (R65). Later that morning, the tug duly took up her position on the firing range, approximately twelve miles west of Portland Bill, drawing behind her the large mesh-type target on a course of 270° and a speed of 8 knots. It was planned that the destroyer would fire a total of fourteen broadsides at the target, the first seven blind, using the ship's radar to direct the shot, followed by a further seven salvos controlled visually.

Blind fire was opened at 1148 with the destroyer on a closing course with the target. At this point, the relative position of *Buccaneer* to *St. James* was 30° abaft the beam at a range of 11,000-12,000 yards. On the bridge of the tug, Commanding Officer, Lieutenant-Commander S.E. Veal MBE, RN (Retd), witnessed the fall of shot as the first of the

*The naval tug HMS Buccaneer in 1938, with a floating target alongside. It was whilst towing such a target off Portland on 25 August 1946 that Buccaneer was accidentally struck by a shell from the destroyer HMS St. James and sank. (Maritime Photo Library)*

salvos straddled the target. The next six salvos also fell close to the target, but with a very slight deflection towards *Buccaneer*.

Aboard the destroyer, the order "Enemy in sight" was given, with which gunnery control was switched to 'Aloft' in preparation for the visual firing phase of the exercise. Course was altered to position the target on the destroyer's beam and the eighth salvo roared from the guns. Seconds later, as the shells were seen to drop close to the *Buccaneer*, "Check fire," was ordered, but the ninth salvo had already been fired.

One shell from the eighth salvo struck *Buccaneer* on the port side under the rubbing strake, at the after end of the engine room, the blast killing an officer, Sub-Lieutenant Colbourne, RNVR. A second shell plunged close to the vessel's counter. In the engine room, water was pouring in through an 18-inch diameter hole near the bulkhead at frame 69. The Chief Engine Room Artificer made a valiant attempt to reach the salvage pump, located in the port after corner of the compartment, but it proved impossible against the force of the water. Reports of the damage in the engine room quickly reached Lt.Cdr. Veal, who immediately set course for land and ordered damage-control teams to breach the gaping wound in his vessel by hanging a collision mat over the side. Unfortunately, the position of the hole, immediately below the rubbing strake, meant that the 9-inch thick protrusion prevented the mat from bowsing in and thereby rendered it ineffective. The closing of watertight doors and hatches leading to the engine room prevented the flood from spreading, but as the level in the engine room rose, water began cascading into No.2 boiler room through an air intake which was not fitted with a watertight shut-off. No.2 boiler was ordered shut down, with limited steam pressure maintained by No.1 boiler.

With the realisation of the terrible incident that had occurred, *St. James* closed at high speed to render assistance to the crippled tug, which was now settling in the water and listing to port. One of the destroyer's portable pumps was quickly rigged and a suction hose led into the after boiler room, whilst on deck towing lines were being prepared. By now, the upper deck was awash up to the engine casing and it was obvious that the tug was sinking rapidly by the stern. Orders were passed to evacuate the engine room and the after boiler room and for No.1 boiler to be shut down. Minutes later all 43 survivors clambered aboard the destroyer. *Buccaneer* finally succumbed at 1220, sinking vertically by the stern, but not before lashing out at her assailant as she plunged beneath the water's surface and damaging the destroyer's starboard propeller.

A Board of Enquiry, held on board the cruiser *HMS Superb* on 28 September. It was established that the first seven salvos had been fired correctly by the *St. James*, with the gunnery director in 'Below' control, the firing circuit changeover switch in the 'Radar Firing' position and the guns fired by the CPU operator. On the order "Switch to aloft control", the control officer had put the 'Aloft/Below' changeover switch from 'Radar' to 'Director'. Consequently, as the 'Permission to Open Fire' lamp was still burning, the CPU operator fired the eighth and ninth salvoes. Unfortunately, the gunnery director layer, believing his part in the exercise was concluded, had taken his eyes from his binoculars, whilst the director trainer simultaneously switched off his yaw stabiliser. These actions allowed the radar, which still had control of the guns, to swing sharply to the left, towards the tug, thereby directing the eighth and ninth salvos towards the unfortunate vessel.

This was not to be an isolated incident. On 23 August 1956, the cruiser *HMS Jamaica* (C44) accidentally sank the Remote Control Boat *RCB4* by gunfire off Malta. *RCB4* was one of two former-MTBs that had been converted to target boats in 1953 and sent to Malta to provide gunnery training to the British Mediterranean Fleet. On 1 January 1968, the Miner-class target vessel *Gossamer* (ex-*Miner II*) was sunk in error off Portland when shells from the Iranian destroyer *Artemiz* struck her. *IS Artemiz* (ex-*HMS Sluys*), having recently received a major refit by Vosper Thornycroft at Southampton, was working up with units of the Royal Navy prior to sailing for Iran.

In July 1968 the 854-ton Samson class tug *RMAS Sea Giant* (A288) was allocated to Portland for target towing duties. Whilst undertaking this task on 24 June 1970, a shell fired by the German destroyer *FGS Schleswig Holstein* (D182) landed in the tug's engine room and injured two of her crew. *Sea Giant* was later repaired and returned to service.

Similar accidents have undoubtedly occurred during exercises all over the world. That such incidents occur during times of conflict may be explained in some cases by lack of time to visually identify the target and the unexpected location or response of the victim. However, during peacetime exercises, detailed planning of a serial should mean that the safety of all participating units is assured. This is not, however, always the case.

On 18 January 1978, having placed an old YOG-type hulk in position at the San Diego bombing range, the Cherokee-class fleet tug *USNS Cree* (ATF-84) was mistakenly bombed by a US Navy A-6E aircraft.

The sinking exercise (SINKEX), planned some months in advance, was to be undertaken by aircraft of Carrier Air Wing 14, based aboard the nuclear-powered aircraft carrier *USS Enterprise* (CVN-65). *Cree* was assigned to tow the target hulk, the ex-*YOG-219*, to the firing range and then to act as the range safety vessel. The exercise was to be run by *Enterprise* and controlled and monitored by an E-2B Hawkeye surveillance aircraft positioned about 45 miles to the north of the target. An SH-3D Sea King helicopter was to be assigned the task of marking the target hulk using smoke bombs and then to act as safety observer, positioning itself directly overhead the tug.

At 0840 on 18 January, *Cree* deposited the hulk in the designated position at latitude 31°44'N, longitude 118°45'W, and an hour later took up station eight miles to the north. Sea and weather conditions were fair, but overcast, with a gentle wind and swell and a visibility of approximately eight miles. Five minutes later the helicopter took up position above *Cree*, having marked the target's position with four Mk.58 smoke flares, which had a burning duration of 45 minutes. *Cree* was lying-to with no way on, two of her four main diesel engines supplying her single electric propulsion motor and diesel generators Nos.1 and 2 supplying electrical power, with No.3 in a stand-by condition.

The exercise was to take the form of two separate 'events', with a third if required, each event consisting of an attack on the target hulk by two waves of A-6E Intruder and A-7E Corsair aircraft, each with a payload of Mk.82 500lb Snakeye bombs.

The first serial of the exercise went according to plan, with two waves of aircraft carrying out 'textbook' bombing runs on the target before returning to the carrier. It was at this stage that a tragic chain of events was set in motion. Having been told to mark the target with further flares, the crew of the safety helicopter reported that they had been unaware that they were to remain on station for the second event. This oversight had also resulted in the helicopter being loaded with five Mk.58 flares and nine of the shorter burn-time Mk.25 flares, instead of the fourteen Mk.58 called for. Soon after

1100 they reported to the E-2B aircraft that they had insufficient fuel to remain on task until 1330, as required. The helicopter was subsequently given a revised time to return to *Enterprise* of 1215 by the Air Operations Watch Officer.

The fact that this would not provide helicopter cover during the entire period of the second event was not passed to the carrier's Commanding Officer or the Operations Officer.

Aircraft of the second event approached the area of the target at 1117, having been vectored in by the Hawkeye, and split into two divisions to over fly and visually identify the target. The helicopter then marked the target using one Mk.58 flare and four 15-minute duration Mk.25 flares, noting that the hulk was listing to starboard and settling by the bow, before returning to its position over *Cree*. Over the next thirty minutes, the two divisions of aircraft successfully carried out their first bombing runs on the hulk.

Whilst the aircraft returned to a holding position 45-50 miles east of the target, the OOD aboard *Cree* was informed that the hulk was only showing intermittently on the ship's radar screen. Two minutes later, at 1156, it disappeared completely. It was later to be realised that the target had in fact sunk, a point not detected by the Hawkeye, whilst aboard *Cree* discussions went on to decide whether or not it had actually sunk.

Meanwhile, the helicopter was departing the area to meet its 1215 rendezvous with *Enterprise*. As the helicopter passed a point a few miles from the position of the hulk at noon, it's crew reported to the E-2B that they could see smoke, but failed to report that they could not see the hulk. A minute later, the first two A-6Es began their second run, vectored in by the Hawkeye and using their onboard navigational computer systems to guide them on their final approach. It was at this point that the Hawkeye reached the end of its patrol leg.

Sure that the A-6Es had been given the necessary final instructions, the Hawkeye began a 180° turn, during which time the aircraft's radar presentation was disorientated and the two vessels, *Cree* and the ex-*YOG-219*, would have been indistinguishable as separate contacts on the aircraft's radar plot.

Furthermore, since the target vessel had been deposited in it's designated position at 0840 that morning, the 15 knots wind blowing from 320° had caused it to drift slowly in a south-easterly direction. *Cree* had also drifted parallel with the hulk, to a position three miles north and four miles east of the target's original position, although the tug had held its relative designated position to the north of the target and at no time moved closer than eight miles to it. By using their navigational computers to guide them to the expected position of the target, the aircraft were actually heading for a point slightly to the south of the *Cree*, but to the north of the target.

As the two Intruders approached the target area at a height of 300 feet, a contact, assumed to be ex-*YOG-219*, was acquired on the lead aircraft's radar. The fact that the radar was being operated in the narrow beam mode meant that no attempt was made to detect other vessels expected to be in the area, namely *Cree*. Popping up a few miles from the estimated target position, the 'target' was spotted visually. In the extremely short time available at this point to establish positive identification, the crew of the A-6E noted the head-on silhouette of a vessel which appeared to match that of the target shown to them during the pre-exercised briefing. There was no sign of a wake astern of the craft, as *Cree* was lying dead in the water. Although the pilot did not spot any smoke, this did not surprise him as on the previous run he had noted that the smoke marking the target was already dispersing. The lack of the expected helicopter above the 'target' also

convinced the pilot he was attacking the hulk. Intruder No.501 began its 420-knot dive-bombing run.

When the crew of *Cree* realised that their ship was the subject of the Intruder's attack, they broadcast a "cease fire" order over the primary strike radio frequency, causing the second aircraft to break off its attack, but too late to prevent the lead aircraft dropping three 500lb bombs. As the second aircraft turned to the south, it's pilot spotted smoke on the water's surface about eight miles to the south, the position at which ex-*YOG-219* had sunk.

The first of the three bombs stuck the water off the *Cree*'s port side, scraped the bow, bilge keel and bilge before detonating beneath the starboard side amidships, sending a huge wall of water crashing over the ship. The second bomb struck the vessel just above the waterline on the port side forward, penetrating the hull and punching it's way through several bulkheads and compartments before coming to rest embedded in the bulkhead at frame 36. Although this bomb failed to explode, the impact was sufficient to render Nos.2 and 3 diesel generators inoperative, although No.1 continued to supply the ship with power with which to run lighting and pumps.

The final bomb struck the vessel's foremast and fell over the starboard side, detonating as it struck the water. The blast peppered the superstructure with shrapnel and caused severe damage to the ship's hull in the vicinity of the Main Engine Room (compartment B-1) and the Main Motor Room (compartment B-2). The motor room began flooding rapidly through the holes punched by the projectiles and through ruptured hull seams and sprung rivets. Minor flooding also occurred in the engine room, partially via a large split which had been wrenched in the lower part of the main watertight bulkhead between the motor room and the engine room by the detonation of the bombs. The ship's two P-250 pumps, as well as portable eductors, were promptly put to task in the motor room in an attempt to control the rising water level and crewmen began plugging holes in the hull with rags and wooden bungs.

Use of the larger fitted salvage pump was thwarted when the increasing depth of water threatened to swamp the pump's motor and so endanger the lives of the damage-control party. Damage-control efforts were interrupted, however, when at 1212, the presence of a live unexploded bomb was discovered. An Explosive Ordnance Disposal team flown to the tug from the *Enterprise* later defused the bomb and jettisoned it and the fuse overboard.

At 1230, it was decided that the salvage pumps located in the ship's hold should be utilised in the motor room. These heavy pumps, as well as the massive hatch cover, had to be shifted manually as the ship's 10-ton boom was out of action due to the severe damage inflicted on the ship's electrical systems - a mammoth task which took the crew nearly three hours to complete before the largest 6-inch suction salvage pump could be put into operation. The pumping capacity provided by this pump was to prove crucial in the ensuing battle by the crew to save their ship from sinking.

By 1305, the water level had reached the windings of the only operable generator, which then had to be shut down rather than risk a fire when the water shorted it out. This left the vessel without electrical power until temporary repairs enabled No.3 generator to be started and put onto the ship's electrical grid at 1445.

Meanwhile, the crew worked continuously to plug holes in the hull and tend the pumps, which persistently lost suction due to the large lift from the motor room to the pumps situated on the weather deck. Additional pumps were also transferred from *US Ships Enterprise*, *Long Beach* (CGN-9) and *John Paul Jones* (DDG-32), along with extra

manpower from the latter. However, of the six P-250 portable pumps transferred to *Cree*, several were defective, necessitating the formation of a five-man repair team to continuously rectify defects on these units.

The fact that this repair action was necessary during an intensive salvage operation, when time is of the essence, betrayed a serious lack of attention to the maintenance of these important items of equipment. This was a shortcoming which had been highlighted time and again during previous emergencies aboard US Navy ships, and was to be mirrored by the poor performance of Rover gas turbine-driven pumps transferred to the British destroyer *HMS Sheffield* (D80) after she was struck by an Argentine Exocet missile during the Falkland Islands conflict of 1982.

Although the rising water level was stalled by about 1530, the crew had to continue their feverish efforts for several hours longer before they reached the stage where the pumping capacity outstripped the volume of water leaking into the ship. As the water level dropped they were able to reach the lower leaks and, as darkness fell, the damage control initiative changed to shoring of the shattered hull.

An attempt by the crew of the *John Paul Jones* to establish a tow of the stricken tug resulted in further misfortune when the towing hawser parted and became entangled around one of the destroyer's propellers. Ironically, this necessitated the despatch of two divers from *Cree* to assist in the removal of the offending obstruction. This task completed, the divers returned to *Cree* and an emergency towing hawser was passed to the *John Paul Jones* about 1730, some three hours after the initial tow had been passed. *Cree* was then towed to San Diego where the damage was surveyed and the inevitable investigations into the incident began.

That no personnel had been killed or seriously injured during the bombing of the *Cree* is nothing short of a miracle. Nevertheless, estimated costs for the repair of the extensive damage inflicted on the tug by the three bombs was in excess of $3,500,000, resulting in the vessel, which had been launched in 1942, being judged as 'beyond economical repair' and decommissioned on 21 April. Following cannibalisation for spare parts for her sisters *USN Ships Ute* (T-ATF-76) and *Lipan* (T-ATF-85), in service with the Military Sealift Command, the ship was herself sunk as a target on 27 August 1978.

The formal investigation into the circumstances surrounding the bombing of *Cree* was extremely thorough and detailed. Although it was determined that all precautions required for the safe execution of the SINKEX had been accounted for in the exercise's planning stage, it was found that not all parties taking part were properly briefed on the morning of 18 January as to their roles in the exercise. In particular, the crews of the helicopter and the E-2B were only briefed on Event 1, resulting in a failure by the helicopter's crew, and the OOD aboard *Enterprise*, to appreciate the essential safety aspects of the helicopter remaining hovered over the tug throughout both events. It was the responsibility of the Commanding Officer of *USS Enterprise,* as Officer Conducting the Exercise, to ensure that all participants were fully briefed on their duties and responsibilities prior to the start of the evolution.

In future, detailed written orders (in the form of a Letter of Instruction) would be prepared and promulgated before all exercises involving the use of live ordnance. The lack of such a document was the single most significant failure that led to the bombing of *USNS Cree.*

Primary blame for the incident rested with the crew of Intruder No.501: for failing to positively identify the 'target' prior to attack; for releasing his weapons even though he had not sighted smoke; for failing to check for more than one return from his radar; and for placing too much faith in the reliability of his aircraft's CAINS weapon systems to guide him on his final approach to the 'target'. However, the strike aircraft should have been more firmly vectored into the area by the crew of the E-2B aircraft, whose responsibility it had been to monitor the progress of the events, especially during the crucial final stages of the attack runs.

The failure of the crews of *Cree*, the helicopter and the E-2B aircraft to promptly report the sinking of the target vessel was also a major factor in the incident. In fact, had this information been passed immediately by any of the participants, then "*the bombing of USNS Cree would, in all probability, not have occurred.*"

The investigation resulted in a large number of officers being found negligent in their particular duties during the SINKEX, primarily in that they did not ensure the efficient flow of information to all those requiring it. The fact that the target hulk was not distinctively marked was also criticised, especially as this was the first SINKEX which was to be executed using actual 'War-at-sea' tactics, that is, a low-level approach and final 'pop-up' dive-bombing attack, relying on very short target verification times. It was recommended that, in future, target craft were to be positively identified prior to the release of any ordnance and that a safety aircraft remain on station throughout the exercise. A suggestion that target craft should be painted a highly visible colour was rejected as being economical ly unfeasible, in favour of methods such as a distinctive marking around the funnel. The fitting of a portable radar beacon and a strobe light aboard vessels involved in target towing activities was also recommended.

Commander Service Group One also stressed that all ships companies should be proficient in, and should practice regularly, towing operations. Had *Cree* not been a salvage vessel with her own trained divers aboard, then the botched attempt by the *John Paul Jones* to establish a tow could have resulted in two crippled vessels requiring assistance.

Almost all naval warships and auxiliaries, from aircraft carriers to tugs, at some time in their active careers act as target towing vessels during naval exercises. This task normally entails the trailing, at a safe distance, of a small 'splash target', comprising of a wooden frame incorporating a water scoop which produces a plume of water as it travels just beneath the surface of the water at which aircraft or warships fire their weapons. Alternatively, small target vessels, incorporating radar reflectors hung on a steel framework and mounted on a barge, are towed behind the ship. Before opening fire on the target, the attacking vessel or aircraft will be required to communicate with the towing vessel and confirm identification of the target. Once ordered to proceed, a single round is usually fired so that should a mistake be made, a full salvo is not loosed in the wrong direction.

In some exercises, a warship may itself act as a 'target', the firing vessel introducing a set throw-off angle into its firing solutions. This angle will be dependant on the calibre of the weapon being fired and the range at which firing is commenced, and will include a ricochet safety angle to prevent bouncing shells endangering the target ship.

Such procedures inevitably involve an element of risk to ships towing, or acting as, targets, especially when exercises involve navies of different countries unaccustomed to operating together or aircraft pilots unfamiliar with naval operations. However, strict adherence to detailed safety regulations will considerably reduce such risk. As an added precaution against mishaps, most weapon firing exercises are carried out only in clear weather and calm sea conditions. However, even in seemingly ideal weather conditions, accidents can happen. For instance, the sinking of a buoy tender by practice bombs from a German Marineflieger Tornado aircraft on a Baltic firing range on 9 February 1995 has been attributed to the pilot being temporarily blinded by the glare of sunlight on his cockpit canopy.

# Chapter Nine

# CAUSE UNKNOWN?

The disappearance of a vessel without trace is a rare occurrence, as there are normally some clues as to the cause of the accident, in the form of distress messages transmitted before the vessel's sinking or from surveys of the wreckage. Occasionally however, little is ever found of the vessel apart from debris floating on the water's surface or washed up on nearby coastlines, which may provide few clues regarding the cause of her demise. Several such unexplained losses remain a mystery, particularly in the case of submarines, which when lost often take all evidence, and crew, to the bottom of the ocean.

Cases of surface vessels disappearing without trace are extremely rare, as there are normally some traces of flotsam or wreckage to be found. Nevertheless, a few craft have disappeared and, although they have never been found and the cause of their loss many never be known, they have been attributed to foundering in storms. These include the Danish patrol cutter *HDMS Alken*, which disappeared with her 9-man crew off Greenland in October 1948 whilst en route from the weather station at Aputiteq to Angmagssalick. Almost exactly ten years later, the Argentine tug *Guarani*, vanished in the Strait of Magellan. In both of these cases neither the craft nor their crews were found, despite extensive air and sea searches.

There have been at least four unexplained submarine losses since 1945. The construction of such craft, with few protrusions and even fewer fixtures to their hulls, may result in a complete lack of flotsam. Even if eventually found after exhaustive searches, the true cause of their loss remains a mystery as the extreme depth at which they lay may preclude detailed examination of the wreck internally.

Mystery still surrounds the disappearance of the Soviet Shch-class submarine *S-117* in the Sea of Japan on the night of 15-16 December 1952. The aged boat, launched in 1934, boat sailed from Vladivostok at about 1100 on 14 December to participate in a naval exercise. Later that afternoon the boat signalled headquarters that it was experiencing problems with the starboard main engine. A couple of hours later, the submarine reported the sighting of a floating mine. The last message received from the boat on the morning of 15 December reported repairs to the starboard engine as complete. *S-117* missed her

*Although the 1948 disappearance of the Danish Navy patrol cutter Alken has been attributed to foundering in a storm off Greenland, the true reason for her demise has never been poitively determined, as no trace of the vessel has ever been found.*

*(Kommandorkapitajn Holm, Marinens Bibliotek)*

next scheduled report at 1700 that evening and nothing more was ever heard from her.

Search operations were conducted over the following week, centred mainly on the area to the west of the island of Sakhalin, between Tomari and Holmsk. Hampered by severe winter weather, extensive searches of the Tatar Strait resumed in the spring, but failed to locate the boat. Despite initial suspicions that she had been sunk in a collision with the steamer *Gornozavodsk*, examinations of ship's hull in dock in January 1953 revealed no significant underwater damage. Various hypotheses have been presented regarding the loss, most recently in an article by Vladimir Shigin in the naval magazine "*Morskoi Sbornik*" (No.12, 1997, "*Secrets of the Vanishing 'Shchuka'*" (pp.86-93)). Theories include that *S-117* had struck a mine, suffered an equipment failure, or had been involved in an incident with a U.S. Navy submarine, but insufficient evidence is available to support any of these theories. To this day, no trace has been found of the boat or her 51 crewmen.

As a direct result of the uncertainty surrounding the disappearance of *S-117*, the Chinese cancelled plans to acquire four Shch-class boats and instead four S-type (Series IX) boats, including *S-52* and *S-53*, and four M-type boats were transferred in June 1965 and June 1966.

This was to be the second disappearance of a submarine in 1952. The Royal Navy S-class submarine *HMS Sportsman* had been lent to the French Navy in 1951 for anti-submarine training and to replace war losses, being re-commissioned under the new name *FS Sibylle* (S614). On 24 September 1952, while engaged in a routine anti-submarine exercise with the ex-US Cannon-class destroyer escort *FS Touareg* (F721) she disappeared near Cape Camarat in position 43.16°N, 6.81°E.

After diving at 0743 that morning, the *Sibylle* was to maintain a safe depth of 30 metres, changing course every ten minutes, in the role of an enemy submarine. *Touareg's* first dummy attack on the submarine, commencing at 0752, went according to plan but during the second attack run ten minutes later contact with *Sibylle* was lost at a distance of 270 metres. The escort began a thorough search of the area and, at 0815, a submarine emergency buoy was sighted and picked up. Further extensive searches failed to find any further signs of the *Sibylle*.

The exact cause of the loss, along with her entire crew of 47 men, remains uncertain, as the boat has never been recovered. The subsequent inquiry examined various theories as to the boat's loss. The possibility of an internal explosion was quickly discounted as neither *Touareg*, nor the submarine *FS Laubie* (S610), submerged in a neighbouring area, had detected any evidence of such an occurrence. Collision was also ruled out, as there were no other vessels, besides the escort, in the immediate area at the time of *Sibylle's* disappearance.

Despite the fact that *Sibylle* had been in contact with *Touareg* almost constantly between the time she submerged at 0743 and the loss of contact nearly twenty minutes later, a diving control-related accident remains the most likely explanation, possibly due to unfamiliarity of the French crew with the newly-acquired boat. A watch change would have been in progress aboard the submarine at the time of her disappearance and various procedures would have been carried out during the hand-over, such as routine opening and closing of the main vents to remove any trapped air from the top of the ballast tanks, followed by minor alterations to the vessel's trim to compensate for any air expelled. It is probable that during these, or similar routines, control of trim was lost, sending the boat into an uncontrolled dive. *Sibylle*'s Commanding Officer would have had two choices: firstly, he could have attempted to surface immediately; or secondly, he may have attempted to regain control of the trim and maintain a safe depth. This second alternative is likely to have been the preferred option, especially with the close proximity of *Touareg* and the very real danger of a collision should she surface unexpectedly. It is obvious that all efforts to regain control failed and as a last resort the vessel's emergency buoy was released.

Another possible cause of the loss was failure of the torpedo tube doors, which were not fitted with safety interlocks. Such interlocks were quickly fitted to all French submarines, a lesson that had been painfully learnt by the Royal Navy with the loss of *HMS Thetis* in 1939. As a consequence of the loss of *Sibylle*, the remaining three boats of the class in service with the French Navy had their torpedo tubes sealed and were relegated to training duties until their disposal in the late-1950s.

This was France's third submarine loss since the end of the war. In September 1945, *FS Minerve* (P26) ran aground off Portland and then, a little over a year later, the French Navy suffered its second loss. The German Type XXIII submarine *U2326* had surrendered to the British at Loch Foyle on 14 May 1945, after which she was commissioned into Royal Navy service as *HMS N35* and, following a series of trials, the boat was ceded to France on 4 June 1946.

From 28 October to 25 November the boat underwent a maintenance period at Toulon. Under the command of Capitaine de Corvette Avon, *U2326* sailed at 0913 on 5 December 1946 and dived 22 minutes later. Nothing more was heard from the boat and she sank with her crew of two officers, thirteen ratings and three passengers, including a Capitaine de Corvette (Lieutenant-Commander) from the Paris General Staff, an engineer and an employee of the DCAN Casselle shipyard.

Although the boat was later raised and scrapped, the cause of her sinking is still unclear. The Type XXIII submarines were well known for their excellent performance, but were at times thought to be too advanced for operation by inexperienced crews, even in German hands.

The loss of the Israeli submarine *Dakar* remained a mystery for over 31 years after her disappearance on 26 January 1968. Dogged perseverance by the Israeli Navy to find the lost boat and discover the cause finally paid off when she was discovered in the Aegean Sea on 28 May 1999, some 270 miles from her intended destination of Haifa. The cause of the submarine's sinking was finally determined to be the result of flooding of her forward compartments following a pipework failure (see Chapter 5).

However, Israel was not the only country to suffer the tragedy of a submarine loss in January 1968. On the 27th - the day after *Dakar*'s disappearance - the French Daphné-class submarine *FS Minerve* (S647) also vanished in the Mediterranean.

Having completed a major refit at the end of 1967, *Minerve* underwent a work-up and training period extending into January 1968. On the 21st of that month, Lieutenant de Vaisseau Fauve, an experienced and respected submarine officer, took command of the boat and in the following days he and his crew were put through their paces by the staff of the Training Officer of the First Submarine Squadron. On completion of a fully satisfactory training period, the training officer was disembarked at Vignettes on the night of Friday, 26 January and *Minerve* proceeded to an area south of Cape Sicie, known as Sector T.65, where she was to take part in exercises with aircraft from the Naval air station at

Nimes-Garon. She was then expected to return to her anchorage at Toulon at 2100 on 27 January. The boat never arrived at Toulon and nothing more was seen of the submarine or her crew of 6 officers and 47 ratings. An extensive search operation was immediately initiated, but no trace of *Minerve* was found.

The sudden and unexplained disappearance of the submarine caused grave concern throughout the French submarine service, not least because the design was relatively new. *Minerve* - commissioned on 10 June 1964 - had been the seventh of eleven boats of the class in service with, or building for, the French Navy at the time. Several boats of the same design had also been ordered for service in the navies of Pakistan, Portugal, South Africa and Spain, and were in various stages of construction. No effort was to be spared in determining the cause of the loss.

The Press Information Service of the French Navy made an announcement on 31 January to update the public on the ongoing search operation for the missing boat, but the following day the search was temporarily suspended, all hope of finding survivors having faded. The primary aim of the search operation was now to find the missing boat and to ascertain the cause of her loss. The immediate search was carried out in Sector T.65 - the area in which *Minerve* had last been contacted. However, the area to be covered was large and accurate survey information scarce.

It was known only that the submarine had dived to snorkel depth at about 0800 on the 27th, in preparation for the exercise, which was cancelled due to a violent mistral, a fierce offshore wind common to the French Mediterranean coast. Communications between the submarine and the Bréguet Atlantic aircraft with which she was to have exercised was broken abruptly at 0755, immediately after the aircraft had informed the boat of the cancellation of

the training serial, at which time the aircraft noted the submarine's position in the south-eastern corner of Sector T.65. The only real clue as to the submarine's fate was a recording made by a seismology station at 23 seconds past 0759 on the 27th, emanating from the east of Sector T.65, which subsequent analysis determined had corresponded with that of an implosion of a large bubble of gas of around 600 cubic metres in volume - the approximate internal volume of a Daphné-class submarine.

Although the combination of this information and the position given by the Bréguet Atlantic should have resulted in a fairly accurate fix of the submarine's location, there was a sizeable discrepancy between the positions given. Consequently, the position given by the aircraft was subjected to close and critical scrutiny and corrected slightly.

Much had been gleaned from the US Navy's experiences in the then recent searches for the nuclear-powered submarine *USS Thresher* in 1963/64 and the search near Palomares, Spain, in 1966 for a nuclear bomb lost from a USAF bomber. However, the French Navy at that time possessed little specialist equipment such as that used in the US search operations or that for *USS Scorpion* later in 1968. The search for *Minerve* was therefore to be divided into two separate phases. The first, using equipment already in service was to be undertaken in the following few months. Should it be necessary, a more detailed search was planned for the following year, utilising equipment in the course of development or enhancement.

Early in the initial search hopes were raised when a large patch of oil was spotted near Toulon, but further investigations failed to link it with *Minerve*, it being suspected that it had originated from a merchant vessel passing through the area. The possibility that *Minerve* had been struck by a surface ship was ruled out after divers surveyed the hulls of all vessels having transited the area south of Toulon on 27 January.

Having found nothing in the initial search area, the scope of the search was extended to cover neighbouring sectors and their approaches and along the coast east and west of Toulon. The large-scale operation, involving dozens of ships and aircraft, had been slimmed down and by now involved the 810-tonne hydrographic vessel *La Recherché* (A758), and the 800-tonne ex-German aviation tender *Marcel Le Bihan* (A759) which carried on board the 65-tonne bathyscaphe *Archimede*, under the operational code-name Reminer.

*La Recherché* first carried out systematic soundings of the search areas at specific intervals of 50 metres, 100 metres or 200 metres. Any contacts found were passed to *Marcel Le Bihan* for more detailed investigation. However, the capability of the German ELAC sounder operated by *La Recherché* was severely limited, with a short range and, although claimed to be capable of detecting items protruding over a metre from the sea floor, only picked out obstructions of at least 4-5 meters. The position, determined by the Trident navigation system, of over a dozen such contacts were passed to *Marcel Le Bihan*, several of which looked exceedingly promising.

The timetable for the operations was extended considerably by poor weather, especially with a number of severe mistrals in August 1968. A series of seven dives were subsequently carried out in September and October to the following formula: firstly, *Marcel Le Bihan* moved into the general area given by *La Recherché*; then, the bathyscaphe, ready to submerge, was towed by *Marcel Le Bihan* to a position a few hundred metres to leeward of the contact; finally *Archimede*, guided by its mother ship and its onboard panoramic sonar, subjected the contact to close scrutiny. The

powerful floodlights of *Archimede*, even at depths of over 2,000 metres, allowed details of the contacts to be picked out and allow positive classification.

The first of these contacts, although initially promising, proved to be an unidentified wreck of a surface ship. Identification of a cargo derrick and a three-bladed propeller resulted in a similar classification of a second contact a few days later. Some of the other protrusions turned out to be no more than large rocks or small cliffs. Another turned out to be a rocket embedded in the soft sediment. None of the contacts proved to be *Minerve* and further operations were planned for 1969. However, much had been learnt of the uneven contours of the seabed in the areas searched and the inadequacies of the equipment used were highlighted.

The initial search by *La Recherché* in March 1969 covered an area of five miles radius, centred on the position given by the Bréguet Atlantic aircraft. Improvements in the accuracy of positioning and the use of magnetometers to determine the existence of metallic objects on the seabed, were incorporated using experience gained by the US Navy in the searches for *Thresher* and *Scorpion*.

This method permitted distinction between seabed undulations or rocks and true metallic contacts such as shipwrecks, thus allowing a more efficient use of the bathyscaphe *Archimede*. A submerged 'fish', towed behind the ship incorporated the magnetometers, magnetometer-triggered cameras, sidescan sonar and an ultrasonic positioning system. Unfortunately, lack of funds meant that specialist equipment was not available in the French Navy and equipment belonging to the famous Commander Jacques Cousteau was utilised.

Although the search continued throughout the year, the determination to find *Minerve* was overtaken by the huge cost of the exercise and the requirement to utilise the resources on other projects.

The loss of the submarine thus remains a mystery. The French Navy gained a great deal of experience in the campaign and set up a new department to correlate the information gained and to formulate detailed procedures for activation in the event of similar incidents in the future.

The year 1968 was the worst ever for submarine losses in peacetime. As well as the aforementioned losses of the Israeli *Dakar* and of the French *Minerve* in January, the Soviet's lost the Project 629A boat *K-129* in April, whilst the US Navy lost the nuclear-powered attack boat USS *Scorpion* the following month. In all, these four accidents cost the lives of almost 300 submariners. Furthermore, the Soviets suffered a nuclear accident aboard the Project 656 boat *K-27* in May of the same year. Tragically, the French Navy was to suffer a further loss of a Daphné-class boat only two years later.

Having been at anchor for 48 hours at Toulon, *FS Eurydice* (S644) set sail at 2300 on 1 March 1970 for Saint Tropez, where she arrived at 1100 on the 3rd, exercising with the experimental vessel (ex-destroyer escort) *Arago* (A607) en route. She sailed again at 0530 4 March for a series of exercises with a Bréguet Atlantic aircraft in the Cape Camarat exercise area. On board was her Commanding Officer, Lieutenant de Vaisseau Truchis de Lays, and 56 crewmen, including a Pakistani officer on board for a familiarisation cruise prior to joining one of his own Navy's boats of the same class.

At 0700 that morning, the aircraft detected *Eurydice* on radar at periscope depth and made radio contact soon afterwards. Contact was broken at 0713 in preparation for the first serial of the exercise, which required *Eurydice* to proceed at periscope depth, using her aerials and snorkel, and to dive as soon as she detected the presence of the aircraft. It was planned that she should regain contact ten minutes later before beginning

the next serial. However, there was no further contact between the submarine and the aircraft and the Préfecture Maritime (Maritime Headquarters) declared a full SubMiss operation two hours later. Further aircraft were dispatched to the area and at 1040 a full-scale search operation was instigated, involving destroyers, frigates and two of *Eurydice*'s sister boats. News of the boat's disappearance was released to the public at 1300 that afternoon.

Despite an extensive search, *Eurydice* was not found for some time. A Toulon laboratory recorded a large explosion on its instruments emanating from the estimated position of the boat, evidence that gave the French Navy its only clue as to the cause of her loss. The wreck was later located by the US Navy ship *Mizar* (AGOR-11), in position 43.16ºN, 8.80ºE - very close to the last known position of the *Sibylle* 18 years earlier. At a depth of almost 100 metres, nothing was retrieved from the shattered vessel.

Once again, suspicion that the boat had been in collision with a merchant ship resulted in the examination of several vessels that had transited the area at the time of the boat's loss, but no such evidence was found. The cause of the boat's loss remains a mystery.

*Eurydice* had been completed in September 1964 and over the next $5^{1}/_{2}$ years had travelled 81,000 miles in 774 days at sea. During this time, 9,010 had been spent submerged, 1,780 of which included the use of her snorkel. The Daphné-class boats were extremely manoeuvrable for their time and one theory voiced for the numerous accidents involving them early in their service lives was that some young Captains in command were tempted to take unnecessary risks. Although the class had by then been sold to several other countries, orders for further boats suddenly dried up from this point. This has probably been the unluckiest class of submarine in the western world as, apart from the loss of *Minerve* and *Eurydice*, *Galatée* was almost lost in collision in 1970 and the two year-old *Siréne* (S651) sank at Derman, Lorient, on 11 October 1972 after flooding through a faulty torpedo tube. The *Siréne* was raised eleven days later, refitted and served until the mid-1990s. The crew of another of the class, *FS Flore* (S645), narrowly averted the loss of their submarine in 1971 when the snorkel developed a serious leak.

It appears from the above that the French Navy has been unable to ascertain the true reasons for several of their submarine losses, although how much they really know about the accidents is probably still classified. Because of the embarrassing nature of such incidents, many countries are loath to release details, whilst the lust for secrecy means that the truth may never be known. Terrifying accounts of some of the Soviet Union's submarine disasters have come to light since the end of the Cold War, but the aftermath of the *Kursk* disaster illustrated that the Russians still have a strong desire for secrecy.

Such a veil of secrecy spread over such incidents by some countries means that it is difficult to ascertain whether or not the true cause of some losses is actually known. For example, a North Korean submarine of the Soviet-built Project 633 ('Romeo'-class) reportedly sank in 350 feet of water off the east coast of Korea on 20 February 1985, along with her entire crew of around 56 men. The cause of the loss, if known at all, has not been revealed.

# Chapter Ten

# SURVIVAL, ESCAPE, RESCUE AND SALVAGE

When a ship sustains damage, by whatever cause, the effects must be countered by prompt and effective damage control measures such as leak stopping, pumping and fire-fighting. Failure to contain the damage will result in the effects of the damage growing out of control and threatening the safety of the vessel and the lives of the crew. Various aspects of damage control have been covered elsewhere in this book and so will not be considered here. This chapter will therefore cover the actions that will follow the failure and cessation of damage-control activities.

When his vessel is in imminent danger of foundering the Commanding Officer's

## SURVIVAL

priority will change to the safety of his crew and consideration may be given to abandoning ship. Rescue services should already have been alerted soon after the occurrence which endangered his ship, in the form of distress signals, such as transmission of SOS messages or the firing of flares and hopefully, help will already be on its way. Each country has its own integrated and centrally controlled organisation to co-ordinate the stages of a rescue operation. Assets available will normally consist of the Coast Guard, Lifeboat Services, Naval and Air Forces, and any other shipping in the vicinity of the ship in distress.

However, even if the ship's distress messages and signals have been detected, it is likely to be some time before rescue services are in position to render assistance. The endangered crew will therefore have to take all steps available to them to ensure their own survival until the rescue services arrive.

During the Second World War Battle of the Atlantic, over 50,000 Royal Navy personnel, as well as about 30,000 British merchant naval seamen, lost their lives, two-thirds of which died after abandoning ship, despite being rescued within 24 hours in almost all cases. The primary cause of death was hypothermia, the result of the lowering of the body core temperature. The normal body temperature is 36.8°C. Unconsciousness will occur around 30°C, whilst a body temperature of below 25°C is usually fatal. Even in sub-tropical waters, prolonged immersion may result in the excessive loss of body heat and the onset

Carley Float

*The Carley float was a simple flotation device intended to merely keep survivors afloat and offered no protection from the elements. Later variants, like this one, provided limited survival rations in a small compartment slung beneath the float.*

*(Author)*

the compartment was slung by a net beneath the flotation ring. Very few ships' boats were carried, particularly on warships, as they were large and unwieldy and occupied valuable deck space required for weapons.

Personal life-saving equipment was largely limited to cork-filled life jackets. These bulky items were not always immediately available to a crewman to don before abandoning ship and would not keep the wearer's face above water should he lose consciousness. These clumsy garments were still in use in the major western navies well into the 1950s and much later in some others, until they were finally replaced by an inflatable design. These more practical items can be stowed in larger numbers, can be easily carried about one's person on a belt or strap, and can be worn in a deflated or partially inflated condition in periods of increased danger without seriously restricting mobility. A survivor can easily inflate them immediately before or after abandoning ship. A further enhancement is some designs is the incorporation of a small compressed air bottle which automatically inflates the life-jacket when the wearer enters the water - a particularly valuable function when the wearer is injured or unconscious.

The prevention of the loss of body heat is paramount to survival. Even ordinary clothing will help to maintain the body's core temperature for a time. Survival suits are now standard equipment aboard most ships. These waterproof garments, generally made of rubberised cotton, totally enclose the body, with the neck and wrists sealed by elasticated bands. Hoods are normally provided to help keep the wearer's head dry, whilst the life jacket usually has a transparent hood and visor that will protect the survivor's face from water spray. The latest version entering service with the Royal Navy is a one-piece suit that covers the entire body, including the hands, with only the

of hypothermia. In water temperatures of 15°C, the average life expectancy of an unprotected survivor is around six hours, but survivability is reduced to only about one hour as the water temperature falls to 5°C.

The life-saving equipment available during the Second World War was totally inadequate by modern standards, most ships carrying only Carley floats or open life rafts that left the unfortunate survivors to the mercy of the elements. These were no more than wooden or cork flotation aids and not nearly enough of them were carried to enable every member of the crew to find space atop one, the majority having to merely cling to the sides in an effort to maintain their heads above water.

The Carley float did include a small compartment containing a meagre amount of emergency rations, but survivors had to dive beneath the water to retrieve them as wearer's face open to the elements; the face will then be kept clear of salt water spray by the visor of the wearer's life jacket. Correctly worn, preferably prior to entering the water, a survival suit will keep a survivor's body and clothing dry and reduce body heat loss dramatically.

Modern life rafts have probably undergone the greatest transformation since the Second World War, evolving from basic flotation aids to fully enclosed and well-equipped self-inflating craft. Enough of these life rafts are normally carried to enable 110% of the crew to be accommodated.

The most common design has a capacity of 25 persons and is stored in upper-deck locations within a weather-tight glass-reinforced plastic container. The NL Mk.1 liferaft, manufactured by Beaufort Air-Sea Equipment Ltd, is fitted to all Royal Navy vessels and has been further improved to incorporate many lessons learned from the Falklands conflict. Viewed as the optimum equipment in terms of life-saving features, the life rafts may be released manually from their stowage or, should the ship sink, a hydrostatic operating mechanism will release it from the ship when a depth of about five metres is reached, allowing the raft to float to the surface. When launched, the craft is inflated automatically by two gas cylinders containing a mixture of carbon dioxide and a small quantity of nitrogen as an anti-freezing agent. A SART (Search and Rescue Radar Transponder) radio beacon, operating on the International Distress Frequency (243 Mhz) is located in each life raft to allow it to be detected by searching aircraft. A basic survival pack is stowed within the life raft, consisting of such useful items as flares, first aid kit, balers, water, glucose sweets and spare survival suits.

The importance of frequent basic sea survival training cannot be overemphasised, as it will prepare crew

NL Mk.1 Life Raft

members psychologically for an emergency and will reduce the mental and emotional shock caused by the fear after abandoning ship. Familiarity with survival equipment and its capabilities will without doubt improve the chances of its user to survive. There is no point in having excellent equipment if the personnel do not know how to use it properly. Personnel should be taught not only how to survive in a life raft for extended periods, but also the basics of how to board or right the craft. Constant maintenance of survival equipment is also of extreme importance if it is to be effective when required for use.

The combination of life jackets that keep a survivor's face clear of the water, even when unconscious or asleep, survival suits that prevent the loss of body heat, the provision of enclosed life rafts which protect survivors from the elements and the fitting of radio beacons to life rafts that searching aircraft can track, means that the chance of survival after abandoning ship is better now than has ever been the case. Nevertheless, the adage that a survivor is not a survivor until rescued, still holds true.

*The latest life raft to enter service with the Royal Navy is the NL Mk1. The availability of such equipment gives shipwreck survivors an immeasurably grater chance of survival over their immediate post-war counterparts.*

*(Author)*

# ESCAPE

Escape from a surface vessel is normally a case of the crewmen, should they be physically capable, proceeding to the upper deck by the quickest or safest route and leaving the vessel before it sinks. Most modern vessels are fitted with emergency lighting and ultraviolet signs to direct personnel to the upper deck via the quickest route, whilst portable emergency life support apparatus in the form of a hood supplied with oxygen from a small bottle, may be provided to enable the crewman to survive in a smoke-filled environment for long enough to reach the open air. However, in the vast majority of cases, there is little chance of escape from a surface vessel once it has sunk, unless the person is trapped within a watertight compartment and the vessel lies in very shallow water.

In the case of submarines however, escape from a boat in distress is seldom so simple. The submarine's natural operating environment means that a submerged boat in difficulties may be incapable of returning to the surface. Even when involved in an incident on the surface, the submarine's delicate balance between displacement and buoyancy may result in the boat sinking so suddenly that the crew will have little chance of escaping before it slips below the surface.

Trapped on the sea bed within their crippled submarine, escape must be in a calm and controlled manner if they are to survive their ordeal. Such escape methods, and the equipment used, have been constantly improved since the early days of the submarine.

The first successful submarine escape took place on 1 February 1851 by the German engineer Wilhelm Bauer and his two man crew from his submersible, *Brandtaucher*, as it lay crippled and flooded in Kiel Harbour in sixteen metres of water. The method they used was simple but effective. By waiting until their boat had flooded sufficiently for the pressure inside to equalise with that outside the hull, they were able to open the hatch and swim to the surface. The boat was salvaged in 1887 and now stands on display in the Berlin Naval Museum.

Despite the steady evolution in submarine design, there was little advance in escape techniques for the rest of the nineteenth century. Then, on 15 April 1909, a young American submariner, Ensign Kenneth Whiting, carried out an escape from the torpedo tube of the submarine *USS Porpoise* (SS-7) by first flooding the tube and escaping through the outer door once the inside and outside pressures had equalised, employing much the same principal as that used by Bauer 58 years earlier.

Reversing this principle, a re-entry into a submarine was later successfully enacted when Ensign Carr entered the torpedo tube of *USS Shark* (SS-8) through the outer door. The outer door was then closed and the torpedo tube drained down to allow him to enter the boat through the tube's inner door. These actions pointed the way to further developments in submarine escape methods. That said, the recognised method of escape for many years to come was to remain the flooding of compartments within the submarine to allow the crew to swim out from the hatch.

Meanwhile, the problem of the presence and build-up of carbon dioxide and chlorine gas in a sunken submarine still had to be overcome. The very nature of the submarine requires that it remains submerged for extended periods, where the submarine's atmosphere is constantly being contaminated by carbon dioxide from the crew's respiration, as well as by smoking, cooking, hydrogen from battery charging, and hydrocarbons from oil from the running machinery. To be totally independent of the surface submarines need to remove all of these contaminants from the atmosphere, which then has to be rejuvenated with a supply of fresh oxygen. Until the advent of more sophisticated systems, rejuvenation relied almost entirely on the use of oxygen candles.

In a flooding boat, contamination of the batteries by seawater will result in large quantities of hydrogen gas, a highly poisonous substance, being produced. Special equipment was therefore required to allow the crew to survive long enough in a crippled submarine to affect an escape before being overcome by the toxic gases.

The development in 1878 of the Fleuss-Davis self-contained breathing apparatus went some way to overcoming this problem. This portable closed circuit system utilised a chemical cartridge to absorb the carbon dioxide emitted from exhaled breath. A high-pressure cylinder then provided a small amount of oxygen to the facemask to revitalise the inhaled air. Although effective, the system was extremely bulky, especially within the confines of the small submersibles then in service.

Almost 30 years later, the British Admiralty patented the Hall-Rees apparatus, which used sodium peroxide to absorb carbon dioxide and produce small quantities of oxygen. However, a major disadvantage of this system was the highly inflammable nature of sodium peroxide when brought into contact with water.

The next design of breathing apparatus to appear was the Drager Lung, developed in Germany in 1912. This portable self-contained apparatus utilised a caustic potash air purification cartridge to filter out carbon dioxide, and remained in service in German Navy U-boats until after World War Two.

In 1929, the Fleuss-Davis equipment was further developed into the smaller Davis Submerged Escape Apparatus (DSEA), which remained in service with several navies for many decades. A small cylinder provided the wearer with a 30-minute supply of oxygen, the exhaled carbon dioxide being directed via the mouthpiece and a diverting valve to a receptacle containing a chemical purifying agent, filtered air then being mixed with fresh oxygen before being inhaled by the wearer. The apparatus also incorporated a buoyancy bag and drogue that would enable the escaping submariner to control his ascent to the surface. A nose clip and goggles were also provided. Besides it's primary use by escaping crewmen, the apparatus could also be used for fire-fighting purposes in a limited capacity.

It was not long before the DSEA was put to the test. On 9 June 1931, the British submarine *HMS Poseidon* (P99) sank after a collision with the merchant vessel *ss Yuta* 21 miles off Wei Hai Wei in the North China Sea. Of the submarine's 55 crewmen, only 27 managed to escape before it sank to the bottom 40 metres below. By flooding their compartment, six of the submariners donned DSEA and successfully escaped to the surface, although two of them died in the attempt. Consequently, the apparatus became standard equipment aboard Royal Navy submarines.

Also in 1929, another portable breathing apparatus based on the Fleuss-Davis closed cycle principle was developed by Momsen, know as the Momsen Lung. This equipment differed from the DSEA by being connectable to a central oxygen ringmain inside the submarine in order to top up the equipment's reservoir just before its use for escape. It saw extensive service with the U.S. Navy.

Also developed around this time was the collapsible twill trunk, which could be pulled down to form an airlock on the underside of the submarine's hatches. This allowed a compartment to be flooded and, once the pressure inside and outside of the hull had equalised and the water level inside the compartment stabilised, would allow the personnel within to duck below the skirt of the twill trunk and swim out through the submarine's hatch to carry out a free ascent escape to the surface. This was known as the compartment escape.

The adoption of twill trunks, coupled with improved training in the use of breathing apparatus typified by the DSEA, the Momsen Lung and the Drager Lung, greatly improved the survivability of submariner's following the sinking of their boats. However, the policy in the Royal Navy remained that submariners should not, unless absolutely necessary, affect an escape until they were sure that assistance was at hand. This policy was changed in March 1934, following an announcement by the First Lord of the Admiralty to the House of Commons that trapped submariners would be allowed to use their own judgement and initiative in determining when it was safe to execute an escape from a sunken submarine. It was also announced that submarine escape training was to be enhanced with the building of escape training towers at Gosport, Hong Kong and Malta.

Later submarines were designed with fore and aft escape chambers and with flooding valves and emergency buoys (of which the Germans had seen the potential as early as 1912). The first U.S. Navy submarines to incorporate floodable escape chambers were the three V-class boats *Barracuda*, *Bass* and *Bonita* (SS163-165), launched in 1924/25. Later submarines of the Royal Navy's T-class were also fitted with two-man escape chambers forward and aft. These cylindrical structures were fitted with three sets of operating controls, allowing their operation from inside and outside the chamber. During the Second World War it became common practice to bolt down some escape hatches to prevent their inadvertent opening during a depth-charge attack.

After the War, the Ruck-Keene committee was set up in Britain to investigate all aspects of submarine safety. Most of their proposals were subsequently adopted, not only by the Royal Navy, but also by most of the world's submarine operating nations. One-man escape chambers were to be fitted in all submarines, immersion suits were to be developed to keep submariners afloat and improve their chances of survival, incorporating a flashing light to aid detection by rescue forces, and the free ascent method of escape was to be further developed, as in the U.S. Navy, phasing out use of the DSEA.

A new 100 foot deep tank, similar to one already in service with the U.S. Navy, was to be built at *HMS Dolphin* in Gosport to train submariners in free ascent escape techniques. The new tower still dominates Fort Blockhouse on the Gosport skyline and has been used to train generations of submariners. In the free ascent escape method, trapped submariners in a stricken boat were to calculate how long they could survive on the available air supplies. If rescue ships did not appear, escapees were to don life jackets and exit the boat through the escape chambers and rise to the surface.

Sadly, none of these innovations could be incorporated before the next tragedy struck the Royal Navy Submarine Service, the loss of *HMS Truculent* (P315) in a collision in the River Thames on 12 January 1950. This disaster accelerated the introduction into service of air purification equipment, immersion suits, indicator buoys, signal ejectors, underwater telephones, detectors to give warning of the presence of dangerous gases and the Built In Breathing System (BIBS). This system has been adopted by a large number of navies, including most of the NATO submarine forces. The pressure hulls of most modern submarines are divided into two separate sections by a watertight bulkhead of similar strength to the pressure hull itself, usually between the control room and torpedo room. Each of the two sections incorporates an escape tower and a self-breathing apparatus. The BIBS comprises of a bank of bottles containing a mixture of 40% oxygen and 60% nitrogen, this mixture being fed through a ringmain to multiple connections around the boat into which the crew's face masks can be plugged, there being enough of these fittings to supply 133% of the crew so that every man should have the use of one in an emergency. Connections are also provided in the escape trunks.

Using this system, an escapee will don a life jacket and enter the escape tower, where he will breathe in as much air as possible as the trunk is flooded. When the pressure inside the tower equalises with that outside the hull the upper hatch is opened and the escapee will carry out a free ascent to the surface, remembering to exhale hard during the ascent to compensate for expansion of the air in his lungs as he ascends and the pressure on his body decreases. The tower is then isolated and drained down before the next man carries out his escape.

The escape chamber was a major improvement over the earlier twill trunk. When using the twill trunk, the escaping crew would don facemasks and plug them into the BIBS. The twill trunk would be unfolded to within a few feet from the deck and the compartment flooded until the pressure inside and outside the hull equalised. The level at which the water inside the compartment stabilised would depend on the submarine's depth. Each of the escapees within the compartment would be subjected to the high pressure pertaining to the submarine's depth for as long as it took for their turn to come to escape as they 'hose fleeted' between BIBS connections one after the other towards the twill trunk. The last men to leave the compartment would therefore spend an extended period subjected to the high pressure and were likely to be subjected to the 'bends'.

The bends is a condition that can occur when oxygen seeps into a person's bloodstream due to external pressure on the body, producing nitrogen bubbles in the bloodstream that will expand as the escapee rises to the surface, causing extreme pain and even death.

However, with the escape chamber, the escapee would be subjected to the extreme pressure for only as long as it would take to flood the chamber - probably only a few minutes - before the upper hatch opened and he rose to the surface. The danger of suffering from the bends was therefore very much reduced.

In the 1960s the Royal Navy carried out a series of trials with the Hood Inflation System (HIS). This system comprises a bank of air reservoirs located outside the boat's pressure hull, feeding compressed air via a series of charging connections and filters inside the submarine to HIS/BIBS inflation connections inside the escape chamber. A cotton fabric hood with a plastic facemask was tested from a depth of 200 feet. Air trapped in the hood would permit an escapee to breath normally during the ascent to the surface. The system could also be used for inflation of immersion suits immediately prior to escape.

The feasibility of escape from a stricken submarine anywhere on the European Continental Shelf was proved in July 1970, when 79 men, using the HIS, carried out a series of free ascent escapes from the submerged *HMS Osiris* (S13) at a depth of up to 600 feet in the Mediterranean while the boat was moving at 3 knots. Subsequently the Royal Navy Escape System has been installed in the submarines of several NATO and foreign navies.

Most of the world's submarine services have now adopted the combination of the escape chamber and the immersion suit. The immersion suit, developed in Britain, is a complete personal survival system, comprising an inflatable quilted suit and incorporating a hood, an integral $CO_2$ bottle and a water activated light.

The escape routine is a simple and frequently practised procedure. Having donned the immersion suit, the escapee will enter the escape chamber, closing the lower hatch behind him. He will then inflate his immersion suit from the tower's air connection via a connector in the suit's cuff. The suit incorporates a relief valve that will open when the pressure inside it reaches a certain level, exhausting into the suit's hood to provide the wearer with a breathable air supply. When this operation is complete the chamber is flooded and the escapee will be subject to a rapid increase in pressure,

up to the stage when the pressure equalises with that outside the submarine.

The upper hatch is then opened and the escapee begins his ascent to the surface at a speed of around 2.5m/s.

His self-sealing cuff connection will be automatically disengaged as he leaves the chamber. Because the bottom of the suit's hood is open, the hood pressure remains the same as that of the sea pressure around it during the ascent and the wearer can breath normally. The outer hatch of the chamber is closed from inside the submarine and the chamber drained in preparation for the next escapee. The immersion suit is designed to retain the wearer's body temperature, and also keeps him floating horizontally, the face visor keeping water from his face. By delaying escape until sure that rescue forces are in the vicinity, the survivor can reduce the amount of time he will have to spend in the water, and so increase his chances of survival even further.

Some submarines, notably those of German design, are provided with an inflatable raft, which can be released from the boat in its pressure-proof container to provide escapees on the surface with a further survival aid.

The Mark 10 Submarine Escape and Immersion Equipment (SEIE), developed from the earlier Mark 8, was introduced into Royal Navy service during 1994 and has been specially designed to allow survival in the bitter temperatures encountered in the North Atlantic in winter. Regarded as the optimum in survival suits, it provides submariners with a means of escape from any depth down to 180 metres and will allow the wearer to survive on the surface for at least 24 hours. It is also suitable for wear when abandoning a submarine on the surface. The hood is inflated with $CO_2$, whilst the separate front and back inflation cavities can be inflated with $CO_2$ from individual cylinders. This latest version also incorporates a single-seat life

*The Mk10 Submarine Escape and Immersion Equipment (SEIE); introduced into Royal Navy service during 1994, has been designed to allow survival in the bitter temperatures encountered in the North Atlantic in winter. A later version also incorporates a single-seat life raft.*
*(Beaufort Air-Sea Equipment Ltd)*

raft, with a gas-inflated buoyancy chamber, a canopy and a water-activated battery/lamp.

The above systems permit escape from depths of around 180 metres, although immersion suits could probably be used from depths of about 230 metres in extreme cases. This will permit escape from most areas of the continental shelves, and so is seen as sufficient by most navies. Where greater depths are involved, the assistance of Deep Submergence Rescue Vehicles (DSRV) will be required. With this in mind, the hatch of at least one escape chamber of most submarines is capable of docking a suitable DSRV.

In addition to the SEIE, the Royal Navy has also introduced the Personal Locator Beacon Submarine (PLB(S)). Three of these devices are stowed in the submarine's forward and aft escape compartments. As the crew conduct their free escape from a stricken boat, assigned personnel will attach the beacon to their belt. The beacon will then transmit a signal to the international COSPAS-SARSAT search and rescue satellite, alerting rescue services to their position.

The need for some form of air purification system became evident during World War Two, when submarines operating in the North Atlantic had to remain submerged for extended periods to avoid detection. A small fan with soda lime canisters in its air-stream was the first such device, absorbing $CO_2$ from the boat's atmosphere.

With the advent of nuclear submarines in the 1950s, which could remain dived for weeks on end, the storage of the large quantities of soda lime became impracticable. One method available to remove $CO_2$ was using a substance of the amine family, monothanolamine, which can absorb $CO_2$ when in a cold state. Air is drawn through monothanolamine-soaked foam absorbers to remove $CO_2$. The monothanolamine is then heated,

when it will release this $CO_2$, which is disposed of via a dedicated $CO_2$ compressor. Thus, the cooling and heating process will provide a regenerative $CO_2$ absorption system. Carbon filters in the plant outlet remove any degradation products such as ammonia and peroxides.

The first four boats of the Royal Navy's Trafalgar-class nuclear-powered attack submarines use Molecular Sieves, in which zeolites (microporous crystalline solids) are used to filter the air, $CO_2$ being removed by a vacuum pump. Later boats use a newer plant that mixes air and monothanolamine in the inlet, the mixture then passing through a dense wire mesh, where the $CO_2$ is absorbed.

Air purification in a submarine disabled on the seabed, when power may not exist, will prevent the use of normal air purification plants. In this case consumable carbon dioxide absorbers will be needed. These include soda lime, sodium hydroxide, baralyme and lithium hydroxide. The first of these is judged to be the most cost effective, and is utilised in the Mk.III carbon dioxide absorption plant fitted in all Royal Navy submarines for use in emergencies. Lithium hydroxide units are used in the submarines of some NATO navies. Sufficient supplies of the substance to provide around a week's survival are usually stored in the vicinity of each of a submarine's escape chambers. New carbon dioxide absorption units are fitted with a cycle-type arrangement to power the unit in an emergency when no ship's power is available.

The Russian Navy uses superoxide air-regeneration cartridges, the superoxide reacting with moisture in the air to absorb $CO_2$ and emit oxygen. However, as was discovered following the *Kursk* tragedy in 2000, contamination of the cartridges with oil-contaminated water may result in a violent chemical reaction and a fire, adding a new threat to the precarious position of survivors. To avoid such an occurrence, the Royal Navy has recently replaced their Mk.V oxygen candles with a safer model, in which the Sodium Chlorate fuel is sealed within the canister, thereby reducing the fire risk from oil contamination.

The charging of batteries, especially in conventional submarines, produces hydrogen and carbon monoxide into the boat's atmosphere. These dangerous substances are removed by a number of catalytic burners distributed around the boat, maintaining a hydrogen concentration of less than 2% by volume. The concentration of carbon monoxide should be less that 15-parts-per-million.

Carbon filters are also fitted to remove hydrocarbons and smells from within the boat.

The employment of such systems means that the crew of a crippled submarine can survive for much longer periods before attempting an escape, giving time for rescue vessels to reach the area and so improve the escapees' chances of survival after escape.

In the 1980s the Soviet Navy fitted some of its submarines with an innovative escape system, the escape capsule. One boat so equipped was the prototype nuclear-powered submarine *Komsomolets*, which tragically sank following a fire off northern Norway in April 1989 with the loss of 42 crewmen. The advanced 40 feet-long escape capsule was built into the submarine's conning tower, with access from the submarine via a hatch in the control room, with passage to the bridge through the capsule. The capacity of the capsule was probably of sufficient size to accommodate most, if not all, of the 69-man crew. Unfortunately, for a variety of reasons, the chamber failed to save the lives of the crew aboard the *Komsomolets*.

Nevertheless, escape chambers are now a common feature in newer classes of nuclear-powered submarines in the Russian Navy, including the Project 941 ('Typhoon'-class), Project 667BDRM ('Delta-IV'-class), Project 949A ('Oscar-II'-class), Project 971 ('Akula'-class) and Project 945 ('Sierra'-class).

The fitting of escape capsules in all future submarines would be a major step forward in the submarine escape world. However, it was perhaps a design flaw that *Komsomolets'* capsule was used as a passage to the boat's bridge. Future designs could be fitted in the after section of the submarine's fin, where its use would be purely reserved for emergencies.

The present trend towards a greater degree of automation aboard modern submarine designs, resulting in the requirements for smaller crews, means that an escape capsule need not be of excessive size. The fitting of the capsule would have to be incorporated at the submarine's design stage. Fairing the equipment into the boat's fin would insure a minimum effect on the vessel's operational efficiency. Combined with the provision of immersion suits for use should the escape capsule be defective or damaged, the chances of survival of submariners aboard a crippled submarine would be substantially improved. Nevertheless, there remain two major drawbacks to the incorporation of escape capsules: the necessary increase in the size of the submarine to accommodate it; and the resultant increase in building cost.

Whether these problems are insurmountable is based on how much insurance a country feels is needed to ensure the safety of its submarine crews. Despite any other failings that the Russian Navy may have, they at least consider the inclusion of such devices worthy of the expense.

RESCUE

Before a rescue operation can be initiated, the rescue services have to be alerted. Most countries have Coast Guards, whose staffs constantly monitor radio channels for any distress or SOS signals. These include the VHF distress circuit on VHF channel 16 (156.8MHz), as well as the other main HF international distress frequency on 2182kHz. The most commonly used distress signal since 1912 has been the transmission in Morse of the letters SOS followed by the ship's position on 500kHz, a frequency monitored by all ships and coastal stations during the 20th century. An alternative was the transmission of the word 'Mayday' on 2182kHz, primarily used today by small coastal craft. Locator beacons also use the aeronautical distress frequency on 243MHz a frequency monitored by aircraft. Submarines have their own dedicated international submarine safety frequency, 8364kHz, on which submarine indicator buoys also transmit.

In 1979 the International Maritime Organisation (IMO) was tasked with the development of a Global Maritime Distress and Safety System (GMDSS). Adopted by almost all of the world's maritime nations, the system utilises a combination of satellite and terrestrial radio services and has largely replaced the use of Morse code. Since 1 February 1999, the Safety of Life at Sea (SOLAS) Convention has required that all ships carry NAVTEX and satellite Emergency Position-Indicating Radio Beacons (EPIRBs). The USA, Canada, Russia and France have also jointly developed a 406MHz satellite EPIRB as an element of the GMDSS designed to operate with the COSPAS-SARSAT system. Now a mandatory fit on all SOLAS ships, including commercial fishing vessels, the GMDSS will automatically transmit identification and position of any ship in distress to a rescue coordination centre on VHF maritime channel 70 (156.525MHz). This automatic system has now negated the requirement of GMDSS-equipped ship's crews to constantly monitor VHF channel 16, although ships are still, at least for the time being, required to keep a listening watch on 2182kHz.

The transmission and reception of any distress signal should bring all available ships in the vicinity to the rescue, usually co-ordinated by the nearest Coast Guard station. Apart from Coast Guard vessels, lifeboats, and naval and merchant ships, the assistance of maritime patrol aircraft and the helicopters of all services may be requested. As well as search and life-saving operations, these assets may be called upon to render fire-fighting and damage-control assistance, which may ultimately lead to the salvage of the damaged vessel.

Until the advent of GMDSS, in cases where a vessel was overwhelmed by an unexpected phenomenon such as a freak wave or an explosion, it may not have been possible to transmit an SOS or 'Mayday' signal before the vessel foundered. In such cases, rescue services were not alerted until the vessel became overdue at its expected position or failed to transmit a routine message to report its position or its Estimated Time of Arrival (ETA) at its intended destination.

It was with such incidents involving submarines in mind that the Royal Navy in 1931 instigated its 'Subsunk' organisation, which required that every submarine signal its position and estimated surfacing time and position immediately prior to submerging. Failure of a submarine to make such a routine 'Subcheck' report after surfacing would result in a 'Comcheck' signal being broadcast in an attempt to regain contact with the boat. An inability to regain contact would result in a 'Subsmash' signal being instigated from the Submarine HQ at Northwood, near London, to the base nearest the incident in order that a search could begin. This procedure was later modified to include a 'Submiss' signal being issued an hour after the submarine was suspected as missing. An hour later, the 'Subsunk' signal would instigate a full air and sea search for the missing boat, involving all vessels and aircraft in the vicinity.

The 'Subsunk' procedure, in continually refined form, is still in use today, having been adopted by almost all of the world's submarine operating navies, including those of the former Warsaw Pact. Most countries have their own dedicated organisations for co-ordinating submarine rescue, which in Britain is the Standing Committee on Submarine Escape and Rescue (SCOSER).

All submarines now carry indicator buoys, which incorporate automatic radio transmitters as well as a flashing light and radar reflector, which can be released from the boat in an emergency. Once on the surface, the indicator buoy will guide searchers to the area, saving the ships or aircraft valuable hours, or even days, and thereby increasing the chances of a speedy and effective rescue operation.

Such a device in was tested by the Royal Navy in 1953 aboard the submarine *HMS Andrew* (S63), with the first boat fitted operationally with the buoy being *HMS Seraph* (S89). Special valves and connections were also fitted on the pressure hull so that rescue vessels could connect an airline through which oxygen could be injected into the stricken submarine, and so sustain the lives of the trapped crew whilst their rescue was affected. This particular component had been fitted to earlier submarines, but the practice had been dropped by the Royal Navy in 1931, an oversight which was to cost the lives of many submariners such as the 99 men who succumbed to carbon dioxide poisoning aboard *HMS Thetis* in June 1939.

Royal Navy submarines carry two Type 639 indicator buoys that can be released from a disabled submarine. On reaching the surface, the radio contained in these buoys will transmit an international distress signal. Type 680 Emergency Communications Buoys are also carried and can be fired from ejectors in the escape compartments. The new Type 2073 underwater telephone/pinger has now been deployed which, mounted in the submarine's escape compartment, transmits a multi-frequency distress signal. The signal frequency of the device can be adjusted to act as an underwater telephone, providing voice communication with rescue vessels. Selected escapees are also provided with personnel locator beacons, which transmit on the same frequency as the communications buoys. Similar locator beacons are carried on ships' lifeboats and inflatable life rafts.

Underwater telephones are fitted to almost all modern submarines and are being continually improved. Working on the same principle as sonar, they generally have a range of several miles, dependant on the presence of thermal layers in the sea.

There are two ways in which a survivor can evacuate a disabled submarine. The first method is by the use of the escape chamber, a method already discussed. However, in deeper waters beyond the continental shelves, the trapped submariners will have to await the arrival on the scene of a dedicated rescue vessel equipped with a diving bell or rescue submersible. With this in mind some navies have tended to concentrate on the development of rescue methods, as well as the survival of crew in a stranded submarine until a rescue can be affected. This period could be up to four days, or even longer if the position of the sunken boat is not known.

In the early 1930s the U.S. Navy began development of Lieutenant-Commander Allen McCann's escape bell. The bell comprises a shell with two vertical compartments that could be lowered to a stricken submarine and attached to one of the boat's hatches. The lower section, open to the sea until sealed to the submarine's hatch and pumped dry, can be used as an airlock, allowing up to eight personnel at a time to be transferred from the submarine to the bell's upper compartment and then winched to safety.

The chamber is connected to the mother ship via a number of umbilicals including lift, air, electricity and communications lines. A haul-down cable, secured to an eye-plate located near to the submarine's hatch, allows the nine-ton rescue chamber to return to the submerged boat time after time under complete control. The other end of the cable is secured to a winch inside the almost spherical 10 feet high by 7 feet diameter lower chamber. Water inside the lower section is displaced into a special ballast tank on reaching the submarine, thus neutralising the positive buoyancy of the chamber. The rescue procedure requires the diving tender to be secured in the same fore-and-aft axis to the stricken boat.

This equipment was first used in an emergency when, on 23 May 1939, the submarine *USS Squalus* (SS-192) sank in 240 feet of water off the Isle of Shoals , New Hampshire, after the failure of a main induction valve. Thirty-three survivors from the crew of 62 were successfully rescued, and *Squalus* was later salvaged, repaired, and re-commissioned as *USS Sailfish*.

A limitation of the McCann rescue bell is that it can only be used if the disabled submarine is relatively intact and within a few degrees of an upright position or else the gasketed skirt will not seal. Moreover, the operating depth of the latest version of the McCann chamber, the Submarine Rescue Chamber (SRC), is restricted to

around 250-metres by the requirement for divers to make the connections to the submarine and guide the chamber. Nevertheless, the SRC is still in use in the US, Italian and Turkish Navies today.

In the summer of 1954 the Royal Navy converted the salvage vessel *King Salvor* into the submarine rescue ship *Kingfisher* (A291), which was equipped with a diving bell. However, her diving bell was never to be used for the purpose originally intended as no submarines were modified to accept it because the alteration of the submarines to accept the bell would have seriously interfered with their internal layout. Instead, the individual free-ascent escape method via escape chambers was

*The US Navy's Submarine Rescue Chamber (SRC) is lowered to the water from the MV Kendrick for a diving and docking manoeuvre with the Japanese submarine Akishio during Exercise Pacific Reach 2000.*

*(US Navy)*

*The US Navy 21-ton Deep Submergence Vehicle Turtle (DSV 3), is raised from the deck of the Military Sealift Command's Submarine Support Vessel MV Dolores Chouest at Naval Air Station North Island, California, following trials in 1990.*
*(US Navy)*

preferred. Also, *Kingfisher*'s low speed of only ten knots would mean that she would take too long to reach the scene of a rescue operation unless she was lucky enough to be in the immediate vicinity at the time of the incident. Consequently, the ship was used primarily for training purposes.

There was clearly a need for a vehicle that could manoeuvre independently of a mother ship and in 1957 the US Office of Naval Research chartered the bathyscaphe *Trieste*, which had been completed four years earlier in the Italian port of the same

name. *Trieste* was purchased outright by the U.S. Navy the following year and refitted with a new pressure sphere to increase its diving depth from 6,000-metres to 11,000-metres, being re-designated a Deep Submergence Vehicle. This new depth capability was proven on 23 January 1960, when it was piloted into the Marianas Trench off Guam. It was then used extensively during the search for *USS Thresher* in 1964, after which it was again rebuilt at Mare Island Naval Shipyard and renamed *Trieste II*. In 1969 it was re-designated *X-2* and again as *DSV-1* in 1971. *Trieste II* was taken out of service in 1984 and is now on display at the Naval Undersea Museum in Keyport, Washington.

A series of other DSVs were built for the U.S. Navy. *Alvin* was completed in 1965 and with a diving depth of over 4,000-metres, it could hold three men in its 6.9-metre long streamlined hull. The next, *Turtle*, was completed the following year and had a 3,000-metres diving depth. The titanium-hulled *Sea Cliff* followed in 1969, with a diving depth of 6,100-metres. These vehicles were re-designated *DSV-2*, *DSV-3* and *DSV-4*

*The Deep Submergence Rescue Vehicle Mystic (DSRV-1) being lowered on to a cradle aboard USS Dallas at Askaz Naval Base in Turkey in August 2000. The craft's skirt, which mates with the submarine's escape hatch, can be clearly seen in this view.*
*(US Navy)*

respectively in 1971.

Two weeks after the loss of *Thresher*, the U.S. Navy formed the Deep Submergence Systems Review Group. In 1966 the first two of a planned series of six Deep Submergence Rescue Vehicles (DSRVs) were ordered from Lockheed Missiles and Space Company in Sunnyvale, California. *Mystic* (DSRV-1) and *Avalon* (DSRV-2) were completed in August 1971 and July 1972 at a cost of $41 and US$23million respectively. Unfortunately, due to their huge cost and financial restraints the other four vessels were cancelled. Each of the 37-ton submersibles has sonar and closed-circuit television, and can accommodate 24 survivors in addition to its three crewmen. Its ingenious skirt can mate with a disabled boat's escape hatch with the submarine lying at an angle of up to 45°. Their triple-sphere pressure hulls, constructed of HY-140 steel, gives them a maximum operating depth of over 1,500-metres. *Avalon* is now laid up, leaving the *Mystic* as the only DSRV available for use to the U.S. Navy.

*Mystic* can be transported to the required area by road, on C-141 Starlifter or C-5 Galaxy transport aircraft, or in piggy-back fashion aboard selected submarines such as the Los Angeles-class nuclear-powered boats *USS Dallas* (SSN-700) and *USS La Jolla* (SSN 701), on a cradle abaft the sail.

Since 1979, the Royal Navy, under a Memorandum of Understanding, has had the opportunity to call on the use of the U.S. Navy's DSRVs, which the Resolution-class SSBNs could carry mated to their after escape towers - a capability that has now been adopted by the new Vanguard-class SSBNs. All US and Royal Navy submarines and French SSBNs can accept the DSRV on their escape towers. From its base in San Diego, the DSRV can be flown to the UK and be teamed with one of the SSBNs within 48 hours, ready to sail to the rescue

area. On arrival in the area the DSRV would disengage from the SSBN, descend to the distressed submarine, mate with one of its escape towers, de-water, embark up to 24 personnel, disengage and return to the mother boat. If decompression of escapees were required then they would enter the mother-SSBN by the forward escape tower. A decompression system that can mate with submarine escape towers is under development.

The Royal Navy has also developed its own submersible, the nine-man *LR5*, which is operated by the commercial contractors James Fisher Rumic Ltd on the Royal Navy's behalf and can be deployed from a variety of vessels. In August 2000, *LR5* was deployed to the Barents Sea aboard the mother ship *Normand Pioneer II* to prepare for the rescue of the survivors of the *Kursk*. Although the LR5 was not utilised during the *Kursk* incident, the Royal Navy Submarine Rescue Service's assistance was again called upon five years later, after a Russian mini-submarine became trapped 190-metres below the surface of Berezovaya Bay, Kamchatka. The highly-skilled team immediately despatched their *Scorpio* Remotely Operated Vehicle (ROV), which was then deployed to cut

*The British rescue submersible LR5 being lowered into the water by a crane from the Finnish ship Fennica during the NATO exercise Sorbet Royal 2005. In August 2000 LR5 was deployed to the Barents Sea in an attempt to rescue survivors of the Kursk.*

*(US Navy)*

up to ten knots and can accommodate up to 25 personnel. An additional feature of *URF-1* is it's lock-out capability, which can support two divers at depths of up to 300-metres.

The navies of Australia, China, France, Italy, Japan, South Korea and Russia operate other rescue submersibles, the South Korean *LR5K* being based on the UK's *LR5*. However, with the exception of the American DSRV, all of the above systems are carried by surface ships, so restricting their deployment in high seas states.

One of the most innovative designs is that of the Australian Navy's *Remora* DSRV. Unmanned, this Remote-Operated Vehicle (ROV) can rescue up to six submariners from a depth of 500-metres, whilst it's ingenious skirt design can mate with a submarine lying at an angle of up to 60°. An enlarged version of the *Remora* is to be built as part of the U.S. Navy's Submarine Rescue Diving and Recompression System (SRDRS) to replace the aging *Mystic* in 2006. The SRDRS is able to rescue fifteen personnel at depths of up to 600-metres and will be transportable in standard ISO containers for rapid airlift to the rescue area.

free the 13-metre long Priz-class boat *AS-28*, which had become entangled in a fishing net during a training mission. On Sunday 7 August 2005, the *AS-28* and her 7-man crew were finally rescued, 76 hours after having become stranded on the seabed.

Other navies have also shown an interest in acquiring their own rescue submersibles, including the Swedish *URF*, launched at the Kockums Yard at Malmö in August 1978. Deployable from the submarine rescue and salvage ship *Belos III* (A211), *URF-1* displaces 50 tonnes and its HY130 steel hull gives it a diving depth of 460-metres, with a collapse depth of twice that figure. The vessel can be towed to the rescue area at

Following several delays in construction, *HMS Challenger* (K07) was commissioned in 1988 for the deployment and support of the Royal Navy's Saturation Diving System. For this purpose she carried a submersible compression chamber, deployable through a moonpool to a depth 300 metres. She could also deploy and recover manned and unmanned submersibles from the large stern A-frame to a depth of more than 3,000 metres. A Dynamic Positioning System, together with Voith Schneider propulsors aft and bow thrusters forward allowed the 7,200-tonne vessel to maintain a set position in up to sea state 5. The ship was also fitted with sonar for detection of objects on the seabed. Omega and Delta Hyperfix 6

navigation systems allow the position of these objects to be plotted with an accuracy of five metres. Beacons dropped to the seabed and hydrophones on the ship's hull could then help the vessel maintain its position. A flight deck was fitted aft, which could handle helicopters of up to Sea King size.

The Saturation Diving System allowed up to twelve divers to be pre-compressed in compression chambers prior to their lowering to the seabed in a submersible compression chamber. Divers could then live between the onboard compression chambers and the submersible compression chambers for several weeks at a time without the need for lengthy decompression after each dive. At the end of the mission the divers could be decompressed slowly, a process which can take up to ten days for decompression from a depth of 300 metres. A manned submersible utilising a diver lock-out facility could, when carried, operate in the same way.

*Challenger* had obvious value in the event of a submarine disaster. Unfortunately, defence cuts forced the Royal Navy to decommission the ship in 1991 and and it was sold to the commercial sector, where she is now (2008) operated as the diamond mining vessel *mv Ya Toivo*. This deprived the Royal Navy of a valuable diving capability and they, along with several other navies, now rely mainly on commercially available ships for search and salvage operations.

The Russian Navy, which still operates one of the world's largest submarine fleets, has developed a number of special salvage and rescue submersibles. Completed in 1979 and 1980, one of two specialist Project 940 ('India'-class) submarines served with the Soviet Pacific Fleet, the other with the Northern Fleet. Each submarine could carry two salvage and rescue submersibles in semi-recessed wells abaft the sail structure. The submersibles, which could be entered and launched directly from the mother submarine whilst submerged, could mate with the escape hatches of most modern Russian submarines. However, the Project 940 boats became victims of the harsh economic climate in the post-'Cold War' Russian Navy and have been scrapped.

Similar submersibles to those that were carried on the Project 940 boats were carried aboard the three Russian Project 537 El'Brus-class salvage and rescue ships completed in the early-1980s, which, with a displacement of over 15,000 tonnes, were the biggest vessels of their type in the world. *El'Brus* was stationed with the Black Sea Fleet and *Alagez* with the Pacific Fleet, whilst a third vessel of the class was handed over to the Ukrainian Navy. However, only the *Alagez* is now considered operational. The decimated Russian submarine rescue service was found totally unprepared to react to the *Kursk* disaster in 2000 and now consists of mainly of one *Bester* and five *Priz* submersibles.

Smaller and less capable salvage and rescue ships are in service with several submarine-operating navies, most of which are equipped with variants of the McCann diving bell and decompression chambers.

The need for stringent economy in defence spending and the occurrence of recent submarine disasters, notably the sinking of the Peruvian submarine *Pacocha* in 1988 and the loss of the Soviet *Komsomolets* the following year, spurred the NATO nations into a joint study for a future submarine rescue system. The pre-feasibility study, concluded in January 1992, involved 42 companies from eight countries, including the UK, Canada, France, Germany, Italy, the Netherlands, Spain and the USA. The aim of the study, under the co-ordination of NATO's Submarine Escape and Rescue Working Party (SMERWP) was to develop a rescue

The Norwegian Coastguard vessel HARSTAD is seen on the Clyde with the new NATO Submarine Rescue System (NSRS) embarked on the stern for initial trials. The orange gantry is the Portable Launch and Recovery System (PLARS), while the Submarine Rescue Vehicle (SRV) itself can be seen on the deck below the gantry.
(Dave Cullen)

system to replace manned rescue submersibles such as the US DSRVs, the French *Licorne*, the Italian *Usel* and the British *LR5*, all of which are nearing the end of their service lives. Originally intended to enter service in 1998, a £47-million contract was finally placed in June 2004 for the NATO Submarine Rescue System (NSRS) for the UK, France and Norway, due to enter full operational service during 2008. The rescue system consists of four components; the intervention remotely operated vehicle (IROV), the Submarine Rescue Vehicle (SRV), the Portable Launch and Recovery System (PLARS) and the Transfer Under Pressure System (TUPS). All four components can be airlifted and deployed on a suitable mothership.

The system is centred around a 27-tonne submersible (SRV), operated by a crew of three, that can dock with stricken submarines at depths of up to 600-metres.

Also included in the contract is an unmanned craft (IROV) to locate the sunken boat, decompression chambers and all of the required support and medical systems. The NSRS is based at the Royal Navy submarine base at Faslane and will be able to be airlifted to a location near the accident and loaded aboard a suitable vessel for response to emergencies worldwide within 72 hours.

The need for co-operation in submarine rescue efforts has also led to several multi-national exercises in recent years, such as 'Pacific Reach 2000', including naval elements from Japan, Singapore, South Korea and the USA, with observers from Australia, Canada, Chile, China, Indonesia, Russia and the UK. During the exercise, a DSRV from the Japanese Navy submarine depot and rescue ship *Chiyoda* (AS405) successfully mated with the South Korean submarine *Choi Muson* (063) and 'rescued' three crewmen. In September 2000, the Italian, Turkish and U.S. Navies took part in 'Sorbet Royal 2000' off southern Turkey. The Royal Navy had also been due to participate, but *LR5* had been diverted to the Barents Sea after the sinking of the *Kursk*. The 'Sorbet Royal' series of submarine search and rescue exercises, the eighth being 'Sorbet Royal 2005', are multi-national exercises involving Canada, Denmark, France, Greece, Italy, Norway, Poland, United Kingdom and the United States, with other nations able to participate as necessary.

Continuing co-operation and exercises will foster familiarity with equipment and procedures essential in the successful rescuing of submariners, so improving the chances of rescuing the crew of the next submarine to sink.

# SALVAGE TECHNIQUES

Salvage operations generally require the employment of specialist personnel using specialist equipment. However, the term 'salvage operation' covers a wide range of tasks, including those carried out by a well-trained crew when involved in damage-control exercises. Well-executed fire-fighting and breaching and pumping operations on a damaged ship will often save the vessel from foundering and remove the necessity for a more specialised salvage operation.

When the crew of one ship render such assistance to another vessel which subsequently prevents its foundering, the rescuing crew have the right to claim recompense in the form of a salvage award, its amount being commensurate with the salved value of the vessel and its cargo and the degree of assistance rendered. For such a salvage situation to exist, the service offered must be voluntary and must apply to maritime property that is in real danger, not just imminent or supposed. Where the Master or Commanding Officer of a ship in distress is still aboard his ship, he has the right to dictate the degree of assistance, if any, rendered by the crew of the vessel offering it. Once assistance is rendered however, a salvage award will only be made if the rescue attempt is successful - 'no cure, no pay'. Before the salvage attempt is commenced, the Commanding Officer of the distressed vessel will usually be called upon to sign a 'Lloyd's Standard Form of Salvage Agreement' so that the salvers can claim recompense later.

The unwillingness of a ship's captain to surrender his vessel to salvers has in the past resulted in the ship foundering. Such was the case in the *Amoco Cadiz* tanker disaster off the coast of Brittany in March 1978. In the case of a vessel whose entire crew has disembarked, there must be a clear intention by them not to return to their ship before the vessel can be legally considered abandoned. Nevertheless, it should be remembered that it is the duty of every mariner to render assistance to fellow mariners in distress.

The next stage of a salvage operation may involve towing of the stricken vessel to a nearby port or anchorage where more permanent repairs or surveys can be undertaken to determine the fate of the vessel. In the case of a badly damaged ship being in imminent danger of foundering before reaching a safe port with good repair facilities, consideration should be given to beaching the vessel. This event in itself presents its own perils as a beached vessel may still be in danger of capsizing or of sustaining further damage in the form of structural collapse or hull damage. If the ship's hull has sustained only minor damage it may be preferable to beach her on a falling tide, rather than drive her onto a beach. The beach should ideally be of soft sand or shingle and of shallow contour. The vessel should not be driven too far up the beach as this may make the re-floating operation more difficult.

Once beached, the vessel should be suitably secured to prevent her being driven farther onshore by the actions of the sea. This can be achieved by means of anchors and cables, or by scuttling her so that the extra weight of the water within her hull holds her firm on the shore.

However, we are not interested here in the basic damage-control type operations as these have been considered elsewhere in this book, but rather those undertaken after a vessel has grounded, been beached or has foundered. Such salvage operations were undertaken on a massive scale in the immediate post-war period to clear hundreds of wrecks from in and around harbours and estuaries all around the world. Many of the same principles still apply today.

Beached or Grounded Vessels

Before any attempt is made to re-float a beached or grounded vessel it will first be necessary to carry out repairs to any damage affecting the vessel's watertight integrity and stability. This may be a simple matter of fitting temporary patches over a breached hull and the removal of floodwater to regain watertight integrity, or the removal of ship's fittings, equipment or cargo high in the vessel to increase buoyancy, so that the vessel may be towed to a nearby port with sufficient repair facilities to effect a more permanent repair or where a detailed survey of the vessel's damage may be carried out. In the case of more seriously damaged vessels, it may require major structural work be carried out on site, or where the vessel is judged a constructive total loss, it may simply involve the breaking up of the wreck where it lays. Whatever the situation, the advice of a specialist construction or salvage officer should be sought to determine the extent of temporary repairs and the salvage method to be employed.

The easiest and most logical method of re-floating a stranded vessel is to haul her off using other ships, ideally tugs of a suitable size, or by the use of ground tackle and the ship's own winches to haul herself off. These operations will be greatly assisted by a high tide. In the vast majority of minor groundings, especially where the vessel is grounded bow or stern directly on to the beach, these methods may prove successful.

Muddy or sandy beaches may silt up around the hull of a beached ship to such an extent that it well be almost impossible to haul her off. There are several methods that have proved effective in removing such silt to enable re-floating of a stranded vessel.

The first method which may be tried if the silt is not too dense is the use of the propeller wash from small vessels or craft to dredge away the silt around the hull, so permitting the stranded vessel to sink lower into the silt until she regains her buoyancy to such an extent that she may be floated or hauled off of the beach at high tide. The removal of as much weight from the ship as possible will greatly increase the chances of success. This method however, may be ineffective where the beach comprises clay, solid mud or rock. In such a case it is likely that the stranded vessel's hull plating will have suffered major damage and have resulted in the flooding of several compartments.

For vessels more solidly embedded in silt a combination of lightening of the vessel and the use of specialised dredging vessels may be the only means of re-floating. The employment of two dredgers will usually be required if the operation is to be carried out quickly and efficiently. This is a much more time consuming and expensive method, possibly requiring the charter of other ships to remove ammunition or liquids, particularly in the case of some naval auxiliaries such as ammunition ships or tankers, and the cost of such an exercise may be prohibitive and outweigh the value of the vessel.

In many cases, the cause of a vessel grounding will have been bad weather and any salvage attempt may be thwarted until any storm has abated. By this time however, the vessel may have been further battered by the sea and have broken up. In such circumstances the hulk may be de-stored and stripped of valuable items of equipment before being sold for scrapping on-site, or even left to rot where she lays where the site is inaccessible or the cost of breaking-up is prohibitive. Nevertheless, in accordance with the latest MARPOL (MARine POLlution) policies for the protection of the environment, all traces of oil, fuel or other chemicals and minerals will have to be removed from the wreck to prevent a pollution hazard.

## Sunken Vessels

The salvage of sunken vessels presents problems that can only be overcome by the employment of specialist personnel and specialised equipment. This ranges from underwater welding and cutting equipment, compressors, pumps and air-driven tools, to trained divers and specially built ships and craft. The complexity of the operation is determined by many factors: the geographic location of the sunken vessel; the depth of water in which she lies; the presence of any peculiar tidal phenomenon; the weather conditions prevailing; the presence of hazardous materials such as ammunition aboard the vessel; the locality of vital shipping lanes; and the extent of damage to the vessel's watertight structure. With such a variety of factors to consider, no two salvage operations will be the same and the course of action will have to be carefully considered by a skilled salvage officer.

Most salvage operations utilise one or more of the three basic principles of salvage: the recovery of internal buoyancy; the addition of external buoyancy; or the use of an external power lift. The simplest situation will be that of a partially submerged vessel sunk in an upright or near upright condition in shallow water in a relatively sheltered location. It will first be necessary, as in the majority of salvage operations, to carry out temporary repairs to any breaches to the watertight integrity of the hull and seal all possible openings below the surface of the water. The water may then be pumped from the hull until it is re-floated.

Where the vessel is entirely submerged, a series of watertight tower structures, constructed of a suitable material such as steel or aluminium plating or wood of suitable thickness to withstand the pressure of water acting on it, can be built over selected openings, sealed to the vessel at the lower end and extending to above the water's surface. Through these towers, known as cofferdams, the water can then be pumped from the hull using either submersible pumps lowered into the vessel or by using powerful pump suctions from units fitted aboard a salvage vessel.

It may not be possible to make the hull completely watertight and so pumps will probably have to be run continuously. By this method the vessel may regain sufficient buoyancy to float to the surface, where she can be towed to a nearby ship repairers or beached whilst further hull repairs are undertaken.

It may be required, even in the simplest of operations to utilise further special equipment to provide additional buoyancy to raise the vessel, such as pontoons or air bags. Pontoons are normally of cylindrical construction, internally subdivided into two or more chambers, with air hose connections at the upper end and sluice valves at the lower end of each chamber. Internal pipes running vertically through the centre-line of the pontoon will allow the lifting hawsers to pass through them.

In a typical salvage operation utilising pontoons, a red marker buoy will first mark the location of the wreck. Divers will then carry out a detailed survey of the wreck to determine the damage to the vessel's hull, the angle at which it is lying and the how best messenger wires may be passed around the hull, after which the salvage officer will analyse this information, together with plans of the vessel, hydrographic survey data and details of tides and currents, to formulate a plan of action.

Two salvage vessels will be moored, bows facing each other, above and abeam of the wreck. A small messenger wire will then be passed from one vessel,

positioned by divers beneath the bows of the wreck, and taken up by the other vessel. By pulling this wire between the two salvage vessels in a seesaw motion, the wire will be worked beneath the hull of the wreck until in the desired position. Further messenger wires can then be passed under the hull as required. These wires will then be used to haul larger wires beneath the hull, gradually increasing in size until lifting wires of sufficient size, determined by the weight of the wreck and possibly over 12-inches in circumference, are in position.

To speed up the process where multiple cables are required to be positioned, a triangular plate, known by some in the salvage profession as a 'Gosunder', one corner connected to one end of an already positioned messenger wire and the other two corners attached to two further messengers, can be hauled under the

wreck, so replacing one cable for two.

Once in position, the lifting wires can then be passed through the passages of the floating pontoons and secured aboard the salvage vessels. These pontoons are then flooded and located alongside on each beam of the sunken hull. The pontoons are then secured to the wires by suitable clamps. Via the hose connections compressed air can now be blown into the pontoon to eject the water from the pontoon's buoyancy chambers. By carefully regulating the air supply to the pontoons, their buoyancy will increase and slowly lift the wreck to the surface under complete control, the slack in the wires being taken up by the salvage vessels as it rises. To provide additional buoyancy, further air hoses may be connected to certain sealed tanks on the wreck, such as ballast tanks on submarines, and compressed air used to

Survival, Escape, Rescue and Salvage

eject some of the water from them.

However, pontoons tend to be large and unwieldy. Special cylindrical or balloon-shaped air bags are now commonly used, being easily transported and attached to the vessel in their deflated condition, where can be easily inflated. Even so, these rubberised fabric airbags tend to have a smaller capacity of up to around 15-tons, whilst pontoon's can have a capacity in excess of 100-tons, therefore more air bags will be required for a given salvage operation, requiring a correspondingly larger number of cables to be attached to, or passed around, the sunken vessel.

In 1980 a British firm developed an ingenious method of raising vessels from the seabed using nitrogen to expel water from the wreck's ballast tanks, thus providing enough buoyancy to allow it to float to the surface. Adapters and hoses attached to the hull of the sunken vessel by divers permitted the nitrogen to be injected into the hull. Initial tests were carried out with models in a swimming pool. The method was later proved on a small vessel intentionally sunk in the English Channel. The 40-foot ketch rose to the surface minutes after the liquid nitrogen was pumped into it. Following this initial success, a further, more ambitious trial was undertaken in September 1980. The 476-ton supply vessel *Bon Venture*, fitted with four massive insulated nitrogen tanks, was sighted over the wreck of the Norwegian ship *Germa Geisha*, which had foundered in the English Channel in 100 feet of water during a storm six months earlier. The idea was to pump super-cooled liquid nitrogen, which on returning to its gaseous state expands to more than 700-times its volume, into the wreck's ballast tanks. Just a few tons of nitrogen was required to successfully raise the ship.

However, the above methods have several serious limitations. They normally require that the sunken vessel be

in a relatively upright condition. Any hull damage must also be easily plugged to allow floodwater to be expelled from the hull once sealed. Capsized vessels may be raised by these and other methods, but are generally only fit for sale to a shipbreakers. It is possible to right a vessel lying on its side by use of additional pontoons or buoyancy bags on the low side of the hull, selective ballasting of compartments, or hauling her into an upright position by use of strong hawsers. It is more likely however that such a vessel will be raised in the condition in which she lies and deposited on a nearby beach for further repair or breaking.

Some salvage operations, particularly where the hull of the vessel is seriously damaged, may require that the wreck be physically lifted from the seabed. Specialist heavy lift vessels can be utilised for this purpose, normally consisting of a large shallow-draught barge incorporating a large number of ballast tanks, powerful winches, a large shear-leg type lifting frame and a clear uncluttered deck area. They can be used to raise wrecks of several thousand tons displacement from most areas within the confines of continental shelves. Very few of these lifting craft are owned by the world's navies, but are normally chartered as required from specialist salvage companies. They are generally used in conjunction with salvage and mooring vessels, a large number of which are in service with the larger of the world's navies or fleet auxiliary services.

The construction of these ships incorporates twin horns overhanging the stem over which cables can be passed to lift quite heavy loads, powerful winches and extensive mooring arrangements. A large uncluttered deck area is also provided for the lay out of cables. A salvage operation utilising these two types of vessel may proceed as follows:
The two salvage vessels position

385

themselves over the wreck and pass messenger wires beneath the vessel's hull, as described in the pontoon method above. The ends of each messenger wire will then be attached to small buoys and the salvage vessels moved clear to allow the heavy lifting craft to be manoeuvred into position, with the jib or shear legs positioned over the wreck, and securely anchored. With the assistance of the salvage vessels and small boats, the messenger wires will be retrieved and used to pass the lifting wires of suitable size under the wreck. The ends of the lifting wires are then folded over to form 'eyes' by the use of huge clamps, connected to the purchase blocks of the lifting frame at water level and all slack taken up by the powerful lifting winches.

Divers will then carry out final checks before the lifting operation commences. The lifting craft's ballast tanks nearest the wreck may be flooded to increase the draught of the vessel, the resulting slack in the lifting wires being taken up by the lifting winches. By then transferring the ballast water to tanks at the other end of the lifting vessel, thereby altering its trim, the tension in the lifting wires may be sufficient to lift the wreck just clear of the seabed.

Once the wreck appears above the water's surface a more detailed survey of the damage can be undertaken and dangerous materials and classified documents removed. The lifting craft may then recover its moorings and slowly manoeuvre its catch towards a suitable shore where it can be beached at high tide. Here, further surveys and repairs can be carried out, floodwater pumped out and all remaining oil, fuel and ammunition removed.

The above methods are of little use however in extreme depths such as those found in the open oceans. Here, the first major problem is the actual location of the wreck, which can drift for great distances on it's descent to the ocean floor. Following the loss of *USS Thresher* in April 1963, the U.S. Navy prepared the decomposing submarine *Toro* (SS-422) for a trial in which she was to be intentionally scuttled to assess the way in

*A starboard bow view of the guided missile frigate USS Samuel B. Roberts (FFG 58) secured on the deck of the Dutch heavy lift ship Mighty Servant II. The frigate was returning to its home port for damage repair after striking an Iranian mine while on patrol in the Persian Gulf in 1988.*
*(US Navy)*

which a boat would sink when out of control, but the trial was later cancelled.

A search operation would be further complicated by the possibility that the sinking vessel may have imploded on reaching collapse depth and be scattered over a large area. The successful execution of such a salvage operation will require the commitment of huge resources in the form of specialist salvage and hydrographic ships, deep submergence vessels and Remote Operated Vehicles (ROVs). For the recovery of the wreck of the Soviet submarine *K-129* after it sank in the Pacific in April 1968, the U.S. Navy ordered the 'mining ship' *Glomar Explorer* to be specially built by the infamous Howard Hughes. In an operation under the command of the CIA, a 35-feet long section of the ballistic-missile submarine was raised from a depth of around 8,000-feet.

However, even where the necessary equipment and technology is readily available, the huge cost of such an operation precludes the salvage of most wrecks sunk in the sea areas beyond the continental shelves. Such expenditure will normally only be committed to the recovery of sensitive equipment, weapons or materials aboard such vessels as nuclear-powered submarines, or to cases where the value of a vessel's cargo makes the venture financially viable.

For severely damaged vessels, there may not always be a shipyard in the area which can carry out the necessary repairs, or it may be desirable to return the vessel to a Naval Base in it's own country. A relatively new design of ship is available which can transport damaged vessels of several thousand tons displacement, the heavy lift dock ship. A Dutch ship of this type was used to transport the badly damaged frigate *USS Samuel B. Roberts* (FFG-58) from the Gulf of Oman to the USA after she was mined in April 1988. Later that year the Type 42 destroyer *HMS Southampton* (D90) was returned to its Portsmouth base aboard another Dutch heavy lift vessel, *Mighty Servant I*, following her severe damage in collision with a British container ship in the Gulf in September 1988. In October 2000, the

*Heavy-lift dock ships are often used to transport damaged vessels to a suitable port for repair. Here, the destroyer HMS Southampton is returned to Portsmouth aboard the Mighty Servant I after her 1988 collision.*
*(L. van Ginderen)*

destroyer *USS Cole* (DDG 67) was heavily damaged in a terrorist attack in the port of Aden and was returned to Norfolk, Virginia aboard a heavy lift ship. Then, in 2002, another Type 42 destroyer, *HMS Nottingham* (D91), was transported back to Portsmouth from Australia aboard the Dutch-registered heavy lifting vessel *MV Swan*.

These heavy lift ships are able to sink in the water by filling their massive ballast tanks so that the after three-quarters of the vessel is submerged. The damaged ship may then be manoeuvred into position over this section in the same way as it would enter a dry-dock. The heavy lift ship's ballast tanks are then pumped out, lifting the damaged ship clear of the water and then transporting it to its required destination 'piggy-back' style.

As with any intricate operation, constant practise is required to enable skills to be maintained, procedures improved and new techniques evaluated. Salvage operations are no different. Some of these exercises take the form of simple training drills, but other more complicated ones which test the organisation and equipment available to the full need to be carried out periodically.

In 1964 the Royal Navy undertook one of a series of salvage exercises. In one, the surplus Royal Navy submarine ex-*HMS Scotsman* (S143) was deliberately sunk in the Kyles of Bute, western Scotland, so that fresh experience could be gained with the two lifting craft stationed on the River Clyde, which had not been used since the Suez crisis. The *Scotsman* was raised in June 1964 and sold to the West of Scotland Shipbreaking Company.

The U.S. Navy carried out a similar trial five years later off the US Atlantic coast using the old submarine ex-*USS Hake* (AGSS-256). The boat was scuttled on 5 May 1969 in Chesapeake Bay in 100 feet of water and was raised by the salvage craft tender *YRST-2* using YSP wooden salvage pontoons and later towed to Norfolk for further trials. The Royal Navy performed another trial when the decommissioned Porpoise-class boat *Narwhal* was intentionally sunk on 2 June 1980 off Portland, England. She was raised again on 26 June as a salvage exercise by the Swedish heavy lift ship *Herbe III* and two RMAS salvage vessels and the hulk was sold for scrapping.

Such exercises are being undertaken by the majority of the world's major countries on a continual basis, not only by the naval and auxiliary services, but also by the private salvage companies for whom an efficient and well-executed operation can mean huge profits. As long as vessels sail on, or aircraft overfly, the world's oceans, seas and waterways there will be a requirement for salvage operations to be undertaken. The speed of such an operation can be paramount in the saving of human lives or the prevention of an environmental disaster.

# Appendix

# NAVAL ACCIDENTS

To qualify for inclusion in this list, the warship or naval auxiliary vessel must have been an active or reserve unit of the relevant fleet and must have been lost or critically damaged by some form of mishap, such as storms, fires, explosions, collisions, grounding or structural failure. Vessels subsequently repaired and returned to active service - either with the original owner or another naval force - are excluded, as are vessels lost due to enemy action during times of conflict.

There will inevitably be vessels that have not been included in this list, as some the circumstances surrounding many instances of ships being paid-off and scrapped, or merely disappearing from fleet lists, have gone unexplained by the owners. Cases of this will be particularly prevalent were small, low-value ships and craft have been discarded following accidental damage.

This list does not claim to include every single warship or naval auxiliary vessel of the world's navies lost or critically damaged since the end of World War Two, but is probably the most complete attempt in existence.

| DATE | CLASS | NAME | PEN No | TYPE | COUNTRY | CAUSE |
|---|---|---|---|---|---|---|
| 1945 | | *Columbia* | | Trans. | Cuba | CTL after stranding |
| 08.09.45 | Pa.No.1 Type | *Pa.No.90* | Pa.90 | PS | Japan | Lost, cause unknown, off Sakate |
| Late-45 | 150-ton Type | *Eisen* | No.709 | ML | Japan | CTL by stranding near Mera, Chiba Per. |
| Late-45 | Pa.No.1 Type | *Pa.No.54* | Pa.54 | PS | Japan | Sank after springing a leak |
| Late-45 | Pa.No.1 Type | *Pa.No.111* | Pa.111 | PS | Japan | Sunk by leakage at Nishiu |
| Late-45 | Pa.No.1 Type | *Pa.No.165* | Pa.165 | PS | Japan | Sank after springing a leak at Yokosuka |
| Late-45 | Yu1 | *Yu10* | Yu10 | SS | Japan | Sank in storm at Kuchinotsu, Nagasaki |
| Late-45 | Yu1 | *Yu12* | Yu12 | SS | Japan | Sank in storm at Kuchinotsu, Nagasaki |
| Late-45 | 150-ton Type | *No.929* | | Aircraft Rescue | Japan | Sank off Shibauro, Tokyo |

| DATE | CLASS | NAME | PEN No | TYPE | COUNTRY | CAUSE |
|---|---|---|---|---|---|---|
| 09.45 | I13 (AM) | *I1* | I1 | SS | Japan | Sank after springing a leak in storm at Kobe (Incomplete) |
| 11.09.45 | PC-461 | *PC815* | PC815 | SC | USA | Cut in two in collision with destroyer *USS Laffey* in San Francisco Bay |
| 14.09.45 | Aloe | *Mahogany* | AN23 | Netlayer | USA | Wrecked during Typhoon Iola at Okinawa |
| 16.09.45 | LST 511-1152 | *LST823* | LST823 | LST | USA | CTL after being driven aground and wrecked in typhoon off Okinawa |
| 16.09.45 | SC Type | *SC632* | SC632 | SC | USA | Driven aground and sunk in typhoon off Okinawa |
| 16.09.45 | YMS-1 | *YMS98* | YMS98 | MSC | USA | Lost in typhoon off Okinawa |
| 16.09.45 | YMS-1 | *YMS341* | YMS341 | MSC | USA | Foundered in typhoon off Okinawa |
| 16.09.45 | YMS-1 | *YMS421* | YMS421 | MSC | USA | Lost in typhoon at Okinawa |
| 16.09.45 | YMS-1 | *YMS472* | YMS472 | MSC | USA | Lost in typhoon at Okinawa |
| 17.09.45 | Kos | *Mandal* | | MSC | Norway | Wrecked by grounding off Farsund |
| 18.09.45 | Cha.1 | *Cha.228* | Cha.228 | SC | Japan | Sank after springing a leak in storm at Sasebo |
| 18.09.45 | Type 103 | *T175* | T175 | LST | Japan | Sank in storm off Imari, Saga Perfecture (Incomplete) |
| 18.09.45 | Type 103 | *T176* | T176 | LST | Japan | Sank in storm off Imari, Saga Perfecture (Incomplete) |
| 18.09.45 | 300-ton Type | *No.1337* | | Aircraft Rescue | Japan | CTL after storm damage off Kobe |

| DATE | CLASS | NAME | PEN No | TYPE | COUNTRY | CAUSE |
|---|---|---|---|---|---|---|
| 18.09.45 | LST 511-1152 | *LST555* | LST555 | LST | USA | Driven aground in typhoon at Wakayama |
| 19.09.45 | Minerve | *Minerve* | P26 | SS | France | Ran aground in bad weather on Portland Bill |
| 19.09.45 | Pa.No.1 Type | *Pa.No.25* | Pa.25 | PS | Japan | Sank in storm at Shimanoseki |
| 19.09.45 | Type A | *CDa.No.1* | CDa.1 | Escort | Japan | Sank after springing a leak (50% complete) |
| 19.09.45 | Type A | *CDa.No.2* | CDa.2 | Escort | Japan | Sank after springing a leak |
| 29.09.45 | Cannon | *Roche* | DE197 | DDE | USA | CTL after striking mine off Eniwetok, en route to Japan |
| 10.45 | Yu Type | *Yu3002* | Yu3002 | SS | Japan | Ran aground and capsized in Sosan Sea, south of Inchon |
| 10.45 | Type 103 | *SB110* | SB110 | LST | Japan | CTL after boiler explosion at Hakata |
| 10.45 | LST(2) | *LST405* | L405 | LST | UK | CTL after collision in Colombo Harbour |
| 03.10.45 | 264-ton Type | Ex-*Othmarschen* | V6507 | MST | Germany | Sunk by mine in Kattegat (GM/SA) |
| 04.10.45 | Hirashima | *Niizaki* | | ML | Japan | CTL after striking mine off Muroran |
| 04.10.45 | Admiralty Type | *HDML1226* | HDML1226 | PC | UK | Sunk by mine north of Dardanelles |
| 05.10.45 | Admiralty Type | *MFV118* | MFV118 | MFV | UK | Lost by fire at Portsmouth |
| 08.10.45 | Momi | *Kuri* | | DD | Japan | Sank after hitting mine off Pusan, Korea |
| 08.10.45 | YMS.1 | *YMS478* | YMS478 | MSC | USA | Driven aground in typhoon at Wakanura, Japan |

| DATE | CLASS | NAME | PEN No | TYPE | COUNTRY | CAUSE |
|---|---|---|---|---|---|---|
| 09.10.45 | Clemson | *Greene* | APD36 | APD | USA | Driven aground and lost in typhoon at Katuka, Okinawa |
| 09.10.45 | Wickes | *Dorsey* | DMS1 | DMS | USA | Wrecked when driven aground in typhoon at Okinawa |
| 09.10.45 | Clemson | *Southard* | DMS10 | DMS | USA | Driven aground on at Tsugen Jima, Okinawa in typhoon |
| 09.10.45 | LST 511-1152 | *LST534* | LST534 | LST | USA | Lost in typhoon at Okinawa |
| 09.10.45 | LST 511-1152 | *LST826* | LST826 | LST | USA | CTL after being driven aground in typhoon at Okinawa |
| 09.10.45 | LST 511-1152 | *LST896* | LST896 | LST | USA | Driven aground in typhoon at Okinawa |
| 09.10.45 | LST 511-1152 | *Nestor* | ARB6 | Repair | USA | Driven aground and wrecked in typhoon at Okinawa |
| 09.10.45 | LSM-1 | *LSM15* | LSM15 | LSM | USA | Sunk in typhoon at Okinawa |
| 09.10.45 | LSM-1 | *LSM137* | LSM137 | LSM | USA | Driven aground in typhoon at Okinawa |
| 09.10.45 | LSM-1 | *LSM361* | LSM361 | LSM | USA | CTL after being driven aground in typhoon at Okinawa |
| 09.10.45 | PGM-9 | *PGM9* | PGM9 | PC | USA | Driven aground and wrecked in typhoon at Okinawa |
| 09.10.45 | PGM-9 | *PGM27* | PGM27 | PC | USA | Driven aground and wrecked in typhoon at Okinawa |
| 09.10.45 | PC-461 | *PC584* | PC584 | SC | USA | Sunk in typhoon at Okinawa |

| DATE | CLASS | NAME | PEN No | TYPE | COUNTRY | CAUSE |
|---|---|---|---|---|---|---|
| 09.10.45 | PC-461 | *PC590* | PC590 | SC | USA | Broken in half and sunk in typhoon at Okinawa |
| 09.10.45 | PC-461 | *PC1126* | PC1126 | SC | USA | Driven aground and wrecked in typhoon at Okinawa |
| 09.10.45 | PC-461 | *PC1128* | PC1128 | SC | USA | Driven aground and wrecked in typhoon at Okinawa |
| 09.10.45 | PC461 | *PC1238* | PC1238 | SC | USA | Capsized and wrecked in typhoon at Okinawa |
| 09-10-45 | Sweeper Type | PCS1418 | PCS1418 | SC | USA | CTL after being driven aground in typhoon at Okinawa |
| 09.10.45 | SC Type | *SC636* | SC636 | SC | USA | Sunk in typhoon at Okinawa |
| 09.10.45 | SC Type | *SCC686* | SCC686 | SC | USA | Sunk in typhoon at Okinawa |
| 09.10.45 | SC Type | *SCC999* | SCC999 | SC | USA | Driven aground and wrecked in typhoon at Okinawa |
| 09.10.45 | SC Type | *SC1012* | SC1012 | SC | USA | Driven aground and wrecked in typhoon at Okinawa |
| 09-10-45 | SC Type | *SC1049* | SC1049 | SC | USA | Driven aground in typhoon at Okinawa. Destroyed 4-12-45 |
| 09.10.45 | SC-Type | *SCC1306* | SCC1306 | SC | USA | CTL after being driven aground in typhoon at Okinawa |
| 09.10.45 | Sweeper Type | *PCSC1461* | PCSC1461 | SC | USA | Driven aground and wrecked in typhoon at Okinawa |

| DATE | CLASS | NAME | PEN No | TYPE | COUNTRY | CAUSE |
|------|-------|------|--------|------|---------|-------|
| 09.10.45 | 1116-ton Type | *Southern Seas* | PY32 | PC | USA | Sunk in typhoon at Okinawa |
| 09.10.45 | Salem | *Weehawken* | CM12 | ML | USA | Driven aground and wrecked in typhoon at Okinawa |
| 09.10.45 | YMS-1 | *YMS90* | YMS90 | MSC | USA | Driven aground and wrecked in typhoon at Okinawa |
| 09.10.45 | YMS-1 | *YMS146* | YMS146 | MSC | USA | Sunk in typhoon at Okinawa |
| 09.10.45 | YMS-1 | *YMS151* | YMS151 | MSC | USA | Driven aground and wrecked in typhoon at Okinawa |
| 09.10.45 | YMS-1 | *YMS275* | YMS275 | MSC | USA | Sunk in typhoon at Okinawa |
| 09.10.45 | YMS-1 | *YMS383* | YMS383 | MSC | USA | Sunk in typhoon off Okinawa |
| 09.10.45 | YMS-1 | *YMS384* | YMS384 | MSC | USA | Driven aground and wrecked in typhoon at Okinawa |
| 09.10.45 | YMS-1 | *YMS424* | YMS424 | MSC | USA | Driven aground and wrecked in typhoon at Okinawa |
| 09.10.45 | YMS-1 | *YMS454* | YMS454 | MSC | USA | Driven aground in typhoon at Tsuken Shima, Japan |
| 09.10.45 | MSc Type | *Industry* | MSc86 | MSC | USA | Driven aground in typhoon at Okinawa |
| 09.10.45 | Mettawee | *Sacandaga* | AOG40 | AOG | USA | Driven aground and wrecked in typhoon at Okinawa |
| 09.10.45 | 9563-ton Type | *Vandalia* | IX191 | Tanker | USA | Driven aground and wrecked in typhoon at Okinawa |

| DATE | CLASS | NAME | PEN No | TYPE | COUNTRY | CAUSE |
|---|---|---|---|---|---|---|
| 09.10.45 | Apache | *Wateree* | ATF117 | ATF | USA | Driven aground and wrecked in typhoon at Okinawa |
| 09.10.45 | Anchor | *Extricate* | ARS16 | ARS | USA | Sunk in typhoon at Okinawa |
| 09.10.45 | 5868-ton Type | *Ocelot* | IX110 | Barrack Ship | USA | Lost after being driven aground in typhoon at Okinawa |
| 09.10.45 | Ailanthus | *Snowbell* | AN52 | Netlayer | USA | Lost in typhoon at Okinawa |
| 09.10.45 | YTB Type | *Ponkabia* | YTB411 | Tug | USA | Lost in typhoon at Okinawa |
| 09.10.45 | ATA.121 | *ATA191* | ATA191 | Tug | USA | Lost in typhoon at Okinawa |
| 09.10.45 | | *Cinnabar* | IX163 | Barge | USA | Driven aground in typhoon at Okinawa |
| 10.10.45 | PC.461 | *PC814* | PC814 | SC | USA | Lost in typhoon at Okinawa |
| 12.10.45 | 352-ton Type | *Loch Eribol* | FY704 | MST | UK | Lost in collision with American *ss Sidney Sharman* off Start Point |
| 17.10.45 | 30-ton Type | *Lord Beaconsfield* | FY608 | MST | UK | Wrecked by grounding off east Scotland |
| 24.10.45 | 254-ton Type | *Pinios* | | MSY | Greece | Sunk by mine off Prevesa |
| 29.10.45 | I361 (D1) | *I363* | I363 | SS | Japan | Mined off Miyazaki Pref. on passage to Sasebo to surrender |
| 29.10.45 | Ha.201 (STS) | *Ha.204* | Ha.204 | SS | Japan | Wrecked by stranding in Aburatsu Bay, Miyazaki Pref. |
| 05.11.45 | LST(2) | *LST199* | L199 | LST | UK | CTL after striking mine off Surabaya |
| 11.45 | LCI-1 | *LCI(L)128* | L128 | LCI | UK | Destroyed whilst leased from US |

| DATE | CLASS | NAME | PEN No | TYPE | COUNTRY | CAUSE |
|---|---|---|---|---|---|---|
| 12.11.45 | Isles | Ex-*Eriskay* | P8 | Trawler | Portugal | Wrecked off Sao Jorge, Azores |
| 16.11.45 | Mikura | *Daito* | | Escort | Japan | Sank after hitting mine, Tsushima Straits |
| 17.11.45 | Natsushima | *Ashizaki* | | Aux ML | Japan | Ran aground and abandoned in storm at Hayakawa |
| 18.11.45 | Natsushima | *Kurosaki* | | Aux ML | Japan | Ran aground and broke up in storm off Hachinohe |
| 12.45 | Air | *Air Mist* | ASR917 | Rescue Launch | Australia | Wrecked |
| 01.12.45 | LST 511-1152 | *LST767* | LST767 | LST | USA | Driven aground and wrecked in typhoon at Okinawa |
| 01.12.45 | LST 511-1152 | *Bellona* | ARL32 | Repair | USA | Lost by grounding on Kama Rocks, Iwo Jima |
| 04.12.45 | Admiralty Type | *MFV1218* | MFV1218 | MFV | UK | Sank after collision with *MFV1161* off North Scroby, Yarmouth |
| 05.12.45 | Flower | *Carabobo* | | Corvette | Venezuela | Wrecked on Gaspe coast, Nova Scotia |
| 10.12.45 | Ch.28 | *Ch.51* | Ch.51 | SC | Japan | Sank in storm at Sasebo |
| 14.12.45 | Cha.1 | *Cha.65* | Cha.65 | SC | Japan | Sank after running aground near Hachinohe |
| 21.12.45 | Type 103 | *LST144* | 144 | LST | China | CTL after collision with *USS Saint Paul* (CA-73) in Whangpoo River |
| 27.12.45 | Type VIIC | *U345* | U345 | SS | Germany | Sunk by mine near Warnemunde |
| 27.12.45 | ZZ | *ZZ13* | ZZ13 | MSC | UK | Capsized and sank in heavy weather in UK waters |

| DATE | CLASS | NAME | PEN No | TYPE | COUNTRY | CAUSE |
|------|-------|------|--------|------|---------|-------|
| 29.12.45 | Raven | Minivet | AM371 | MSF | USA | Capsized after striking mine in Tsushima Straits |
| 30.12.45 | LST 511-1152 | *LST814* | LST814 | LST | USA | CTL after severe damage by grounding off Sasebo, Japan |
| 1946 | LCS(L)(3)-1 | LCS(L)(3)-31 | LCSL31 | LCS | USA | CTL after grounding on reef |
| 1946 | YU1001 | *YU1007* | YU1007 | SS | Japan | Sank in storm off Mikiriya |
| 1946 | YU1001 | *YU1011* | YU1011 | SS | Japan | Sank in storm off Mikiriya |
| 1946 | YU1001 | *YU1013* | YU1013 | SS | Japan | Sank in storm off Mikiriya |
| 1946 | YU1001 | *YU1014* | YU1014 | SS | Japan | Sank in storm off Mikiriya |
| 01.01.46 | Snake | *Alatna* | AM1475 | Workboat | Australia | Sunk in collision |
| 14.01.46 | Kaikoban Type D | *CD62* | CD62 | Escort | Japan | Sank after springing a leak in Kure Harbour |
| 25.01.46 | Cha.1 | *Cha.248* | Cha.248 | SC | Japan | Sunk by mine in Iki Sound |
| 27.01.46 | YTB Type | *Tamaroa* | YTB136 | Tug | USA | Sunk in collision with *USS Jupiter* (AVS-8) in San Francisco harbour |
| 28.01.46 | Admiralty Type | *MFV1512* | MFV1512 | MFV | UK | Lost on passage from Cochin to Penang |
| 29.01.46 | 1001 Series | *ME1016* | ME1016 | MSC | Denmark | Wrecked in fog on east coast of Jutland |
| 30.01.46 | Fairmile D | *MTB633* | MTB633 | MTB | UK/Egypt | Sank under tow in storm off Benghazi |
| 30.01.46 | Fairmile D | *MTB634* | MTB634 | MTB | UK/Egypt | Sank under tow in storm off Benghazi |
| 30.01.46 | Fairmile D | *MTB637* | MTB637 | MTB | UK/Egypt | Sank under tow in storm off Benghazi |
| 30.01.46 | Fairmile D | *MTB638* | MTB638 | MTB | UK/Egypt | Sank under tow in storm off Benghazi |

| DATE | CLASS | NAME | PEN No | TYPE | COUNTRY | CAUSE |
|---|---|---|---|---|---|---|
| 30.01.46 | Fairmile D | *MGB642* | MGB642 | MGB | UK/Egypt | Sank under tow in storm off Benghazi |
| 30.01.46 | Fairmile D | *MGB643* | MGB643 | MGB | UK/Egypt | Sank under tow in storm off Benghazi |
| 30.01.46 | Fairmile D | *MGB658* | MGB658 | MGB | UK/Egypt | Sank under tow in storm off Benghazi |
| 30.01.46 | Fairmile D | *MGB659* | MGB659 | MGB | UK/Egypt | Sank under tow in storm off Benghazi |
| 30.01.46 | Fairmile D | *MTB670* | MTB670 | MTB | UK/Egypt | Sank under tow in storm off Benghazi |
| 30.01.46 | Fairmile D | *MGB674* | MGB674 | MGB | UK/Egypt | Sank under tow in storm off Benghazi |
| 30.01.46 | Fairmile D | *MTB698* | MTB698 | MTB | UK/Egypt | Sank under tow in storm off Benghazi |
| 30.01.46 | Fairmile D | *MTB700* | MTB700 | MTB | UK/Egypt | Sank under tow in storm off Benghazi |
| 02.46 | T51 Type | *Gyoraitei No.13* | | MTB | Japan | Destroyed by fire at Uraga |
| 03.02.46 | 766-ton Type | *Captive* | W148 | Tug | UK | Sank in Potomas Bay |
| 13.02.46 | 690-ton Type | *Inn* | DW35 | Mine Transport | Germany | Sank after striking mine near Elbe River |
| 03.46 | LST 511-1152 | LST1005 | LST1005 | LST | USA | CTL after grounding. Decommissioned 06.04.46 |
| 04.03.46 | Admiralty Type | *MFV411* | MFV411 | MFV | UK | Lost at Brisbane |
| 04.03.46 | Admiralty Type | *MFV412* | MFV412 | MFV | UK | Lost at Brisbane |
| 06.03.46 | | *Osashi* | | Target | Japan | Sank at Yokohama due to hull leaks |
| 25.03.46 | 325-ton Type | Ex-*Schwarzburg* | DB30 | Lightship | Germany | Sunk by mine on Elbe River |
| 25.03.46 | Cha.1 | *Cha.180* | Cha.180 | SC | Japan | Destroyed by fire in Osaka Harbour. Scuttled at sea |

| DATE | CLASS | NAME | PEN No | TYPE | COUNTRY | CAUSE |
|---|---|---|---|---|---|---|
| 25.03.46 | Kaikoban Type D | *CD116* | CD116 | Escort | Japan | Ran aground off Makurazaki, Kyushu |
| 29.03.46 | LCI-1 | *LCI(L)4* | LCI(L)4 | LCI | UK | Lost |
| 04.46 | Cha.1 | *Eisen No.1649* | Cha.1649 | SC/Tug | Japan | Burned out and sank at Uraga |
| 14.04.46 | YP Type | *YP280* | YP280 | YP | USA | Lost |
| 16.04.46 | Ha.101 (SS) | *Ha.110* | Ha.110 | SS | Japan | Sank after springing a leak at Kawasaki |
| 18.04.46 | Cha.1 | *Cha.81* | Cha.81 | SC | Japan | CTL after grounding off Matsushita |
| 18.04.46 | Pa.No.1 Type | *Pa.No.137* | Pa.137 | PS | Japan | Sank after running aground near Yoshimi |
| 18.04.46 | Pa.No.1 Type | *Pa.No.176* | Pa.176 | PS | Japan | CTL after grounding in rough weather near Yoshim |
| 21.04.46 | Empire | *Empire Christopher* | | Tug | UK | Sank after striking drifting mine in Maungmagon Bay |
| 30.04.46 | Buckley | *Solar* | DE221 | DDE | USA | Destroyed by internal explosion at Leonard, New Jersey |
| 03.05.46 | Alligator | *Crocodile* | W88 | Tug | UK | Wrecked by grounding off Sind coast |
| 05.05.46 | ZZ | *ZZ12* | ZZ12 | MSC | UK | Capsized and sank in heavy weather in Firth of Forth |
| 04.06.46 | Shumushu | *Kunashiri* | | Escort | Japan | CTL after stranding on reef off Omaezaki, Suraga Wan |
| 07.06.46 | Kamikaze | *Kamikaze II* | | DD | Japan | CTL after grounding near Omaezaki, Shizuoka Pref. |
| 27.06.46 | C | *C4* | C4 | SS | Spain | Sank after being rammed by destroyer *Lepanto* off Balearic Islands. |

| DATE | CLASS | NAME | PEN No | TYPE | COUNTRY | CAUSE |
|---|---|---|---|---|---|---|
| 07.46 | Seishu | *Seishu* | | Repair | Japan | Sank in typhoon in Hong Kong area |
| 20.07.46 | YOG Type | *YOG74* | YOG74 | YOG | USA | Lost |
| 30.07.46 | Kaikoban Type C | *CD59* | CD59 | Escort | Japan | Sank after colliding with wreck of battleship *Hyuga* at Kure in storm |
| 08.46 | Ch.51 | *Eisen No.1651* | Cha.1651 | SC/Tug | Japan | Sank by flooding caused by leaks |
| 05.08.46 | MAS438 | *AS26* | AS26 | SC | Italy | Sank after fuel tank explosion off Cape Miseno |
| 25.08.46 | Brigand | *Buccaneer* | W49 | ATF | UK | Sank after being hit by shellfire from DD *HMS St James* during target practice |
| 27.08.46 | ATA Type | *Beaverton* | | Tug | Canada | Sunk in collision off Quebec |
| 09.46 | ZZ | *ZZ16* | ZZ16 | MSC | UK | CTL after fire at Port Said |
| 01.09.46 | Cha.1 | *Cha.174* | Cha.174 | SC | Japan | Lost by fire at Otake |
| 18.09.46 | YO Type | *YO184* | YO184 | Oiler | USA | Lost in gale |
| 20.09.46 | TID | *TID62* | TID62 | Tug | UK | Sank under tow of *HMS Tenacity* off Beachy Head |
| 25.09.46 | Type 1 | *T20* | T20 | LST | Japan | CTL after grounding at Kitsubai Sho in the Pescadores |
| 22.10.46 | S | *Saumarez* | D12 | DD | UK | CTL after striking mine in Corfu Channel. |
| 02.11.46 | LSM.1 | *LSM459* | LSM459 | LSM | USA | CTL after running aground off Alaska |
| 02.11.46 | T31 Type | *Gyoraitei No223* | | MTB | Japan | Sunk in Tsunami at Toba |
| 07.11.46 | YTB Type | *Saguanash* | YTB288 | Tug | USA | Lost off coast of Washington |

| DATE | CLASS | NAME | PEN No | TYPE | COUNTRY | CAUSE |
|---|---|---|---|---|---|---|
| 19.11.46 | | *Walcheren* | MV18 | MSC | Netherlands | Sank after striking mine near Balik Papan |
| 02.12.46 | Algerine | *Middlesex* | J328 | MSO | Canada | Wrecked on Half Island Point, near Halifax |
| 05.12.46 | Type XXIII | Ex-*U2326* | | SS | France | Lost off Toulon, cause unknown |
| 06.12.46 | YTB Type | *Lone Wolf* | YTB179 | Tug | USA | Sunk in collision in Narragansett Bay |
| 20.12.46 | River | *Aire* | K262 | FF | UK | Wrecked by grounding on Bombay Reef |
| 21.12.46 | Envoy | *Enticer* | W166 | Tug | UK | Foundered in China Sea |
| 1947 | Flower | Ex-*Asbestos* | C106 | Corvette | Dominican R | Wrecked on Cuban coast during delivery from Canada |
| 11.01.47 | LSM.1 | *LSM432* | LSM432 | LSM | USA | Abandoned after running aground on east coast of Babuyan Island, Philippines |
| 31.01.47 | YO Type | *YO132* | YO132 | Oiler | USA | Lost |
| 02.47 | YO Type | *YO163* | YO163 | Oiler | USA | Lost |
| 19.03.47 | Flower | *Fu Po* | | Corvette | China | Sunk in collision with merchantman in Formosa Strait |
| 21.03.47 | 175-ton Type | *Onyx* | Z79 | Drifter | UK | Foundered in Bermuda dockyard basin |
| 04.47 | 105 | *MMS107* | M1607 | MSC | UK | Mined off Singapore |
| 05.47 | PC-461 | Ex-*PC493* | PC493 | PC | Thailand | Lost in typhoon at Manilla Bay shortly after transfer from US Navy |
| 14.05.47 | 1118-ton Type | *Kosai* | | Ferry | Japan | Wrecked by grounding at Omaezaki en route Osaka to Yokosuka |

| DATE | CLASS | NAME | PEN No | TYPE | COUNTRY | CAUSE |
|---|---|---|---|---|---|---|
| 06.06.47 | LCT4 | *LCT1068* | L1068 | LCT | UK | Sank in Stokes Bay two days after being hit by shell during target trials |
| 01.07.47 | Buffoluto | *Panigaglia* | | Lighthouse Tender | Italy | Destroyed by explosion in San Stefano harbour |
| 08.47 | HDML Type | *Dingo* | RP113 | PC | Netherlands | CTL off Suarabaja, New Guinea |
| 21.08.47 | VAS Type | *VAS246* | | PC | Italy | Destroyed by fire at Venice |
| 09.47 | YO Type | *YO188* | YO188 | Oiler | USA | Lost |
| 27.09.47 | YTB Type | *Pokagon* | YTB274 | Tug | USA | Capsized and sank under tow en route to Green Cove |
| 01.10.47 | | *Dom Joao de Castro* | | AGS | Portugal | Wrecked off Cape Verde Islands |
| 1948 | HDML Type | *Bever* | RP110 | PC | Netherlands | CTL after stranding |
| 19.01.48 | Empire | *Oriana* | | Tug | UK | Hit mine and sank in River Blackwater |
| 26.01.48 | LCI.1 | *LCI(L)124* | L124 | LCI | UK | Lost whilst leased from US |
| 21.02.48 | AMS Type | *Kayung San* | AMS515 | MSC | South Korea | Sunk by grounding |
| 23.03.48 | LST 511-1152 | *LST1130* | LST1130 | LST | USA | Abandoned as CTL after grounding at Yap, Caroline Is. |
| 14.03.48 | HDML Type | *VP61* | VP61 | CPC | France | Sunk in hurricane |
| 14.03.48 | HDML Type | *VP63* | VP63 | CPC | France | Sunk in hurricane |
| 18.03.48 | MAL Type II | *MAL44* | MAL44 | LCL | Germany | Capsized in tow of tug *Fairplay XIV* off Terscelling |
| 18.03.48 | MAL Type II | *MAL46* | MAL46 | LCL | Germany | Capsized in tow of tug *Fairplay XIV* off Terscelling |
| 07.05.48 | AMS Type | *Tong Chun* | AMS311 | MSC | South Korea | Lost with all hands |
| 15.05.48 | YMS-1 | *Go Won* | MSC517 | MSC | South Korea | Lost with all hands |

| DATE | CLASS | NAME | PEN No | TYPE | COUNTRY | CAUSE |
|---|---|---|---|---|---|---|
| 06.07.48 | LSM-1 | *LSM5* | LSM5 | LSM | USA | CTL after grounding on beach at Saipan |
| 27.08.48 | SC.497 | Ex-*SC723* | | PC | Taiwan | Sunk in typhoon under tow from Philippines to Taiwan |
| 11.09.48 | YTB Type | *Mahackeno* | YTB223 | Tug | USA | Foundered under tow off Cape Hatteras, North Carolina |
| 10.48 | Maagen | *Alken* | | CPC | Denmark | Disappeared off coast of Greenland in gale |
| 18.10.48 | HDML Type | | RP138 | PC | Netherlands | Sunk in Westervaarwater |
| 17.11.48 | Tacoma | Ex-*USS Belfast* | EK3 | FF | USSR | Foundered off Petropavlosk |
| 23.11.48 | Fairmile D | *Hauk* | | MTB | Norway | Sank after explosion off Bergen |
| 06.12.48 | Ailanthus | *Whitewood* | AG129 | Auxiliary | USA | CTL after being holed by ice |
| 08.01.49 | YTB Type | *Poquim* | YTB285 | Tug | USA | Sank under tow off San Diego |
| 22.01.49 | Azevia | *Fataga* | F | GB | Portugal | Wrecked |
| 24.02.49 | YMS.1 | *Ka Ya San* | MSC511 | MSC | South Korea | Sunk by grounding |
| 12.04.49 | Flower | *Libertad* | | Corvette | Venezuela | CTL after grounding off Western Venezuela |
| 11.05.49 | YMS.1 | *Kang Hoa* | MSC508 | MSC | South Korea | Lost with all hands |
| 23.05.49 | Pa.No.1 Type | *MS27* | MS27 | MSO | Japan | Sank after hitting mine near Manju Islands |
| 06.49 | | Ex-*F212* | 212 | Naval Ferry | Germany | Sunk by mine at mouth of Weser River |
| 09.08.49 | YMS.1 | *Simon Newcomb* | AGSc14 | AGS | USA | CTL after being driven aground off Labrador |
| 26.08.49 | Baloa (GUPPY II) | *Cochino* | SS345 | SSK | USA | Sank north of Norway after battery fire |

| DATE | CLASS | NAME | PEN No | TYPE | COUNTRY | CAUSE |
|------|-------|------|--------|------|---------|-------|
| 22.09.49 | Bouchard | *Fournier* | | MSO | Argentina | Sank after striking uncharted rock at entrance to San Gabriel Channel |
| 07.10.49 | Patapsco | *Chehalis* | AOG48 | AOG | USA | Sank after fire and explosion at Tutuila, Samoa |
| 23.12.49 | | *RS21* (Ex-*M1*) | RS21 | Tug | Netherlands | Lost in gale near Norderney |
| 1950? | Halcon | *La Paz* | | PB | Mexico | Wrecked |
| 12.01.50 | T | *Truculent* | P315 | SS | UK | Sunk in collision with Swedish tanker *mv Divina* in Thames Estuary |
| 25.01.50 | LST3 | *Tarakan* | LST3017 | LST | Australia | Irreparably damaged by petrol explosion at Garden Island, Sydney Harbour |
| 26.07.50 | BYMS-1 | *Gaza* | | MSC | Egypt | Sank after fuel tank explosion off Mersa Matrouh |
| 25.08.50 | Haven | *Benevolence* | AH13 | AH | USA | Sank after collision with freighter in San Francisco Bay |
| 15.09.50 | LST 511-1152 | *Munsan* | LST | | South Korea | Grounded and broached north of Pohang |
| 16.09.50 | Tacoma | *Laplace* | F13 | FF | France | Exploded and sank off Cape Frehel striking a mine |
| 10.10.50 | Cha.1 | *MS14* | MS14 | MSO | Japan | Struck mine in Yong Hung Bay |
| 27.10.50 | Pa.No.1 Type | *MS30* | MS30 | MSO | Japan | Wrecked on reef near Koriyama |
| 30.10.50 | Pa.No.1 Type | *MS28* | MS28 | MSO | Japan | Wrecked on reef off Suzaki |
| 30.10.50 | | *Voroshilovsk* | | ML | USSR | Lost with 20 lives |
| 07.01.51 | Flower | *Prasae* | | FF | Thailand | Destroyed after grounding on Korean coast in snowstorm |

| DATE | CLASS | NAME | PEN No | TYPE | COUNTRY | CAUSE |
|---|---|---|---|---|---|---|
| 14.02.51 | | *Garo* | | PC | Portugal | Sank after collision with Portuguese warship off Portugal |
| 17.04.51 | A | *Affray* | S20 | SS | UK | Sank after flooding through fractured snorkel in Hurd Deep |
| 27.04.51 | Bedenham | *Bedenham* | | Armament Carrier | UK | CTL after ammunition explosion at Gibraltar |
| 19.05.51 | LST 511-1152 | *Adour* | L9007 | LST | France | Exploded and sank after grounding in Nha Tang |
| 11.51 | MMS Type | *Vlieland* | M867 | MSI | Netherlands | Sunk near Hollandia, New Guinea |
| 1952 | PC461 | *Volontaire* | | PC | France | Hulked after critical grounding damage |
| 1952 | LCT-6 | *LCU1460* | LCU1460 | LCU | USA | Lost at sea |
| 1952 | Project 73-K (Poluchkin) | *T-450 Pavel Golovin* | | MSO | USSR | Wrecked in storm near Taupse (Black Sea) |
| 23.01.52 | LST 1-510 | *Andong* | LST803 | LST | South Korea | Wrecked by grounding during typhoon |
| 31.01.52 | Saunders-Roe 75ft Type | *MTB1602* | MTB1602 | MTB | UK | Foundered under tow in gale off Anglesey |
| 28.03.52 | Vosper 73ft Type | *MTB1030* | MTB1030 | MTB | UK | Sank after collision with *FPB1032* off the Hook of Holland |
| 26.04.52 | Bristol | *Hobson* | DMS26 | DD | USA | Sunk in collision with *USS Wasp* (CVA-18) west of Azores |
| 21.05.52 | Tacoma | *Apnok* | PE62 | FF | South Korea | CTL after collision. Returned to US, expended as target |
| 02.06.52 | MMS1 | *MMS1534* | MMS1534 | MSC | UK | Destroyed by fire off coast of Tunisia |

| DATE | CLASS | NAME | PEN No | TYPE | COUNTRY | CAUSE |
|------|-------|------|--------|------|---------|-------|
| 05.06.52 | Fairmile B | *ML2582* | ML2582 | PB | UK | Sank after NATO aircraft crashed on her off Dutch coast |
| 05.08.52 | Admiralty Type | *SMDL1322* | SMDL1322 | PC | Australia | Wrecked off Sydney after breaking tow |
| 18.09.52 | Ex-US Type | *Olpamei* | PT26 | FAC(T) | South Korea | Destroyed by fire |
| 24.09.52 | S | *Sibylle* | S614 | SS | France | Lost near Toulon, cause unknown, with all hands |
| 21.10.52 | MMS1 | *MMS288* | M1788 | MSC | UK | Foundered in heavy weather off Winterton Ness |
| 22.10.52 | Huemel | *Contramaestre Brito* | | Tug | Chile | Sank after grounding near Quintero |
| 15.12.52 | Grommet Reefer | *Grommet Reefer* | T-AF-53 | AF | USA | Driven aground gale off Leghorn, Italy, and broke in two |
| 16.12.52 | Shch | *S.117* | | SS | USSR | Disappeared in Sea of Okhotsk |
| 01.02.53 | Castle | *Berkeley Castle* | F387 | FF | UK | CTL after capsizing in dry dock at Shearness during floods |
| 01.02.53 | S | *Sirdar* | S76 | SS | UK | CTL after being flooded in dry dock at Shearness during floods |
| 07.03.53 | Bangor | *Sollum* | | Corvette | Egypt | Sank in heavy weather off Alexandria |
| 03.04.53 | Baloa | *Dumlupinar* | S339 | SS | Turkey | Sunk in collision with Swedish *mv Naboland* in Dardanelles |
| 17.04.53 | 105 | *MMS58* | M1558 | MSC | UK | Sank after fire 15 miles off Dunkirk |
| 16/17.05.53 | Flower | *Misr* | | FF | Egypt | Sunk in collision south of Suez |

| DATE | CLASS | NAME | PEN No | TYPE | COUNTRY | CAUSE |
|---|---|---|---|---|---|---|
| 17.05.53 | Vosper 73-foot Type | *MTB1023* | MTB1023 | MTB | UK | Caught fire and blew up in Aarhus Harbour |
| 08.53 | LCU.1466 | *LCU1503* | LCU1503 | LCU | USA | Lost |
| 09.09.53 | 565-ton yacht | *Esmereldas* | | PC | Ecuador | CTL after grounding near Guayaquil on Guyas River |
| 03.10.53 | Sprangaren | *Sokaren* | V47 | PC | Sweden | Sank after grounding near Ingarolandet |
| 22.10.53 | Admiralty Type | *Ricasoli* | MFV26 | MFV | UK | Foundered off Malta |
| 25.03.54 | Bidasoa | *Guadalete* | DM2 | MSO | Spain | Sank in gale 20 miles east of Gibraltar |
| 02.05.54 | LCT4 | *LCT565* | L565 | LCT | UK | Wrecked on Lundy Island after breaking tow |
| 26.09.54 | Kaikoban 1 Type | *Chang An* | | Escort | Taiwan | CTL after grounding on Pescadores Is. |
| 04.10.54 | Bicudas | *Barreto de Menezes* | F6 | AGS | Brazil | Grounded, lost in quicksand 17.10.54 |
| 21.11.54 | Admiralty Type | *Pomona* | MFV1163 | MFV | UK | Grounded and lost on Carness Point |
| 02.55 | | *Rio Blanco* | | Tug | Mexico | Lost in Gulf of Mexico |
| 02.02.55 | MSB.5 | *MSB23* | MSB23 | MSB | USA | Destroyed by fire during build |
| 16.05.55 | S | *Sidon* | S59 | SS | UK | Sank after torpedo explosion at Portland |
| 14.10.55 | Graadyb | *Graadyb* | M568 | MSI | Denmark | Destroyed by explosion in Copenhagen Naval Dockyard |
| 15.10.55 | YMS-1 | *Kosung* | MSC518 | MSC | South Korea | CTL after collision |
| 29.10.55 | Conte di Cavour | *Novorossisk* | | BB | USSR | Sunk by German mine at Sevastopol |
| 1956? | LCT6 | *Samana* | LA2 | LCT | Dominican R | Lost in bad weather |

| DATE | CLASS | NAME | PEN No | TYPE | COUNTRY | CAUSE |
|---|---|---|---|---|---|---|
| 1956? | APC Type | *Vertieres* | GC6 | LCT | Haiti | Lost at sea |
| 1956 | Ex-USCG 83ft | | MGB103 | MGB | Burma | Sank in heavy seas off Fenessarin coast |
| 1956 | Capitan Alsina | ? | LR102 | CPC | Dominican Republic | Lost |
| 1956 | | *Hercules* | R2 | Tug | Dominican Republic | Lost |
| 1956 | 110ft SC Type | *Alert* | PY54 | PC | Philippines | Sunk |
| 1956 | Shch (Series V) | *Sazan* | Shch201 | SS | USSR | Believed wrecked accidentally off Poti |
| 28.03.56 | 45ft TB Type | *TB6* | TB6 | Tug | Australia | Sank under tow |
| 17.05.56 | Project 617 | *S-99* | | SS | USSR | CTL after machinery explosion whilst submerged in Baltic |
| 23.07.56 | YMS-1 | *T-526* | | MSC | USSR | Destroyed |
| 09.08.56 | Wave | *Wave King* | A264 | AO | UK | CTL after striking rocks off Brazil |
| 29.09.56 | Ley | *Broadley* | M2006 | MSI | UK | Critically damaged by fire at Gosport |
| 29.09.56 | Ham | *Bisham* | M2607 | MSI | UK | Destroyed by fire at Gosport |
| 29.09.56 | Ham | *Edlingham* | M2623 | MSI | UK | Destroyed by fire at Gosport |
| 21.11.56 | Project 96 (Malyutka V) | *M-200 Myest* | | SS | USSR | Sank after collision with destroyer *Statnyi* in Tallin Bay |
| 1957 | Matsu | *Hui Yang* | | DD | Taiwan | CTL after running aground |
| 1957 | Ashville | *Juan Pablo Duarte* | F102 | FF | Dominican Republic | Wrecked |

| DATE | CLASS | NAME | PEN No | TYPE | COUNTRY | CAUSE |
|---|---|---|---|---|---|---|
| 1957 | Project A615 (Quebec) | *M-296* | | SS | USSR | Sank. Raised and erected as memorial in Odessa |
| 25.01.57 | 82-ton Type | *Ternen* | Y381 | PC | Denmark | Sank due to weight of ice off west Greenland |
| 07.03.57 | Mission | *Mission San Francisco* | T-AO123 | AO | USA | Broke in two and sank after collision with *ss Elna II* in Delaware River |
| 02.07.57 | 45ft TB Type | *TB11* | TB11 | Tug | Australia | Sank under tow near Port Moresby |
| 01.08.57 | YMS.1 | *Delfin* | T33 | MSC | Poland | Wrecked north of Gdynia, Poland |
| 04.09.57 | Gribben | *Hogen* | P555 | MTB | Denmark | Sunk in collision with MTB *Flyvefisken* in the Store Baelt |
| 26.09.57 | Project A615 (Quebec) | *M-256* | | SS | USSR | Sank after fire near Tallin with 35 crewmen |
| 08.10.57 | Mission *Miguel* | *Mission San* | T-AO129 | AO | USA | CTL after grounding on Maro Reef, Hawaiian Islands |
| 17.10.57 | Churruca | *Ciscar* | 41 | DD | Spain | Ran aground in fog off El Ferrol and broke her back |
| 12.57 | Stalinets | *S-104* | | SS | USSR | Wrecked by grounding on Paramashiro Island |
| 13.01.58 | Bar | *Barcombe* | P216 | Boom Defence | UK | Wrecked by grounding at Loch Buie |
| 29.05.58 | Baloa (GUPPY IIA) | *Stickleback* | SS415 | SSK | USA | Sank off Pearl Harbour after collision with destroyer |
| 01.06.58 | LST 511-1152 | *Chittenden County* | LST561 | LST | USA | CTL after grounding off Kauai, Hawaii |
| 23.08.58 | Aggressive | *Prestige* | MSO465 | MSO | USA | CTL after stranding in Naruto Straits, Inland Sea, Japan |

| DATE | CLASS | NAME | PEN No | TYPE | COUNTRY | CAUSE |
|---|---|---|---|---|---|---|
| 15.10.58 | Ona | *Guarani* | | Tug | Argentina | Lost without trace in Straits of Magellan |
| 1959 | AOG Type | *Yu Chaun* | AOG303 | Oiler | Taiwan | CTL after grounding |
| 1959 | YTL Type | | Y1057 | Tug | Turkey | Sunk |
| 18.02.59 | 208-ton Type | *Hermodur* | | OPV | Iceland | Foundered in bad weather off southwest Iceland |
| 25.08.59 | Battle | *Hogue* | D74 | DD | UK | Scrapped after severe damage sustained in collision with Indian cruiser *Mysore* off Ceylon |
| end-59 | Riga | | KSS44 | FFL | E.Germany | Gutted by explosion and fire in Rostock soon after delivery |
| 1960s | Type 103 | *Lu Shan* | | LST | Taiwan | CTL after running aground |
| c.1960 | Type 7 (Ex-DD) | *Razumny* | | AGI | USSR | Driven ashore and wrecked in storm near Murmansk |
| 19.07.60 | Fletcher | *Ammen* | DD527 | DD | USA | CTL after collision with *USS Collett* off Newport Beach |
| 11.10.60 | Woomera | *Woomera* | | Armament Carrier | Australia | Blew up and sank 23 miles from Sydney |
| 15.12.60 | Kave | *Kave 5* | Kave 5 | LCU | Finland | Lost under tow |
| 11.01.61 | Ex-Ger R157 | *Egenaes* | MR157 | PC | Denmark | Wrecked by gounding east of Odden Havn, Zealand |
| 27.01.61 | Project 644 (Whiskey Twin Cylinder) | *S-80* | | SSG | USSR | Sank by flooding through snorkel with crew of 68 |
| 16.04.61 | Gleaves | *Baldwin* | DD624 | DD | USA | Ran aground off Montauk Point, Long Island, after breaking tow |
| 17.04.61 | PC-461 | *Baire* | PE203 | PC | Cuba | Sank at Isla de Pines (during coup) |

| DATE | CLASS | NAME | PEN No | TYPE | COUNTRY | CAUSE |
|---|---|---|---|---|---|---|
| 06.05.61 | Ex-US PT Type | *R43* | R43 | CPC | Cuba | Sank after hitting submerged object off western Cuba |
| 26.09.61 | Type VIIC | *Laubie* | S610 | SS | France | CTL after damage by collision |
| 26.09.61 | Maumee | *Potomac* | AO150 | AO | USA | Destroyed by explosion at Morehead City, North Carolina |
| 26.12.61 | 110ft SC Type | *SC33* | SC33 | PC | Thailand | Destroyed by explosion and fire at Bangkok and beached to prevent sinking. Scrapped 08.03.62 |
| 11.01.62 | Project 641 (Foxtrot) | *B-37* | | SS | USSR | Lost by torpedo explosion at berth in Northern Fleet area |
| 11.01.62 | Project 633 (Romeo) | *S-350* | | SS | USSR | Sunk by explosion of *B-37* |
| 06.03.62 | Fletcher | *Monssen* | DD798 | DD | USA | CTL after grounding in storm whilst under tow |
| 06.62 | Buckley | *Rajah Soliman* | D66 | Command | Philippines | Capsized in typhoon at Bataan Ship National Shipyard |
| 02.08.62 | Weapon | *Battleaxe* | D118 | DD | UK | CTL after collision with *HMS Ursa* in Clyde Estuary |
| 30.09.62 | Schwalbe | *Sternberg* | 422 | MSB | E.Germany | Sank after collision |
| 29.10.62 | TID | *TID97* | TID97 | Tug | UK | Girded and sunk at Chatham whilst berthing *RFA Hebe* |
| 11.11.62 | PC 461 | *Han Ra San* | PC705 | PC | South Korea | Sunk in Typhoon Karen at Guam |
| 11.11.62 | PC 461 | *Negros Oriental* | C26 | PC | Philippines | Sunk in Typhoon Karen at Guam |

| DATE | CLASS | NAME | PEN No | TYPE | COUNTRY | CAUSE |
|------|-------|------|--------|------|---------|-------|
| 17.11.62 | Ranger | *Green Ranger* | A152 | AO | UK | Wrecked in gale at Hartland whilst under tow for refit |
| 1963 | LST 511-1152 | *Teluk Dadja* | LST2 | LST | Indonesia | CTL after grounding |
| 26.02.63 | LSM 1 | *Dokdo* | LSM603 | LSM | South Korea | CTL after grounding |
| 27.03.63 | Gribben | *Tranen* | P567 | MTB | Denmark | Sank after collision with Norwegian fishing cutter in Stavangar Fjord |
| 04.63 | BYMS-1 | *Djebel Aures* | | MSC | Algeria | Wrecked off Algiers |
| 10.04.63 | Thresher | *Thresher* | SSN593 | SSN | USA | Sank 220 miles east of Boston |
| 05.63 | YTB Type | *Iona* | YTM220 | Tug | USA | Sunk in collision off the Philippines |
| 21.09.63 | YMS.136 | *Grouse* | MSC(O)15 | MSC | USA | Destroyed after grounding at Rockport, Maine |
| 01.10.63 | Cook | *Cook* | A307 | AGS | UK | Scrapped as a result of damage sustained in grounding in Fiji Islands. |
| 10.02.64 | Daring | *Voyager* | D04 | DD | Australia | Sunk in collision with *HMAS Melbourne* |
| 19.05.64 | YTM Type | *Ala* | YTM139 | Tug | USA | Sank after grounding in Kulak Bay, Adak, Aleutian Is. |
| 25.05.64 | Galvez | *Yagan* | YT126 | Tug | Chile | Capsized and sank in Punta Arenas whilst assisting merchant ship on sandbank in storm |
| 22.11.64 | FS Type | *Ruminahui* | YO123 | Oiler | Ecuador | Foundered in Caribbean |
| 22.12.64 | Ford | *Kotiya* | | PC | Sri Lanka | Sank in Trincomalee Harbour during cyclone |
| 22.12.64 | Algerine | *Viyaya* | M370 | MSO | Sri Lanka | Beached and broached in Trincomalee Harbour during cyclone |

| DATE | CLASS | NAME | PEN No | TYPE | COUNTRY | CAUSE |
|---|---|---|---|---|---|---|
| 22.12.64 | Tanac | *YTM1* | YTM1 | Tug | Sri Lanka | Sank in Trincomalee Harbour during cyclone |
| 22.12.64 | Tanac | *YTM2* | YTM2 | Tug | Sri Lanka | Sank in Trincomalee Harbour during cyclone |
| 22.12.64 | Tanac | *YTM3?* | YTM3? | Tug | Sri Lanka | Sank in Trincomalee Harbour during cyclone |
| 22.12.64 | Empire | *Behest* | | Tug | Sri Lanka | Sank in Trincomalee Harbour during cyclone |
| 1965 | PGM Type | *Masbate* | PG52 | PC | Philippines | Sunk |
| 02.08.65 | Lautaro | *Leucoton* | PP61 | PC | Chile | CTL after grounding on sandbank in storm |
| 15.08.65 | Apache | *Janequeo* | AGS65 | AGS | Chile | Sank in storm during salvage of *Leucoton* |
| 02.66 | Cannon | *Beberibe* | D19 | DDE | Brazil | Stricken and scrapped after grounding |
| 25.02.66 | Audaz | *Ariete* | D36 | DD | Spain | CTL after grounding on rocks at entrance to River Muros |
| 21.04.66 | Crosley | Ex-*USS Walter B. Cobb* | Ex-APD1006 | FF | Taiwan | Foundered under tow from US to Taiwan after collision with sister *Wen Shan* (Ex-*USS Gantner*) |
| 07.05.66 | Skarven | *Skarven* | Y382 | OPV | Denmark | CTL after grounding in the Faeroes |
| 25.06.66 | Aggressive | *Stalwart* | MSO493 | MSO | USA | Capsized and sank after fire at San Juan, Puerto Rico |
| 14.09.66 | Type XXIII | *Hai* | S170 | SS | W.Germany | Sank in storm off Dogger Bank |
| 15.11.66 | Swift | *PCF77* | PCF77 | PC | USA | Sank in heavy weather off South Vietnam |
| 01.01.67 | LST 511-1152 | *Mahnomen County* | LST912 | LST | USA | Broke in two after stranding off Chu Lai, Vietnam |

| DATE | CLASS | NAME | PEN No | TYPE | COUNTRY | CAUSE |
|---|---|---|---|---|---|---|
| 14.01.67 | MSB-5 | *MSB14* | MSB14 | MSB | USA | Sunk in collision with freighter *Muifinh* in Long Tau River near Saigon |
| 20.01.67 | MSB-5 | *MSB43* | MSB43 | MSB | USA | Sank after collision with dolphin at Charleston! |
| 08.03.67 | PBR Mk.1 | *PBR20* | PBR20 | PC | USA | Cut in two and sunk in collision with British merchant ship in Saigon channel |
| 10.67 | Swift | *PCF14* | PCF14 | PC | USA | Sank in heavy weather off South Vietnam |
| 10.67 | Swift | *PCF76* | PCF76 | PC | USA | Sank in heavy weather off South Vietnam |
| 25.01.68 | T | *Dakar* | 77 | SS | Israel | Sank after flooding in eastern Mediterranean |
| 27.01.68 | Daphne | *Minerve* | S647 | SS | France | Disappeared in western Mediterranean |
| 06.02.68 | Fletcher | *Bache* | DD470 | DD | USA | Wrecked by running aground on Rhodes. Scrapped in situ |
| 11.04.68 | Project 629A (Golf II) | *K-129* | PL722 | SSB | USSR | Foundered after explosion in Pacific |
| 22.05.68 | Skipjack | *Scorpion* | SSN589 | SSN | USA | Sunk by own torpedo, 400 miles south-west of Azores |
| 24.05.68 | Project 645 (November) | *K-27* | | SSN | USSR | CTL after reactor accident which killed 9 crewmen. Scuttled near Novaya Zemlya 1983 |
| 16.06.68 | Swift | *PCF19* | PCF19 | PC | USA | Sunk accidentally by US aircraft off South Vietnam |
| 20.10.68 | Nasty | *Iniochos* | P22 | FAC(T) | Greece | Foundered after grounding in storm near Piraeus |

| DATE | CLASS | NAME | PEN No | TYPE | COUNTRY | CAUSE |
|---|---|---|---|---|---|---|
| 11.11.68 | Empire | *Empire Ace* | | Tug | UK | Wrecked by grounding on Mull of Kintyre |
| 23.12.68 | LST 511-1152 | *LST600* | T-LST600 | LST | USA | CTL after grounding in storm off Okinawa |
| 1969 | Project 527 (Prut) | *Altai* | | ASR | USSR | Burned under repair at Murmansk (Sudo-Ryemontiy Yard) |
| 1969 | PC-461 | *Han Kiang* | PC124 | PC | Taiwan | CTL after grounding |
| 03.06.69 | A M Sumner | *Frank E Evans* | DD754 | DD | USA | Sunk in collision with *HMAS Melbourne* |
| 16.06.69 | LSM-1 | *Mei Hwa* | LSM341 | LSM | Taiwan | Sunk in collision with merchant ship *Ta Tung* in dense fog |
| 10.69 | PC-461 | *Ogoya* | | PC | Nigeria | Wrecked off Brass (Niger Delta) |
| 06.10.69 | Aggressive | *Avenge* | MSO423 | MSO | USA | CTL after fire damage in dry dock at Baltimore |
| 1970 | Project 705 (Alfa) | *K-377* | | SSN | USSR | Scrapped following reactor meltdown |
| 01.70 | A M Sumner | *Soley* | DD707 | DD | USA | CTL after grounding. Sunk as target 19.09.70 |
| 03.70 | Aggressive | *Sagacity* | MSO469 | MSO | USA | CTL after grounding at entrance to Charleston harbour |
| 04.03.70 | Daphne | *Eurydice* | S644 | SS | France | Sank after internal explosion |
| 12.04.70 | Project 627 (November) | *K-8* | | SSN | USSR | Foundered after electrical fire |
| 05.70 | Kagero | *Tan Yang* | 12 | DD | Taiwan | CTL after running aground in typhoon |
| 05.70 | Gleaves | *Hsuen Yang* | 16 | DD | Taiwan | CTL after severe grounding and scrapped |

| DATE | CLASS | NAME | PEN No | TYPE | COUNTRY | CAUSE |
|---|---|---|---|---|---|---|
| 01.06.70 | Dale | *Ennerdale* | A213 | Oiler | UK | Sank after striking submerged reef |
| 09.10.70 | Bluebird | *Bach Dang II* | HQ116 | MSC | S.Vietnam | CTL after grounding |
| 01.71 | Project 641 (Foxtrot) | | | SS | USSR | CTL after collision with merchantman |
| 21.05.71 | Bluebird | *King Bird* | MSC194 | MSC | USA | CTL after severe collision damage at Pensacola |
| 24.05.71 | Chun-ji | *Poochun* | AO3 | AO | South Korea | Lost by grounding |
| 25.05.71 | USCG 95-ft Type | *Albbami* | PB7 | PC | South Korea | CTL after grounding |
| 06.71 | LSM-1 | *Batanes* | LP65 | LSM | Philippines | CTL after running aground. Scrapped 1972 |
| 06.06.71 | Surcouf | *Surcouf* | D621 | DD | France | Forward section sank after collision in Mediterranean |
| 01.07.71 | A | *Artemis* | S49 | SS | UK | Sank alongside at Fort Blockhouse, Gosport |
| 16.08.71 | Denebola | *Regulus* | AF57 | AF | USA | CTL after grounding in typhoon off Hong Kong |
| 23.10.71 | Ton | *Belton* | M1199 | MSC | UK | CTL after grounding in Loch Maddy |
| 04.12.71 | Tench | *Ghazi* | S130 | SS | Pakistan | Sank after internal explosion off India |
| 1972 | Apache | *Felipe Larrazabal* | R11 | ATF | Venezuela | CTL after grounding |
| 1972 | Project 206 (Sherschen) | | | FAC(T) | USSR | Destroyed by fire in Northern Fleet area |
| 1972 | Project 206 (Sherschen) | | | FAC(T) | USSR | Destroyed by fire in Northern Fleet area |
| 1972 | Project 206 (Sherschen) | | | FAC(T) | USSR | Destroyed by fire in Northern Fleet area |

| DATE | CLASS | NAME | PEN No | TYPE | COUNTRY | CAUSE |
|------|-------|------|--------|------|---------|-------|
| 09.01.72 | YTL Type | *YTL432* | YTL432 | Tug | USA | Lost off transport *General Meigs*, which grounded whilst under tow off Cape Flattery, Washington |
| 16.01.72 | Rudderow | *California* | B3 | FF | Mexico | Wrecked by grounding on Bahia Peninsula |
| 23.04.72 | Suamico | *Cowanesque* | T-AOT79 | AO | USA | Sank after grounding at Kin Bay, Okinawa |
| 15.11.72 | LSM-1 | *Ypoploiarchos Merlin* | L166 | LSM | Greece | Sunk in collision with supertanker |
| 16.11.72 | Tucumcari | *Tucumcari* | PGH2 | PGH | USA | Wrecked by grounding on reef at Caballo Blanco |
| 1973 | Ushuia | *Ushuia* | Q10 | AGS | Argentina | Sunk in collision |
| 1973 | V4 | *R4* | IA14 | Tug | Mexico | Sank in heavy weather |
| 1973 | Project 527 (Prut) | *S-44* | | ASR | USSR | Lost by grounding on rocks in Pacific during salvage Operation |
| 07.04.73 | YTM Type | *Nanigo* | YTM537 | Tug | USA | Sank in heavy weather whilst under tow to Bremerton |
| 24.04.73 | Aggressive | *Force* | MSO445 | MSO | USA | Sank at sea after fire west of Guam |
| 25.09.73 | Lt James E. Robinson | *Sgt. Jack J Pendleton* | T-AK276 | AK | USA | Wrecked on Triton Island, Paracel Islands |
| 19.12.73 | Lt James E. Robinson | *Pte. Joseph F Merrell* | AK-275 | AK | USA | CTL after collision off Carolina |
| 1974 | MSC268 | *Shahbaz* | 32 | MSC | Iran | CTL after collision and fire |
| 09.01.74 | Holland | *Noord Brabant* | D810 | DD | Netherlands | CTL after collision with *mv Tacoma City* off Flushing |
| 07.74 | P4 or R | ? | ? | FAC | Cyprus | Stranded and lost |

| DATE | CLASS | NAME | PEN No | TYPE | COUNTRY | CAUSE |
|------|-------|------|--------|------|---------|-------|
| 22.07.74 | Gearing | *Kocatepe* FRAM II | D354 | DD | Turkey | Sunk in error by Turkish Air Force off Cyprus |
| 30.08.74 | Project 61 (Kashin) | *Otvazhnyy* | 530 | DDG | USSR | Sank after explosion and fire in Black Sea |
| 25.12.74 | Attack | *Arrow* | P88 | PC | Australia | Sank in Cyclone Tracy at Darwin |
| 13.02.75 | Sotoyomo | *Bahia Honda* | RM74 | Tug | Colombia | CTL after grounding |
| 19.08.75 1976 | PTF Type Rudderow | *PTF22* *Papaloapan* | PTF22 B4 | PC FF | USA Mexico | CTL after grounding Lost by gounding |
| early-76 | Komar | *Hardadali* | 610? | FAC(M) | Indonesia | Sank after hitting underwater obstacle |
| 10.01.76 | Cherokee | *Comm.General Zapiola* | A2 | PC | Argentina | Capsized and sank after grounding in Morton Strait, Antarctica |
| 10.08.76 | Bustler | *Reward* | A264 | PC | UK | Sunk in collision with *ss Plainsman* in Firth of Forth |
| 09.76 | YTL.422 | Ex-*YTL748* | | Tug | Philippines | Lost overboard from transport on delivery voyage from Japan |
| 14.09.76 | Gearing | *Bordelon* | DD881 | DD | USA | CTL after collision with *USS John F. Kennedy* (CV67) during refuelling. Wreck sold to Turkey for spares |
| 20.09.76 | Ton | *Fittleton* | M1136 | MSC | UK | Sunk in collision with *HMS Mermaid* in North Sea |
| 27.12.76 | SX404 Type | | | SS(M) | Pakistan | Sank off Karachi. Crew of 8 killed |
| 17.01.77 | LCM-6 | ? | ? | LCM | USA | Sunk in collision with Spanish merchant ship *Uriea* in Barcelona Harbour. 48 killed |

| DATE | CLASS | NAME | PEN No | TYPE | COUNTRY | CAUSE |
|------|-------|------|--------|------|---------|-------|
| 24.02.77 | LST 1-510 | *Comandante Toro* | R88 | LST | Chile | CTL after running aground off Isla San Felix |
| 22.08.77 | Gearing FRAM I | *Chao Yang* | 912 | DD | Taiwan | CTL after grounding under tow from US |
| 24.08.77 | PGM9 | *A. Pezopoulos* | P70 | PC | Greece | CTL after collision with ferry in Pserimos Strait |
| 1978 | 15000-ton Type | | AFD109 | Floating Dock | Peru | Lost under tow during delivery voyage. Replaced |
| 18.01.78 | Cherokee | *Cree* | ATF84 | ATF | USA | CTL after being bombed in error by US aircraft |
| 08.78 | Luda | | 160 | DDG | China | Destroyed by explosion at Guangzhou |
| 14/15.09.78 | Polnochny C | *Ibn Al Qis* | 113 | LSM | Libya | Wrecked by fire during landing exercises |
| 28.12.78 | Brooke Marine | *Al Bushra* | B1 | FAC(M) | Oman | Swept overboard from heavy 37.5 metre Typelift ship in Bay of Biscay and sank |
| 1979 | PCE-827 | *Leyte* | PS30 | Corvette | Philippines | Foundered after grounding |
| 1979 | Brooke Marine 45-ft Type | *Chatoyer* | | CPC | St Vincent | Lost in hurricane |
| 1979 | Vosper 101 Type | | PB101 | PC | Sri Lanka | Sunk in collision |
| 1979 | Project 771 (Polnocny B) | *SDK-84* | | LSM | USSR | Scrapped following accidental damage in Pacific |
| 02.79 | Goryn | *Bolshevetsk* | | Tug | USSR | Lost off Japan |
| 24.04.79 | Redwing | *Llobregat* | M22 | MSC | Spain | CTL after fire |
| 1980 | Storm | *Pil* | P976 | FAC(M) | Norway | Condemned after grounding |
| 1980 | Project 675 (Echo II) | *K-10* | | SSGN | USSR | Scrapped after collision with Chinese submarine |

| DATE | CLASS | NAME | PEN No | TYPE | COUNTRY | CAUSE |
|---|---|---|---|---|---|---|
| 1980 | KM-1 | | | WIG | USSR | Sank in Caspian Sea |
| 10.04.80 | LST 511-1152 | *Aguila* | ARV135 | LST | Chile | Scuttled after grounding in storm at Valparaiso |
| 10.05.80 | Vosper 103-ft Type | *Flamingo* | P02 | PC | Bahamas | Mistakenly(?) sunk by Cuban aircraft |
| 20.08.80 | Project 659T (Echo I) | *K-66* | | SSN | USSR | Scrapped after reactor accident and fire off Japan |
| 22.08.80 | Keith Nelson 60-ft Type | *Acklins* | P21 | PC | Bahamas | Destroyed by engine room explosion |
| 25.09.80 | Jaguar | *Kataigis* | P51 | FAC(T) | Greece | CTL after engine fire off Saronikos |
| 1981 | Project 904 (Orlan) | *S-23* | | WIG | USSR | Scrapped following accidental damage |
| 09.06.81 | Ham | *Thornham* | M2793 | MSI | UK | CTL after mobile crane fell on her at Aberdeen |
| 19.09.81 | Kutter | MHV68 | MHV68 | CPC | Denmark | Sank off Laesoe, Kattegat, after grounding the previous day |
| 20.09.81 | Cannon | *Datu Kalantiaw* | PS76 | FF | Philippines | Grounded in Typhoon Clara and capsized |
| 21.10.81 | Project 613V (Whiskey I) | *S-178* | | SS | USSR | Sank after collision off Vladivostok |
| 25.11.81 | Keith Nelson 60-ft Type | *San Salvador* | P24 | PC | Bahamas | Destroyed by fire off the Berry Islands |
| 82 | Project 205 (Osa) | *R-2* | | FAC(M) | USSR | Lost by fire in Pacific |
| 19.01.82 | SRN-6 | *XV617* | P237 | Hovercraft | UK | CTL after grounding off Hong Kong |
| 16.02.82 | Mekhanik | *Mekhanik Tarasov* | | Ro-Ro | USSR | Foundered in heavy weather off Newfoundland |

| DATE | CLASS | NAME | PEN No | TYPE | COUNTRY | CAUSE |
|---|---|---|---|---|---|---|
| 18.02.82 | President | *President Kruger* | F150 | FF | South Africa | Sunk in collision with *Tafelberg* southwest of the Cape |
| 07.03.82 | | *Golden Dolphin* | AO/T8 | Tanker | USA | Exploded and sank in Atlantic |
| 12.04.82 | Cherokee | *Antonio Picardi* | R22 | ATF | Venezuela | CTL after grounding |
| 15.08.82 | Ex-trawler | *Rigel* | | PC | Colombia | Lost |
| 01.83 | | *Rosendo Melo* | EH173 | AGS | Peru | Scrapped after fire damage |
| 23.03.83 | Project 205 (Osa) | *R-82* | | FAC(M) | USSR | CTL after fire as a result of being struck by missile |
| 24.06.83 | Project 670 (Charlie I) | *K-429* | | SSGN | USSR | Foundered off Kamchatka Peninsula. Raised, but sank again 13.09.85 |
| 24.06.83 | Goulandris | *N I Goulandris II* | P290 | PC | Greece | Blew up and sank south of Lesbos |
| 08.83 | LCM-8 | *CTM11* | CTM11 | LCM | France | Sank in heavy weather |
| 21.08.83 | Project 659T (Echo I) | *K-122* | | SSN | USSR | CTL after major fire. 14 killed |
| 1984 | 18.2m Type | *Port Harcourt* | P213 | PC | Nigeria | Sank |
| 1984 | Project 860 (Samata) | *Anadyr* | | AGS | USSR | CTL after grounding |
| 01.84 | Kedah | *Sri Perek* | P3140 | PC | Malaysia | Foundered |
| 25.02.84 | 28.2m Type | *El Tayacan* | | PC | Nicaragua | Sunk by mine at El Bluff |
| 04.84 | Nampo | | | PC | Madagascar | Lost in typhoon |
| 04.84 | Nampo | | | PC | Madagascar | Lost in typhoon |
| 04.84 | Nampo | | | PC | Madagascar | Lost in typhoon |
| 02.05.84 | Gearing FRAM II | *Tinaztepe* | D355 | DD | Turkey | CTL after being badly damaged in collision |

| DATE | CLASS | NAME | PEN No | TYPE | COUNTRY | CAUSE |
|---|---|---|---|---|---|---|
| 21.06.84 | LSM-1 | *Los Frailes* | T23 | LSM | Venezuela | Scrapped after fire |
| 1985 | Xia | ? | ? | SSBN | China | Reportedly lost in accident (unconfirmed) |
| 09.01.85 | 130-ton Type | *Romaleos* | A418 | Tug | Greece | Girded and sunk in Suda Bay, Crete |
| 30.01.85 | C119 Type | | C136 | LCU | Turkey | Sank in storm |
| 20.02.85 | Romeo | | | SS | N.Korea | Reported sunk off east coast of Korea, cause unknown |
| 11.04.85 | Ashville | *Yilderim* | P338 | PC | Turkey | Lost following explosion near Lesbos |
| 10.08.85 | Project 675 (Echo II) | *K-431* | | SSGN | USSR | Destroyed by explosion during reactor refuelling in Chazhma Bay |
| 25.09.85 | Kartal | *Meltem* | P325 | FAC(M) | Turkey | Cut in two in collision with Soviet training ship *Khasan* near Istanbul |
| 1986 | Ro/Ro Type | *El Timsah* | | Transport | Libya | Burned out and lost |
| 1986 | Tyler Vortex 13-metre Type | *QRB1* | Q1 | FIB | Oman | CTL after grounding |
| 1986 | 6000-ton Type | *Erkin* | A590 | AS | Turkey | CTL after engine-room fire |
| 05.02.86 | Vigilant | *Heron II* | | PC | St Lucia | Destroyed by fire |
| 03.86 | Polnochny A | | 138 | LSM | S.Yemen | Destroyed by fire (during coup?) |
| 22.03.86 | YTL422 Type | *Secota* | YTM415 | Tug | USA | Sunk in collision with *USS Georgia* (SSBN-729) off Midway Is. |
| 06.10.86 | Project 667A (Yankee I) | *K-219* | | SSBN | USSR | Sank after explosion in missile section |
| 1987 | Dorina | *Dorina* | F81 | Corvette | Nigeria | Sank at moorings. Raised 18.05.87 and hulked |

| DATE | CLASS | NAME | PEN No | TYPE | COUNTRY | CAUSE |
|---|---|---|---|---|---|---|
| 1987 | Osprey | *In Ma* | FV56 | OPV | Myanmar | Sank. Not raised |
| 1987 | Project 1124A (Grisha II) | *Sapfir* | | FFL | USSR | Sank in storm near Nevyel'sk |
| 28-02-87 | Sirius | *Capella* | M755 | MSC | France | CTL after collision with Guatemalan merchant ship |
| 30.03.87 | Type 207 | *Stadt* | S307 | SSK | Norway | CTL after grounding. (Stricken beyond repair) |
| 16.04.87 | Project 1234-1 (Nanuchka III) | *Musson* | | Corvette | USSR | Sank after fire as a result of being struck by target drone |
| 26.05.87 | Bowditch | *Bowditch* | T-AGS21 | AGS | USA | CTL after severe storm damage. Laid up at New Orleans |
| 1988 | Krogerwerft Type | *P1552* | P1552 | Air/Sea Rescue | South Africa | Sank after grounding in Saldanha Bay |
| 1988 | Project 206M (Turya) | *T-116* | | FAH(T) | USSR | Sank near Russkiy Island |
| 1988 | Project 1206 (Lebed) | *D-379* | | Hovercraft | USSR | Destroyed by fire |
| 1988 | Project 1206 (Lebed) | *D-633* | | Hovercraft | USSR | Destroyed by fire |
| 24.04.88 | Barbel | *Bonefish* | SS582 | SSK | USA | Written off after battery explosion and fire in Caribbean |
| 02.06.88 | LST 511-1152 | *Aurora* | LT518 | LST | Philippines | CTL after grounding |
| 26.08.88 | GUPPY 1A | *Pacocha* | S48 | SSK | Peru | Sank after collision with Japanese ship |
| 22.10.88 | LST 511-1152 | *Davoa Oriental* | LT506 | LST | Philippines | Sank? |
| 22.10.88 | ? | *Pag-Ibig* | AH81 | ? | Philippines | CTL after grounding |
| 28.01.89 | Bahia Paraiso | *Bahia Paraiso* | Q6 | Polar | Argentina Supply | Grounded in Bismarck Strait. Capsized 02.02.89 |

| DATE | CLASS | NAME | PEN No | TYPE | COUNTRY | CAUSE |
|---|---|---|---|---|---|---|
| 21.02.89 | YO Type | *Capitan W Arvelo* | BT4 | Tanker | Dominican Republic | Sank |
| 26.02.89 | 1200-ton Type | *Humboldt* | | Survey | Peru | CTL after grounding |
| 07.04.89 | Project 685 (Mike) | *Komsomolets* | | SSN | USSR | Sank after fire in Norwegian Sea |
| 25.06.89 | Project 675 (Echo II) | *192* (Ex-*K-131*) | | SSGN | USSR | CTL after reactor fire north of Norway |
| 19.08.89 | Project 266 (Yurka) | | | MSO | USSR | Sank after explosion in Black Sea |
| 30.08.89 | LST 1-510 | *Tuk Bong* | LST672 | LST | South Korea | CTL after grounding |
| 10.89 | Zhuk | | ? | CPC | Nicaragua | Sank in hurricane |
| 10.89 | Zhuk | | ? | CPC | Nicaragua | Sank in hurricane |
| 10.89 | Sin Hung | | ? | CPC | Nicaragua | Sank in hurricane |
| 10.89 | Yevgenya | | 512 | MSI | Nicaragua | Sank in hurricane. Raised and scrapped |
| early-90s | Okean | *Ekholot* | | AGI | USSR | Destroyed by fire in Pacific |
| 1990 | Damen 15 m Type | | T1 | Tug | Oman | Swept overboard from transport on delivery voyage and sank |
| 1990 | Anchova | *Rio Reque* | PP234 | CPC | Peru | Wrecked |
| 1990 | Project 1206T (Pelikan) | | | MSI | USSR | Wrecked in Black Sea |
| 1990 | Project 364 (Pozharny I) | *PDK-70* | | Tug | USSR | Sank in Black Sea |
| 1990 | Project 1806 (Onega) | *SFP-340* | | SFP | USSR | Destroyed by fire in Pacific |
| Mid-90 | Shanghai II | *P101* | P101 | PC | Zaire | Sank at moorings |
| 22.08.90 | Petya II | *Andaman* | P74 | FFL | India | Sank in heavy seas in Bay of Bengal |

| DATE | CLASS | NAME | PEN No | TYPE | COUNTRY | CAUSE |
|---|---|---|---|---|---|---|
| 11.90 | Project 513 (T-43) | *GKS-23* | | AGS | USSR | Destroyed by fire in Pacific |
| 1991 | Swift Mk.I/II | | PCF304 | CPC | Philippines | Sank |
| 1991 | LCM-6 | | | LCM | Philippines | Sank |
| 1991 | Koln | *Gemlik* | D361 | FF | Turkey | CTL after engine-room fire |
| 1991 | Project 1231-1 (Aist) | | | Hovercraft | USSR | Destroyed by fire in Leningrad |
| 01.91 | 8.8m Type | | P106 | CPC | Bahamas | Sunk in hurricane during search-and-rescue mission |
| 26.01.91 | Project 641 (Foxtrot) | *B-33* | | SSK | USSR | Sank at Vladivostok |
| 29.04.91 | Hegu | ? | ? | FAC(M) | Bangladesh | Wrecked in typhoon at Chittagong |
| 29.04.91 | Huangfen | ? | ? | FAC(M) | Bangladesh | Sank in typhoon at Chittagong |
| 29.04.91 | Hainan | *Durjoy* | P811 | FAC(P) | Bangladesh | Irreparably damaged in typhoon. Scrapped 1995 |
| 29.04.91 | Yushin | *L103* | L103 | LCT | Bangladesh | Irreparably damaged in typhoon. Scrapped 1994 |
| late-91 | Vihuri | *Vihuri* | 541 | Launch | Finland | Destroyed by fire |
| late-91 | Ham | *Olib* | ML144 | MSI | Yugoslavia | Lost by grounding on south coast of island of Hvar |
| 23.12.91 | LST 1-510 | *Eastern Samar* | LT502 | LST | Philippines | Sank |
| 1992 | Ming | | | SSK | China | CTL after fire. Scrapped |
| 1992 | Ro-Ro 1300 Type | *Ofiom* | LST1313 | LST | Nigeria | Seriously damaged by grounding and scrapped |
| 1992 | Project 1783A (Vala) | *TNT II* | | Tanker | Russia | Sank |

| DATE | CLASS | NAME | PEN No | TYPE | COUNTRY | CAUSE |
|---|---|---|---|---|---|---|
| 1992 | Project 1206 (Lebed) | *D-435* | | Hovercraft | USSR | Destroyed by fire |
| 1992 | Mal | ? | ? | PC | Somalia | Sank at berth after being ransacked during 1991 revolution |
| 1992 | Mal | ? | ? | PC | Somalia | Sank at berth after being ransacked during 1991 revolution |
| 1992 | 15.9m Type | | P115 | CPC | Spain | Scrapped after major fire |
| 17.02.92 | Project 1155 (Udaloy) | *Admiral Zakharov* | | DDG | Russia | CTL after major fire off Vladivostok |
| 09.92 | Dore | *Amurang* | 581 | LCU | Indonesia | Sank 900km south-east of Jakarta. 1 dead, 13 missing |
| 10.92 | Vosper 33 m Type | *Kandula* | L837 | LCM | Sri Lanka | Sank in storm off Kalpitiya coast.  Raised but beyond repair |
| 02.10.92 | Robert H Smith | *Mauvenet* | DM357 | DD | Turkey | CTL after mistaken missile attack |
| 22.10.92 | 2180-ton Type | *Almirante Alvaro Alberto* | H43 | AGS | Brazil | Sank after fire in Lagos dos Patos |
| 1993 | Romeo | | | SSK | China | Sank during training exercise (CO Qualifying Course) |
| 1993 | Jianghu | *Kaifeng* | 520 | FFG | China | Scrapped after accidental damage? |
| 1993 | 2900-ton Type | *Xiangyang Hong 16* | | Research | China | Sunk in collision at sea |
| 1993 | Project 904 (Orlan) | *S-21* | | WIG | Russia | Scrapped following accidental damage |
| 1993 | Namacurra | *Y1506* | Y1506 | CPC | South Africa | Sank at sea |
| 22.02.93 | 580-ton Type | *ADRI XXXI* | | LCL | Indonesia | Sank in position 08.02°S, 125.35°E |

| DATE | CLASS | NAME | PEN No | TYPE | COUNTRY | CAUSE |
|---|---|---|---|---|---|---|
| 10.03.93 | PC 461 | *Nueya Viscaya* | PS80 | PC | Philippines | Sank in typhoon at Cebu, Philippines |
| late-93 | Timsah | | 03 | PC | Egypt | Sank |
| 24.01.94 | Oslo | *Oslo* | F300 | FFG | Norway | Sank after grounding following engine failure |
| 06.94 | Adjutant | ? | ? | MSC | Taiwan | Destroyed by fire |
| 1995 | SX756 Type | | | SS(M) | Pakistan | Sank |
| 1995 | Project 572 (MP6) | *Vologda* | | AK/AE | Russia | Sank |
| 1995 | Seal | *Porpoise* | 2002 | Diving Tender | Australia | Scrapped following grounding |
| 27.05.95 | Botved | *Y375* | Y375 | CPC | Denmark | Sank after fire in the Kattegat. Salvaged and scrapped. |
| 05.10.95 | LST 511-1152 | *Chung Sheng* | LST222 | LST | Taiwan | CTL after grounding near Keelung. Scrapped on site. |
| 18.09.96 | Sang-O | | | SS(M) | N. Korea | Abandoned after grounding 9km south of Kangnung, South Korea |
| late-96 | Gearing FRAM I | *Piyale Pasa* | D350 | DD | Turkey | Seriously damaged by grounding. Scrapped 1999 |
| 04.11.96 | La Combattante IIIN | *Antipliarchos Kostakos* | P25 | FAC(M) | Greece | Sunk in collision with Greek ferry. Four killed |
| 12.11.96 | Imperial Marinhiero | *Forte de Coimbra* | V18 | PC | Brazil | CTL after stranding on Baixinha reefs near port of Natal |
| 1997 | Shanghai II | *Naimbana* | | FAC(G) | Sierra Leone | Sank. Replaced with identical unit with same name |
| 28.03.97 | PO-2 | | A451 | PC | Albania | Capsized and sank after collision with Italian corvette *Sibilla* in Adriatic |

| DATE | CLASS | NAME | PEN No | TYPE | COUNTRY | CAUSE |
|------|-------|------|--------|------|---------|-------|
| 30.04.97 | La Prudente | *La Fidelle* | Y751 | Netlayer | France | Sank after explosion whilst transporting ammunition 5 miles off Cherbourg |
| 25.09.97 | Gong Bian | *Gong Bian* | 4406 | PC | China | Abandoned off Hong Kong after fire |
| 11.97 | Project 61 (Kashin) | *Skoryy* | | DDG | Russia | Scrapped after sinking alongside in Sevastopol |
| Late.97 | Hoijan | | | FAC(M) | China | Sank off Hong Kong |
| 1998 | 18m Type | | P25 | CPC | Malta | Wrecked |
| 1998 | 4500-ton Type | *Rio Balsas* | A23 | AKS | Mexico | Scrapped after major fire |
| 22.06.98 | Yugo | | | SS(M) | N. Korea | Abandoned after becoming entangled in nets 11 miles off Sokcho, South Korea. Later sank under tow |
| 08.98 | Sotoyomo | *Comodoro Somellara* | A10 | PC | Argentina | Sunk in collision at Ushuaia. Refloated and scrapped |
| 09.98 | Manta | *Tulcan* | LM28 | FAC(M) | Ecuador | Sank after collision with tug |
| 09.05.99 | LST 511-1152 | *Sierra Madre* | LT57 | LST | Philippines | CTL after stranding on rocks in Spratley Islands. Paid off and used as observation post |
| 17.05.00 | T-43 | *Pulau Ratewo* | 702 | MSO | Indonesia | Sunk in collision with merchant ship Iris near Madura Is. |
| 06.08.00 | Kondor II | *Valiente* | 32 | MSC | Uruguay | Cut in two and sunk in collision with freighter 150 miles east of Montevideo |
| 12.08.00 | Project 949A (Oscar II) | *Kursk* | K141 | SSGN | Russia | Sank after explosion in torpedo compartment |
| 12.09.00 | Newport | *La Moure County* | LST1194 | LST | USA | CTL after running aground on a reef of coast of Chile |

| DATE | CLASS | NAME | PEN No | TYPE | COUNTRY | CAUSE |
|---|---|---|---|---|---|---|
| 06.11.00 | Ribnazor-4 | *Spulga* | KA02 | PC | Latvia | Sank after being re-floated following grounding |
| 16.11.00 | | *Khakhwe* | 207 | ? | Myanmar | Blew up and sank |
| 24.12.00 | Oberon | *Tonelero* | S21 | SSK | Brazil | San alongside at Rio de Janeiro. Raised and paid off |
| early 12.02 | Moma | *Artktika* | | AGS | Russia | Capsized and sank due to heavy ice at Novorossisk |
| early 12.02 | Nuryat | *BGK-775* | BGK-775 | Tender | Russia | Sank due to heavy ice at Novorossisk |
| 19.11.02 | Alta | *Orkla* | M353 | MSC | Norway | Destroyed by fire |
| 01.09.03 | Lago | *Lago de Cuitzeo* | PC323 | RPC | Mexico | Capsized and sank off Costa Maya with loss of 12 crew |
| 12.10.04 | ? | ? | ? | FIB? | South Korea | Capsized and sank 37km off Ulsan with loss of 4 crewmen |
| 12.04 | LST 511-1152 | *Lanao del Norte* | LT504 | LST | Philippines | Ran aground and abandoned in Spratly Islands. |
| 26.12.04 | Haiqing | *Parakramabahu* | P351 | CPC | Sri Lanka | Sank at Galle during tsunami. Raised 15.05.05. Never repaired. |
| 26.12.04 | T213 | *T215* | T215 | CPC | Thailand | Sank near Thap Lamu during tsunami |
| 19-12-05 | Baleares | *Extremadura* | F75 | FFG | Spain | CTL after boiler-room explosion |
| 03.05.06 | SKA11 | *SKA11* | SKA11 | Survey | Denmark | Sank after grounding in Arsuk Fjord, Greenland, 27 April 2006. |
| 22.06.06 | Houjian | *Hiangjiang* | 774 | FAC(M) | China | Sank in collision with 18000-ton freighter off Guishan Island. |

| DATE | CLASS | NAME | PEN No | TYPE | COUNTRY | CAUSE |
|------|-------|------|--------|------|---------|-------|
| 22.06.06 | Veer (Tarantul) | *Prahar* | K98 | Corvette | India | Sank after collision with merchant ship off Goa. |

## Key to Abbreviations

| | |
|---|---|
| AE | Ammunition Ship |
| AF | Stores Ship |
| AG | Miscellaneous Auxiliary Vessel AGI - Auxiliary, Intelligence Gathering |
| AGS | Survey Ship |
| AH | Hospital Ship |
| AK | Cargo Ship |
| AKS | General Stores Ship |
| AO | Fleet Oiler |
| AOG | Gasoline Tanker |
| APD | High-speed transport |
| AS | Auxiliary, Submarine Tender |
| ASR | Auxiliary, Submarine Rescue |
| ARS | Auxiliary, Rescue and Salvage |
| ATA | Auxiliary, Fleet Tug |
| ATF | Auxiliary, Tug, Fleet, Oceangoing |
| BB | Battleship |
| CPC | Coastal Patrol Craft |
| CTL | Constructive Total Loss |
| DD | Destroyer |
| DDE | Destroyer Escort |
| DDG | Destroyer, Guided-missile armed |
| DMS | Destroyer Minesweeper FAC(G) - Fast Attack Craft (Gun-armed) |
| FAC(M) | Fast Attack Craft (Missile-armed) |
| FAC(P) | Fast Attack Craft (Patrol) |
| FAC(T) | Fast Attack Craft (Torpedo-armed) |
| FAH(T) | Fast Attack Hydrofoil (Torpedo-armed) |
| FF | Frigate |
| FFG | Frigate, Guided-missile armed |
| FFL | Frigate, Light |
| FIB | Fast Interceptor Boat |
| GB | Gunboat |
| LCI | Landing Craft, Infantry |
| LCL | Landing Craft, Logistic |
| LCM | Landing Craft, Mechanised |
| LCT | Landing Craft, Tank |
| LCU | Landing Craft, Utility |
| LSM | Landing Ship, Mechanised |
| LST | Landing Ship, Tank |
| MFV | Motor Fishing Vessel |
| MGB | Motor Gun Boat |
| ML | Minelayer |
| MS | Minesweeper |
| MSB | Minesweeping Boat |
| MSC | Minesweeper, Coastal |
| MSF | Minesweeper, Fleet |
| MSI | Minesweeper, Inshore |
| MSO | Minesweeper, Ocean |
| MST | Minesweeping Trawler |
| MSY | Minesweeping Yacht |
| MTB | Motor Gun Boat |
| MTB | Motor Torpedo Boat |
| OPV | Offshore Patrol Vessel |
| PB | Patrol Boat |
| PC | Patrol Craft |
| PGH | Patrol Gunboat Hydrofoil |
| PS | Patrol Ship |
| Ro-Ro | Roll-on, Roll-off Cargo Ship |
| RPC | River Patrol Craft |
| SC | Submarine Chaser |
| SFP | Ship of Physical Fields (Acoutsic Measurement Ship) |
| SS | Submarine |
| SSB | Submarine, Ballistic-missile armed |
| SSBN | Submarine, Ballistic-missile armed, Nuclear-powered |
| SSG | Submarine, Cruise-missile armed |
| SSGN | Submarine, Cruise-missile armed, Nuclear-powered |
| SSK | Submarine, Hunter-killer |
| SS(M) | Submarine (Midget) |
| SSN | Submarine, Nuclear-powered |
| Trans | Transport |
| WIG | Wing-In-Ground-Effect craft |
| YOG | Yard (Harbour) Tanker |
| YP | Auxiliary Patrol Craft |
| YTB | Harbour Tug, Large |
| YTM | Harbour Tug, Medium |

# General Index

# Ship Name Index

**United States of America**